THE OXFORD HISTORY OF
MEXICO

THE OXFORD HISTORY OF
MEXICO

Edited by

MICHAEL C. MEYER *and*

WILLIAM H. BEEZLEY

OXFORD

UNIVERSITY PRESS

OXFORD
UNIVERSITY PRESS

Oxford New York

Athens Auckland Bangkok Bogotá Buenos Aires Calcutta Cape Town
Chennai Dar es Salaam Delhi Florence Hong Kong Istanbul Karachi
Kuala Lumpur Madrid Melbourne Mexico City Mumbai Nairobi
Paris São Paulo Singapore Taipei Tokyo Toronto Warsaw

and associated companies in

Berlin Ibadan

Book design by Charles B. Hames

LIBRARY OF CONGRESS CATALOGING-IN-PUBLICATION DATA
The Oxford history of Mexico / Michael C. Meyer and William H. Beezley, [editors].
   cm.
Includes bibliographical references and index.
ISBN 0–19–511228–8 (alk. paper)
1. Mexico—History.
   I. Meyer, Michael C.   II. Beezley, William H.
   F1226.O94   2000
   972–dc21
   99–056044

10 9 8 7 6 5 4 3 2 1

Printed in the United States of America on acid-free paper.

Contents

✦ ✦

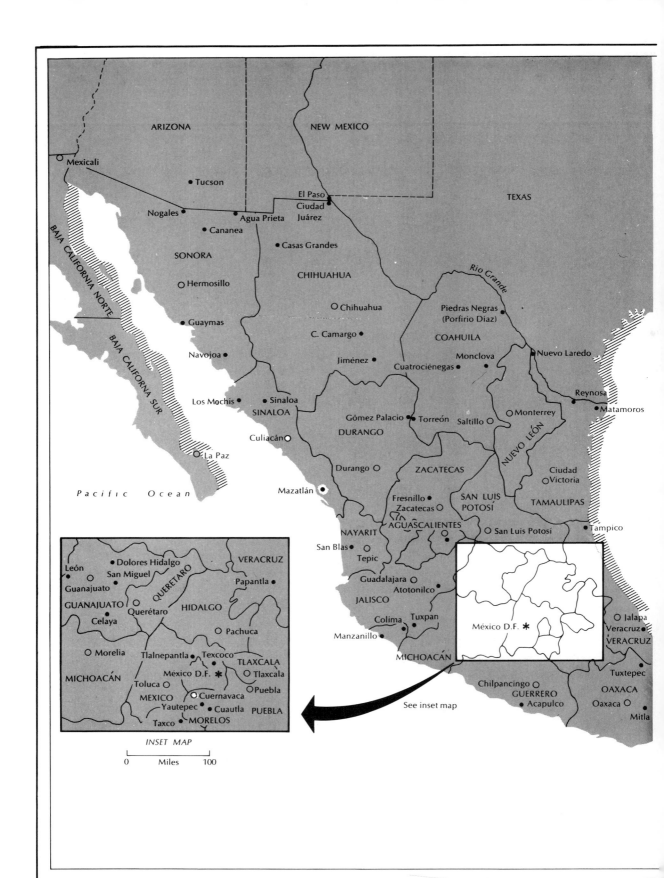

ARIZONA

NEW MEXICO

Mexicali

TEXAS

• Tucson

El Paso

Nogales

Agua Prieta

Ciudad
Juárez

• Cananea

• Casas Grandes

BAJA CALIFORNIA NORTE

SONORA

Rio Grande

○ Hermosillo

CHIHUAHUA

○ Chihuahua

Piedras Negras
(Porfirio Díaz)

• Guaymas

C. Camargo •

BAJA CALIFORNA SUR

Navojoa •

Jiménez •

COAHUILA

Monclova

Nuevo Laredo

Cuatrociénegas •

Los Mochis •

• Sinaloa

SINALOA

Reynosa

Gómez Palacio • • Torreón

Saltillo ○

○ Monterrey

Matamoros

Culiacán ○

DURANGO

NUEVO LEÓN

○ La Paz

Durango ○

ZACATECAS

Ciudad
○Victoria

Pacific   Ocean

Mazatlán ○

Fresnillo •

SAN LUIS
POTOSÍ

TAMAULIPAS

Zacatecas ○

NAYARIT

AGUASCALIENTES

○ San Luís Potosí

Tampico

San Blas ○

Tepic •

México D.F. ✴

Guadalajara ○

○ Jalapa

JALISCO

Atotonilco •

Veracruz •

Colima •

Tuxpan •

VERACRUZ

Manzanillo •

Tuxtepec

MICHOACÁN

See inset map

Chilpancingo ○

OAXACA

GUERRERO

• Acapulco

Oaxaca ○

Mitla

INSET MAP

León •

• Dolores Hidalgo

• San Miguel

VERACRUZ

Guanajuato ○

QUERÉTARO

Papantla • •

GUANAJUATO

HIDALGO

Querétaro ○

Celaya •

○ Morelia

Pachuca ○

MICHOACÁN

Tlalnepantla •

Texcoco •

TLAXCALA

México D.F. ✴

○ Tlaxcala

Toluca ○

• Puebla

MEXICO

○ Cuernavaca

Yautepec

• Cuautla

PUEBLA

Taxco •

MORELOS

INSET MAP

0   Miles   100

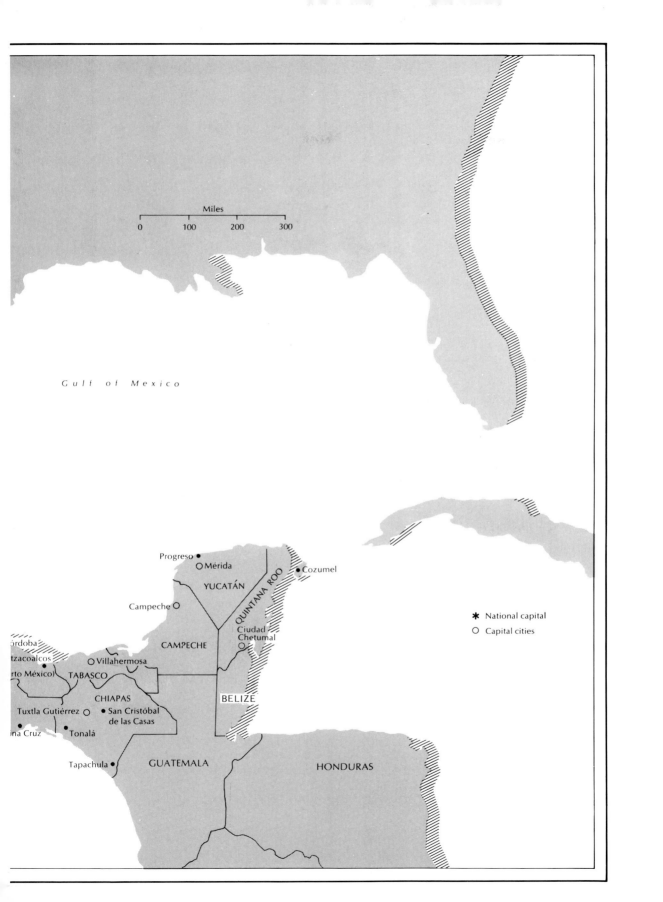

Miles

0   100   200   300

Gulf of Mexico

Progreso ●
○ Mérida

● Cozumel

YUCATÁN

QUINTANA ROO

Campeche ○

Ciudad
Chetumal
○

CAMPECHE

órdoba

tzacoalcos

○ Villahermosa

rto México

TABASCO

CHIAPAS

BELIZE

Tuxtla Gutiérrez ○   ● San Cristóbal
de las Casas

na Cruz   ● Tonalá

Tapachula ●

GUATEMALA

HONDURAS

✳ National capital
○ Capital cities

Introduction

✦ ✦

The distinct races of the world tend to mix more and more until they
form a new human type. . . . Even the most contradictory mixtures can
always be beneficially resolved because the spiritual factor in each serves
to elevate the whole.

JOSÉ VASCONCELOS (1882–1959)
La raza cósmica

Mexico is the product of a collision between, and ultimately a
fusion of, two vastly different worlds. In the early 16th century,
a generation after Christopher Columbus bumped into Watling
Island in the Bahamas, Spain encountered a bewildering kaleidoscope of
Mesoamerican cultures in what later became southern and central Mexico. And
more would be found in the decades ahead as a series of frontiers were pushed farther and farther to the north. Although the Spaniards were not strangers to the
notion that racial and ethnic confrontations could be followed by accommodation, reconciliation, and the blending of ideas, they were not prepared for the
remarkable civilizations they encountered. The Native American community
found itself surprised and unprepared as well. Neither party to this epic ren-
dezvous would again be the same. Mexican historian Enrique Krauze captured the
essence of this historical moment perfectly in a recent description of the first
meeting of Hernán (Fernando) Cortés and Moctezuma (Moteuczoma, or Montezuma): "They created a new nationality at the instant they met."

Once the physical conquest played itself out, shattering the status quo and
defining history's latest victors and vanquished, both the conquerors and the conquered set out to test each other's tolerance levels and devise strategies of acceptance and rejection. This process itself was of such a magnitude that it has already
taken more than four full centuries and is not yet completed. In their appraisal of
the Native American civilizations, the Spanish philosophers, theologians, and
bureaucrats had to decide what could be warmly embraced, what might be indif-
ferently allowed, and what was so noxious to Spanish notions of polity and Christian ethic that it had to be brazenly suffocated. Where persuasion failed, coercion
followed.

Similar choices confronted the Native American communities, whether they
were found in the southern rain forests or the northern deserts of what came to be

called New Spain. While they certainly maintained a degree of autonomy, as subject peoples they nevertheless lost much of the independence they had previously enjoyed. With less control of their own destinies they still had to determine what innovations were to be welcomed, which would be accommodated (albeit with little enthusiasm), and which were so foreign to their worldview that they invited subterfuge, ridicule, creative resistance, and, on occasion, open rebellion, even when it unleashed punitive retribution.

Even in the late 18th century, as Spain's hold on her Mexican empire was being challenged and the old colonialism was drawing to an end, the pivotal lines of acceptance and rejection were still being defined and legitimized. The viceroyalty of New Spain had by then been incorporated into a vast imperial system, and the Roman Catholic Church had fashioned and refined the contours of its apostolic presence. But colonial society remained in perpetual flux. In spite of the best efforts of Spain's conquerors, clergymen, petty officials, and colonists, the Native American presence proved much too strong to be totally absorbed. As a result, Mexico never became completely Hispanicized. Ultimately, according to the brilliant if controversial Mexican savant José Vasconcelos, there emerged a synthetic ideal, a *raza cósmica*, or cosmic race, in which the parts assumed the integrity of the whole.

The subtle composite that began to emerge as Mexico in the late 18th and early 19th centuries was given its unique form, color, and texture as further pieces of tile were superimposed on the still-emerging racial mosaic. Testing the compatibility of competing values, these fragments fashioned relationships between the classes, between men and women, between church and state, between humans and their natural environment, and—somewhat later—between Mexico and the outside world. Mercifully, the adhesive holding the pieces together took a long time to solidify, making it possible to have constant adjustment, the altering of proportion, the tempering of exaggeration, and on occasion even redefinition of the design itself.

Because the Mexico that emerged as an independent nation in 1821 had been given so little preparation in self-government, the process of forming a state, or *forjando patria*, was difficult in the extreme. It is now well accepted that the independence leaders of the early 19th century too often underrated the gravity of the task that lay ahead. It had been easy to exalt the principles of freedom and self-determination, but the goal of seeking that singularly perfect union proved elusive. Inevitably, as fledgling politicians tried to replace old measures of authority with new ones, costly errors were made. Liberals and conservatives, federalists and centralists, fought incessantly over how to give meaning to the newly won independence, resulting in decades of unfulfilled promises. Clashing interests strained relations between church and state, while efforts to compromise were relegated to contempt. Experimentation, strategic maneuvering, and a significant amount of financial mismanagement produced a weak and divided country, which seemed not only to invite external aggression but to make it irresistible.

In the middle of the 19th century, only one generation after its independence from Spain, Mexico found itself at war with a much stronger United States. At the war's conclusion a Mexican citizenry already rendered despondent by government mismanagement would soon learn that the country had lost half its land and much of its wealth to the territorial appetites of a belligerent northern neighbor. From the Mexican perspective the covenant that ended the war, the Treaty of Guadalupe Hidalgo (1848), did not dictate merely a loss of territory but rather an amputation, a painful surgery designed only to conserve what was left. The Mexican War could easily have been avoided, but too few strong voices on either side were willing to prevent it.

In the aftermath of that devastating defeat, Mexican politicians and intellectuals began seriously to reassess Mexico's progress, or lack of it, since emerging as an independent nation. The positivists, or *científicos*, led by Dr. Gabino Barreda, believed that science and the scientific method should dominate public discourse. They lamented the irrational disorder and violence the Mexican nation had witnessed for more than a generation. Banditry seemingly could not be repressed. Mexico had fallen increasingly behind a rapidly modernizing Western world as the country had scarcely been touched by the 19th–century technological innovations that had begun to transform western Europe and the United States.

By the late 1860s and early 1870s the need to nurture modernization had begun to suffuse social thought. Benito Juárez, a Zapotec Indian, not only became an example for other members of the Native American community but set a proper moral tone for the nation with his honesty, resolve, and firmness of character. It was he who launched the double process of containing disorder and transforming society. But while the Juárez administration ushered in an important period of transition, he was not to lead his country to the promised land of 19th–century modernity. For that another self-made politician, Porfirio Díaz, waited in the wings, eager to secure his country's future to this new and powerful impulse toward modernization.

Díaz controlled Mexico's fortunes for 35 years, from 1876 to 1911, kept the peace, and implemented a series of structural reforms that transformed the face of the country. With the infusion of foreign capital, railroads tied Mexico City to the U.S. border and began to push wooden carts and human carriers of goods off the roads. Streetcar systems replaced horse-drawn carriages on urban thoroughfares. Telephones, telegraphs, and an efficient postal service revitalized communications. Newly dredged harbors and improved dock facilities welcomed large foreign commercial vessels for the first time, making it possible for Mexico to enter the global economy. The introduction of the thresher and the reaper rejuvenated agriculture, and quantum leaps in the oil industry made Mexico a major international exporter of energy.

The Mexico of 1910 scarcely resembled that of 1876, but modernization did not come free. In subjecting the country to his master plan, Díaz expunged any trace of a free press, exiled intellectual dissidents, jailed opponents without benefit of trial, and trampled on democratic freedoms, all with seeming impunity. His intolerance of any form of opposition negated much of his achievement. The científicos who surrounded him were seen as increasingly subservient to foreign interests, and there was much truth in these accusations. In 1910, most of the largest businesses in Mexico were owned by foreign nationals, primarily by citizens of the United States and Britain. Foreign interests also owned 20 percent of Mexico's land.

The devastating epidemics of social maladies that always seem to spread rapidly during the early stages of industrialization took their toll as well. The gap between rich and poor, evident throughout Mexican history, widened as those most in need found themselves without protections of any kind. Workers were forbidden by law to organize collectively or go on strike. Peones (peasants) on the nation's haciendas (landed estates) found themselves subject to the "justice" of local resident managers. Forgotten at best and abused at worst, the rural and urban poor alike found little to allay the tedium of their lives and give them hope of escaping poverty.

For a time, critics excused the many excesses of Porfirian Mexico as the inevitable price of modernity. Porfirio Díaz was, after all, the irreplaceable president. But ultimately such rationalization could not carry the day. Díaz's reputation does not fare well if judged only by the enemies he made. It is of course possible that his faults loom larger from our historical perspective than they did at the time, but if we allow ourselves to embrace such a theory, we are left without an adequate explanation for the outbreak of the Mexican Revolution on November 20, 1910.

In the fall of 1910, Francisco I. Madero, the leader of the struggle against the dictatorship, having already experienced prison for his political beliefs, raised a citizen's army that overthrew Díaz by force. He then sought to mobilize Mexico's democratic energy to construct a new political infrastructure that would finally give voice to those without access to power. Madero was not calling for a redistribution of wealth. His agenda was narrowly political, but even with its modest goals he enjoyed scant success, as did his immediate successors in the presidential chair. His vision for a democratic Mexico would ultimately survive, but only in a tarnished form.

For ten full years, from 1910 to 1920, Mexico underwent a series of violent internal struggles that claimed a tremendous toll in human life, caused incalculable suffering, and sapped the country's strength. It was a time of self-proclaimed generals. Civilians were threatened with a terror unimpeded by law or compassion. As many as 1 million Mexicans may have sacrificed their lives to goals that remained ambiguous at best. The economy lay in ruins as mines were abandoned and factories closed their doors. Classrooms from the primary school level to the universities were empty for lack of teachers. It was a difficult period in which to preserve any measure of faith, but the Mexican people somehow retained their resilience. Out of that gigantic civil war the country gained a roster of genuine revolutionary heroes while assigning others to historical disgrace. In 1920, it was far from clear whether the movement unleashed with such idealism only a decade earlier had brought the Mexican world a blessing or a curse.

It was not until the 1920s and 1930s, with the resurgence of civility and accommodation, that the Mexican Revolution (with a capital, to distinguish it from the many revolts of the past) underwent a metamorphosis so startling that Madero himself would not have recognized it as the movement he had initiated. Its vision broadened and its goals changed, from political reform to social transformation. A product of competing ideas, the Revolution imbued Mexicans not only with new notions of progress but with a new sense of urgency.

For the first time, the country became hostile to the private concentration of economic power. In the interest of providing a safety net for the most vulnerable in Mexican society, laissez-faire capitalism gave way to increasing social regulation, trade union participation in public life, and active state intervention in the economy. Monumental efforts were undertaken to improve life in rural Mexico through the *ejido*, or collective farm, financed by the state. And programs were designed to provide classrooms and teachers for all the nation's children. These profound changes were designed with the expectation that a fuller and better life for the Mexican masses was finally within reach. Mexico City had always been the focal point of Mexico's political, social, and economic life, but now, with this planned economy, greater and greater power was concentrated in the nation's capital.

The ambitious governmental undertakings of the 1920s and 1930s were accompanied by an outburst of creative vitality in literature and the visual arts. The unique artistic aesthetic in the 1920s and 1930s insisted that the creative arts embrace the accepted revolutionary credo of the day. The art was unusually communicative and unashamedly associated with politics in its defiant condemnation of social injustice in any form. In that art one can find criticism of the administrations that actually subsidized it, but it was a muted criticism at best, one designed to highlight deviations from revolutionary goals. Art designed to convey a social message, as happened at this time in Mexico, is not always good art, but in this case the flowering of Mexican mural painting was so innovative in its conception, so imposing in its dimensions, and so distinguished in its execution that it would win the artists and the country itself world acclaim.

In an obvious challenge to the economic orthodoxy of the 1920s and 1930s, as well as to a generation of politicians whose only goal, some argued, had been to redistribute wealth, post-World War II Mexican policy planners placed their faith in a more expansive economy. Industrialization became an impressive fact of Mexican life, to the degree that by the 1970s and early 1980s at least some sectors of society could revel in the exhilaration of the country's "economic miracle." The robust economy proved short-lived, however. The postwar economic system was riddled with abuses. Mexico's impressive growth in this period was so predicated on deficit spending that the results were predictable. Moreover, even before utter bust followed boom in the later 1980s, it was clear that the economic elixir had failed to trickle down to the vast majority of Mexicans. Because it had not been designed to accelerate the circulation of wealth between classes, it never really challenged the plight of the Mexican poor.

Only in the last quarter of the 20th century did Mexico thoroughly reassess its place in a world that within human memory had split the atom, placed a man on the moon, cloned animals, invented microchips, connected millions of individuals by networking them with computers, and witnessed first the dissolution of the Soviet bloc, then of the Soviet Union itself. But the issues that Mexicans contemplated were the same universal concerns that had occupied the philosophers from Plato to John Locke to Karl Marx: how to marry individual rights to social justice, and how to ensure genuine democratic participation in the choice of leadership. All countries have encountered resistance in their attempts to widen the base of prosperity among their citizens; the Mexican experience in this regard is not unique. But Mexico seems to have encountered greater than average roadblocks in the equally monumental effort to make ruling authority responsive to the popular will. At the end of the 20th century, the Mexican solutions to these most vexing of human problems were far from clear.

More than in most countries, the passage of time has been a factor in the Mexican experience. Continuities from the past in Mexico leave an indelible imprint on the present. Like the living splendors of Greece and Rome, the artifacts of classical antiquity that engulf Mexico assault one's historical consciousness and conjure up powerful images of times gone by. Like Egypt, Mexico has its ancient pyramids; like Spain, its ancient aqueducts; like Persia, its ancient hieroglyphics; like China, its collections of ancient art. Public murals, frescoes, and statuary, all attentive to history and all with unmistakable messages, as well as cultural programming on radio, television, and film, reinforce these powerful legacies of Mexico's ancestry. The collective memory strongly reflects the heritage bequeathed by the centuries. Moreover, it permits a wonderfully personal engagement with the nation's past. The very name of the country is taken from the original Aztec tribal designation (*mexica*), while its quintessential symbol, the national flag, depicts an eagle perched on a nopal cactus devouring a serpent, reproducing the Aztec legend of the founding of their capital of Tenochtitlán, the site of the sprawling megalopolis that is today Mexico City.

To be sure, historical analogies are at best complex, at worst precarious. Because ancient artifacts are inert, they can camouflage the complex process of history, but properly appreciated, they can also illumine it. The past can of course be invented, anthropology and history can be manipulated, and chaos can be reduced to a false kind of order; such untoward uses are not unknown to scholars of Mexico. But it is a genuine historical awareness that makes it possible for Mexico's citizens to reconcile contemporary reality with tradition. This understanding clearly helps them cast the moral arguments used in daily discourse. Even if they now seem willing to forgive previous misdeeds of previous leaders, they will not easily agree to the repetition of similar transgressions in the future. In short, the past continues to weigh heavily on Mexico at the beginning of the 21st century but is without question one of its pillars of strength.

The chapters in this volume, none of which has appeared in print previously, depict a Mexican history that is rich and varied. The contributors, all with impeccable scholarly credentials and all well-established professionals in their respective areas of inquiry, have collaborated on a volume that would have had a very different look had it been written even 10 or 15 years ago. There has been an explosion of historical knowledge in recent years. Although many of the most noteworthy innovations have been recorded in the field of social history (for example, in studies of race, class, and gender) a number of interesting breakthroughs have altered our appreciation of Mexico's political, economic, and cultural history as well. Access to previously unavailable archival sources and new collaborations by U.S. and Mexican scholars have yielded results challenging traditional periodizations, reassessing Mexico's role in the international community, and probing the urban-rural dichotomy. A series of new regional studies has brought into question older generalizations that now seem too facile about Mexico as a whole. New questions, and new answers to old questions, combine to provide a more nuanced appreciation of Mexico's historical experience and form the basis of the synthesis found in each chapter.

The course of Mexican history, as with that of any other nation, demonstrates amply that sincerity and guile can occupy the same stage. There is much in the Mexican experience to command admiration and ennoble the human spirit, even if on a few occasions it might also cause an eyebrow to be raised. The historical triumphs Mexico has witnessed have too often been neutralized by disappointments and defeats. But those who study the past know that the lines of historical progress are seldom straight. In the last analysis it is the indelible record of a unique and vital history that makes it possible to best interpret the Mexican present and, while not trespassing on the boundaries of prophecy, to imagine the Mexican future and ponder Mexico's prospects as it enters the morning of a new millennium.

MICHAEL C. MEYER
WILLIAM H. BEEZLEY

The Great Encounter

✦ ✦

Throughout the Americas, October 12 marks the arrival in the Western Hemisphere of Christopher Columbus (or Cristóbal Colón), a native of Genoa, Italy, sailing in search of the spice islands for the Spanish kingdom of Castile. This date in much of western Europe commemorates the same event, but in Spain it refers to much more. October 12 stands as the anniversary in Spanish Christianity of the appearance of the Virgin to Saint James (Santiago), which began the Christian evangelization of the Iberian Peninsula. As a result, Santiago became the patron saint of the Spanish kingdoms. Spain's imperial politics in the Western Hemisphere would thus be shaped in terms of evangelization throughout the colonial era.

The encounter Columbus initiated is distinguishable from earlier European and Asian voyages to the Americas by the size of the migration it inaugurated and the indelible impact it had on the New World's social, economic, and political life. Other voyages—by solitary Asian sailors, daring Viking seamen, and adventuresome South Pacific seamen—although important, did not have the effect of leading to further migrations.

Columbus's voyages served as a prelude to the dramatic meeting in the Aztec capital city, Tenochtitlán, which became Mexico City, between the Spanish adventurer Hernán Cortés and the Aztec emperor Moctezuma II. This encounter cannot be overdramatized, because in some sense it brought together peoples from Europe, America, Africa, and Asia. Moctezuma, the most powerful leader in the Americas, ruler of dozens of different cultural and linguistic groups, received Cortés, a European interloper, and his expedition, which counted among its members at least one African conquistador. Present at the meeting, as a dream, was Asia. Cortés, like Columbus a generation before him, dreamed of reaching the spices of Asia. He sent out several expeditions to find a route from Mexico to the Far East.

This encounter also set the stage for the colonial era in the Americas, in which Europeans and Americans played the dominant role, with Africans (both slave and freed) active in economic and cultural ways and the trickle of Asians participating in minor ways. Mexican silver would distort the Spanish economy, and to a lesser extent the other European economies, and would completely reshape various Asian economies.

The encounter between Cortés and Moctezuma did not initiate an ethnic and cultural melting pot. Both the Spanish kingdoms and the Aztec empire represented cauldrons of biological, cultural, and ethnic diversity. To refer to the peoples and kingdoms of the Iberian Peninsula as Spain during the era before Columbus and for as long as three centuries afterward is more a useful device for historians than actual fact. The region's religious (Christian, Jewish, and Islamic), ethnic (north and south European, and north and west African), and linguistic (Spanish, Catalán, Basque, and Arabic) contributions created a complex multicultural population.

The peoples of the Aztec Empire were even less culturally uniform, although because of their isolation they did share common biological characteristics such as bone structure, hair texture, and blood type. The Aztecs required tribute payments and some religious unity, but otherwise those they had conquered continued their own cultural traditions. Ultimately, then, the meeting of Cortés and Moctezuma only intensified patterns of cultural and ethnic intermixing that had begun centuries before. Nevertheless, the intensity and endurance of this mixture, which resulted in the modern Mexican population, justifies the label the Great Encounter for this meeting of cultures.

Two of our contributors, Professor Susan Schroeder (Chapter 2) and Ross Hassig (Chapter 3) are specialists in Nahuatl, the language of the Aztecs and the dominant language of central Mexico. In their effort to be faithful to the scholarly conventions of Nahuatl linguistics they have chosen to render Native American words without Spanish-language diacritical marks, spelling, or alterations dictated by modern usage. In the interest of clarity for the reader, however, the modern designation is also offered parenthetically immediately after the first usage of the Nahuatl word or phrase.

1

The Spain That Encountered Mexico

HELEN NADER

Urban life occupied center place in the minds of the Spaniards who first encountered Mexico. Scenes of city, commerce, and market-place predominate in the reports and memoirs written by the Spanish conquerors. As the Spanish expedition began marching inland from Veracruz, on the Gulf of Mexico, in August 1519, its captain, Hernán Cortés (1485–1547) paused to describe the first Mexican city he saw, Cempoala. In a letter to the emperor that he wrote on the spot, Cortés estimated that 30,000 people came to buy and sell in Cempoala's marketplace every day. The town's commerce in precious stones, food, medicines, clothing, and footwear was, Cortés claimed, more bountiful than that of Granada when King Ferdinand and Queen Isabella took it and ended Muslim power in Spain in 1492.

Cortés may have been exaggerating, perhaps, but he knew exactly what news would impress Emperor Charles V (king of Spain from 1516 to 1556). He wanted to persuade his emperor that the expedition, which the conquerors, or conquistadores, had undertaken on their own initiative without the emperor's knowledge, deserved royal approbation and rewards. Cortés's companions shared his enthusiasm and his urban focus. One of the hardiest of them, Bernal Díaz del Castillo (1496–1584) recalled the thrill when they caught their first glimpse of Moctezuma's capital, Tenochtitlán, on November 7, 1519: "When we saw all those cities and villages built in the water and other great towns on dry land, and that straight and level causeway leading to Tenochtitlán, we were astounded."

Díaz and Cortés rejoiced at the sight of Mexico's cities, towns, and villages; its stone temples and buildings; its water tamed by and for the community. Díaz reported that "these great towns, temples, and buildings, all made of stone and rising from the water, seemed like an enchanted vision. . . . Indeed, some of our soldiers asked whether it was not all a dream." Above all, the Spanish conquerors described in gleeful detail the great marketplace crowded with people, with its merchandise of every sort being sold from stalls arranged in an orderly manner.

The conquerors knew what to write to the emperor because they shared a common purpose—the discovery of a route to Asia, with its fabled cities and teeming marketplaces. Mexico seemed much like what generations of European merchants and rulers had dreamed of reaching—permanent cities like those in the Old World of Europe. Surely, the similarities suggested that Asia could not be far away.

For Spaniards, cities, towns, and villages formed the heart of civilization because commerce and political life took place in urban marketplaces (plazas). When they toured Tenochtitlán as Moctezuma's guests the next day, they climbed to the top of a temple and looked out over the city's largest marketplace, Tlatelolco. Díaz reported that the marketplace fulfilled a merchant adventurer's dreams: "We turned back to the great market and the swarm of people buying and selling. The mere murmur of their voices talking was loud enough to be heard more than three miles away. Some of our soldiers who had been in many parts of the world, in Constantinople, in Rome, and all over Italy, said that they had never seen a market so well laid out, so large, so orderly, and so full of people." Though they thought Tlatelolco larger, better, and more crowded than any market in Europe, it reminded the conquerors of home. Cortés thought it was twice as large as the principal marketplace in Salamanca, where he had studied Latin as an adolescent. Díaz admitted that Tlatelolco outdid the marketplace of his hometown, Medina del Campo, the site of Europe's annual international wool fair: "You could see every kind of merchandise to be found anywhere in New Spain, laid out in the same way as goods are laid out in my hometown . . . where each line of stalls has its own particular sort. So it was in this great market."

Díaz thanked God that he and his 400 companions had survived so many obstacles on the long trek to this great city. But the success of these Spaniards who first encountered Mexico culminated a much longer journey—Castile's emergence from collapse in the 14th century to this achievement of the European dream.

The conquerors grounded their aspirations in the historic past, not in chivalric novels or imaginative leaps into an unknown world. Their historical memory focused on the Middle Ages, when Europeans had carried on regular long-distance commerce with Asia. During that era, trade with Asia had been monopolized by consortia of merchants from Italian city-states. By galley fleets the Italian merchants shipped European merchandise east through the Mediterranean and Aegean seas to the Black Sea. There they sold heavy wool cloth manufactured by men and women in every part of Europe. With the profits they bought spices, precious stones, silk, and slaves from Asian businessmen, who brought merchandise overland by caravan along what became known as the Silk Route from central Asia, China, and India.

Exchange between Asian and European merchants began to decrease during the 14th century as political turmoil made the overland trade routes dangerous.

Kublai Khan granted the Polo brothers passports to Mongolia. Although the legends surrounding the fabled silk route to China exaggerated the economic importance of silk in European commerce, the popularity of Marco Polo's narrative attests to the central role Asia played in European trading patterns and aspirations.

After bubonic plague in 1347 shattered the Mongol order that had made the long-distance caravans safe, the Ottomans captured the Italian trading outposts on the Black Sea. Italy's merchants were forced to withdraw to their trading posts in Constantinople (now Istanbul) and their islands in the Aegean Sea. Europeans watched helplessly as these mercantile enclaves fell to the Ottomans by the mid-15th century and Genoa lost its last islands in the eastern Mediterranean by the 1470s. Only the republic of Venice continued to trade with Asia, having negotiated a monopoly with the Ottoman rulers of the eastern Mediterranean.

The generation of Europeans born in the middle of the 15th century grew up with an acute sense of how much had been lost. Among these were King Ferdinand of Aragon (1452–1516), Queen Isabella of Castile (1451–1504), and Christopher Columbus of Genoa (1451–1506). They were consumed with a desire to find another way to reach the great commercial cities of Asia. When they were born, few Europeans could have predicted, or even imagined, that Spain would be one of the leaders in finding a new trade route, let alone a continent previously unknown to Europe. Yet this generation's children would be the Spaniards who first encountered Mexico.

Spain achieved its goal of exploration by refashioning itself out of the disasters that put an end to medieval Europe's trade with Asia. The first catastrophe was a change in climate, the Little Ice Age. In Spain and other parts of Europe that had been planting drought-resistant wheat since ancient Roman times, heavy rainfall beginning in 1315, known as "the first bad year," brought food crises. The wheat failed to germinate or did not reach maturity for three years in a row. For the first time in centuries, crop failures and famine devastated large areas of western Europe. To meet the demand for this essential dietary element, as rainy years recurred, Italian merchants imported wheat—and with it plague-infected rats—from the Black Sea. The result was bubonic plague epidemics, depopulated towns, business bankruptcies, dynastic instability, and civil wars.

Spain's medieval society, organized for war against Muslim city-kingdoms in the peninsula, crumbled under the impact of these disasters. The walled cities it had captured from the Muslims, Castile's fabled prizes of the Reconquest, lost population. Frightened citizens fled the cities to escape epidemics. They formed squatter settlements in the countryside, where they could secure a food supply by growing their own. Out of the ruins of the medieval cities organized around war, Spain created towns and villages centering instead on production and commerce. The innovation and stability that enabled Spain to explore and settle the Americas grew out of its experience during the Renaissance as a society reconstructing itself for peace.

Spain suffered the same diseases as the rest of Europe during the Renaissance, an age of unprecedented epidemics. The Black Death epidemic of bubonic plague in 1348–50 caused as much as 40 percent overall mortality in Europe's cities and as much as 60 percent mortality in its smaller towns and villages. Bubonic plague (*Yersinia pestis*) is a bacterial disease transmitted by a vector, the rat flea (*Xenopsylla cheopis*). After the local population of rats (*Rattus rattus*) dies of the infection, the rat flea, in search of a new blood supply, moves to humans and transmits the disease through biting an exposed area of skin, often on the wrist or ankle. The skin around the bite becomes necrotic, forming a hard black plaque from which the initial epidemic in 1348 received its name, the Black Death. The bacillus injected through the flea bite multiplies most rapidly in the capillaries near the lymph nodes, forming a huge, extremely painful bubo, from which the name bubonic plague is derived. Before the discovery of antibiotics, 60 percent of those infected died, regardless of their state of nutrition. The great city of Barcelona never recovered from the population, manufacturing, and commercial decline it suffered as a result of bubonic plague in the 14th century. Castile, too, suffered huge population losses from plague epidemics in 1575–77, 1596, 1601–2, and 1630.

Plague and its secondary infections killed infants at a higher rate than it did adults, but other endemic ever present infectious diseases year after year had equally disastrous effects. In nonplague years, one-quarter of all children died before the age of six of measles, scarlet fever, diphtheria, whooping cough, and diarrhea. No segment of the population escaped the ravages of these diseases.

A new infectious disease, typhus (caused by bacteria-like rickettsia), entered Spain and Italy in the late 15th century. Typhus epidemics typically broke out in crowded shipboard conditions and may have developed in the galley fleets during the new warfare against the Ottomans in the western Mediterranean. Andrés Bernáldez and most of his parishioners in the town of Los Palacios near Seville suffered this new disease in 1507, during an epidemic that swept through Castile killing about 40 percent of the population in the cities and towns it reached. In the Extremadura farm town of Cabeza de Vaca so few citizens survived the typhus epidemic that they declared the place unhealthful, tore down the houses, salted the ground (to make the land sterile and therefore prevent any future crop cultivation), and moved to other towns.

The record showing epidemics of smallpox (a viral disease) in Europe, including Spain, is negligible before the 1560s; a milder form of pox probably prevailed. The modern notion that Europeans were innately immune to bacterial and viral infections is both biologically and historically incorrect. Virulent smallpox entered Spain in the early 17th century and held a prominent place among the diseases of the 17th and 18th centuries. Whole families of aristocratic children, for example, died of smallpox, leaving a handful of lucky distant cousins to inherit multiple noble titles and vast fortunes. Every level of society, from kings to paupers, was touched by smallpox.

An influenza pandemic (widespread outbreak) in 1580 resembled the devastating influenza of 1918 in that morbidity and mortality were especially high among young adults. Hundreds of young Castilian men, in a vast army invading Portugal in 1580, died of influenza without ever seeing battle. In contrast to the usual high mortality among infants and the elderly in most flu epidemics, this pandemic killed young adults, leaving a reduced number of adults of childbearing age to replace the population lost to bubonic plague and smallpox over the next 50 years. The combined effects of epidemics and a low birth rate resulted in a Spanish population that was one-third lower during the 17th century than in the century before.

These population losses opened the way for new political and economic leaders, who faced among themselves the problems of disease and early death. High infant mortality led to dynastic instability in monarchical societies. The Trastamara monarchs of Spain (1369–1516) were afflicted with tuberculosis, which carried them off at an average age of 37. Their successors, the Habsburgs (1516–1700), suffered agonies with tubercular joints and respiratory crises, and more than a dozen royal children died before reaching adulthood. Early deaths—together with a high rate of insanity, heirless kings, incompetent male heirs, and wars of succession that bedeviled the monarchies of England, France, and Spain during the Renaissance—gave rise to new ruling families.

Six separate medieval monarchies coalesced during the 15th century to form Spain. An illegitimate branch of the Castilian royal family, the Trastamara, bound them together. The founder of the dynasty, Henry II (ruled 1369–79), seized the throne of Castile during a brutal civil war in 1366–69. Henry, the third of Alfonso XI's illegitimate sons, could not be considered legitimate by any standards. And, having killed his half-brother King Peter, he was both a regicide and a fratricide. In 1412, after the death of the last legitimate male heir to the crown of Aragon, electors chose a brother of the Trastamara king of Castile, Ferdinand I (ruled 1412–16), as king of Aragon and Valencia and prince of Catalonia.

When Isabella, princess of Castile, married Ferdinand, prince of Aragon, in 1469, neither had a clear legal right to inherit their respective kingdoms. (Isabella did acquire her kingdom through civil war, five years after the marriage, and Ferdinand inherited his five years after that.) Nevertheless, together they reunited the Trastamara dynasty and went on to conquer the Muslim kingdom of Granada in 1492.

In 1512, Ferdinand conquered a sixth monarchy, the kingdom of Navarre, to which he claimed rights by inheritance. The individual monarchies in the union retained their own separate laws, customs, and languages, while their combined strengths enabled the Trastamara monarchs to pursue a single-minded policy of expansion.

The same physical afflictions that had wiped out so many ruling families earlier now set the stage for a new dynasty, the Habsburgs, to plunge Spain into the politics of northern Europe. The only son of King Ferdinand and Queen Isabella died at the age of 18, leaving a pregnant widow who gave birth to a stillborn child. The devastated monarchs summoned back to Castile from Portugal their cherished eldest daughter, Isabella. She had been widowed weeks after her marriage to one Portuguese crown prince, then married to another, and would die in childbirth just days after receiving the oath officially acknowledging her as the heiress apparent. Her child, Miguel, died at the age of two.

Succession to the Spanish kingdoms then passed to the monarchs' second daughter, Juana, married to Philip of Burgundy, son of the Holy Roman Emperor, a Habsburg. Because they had six living children, the succession seemed secure in Juana and Philip. Juana's behavior became so erratic, however—modern writers nicknamed her Juana la Loca (Juana the Madwoman), that she was incarcerated permanently as, apparently, a schizophrenic. Charles, her eldest son, came to Spain for the first time in 1518, when he was 18 years old, to receive the oath of the Cortés (parliament) acknowledging him as king. With Charles, heir presumptive to his paternal grandfather, the Habsburg archduke of Austria and Holy Roman Emperor, came a whole range of new possibilities for expansion.

The part of Spain that refashioned itself most successfully throughout these crises was the kingdom of Castile, which became one of the most dynamic countries in Europe. By 1530, Castile's population numbered 6 million, while all the other Spanish kingdoms together counted one-half million inhabitants. The most important reason behind Castile's growth was a legal fact: Castilians were free men and women. Serfdom had never developed in Castile, and King Ferdinand extended this freedom to the serfs of Aragon in 1485. By the mid–15th century, European monarchs had achieved consensus that their subjects could not be enslaved. By royal decree in 1500, Queen Isabella guaranteed this legal freedom to Castile's American Indian subjects with the exception of those who rebelled against the Spaniards, who were cannibals, or who were already slaves to other Indians. The royal policy toward nonsubjects was the opposite, however: Non-Christians captured in war in Europe could be enslaved, as could subjects who rebelled against the royal sovereignty anywhere. In addition, European monarchs permitted the purchase of enslaved Africans from the Portuguese, who held a monopoly on slaving in sub-Saharan Africa.

Spaniards were free citizens, *vecinos*, of their home cities, towns, and villages. Virtually every notarized document of the period begins "I, John Doe, citizen of

the town of X, and I, Jane Smith, his wife and citizen of the town of X, do hereby
. . . " These citizens governed themselves through democratic town meetings and
elected town councils and judges. Each citizen household possessed a vote, but
only the married men had the right to cast the vote in a town meeting and could
hold municipal office. Women could speak in town meetings, and widows possessed the vote of their household. But women could not hold office or vote, and
widows had to ask a male proxy—usually a son or the town judge—to cast
their votes.

Whether noblemen or freemen, clergy or farmers, Spaniards lived in cities,
towns, and villages. Farmers walked from their homes in the residential district
to their fields and back daily. The isolated farmhouse in the countryside was the
rare exception. The few people whose occupations required them to live outside
the towns—millers, roadside-inn keepers, and shepherds, for instance—were
regarded as outside the norms of society. Popular and high literature alike often
depicted these exceptions to the rule as lecherous, venal, and violent. The fictional
Don Quixote's bizarre adventures, first published in 1605, could take place only
outside the norm of municipal life.

The most dramatic sociological innovation of the age of plague took place
during the 15th century, in the form of thousands of new towns and villages. The
greatest expansion of that century unfolded within Spain itself, initiated by and
implemented through ordinary people. In 1492, when Columbus launched his
momentous voyage from the seaport of Palos, the town was barely a century old.
In this, it was typical of the new settlements in Castile. Palos first appears in a
Spanish document dated 1380, when it was a squatter settlement within the
municipal territory of the town of Moguer. That year, King John I of Castile
legally separated the village of Palos from the town of Moguer, made it into a
town, and sold it to a nobleman from Seville, Alvar Pérez de Guzmán.

Alvar Pérez, as *señor* (lord) of Palos, proceeded to develop the economic infrastructure of his new town in order to attract families. First the king exempted
from all royal taxes the first 50 families that would come to settle in Palos.
Because almost no land was suitable for cultivating wheat, Alvar Pérez planted
olive trees and built a warehouse on the shore, where the seamen of Palos could
auction their fresh fish. He drew up municipal ordinances and delegated his judicial and executive authority over Palos to the town council. This council, elected
annually by the voting citizens, took the oath of office in the presence of the lord
or his proxy and received from him the *varas* (staffs) of justice. After Alvar Pérez
died in 1394, his daughters Isabel and Juana authorized the building of a Franciscan monastery, Santa María de La Rábida, within the town's borders.

The town council and its judges developed the new town's economy further.
By the mid–15th century, Palos had a municipal shipyard and an extensive salt
extraction industry; the town trapped seawater at high tide in shallow ponds (salt
pans), which evaporated quickly in the summer heat, leaving a thick crust of salt
for the men of Palos to harvest. With this municipal income, the town council
built a parish church as well as a civic marketplace where the citizens carried on

their everyday business. The town's sole financial obligation to its lord was to pay a 5 percent sales tax on the fish auctioned on the beach to wholesalers.

The prosperity of Palos attracted new settlers, even though these latecomers did not receive the royal tax exemptions the first ones had. Most of the town's citizens made their living from the sea as fishermen, import-export merchants, shipbuilders, and pirates—the latter, almost a standard occupation in fishing communities. Fish, olive oil, and salt—the trinity of the preserved-fish industry—were the town's major exports, wheat its main import. By 1478, the town's population had grown to 600 households.

On May 23, 1492, the men of Palos responded to a royal summons to attend a town council meeting in the parish church of San Jorge. There the town crier read a letter from Queen Isabella ordering Palos to contribute two caravels (shallow-drafted ships that could safely enter inlets and coastal waters) for three months' royal service. The town clerk, Francisco Fernández, recorded the reading of the royal order. He certified that two noncitizens were present: a Franciscan from the monastery of La Rábida, Juan Pérez, and a foreign businessman, Christopher Columbus, as well as the usual town judge and three town councilmen. The customary practice then was for most city and town councils to pledge to obey royal decrees but not execute them until they could negotiate better terms. But in this instance Palos had to comply, because its seamen had been charged with violating Portuguese waters and the Spanish monarchy had paid heavy fines. Now Palos either had to reimburse the royal treasury or see its citizens imprisoned.

Under these circumstances, the town council paid the cost of leasing two caravels, the *Niña* and the *Pinta*. The local businessmen who owned these ships, members of the Pinzón family—probably the trespassers who had wrongly entered foreign waters—agreed to captain the two ships. Thus the seamen of Palos sailed into the pages of history. A few days later, in the port of Sanlúcar de Barrameda, Christopher Columbus leased a large Basque cargo ship, *Santa María*, from her owner, Juan de la Cosa, who agreed to captain her.

The interplay here between the town of Palos and the Spanish monarchy reveals the normal relationship at the time between local and royal government. Because the Trastamara dynasty had seized power through extraordinary measures, it had to be innovative to maintain itself in power. The illegitimacy of the Trastamara impelled them to seek support aggressively from nontraditional sources: the small towns and villages that were flourishing while the cities languished. Any growing village that found itself chafing under the rule of its governing city welcomed the Trastamara policy of conferring municipal autonomy on villages and giving them to nobles as *seigneurial* (subject to a lord) towns.

Lords and kings delegated the governing of their towns to the towns' councils and rarely interfered, with the result that towns enjoyed nearly as much autonomy as cities. The town sheriff, for instance, arrested suspects and brought them before the town judge, who heard cases, pronounced sentence, and imposed fines and punishments. Town judges held jurisdiction over all criminal and civil cases

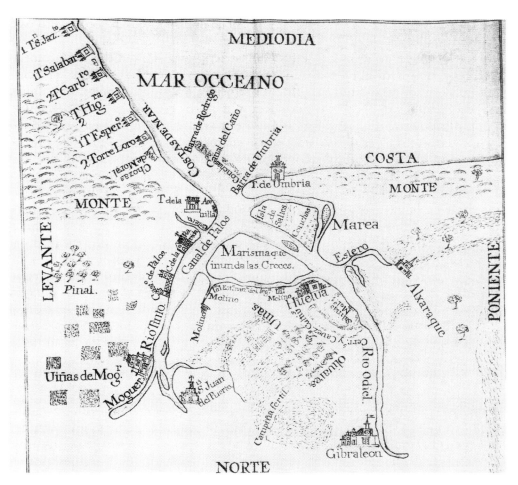

This 16th-century map of the Odiel River region served as a tool for navigating the ever-changing channel of the estuary. The mapmaker highlighted the major landmarks on the coast. The two tallest buildings in the town of Palos, the *castillo* (watchtower) around the squatter settlement, which was first developed in the 14th century, and the convent of La Rábida, would have been visible to ships entering the estuary. The castillo is labeled *Cast. de Palos* and is near the center to the left; the convent is above the castillo and is labeled *C. de la Ravida.*

arising within the town boundaries and exercised the power of capital punishment. Town councils owned and administered the municipal commons, such as the salt mines of Palos. For this autonomy the citizens of seignorial towns cooperated with the Trastamara monarchs.

In order to prevent themselves from being overthrown by neighbors with more legal right to inherit the throne, the Trastamara dynasty simply absorbed adjacent realms. These acquisitions by the Trastamara dynasty shaped local government in most of the Iberian Peninsula. There were in fact no regional governments—provincial governments were not created in Spain until the 19th century. Instead the monarchy depended on, and communicated directly with, municipal governments to carry out royal policy and collect taxes. The city and town councils wrote directly to their kings and queens when carrying out their administrative duties on behalf of the monarchy or requesting favors in return. This correspondence between small municipalities and their monarchs has left us a vast treasury of testimony about the details of everyday life witnessed by ordinary citizens.

The Column of Justice stands in the marketplace of Villalar, Spain, in front of the town hall on the right. Members of the town council took turns standing on the steps of the column (called a *picota* or *rollo*) to preside over the market, inspect weights and measures, witness contracts, set maximum prices, and adjudicate disputes.

Rulers and ruled alike shared the most basic assumption in Spanish society — that municipalities were the fundamental, indispensable units of civilization, the cells that made up the body politic. Such a cell was a complex system of parts and events, all interconnected in a dynamic system of relationships. Citizens, lords, monarchs, and clergy shared a detailed — and usually unexpressed — knowledge of the internal mechanisms of the municipality and its natural course of development. They took for granted the internal workings and political competence of the town councils. They understood the legal constraints of the system but knew how to maneuver around them to achieve their goals. Spain, the most powerful absolute monarchy in 16th-century Europe, governed itself through direct connections between the king and thousands of minute municipal corporations.

Every city and town had its own *fuero* (constitution) that defined its relationship with the king or lord and contained the local laws governing commerce, contracts, and inheritance. Despite the number and diversity of the different codes of law, an ideal of equality prevailed in the inheritance laws throughout the Spanish kingdoms. The only inheritance subject to the rule of primogeniture (inheritance by only the oldest son) was succession to the monarchy.

The common notion that younger sons emigrated to the West Indies because they would not inherit has no basis in Spanish law or practice. In general, all the children of a marriage — both male and female — had the right to inherit equitable portions of their parents' property. Parents could not exclude a child, except in extreme cases such as if a child attempted to murder a parent. Because the laws mandated, and the towns' judges enforced, the partition of inheritance, parents had no need to draw up wills, which were extremely rare in the 15th century. In Mexico, wills would become more common, even though partible inheritance remained the rule because of the great distance between family members on both sides of the Atlantic.

Spaniards from the king on down to the farmer-citizen of the smallest town shared a widespread commitment to a participatory tradition of town government. In Castile, towns and villages averaged about 150 households and held town meetings regularly. But once a town grew to more than some 300 or so households, factions became too powerful for town meetings to arrive at a consensus. The larger towns and cities thus came to dispense with town meetings in favor of decision making by the town council.

These practices of municipal government became entrenched in Castilian society not just because they seemed indispensable and natural but also because they were automatic. That which is most habitual most strongly resists change— and also escapes notice. Many historians tell us, for example, that the Spaniards were very litigious, and they are right. Few notice, however, that it was the towns that initiated the overwhelming majority of lawsuits, and that every such lawsuit began with a town meeting in which the citizens voted unanimously to give their power of attorney to a specific lawyer. The very depth at which municipal democratic habits were embedded in Castilian society makes them almost invisible.

Spaniards found that their need for power over their daily lives could be satisfied only by participating in municipal government. Castile's citizens rose up in protest against anyone who tried to deprive them of this essential right. In the town of Medellín, the citizens who were knights and noncommissioned officers in the municipal militia traditionally elected the town judge and town councilmen. But in 1480, the lord, the Count of Medellín, began to choose these officials himself. By 1488, the traditional electors were so upset with this infringement on their powers that they protested to King Ferdinand and Queen Isabella. Among the 26 signatories of the protest were Martín Cortés, father of the infant Hernán Cortés, and eight women. In such cases the monarchs nearly always sided with the citizens and against the lord, as happened in this case.

Spaniards' hunger for land and water also bound them to urban life. By 1500, all the land of Spain was incorporated into more than 32,000 cities, towns, and villages. Farmers owned their own fields and gardens as private property, but the *montes* (uncultivated commons) and its resources belonged to the *común*, the municipal corporation. This town council controlled all the standing and running water, the forests, pasture, game, wild fruits and herbs, and quarries. The town councils owned the commons, so the judges and councilmen not only administered local justice but also managed the natural resources of the municipal territory.

The town councils provided for the common welfare by setting prices and inspecting weights and measures in the plaza, hiring the town schoolteacher, and building bridges, fountains, laundries, and churches. The council developed and managed the infrastructure of the town's farmland by constructing dams and irrigation systems, terracing hillsides, and clearing sections of the commons to expand cultivation.

Agriculture and commerce expanded as Spain's population grew; in fact, the two were indistinguishable. Spanish farmers owned their own farms and in slack seasons worked as artisans, teamsters, and retail merchants. Urban wholesalers and bureaucrats owned farms. With growing demand for food and wine, Castilian farmers increased and diversified their production. They added more land to cultivation by planting hillsides with perennials, especially grapevines and olive trees. In response to rising demand for textiles, rope, and paper, farmers planted flax and hemp, and increased the size of their transhumant (migratory) sheep flocks. Farm towns built processing facilities to turn these crops into market commodities. Typically, town councils constructed threshing grounds, wool-washing stations, flax- and hemp-soaking ponds, and fulling mills.

Some of Spain's most spectacular fortunes in wool, international trade, and land started from modest beginnings in the early 15th century, when Castile regained its pre-Black Death population levels and embarked on nearly a century of domestic growth. With rising fortunes came upward social mobility. Successful farmers became wealthy businessmen who used their plow mules and oxen to transport their produce, sold it in the cities, used the profits to buy city goods, and sold these back in their hometowns.

Citizens of the largest cities and the smallest farm towns alike saw town life as the goal worth striving for and thought it indispensable for their commercial agrarian economy. Each town prudently undertook to provide its citizens, individually and communally, with the infrastructure of commerce: plazas, roads, bridges, ferries, hospitals, and roadside inns for traveling merchants. Our modern distinctions between rural and urban, agrarian and commercial did not exist in their world or in how they designed their towns and cities.

Just as Spain was a monarchy of cities and towns, a noble estate was a cluster of towns. The Trastamara monarchs gave away the right to govern towns as hereditary property to military leaders who had helped them gain the throne in the civil war. To ensure that these new seigneurial towns would remain in loyal hands, the Trastamara monarchs required that they be placed in *mayorazgos* (perpetual trusts), of which the monarchs were the trustees and the new lords the beneficiaries.

After 1400, the monarchs introduced another innovation, giving hereditary titles of nobility to the lords of seigneurial towns. In 1400, Castile had fewer than a dozen noble titles, none of them hereditary. By the end of the century, the kingdom boasted more than 100 hereditary titles of nobility.

These titles did not transfer lordship from the monarchy to a lord; instead, each grant of a noble title ended lawsuits or feuds that had erupted after the untimely deaths of direct heirs to an already existing *señorío* (lordship). For this reason, each noble title was the name of a town whose lordship had been in dispute between rival heirs. The first hereditary title was Count of Alba, granted in 1439 by King John II and elevated to Duke of Alba in 1465 by King Henry IV. In 1520, Charles V ranked the titled nobles and designated the wealthiest as grandees. The dates when those hereditary noble titles were created, and the size of their annual incomes by 1520, shown in the table below, indicate how quickly the nobility was changing and how widely noble incomes diverged from one another in 15th–century Castile.

Top Grandees of Castile in the Order Established by Emperor Charles V in 1520

Title	Date Created	Family	Annual Income in Ducats
Constable of Castile	1492	Velasco	50,000
Admiral of Castile	1405	Enríquez	32,000
Duke of Alba	1465	Toledo	30,000
Duke of Infantado	1475	Mendoza	30,000
Duke of Medina Sidonia	1445	Guzmán	50,000
Duke of Béjar	1485	Zúñiga	24,000
Duke of Medinaceli	1479	La Cerda	16,000
Duke of Alburquerque	1464	La Cueva	24,000
Duke of Arcos	1493	Ponce de León	30,000
Duke of Escalona	1472	Pacheco	24,000

Most nobles lived in cities, where they sought to increase their fortunes by, among other pursuits, acting as international merchants. These lords had surpluses to sell because their seigneurial towns paid them annuities half in cash and half in commodities such as wheat, barley, wine, olive oil, cheese, silk, and honey. Nobles incurred no stigma by engaging in wholesale or international commerce (though this would change, in theory at least, during the Bourbon period, the 18th century). Most of them tried to capitalize on their in-kind revenues by building various facilities in the cities where they lived. The second Count of Tendilla (1442–1515), captain-general of the newly conquered kingdom of Granada, invested in that city by purchasing buildings in the heart of the city and renting out their ground floors as shops and upper floors as apartments. He bought flour mills on the city's two rivers, a teamsters' inn at the juncture of the city's two busiest streets, and a tavern just outside the principal city gate, Bibrambla. He bought a galley ship to transport the horses he bred and sold to Castilian garrisons in North Africa. Foolishly, however, he did not buy marine insurance and thus lost his investment when the ship sank off Gibraltar in a pirate attack. Other nobles who had more success with maritime ventures built their own fleets or ports.

The most notable international shipping magnates of Castile, the dukes of Medinaceli and Medina Sidonia, combined their military and commercial roles, to the advantage of themselves and the monarchy. These two titled nobles possessed as royal monopolies the tuna catch off Spain's southwestern Atlantic coast. There they built packing facilities on shore and purchased fleets to transport the

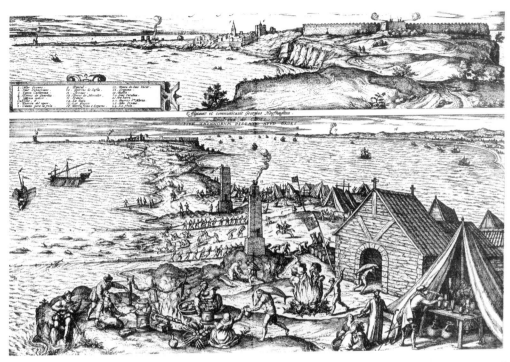

The annual *almadraba*, or tuna catch, produced the major income for the Cádiz region and the dukes of Medina Sidonia. Two rows of men pull nets full of live tunas onto the beach, while others kill the fish with harpoons. In the foreground, women cook some of the catch, and a man carries a tuna on his back into the warehouse. The dukes of Medina Sidonia shipped the preserved tuna, packed in salt or olive oil, to markets in Italy, France, and northern Europe.

preserved tuna to markets throughout Europe. But Muslim piracy in the Strait of Gibraltar, between Africa and Spain, either by North African or Granadan ships, posed a serious threat to their export business.

To counter this threat, in 1462, the second Duke of Medina Sidonia financed and led a force that conquered Gibraltar. The third duke, Juan de Guzmán (1466–1507), financed a fleet and army that conquered Melilla from the Muslim king of Tlemcén in 1496. Holding this North African entrepôt (trading outpost) as his own territory, Medina Sidonia commanded an advantage in maritime shipping through the Strait of Gibraltar. Meanwhile, the Duke of Medinaceli decided to build his own port and warehousing facilities in his town of Puerto de Santa María, across the bay from Cádiz. During this period of expansion he employed a Genoese merchant named Christopher Columbus in his export business. Through such individual, privately financed initiatives Spain grew in power and wealth throughout the 15th century, creating a society of merchant farmers and noble merchants eager to engage in world commerce by land and sea. The grandees of Castile were a new nobility actively engaged in domestic and international trade.

Ferdinand and Isabella refused to give hereditary lordship to anyone in the Americas, Spaniard or Indian, in order to retain the seigneurial income of the New World for their royal treasury. Their grandson, Charles V, gave conquerors in the Americas *encomienda* (lifetime lordship) over some Native American towns. He also bent the royal policy in exceptional cases, granting two hereditary lordships in the Americas. In 1529, he gave the conqueror of Mexico, Hernán Cortés, hereditary lordship over the valley of Oaxaca, with the title Marquis of the

expectation of equality, the entrenched elite and longtime Christians who hoped to advance socially and politically erected formidable barriers.

Municipal office was the most avidly sought route to social and political status. In Toledo conflict over eligibility for city offices erupted during a tax revolt in 1449 when the city council passed a statute to prohibit those whose ancestors had been Jews from holding public office. This tactic was part of the council's stated intention to protect the Christian faith from converts who, it claimed, were likely to relapse. At the time, many of Toledo's city councilmen and municipal officials, including tax collectors, were converts. Both pope and king disapproved of this "statute of pure blood," but the city passed it several times during the last half of the century, and by 1566, the monarchy had also begun advocating it. The statute did not keep converts off the city council; it just made such offices more expensive and complicated to buy. Men who were popularly known or suspected to be of Jewish heritage continued to buy seats on the city council and grants of tax exemption called *hidalguías* from the crown municipal office.

Religious tension in Toledo and many other cities intensified when cathedral chapters engaged in power struggles with their bishops or cathedral deans. Prejudice against converts and against men of low social class often shaped attitudes among the canon priests on Toledo's cathedral staff, for example. During the 15th century, the Castilian monarchs had usurped the traditional right of cathedral chapters to nominate new bishops and, to avoid the problem of ending up with prelates from aristocratic families who wielded too much power, began nominating men of lesser social status. In the mid–16th century, the canons of the cathedral, many of them members of local elite convert families, resented the rude, heavy-handed manner of their new archbishop, Cardinal Juan Martínez de Silíceo, which they attributed to his nonaristocratic background and foreign education. The unpopular archbishop and his intransigent canons showed their disdain for each other in a protracted dispute over the qualifications for new appointees; the archbishop wanted to eliminate men of lower social class. In the end, they compromised by excluding persons from each other's backgrounds; the new cathedral statute stated that in the future only men of high social status and old Christian heritage could hold cathedral offices.

Tensions simmered wherever friars preached. In the last decade of the 14th century, massive conversions to Christianity followed urban violence against Jews, inspired by Franciscan friars fired with a vision of total conversion. Then, in the 15th century, itinerant Dominican preachers set off popular riots attacking new converts. As a result, in 1478 the monarchs, in an effort to defuse popular violence toward converts, instituted the Spanish Inquisition.

This ecclesiastical court moved into a city or town, invited Christians to confess their lapses, imposed penance, and then used information gained from these voluntary confessions to apprehend and interrogate others. From 1540 (the earliest period for which documentation survives for all of Spain) to 1700, Inquisition tribunals tried 44,000 cases, an average of 275 per year. Some 22,000 of these cases were tried during the height of the Inquisition's activity, from 1560 through 1614. Executions in effigy of those tried in absentia or postmortem averaged 2 percent of those tried, and actual executions averaged 2.3 percent of those tried. The Inquisition tribunal in the kingdom of Aragon led with 29 percent of all those executed. Tomás de Torquemada, the Dominican inquisitor-general for Castile and Aragon, persuaded King Fedinand and Queen Isabella to expel the Jews from Spain in 1492.

The Inquisition policed the beliefs and practices of those who claimed to be Christian. By this time, Franciscan and Dominican preachers moving from city to city had succeeded in publicizing their ambition to convert all Spaniards to Christianity. But the Inquisition never achieved this objective. In fact, Torquemada concluded from evidence extracted in Inquisition trials that unconverted Jews were actively encouraging converts to relapse. The monarchs decided that the only way to protect converts was to expel the Jews. Accordingly, they issued a royal decree to this effect in January 1492, requiring all Jews to convert to Christianity or leave Spain by the end of July. About one-half of the Spanish Jewish population quickly converted, while the remainder—perhaps 50,000 Jews— traveled by sea and land to Portugal; Navarre, on the French border, and North Africa. Then, not content with limiting their activities to Spain, the Franciscans expanded their ambitions to converting Africa—a special enthusiasm of the monastery at La Rábida in Palos. When that project failed, they shifted their sights to the Americas.

The monarchs meanwhile poured their resources into conquering the kingdom of Granada, the one Muslim government still remaining on the Iberian Peninsula. Their decision to conquer Granada was driven by commercial ambition. Spain had long been one of the great seafaring nations of Europe. By the end of the 15th century it had become a leader in the new enterprise of exploring the Atlantic. As noted earlier, the Trastamaras wanted to expand their empire by entering into commerce with Asia. Ferdinand's kingdom of Aragon was expanding east into the Mediterranean, engaged in an ongoing sea war against ships from Genoa, Italy, to control the shipping lanes to Corsica, Sardinia, and Sicily. Ferdinand himself initiated the war of territorial conquest that won the kingdom of Naples for Aragon.

In contrast, Castile's fishing and merchant fleets were expanding west into the Atlantic. Though they had ports on both the Mediterranean and Atlantic, Castilian ships that tried to bring cargoes from the Mediterranean to north European ports through the Strait of Gibraltar met two formidable obstacles—the Muslim kingdom of Granada on the Iberian Peninsula and the Portuguese fleet on the Atlantic.

The Trastamara rulers had a powerful economic reason to maintain their alliance with Granada. Every year, the king of Granada paid about one-quarter of his royal income, approximately 12,000 gold doubloons, in tribute to the monarch of Castile. Furthermore, the Castilian trade with North Africa flowed fairly smoothly through Granadan and Italian middlemen. A treaty dating back to 1279 with a consortium of Genoese merchants gave them a monopolistic trading post in Granada's seaport of Málaga.

King Ferdinand and Queen Isabella, on the other hand, had powerful commercial reasons to try to gain control of Granada. For one, they wanted to protect Spanish shipping, which remained vulnerable to attack from North Africa by sea and from Granada by land. More urgently, the fabled silk markets of Granada and Málaga lured these monarchs to opt for potential commercial profits over the more secure tribute. With this aim, in 1482, they began annual war campaigns against the kingdom of Granada. From that year until the end of 1485, the Castilian policy of frontal attacks against the city of Granada itself failed. The surrounding terrain proved too rugged for a rapid advance, and the supply line was too long through hostile territory to support a prolonged campaign.

Finally, Ferdinand and Isabella isolated the city from its seaports and surrounding farmland. In 1487, they besieged and captured Málaga and enslaved 11,000 to 15,000 of its citizens because they had resisted so fiercely. The lesson was not lost on the people of Granada. As one port after another fell to the Christian armies, the citizens of the capital escaped to Africa. Granada surrendered without a fight and received favorable terms for doing so. The defeated Muslim ruler transferred sovereignty to King Ferdinand and Queen Isabella on January 2, 1492, and the Castilian monarchs officially entered the city on January 6.

The first task facing the victors was to appraise the booty. Royal treasury secretary Hernando de Zafra's massive survey of property in the city and its countryside lasted until 1497. This review shaped how the city would be rebuilt by identifying and appraising each abandoned house, parcel of land, tax, and endowment to transfer them intact to the victors.

The monarchs distributed the spoils in the centuries-old process of *repartimiento* (distribution). In Granada, the Catholic monarchs took for the royal domain all the taxes, land, palaces, fortresses, and city walls that had previously been the property of the Muslim royal family. They gave to the church the endowments that had previously supported Islamic religious and charitable foundations. They also gave certain public properties, such as Muslim cemeteries, livestock and fish markets, water reservoirs, fountains, public baths, sewer systems, streets, and the surrounding pastures and wilderness to the municipal corporation of Granada. These public properties became the commons, owned by the city council. Finally, the monarchs distributed the abandoned lands and houses to individual conquerors. The city and the monarchs amended and redefined the terms of the distribution for several years as they became aware of unexpected needs and found resources that had been overlooked.

After distributing the spoils, the victors repopulated the conquered city. They brought their wives and children to Granada and occupied its formerly Muslim buildings. The second Count of Tendilla's wife and young children joined him and set up housekeeping in the Alhambra, of which he was the royal commander.

Queen Isabella, along with King Ferdinand, searched for new sources of income after their conquest of the Kingdom of Granada ended the annual tribute that the Muslim kingdom had paid to the monarchs of Castile for more than a century. The urgency of their financial needs emerges clearly in the business partnership they signed with Christopher Columbus, the Santa Fe Capitulation. They were willing to take great risks to gain access to Asian markets.

Their first child born in this new home, Antonio de Mendoza, would one day be the first viceroy of New Spain, the representative of the king himself.

Under the terms of the capitulation agreement, the Islamic inhabitants of Granada were allowed to retain their religion, laws, and customs. But the same taxes they used to pay to the Muslim ruler they now paid to the Christian monarchs. During this transitional period, Muslim officials collaborated with Christian royal officers in administering the city. All indications are that the royal administrators treated the Muslim population with tolerance and tried to accommodate the city's bicultural population. It is clear that the Muslims vastly outnumbered the Christians.

By 1497, enough Christians had established residence in the city to establish a municipal government. The first city council meetings of Granada, begun in 1497, have continued to the present day. Nevertheless, the city failed to prosper.

The first problem erupted when the new archbishop of Toledo, Cardinal Francisco Jiménez de Cisneros, visited Granada in late 1499 and began baptizing Muslim orphans. Infuriated by what they perceived to be a violation of the peace agreement, some Muslims rioted and killed two sheriffs. The violence in the city stopped only after diplomatic intervention by the Count of Tendilla. But by this time the uprising had spread to the surrounding mountain villages. Royal troops directed by King Ferdinand eventually put down the revolt. Ferdinand and Isabella considered that the agreement had been irretrievably broken by this revolt and required the Muslim population to convert to Christianity by the beginning of the year 1501. The preconquest population of Granada, estimated at about 100,000, declined after this as Muslims moved to Africa rather than convert.

The city was further devastated by typhus in 1507, which carried off Archbishop Hernando de Talavera and the Count of Tendilla's wife and youngest children. By 1512, the total population of Granada had dropped to some 80,000 and continued to decline throughout the 16th century. Its conquest by Christian forces transformed Granada from the capital city of the last Muslim kingdom on the Iberian Peninsula into a defeated, deeply divided outpost on the periphery of Castilian political affairs.

✦ ✦ ✦

The secret of the Portuguese maritime expansion of the years 1400–1580 lay in its being a significant departure from the Italian model. Instead of working through consortia of businessmen as the Italians had, the Portuguese expansion made use of the royal monopoly. The king or other members of the royal family commissioned each voyage and selected which ship owner was to captain the venture. After a successful voyage, the monarch divided the profits with the captain, who in turn distributed a share of his profits to the crew.

Portuguese merchants, like their Italian predecessors, did not treat their trading stations as colonies. Only military and royal administrators were on hand in foreign outposts to protect merchants as they arrived, unloaded their cargoes, loaded their purchases, and departed. In Africa, India, South Asia, Japan, and Brazil the Portuguese established trading posts without family households, a civilian community, or civil governments.

Within this mold, Portuguese expansion in the Atlantic evolved throughout the 15th century. One of the royal princes, Henry the Navigator (1394–1460), took a prominent role in the capture of Ceuta, opposite Gibraltar, in 1415, then sponsored voyages of commercial exploration in the Atlantic and south along the west coast of Africa. One of his ships brought back the first slaves and gold from Guinea. In 1448, Henry built a fort and warehouse on the island of Arguin (in modern Mauritania). A few years later this trading post was successfully exploiting the Guinea trade; an Italian traveler reported that many Portuguese ships arrived every year bringing wheat, cloth, and horses and taking away gold, some 700 or 800 slaves, silk, and cotton. But on the African coast, the Portuguese were not able to take the territory by force. They were repeatedly repulsed by armed native forces in canoes who attacked Portuguese landing crews and prevented them from reaching the shore.

Instead of attempting conquest, the Portuguese royal family negotiated with local rulers to gain for themselves a monopoly on trade between African ports and European merchants. In their most important African market, the Saharan port of Safi (now in Morocco), terminus of a caravan route where traders from the interior sold raw wool and bought salt and wool cloth, they acquired exclusive European trading rights. When Genoese merchants tried to trade in Safi in 1454, for example, the Portuguese judge there found them guilty of violating the monopoly and cut off their hands. It seems safe to assume that when Christopher Columbus's father dealt in raw wool from Safi a few years later, he bought it from a Portuguese vendor.

In 1480, King John of Portugal negotiated to establish a trading post on the Guinea mainland near a native gold-mining operation. The local ruler agreed to give the Portuguese sole trading rights in the area and allowed John to build a fortified trading post there, Saint George of the Mine. The profitability of this particular post became legendary. The point that royal sponsorship and protection were necessary for business success when dealing with overseas governments was not lost on other rulers.

Royal monopolies garnered huge profits. The Portuguese trade monopoly in West Africa became the envy of every ruler in Europe, especially the Castilian kings, who proceeded to compete with and imitate them. Ferdinand and Isabella incorporated the key elements of Portuguese success into the contract that launched their enterprise in the Americas. In the contract called the Santa Fe Capitulations, signed on April 17, 1492, Ferdinand and Isabella formed a business partnership with Columbus to engage in trade and commerce with Asia.

As the monarchs' sole partner, Columbus had the right to supply one-eighth of the cargo on all voyages to Asia and take one-eighth of the profits. The monarchs determined the destination and route, chose Columbus to command the voyage and manage the trading, and provided the ships, crew, provisions, and cargo. The king and queen supplied Columbus with letters of introduction to Asian rulers and empowered him to negotiate trade treaties with these rulers on behalf of the Castilian monarchy. Thus, from the very beginning, the Spanish voyages were not to be carried out on the traditional Genoese model. Instead of a consortium of merchants, there were trade agreements between sovereign rulers. The old world of Italian overseas expansion ended before it even started in the Americas. The Portuguese model was the one that Ferdinand and Isabella chose.

Columbus implemented the Portuguese model on his very first voyage. The opportunity arose on Christmas day of 1492, when his flagship *Santa María* ran aground off the north shore of the island of La Española (now Hispaniola, the modern republic of Haiti and the Dominican Republic). He and the crew saved most of the cargo, but his remaining ships, *Niña* and *Pinta*, did not have enough room to take everyone back to Spain. So Columbus established a stockaded trading post, which he named La Navidad. The parallels of this operation with those of the Portuguese are striking: Columbus departed for Spain, leaving behind merchandise, equipment, provisions, and 38 men under the command of the fleet marshal. All the men, whether they stayed in La Navidad or returned to Spain, were salaried employees of the Spanish Crown.

Ferdinand and Isabella feared Portuguese interference with their new trading post on the supposed route to Asia. Consequently, on Columbus's second voyage, in 1493, they insisted on sending cavalry to protect the trading post. When Columbus returned to La Navidad, however, he found all the Europeans dead. The natives, whom Columbus had described as meek and friendly, turned out to be just as hostile and competent in war as the Africans fighting the Portuguese. Columbus's almost immediate strategy of using cavalry against the natives in the rugged interior only caused damage to the horses and created disgust among the Spaniards.

Columbus abandoned the site of La Navidad and constructed a new trading post that he called La Isabela, for his royal sponsor. Here he built a stone structure to serve as the royal storehouse, all trade being a royal monopoly. Columbus held not only the office of admiral but also the legal rights to profits as the business partner and commercial agent of the monarchs. The salaried employees—1,200 on the second voyage—would have to buy their European food, equipment, and clothing from the royal storehouse. This at least was the plan, patterned on Saint George of the Mine.

The era of royal monopolies and trading posts with salaried employees ended quickly. The years between the first Columbian voyage in 1492 and Columbus's death in 1506 were the most complex and volatile ones in the encounter between the New World and the Old. In these first few years the Spanish monarchs adapted to the American reality. Ferdinand and Isabella reassessed their relationship with Columbus, reformed their commercial policy, and transformed the Spanish and Indian settlements in the Americas. Their growing awareness of the Americas forced an end to the old period of European exploration and expansion.

By early 1494, a resupply fleet returning to Spain had brought a report from the La Isabela trading post that made Ferdinand and Isabella understand that the Portuguese exploration model would not work in the Americas. They had sent Columbus on a second voyage designed to fortify and expand the trading post into a supply station. But it quickly became apparent that the Spaniards at the post could not produce enough food and fodder there for themselves and their cavalry. The European crops that they planted did not come to maturity, and the food supplies that the monarchs sent from Spain spoiled en route in the tropical climate of the Caribbean.

The Spanish monarchs responded by innovating. Whereas the Italians and Portuguese had sent one or two cargo ships to their trading posts every four or five years, Ferdinand and Isabella began sending several ships each year. Between February 1494 and October 1496, they sent four resupply fleets across the Atlantic to their new trading post. Such a steady stream of traffic between the homeland and its colonies became characteristic of Spanish colonization. Except for 1497, ships have crossed between Spain and the Americas every year since 1492. This continuous contact and interaction linked the Americas, Africa, and Europe (and later Asia) together into a single new world.

The next change came in the partnership agreement between Columbus and the monarchs. Ferdinand and Isabella wanted Columbus to find a route around the new continent to Asia but realized that he could not do that and manage their partnership at the same time. However, they were disturbed by the many reports from returnees about Columbus's mismanagement of the post's royal storehouse and his adversarial relations with the Spanish and Indian residents of the islands. Accordingly, in late 1497, they suspended the Santa Fe Capitulations for 1498, 1499, and 1500 until the accounts from the first two voyages could be audited.

Once again, in the face of the new American reality, the monarchs innovated. While the Santa Fe Capitulations were suspended, Ferdinand and Isabella authorized joint-stock companies in Seville to finance exploratory voyages to South America. The monarchs, as the majority stockholders, invited Andalusian investors to buy shares of stock in this unincorporated business enterprise—a new form of capitalization that would become the norm for later French, English, and Dutch ventures in the New World. The stockholders meeting in Seville in 1497 instructed their expedition to explore, map, and colonize the coast of this continent that Columbus had described as "another world." Eleven voyages under the command of various Spanish captains had mapped the coast of South and Central America, from modern Brazil to Panama, by 1503. Hundreds of Spanish men and women emigrated as colonists on these voyages but suffered an appalling rate of death by shipwreck, starvation, disease, and warfare with the Native Americans.

The urgency of the food shortage on the island of Hispaniola meant that the resupply fleets could not be delayed in Seville or Cádiz waiting for Columbus in the Caribbean to invest his share of the cost. So in their 1497 instructions for Columbus's third voyage, Ferdinand and Isabella laid out their plans to colonize the Americas on the same model the Castilians employed in Spain. Thirty Spanish farmers went to Hispaniola on Columbus's third voyage, sent to cultivate European crops to feed the trading post staff and resupply ships that would, they hoped, soon be trading with the Asian mainland.

The monarchs instructed Columbus to establish regular free towns, as opposed to trading posts, with private farms and common lands, and to take Spanish women to the colonies. The names and identities of just four of these pioneer women are known: Catalina de Sevilla accompanied her husband, a noncommissioned officer named Pedro de Salamanca; Gracia de Segovia may have been single and traveling alone; Catalina de Egipcio and María de Egipcio, gypsy women convicted of murder, emigrated to take advantage of a royal offer to commute their sentences after they had put in ten years of unpaid service in the Americas.

The monarchs' doubts about Columbus's administrative abilities meanwhile intensified. As soon as they landed in 1498, the colonists on his third voyage rebelled against his attempts to prevent them from establishing new towns. But Columbus was unwilling to set up towns because a town would have a free marketplace that would compete with his monopoly. He tried to negotiate some sort of arrangement with the settlers that would preserve his interests in the company store, which by now had been moved to Santo Domingo, a new town on the south coast.

Conflicts immediately erupted, however, because in the minds of the Spanish settlers this was not an issue for negotiation; they believed that the workings of the municipal tradition of Spain had been implicit in their contracts. In this revolt they won the support and leadership of the island's highest legal officer appointed by Columbus, the appellate judge, Francisco de Roldán.

The colonists' complaints to the monarchs about Columbus's uncompromising determination to control all importing and exporting of merchandise through the company store and to prevent the functioning of free town marketplaces led the monarchs to send an investigative judge to the island in 1500. He stripped Columbus of his offices and sent the admiral and his brothers back to Spain to be judged by the monarchs. They gradually reinstated Columbus in some of his offices and privileges but appointed a new governor and a new manager.

Furthermore, the monarchs' faith in Columbus as a businessman appears to have been permanently destroyed by the audits of his first two voyages. Their disillusionment shaped their instructions to the new manager of the trading post, Fernando de Monroy. Columbus and his Genoese contractors in Seville had been responsible for deciding what to send for their one-eighth of the cargo carried by the huge fleet that transported the new governor, Nicolás de Ovando, to Hispaniola in 1500. The merchandise included heavy English wool broadcloth. At the end of 1501, Ferdinand and Isabella commended Monroy for not having accepted this merchandise: "We have seen what you wrote us about the merchandise that they sent you as part of Admiral Christopher Columbus's one-eighth according to the Capitulation. . . . And because these were things that could not be sold quickly there and were over priced, you did well not to accept them." In short, Ferdinand and Isabella understood the reality of the Caribbean climate, but Columbus and his fellow Italians were still trying to carry on a traditional Europe-to-Asia trade in wool cloth.

By 1501, the monarchs were insisting that Spaniards in the Caribbean live in towns: "It is our wish that the Christians living on the island of La Española shall not live dispersed from now on. Make sure that no one lives outside of the towns that have been established on the island and that each can have a hut or cabin on his fields where he can stay when he goes to inspect or plow his land." The founding of free towns had by this time taken precedence over all other considerations in royal policy. Profits from the royal monopoly, contracts with Columbus, the company store—all were intolerable to the colonists. They had come to the Americas with the understanding that they would be free citizens of Spanish towns, and they knew exactly what that involved. They expected to have their own farms as private property, live in a town nucleus with its free marketplace for the sale of their produce and manufactures, and govern themselves, their marketplace, and their commons through democratic town meetings and an annually elected town council.

The practice of having a royal company store and monopoly continued to be a disincentive to emigration and an impediment to peaceful government in the colony. In 1503, the colonists sent a delegation to Ferdinand and Isabella to complain about the company store's inappropriate merchandise and its excessively high prices. By the end of the year, the monarchs concluded that colonization could not be successful as long as the colonial towns were not permitted to trade in European goods in their own marketplaces. Towns, they decided, were more important than profit.

Ferdinand and Isabella never renewed the partnership with Columbus after it expired in 1500, nor did they form partnerships with other businessmen. The risks of the American trade proved too high to be limited to just a few individuals or joint-stock companies. The Americas trade could be profitable only with a high volume of transatlantic traffic and sales. The monarchs therefore needed to attract as many investors as possible.

Ferdinand and Isabella decided to end the royal monopoly and open the Americas to free trade for all Spaniards. A decree to that effect went into effect on July 28, 1504. Instead of profiting from a monopolistic partnership, the monarchs now profited by imposing royal fees and import-export taxes collected from all passengers and merchandise passing through closely regulated ports in Spain and the Americas. The next year, on March 5, 1505, King Ferdinand opened the Americas to free trade by foreign residents of Spain, as long as their partners and agents in the Americas were royal subjects.

To Columbus this was the unkindest cut of all. Back in Spain in 1504 and 1505 he wrote frequently to his son Diego at court, railing against free trade and complaining that anyone could now send merchandise to the Indies without having a partnership or a contract with him. He instructed Diego to lobby friends at court to reverse free trade, but the monarchy refused. Free trade for all Spaniards remained the colonial policy.

The transformation from royal trading post to free towns, from company store to town marketplace, attracted a new type of settler. The new colonial towns, with their growing families, changed the nature of Spanish commerce. Packed in among their boxes of weapons and barrels of gunpowder, ships from Spain now carried supplies for family life. In 1509, for example, Dr. Diego Alvarez Chanca (about 1463–about 1515) and his wife, Ana de Zurita, formed a commercial company in Seville to export merchandise to the colonies. Their bills of lading demonstrate how much had changed in the ten years since Ferdinand and Isabella had initiated their colonial policy. Now the exports included items of women's clothing and adornment: married women's caps, ladies' neckcloths, hair nets, and chemises. Furthermore, Dr. Chanca and his wife sent supplies for the care of the sick, which was traditionally the wife's responsibility: 150 boxes of quince paste (renowned as a laxative), ten casks of white wine, three casks of fine wheat flour, two barrels of honey, medicinal herbs, and drugs.

Ferdinand and Isabella responded creatively and appropriately to rapidly changing realities. The necessity of innovating came out of the American environment, from the interactions of natives and Europeans, from the new world that was being created year by year in the Caribbean. Those who did not adjust fell behind, which is what happened to Christopher Columbus. By the time he died in 1506, the old world of monopolies in which he had carved a place for himself was gone. He had not found a way to play an equally important role in the new world of free markets. When the Spanish interest shifted to the Mexican mainland, innovations had already shaped the Spanish colonies on the Caribbean islands. These colonies had by then become a world of family farms; of households of men, women, and children; of local civic government; of free trade.

The degree to which concerns regarding municipal society and citizenship dominated the thoughts of even the most rebellious Castilian can be seen in the actions of the Cortés expedition. Historians now recognize that the expedition's decision to march on Mexico City (Tenochtitlán), to confront the emperor Moctezuma, was an act of rebellion against the Spanish royal governor in Cuba. The rebels rejected the governor's instructions for the expedition, which were to return to Cuba after exploring the coast and rescue enslaved Spaniards. They set up their own government by establishing the town of Veracruz—against the governor's orders—and appealed directly to Emperor Charles V for recognition. They did not organize themselves into a county, a kingdom, or an empire but instead created the same sort of municipal government they were familiar with as citizens of Castilian towns. They took it for granted that the king would want his royal dominions on the American continent to be organized into municipalities. They also needed an excuse to evade their governor's instructions and do what they wanted to do—march on the Mexican capital of Tenochtitlán. For this purpose they decided to form a municipal militia. To do this, however, they first needed to establish a municipality, which is how Veracruz came about.

Cortés's plan to establish a town in order to set up a municipal militia that could attack Tenochtitlán was a rebellious act that aroused controversy among his fellow Spaniards. Those who were allies of Governor Diego Velázquez wanted to return to Cuba, arguing that they had accomplished the objectives of the expedition. They pointed out that the governor had not authorized the expedition to establish a settlement, as Cortés had advertised in Cuba; the governor's written instructions to Cortés authorized the expedition only to explore the land and ransom shipwrecked Spaniards (who had been enslaved by Indians). Not only did the Spaniards lack the supplies and people to settle, argued the dissenting members of the expedition; they did not have even the possibility of future support from Cuba. Cortés appeared to go along with this argument.

But secretly Cortés and his allies had decided to resist any move to abandon the mainland. They initiated discussions with individual members of the expedition, lobbying for votes in preparing for a town meeting. During the night, several leaders came to solicit Bernal Díaz del Castillo's vote, pointing out the futility and waste of expeditions that came only to ransom and explore without settling. But to settle in defiance of the governor's instructions would make them outlaws. The solution they proposed was to form a town council and petition the king for recognition of it as a municipality, bypassing the governor's authority. Cortés's men argued to Díaz that if the allies elected Cortés as the captain of their municipal militia in a town meeting, then Cortés, instead of being the governor's appointed commander, "could do it in the king's name and then send the news directly to the king our lord in Castile. And be sure, sir, to cast your vote, so that all of us elect him unanimously as captain, because it will be to the service of God and the king our lord."

The next day, a meeting convened and demanded that Cortés found a town. The men complained that it had been wrong to bring them under false pretenses, that in Cuba Cortés had announced that he was going to settle but instead had come to ransom, and they demanded for the sake of God and the king that he settle a town immediately. They added other good arguments, pointing out that the natives would not let them land in peace again, that other soldiers would certainly come from the islands to help them if the land were settled by Spaniards, and that Governor Velázquez had knowingly sent them on a fool's errand by advertising that he had authority from the king to settle when the contrary was true. Finally, the rebels said they "wanted to settle, and whoever did not want to could go back to Cuba."

Cortés agreed finally to settle a town, but only after a great show of "beg me to do what I want," as the Spanish saying goes, and on condition that they would elect him interim judge and captain-general and agree to give him one-fifth of all the gold they might acquire after setting aside the royal fifth. The harshness of this last condition gave rise to heated discussions that prolonged the meeting over several days. But the men finally agreed to Cortés's terms in order to get their town. Then a royal notary, Diego de Godoy, drafted a letter to the king, in which they explained this rebellious act in the most loyal and traditional terms: "It seemed to all of us better that a town with a court of justice be founded and inhabited in your royal highnesses' name so that in this land also you might have sovereignty as you have in your other kingdoms and dominions. For once the land has been settled by Spaniards, in addition to increasing your royal highnesses' dominions and revenues, you may be so gracious as to grant favors to us and to the settlers who come in the future."

Cortés then proceeded to found a town, which exists to this day on the Gulf of Mexico directly east of Mexico City. He appointed the usual municipal officials — two judges, a sheriff, a treasurer, an accountant, and councilmen — erected the symbols of town jurisdiction (a column of justice and a gallows), and named the town Veracruz (true cross), because they had disembarked on Good Friday, April 22, 1519. The founding citizens began improvising homes while exploring the surrounding areas and forming alliances with some 30 Indian towns.

Having carried out a rebellion, they contrived to lend it legitimacy by acting as a town. The town council convened and demanded that Cortés show them the written instructions in which Governor Velázquez had authorized him to come to the mainland. In the process they discovered that Cortés's commission had expired, and he could no longer exercise the offices of captain or appellate judge. The council, which now found itself the only legitimate Spanish authority on the mainland, appointed Cortés as the town militia's captain and interim judge. Then they sent a letter to the emperor explaining what they had done: "We appointed Cortés . . . and received from him the customary oath in the service of your majesties, and we accepted him in our town meeting and council as interim appellate judge and captain in your royal name."

While this letter was traveling back to Spain, a matter of six or seven weeks, Cortés and the expedition members began building the new town's residential nucleus to make good their claim of having settled a new municipality. According to Díaz, "Everyone from Cortés, who was the first to start digging out dirt and stones for laying the foundations, down to every captain and soldier set to it and worked to finish the town and fortress quickly, some working on the foundations, others on building walls, others bringing water, some working in the lime pits and in making bricks and tiles, others looking for food, or sawing lumber, the blacksmiths at their anvil, because we had two blacksmiths. In this way we worked on it without stopping from the greatest to the least, along with the Indians who helped us until the church and houses were roofed and the palisade built." As soon as the town was built, the municipal militia packed up their gear and, with their Indian allies, moved inland and began their march on Tenochtitlán.

The greatest problem that conquerors anywhere have faced has occurred whenever they have not had an opportunity to build from the ground up. Normally, when Christians conquered a Muslim city they were limited to an already existing town layout. As a result, there were two basic types of towns in Castile: the jumbled, unfocused warrens of towns and cities taken from the Muslims, such as Seville, Granada, and Madrid; and the newly founded towns and villages centered on an open plaza in the style of ancient Rome. While we tend to think of Granada as a typical medieval city, the Spaniards themselves found these Muslim urban agglomerations unnatural and never stopped trying to straighten them out. The city council minutes of Granada are discourses that go back centuries on widening and straightening streets, rationalizing city blocks, and opening up large, rectangular plazas.

In Granada the new city council organized after the conquest set itself to creating a rectangular open plaza and widening the streets. Muslim cities did not have open markets within the city walls; instead, their merchants carried on livestock markets in the open spaces outside the city's walls. Within the city walls, retailers and artisans conducted their trade in small shops on the ground floors of their homes, along streets that were often so narrow and crooked that goods could be brought in only by humans or on pack animals. Granada's commercial district under the Muslims was Elvira Street, which led from the city gate to the silk and wheat exchanges in the most narrow, crowded streets of the central city.

After the departure of the Muslims, the city council decided to enlarge a space in front of the city gate, called Bibrambla, to create a proper Castilian plaza. Demolishing the existing houses and shops to make room for this project and compensating their owners took years and cost a fortune. Typically, the council appointed four of its members to accompany the royal appeals judge on an inspection tour of the targeted buildings in order to appraise them "so that the city can pay their owners for them, in order to make the plaza." But it soon became clear that the Plaza Bibrambla as originally envisioned would not be enough. As soon as a new section of the plaza was opened, it filled up with merchants' stalls.

The continuity between Old and New World cities was this tradition of the medieval Spanish municipality designed for commerce. Granted, the similarities between Granada and Mexico City have not seemed striking to historians. For one thing, the members of the Cortés expedition were much too young to have participated in the conquest of Granada. Furthermore, other cities of the Iberian

After the Christian city council began meeting in 1497, it effected the most important change in Granada's landscape: the creation of the central marketplace, Granada's Plaza Bibrambla (bottom center). Bordered by the silk market and the city hall, Plaza Bibrambla became the center of civic life. When Cardinal Cisneros staged a bonfire to destroy the Korans and other Muslim books, the plaza served as the stage for his propaganda effort.

Peninsula seemed to have closer ties with Mexico: Most of the trade and official correspondence for Mexico came from the city of Seville, and Mexico City's new fuero was modeled on that of the city of Toledo. Yet 30 years is historically a very short time, and several of the Spanish conquerors of Mexico boasted that their fathers and other ancestors had participated in the campaign against the Muslims of Granada. There thus seems every reason to suppose that the members of the Cortés expedition would have Granada on their minds when confronted with the task of remodeling and reorganizing the Mexican capital. The continuity of traditions cannot be clearer than to note that one of the city councilmen of Granada in 1513 was the young Antonio de Mendoza, who was already learning the art of creating plazas and widening streets in the Castilian tradition, to accommodate commercial activity. When Mendoza arrived in Veracruz in 1535 as the first viceroy of New Spain, his first act was to instruct the city council of Mexico City to straighten out and widen the city streets and build covered colonnades (*soportales*) around the city square to protect merchandise from the rain.

Conquest, of course, destroys the very prize it seeks to gain. The successful conqueror destroys walls, buildings, bridges, water systems, and people. Thus, only to the degree that conquerors are able to rebuild, repopulate, and govern does a prize city become worth the destruction. In August 1521, almost 30 years after the fall of Granada, Hernán Cortés conquered the city of Tenochtitlán, capital of the Aztec empire. Throughout the following centuries Spaniards remodeled the conquered city, reorganized its government, and converted the defeated population to Christianity. The Spaniards held a common ideal of what a city

Sixty years after the first encounter between the Spaniards and the Aztecs, the marketplace of Tlaxcala blended Spanish and indigenous elements. The town hall, jail, tavern, and royal offices surrounded the communal fountain and column of justice. The design of the buildings combines Spanish and Native American decorative elements. While a European cornice crowns the government buildings, the private buildings on the other sides of the square display distinctive indigenous design.

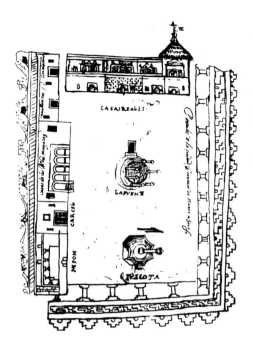

should look like and rebuilt both Granada and Tenochtitlán to fit that ideal. These were parallel actions, but they did not have parallel results. The difference lies in the affection we hold for any preconquest city.

The conquest of Tenochtitlán is usually told in a more savage way than that of Granada: as a tale of a fabulous metropolis, with monumental architecture and sophisticated technology, succumbing to the savagery of an insensitive, intolerant conquering society. In genres other than history, Tenochtitlán appears as a sort of floating fairyland, which first enchanted the Spaniards but then sank under their destructive embrace.

With Tenochtitlán, Cortés faced a uniquely difficult task of reconstruction, for the Aztec capital was destroyed by his troops as no other had been in the long history of Spanish conquest. Certainly, the level of destruction in Granada, the most important conquest of the previous generation, could not compare with Tenochtitlan's. Granada was indeed a fabled metropolis of exquisite architecture and sophisticated technology, but it suffered little physical damage because it surrendered in the early stages of the siege. Yet, despite Granada's nearly intact state, its Christian city council soon began demolishing buildings to create large plazas, straight streets, and a cathedral. In short, Granada, so different in the manner of its conquest, experienced the same degree of rebuilding as Tenochtitlán. The Spaniard's traditional sense of what a city should be could not tolerate the chaotic warren of city streets the Muslims left behind in Granada any more than it would have been able to accept Tenochtitlán's market transport system based on canals. Urban historians have often explained the orthogonal city plan as an attempt to impose upon the town new Renaissance concepts of rationality and rectilinearity.

The history of Spanish town planning in the Middle Ages suggests quite the opposite, however: Spaniards built towns in the New World in the same way they had built them for centuries in the Old. The rectangular plaza shaped Spanish towns and villages from ancient Roman to modern times; this design was not a Renaissance innovation imposed by royal fiat. Spanish towns often did not end up with straight streets, square blocks, or rectangular plazas, but town councils struggled for centuries to achieve this ideal.

Central Mexico fulfilled many of the aspirations and hopes of the Spaniards because it was civilized—a society that lived in cities. Since the organization and government of native cities did not fit European legal definitions of "city," "town," or "village," the conquerors referred to them with the Spanish generic term *"pueblo"* (municipality). As the Spaniards moved north, however, they encountered the same conditions they had explored in the Caribbean, Central America, and the east coast of South America, where transhumant peoples migrated from coastal settlements to inland villages with the seasons and the weather, never erecting permanent buildings or organizing pueblos. To the Spaniards, these were not civilized people.

Even their great champion Bartolomé de Las Casas (1474–1566) regarded the Caribbean islanders as primitives on this basis. On every other ground of comparison—religious sophistication, familial relations, economic productivity, native intelligence, capacity for war—he regarded the islanders as civilized. But they lived, as he noted in his *Apologética historia sumaria* (Brief Historical Defense), "scattered and isolated, not in settlements with the form of cities, and others did not even live in large or small settlements but wandered without order like savages." The nonurban character of the Caribbean Indians demonstrated, Las Casas suggested, that they lacked the essential political experience of civilized societies. In this respect, as in many others, Las Casas drew his argument from Aristotle, who had written in his treatise *On Politics*: "It is evident that the polis [Greek, "city," as in "metropolis"] belongs to the class of things that exist by nature, and that man is by nature an animal intended to live in a polis. He who is without polis, by reason of his own nature and not of some accident, is either a poor sort of being, or a being higher than man; he is like the man of whom Homer wrote in denunciation, 'Clanless and lawless and heartless is he.'"

Las Casas devoted his life to combating the idea that the Caribbean islanders lacked towns by reason of their own nature. Instead he argued that an accident of historical development accounted for the islanders' lack of towns. He ignored his own earlier theological arguments and resorted instead to historical anthropology. By arguing that all social and cultural institutions, including those of the Europeans, develop through human experience over time, Las Casas could attribute the lack of towns on the islands to anthropological or developmental causes rather than defects in native intelligence. He explained that because the islanders had been encountered at an early stage of development common to all cultures, they only needed time and an appropriate example to achieve self-government in towns.

The role of the Spaniards, Las Casas argued, should be to bring the islanders together to live in nuclear towns and then, by teaching and example, develop the natives' skills until they, too, could form self-governing towns: "If any more should be discovered like those who were found on the mainland that we call Florida," he wrote, "they should be considered rational beings, reducible to order and reason." What the Spaniards must not do, Las Casas claimed, was to use slavery or physical force, which would prevent the potential development of the Caribbean natives into good citizens: "When such isolated and primitive people are found in the future, they should, with energy and discretion, love and tenderness, be induced to live together in society so that they may experience themselves the benefits of living a life of self government." The next generation of evangelizing priests tried to achieve this goal by creating in northern Mexico a new institution that had never existed in Spain, the mission church.

Much of the contrast between Cortés and Las Casas during their own lifetimes can be explained by how they each applied the same core of values to Native Americans with widely different lifestyles. Cortés moved decisively to the mainland, accepted the indigenous organizations as valid Indian municipalities (pueblos), and injected new Spanish towns among them. At the end of the 16th century, there were about 100 Spanish towns in New Spain and the Caribbean. They had come into being in the same way as Palos and Veracruz, founded by squatters in between already existing towns, although in Central Mexico those preexisting towns were Indian. The process and structure were the same in the Old World and the New because the intent was the same—to create a society of self-governing towns whether Indian or European.

Las Casas limited his experience to the islands of the Caribbean and parts of Central America. Because he held the same values of civilization that Cortés did, however, he could not recognize as valid the nonurban migratory life of the people he loved. He therefore kept inventing one scheme after another to organize them into self-governing towns.

The different backgrounds of the conqueror Cortés and the churchman Las Casas shaped their aspirations for Mexico. In Mexico, just as they did in the home country, the clergy single-mindedly pursued a program of converting people to a Christian lifestyle similar to their own priestly ideals. But lay people such as Bernal Díaz and Hernan Cortés took their religion for granted except in times of crisis. The chasm between these two groups—laypeople and clergy—had divided the Spaniards long before they encountered Mexico. Knights and municipal militiamen who fought against the Muslims in these battles described them as wars of territorial conquest and booty; the clergy described them as religious crusades.

The laypeople who initiated and carried out Spain's program of expansion never wavered in their purpose: Whether monarch, merchant, soldier, or royal administrator, commerce was their major motive for exploring west to the Americas. By 1519, they felt frustrated by a previously unknown continent blocking the way to Asia and were bitterly disappointed in the cultures and economies they had encountered in the Americas. Their explorations of the Caribbean and the coasts of Central and South America had brought welcome mineral resources but nothing of what they had expected to find in Asia: no stone buildings or cities or great marketplaces.

Tenochtitlán had all of these. Bernal Díaz seemed overcome: "It was all so wonderful that I do not know how to describe this first glimpse of things never heard of, seen, or dreamed of before." Fortunately, he described it anyway, focusing on the goods for sale in Tenochtitlán's largest marketplace, Tlatelolco. Beginning with the most valuable merchandise—gold, silver, precious stones, feathers, cloaks, embroidered goods, male and female slaves, cloth, and chocolate—Díaz proceeded to list a total of 65 different types of merchandise. He saw Tenochtitlán as a great emporium, a well-stocked marketplace humming with buyers and sellers.

Through its Renaissance transformation into a society organized for commerce, Spain went beyond conquest to take the lead in colonizing the Americas. The institutions and customs that were most effective in rebuilding Castile went on to shape Spanish settlement in America. Because town life was the norm for Spaniards, they could not conceive of a civilization without municipalities. When they found great cities in central Mexico, they rejoiced in this discovery of a civilization previously unknown to Europeans. With few exceptions, they did not destroy Indian pueblos but instead founded new Spanish towns in between the established pueblos. Mexico therefore came to be, like Spain itself, patterned with a few large cities surrounded by thousands of smaller autonomous towns.

2

The Mexico That Spain Encountered

SUSAN SCHROEDER

Imagine the pleasure experienced by the Spaniards reconnoitering the waters between Honduras and the Yucatan (Yucatán) Peninsula in 1502 upon finally sighting a Maya trading vessel loaded with cargo. The vessel, called a *canoa*, or canoe (a term borrowed by the Spaniards from Caribbean Island Arawak natives), was transporting finely woven cloth, pottery, metalware, weapons, cacao, and probably female slaves for sale or exchange with coastal Yucatan populations. Such canoes, sometimes 40 feet in length and capable of accommodating huge loads and many passengers, were a primary means of transportation for numerous native peoples in the Americas and provided but one clue for the Spaniards as to indigenous technology. Even more impressive, however, was the handsomely outfitted Maya official at the helm and a number of slaves, bound together with cord around their necks, who manned the paddles that propelled the boat. Other Mayas along the shore gathered to watch and try to make sense of the strange Spanish ships. Later they would furnish the newcomers with food; water; fodder for the horses, pigs, and chickens the Spaniards had on board; and other items that the Spaniards demanded, at least for a while. However, this initial encounter with the Mayas was indicative enough of both the wealth and the sophistication of local societies to warrant further Spanish exploration and penetration of the mainland.

The Spaniards' later reports of their early experiences with the Mayas of Yucatan were encouraging, for most often they were desperate for the natives' hospitality while dazzled by the coastal Mayas' "towers," or stone-hewn temples and palaces at places such as Tulum, a major trade entrepôt (trading outpost) at the time. They had little way of determining for certain, however, the existence of additional highly advanced societies located farther inland or the extraordinary terrain that they inhabited.

The Yucatan Peninsula is a flat limestone shelf extending into the Caribbean Sea. With shallow topsoil, insubstantial vegetation, and little in the way of reliable freshwater sources, the peninsula is a stark contrast to its base, which projects into extensive rain forest and wetlands. Here potentially rich soils have their nutrients continuously leached out by heavy rainfall. Beyond this region, in the highlands of what is today Guatemala, the land is distinguished by high and often active volcanoes, large lakes, and fertile but rugged alluvial plains created where runoff water has deposited soil from the mountainsides. Occupied for centuries by linguistically diverse Maya populations whose territory encompassed approximately 400,000 square kilometers (155,000 square miles) extending from the southeastern state of Tabasco to western El Salvador, this challenging topography was nonetheless conducive to the development of one of the most extraordinary civilizations in all the Americas.

Indeed, Mexico's spectacular landscape (as claimed for the Spanish Crown) extended as far north as the upper reaches of California and New Mexico and south to Costa Rica's borders. Millions of indigenous people had either traversed or settled in prime regions of this vast territory since their first migrations from Eurasia perhaps 40,000 years before. These earliest natives, representing only five linguistic phyla, diversified and settled as distinct culture groups in thousands of different locations. Just one example of the complexity of local social and environmental adaptations is California, where abundant marine, forest, and river-plain resources resulted in indigenous culture enclaves representing some 120 divergent languages.

For present purposes, though, we are concerned with the natives who lived within or near the boundaries of modern Mexico, Guatemala, and Honduras. Most familiar are the extraordinary accomplishments of the classic Mayas (about A.D. 250 to 900 or 1000) in tropical and highland Guatemala and the Aztecs (about A.D. 1428–1521) in central Mexico. Both civilizations developed and flourished, for the most part, in close proximity to fertile volcanic alluvial soils, woodlands, and large dependable lakes and rivers, with food supplies augmented by raised-field agriculture in wetlands areas. The Aztecs were especially well known for what may have been a similar form of raised-field agriculture, called *chinampa*, which is discussed below. It is in these regions that dietary basics such as corn, beans, squashes, and chiles grew in profusion. With only the turkey, the bee, and small dogs as domesticated animals, the natural flora and fauna, as hunted and gathered, supplemented nutritional and other domestic needs. Deer, mountain lions, peccaries, hares, fowl, iguanas and other reptiles, and insects abounded, along with a full spectrum of edible fruits and vegetables. Even lake scum was harvested, cooked, and eaten for its nourishment.

Although marked by sharp ethnic differences as well as differences in their sociopolitical organization, both zones supported densely populated settlements with, by proportion, increasingly thinning populations the greater the distance from the two centers. In Mexico, with fewer lakes and rivers in the north and south, the terrain becomes progressively rugged and arid. Broad flatlands of cactus, scrub, and scant grasses are cut by stark sierras. Rainfall in the northern reaches is seasonal at best. Correspondingly, the native populations tended to be sparse and, with the exception of the Pueblo peoples of New Mexico and Arizona, only semi-sedentary in nature. Seasonal hunting and gathering typically supplied the necessary food. A notable exception was the Zapotec- and Mixtec-speaking peoples in south-central Mexico who, like the Aztecs and Mayas, established impressive political centers in the valleys of their own seemingly limitless mountain ranges. Nevertheless, in spite of great geographic, ethnic, and linguistic diversity, most indigenous societies shared many common cultural characteristics in terms of diet and intellectual and technological achievements. To distinguish these remarkable peoples from other native groups in North America, anthropologist Paul Kirchhoff proposed in the early 1940s that the region as well as the societies and cultures within it be designated "Mesoamerica" (see Table 1, page 76, for a general chronology of Mesoamerican culture epochs).

Yet all the reliable evidence indicates that each of these major centers, their linguistic and ethnic differences notwithstanding, could likely trace many key characteristics of their societies to a common cultural ancestor and locale along the wet, lowland Gulf Coast region of Veracruz. Known today as the Olmec (in Nahuatl, the Aztecs' language: "people of the place with rubber [*olli*]") heartland, its inhabitants warrant recognition for establishing what traditionally has been described as the mother civilization of Mesoamerica.

In addition to having a sociopolitical system that channeled at least part of its energies into developments such as monumental architecture, fine art, and esoteric religious concepts, the Olmecs contributed a practice of profound importance to later generations—the practice of employing graphic symbolic forms to convey a unified construct of their worldview, aesthetics, and concept of kingship. Subsequently, over the centuries historical writing expressed by means of pictographs, hieroglyphs, and portraiture in books, stone, bone, wood, and ceramics was institutionalized by Maya, Zapotec, and Aztec rulers to exalt and validate royal authority.

Settled around 1500 A.D., probably by speakers of the ancestral Mixe-Zoquean linguistic group, the two best-known sites where the Olmecs flourished were San Lorenzo (about 1200–900 B.C.) and La Venta (about 900–400 B.C.), which functioned as political, religious, and economic centers. There earthen pyramids and numerous platform mounds and altars were built as part of administrative and ceremonial complexes, with stelae, large stone pillars, carved in low relief to commemorate what are believed to be authoritative individuals and their activities. However, there was far more to Olmec culure than a few ceremonial centers, for strategic regional settlements played key roles in territorial integration and overall development. Ongoing archaeological excavations indicate greater diversity as well as sophistication among the various Olmec people than heretofore thought.

Rubber, a natural resource in the Veracruz area, had many uses, one of the most important being the manufacture of rubber balls. Such balls trace back at least to 1200 B.C. at El Manatí, Veracruz, where they were included in out-of-the-way caches as ritual offerings. Later the Olmecs exported them by the thousands. At distant Olmec-influenced Izapa, south toward the Pacific coast of the state of Chiapas, there is evidence of the earliest Mesoamerican ball game. But the sport was soon ubiquitous. Subsequently, rules, equipment, and the architectural playing fields for ball games varied according to the indigenous peoples who played them. Archaeological evidence for the existence of ball courts is found throughout Mesoamerica and beyond, in Puerto Rico as well as in Arizona.

The ball courts were large and impressive, with daunting stone walls. Typically, they were built adjacent to civic or religious facilities and were used by rulers on occasions of high ceremony. At least three different kinds of ball games were played. From oral histories it is certain that wagers could be costly and contests brutal, with defeated players suffering harsh penalties, some possibly even losing their lives.

Little is known of the Olmecs' place of origin, but their influence, as with the ball game, was widespread. Their trade routes for coveted jade and obsidian extended north and west to the region of Teotihuacan (Teotihuacán) and south to Oaxaca and Guatemala. Considering that there were no beasts of burden in North America, only human carriers, either destination was a considerable trek, to say nothing of making such a journey with a burden of heavy stone.

The more immediate indigenous native art and architecture styles of the Olmecs, who were by no means the only native group that settled in Central Mexico, spread to numerous locales, where Olmecoid ceramic, shell, and stone vessels and figurines appear. Their products in wood, paper, and cloth have since perished from the archaeological record for the most part. Of the numerous Olmec artistic motifs, the jaguar faces on otherwise human and animal representations is the most common. Additional distinguishing features of Olmec ware are deliberately deformed skulls with a cleft in the forehead, a warrior-type figure with a helmet or cap, and tripod rattle-footed (hollow, except for a bead rattling inside each of the supporting legs) vessels. Whether these were brought in as trade items or were of Olmec-influenced local manufacture has yet to be determined.

Among the most distinctive of all Olmec survivals found in what are believed to be their original settings are the huge basalt heads found throughout southern Veracruz. Quarried at a considerable distance and transported to the coast by raft or canoe, these blocks of basalt had distinctive faces and headdresses carved on them and were positioned at important locales. The sculptured heads could stand as tall as a human being. They may have been portraits and thus emblematic of Olmec kingship, but their purpose is otherwise not known. Some scholars believe that the stones were originally altars or thrones, then were refashioned to commemorate the likeness of a recently deceased ruler. Upon the collapse of Olmec civilization around 400 B.C., the stone heads were defaced and toppled from their imposing perches. Researchers continue to speculate whether the Olmecs' decline can be attributed to internal upheaval or invasion by outsiders.

Yet there is little evidence of large-scale warfare or even substantial sustained long-distance trade on the part of the Olmecs. The difficulty of crossing long stretches of countryside by foot without dependable food supplies limited all such activity—until the invention of the tortilla. The appearance, finally, at late-Olmec sites such as Tlaxcallan (Tlaxcala) and Chalcatzingo, of the *comal*, a ceramic or stone griddle for grilling tortillas and the manufacture of portable comestibles, did not, however, revolutionize Olmec life, for the Olmecs' dominance of the region began to wane shortly thereafter. It remained for their successors to take full advantage of this handy artifact for empire building.

Obviously, the eclipse of Olmec civilization did not signal an end to developments elsewhere. The decline of one region typically was followed by first the gradual, then the extraordinary, development of others. Contemporaneously, native peoples across Mesoamerica were capitalizing on their rich local soils as well as the intellectual and technological legacy of the Olmecs. Smaller in scale but no less important in Mexico's central zone were sites of industry, trade, and other activities at Cuicuilco, Chupícuaro, and Tlatilco. Archaeologists number such sites in the hundreds. Essentially, this was a time of transition, marking the end of the formative era. Likewise, new social groups were establishing centers in new regions that included increasing numbers of subject populations. Eventually, grandiose political capitals such as Teotihuacan, El Tajin, Monte Albán, Tikal, and Kaminaljuyu began to dominate their respective landscapes, signifying the beginning and later heyday of the classic era in Mesoamerican history.

Already in southern Mexico and lowland Guatemala numerous Maya societies were actively involved in consolidating into regional kingdoms. Surely refugee Olmecs or colonists from the Gulf Coast influenced local inhabitants at some point. Over time, these settlements had refined their techniques for land use, especially for food production. In some Maya regions, swidden, or slash-and-burn agriculture in which short-term growing plots are produced by burning off the land, was practiced, and soil fertility was thus short-lived. Depending upon the terrain, fields were left fallow for anywhere from 2 to 20 years. In other regions, raised fields were formed in areas of wetlands, or the latter were drained for more efficient crop management. Here, as elsewhere in Mesoamerica, with the use of a wooden digging stick called a *coa* (*huictli*) fields of maize, beans (small black ones for the Mayas), squash, and chiles produced such quantities as to generate and support an entire hierarchy of rulers, priests, and other specialists. Orchards of fruit, copal (a resin), and cacao were also products natural to the Mayas' farms. Cacao, in particular, was unique to a very select zone of early Maya habitation and thus became the special preserve of the nobility.

During the early classic period, Maya kingdoms such as Tikal (about A.D. 375–600) and Kaminaljuyu (about A.D. 400–650) enjoyed authority over numerous subject populations in the hinterlands of their capitals. Society was essentially made up of two classes: the nobility and the commoners, with slaves as a special category. Along with their role in food production, Maya commoners and slaves were responsible for myriad tasks, not the least of which was the construction and maintenance of sky-soaring pyramid-like temples of stone as well as palaces and other ceremonial structures. Additionally, some of the Maya nonelite worked as artisans and merchants. However, the great majority of any Maya kingdom was made up of commoners, who tended their fields to provide sustenance for all.

The Maya rulers' authority was conveyed through their lineage, advantageous marriages with the right royal partner being secured through traditional succession practices. Additionally, since polygyny (having multiple wives) was practiced by the male nobility, royal heirs who were not in a direct line for succession often optimized their situations by marrying the offspring of political allies, which served to further unite the kingdom. Both the royal daughters and the royal sons, it seems, participated in the politically motivated practice of making marriage alliances.

In some Mesoamerican monarchies, women succeeded to the office of and officiated as queens. Moreover, Tikal's and Kaminaljuyu's positions were enhanced due to their trade affiliation with the thriving kingdom of Teotihuacan in central Mexico. It is possible that the exchange of noble brides served, at least initially, to enhance this long-distance relationship. But obsidian was the principal commodity, and whether by means of warfare or by holding a monopoly on the product, merchants from Teotihuacan made a lasting impression on the highland Mayas. In addition to making biological contributions to the Maya gene pool through bride exchange, Teotihuacan contributed deities and art and architectural styles that were incorporated into Tikal's and Kaminaljuyu's public space and became a very real part of Maya culture.

In turn, because of their enhanced wealth and power, the local Maya rulers waged war successfully on neighboring kingdoms, thus adding to their dependencies. Tikal's and Kaminaljuyu's holds would wane only with the decline of Teotihuacan and the loss of resources from central Mexico. Already, though, major dependencies like Yaxchilan and Copan (Copán) had become dominant hegemonic capitals in their own right. Numerous other Maya kingdoms would flourish at about the same time, especially in the tropical forests of the Peten (Petén), in present-day Guatemala.

Lineage and territory were integral to classic Maya kingdoms. Boundaries were known, warfare a fact of life as rulers ruthlessly waged war against neighboring polities for booty and probably slaves. Conquered kingdoms were not necessarily destroyed but rather became new dependencies obligated to pay tribute. But each entity was essentially ethnically self-centered and autonomous, with its own state hierarchy, congeries of subject peoples, and local customs.

Empire formation, for both social and geographic reasons, seems not to have been practicable. Certainly, the extremes of topography—namely mountain ranges, forests, lakes, and swamps—played a role in limiting the political unification of the region. More likely, however, empires did not arise simply because of the prevailing sociopolitical practices. Warfare was the province of a kin-linked nobility whose entitlement limited the number privileged to engage in battle as well as the distribution of the spoils. Not only did the Maya aristocracy comprise an exclusive warrior corps but they dominated trading ventures as well. Therefore, opportunities for the nonelite to profit through warfare or commerce and thus to advance socially apparently did not exist. Although everyone in the polity considered themselves kin, however distant, and thus fellow citizens and patriots, control of each kingdom's resources was vested in a cohort of more closely related elite men and women. Because of this exclusivity, imperial pretensions were self-limited. The royal policy of reciprocating prosperity and protection for the nonelite must have been enough to warrant their continued collective allegiance.

The fact of political independence is not to suggest either simplicity or stasis, though, for the Mayas enjoyed unparalleled intellectual achievements during this period. Their trade networks among their own kingdoms as well as abroad to central Mexico also expanded significantly in these same years. Maya luxuries—feathers, pottery, animal skins, salt, chocolate, jewelry, and slaves—continued to be exchanged for obsidian, shells, rock crystal, alabaster, and other exotica from distant trading entrepôts. In addition, ideas and language accompanied these goods as they moved through the trade corridors. As the Maya kingdoms increased in grandeur, the inclination was for them to compete and to fight one another. But none apparently ever had a grander objective whereby a ruler prevailed by subjecting and integrating all the others beyond his sphere.

There are further remarkable features that characterize the classic Maya kingdoms. One of the first that must be emphasized is the quality of their workmanship in stone, which nearly exceeds imagination. Following Olmec precedents, Maya architects and engineers in places like Palenque, Copan, Yaxchilan, and Piedras Negras, to name a few, designed and constructed enormous pyramids and palaces, many of which were truly magisterial. Craftsmen typically built these structures with dramatic frontal staircases ascending steeply to sculpted roof-comb temples at the top. At Copan a staircase was added faced with intricately worked hieroglyphs now thought to have been a piece of historical propaganda on the part of the ruler to assuage the feelings of Copan's citizens for a recent loss in battle.

Buildings' facades were embellished with handsome portrayals of royalty in high and low relief. Lintels, altars, stelae, and statuary were exquisitely carved and documented with relevant inscriptions in the form of epigraphic, or hieroglyphic, texts, all as part of the court complex. Characteristically for the Mayas, arches took the form of a pointed corbel vault. A corbel arch, a diagnostic of this culture, is a pointed vault used as a roof, often but not always to cover a burial chamber.

Both the exteriors and interiors of Maya buildings were painted, sometimes as fresco, and the walls of inside rooms might be covered with murals depicting Maya life. Of all extant Maya wall paintings, those in three rooms at Bonampak are the most exciting, for these brilliantly painted murals portray the cycle of Maya kingship—from the presentation of a male child as heir to the court and

The discovery of Bonampak in 1946 included this brightly painted mural from Room 2 at the classic Maya site in Chiapas. The image from c. A.D. 800 depicts the victorious aftermath of battle. At the top of a stepped temple Maya rulers are shown in all their jaguar finery, jade jewelry, and magnificent headdresses. Women and numerous high-ranking men, identified by the inscriptions above their heads, form part of the retinue. Captives have been stripped. At least one is dead, and the others, wounded and bleeding, wait to learn their fate.

the murderous warfare necessary to secure that office, to the majesty of rulership in the aftermath of victory.

From these paintings and the enormous variety of stone carvings that have survived we can also determine the appearance of upper-class Mayas and observe what they wore. The nobility of this era enjoyed many luxuries, which included beautifully fashioned jade jewelry in the form of earrings, labrets, necklaces, bracelets, and rings. Their clothing consisted of finely woven and decorated cotton hip- and loincloths for men as well as pectorals, belts, sashes, capes, robes, sandals, and feather-and-jewel headdresses of such variety and magnificence that they practically defy description. The women dressed well, too, and wore a great variety of blouses, skirts, capes, and long gowns, some even brocadelike in their design and texture; nor did they want for fine jewels and beautiful hairpieces.

Beauty truly was in the eye of the Maya beholder. But surely the finest adornments were little appreciated if the wearer had not paid careful attention to the physical as well. Maya aesthetics required that the cranium be molded in a certain manner. Ideally, the forehead was flattened to be in line with the plane of the nose. Crossed eyes were thought to be attractive, especially for women, and both men and women pierced their noses, earlobes, and lips to display precious gems. Tattooing, or face painting, on the cheeks and chin was another cosmetic device, and one's smile was considered beautiful only if the teeth had been filed with ridges or drilled and inlaid with exquisite jewels. Hair was done up and often covered with an elaborate headdress. At other times women wore it tied or hanging long and straight down their backs.

Most Maya elites were trim and stately, although some of the men were definitely hefty, with large potbellies. Seniority did not exclude one from the court, for elders were valued for their wisdom. Rulers sat on jaguar-skin-covered thrones in their palaces with staffs of authority and other royal paraphernalia about. They were attended by an elaborate retinue of regal lesser nobles, each with his or her own insignia, many if not all no doubt related in some manner. When the king left the palace on official occasions, he was usually transported in a litter. His wives, who were an important part of the court, too, were usually close by, fixing him a drink of chocolate, fanning themselves, or looking admiringly in mirrors. Female slaves taken in raids or battle were likely responsible for attending to a range of domestic duties on behalf of the nobility.

The Mayas' cuisine was based on corn (maize), beans, and a variety of other vegetables, along with as much meat and fish as local hunters could supply. The comal for preparing tortillas did not exist in Maya households. No one knows exactly why the Mayas did not use the comal. Rather, it is thought that tamales and maize-based gruels and stews were preferred dishes. Banquets and feasting were an important part of ceremonies, whether social or religious. After successful battles, rulers typically shared some of their goods, including food, with their subordinates, who presumably distributed what was left among the commoners. Women were the cooks and servers, and royal women most often dined apart from men.

Balche, an intoxicating beverage made from local bee's honey fermented with bark, was consumed by nobles and commoners alike. However, following a meal, only royalty partook of the frothed chocolate beverage thought to be such a delicacy. Drunk from a ceramic vessel designed especially for the occasion, and sometimes seasoned with chile powder, *achiotl* (similar to allspice), or vanilla, chocolate in all its consummate elegance completed the repast. Other stimulants and intoxicants, such as nicotine and local hallucinogens, might also be taken on ceremonial occasions as inhalants or instilled as colonics.

Music was always a part of Mesoamerican pageantry, and professional musicians as composers and instrumentalists doubtless enjoyed special status and rewards for their contributions. It seems to be the case that they were members of an aristocratic subculture along with advisors, scribes, priests, and other artists and craftspeople. Mayan musical instruments were of two genres, wind and percussion, with song and dance a part of every performance. At Bonampak, drums, trumpets, and gourd and tortoise-shell rattles were played in heraldic concert, but whistles, flutes, rattles, and rasps—ingeniously fashioned from shell, bone (sometimes human), wood, and clay—were also among Mesoamerica's musical instruments.

Kingship was the centerpiece of Maya life and empowerment derived from history, which was understood as local sacred knowledge invested in and manipulated by the ruler. Sacred knowledge included understanding time and the universe and the Mayas' relationship to both. Over the centuries, most Mesoamericans had worked out for themselves a nearly exact calendar system with a 52–year count based on astronomical observations and mathematical calculations. Very likely because of their need to determine optimal periods for planting and harvesting crops, indigenous scientists devised a means to reckon time based upon two calendar cycles.

One cycle was of 260 days, organized in a series of months from 1 to 13, each with 20 named days. The second cycle was of 365 days (the solar year) with 18 named months of 20 days each, followed by 5 "unlucky days" at the end. These calendars operated like two wheels of days, one somewhat larger than the other, that moved together and past each other in a steady rhythm. A given day in the 260–day calendar also had a position in the 365–day count, and every 52 years the two would coincide.

Maya intellectuals kept careful track of these time spans and elaborated their calculations in a long count that allowed them to date events of the past, present, and future with great accuracy. Reckoning by vigesimal multiples, or the counting by units of 20, rather than the more familiar decimal multiples, or units of 10 familiar today in the United States, they also established a sophisticated number system and used dots (one equal to 1) and bars (one equal to a count of five) to quantify Maya time and material culture.

The march of time for the Mesoamericans was intimately related to their cosmology, in which both the deities and men played vital roles. Months were named and had specific characteristics. Moreover, each month was associated with a particular deity whose duty it was to bear the burden of that period of time from beginning to end. Prophecy played a major role in interpreting time and the significance of the date of one's birth could prognosticate one's entire future. Celestial and environmental phenomena such as comets, earthquakes, floods, and famines were recorded and juxtaposed with other historical events.

The Mayas' religion was complex, for there was a full pantheon of deities to be reckoned with on a regular basis. The Maya world was divided into three horizontal strata. A series of layers of heavens lay uppermost. This sphere was followed by a middle one with all the trees and earthly things the Maya knew so well. Below that was an underworld, Xibalba, of nine planes. These three zones were sacred and connected with one another, but only Mayas who died in battle, while giving birth, or as victims of sacrifice were exempted from the dreaded Xibalba. All the others, as in Dante's *Divine Comedy*, were consigned to descend to the underworld and meet again forever in a Mayan afterlife.

The Mayas believed the creator of man to be an entity they called Hunab Ku, an abstract, elusive deity. He was the father of almighty Itzamna, god of the sky, the day, and the night. But the cosmos was not all beyond the reach of ordinary Mayas, for they believed that four *batabob* (lords) representing the cardinal directions and sacred colors (east—red; west—black or blue; south—yellow; north—white) held up the sky. A fifth direction, the center, was green. The sun, above all, literally, with its many theological attributes, was life and renewal as it made its daily round, cutting through all the spheres while keeping the Maya world whole.

Information about the kingship, time, and their deities was made available to the Maya public on the facades of palaces, temples, and stelae. Sacred knowledge was also recorded as history in codices, or books, with beautifully executed inscriptions and other images on screenfold (long sheets that were folded together as one does a screen or stretched open for reading) pages of bark or deerskin, which were paperlike products. Such sages as priests, kings, and scientists hoarded these books and copied and elaborated on their texts according to the occasion.

The Mayas had a rich syllabary language that greatly facilitated their production of written texts. Spoken words could be elaborated with signs, or logographs. Many such literary or spoken devices were inordinately complex in meaning, and not all of the texts have been translated even today. And doubtless not all Mayas could read these histories at the time they were produced, but their significance would have been made known to everyone at ceremonies when the kings and queens came before their fellow Mayas.

Ancestral privilege, prescribed as sacrosanct in the texts, conferred divine authority. Maya rulers drew upon these histories for consolation in periods of hardship and for inspiration when it was time to wage war. Invoking their subjects and their deities by means of gruesome self-mutilation—drawing blood with razorlike slashes on their ears, tongue, and penis—along with the intensity of ritual song and dance, burning torches and incense, and dramatic rhetoric, Maya rulers became the kingdom incarnate through blood sacrifice. Even commoners in locales too distant to permit firsthand participation at royal performances knew the ceremonies, understood that they were presented on their behalf, and felt their membership in the body politic to be secure.

Nevertheless, some things, such as a shift in economic power that occurred during the later years of the classical era in central Mexico, were beyond the control of the Maya kings, and by the end of the ninth century their influence was declining. Theories abound regarding reasons for the "classic Maya collapse," including epidemic disease, invasion, soil exhaustion and drought prompting agricultural collapse, and internal upheaval. Even a shift from the use of overland trading routes to new commercial waterways may have contributed to the Mayas' downfall. At any rate, the centers of the great Maya ethnic states were gradually abandoned one after the other, never to flourish again. The surviving Mayas dispersed, some emigrating to join native groups on the Yucatan Peninsula, which became the locus of control for trade between Mexico and areas south to Panama. Other Mayas moved into the volcanic highlands.

By the 11th century, well into what is described as the postclassic era, Maya settlements came under the influence of a series of invaders from various regions in central Mexico: the Chontal Mayas, Putuns, Toltecs, and others. Presumably, peninsular and highland Mayas had been trading with many of these groups for centuries. But exactly what prompted their large-scale move into the region is not

This is a masterpiece of classic Maya stone carving from a lintel at Yaxchilan, in lowland Guatemala, c. A.D. 725. King Shield Jaguar holds a burning torch while his kneeling queen, Lady Xoc, passes a thorn-embedded rope through her tongue as a blood offering. The finery of her robe, heavy jade pectoral, and bracelet and the elaborate headdresses of both rulers are especially ornate details. Hiero-glyphic inscriptions record the names and titles of the individuals, the date (28 October A.D. 709), and the event.

known. In Yucatan, the newcomer Itzas established their capital at Chichen Itza (Chichén Itzá), which is distinguished by its stunning architecture, stelae, ball courts, feathered serpent motif, and other features that are close in style partly to postclassic period structures at Tollan (believed to be modern-day Tula) in central Mexico but overall in most ways now considered to be distinctively Maya. Ethnically far more heterogeneous than any classic Maya rulership, and thus able to take great advantage of a range of innovative social and political practices, the Itzas would hold sway in northern Yucatan for close to two centuries.

Ultimately, however, the ancient tradition of Mayan lineage-based kingship prevailed. An alliance of dominant kin groups asserted itself and in 1221 successfully overthrew the Itzas. Centralized authority thus shifted from Chichen Itza to Mayapan (Mayapán), where several royal lineages that were in league, yet borrowing innovations from Chichen Itza, changed the prevailing art and architectural styles once again while they revitalized historical writing practices in the form of hieroglyphic inscriptions.

The *castillo* from the Temple of the Warriors is one of the most impressive structures at Chichen Itza, a Maya site. The Mayas dominated Yucatan for nearly two centuries until losing authority to Mayapan in 1221.

Thus, from 1221 to 1440 classic-style Maya lineages enjoyed dominance in Yucatan, at least until one group overthrew the others, shattering the confederacy. Subsequently, the governance of Yucatan broke into some 16 warring factions that fought one another for control of such local resources as salt and cacao but probably also continued to participate in long-distance trade networks. In the Maya highlands, the Quiche and Cakchiquel peoples claiming descent from central Mexico's much mythologized Toltec ancestors developed into formidable warring kingdoms, unifying and dominating the region until the 16th century.

It is about these Mayas that the Spaniards first wrote home, and it was Tulum's towers and palaces high on the cliffs above the Caribbean, one of the trade centers that succeeded Mayapan, that so impressed them. Appalled though they were at some of the Mayas' religious and social practices, the Spaniards nevertheless (and perhaps inadvertently) wrote favorably of the native peoples they met. It is from these reports that we cull critical historical information regarding the lives of the ordinary Mayas: their household living compounds; sizable, well-organized towns with adjacent cultivated fields; local government; cuisine; dress; tools and weapons; language, and, above all, their inordinate hospitality. Cycles of conquest were nothing new to Maya history. The Maya peoples still cherished and consulted their codices. That the Spaniards had similar sources of sacred knowledge seemed not to have been particularly remarkable to these Mesoamericans who had long perfected their own to rationalize nearly all the phenomena in the cosmos.

Contributing significantly to the formation of the Mayas' great rulerdoms was their connection through trade and perhaps marriage alliances with Teotihuacan (about A.D. 1–700), a contemporary classic-era site and society in north-central Mexico. By A.D. 200, Teotihuacan was a full-fledged indigenous metropolis with a commercial empire that facilitated first the development and then later the unification of numerous major polities that came to encompass peoples as far away as the Gulf Coast as well as Mexico's southernmost regions.

By all accounts the city of Teotihuacan was unique. Vast yet urbane, Teotihuacan has no known precedent in terms of sheer size, aesthetic refinement, or political ideology in all Mesoamerica. At its height, Teotihuacan epitomized all the best of the classic era's sophistication. Legend holds that Teotihuacan (a Nahuatl term signifying "where the gods lived") was where native deities first sacrificed themselves for the benefit of humans. Pyramids built upon or enclosing womblike caves corroborate local creation myths about the societies who first populated the region. There was in Teotihuacan an intimate association between gods and humans, and certainly their deities had a major influence on the lives of the large number of people who inhabited Teotihuacan over the course of at least five centuries. Indeed, their pyramids, temples, statuary, and murals commemorate a near pantheon of spiritual beings. In fact, and contrary to practices elsewhere in Mesoamerica, religion outweighed dynastic politics at Teotihuacan. No longer is the city believed to have been an idyllic paradise free of strife and violence of any sort. But neither was a warmongering lineage-based dynasty the center of life at Teotihuacan.

Although the people of Teotihuacan were surely ruled by native kings, who at one point dominated a population numbering close to 200,000 citizens, they apparently felt no great need for permanent public display of either their sovereignty or their individual accomplishments. Rather, if they appear at all in visual or oral history records, humans are most often deity impersonators. In beautifully painted murals of Teotihuacan-like universes, miniature figures with scroll-shaped designs in front of their mouths representing speech sing in praise of the munificence of the city's gods, who provided an abundance of rain and sunshine, flora and fauna. While familiar Mesoamerican counting and calendar systems were known and used in Teotihuacan, it seems that most other sacred knowledge there was theologically oriented. Even their monolithic stone sculptures, temple facades, and ceramicware were fashioned after deities.

Prevailing in the pantheon were images of a rain god (Tlaloc or Tláloc) and a water goddess (Chalchihuitlicue) a sun god and a moon goddess, an old fire god, and, of course, the omnipresent feathered serpent (Quetzalcoatl or Quetzalcóatl). Most ominous was Xipe Totec (Our Flayed Lord), the god of spring and renewal, whose deity impersonator actually wore the flayed skin of a sacrificed human.

This pervasive interest in religion should not be taken to imply that Teotihuacan was without the usual top-heavy bureaucracy of rulers and priests, along with cadres of councillors, merchants, and artists. The city monopolized obsidian along with other valuable commodities that were exchanged within the extensive trade emporium. Not uncommonly, guilds of craftsmen from distant centers at Monte Albán or Veracruz were relocated to Teotihuacan, where they oversaw the production of exotic goods that were otherwise unavailable domestically. As expatriates they made important contributions to the heterogeneous culture of the cosmopolitan city. At least one major district was set aside for the enterprise of Zapotec artisans.

Of all Teotihuacan's contributions to Mesoamerican culture, however, the most lasting was that of urban planning and architecture. Many indigenous societies in Mexico considered the number four to be a sacred quantity. Based upon what became the pattern for many successor states, some researchers postulate that Teotihuacan was divided into city quarters. Archaeological evidence indicates that the huge pyramids of the sun and moon were erected first along a central north-south axis, following a grid pattern.

Construction priorities in Teotihuacan then shifted to residential and temple structures. Each subdivision was made up of large square apartment complexes, some comprising as many as 175 units. Low-roofed, single-storied, and windowless, these apartments had fabric-covered doorways that opened onto well-ventilated, well-lit patios, which doubtless served a great variety of social functions. Each apartment had stately columned foyers that led to spacious lower-level courtyards. The buildings' stone facades were wonderfully worked with low-relief decorative designs.

These apartments were likely extended family compounds or clusters of accommodations for kin housed separately around a single patio. We know little of daily life in and around Teotihuacan, but most individuals were certainly involved in farming and other such activities in support of the city. The average man at Teotihuacan is thought to have been about 1.61 meters tall (about 5 feet 3 inches); a woman's height was approximately 1.45 meters (about 4 feet 9 inches). Their life expectancy is somewhat generously estimated to have been between 35 and 40 years.

The city's rulers probably lived in a separate area adjacent to the temple dedicated to the worship of Quetzalcoatl, now called the Ciudadela. A palace structure often included as many as 45 rooms along with atriums and courtyards, with ceremonial platforms nearby. It is in the palaces that the most exquisite murals are found, telling reminders of the inhabitants' ongoing preoccupation with the profound relationship of their deities to the natural world.

The center of the classic-era city of Teotihuacan (Teotihuacán) encompassed some seven square kilometers. This diagram reveals urban planning around the central "Street of the Dead," or "Great Avenue," along with numerous palaces, temples, courtyards, and residential and manufacturing districts as well as the famed Temple of the Feathered Serpent.

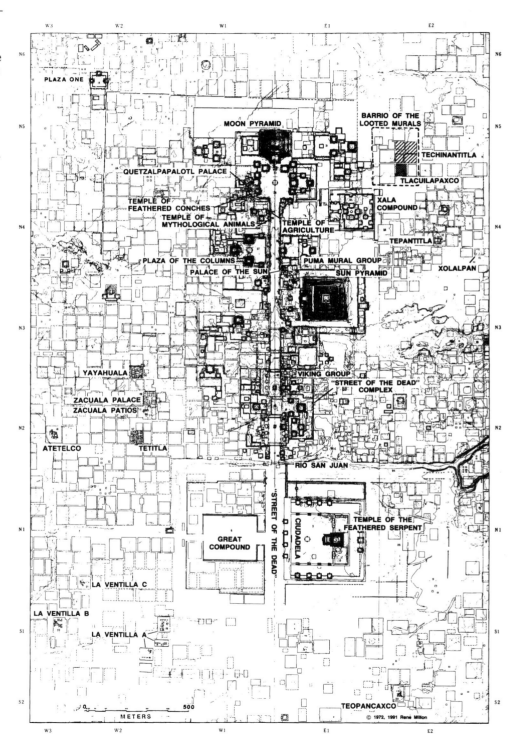

W3 W2 W1 E1 E2

N6

PLAZA ONE

N5 MOON PYRAMID

BARRIO OF THE LOOTED MURALS

TECHINANTITLA

QUETZALPAPALOTL PALACE

TLACUILAPAXCO

TEMPLE OF FEATHERED CONCHES

XALA COMPOUND

TEMPLE OF MYTHOLOGICAL ANIMALS

TEMPLE OF AGRICULTURE

N4 TEPANTITLA

PLAZA OF THE COLUMNS

PUMA MURAL GROUP

XOLALPAN

PALACE OF THE SUN

SUN PYRAMID

N3

YAYAHUALA

VIKING GROUP

"STREET OF THE DEAD" COMPLEX

ZACUALA PALACE

ZACUALA PATIOS

N2

ATETELCO TETITLA

RIO SAN JUAN

N1

GREAT COMPOUND

"STREET OF THE DEAD"

CIUDADELA

TEMPLE OF THE FEATHERED SERPENT

LA VENTILLA C

LA VENTILLA B

S1 LA VENTILLA A

500

S2 TEOPANCAXCO

METERS © 1972, 1991 René Millon

W3 W2 W1 E1 E2

Other motifs portray disquietingly fierce coyotes and jaguars, symbols that may be indicative of a militancy that would be institutionalized during the post-classic period. Other sectors of the city were designated solely for the manufacture of a plethora of items for trade and domestic consumption. However, the importance of obsidian during the classic era cannot be overstated, for at Teotihuacan at least 350 shops to work the material are known to have existed.

Shortly after A.D. 500, Teotihuacan's large population began to contract, and within a century key areas of the city were defaced by fire. What precipitated the downfall of a city of such grandeur and magnitude has yet to be determined. Whether directly related or not to Teotihuacan's decline, the influence of other quite extraordinary classic-era sites, such as Cholollan (today's Cholula), to the east, and Monte Albán, in the south-central region, among many others, also diminished over time. As with the great classic Maya capitals, these centers lost their influence and shrank demographically and territorially.

Over time, displaced groups, some migrating from the north, moved into the region and began to fill the void with their own still evolving and quite foreign social and political practices. Eventually, though, the outsiders would establish new capitals and dominions. Into what is known as the postclassic period, Mesoamerican society would never again achieve the general level of cultural sophistication that exemplified classical Teotihuacan or any of its contemporaries. Mexico's golden age was already in the past.

As had been the case in central Mexico since the beginnings of the Olmec civilization about 1500 B.C., a particular state might prevail politically and economically, but its preeminence depended upon the prosperity of a full complement of other polities for their trade, tribute (in some instances), and social alliances. For many, this was an advantageous relationship, jeopardized only when outsiders threatened the status quo.

The years following the fall of Teotihuacan were marked by cycles with influxes of outsiders who spoke different languages and had distinct cultures. No one knows the origin of these newcomers, called Chichimeca (Chichimecs)—a term of disputed definition—by the settled, more sophisticated societies in central Mexico. Nahuatl legends state that the Chichimeca came from Mexico's northern frontier, where human survival depended on hunting and gathering, sometimes over great distances. Characterized as a "desert culture," the Chichimeca subsisted with rudimentary material goods and by moving from place to place. Each group set out on its own, some already having leaders, one of whom was a "god carrier" with a deity bundle on his back. Of course, the Chichimeca also carried bows, arrows, and other weapons for hunting as well as for defense against marauders.

These natives might stay at a place for a few years to plant and harvest crops before pressing on. And following their calendar system—with regularity, apparently—they conducted their sacred fire ceremonies and "tied up their years" as part of the 52-year cycle described earlier. Their indigenous histories, called annals, are filled with stories of their trials and tribulations in the decades and even centuries of their peregrinations as various of the groups worked their way toward the fertile lands in central Mexico. Centuries later, the great kingdoms of Tetzcoco and Chalco would exalt the qualities of the Chichimeca—ruggedness, fortitude, success—and resurrect the name to dignify their highest-ranking lord and king, who became the "Chichimeca lord."

What distinguished these intruders from their classic-era predecessors was their militancy. Most notable among the intruders were the Toltecs, who established their capital at Tollan (Tula) a site some 60 kilometers (35 miles) southwest of Teotihuacan. The mythohistories tell of early Tula's patrician ruler-priest Topiltzin, who was devoted to the worship of the peace-abiding cult of Quetzalcóatl. Benevolent and well loved by his subjects, Topiltzin Acxitl Quetzalcóatl, as he came to be known, was nevertheless tricked by the vengeful, ruthless deity Tezcatlipoca. It is said that, most unbecomingly, Topiltzin committed incest and engaged in other lascivious activities. Ashamed because of the dishonor he brought on Tula's rulership, the king went to the Gulf Coast and departed by sea to exile sometime toward the end of the 10th century. In another version he was cremated upon arriving at the coast, then appeared in the heavens as Venus, the morning star.

These popular accounts convey little about the Toltec warrior cults, their actual warfare, or the practice of human sacrifice that was becoming commonplace. They do tell, however, of social conflict and factionalism, and help to explain in part the fall of Tula. As mentioned, when the Toltecs dispersed, some sectors joined forces with the Mayas and other central Mexico-influenced groups to establish their rule at Chichen Itza in Yucatan. Other Toltec descendants participated in the formation of the Quiche and Cakchiquel kingdoms that dominated the highlands of Guatemala well into the 16th century. The majority of the Toltecs, though, apparently stayed in central Mexico, relocating to sites such as Cholula (Cholollan), where they joined already settled groups and constructed one of the largest pyramids in all the Americas to perpetuate the worship of Quetzalcoatl.

It is the Toltec capital itself that exemplifies the indigenous beliefs and practices in the postclassic period (about A.D. 900–1150). Almost standard in Mesoamerica by this time were its pyramids, temples, ball courts, residential structures, altars, and monolithic stone columns or stelae. But at Tula the dramatic stone pillars are in the form of fearsome serpents and intimidating human warriors in full regalia. Even more awesome are the larger-than-life Chacmool, stone-carved humans holding basins to receive human hearts. Decorative motifs on temple walls portray images of Toltec military legions and their orders of the eagle, jaguar, and coyote. Skull racks and a painted serpent wall depict human sacrifice and cannibalism.

Gone were the reverential deity impersonators singing in glory of life and nature from the days of Teotihuacan. There was now no place for such worship at Tula, as was seen by the outcast king Topiltzin Acxitl Quetzalcoatl. These gods demanded more: War was the lifeblood of the Toltecs.

As at Teotihuacan, obsidian was the Toltecs' economic mainstay. Especially important by this time were the sharp glasslike points for weapons such as the *atlatl*, darts, and clubs, as well as the finely worked ceremonial knives that were used to extract hearts from sacrificial victims.

Toward the end of the 12th century, it is probable that internal strife combined with new waves of invaders from the north contributed to the end of Toltec supremacy. Tula had already been pillaged and burned, but its greatness remained permanently committed to the historical memories of its successors.

Although it was much influenced by Teotihuacan and its obsidian empire, the contemporary capital of Monte Albán in south-central Mexico was somewhat off the beaten path and thus in some ways suffered less of a chronological and cultural break than other such centers at the end of the classic period. Long inhabited by Zapotec speakers who independently and very early developed their own writing system, Monte Albán was first among numerous Zapotec capitals in Oaxaca. Architecturally, the Zapotecs' temples, platforms, and altars reflect a classic but somewhat modified *talud-tablero* pattern (an architectural feature where progressively sloping walls are interrupted with horizontal panel insets at each level), enhanced with elaborately worked exterior geometric designs.

As one might expect, most of the deities were similar to those at Teotihuacan and elsewhere, but with Zapotec names. Additionally, Monte Albán is known for the Danzantes, an arresting formative period parade of stone-carved wall panels showing some 150 representations of dead nude male figures. Perhaps signifying the conquest of former kings and thus serving as a warning for everyone else, the Danzantes are haunting reminders of the cycles of violence and upheaval that societies suffered even during the earliest years of Mesoamerican history.

Monte Albán ceramicware was as rich and varied as any, with many pieces taking the form of urns fashioned after local deities. Not uncommonly, vases, urns, and other pottery were included as funeral offerings in burial chambers, along with the immolated remains of humans. The Zapotecs' tombs, more than 170 of which have been excavated, are especially revealing of these people's worldview, for the chambers were lavishly decorated and filled with splendid gifts. Murals cover the walls in commemoration of their gods and the dignity of the recently deceased ruler. Moreover, written inscriptions in the form of hieroglyphs were ubiquitous at Monte Albán from formative times, although most of the glyphs have yet to be deciphered. Quite clearly, Zapotec intellectual developments influenced numerous societies, such as the Mayas in the south and in the east near Cacaxtla and Tlaxcallan, as well as other groups at their satellite manufacturing center in Teotihuacan.

Within their own sphere, the Zapotecs had established political alliances with another powerful group, the Mixtecs, in order to wage war against an enemy kingdom in Tehuantepec. Later the ties between the Zapotecs and the Mixtecs were secured through marriages between the royal houses of the two groups. Ultimately, as successors to the Zapotecs' realm, it was the Mixtecs who seemed to perfect the practice of marriage across political boundaries as a principal means of

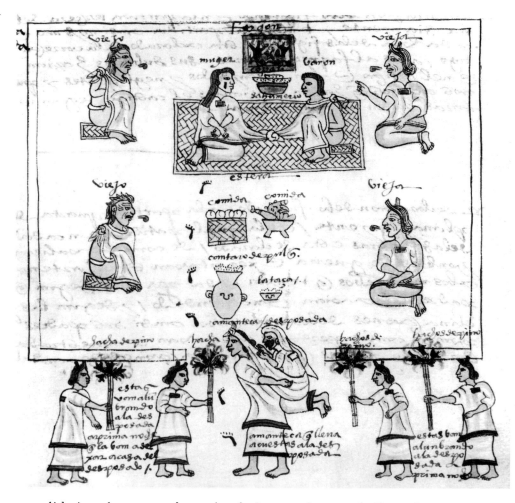

An early 16th-century Mexica Tenochca marriage scene. The bride and groom literally "tie the knot" as elders give advice to the couple. The marriage between the fifteen-year-old girl and the significantly older man was arranged by a matchmaker.

consolidating the area under each ethnic group's control. Once that was accomplished, lineages became so exclusive that, often enough, siblings married each other to singularize dynastic rule.

In postclassic Mesoamerica, Mixtec intellectuals—artists, architects, and scholars—established prestigious powerful enclaves in which they elaborated upon the legacy of their predecessors. At Mitla, for example, the intricate design and ornamentation of the temple complex were unparalleled. Their decorative art, whether in crystal, jade, gold, bone, or ceramic, was delicate and refined. And their codices were masterpieces in the manner of literary texts providing a history of their personal and political development. Some that have survived serve as precious, lasting records of Mixtec high society.

As with the ruler of the Mayas, the Mixtec rulers' authority derived from the culture's sacred books, written historical and genealogical accounts that typically traced back over centuries. It is likely that each dynastic house maintained its own records and used them to legitimate the lineage, keep track of time, and

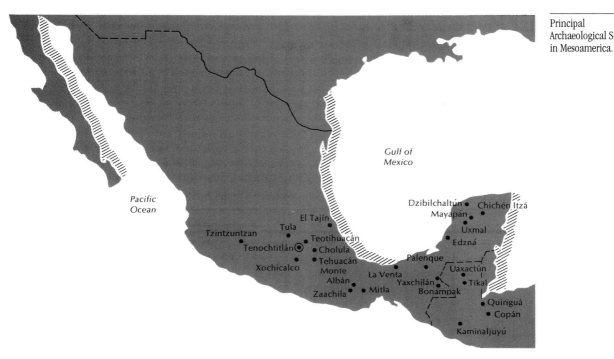

Principal
Archaeological Sites
in Mesoamerica.

follow the mandates of their deities. Mostly pictographic, the images in these texts likely served as encoded mnemonic devices for a king, priest, or laureate who elaborated the records in a high discursive style at political and religious ceremonies. During these grand occasions, musical festivities in the form of song and dance were still traditionally a part of each auspicious presentation, and everyone was brought into the celebration in one way or another as they not only shared in the retelling of their glorious history but also doubtless learned about all that was new for their society on that particular day.

Apt successors to and purveyors of infamous Toltec legend, the Mexica (who in the 15th century were instrumental in forming what is popularly called the Aztec Empire), or Aztecs, as they came to be known, were among a series of newcomers to central Mexico in the 13th century. According to native annals, they were one of several groups (the Chalca, Xochimilca, Tepaneca, and other peoples) who set out from the legendary remoteness in the north called Chicomoztoc, "Place of Seven Caves," in A.D. 1064. The cosmogony of the Mexica and their contemporaries was similar to that at Teotihuacan, where both deities and humans symbolically emerged from caves. The stories about the Mexica and their odyssey across the land and waters from the north are the best known, but all seven groups of Chichimeca travelers eventually made their way to Mexico's fertile central basin and established themselves in or near locales many of which have similar place-names today.

Mexica men, women, and children made up the party. Along with a succession of leaders, one or more priests carried their principal god from one place to another, appeasing the spiritual pantheon with appropriate ceremonies as they journeyed. These rituals did not exempt the travelers from hardship, however, which included warfare with other groups as well as horrific, competitive battles among their deities. At a site called Coatepec, near Tula, the god Huitzilopochtli prevailed, but only after first being forced to slaughter his malicious sister, Coyolxauhqui, immediately after his birth, when he was already a fully outfitted adult warrior, then consume the heart of their priestess-mother, Coatlicue, whom his sister had killed. According to their legends, it was through Huitzilopochtli's counsel that the Mexica ultimately arrived at their promised land and later established their rule as the Aztecs over much of Mexico from 1428 to 1521. The Mexica were thus obliged to their god thereafter.

But the Mexica had to prove themselves first, for as crude Chichimeca they were not welcomed by the long-settled, culturally refined peoples in any region. Accordingly, among various strategies to secure themselves a prime place to live, the Mexica offered themselves to the rulers of Toltec-connected Culhuacan (Colhuacan) as mercenaries against a rival government, and as proof of their prowess they brought back bags filled with the ears of their victims.

The records are legion regarding the Mexicas' exploits during these early years. The following example of an attempt to secure their relationship with Culhua royalty, while surely the most vivid, also foreshadows things to come. Subscribing to the popular myth of Toltec supremacy, the Mexica aspired to try to establish an ancestral affiliation with them through a marital alliance of one of their young men with the daughter of the king of Culhuacan, only to sacrifice the bride-princess, flay her, and have one of their deity-impersonator priests don her skin and display himself before her terrified father at a ceremony in honor of Xipe Totec. Of course, all the Mexica were banished from Culhuacan.

Undaunted, the Mexica followed Huitzilopochtli's prophecy that they should persist until they saw the symbol of an eagle with a serpent in its beak perched on a tall cactus. Thus, in A.D. 1324, while still much in disfavor, they settled on a rattlesnake-infested island, apparently the only place left for them. They named their home Mexico Tenochtitlan, "Place Next to the Prickly Pear Cactus," and the serpent and the eagle became permanent icons of Mexica culture.

But now that they were subject to the powerful rulers of the Tepanecas, whose capital was at Azcapotzalco, the Mexica were obligated to pay tribute and supply warriors to aid the Tepanecas in their conquests of additional peoples and territories. The Mexica also labored diligently to gentrify their Chichimeca ways by emulating the social manners of others with whom they came in contact.

Yet all the while the Mexica were developing their own social and economic situation at Tenochtitlan by means of *chinampa* agriculture. *Chinampas* were raised fields usually located in swampy areas or on the margins of lakes surrounding an island. Raised fields were formed from muck scooped from the lake bed and piled high in rows that could be easily irrigated and cultivated. This was an intensive form of agriculture, and since the soil was unusually fertile, specialty crops often were the preferred produce.

9ª. guerra de Azcaputzalco

The Mexica conquered the kingdom of Azcapotzalco under the leadership of Itzcoatl and Tlacaelel Cihuacoatl. The artist depicts weapons, warrior attire, and battle protocol along with the defeated, stripped warriors at the foot of the conquered ruler's palace. In this painting, even women take up arms.

It is likely that by the mid–1350s Nahuatl, the language of the Aztecs, was the dominant language in central Mexico, although Otomi, Pinome, and numerous other languages were also spoken. Best described as Nahuas in a general sense and because their language was largely the lingua franca of Mesoamerica, all the peoples in central Mexico nonetheless cultivated ethnic-based group identities. The independent Nahua political groupings were known as the *altepetl*, a compound of *atl* (water) and *tepetl* (mountain) that metaphorically signified the indigenous concept of kingdom or ethnic state, each with its own distinct name, territory, rulership, and society. These sovereign Nahua polities sought to enhance their wealth and prestige through trade, marital alliance, warfare, and subjugation.

The Mexica, still striving to establish their legitimacy through pointing up their Toltec ancestry, once again solicited a royal marriage with a Culhua woman. The offspring of this union, a son named Acamapichtli, thus ennobled, became the founder of and the first *tlatoani*, "He Who Says Something," in effect the king of the Mexica dynasty (see Table 2, page 77, for a list of the Mexica and Aztec leaders and kings). Acamapichtli enriched Mexico Tenochtitlan's human and material resources considerably, making it possible for his son Huitzilihuitl and then his grandson Chimalpopoca to succeed him and continue to expand the *altepetl*.

But it was Chimalpopoca's uncle, Itzcoatl, who took the kingdom to its apex while laying the foundation for the Aztec empire. With the assistance of other rulers, Itzcoatl conquered Azcapotzalco and created new alliances with the Tepanecas, the former overlords of the Mexica. Under this new regime succession to Mexica rulership depended not only on meritorious personal character and stalwart behavior on the battlefield but on the official approval of one's royal cohorts as well.

It cannot be said that the Mexica were necessarily innovators. Rather, their genius lay in appropriating established ideologies and practices and employing them for their own exaggerated purposes. The Mexica worldview—whether in religion, politics, economics, or society—fundamentally mirrored that of their predecessors. Theirs was a fourfold universe as well; they structured their lives after that sophisticated and complex cosmic principle.

Ideally, and following established Mesoamerican precedents, Mexica society was composed of two classes: nobles and commoners. But success as a warrior or merchant, or a good marriage, afforded considerable social mobility, and there were many exceptions to the rule. Likewise, Mexico Tenochtitlan was divided into four ranked cardinal Mesoamerican quadrants: Moyotlan in the southwest, Teopan in the southeast, Atzacualco in the northeast, and Cuepopan in the northwest. However, east, always the principal Mesoamerican direction, no longer ranked first.

The quarters of the altepetl were further divided into subunits called *calpolli*, which are more generally thought to be made up of commoners. Each *calpolli*, usually four or six in number, was headed by a lord-ruler who saw to the general well-being of the community, the collecting of tribute, the fulfillment of *calpolli* religious obligations, and the periodic channeling of required goods and labor to the *altepetl tlatoani*, or king, who in turn directed a portion of the commoners' obligations on to the *huey tlatoani*, or great king, the Aztec emperor. Each subunit was a self-contained, separate, equal unit with its own name, space, leader, deity, and society that mimicked the kingdom writ small. Efficiency in organization and operation was achieved by ranking the polities and the rulers of each constituency and systematically rotating their duties.

The Nahua household was the *calpolli* and *altepetl* in microcosm. The Nahua lacked a term for the family. At this most intimate level Nahua social organization was typically based upon a cluster of any number of houses opening onto a common patio, with sometimes several generations of occupants related by blood and marriage. Kinship, then, in one way or another bound the unit together, with an adult male probably serving as head of the overall household. Grandparents and parents, possibly widowed, with their children, siblings, nieces, nephews, and orphans (in no set pattern, it seems) might live in a particular house. Grouped together in a common territory, several clusters could make up a *calpolli*.

Marriages within and across group boundaries created as well as helped to maintain confederations of households, subunits, and kingdoms intact. Even in the grandest manifestation of the Aztec empire, its nexus was in large part its bringing of royal daughters from distant altepetl as brides for imperial kings, with their offspring often becoming rulers in the newly affiliated polity. Aztec kings reportedly had dozens of wives and at least as many children, but such practices were the privilege of the nobility, monogamy being the rule among the Nahua majority.

Indeed, marriage was a key event in the Nahuas' life cycle. Because marriage was considered to be a sacred covenant, brokers representing the families of the prospective bride and groom negotiated on their behalf. Such things as property, residence, and the ceremony itself were doubtless among the topics considered. Once all were in agreement, the bride was secluded and prepared for her marriage. A significant part of the wedding ceremony was the ritual "tying the knot"—literally joining together the bride's blouse or shirt and the groom's cape in a common knot at the shoulder.

The husband's responsibilities included providing for his family—whether by tending to his fields or working as a merchant or an artisan—and, of course, being ready to serve as a warrior when called upon. The wife's duties were just as important, for she had charge of the household, which included nurturing the family, planting and harvesting some crops, maintaining the home, performing certain sacred domestic rituals to foster prosperity, and weaving the textiles to clothe her family, satisfy tribute obligations, and perhaps exchange at the market.

The birth of a child was occasion for celebration and more ceremony. Among the rituals was one of burying the placenta in the dirt floor of the house. In the case of daughters, their umbilical cords were buried adjacent to the hearth. A priest was consulted to divine the baby's future and name her, and there was a presentation of symbolic gender-related tokens as gifts. Baby girls received kits of cooking tools and weaving swords; boys received farm tools, weapons, and other items to ensure success in the battles that likely lay ahead.

Children were cherished among the Nahuas, and most had strict upbringings. Both boys and girls attended school during their formative years. There was a school for commoners and another for children of noble families. Their parents instructed them as to their respective household roles. Females interested in serving as temple priestesses might attend a special school. Education was to ready one for the many responsibilities in life, and noble children especially were to prepare themselves for leadership as rulers, priests, scholars, scientists, jurists, or artists.

The Nahuas' social protocol was such that their language was rich in formulas and modes of eloquent high speech. Males used a special linguistic style to address one another. In their formalized speeches, elders admonished children to practice moderation in all behavior and to be respectful of their superiors. The ideal personality was described as a well-formed "face and heart." During the 15th and 16th centuries, Mexica society was nearly overburdened with well-bred nobles, intellectuals, and other specialists whose influence and contributions were believed critical for the continued well-being of the kingdom.

Mexica society had benefited extraordinarily from the political collaboration of King Itzcoatl and his half-brother Tlacaelel, a wizard of sorts when it came to setting the altepetl on course for greater expansion. Tlacaelel quickly earned the ominous title Cihuacoatl (woman snake), because he helped mastermind the interplay of Mexica theology, economics, and warfare to generate unheard-of wealth and prestige. It was under the joint leadership of Itzcoatl and Tlacaelel Cihuacoatl that the Aztec empire was established. The king and his Cihuacoatl even rewrote history as they launched new, extensive trade networks that brought in not only the supplies needed to sustain the Mexica, with a surplus for redistribution, but also a greater store of luxury items than had been known before.

Access to such resources most often depended on an elite cadre of merchants called *pochteca*, who traveled to both known and unknown territories to gain strategic intelligence and promote trade. Inevitably, warfare became necessary when alien peoples resisted Aztec intrusions. Once conquered (and only a few were able to withstand Aztec warfare over the long term), new subjects were required to furnish tribute in the form of whatever local specialty goods were desired and to provide allocations of young men and women for labor or ritual sacrifice. For example, by the 16th century 16,000 rubber balls from Tochtepec, near Veracruz, were required annually for games with them in the empire. Otherwise, except for an occasional exaction to support extraordinary imperial events in Mexico Tenochtitlan, apparently little else changed.

One major benefit of the extensive Aztec empire was the development of local and regional markets. Food, crafts, textiles, medicines, exotica, and slaves are only a few of the items available there for sale or exchange. By far the largest and most important market was at Tlatelolco, a co-kingdom of sorts on the island of Mexico Tenochtitlan. Some 50,000 people visited on major market days, and there was such an abundance and variety of items available that magistrates were appointed to guarantee their fair exchange. Currency was most often in the form of lengths of woven cloth or given quantities of cacao beans, which on more than one occasion were discovered to have been counterfeited, with soil or meal substituted for the flesh of the beans.

In addition to enjoying ostentatious displays at the markets, the Aztecs patronized guilds of artists and craftspeople to fashion many of the most precious items into exceptional works of art. The Aztecs likened their style and subject matter to those of Toltec arts, but in truth Aztec artists had as distinctive a style as any of their predecessors. Firsthand accounts by conquerors as well as native survivors attest to an Aztec signature style in the decorative arts. For example, work with feathers from many regions of Mesoamerica was exhibited in exquisite headdresses, shields, fans, and courtly attire, and no doubt feather tapestries and the like decorated palaces, temples, and residences. Other luxuries were finely worked ceramics, mosaics, gold, silver, and copperware, and precious stones, jade and turquoise being among the most coveted.

Almost in deliberate contrast to their delicate fine art was the Aztecs' stone statuary. Great numbers of massive—usually terrifying—images of some of their more haunting deities were sculpted with nothing but stone tools. Their representation of Coatlicue, Huitzilopochtli's mother, for example, is estimated to weigh as much as 16 tons. These imposing sculptures were then strategically positioned to reaffirm the Aztecs' devotion to their gods. Their street corners, temple plazas, and most other landmarks were adorned with such creations as enormous fanged serpent heads, stone skulls, skeleton figures, and tall, stark human standard-bearers.

Without doubt, the highest Aztec aesthetic expression came in literature and music. Each Nahua *altepetl* had its own literary tradition derived from annals; philosophical, theological, and astronomical treatises; dynastic genealogies; and oral histories. Moreover, it exalted its own heritage and accomplishments to the exclusion of almost everyone else's. *In tlilli in tlapalli* (the black the red) was the Nahuatl metaphor for writing, but in truth their books were filled with brightly colored pictorial images. Recorded on paper made from the bark of a native tree (the *amaquabuitl*, or "paper tree"), the Nahuas stored their precious books, along with maps, tribute records, and other official and personal accounts, in royal libraries.

But notwithstanding their other literary accomplishments, the Aztecs became masters of history and oratory. Among the population at large, the prevailing wisdom of their sages was presumed to supersede that of everyone else. Rulers, priests, scholars, scribes, and artists collaborated to create an Aztec literary canon. Success in war, the installation of a new king on the throne, festivities in honor of a particular deity, and events called for by the ceremonial calendar were all occasions when the books were brought before the public and the privileged information contained therein was revealed. The images in the texts were memorized and, in concert with instrumental music, dancing, and burning incense, the Nahuatl song-liturgy repeatedly brought to life the full pageant of Aztec culture.

By 1428 the long reach of the Mexica and their great prosperity warranted centralizing their operations into a three-way power structure with two other powerful *altepetl*—Tetzcoco and Tlacopan, thereby launching what is now referred to as the Aztec Empire. Tlacaelel Cihuacoatl survived Itzcoatl and two of his successors. In league with the additional rulerdoms, the Triple Alliance greatly expanded Aztec territory with its combined military might. In its own way, Aztec warfare must have been a sight to behold, for many warriors joined highly esteemed knightly orders, each with its own special heraldic insignia, banners, costumes, privileges, and protocol in battle. The orders of the eagle and the jaguar knights are thought to have been the most prestigious.

In this period Mexico Tenochtitlan became a showplace. Along with statuary, magnificent palaces and temples were constructed, and elaborated upon by successive rulers. It is estimated that the combined urban area of Tenochtitlan and Tlatelolco was close to 16 square kilometers (6 square miles). By the 16th century, the imperial court was a walled compound enclosing numerous warehouses to store the tribute and plunder from warfare, plus apartments, ball courts, a skull

Moteuczoma Xocoyotl (Moctezuma Xocoyotl) stands in traditional dress before a Romanesque landscape in this fanciful late 16th- or early 17th-century European depiction.

rack, palaces for rulers and their families, a zoo, gardens, libraries, tribunals, and an armory. Serving the needs of the Aztecs' court required hundreds of people every day, and its glitter and sumptuousness surpassed all else known in native North America.

Moteuczoma Xocoyotl (popularly called Montezuma), the Aztec emperor fated to negotiate with Hernán Cortés and the Spaniards on behalf of Aztec America, was a ruler without peer. In his intelligence, personal style, and leadership he personified all that was ideal for his time, as well as its traditions. Within his court were the twin temples, or *Templo Mayor*, dedicated to Tlaloc, the rain god, and Huitzilopochtli. The Templo Mayor was possibly conceived as the center of the Aztec universe and was thus a sacred, powerful precinct. Archaeologists, art historians, and religion specialists tend to support the interpretation that the Templo Mayor was constructed in stages to commemorate Huitzilopochtli's savage creation experience with his mother and sister at Coatepec (Snake Mountain) centuries before. A serpent staircase with a massive grotesque sculpture of a dismembered Coyolxauhqui positioned at its foot, the symbolic details embellishing the temple, the Chacmool, the buried caches of offerings representative of the wealth and expanse of the empire, and a variety of firsthand accounts corroborate the public reputation of the omnipotence of the Aztecs' god. In fact, Tlacaelel and successive Aztec rulers had done much to cultivate the idea that an inexorable Huitzilopochtli controlled their lives.

The Aztecs thus believed that the universe and time were measured by epochs, or suns, and were subject largely to the whimsy of cosmic deities. Four previous suns had ended cataclysmically, and the present, the fifth, would be the last, ending in a a violent earthquake. Every 52 years on a given date the Nahuas re-enacted their much-hallowed fire ceremony in anticipation of initiating another calendar cycle. With great reverence and atonement all fires were extinguished. Houses were meticulously cleaned, old items discarded. Then, as night approached, a victim was sacrificed and everyone waited as deity impersonators climbed a mountain south of the capital and, using drills, attempted to kindle a new fire in the gaping chest of the sacrificed person. A flame ensured life for everyone else once again.

Politics still prevailed in the Aztecs' capital, with religion playing a close second. Emperors frequently consulted temple priests to determine propitious times to go to war, as well as to interpret ominous celestial and environmental signs, such as a comet or smoke from the volcanoes. The Aztecs' theologians mandated a collective, all-pervasive religion, with life after death far less a concern than the here and now. Human existence on earth was elusive and transitory, as is reflected in the Aztecs' philosophy and poetry, which often equated life with the blossoming of a beautiful flower that fades and disappears into the earth all too soon.

To be certain that one would have the opportunity to enjoy life at all, it was necessary to follow imperial prescriptions designed to regulate everything from adultery and the consumption of *pulque* (an alcoholic beverage made from the maguey) to when and against whom war would be waged. An elaborate assortment of ceremonies celebrated a galaxy of deities from the past as well as those assimilated in the course of their conquests, but the most onerous requirement was the sacrifice of a given quantity of humans whose hearts were offered to Huitzilopochtli, the warrior-deity emissary to the sun. The Aztec clergy claimed that from time to time it was necessary to sacrifice a number of humans. Therefore, warfare was frequently followed by sacrifice to satisfy any number of ends. Human sacrifice was also used by emperors to intimidate subject kingdoms. Reportedly, in the late 1480s more than 80,000 men were killed on one such occasion.

By the era of Moteuczoma Xocoyotl (1502–20), Aztec economics, politics, and religion were closely interwoven. But the emperor's authority always prevailed, and when he took to the field in battle or joined his priests at the top of the Templo Mayor and deftly cut out the heart of a war captive, it was as much for political control as it was for the glory of the gods and the enrichment of the state. His orthodoxy was profound, but Moteuczoma Xocoyotl brought into play the cumulative knowledge and practices of his forebears when confronted by circumstances that had no explanation in the Aztecs' sacred texts, such as the strangeness of Spanish ships reconnoitering off Veracruz; the unfamiliarity of horses, vicious dogs, and guns; and the inexplicable violence of the Spaniards themselves.

Aztec protocol demanded diplomacy and negotiation; reciprocal gift giving, including women; propitiation of their deities; and combat. But even many centuries' worth of Mesoamerican tradition was no match for European institutions and technology, to say nothing of the urgency of otherwise very humble Spaniards who felt the necessity of making something of themselves off Aztec spoils. Moteuczoma Xocoyotl's vast empire and the majesty of his metropolis, Mexico Tenochtitlan, were all and more than Cortés and his followers could have ever imagined.

TABLE 1
General Chronology of Mesoamerican Culture Epochs

Classification		
Archaic		c. 1500 B.C.
Preclassic, or Formative	c. 1500 B.C.	c. A.D. 100
Classic		
Central Mexico	c. A.D. 1	c. A.D. 900
Maya	c. A.D. 250	c. A.D. 900–1000
Postclassic		
Central Mexico	c. A.D. 900	c. A.D. 1521
Maya	c. A.D. 900–1000	c. A.D. 1540

TABLE 2
Mexica/Aztec Leaders and Kings

Order	Name	Rule*	Title
1.	Moteucçoma	n.a.	
2.	Chalchiuhtlatonac	n.a.	
3.	Quauhtlequetzqui teomama	1168–1205	*teyacanani* (leader)
4.	Acacitli	1205–1219	teyacanani
5.	Citlalitzin	1219–1234	teyacanani
6.	Tzinpan	1234–1235	teyacanani
7.	Tlaçotzin	1235–1239	teyacanani
8.	Tozcuecuextli	1239–1278	teyacanani
9.	Huehue Huitzilihuitl	1278–1299	*tlatoani* (king) of the Mexica Chichimeca
10.	Tenochtzin	1299–1363	teyacanani, *quauhtlatoani* (interim ruler)
11.	Acamapichtli	1367–1387 (1376–1396) Tenochtitlan	tlatoani, first king of Mexico
12.	Huitzilihuitl	1391–1415 (1397–1417)	tlatoani
13.	Chimalpopoca (1417–1427)	1415–1426	tlatoani
14.	Itzcoatl	1427–1440	tlatoani
15.	Huehue Moteucçoma Ilhuicamina Chalchiuhtlatonac	1440–1468	tlatoani
16.	Axayacatzin	1469–1481	tlatoani
17.	Tiçoc	1481–1486	tlatoani
18.	Ahuitzotl	1486–1502	tlatoani
19.	Moteucçoma Xocoyotl	1502–1520	*huey tlatoani* (great king)

*There is some discrepancy in dates in the various annals. Alternative dates are given in parentheses.
Source: Don Domingo de San Antón Muñón Chimalpahin Quauhtlehuanitzin, "The Diario," Bibliothèque Nationale, Fonds Mexicain 220, pp. 72–75, 104–106. See also Elizabeth Hill Boone, *The Aztec World*. Montreal and Washington, D.C.: St. Remy Press and Smithsonian Books, 1994, p. 47.

Don ferdinando Cordeisny 1 5 z 9 semes
altere   Jm 4 z diser hat der kay
azter   karoius dem fimften
herr   ach hann zJndiann
                                  gewunnen.

3

The Collision of Two Worlds

ROSS HASSIG

The Spanish conquest of Mexico is not merely another instance of history being written by the victors but one in which the sole first-hand accounts were theirs, inexorably channeling our understanding along the contours they first plotted. Moreover, the conquistadores' accounts were written for patently political purposes: to justify their actions, to conform to Spanish understandings of legitimate conquest, to secure the support of the king of Spain, and to receive lands and wealth for their deeds.

Spain's expansion into Mexico was a logical extension of its exploration and colonization of the Indies. Authorized by Governor Diego Velásquez de Cuellos, Francisco Hernández de Córdoba left Cuba on February 8, 1517, with three ships and 110 men. Reaching Cape Catoche, Yucatan three weeks later, he saw for the first time native cities and sophisticated civilizations. But Spanish claims of ownership under the king of Spain clashed with those of indigenous rulers, and the heavily armed Spaniards soon found themselves engaged in combat. Despite two dead and many wounded, the Spaniards prevailed and looted the gold from the town once it was abandoned.

Córdoba quickly sailed along the Yucatan coast, landing often to replenish his food supplies. But since rainfall quickly drains into the limestone slab that is the Yucatan (Yucatán) Peninsula, the only fresh water available was from *cenotes* (natural wells). There being no visible streams carrying water into the ocean, the Spaniards knew there were wells only when they saw Mayas cities. Sometimes, as at Campeche, the Mayas allowed the Spaniards to take water, but often they resisted.

At Chanpoton (Champotón), thanks to their superior arms the Spaniards managed to fight off the surrounding Mayas, but 50 were killed, 2 captured, and all but 1 wounded. Córdoba sailed back to Cuba, which he reached on April 20, where he, too, died.

After leading the Spanish Conquest of Mexico, Cortés returned to Spain and, in 1522, obtained the coveted office of governor of Mexico. Charles V also granted him hereditary lordship (*señorío*) of the Valley of Mexico with the title of Marquis of the Valley of Oaxaca.

Thus alerted to the wealth of this newly discovered land, Velásquez dispatched a second expedition, under Juan de Grijalva, who reached Cozumel on May 3, 1518, with 200 men. A cautious man, Grijalva reconnoitered the coast but avoided battle with the Mayas, though when attacked—often while attempting to secure supplies—he defended himself with artillery. Avoiding further hostile attack, these Spaniards sailed along the coast as far as central Veracruz before retracing their route and returning to Cuba on April 20, 1517.

Neither Córdoba nor Grijalva appear to have caused much long-term or fundamental change in the groups they encountered. But Grijalva's expedition did make the first direct contact with Aztecs in Veracruz, and word of his arrival reached King Moteuczoma Xocoyotl in his capital of Tenochtitlan (now Mexico City). This arrival was thoroughly discussed by the king and his advisors, who decided to take no direct action but to dispatch watchers to the coast.

The Aztecs drew on their own background to interpret the Spanish arrival in a meaningful way. Because the Spaniards were unlike any people they had seen before and they possessed what seemed godlike technological capabilities (cannons, harquebusiers, sailing ships, horses, metal armor), a supernatural origin for them had to be considered, but that they were thought to be the god Quetzalcóatl is probably an ex post facto rationalization of events. Whether the invaders were gods or men, there was little the Aztecs could do. Unlike armies, whose timing and probable avenues of approach could be predicted, the Spanish ships offered little warning and could land anywhere along hundreds of miles of coast, and it was not possible to defend the entire coastline.

Meanwhile, even before Grijalva returned to Cuba, Governor Velásquez appointed Hernan Cortés to lead a third expedition to Mexico. A controversial choice for commander, Cortés owed his selection in large part to judicious lobbying by the governor's secretary, Andrés de Duero, and the king's accountant, Amador de Lares, both of whom were his secret allies.

More than 350 men had been recruited for the expedition when rumors about Cortés's intentions not to adhere strictly to Velásquez's orders turned the governor against him. Forewarned of Velásquez's plans to remove him from command, Cortés hurriedly left Santiago de Cuba and sailed first to the port of Trinidad, then to Havana, where he secured more men and supplies. Though Velásquez ordered the local authorities to seize and imprison him, Cortés's force was too formidable. He sailed for Yucatan on February 10, 1519, and arrived with 11 ships, as many as 450 soldiers (including 13 harquebusiers and 32 crossbowmen), four small cannons called falconets, 10 brass cannons, and 16 horses. He landed at Cozumel, where Grijalva's expedition had gone ashore, and there made one of a series of fateful decisions that would crucially influence the outcome of his expedition. First he dispatched a ship to hunt for Spaniards rumored to be held among the Mayas. Of 18 Spaniards shipwrecked off the Yucatan coast in 1511, 2 still survived. One, Gonzalo Guerrero, now bore native tattoos, had married an Indian woman and raised a family, and had risen to high rank in Maya society. Thus assimilated, he refused to return. But the other, Gerónimo de Aguilar, joined Cortés and was to serve as a trustworthy translator of Maya throughout the Conquest.

Cortés then sailed around the coast of Yucatan to Potonchan, where he landed. Met by armed warriors, Cortés ordered Aguilar to read the *requerimiento* (summons) in Maya to the opposing forces, demanding that they recognize the authority of the church, pope, and king, on penalty of subjugation. Then his forces routed the Indians in battle and took possession of the town.

After a subsequent battle in which more than 35 Spaniards were lost, the Mayas pledged fealty and gave them gifts, including 20 women. Among these was one from the Coatzacoalco (Coatzacualcos) region of the southern Gulf Coast who has become known as La Malinche, or Doña Marina, as she was baptized by the Spaniards.

Marina, who spoke both Maya and Nahuatl, is often credited in her role as Cortés's translator with playing a key role in the Conquest. However, her importance as interpreter has been considerably overstated. First, there were many Maya and Nahuatl speakers on the southern Gulf Coast where these two languages abutted, any one of whom could have served as translators as easily as Marina. Second, at least two Spaniards—Orteguilla and Juan Pérez de Artiaga—learned Nahuatl before the fall of Tenochtitlan, thereby reducing the importance of Marina's presence. And third, as useful as a Maya and Nahuatl translator was, the truly crucial linguistic leap was not between two indigenous languages but rather between a European and an indigenous one. This connection was achieved not by Marina but by Gerónimo de Aguilar, who spoke both Spanish and Maya and accompanied her throughout the Conquest.

Having defeated the Mayas at Potonchan, Cortés removed the statues of their gods there and replaced them with a cross, setting a pattern of nominal conversion to Christianity only after subordination that he was to follow thereafter throughout the Conquest. Staying near Potonchan, the Spaniards tended their wounded for five days before sailing on to Mexico, which the Maya had identified as the source of their gold and jewels.

On April 21, Cortés reached San Juan de Ulúa, which Grijalva had made his harbor on the central Veracruz coast. There his ships were met by canoes full of Indians sent by the Aztec governor of the region, Tentlil. After receiving food and trade goods, the Indians departed and Cortés landed his men, artillery, and horses, and fortified a camp. The following day, Tentlil and 4,000 men arrived from Cuetlachtlan (Cotaxtla) laden with food and gifts, including many gold objects, which, for the Spaniards, confirmed the Maya reports. But the Aztecs' real purpose was to gather information for Moteuczoma, and the artists who accompanied them drew pictures of everything they saw. In what was probably an attempt at psychological one-upmanship, the Spaniards demonstrated their weapons, charged their horses, and fired their cannons. The Aztecs encamped near the Spaniards and provided them with food while awaiting Moteuczoma's response.

A week later, Tentlil returned with still more lavish gifts from Moteuczoma and a request that the Spaniards remain on the coast and not come to Tenochtitlan.

Moteuczoma's emissaries brought food to the Spaniards. They presented them with tortillas sprinkled with human blood, which the Spaniards refused. But they did eat other tortillas, turkey eggs, turkeys, and a variety of fruit and vegetables. The messengers included wizards who had been charged with casting spells on the Spaniards, but whose efforts failed.

The king also asked that the Spaniards move their camp to a village six or seven leagues away. Both requests were refused, making it clear that the Spaniards were not settling comfortably into a recognized, limited relationship with the Aztecs. Left uncertain about who the Spaniards were and how they related to the Aztecs, Moteuczoma dared not challenge them directly. But his Aztecs did decamp on May 12, leaving the Spaniards equally uncertain and fearful of attack.

Once Moteuczoma's conditions had been so thoroughly rejected by the Spaniards, for him to continue to feed, house, and support them would have been, in effect, an acknowledgment of his own subordination to them. So politically Moteuczoma had little choice, but in breaking off contact he also relinquished control of the situation. By keeping watch for the Spaniards and immediately sending envoys, the Aztecs had ensured that they alone would have contact, because their presence kept any local groups at bay. But once the failure of their political negotiations forced the Aztecs to withdraw, nothing prevented other groups from making contact. Within three days, the local Totonacs visited the Spaniards, giving Cortés his first hint that the Aztecs had enemies.

Just as important as establishing ties to local disaffected Indians, however, was consolidating Cortés's support among the Spaniards. Many wanted to return to Cuba, especially those loyal to Velásquez. But by legal sleight of hand Cortés established the town of Villa Rica de la Veracruz, complete with a city council that claimed its authority directly from King Charles V. This legal fiction bypassed the governor, at least in theory, allowing the handpicked town council to reappoint Cortés captain under the king's authority, thus freeing him from the restraints imposed by Velásquez.

Leaders in the New World were accustomed to considerable autonomy, because inquiries to the Crown typically required at least a full year for a response as a result of the distance and the limited number of favorable sailing times. Cortés used this delay to his own advantage. Before he could be stopped, either by force or by unchallengeable, direct royal edicts, he would either have conquered Mexico or failed, and his own actions would have decided his fate. Failure meant a likely charge of treason against the Crown and its officials, but success meant land, wealth, and the king's support, regardless of Velásquez's objections.

Cortés's legal maneuver was therefore not intended to legitimize his actions as much as it was to delay complying with Velásquez's orders, provide a pretext for his own actions, and permit future legitimization if he succeeded. Nevertheless, Velásquez's supporters protested when they discovered what Cortés had done, so he mollified them by saying that anyone could return to Cuba if they wished. He never had to keep this promise—and probably never intended to—because he eventually won over Velásquez's supporters by promising to increase their share of the booty.

Having thus solidified his standing among the Spaniards, at least temporarily, Cortés now turned to the matter of Indian support. He marched to nearby Cempohuallan (Zempoala), from which the Totonacs had come, reaching the town on June 3, where he was greeted with gifts of food and lodging. There the local ruler expressed his displeasure with the Aztecs, to whom he paid tribute, and indicated his desire to ally himself with the Spaniards against them, although how much of this was divulged freely and how much was prompted by Cortés is unclear. This offer of an alliance was the first evidence Cortés had that there were significant disaffections and political cleavages among the Aztec tributaries, which he exploited quickly.

Cortés may in fact have been led somewhat astray by the Totonacs' expression of disaffection. In Europe such outspoken opposition by a vassal was considerably more serious than in Mexico, because of the deep differences that underlay the superficial similarities in the Aztec and Spanish empires. Instead of conquering new areas and consolidating their hold over them so they could extract large quantities of tribute (though at a high administrative cost in replacing local rulers and maintaining troops in the European fashion), the Aztecs conquered cities but left the local regimes intact. This hegemonic approach produced less tribute than the European model because it exerted less control, but it also freed soldiers for further expansion.

What kept such an indirectly ruled system operating was simply power—the perception that the Aztecs could enforce their goals—rather than force, direct physical action. Aztec tributaries policed themselves, but the success of the overall system depended on having a strong king, because the empire was vulnerable to collapse if he was weak or indecisive. Thus, the king's military prowess was not simply a matter of ideology or honor but was essential to sustain the empire. The death of a king could disrupt the system if a strong successor was not chosen. Therefore, while the Totonacs were tributaries of the Aztecs and owed them fealty and tribute, their own political system and functionaries remained otherwise intact. The appearance of the Spaniards altered the political equation on which the Totonacs based their compliance, just as their emerging alliance altered the power balance for the Spaniards.

There was no possibility that Cortés could conquer the Aztec empire, regardless of his technological superiority. The Spaniards were so few that they could be overwhelmed and destroyed by sheer numbers, and enlisting more Spanish troops from the Indies was not feasible, given Cortés's political situation. The alternative was to divide the Indians, which was the course of action Cortés followed throughout the Conquest. He began by promising to aid the Totonacs against the Aztecs.

During the weeks he stayed with the Totonacs, Cortés found other cities with similar complaints against the Aztecs. These cities, too, he promised to help. When five Aztec tribute collectors reached Cempohuallan, Cortés ordered the Totonacs to seize them and refuse to pay any more tribute or obey Moteuczoma. The Totonacs did so, though it is unclear whether Cortés actually planned this or merely took credit for it in his account to the king. In any event, the Totonacs seized the tribute collectors. By his own account, Cortés later pleaded ignorance of this action to the tribute collectors and released two of them to assure Moteuczoma that the Spaniards remained friends. When the Totonacs were understandably upset, Cortés feigned outrage that the two collectors had "escaped," yet he subsequently (and secretly) freed the remaining three Aztecs as well.

Cortés was certainly capable of duplicity, and his own account of these events, written some three years later in 1522, presents these actions as deliberate, which they may have been. But there is reason to believe otherwise. First, Cortés could not have fully understood the political situation, because he did not grasp the powers and limitations of either the local kings or the Aztec emperor. Second, he did not know the size of the forces arrayed against him. Third, he did not understand their military potential, inasmuch as his only battles thus far had been against the less organized Mayas. And fourth, if his role in seizing and then releasing the five Aztecs and denying this to the Totonacs was a knowing one, it indicates a level of duplicity unmatched in his relations with any subsequent native allies. If he in fact did as he claimed, his actions might have been born of an ignorance that his subsequent experiences tempered. But the potential for misunderstanding between the Spaniards and the Totonacs was so great that Cortés gained the Totonacs' fealty without yet breaking with the Aztecs.

Although Cortés may have placed little faith in his own pledge of fealty to the Aztecs, the same was likely true of the Totonacs, in that realpolitik dominated the region's political ties. If their alliance with Cortés proved ineffectual, the Totonacs would have quickly had to resubmit themselves to the Aztecs. But given the potential consequences of shifting one's allegiance, the Totonacs must have seen the Spaniards as powerful, however much the seizure of the tribute collectors, regardless of who instigated it, forced the situation.

Forging alliances was crucial to the Spaniards. Once they had secured allies, however, the Spaniards began building and fortifying the city of Villa Rica de la Veracruz. During this period Cortés had contact with Aztec emissaries, which must have made his Totonac allies wary. So with their request that he help assault an Aztec garrison at Tizapantzinco, Cortés was placed in the awkward position of not wanting to alienate the Aztecs but needing Totonac support to march inland, or even to stay where he was. The latter being a crucial need, he dispatched virtually his entire force of 400 soldiers to accompany the 4,000 Indian warriors. However, the Aztecs had already left Tizapantzinco when the joint army arrived, something the Totonacs surely knew, but Cortés's act demonstrated his commitment to them. In any case, this overt action cemented Cortés's Totonac alliance, and he was given eight of their women, all daughters of kings and nobles.

Intermarriage between the ruling families of allied towns was a common way of strengthening political ties in Mesoamerica. Even if this significance was lost on the Spaniards, it was important to the Cempohualtecs. With the Totonacs tied to the Spaniards, Cortés now bound Cempohuallan's rulers to him through religious conversion, which was done for thoroughly political reasons.

Some religious motivation may have underlaid Cortés's attempt at converting the Cempohualtecs, because he had sought the release of slaves being held for sacrifice when he had first reached Cempohuallan. But when rebuffed, he subordinated these religious concerns to the more immediate political ones of forging alliances. Only after these were secure did Cortés impose his religion and destroy the Totonac idols. The placing of Christian objects in the temples of Cempohuallan was vigorously opposed by the native commoners as well as priests, and any conversions must have been superficial at best. But deferring the conversions until the local rulers could be made politically dependent on the Spaniards suggests a political purpose, both in justifying Cortés's own actions to the Spanish throne and in forcing Cempohuallan's leaders to accept the destruction of their old gods and the introduction of new ones or risk losing Spanish support, which would invite Aztec retribution.

Throughout the Conquest, other Spanish ships reached Mexico. One arrived at this point, bringing news that King Charles had authorized Velásquez to trade with and establish settlements in Mexico. Having this to bolster his own claim, Cortés dispatched a ship to Spain on July 6, with not just the king's royal fifth but all the gold collected thus far. But when, against his orders, the ship first stopped in Cuba, word of Cortés's perfidy reached Velásquez, prompting the governor to ready a fleet to capture him.

At this point Cortés again had problems with some of his men, perhaps because they were now having second thoughts, or because he had sent all their booty to the king, or because they now had a fuller appreciation of their precarious position. Therefore, claiming that Velásquez loyalists had conspired to seize a ship and sail to Cuba, Cortés arrested them, ordered the two principal conspirators hanged, the pilot's feet cut off, and the others given 200 lashes each, though not all of these sentences were carried out. Whether or not there actually was such a plot, Cortés used it to justify secretly stripping the 10 remaining ships and sinking them, leaving his men no way to escape. He then forged ahead with his plan to march inland, left Juan de Escalante in command of Veracruz with 60 to 150 soldiers, and solicited 40 or 50 warriors and 200 porters from the Totonacs, and left Cempohuallan on August 16 with 300 Spanish soldiers.

The Aztecs did not react to these events in any overt way, though Moteuczoma could not have remained ignorant of them. Moreover, he had been consulting with his advisors about how the Spaniards should be treated ever since Grijalva had landed, and once the decision had been made to take no action any change, even by the king, could have undermined the political consensus upon which his support depended. So Cortés's force was allowed to proceed unmolested.

Following the advice of the Cempohualtecs, Cortés marched toward Tlaxcallan (Tlaxcala), even though it was hostile to the Aztecs, who had thus far been helpful and friendly. The Tlaxcaltecs must have known of the Spaniards' landing, of their trek inland, and that they were accompanied by loyal Aztec tributaries as well as Totonacs, and must have been aware that they had been lodged and fed along the way in towns allied with the Aztecs. Thus, they had every reason to believe the Spaniards hostile.

As they approached the border of Tlaxcallan, the Spaniards saw a small party of armed Indians, which they tried to capture. But they were resisted, and several horses and riders were wounded. The Spaniards pursued them but were drawn into an ambush, from which they narrowly escaped, though with more wounded and one dead.

The Tlaxcaltec army was the first professional force that Cortés had encountered in Mesoamerica, and he had seriously underestimated their threat, though the danger was as much political as military. If Cortés were defeated or even repulsed, his allies would see him as weak, cease all aid, and, most likely, turn on him. Whether he fully realized it or not, Cortés had gambled that he could overcome all adversaries. The possible consequences for his alliances thus prevented him from following the most prudent military course—withdrawal.

Another battle began the next day, despite Cortés's entreaties. If he could not negotiate a way out of the situation, Cortés would eventually lose, regardless of his technological advantages, because his enemies' numbers were just too overwhelming. In the short term, the Spaniards could keep the Tlaxcaltecs at bay with cannon, harquebus, and crossbow fire, but they were too hard pressed to take effective offensive action.

Although the Spanish firepower finally drove the tightly massed Tlaxcaltecs back, the Spaniards' position was precarious in that they could not allow the battle to degenerate into a war of attrition they would inevitably lose. Accordingly, they directed their offensive at nearby towns in hopes of replenishing their food, but they found none, thanks to the Tlaxcaltecs' "scorched earth" tactics.

The Spaniards had only a few days' supplies remaining, so they once again offered peace, though no more successfully than before. The next day saw another attack, which Cortés beat back only by dividing his men so that some could reload their crossbows and harquebuses while others fired, to concentrate the effect of the weapons against the Tlaxcaltecs' formations.

The standard Mesoamerican tactics were by now proving costly to the Tlaxcaltecs as well, so they next launched a night attack. Communications and military formations are difficult to maintain in the dark, so the use of a night attack suggests that a heavy toll was taken by the Spaniards' cannons, harquebuses, and crossbows, all of which had greater effect and longer ranges than the Indians' weapons. When the Tlaxcaltecs eventually closed for hand-to-hand combat, they did so through a lethal field of Spanish fire that extended much farther than could their own. But the night attack reduced this Spanish advantage by concealing their targets in the darkness.

The Tlaxcaltecs' attack was led by General Xicotencatl who, in Spanish eyes, was to gain a reputation as a duplicitous traitor. Archers, slingers, and atlatls (spear-throwers) attacked the hemmed-in Spaniards on three sides while Tlaxcaltec swordsmen quickly rushed across the killing zone and engaged them hand to hand. These tactics minimized the Spanish advantage in firepower, but mounted lancers managed to disrupt the Tlaxcaltec lines, and, unable to reassemble in the dark, the Indians withdrew.

Since leaving Veracruz, more than 45 Spaniards had been killed, another dozen were ill, several of the 16 horses had been slain, and their food supplies were dwindling, as were their bolts, shot, and powder. So once again Cortés sent messages of peace, coupled with threats of impending destruction, though he knew these were beyond his ability to carry out. Both sides made every effort to conceal the extent of their losses, and neither had a completely accurate picture of the others' capabilities, but it had become clear that the Tlaxcaltecs could defeat these strangers, albeit at a huge cost to themselves. Given their losses, diminishing supplies, and likely annihilation, Cortés's men were near mutiny, though he managed to persuade them to stay through cajoling and promises.

Once again Cortés took the offensive, sacking a couple of minor towns nearby. But by this time his forces were reduced to approximately 250 Spaniards (not all fit), 10 horses (all wounded), 200 noncombatant porters, and fewer than 100 allied Indian warriors. Only the number of casualties among the Tlaxcaltecs was now in doubt, not the ultimate outcome.

But the Tlaxcaltecs, too, were reconsidering their position. Some of this rethinking doubtless arose from the results of the battles thus far, but much of it emerged from Tlaxcallan's complex political situation. Tlaxcallan did not have one paramount ruler who could make authoritative decisions about war but was instead ruled by four confederated provinces, each with its own king.

The provinces of Quiyahuiztlan, Tepeticpac, Ocotelolco, and Tizatlan were ruled, respectively, by Citlalpopocatl, Tlehuexolotl, Maxixcatl, and Xicotencatl the Elder. The lines of succession to the specific provincial thrones were flexible,

and while legitimate succession was the usual pattern, the history of the king-
ships of Tlaxcallan was also marked by discord, assassinations, usurpation, and
fluctuating power relations among the provinces. When Cortés arrived, the two
most powerful provinces were Ocotelolco and Tizatlan. The competition seen
throughout the Conquest between their respective rulers, Maxixcatl and Xicotencatl the Elder, reflected a struggle for dominance. Xicotencatl was old and blind,
and the younger, more vigorous Maxixcatl's position was growing stronger, but
Xicotencatl had essentially ceded the leadership of the province to his son, Xicotencatl the Younger (Xicotencatl Axayacatl), who was also the commanding general of the Tlaxcaltec army. Once Xicotencatl the Younger formally assumed the
throne, he would likely dominate Maxixcatl and the entire confederacy.

Both Xicotencatls supported fighting the Spaniards, which became the Tlaxcaltec policy, though the records are unclear on the positions of the other three
rulers. But when Xicotencatl the Younger failed to win quickly, a split developed
among the rulers, perhaps based on the merits of the competing actions but certainly along the lines of the preexisting political cleavages. In any case, a major
consequence, if not an objective, of shifting the policy seems to have been to
weaken Xicotencatl the Younger internally, because the forces allied with Maxixcatl had already abandoned him in the field, as had those from the allied city-state
of Huexotzinco.

Tlaxcallan decided to seek peace with the Spaniards. They could have continued the battle until decisively defeating the Spaniards, which was certainly
within their power; they could have stopped fighting in hopes that the Spaniards
would simply go away; or they could have sought an alliance with them.
Although this decision reflected longstanding political realities, making peace
was in fact in Tlaxcallan's interests.

The Tlaxcaltecs had been at war with the Aztecs for decades. But now, completely encircled by Aztec tributaries, their defeat was only a matter of time. At
this point the Spaniards presented a means to shift the balance of power. Spanish
cannons, harquebuses, crossbows, and horsemen could all disrupt enemy formations much more easily than could the usual Mesoamerican arms, and though the
Spaniards were too few to exploit these breaches effectively by themselves, in conjunction with large Indian armies they could, wreaking havoc on the enemy.

Intimately familiar with the other Mesoamerican armies and their tactics, the
Tlaxcaltecs would have readily seen the advantage of an alliance in which the
Spaniards would serve as shock troops for their own vastly larger Indian forces.
Whether the Spaniards also recognized these advantages as quickly is unimpor-
tant, because the decision to ally one force with another lay with the Tlaxcaltecs.
They could have defeated the Spaniards or simply withdrawn. The decision to
seek an alliance was a deliberate choice, and it was theirs alone.

This decision was the consensus of the three other rulers but was opposed by
Xicotencatl the Younger. Despite being ordered by them to stop fighting, he
refused. Only by their ordering his subordinates not to obey him and after sending their demands to him three times did he desist.

Tlaxcallã

Cortés sent Cempohuallan messengers to Tlaxcallan (Tlaxcala). This messenger (shown standing) spoke to the Tlaxcallan leaders, who probably represented the four districts, though no glyphs identify them.

The Tlaxcaltecs then sent four nobles to the Spanish camp, claiming that they believed the Spaniards were allied with the Aztecs and arguing also that the initial fighting had been started by the Otomies (Otomí), unbeknownst to the Tlaxcaltecs. These allegations, which were at least partly true, more importantly allowed the Tlaxcaltecs to offer, and Cortés to accept, a peace as nominal equals.

The Aztec emissaries who were accompanying Cortés asked him to wait for word from Moteuczoma before proceeding, and he agreed. The Spanish accounts claim that Moteuczoma asked Cortés not to go to Tlaxcallan and offered to become his vassal and pay him tribute, but given subsequent events this was doubtless an inflated interpretation. Nevertheless, any Spanish agreement with the Aztecs would put the Tlaxcaltecs in a dangerous position, so some of their kings traveled to the Spaniards' camp to negotiate with them. On the following day, September 23, Cortés entered the city of Tlaxcallan.

When they reached the city, Cortés was given one of Xicotencatl's daughters, though he passed her on to Pedro de Alvarado. Maxixcatl's daughter was given to Juan Velásquez de León, and other nobles gave daughters to the various Spaniards, supposedly more than 300 women in all. Whether or not the fact that Cortés gave Xicotencatl's daughter to Alvarado suggested any alignment, the Spaniards were housed at Maxixcatl's Ocotelolco rather than Xicotencatl's Tizatlan, reflecting Maxixcatl's now greater prominence as leader of the pro-Spanish faction.

Although Cortés could not force Christianity on the Tlaxcaltecs, he was allowed to erect a cross and an image of the Virgin in one of the temples. They also let him baptize the daughters of the rulers, which was less a sign of religious conversion than a response to the fact that the Spaniards were nominally not permitted to have sexual intercourse with native women until they became Christians. In Tlaxcallan, Cortés was told about the power of the Aztecs, their army, and Tenochtitlan and its defenses. But since Moteuczoma had not conquered Tlaxcallan despite years of war, Cortés probably believed that the Tlaxcaltecs were therefore roughly comparable in power to the Aztecs. What he did not realize was that the Tlaxcaltecs were engaged not in a conventional war but in a flower war.

The goal of a flower war was to pin down strong opponents, then encircle them slowly and strangle them. Thus, outright conquest was not sought, even though a flower war against Tlaxcallan had been under way for decades. Once the Aztecs had Tlaxcallan completely isolated, it would be crushed. But Cortés's assessment ignored this crucial distinction in types of wars, and he was, accordingly, wrong, though he must have been encouraged in this view by Moteuczoma's continued gift giving and failure to attack.

Gifts were given to acknowledge vassalage, and the Aztecs had brought the Spaniards gifts from the outset. But those of the Aztecs were offered in homage to possible gods, not in political vassalage. The fact that the Aztecs had failed to attack them suggested to the Spaniards that they were correct in their assumption that the Aztecs saw themselves as vassals, though other considerations actually kept them from attacking. For one thing, Moteuczoma was still uncertain about the Spaniards' intentions. For another, when the Spaniards landed on the coast and marched inland, that served to diminish Moteuczoma's political support from that area. And finally, this was September and the Aztecs generally waged war only during the dry season—from December through April—following the harvest, when more men were available, food was plentiful, dirt roads were passable, and streams were fordable. But Moteuczoma's failure to attack was misinterpreted as weakness by the Spaniards.

Cortés left Tlaxcallan after 17 days and marched to Cholollan (Cholula) for the stated purpose of gathering supplies. When Cortés demanded entry to their city, the Chololtecs reluctantly invited the Spaniards in, accompanied as they were by between 5,000 and 6,000 Tlaxcaltec warriors. Cortés's actual reasons for going to Cholollan were in fact not logistical but strictly political and military. Cholollan had traditionally been allied with Tlaxcallan and Huexotzinco but had recently joined the Aztec camp. Thus, whatever the Tlaxcaltecs told Cortés about Cholollan was doubtless tinged with hostility about their perceived betrayal. Cortés was not primarily interested in fighting the Indians' battles, but there were sound military reasons to want to conquer Cholollan, which he accomplished through treachery.

Cortés covered most of the five leagues to Cholollan before making camp for the night, where he was welcomed by nobles bringing food. At the request of the Chololtecs, the Tlaxcaltecs remained in camp and the Spaniards entered Cholollan the next morning, accompanied only by the Cempohualtecs and the

Tlaxcaltecs, carrying the cannons. There they were well housed and fed for two days before the food inexplicably stopped arriving.

According to Spanish accounts, the translator Doña Marina learned of a Chololtec plot to massacre the Spaniards, aided by a hidden Aztec army, variously reported to be from 20,000 to 30,000 or even 50,000 men strong. Thus alerted, Cortés acted first. He assembled the Chololtecs in the main courtyard, placed armed Spaniards at every entrance, then massacred the enclosed and unarmed Indians.

Despite nearly unanimous Spanish support for this account of the Chollollan massacre, it simply does not ring true. In the first place, there probably was no Aztec army, because it is unlikely that Moteuczoma had tens of thousands of soldiers available to send to Chollollan, since it was the agricultural season. And even if the soldiers had been available, only three days elapsed between Cortés's arrival in Chollollan and the alleged reports of the appearance of that army—barely enough time for a message to be sent to Tenochtitlan, much less to raise, arm, supply, and dispatch an army. Thus, an armed Aztec threat does not seem credible, although Cortés may well have accused Moteuczoma of sending one to keep him on the defensive. Moreover, the Spaniards also claimed to have been alerted by the presence of barricades and stones piled atop houses in the city and of concealed pits with sharpened stakes outside the town. The former are entirely to be expected, since nearby Tlaxcallan was now its enemy, but the latter is almost certainly a Spanish projection or misinterpretation. Concealed pits are relatively ineffectual against infantry but were the standard European counter to cavalry. So while the mounted Spaniards might expect to encounter pits, their use is otherwise unattested in the historical sources, and they would have been entirely alien to Mexico, where there were no horses before the Conquest.

There was indeed a massacre, however—but of the Chololtecs. It was probably an intentional act by Cortés to destroy their leaders as a warning to other cities. Chollollan, straddling the main route between Tenochtitlan and Veracruz, posed a major danger to any communications between the two and would have threatened Cortés's rear once he marched on to Tenochtitlan. His need for reliable supply lines to Veracruz had been brought home to him by the rapid exhaustion of his shot and gunpowder in the battles with Tlaxcallan. Veracruz being the only available source for these essential armaments, access from there could not be impeded. Moreover, having established an alliance with Tlaxcallan, Cortés felt less constrained in his dealings with Aztec tributaries.

In short, there was no sound logistical reason to go to Chollollan. But the animus that had built up between that city and his new ally Tlaxcallan threatened Cortés's plans. Thus, his decision to go to Chollollan can best be understood as political—to secure his rear and his lines of resupply, but also to chastise his friends' enemies. Cortés's actions cannot be seen exclusively in terms of his own interests, however. He had no firsthand knowledge of the Chololtecs and no compelling need to attack them for his own purposes, but the attack may well have been orchestrated by the Tlaxcaltecs as a litmus test of Spanish loyalty. If they attacked the Chololtecs, they would prove themselves by undermining a now despised enemy. But such an assault would also be one on an Aztec ally, so it would put the Spaniards in opposition to Moteuczoma, a position from which they could not easily withdraw. This conundrum forced the Spaniards to demonstrate their loyalty to the Tlaxcaltecs at a point when the latter had risked nothing.

The attack thus cemented Cortés's relationship with the Tlaxcaltecs and was probably instigated in retribution for Cholollan's recent shift in allegiances. In a single stroke Cortés killed the king, much of the political leadership, and the cream of the Chololtec army. After the massacre, he appointed a new king and forced an alliance between the Tlaxcaltecs and the Chololtecs. At the same time, he laid the blame for the massacre on Moteuczoma.

Even though the Spaniards described themselves as the motivating force behind the events of the Conquest, it is highly improbable that Cortés understood the situation well enough to have known the weak points in the system and to have exploited them. The most significant of these features was the practice of royal succession.

As we have seen, in Mesoamerican kingship was not typically locked into a strict hereditary succession system such as that of male primogenitures. Kings came from among the upper nobility—often the king's sons—but which one was chosen depended on the political support from both that city and its allies. And even after a candidate for king was selected, there were still other contenders for the throne. These divisions were probably strongly felt in Cholollan, which had shifted its fundamental alliance away from the Tlaxacaltecs to the Aztecs. The Chololtec king must have been the primary supporter and beneficiary of this switch, but there were doubtless other nobles with political and kin ties to Tlax-callan, many of whom were legitimate contenders for the throne.

Cortés also could not have known how the institution of kingship operated in Mesoamerica or who among the Chololtecs fell into what camps, but the Tlaxcaltecs did. When Cortés claimed to have chosen a new ruler, he may have thought himself a kingmaker, but it is likelier that he was serving as a pawn in Tlaxcaltec and Chololtec factional politics. Killing the king and many of his noble supporters left the field clear for a successor with pro-Tlaxcallan sympathies and political support, one who might have actually played a role in preceding events. Cholollan's shift in allegiance was not the agonizing movement of a monolith from one position to its opposite but a subtle shift that allowed an existing faction to take power. In this coup a Spanish hand was on the sword but Indian minds guided it, for only they understood the distribution of power in Cholollan and knew who would support the insurgents' position.

Moteuczoma must have been thoroughly dismayed at this attack on, and wanton destruction of, his allies, who had peacefully received the Spaniards. It can only have reinforced his reluctance to have Cortés come to Tenochtitlan.

Tlaxcallan nobles and Indian porters accompanied Cortés on his expeditions. The foot and hoof prints in this drawing indicate a march, and the house identifies Chalco, where the expedition rested. The stones in the house may represent either stones or trinkets. There is a Spanish dog in the background and the volcano Popocatepetl is in the foreground.

Moteuczoma dispatched a delegation of nobles to greet Cortés and learn his true intentions, but he also sent soothsayers and magicians to stop him supernaturally. When these had no effect, having exhausted both diplomacy and magic, Moteuczoma ordered the main road from Cholollan to Tenochtitlan planted with magueys (century plants). This traditional means of sealing off roads and signaling a breach in relations was a last-ditch effort to deter the Spaniards.

After two weeks, Cortés left Cholollan and chose to march to Tenochtitlan by the more southerly of the two routes. He supposedly made that choice after being warned that the Aztecs had set up ambushes along the northerly one. This explanation seems unlikely because the route Cortés followed was narrower and more tortuous, and could more easily conceal an ambush.

The advantage of the southern route was that it led to the Chalca city-states which, though tributaries, were deeply hostile to the Aztecs, whereas the northern route led to Tetzcoco (Texcoco), ruled by a strongly pro-Aztec king. In any event, the Spaniards marched through the Chalca area, crossed the Cuitlahuac causeway, passed through Ixtlapalapan (Iztapalapa), and, on November 8, entered the island-city of Tenochtitlan, where they were greeted by Moteuczoma.

Some 300 Spaniards and a few thousand Indian allies walked unhindered into the capital of the most powerful empire in Mesoamerica. Moteuczoma allowed them to enter because he knew about the events at Cholollan and his own city was politically divided, harboring dissident factions. He feared that opposing Cortés might encourage these groups and lessen his own support. Moreover, as it was not

This image of Moteuczoma and the Aztec nobles receiving Cortés captures the encounter of the Europeans and Indians, and perhaps Africans as well. The man holding Cortés's horse and spear appears to be an African servant.

the war season, Moteuczoma's forces were not yet mobilized, but once Cortés was inside Tenochtitlan he would be vulnerable.

Cortés may have been emboldened by his success thus far, but he had doubtless miscalculated the strength of Tenochtitlan, which was far larger than any city he had seen previously in Mexico or, for that matter, in Europe. Tenochtitlan had at least 200,000 people and was the center of a valleywide population of between 1 million and 2.65 million people. Once he had entered the Valley of Mexico, Cortés could not retreat, being as he was almost entirely dependent on Indian supplies, labor, and troops. If he faltered, his allies would abandon him.

So whether by plan or miscalculation, the Spaniards found themselves in Tenochtitlan, where Moteuczoma gave them gifts and food, and housed them in the palace of Axayacatl. Perhaps he wanted Cortés inside Tenochtitlan, where he could be the more readily seized and killed, or he may have been waiting until he could again raise a large army. Whatever his motives, publicly he embraced Cortés.

Tenochtitlan was an enormous island-city connected to the mainland by three major causeways, all with removable bridges. The danger of the Spaniards' position quickly became apparent. Most of the Tlaxcaltecs had remained outside the city, and the few hundred Spaniards within it could easily be overwhelmed and destroyed.

Within days of Cortés's arrival in Tenochtitlan, word reached him that the Aztecs had attacked the Totonacs on the Gulf Coast, and although the Spaniards at Veracruz had come to their aid, the Aztecs had been victorious. Because Cortés could not leave Tenochtitlan, whether in reaction or as a pretext, he seized Moteuczoma. Now the Aztecs could be controlled. Cortés held the king captive for the remaining eight months he was in Tenochtitlan, effectively ruling through him. Why Moteuczoma put up with this situation is uncertain, although his personal safety may well have been one concern. Another is that refusing to cooperate with Cortés would have paralyzed the government and encouraged the Aztecs who had opposed admitting the Spaniards, in the end perhaps even costing him his throne.

The degree of Moteuczoma's co-optation was immediately evident when he ordered the leader of the Aztec army that had attacked the Totonacs to be brought to Tenochtitlan. When the captain denied that Moteuczoma had ordered the attack, the king had him burned to death, at Cortés's insistence. Although Moteuczoma did Cortés's bidding, his doing so and being held in obvious captivity made the king appear weak and eroded his control. Furthermore, his actions contrary to the interests of the state did not affect him alone but also struck at the interests of the nobles who depended on the steady flow of tribute that would stop if the king did not respond decisively.

The first to rebel was King Cacama of Tezcoco who, along with the kings of Coyohuacan (Coyoacán), Tlacopan (Tacuba), Ixtlapalapan, and Matlatzinco, plotted an attack on the Spaniards. When word of the plan reached Moteuczoma, he told Cortés. Moteuczoma then sent six loyal nobles to Tetzcoco, who were able to capture Cacama, thanks to help from Tetzcoca dissidents, and had him brought to Tenochtitlan. The rulers of Coyohuacan, Ixtlapalapan, and Tlacopan were also seized. Nevertheless, Moteuczoma's support among both the Aztec people and the nobility was declining, though it is unclear if Cortés knew or appreciated this.

Meanwhile, Cuba's Governor Velásquez had assembled a fleet of 19 ships with crews, more than 800 soldiers, 20 cannons, 80 horsemen, 120 crossbowmen, and 80 harquebusiers, under the command of Pánfilo de Narváez, which he dispatched to Mexico with orders to capture Cortés and return him to Cuba. Around April 20, 1520, Narváez landed at San Juan de Ulúa. When Cortés learned of this from Aztec messengers, he moved to counter him. Leaving Pedro de Alvarado in charge of 80 soldiers in Tenochtitlan, Cortés and 266 Spaniards marched to the coast, reaching Narváez's camp at Cempohuallan about May 27. By Cortés's account he launched a surprise midnight attack, captured Narváez, and forced the surrender of his men. This feat appears to owe more to treachery than to military skill, however. Cortés had begun negotiating a peaceful settlement with Narváez, who was thus not expecting an attack. When it did come, many of the defenders did not fight, nor were the cannons fired, because Cortés had also paid bribes to and sown dissension within Narváez's camp. Once Narváez was imprisoned in Veracruz, his men joined Cortés.

Back in Tenochtitlan, Alvarado led a massacre of thousands of Aztec nobles during the festival of Toxcatl, which the Spaniards had already given permission to hold. He maintained that the Aztecs were plotting an attack on the Spaniards, but this was almost certainly untrue. The festival of Toxcatl, the most important of 18 monthly celebrations, was held in the courtyard of the Great Temple, which was accessible through only four entrances. While the festival was under way, Alvarado blocked these, entered with his fully armed Spaniards, and began slaughtering the unarmed Aztecs. How many died is uncertain, though the 16th-century priest Diego Durán estimated that most of the 8,000 to 10,000

While Cortés was away from the Aztec capital, his lieutenant, Pedro de Alvarado, had the Spaniards and their Tlaxcallan allies attack the Aztecs during the ceremony to honor Tezcatlipoca. Perhaps he believed the Aztecs planned to use the fiesta as an opportunity to rebel against the Spaniards. As a result of the massacre, the Aztecs did attack the Spanish quarters and lay siege to Alvarado's forces. This drawing shows the defenders—the Spaniards, the Tlaxcallans, and Doña Marina—and their cannon. At the upper left is an effigy of Tezcatlipoca. The scattered body parts indicate the ferocity of the fighting.

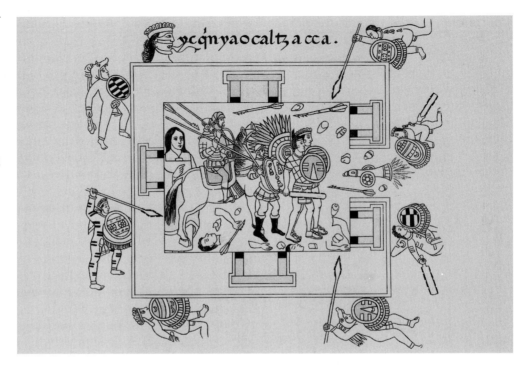

participating nobles were killed. As the populace learned of the massacre, they gathered their arms and attacked the Spaniards, killing seven, wounding many others, and driving the rest back to their quarters, where their artillery held the attackers at bay.

Alvarado's actions were either a complete misunderstanding on his part that initiated a tragic sequence of events or were deliberate. If the latter, Alvarado was unlikely to have undertaken so drastic an action on his own and was probably following Cortés's instructions. In either case, Alvarado, now beseiged, sent two Tlaxcaltecs to tell Cortés what had happened. While the Spaniards' relations with the Aztecs had taken a decided turn for the worse, the massacre had decimated the Aztecs' seasoned veterans and noble warriors who had participated in the festival and destroyed much of the army's command structure.

Under siege, even the Spaniards' superior firepower could not prevail against the Aztecs, but they were still protected from outright assault by Moteuczoma's presence. However, each time he acted on behalf of the Spaniards he lost more support, the Toxcatl massacre being the ultimate outrage.

When Cortés learned of these events, he began the march back from Veracruz. With 1,300 Spaniards, 96 horses, 80 crossbowmen, and another 80 harquebusiers, and joined by 2,000 Tlaxcaltec warriors en route, he reached Tenochtitlan on June 24, entering the city unopposed. Whether intentionally or not, Tenochtitlan's streets were completely deserted, perhaps to show the Aztecs' opposition and displeasure, as they later claimed, but allowing Cortés back into the city had military implications, too. Outside he could move about at will, but once inside Tenochtitlan, Cortés could no longer do so, or use his horses effectively, or receive military and logistical support from his allies. He must have recognized this, yet he continued to pin his hopes on Moteuczoma's intervention.

Once inside the city, Cortés and his men were besieged. Every Spanish sally was forced back, with serious losses. In desperation, Cortés built three war machines: large movable towers from which 20 to 25 men could fire in relative safety. But these machines were destroyed in battle, and the Spanish attempts to burn the city were frustrated by its many canals. With few military options left, Cortés took Moteuczoma up onto the roof to speak to his own people.

The Spanish accounts claim that Moteuczoma was struck by stones thrown from below while pleading with his people to stop the attacks. The Aztec accounts claim he was killed by the Spaniards. Both versions are plausible. On the one hand, ineffectual Aztec kings had been killed by their people before. On the other, Moteuczoma had become a liability to the Spaniards in that his captivity could still inspire Aztec attacks and his release might unite the Aztecs against the Spaniards. The Aztec account seems the more probable.

Running short of food, water, and gunpowder, the Spaniards had to escape. Besieged as they were in the center of the city, they would have to fight their way out in whatever direction they chose. The causeway that ran west to Tlacopan was the shortest and thus offered the least chance of detection.

The Aztecs had removed the causeway bridges to keep the Spaniards bottled up, so Cortés had a portable wooden bridge built. Just before midnight on June 30, in a heavy rainstorm, the Spaniards began their escape. At the second breach they were seen, an alarm was raised, and they had to abandon their portable bridge. Attacked on all sides, one group of Spaniards, including Cortés, fled. This forward element finally reached Tlacopan. Suspiciously, all of their noble prisoners were killed, along with most of Narváez's men, the Tlaxcaltecs, and the Huexotzincas. Cut off and unable to flee, the rear-guard Spaniards retreated to their quarters, where they were besieged for some days before being killed.

The escaped Spaniards had to go around the area's lakes to reach Tlaxcallan, so Cortés marched north. Although the Spaniards suffered some assaults throughout their flight, the fighting was relatively light during most of the transit around the northern lakes, perhaps because of the prescribed four days of mourning that had to be observed for the nobles killed during Cortés's flight, including Cacama and the sons and daughters of Moteuczoma. But the fighting may also have been light because the Aztecs were not equipped to dispatch and support large forces during what was now the agricultural season. Thus, most of the soldiers the Spaniards fought were drawn from the cities they passed, which were few and small in the north.

Once the Spanish reached the eastern side of the valley, however, the attacks grew more ferocious, culminating in a battle at Otompan (Otiemba), which the Spaniards narrowly survived. The next day they reached the territory of

Tlaxcallan. Seriously weakened by the loss of more than 860 Spanish soldiers, 5 Spanish women who had arrived with Narváez, and 1,000 Tlaxcaltecs, they were anxious about their reception.

Having fled in the face of certain defeat, Cortés found his alliances now unsure, because his military superiority had been decisively undermined. Acutely aware of his precarious political position, Cortés ordered his men not to seize anything from the people along their route, despite their desperate need. They entered Tlaxcaltec territory and reached the Otomí town of Huei-Otlipan (Hueyotipa), where they were received and fed but had to pay for it—signaling an ominous shift in the Spaniards' relationship with the Tlaxcaltecs.

Opinion regarding the Spaniards was divided in Tlaxcallan, as in Tenochtitlan. General Xicotencatl had always opposed the Spaniards and was even more opposed after they fled Tenochtitlan. Had Tlaxcallan been a defecting Aztec ally, they would probably have shifted their allegiance back, but they were an independent enemy state and thus had few options. Their own political position had been eroding long before Cortés arrived. Short of becoming an Aztec ally—likely a subservient one—their best choice was to continue their support of the Spaniards.

After deliberating for several days, the rulers of Tlaxcallan and Huexotzinco went to Huei-Otlipan and re-cemented that alliance. However, the balance of power had clearly shifted. The Tlaxcaltecs now demanded greater concessions from Cortés for their continued help should he defeat the Aztecs. Among their demands were the receipt of Cholollan, Huexotzinco, and Tepeyacac (Tepeaca) as tributaries, command of a fortress to be built in Tenochtitlan, half of the spoils received from all the towns and provinces conquered, and permanent freedom from tribute themselves. In short, these new conditions reflected not just a harder bargain to continue the same support as before but a commitment by Tlaxcallan to support the conquest of Tenochtitlan, a significant enlargement of their own kingdom, and equal status as co-conquerors.

Cortés arrived in Tlaxcallan on July 11 with 440 Spaniards, 20 horses, 12 crossbowmen, and 7 harquebusiers. Everyone was wounded, but they could rest and mend there in safety. Dispirited, some argued for returning to Veracruz, but once again Cortés cajoled them into staying.

Tenochtitlan was in chaos, as Moteuczoma and many other rulers were dead. Cuitlahua, Moteuczoma Xocoyotl's brother, son of King Axayacotl, had been selected as king but had not been crowned, nor had he consolidated his position. Because tributary kings were typically left in place as long as they fulfilled their new obligations of paying tribute, their allegiance to Tenochtitlan depended on their perception of the Aztecs' ability to enforce their will. And while established kings were rarely challenged, new rulers had to prove themselves. Thus, each Aztec king-elect normally led his army on a campaign prior to his coronation for the ostensible purpose of securing victims to sacrifice at the investiture. But the underlying reason was to demonstrate his military prowess. An effective show of force would ensure that all the tributary kings would attend the coronation and repledge their fealty, thus eliminating the need to reconquer them all. But the events in Tenochtitlan and the fact that it was not yet the war season prevented Cuitlahua from immediately demonstrating this prowess. At the same time, Tlaxcallan and the Spaniards offered a powerful alternative alliance partner. So the empire Cuitlahua had inherited was rapidly losing its cohesion.

Cortés's attempt to control Tenochtitlan from within had been a failure and, now that there was no longer a compliant king on the throne, was unrepeatable. If Tenochtitlan were to fall, it would have to be assaulted from outside, which meant that Cortés would have to protect his rear, reestablish his Indian alliances, and secure a reliable source of food, all of which had previously been guaranteed by Moteuczoma. Dangerously low on men and equipment, Cortés sent to Veracruz for more. While the coast was to prove a good, though episodic, supplier of both, at this point only seven men were available, but they soon joined his forces.

However modest his Spanish forces, Cortés enjoyed considerable Tlaxcaltec support, and if he could conquer an Aztec tributary and promise it protection from reprisals, getting it to shift its allegiance would be easy, given the structural nature of the Aztec empire. During the siege in Tenochtitlan, a party of Spaniards from Veracruz had been attacked and killed in the province of Tepeyacac, so it became Cortés's first target, either in retaliation or to fulfill Cortés's pledge to the Tlaxcaltecs or to ensure their support for his war on Tenochtitlan.

The Spanish accounts claim that the Aztecs dispatched troops to the Tlaxcaltec region, but because Cortés's attack on that area had taken place less than a month after his flight from Tenochtitlan and it was still well before harvest, any soldiers sent out would have been few. In any event, around the first of August, Cortés marched against Tepeyacac with 420 Spaniards, 17 horses, 6 crossbowmen, and 2,000 Tlaxcaltecs.

Cortés camped three leagues from the town and sent it a message demanding surrender. When it was rejected, he engaged Tepeyacac's army and routed it with no Spanish losses. How serious this battle eventually was is uncertain. This was still the rainy season, so neither side would have been well prepared or able to field a full army. But, more importantly, Tepeyacac had been allied with Tlaxcallan until they were conquered by the Aztecs as recently as 1467, and various titles, including kinship, that might have favored a realliance with Tlaxcallan may have persisted, so the battle may have been more for show than for effect. In any case, Tepeyacac's rulers pledged fealty to the Spaniards, after which Cortés and his allies continued their conquest of the region, subduing it in a matter of weeks. Cortés then founded and fortified the town of La Villa de Segura de la Frontera at Tepeyacac to secure the region. After a series of battles, Cortés's forces controlled most of the major towns along the main route from Cholollan to Veracruz. More men and supplies now reached Cortés from Veracruz—14 men and 2 horses from one ship, and 9 men and one horse from another one eight days later.

In an effort to thwart further Spanish expansion, Cuitlahua sent troops to Cuauhquecholan and Itzyocan (Izucar) to block the main pass from Cholollan into Morelos and thence into the Valley of Mexico. But Cortés sent out a counterforce

Tepeyacac (Tepeaca), located between the Gulf Coast and Tenochtitlan, was the station for a large and well-armed Aztec garrison. Cortés determined to defeat these warriors and use the site as a base for his expedition. The image of the face with the enormous nose is the glyph for Tepeyacac.

that, with the help of the rulers of Cuauhquecholan, routed the Aztecs. They fell back to Itzyocan, but again the Spanish forces prevailed. This time Cortés replaced the unrepentant rulers of both towns with new kings loyal to him.

Cortés repeatedly claimed that these rulers pledged their loyalty to him, but while this probably happened it glosses a larger reality. In this particular campaign Cortés had, although by no means atypically, 200 Spanish infantry and 13 horsemen plus 30,000 Indian allies. Thus, important as the Spaniards were, the main power was undeniably Tlaxcallan, so if the other rulers pledged fealty to Cortés, they did so in a cosmetic act that avoided their submission to a traditional enemy.

Shortly after these victories, three more Spanish ships reached Veracruz in rapid succession, adding 145 men and 19 horses to Cortés's forces. At the same time, Mexico suffered a devastating epidemic. One member of Narváez's forces was infected with smallpox. Smallpox was unknown in Mexico, and exposure to it proved devastating to the Indians. Two factors resulted in a particularly deadly outbreak: The Indians had not been exposed to it previously, so they lacked any immunity to the disease, and the degree of genetic variation among the Mesoamericans was relatively small, so while the first infections were bad enough, the smallpox virus adjusted itself to the hosts and, effectively preadapted to that genetic structure, made subsequent infections significantly deadlier. The smallpox plague reached the Valley of Mexico after mid-October, lasted 60 days in Tenochtitlan, and ended by early December. Some 40 percent of the indigenous population of central Mexico died in less than a year, among its victims Cuitlahua, who died in early December, having ruled only 80 days. Moreover, the disease's pathology would have ensured that he would have been incapacitated for the previous two weeks, leaving the empire in effect leaderless during the crucial period when the Aztecs would normally be preparing for war.

Smallpox did in fact affect the course of the Conquest, but not simply through massive Aztec deaths. Groups friendly to the Spaniards were also devastated, so the numbers were reduced on both sides, but smallpox's effect on the Aztec leadership was greater. New leaders emerged, but they were less experienced than their predecessors and needed yet more time to solidify their positions. Some pro-Spanish rulers were also lost, but the Spaniards, having greater immunity, survived and their leadership remained intact.

Cuauhtemoc (Cuauhtémoc), son of King Ahuitzotl, was chosen to succeed Cuitlahua, though his formal coronation did not take place until February 1521, more than two months after the death of his predecessor. Again the empire had been without a ruler, and once more, Cuauhtemoc had had no time to consolidate his rule. The new king gave lavish gifts to some rulers and remitted the tribute of others, as had Cuitlahua, but this failed to shore up his domain and may even have been perceived as weakness.

After Cortés fled Tenochtitlan, neither Cuitlahua nor Cuauhtemoc took direct action against the badly mauled Spaniards. Much of this may have been the result of the political turmoil in Tenochtitlan, the smallpox epidemic, and the unfortunate timing, though the Aztecs may have believed the Spaniards would not return. But there were also sound military reasons for these leaders to remain in the Valley of Mexico. The Aztecs could muster an enormous army in and around the valley, so remaining there left them in their most powerful position. But marching elsewhere would have been extremely costly. If procuring local supplies could not be ensured, as indeed it could not in enemy territory, all foodstuffs would have had to be carried with the army by human porters at a rate of about 50 pounds per porter. At the most favorable ratio recorded of one porter for every two soldiers, this would have meant being able to carry only eight days' worth of food. Such logistical constraints kept the Aztecs from dispatching all but a portion of their army for any appreciable distance, so they might not have been able to send a large enough force to Tlaxcallan to defeat virtually the entire adult male population of the region.

Remaining in Tenochtitlan, however, reversed this situation, leaving Cuauhtemoc all his soldiers while forcing his enemies to bear the manpower reductions involved in coming to him. Moreover, remaining in and around Tenochtitlan allowed the Aztecs to use canoes and thus enjoy greater mobility and shorter interior lines of communication, whereas the Spaniards would be forced to march around the valley along the shore. Canoes also allowed the Aztecs to mobilize, concentrate, and support troops anywhere in the valley, depriving the Spaniards of a secure rear area and forcing them to defend themselves everywhere at once. Moreover, a lake-centered defense minimized the effectiveness of the Spanish horses. And any land assault would have to be channeled along one or more of the three major causeways, where there was little room to maneuver and the Spaniards could more easily be hemmed in and defeated. Such a plan also minimized the number of allied troops that could be used. While, in retrospect, the Aztec defensive posture seems foolish, it did minimize Cortés's main advantages and force him to take greater risks.

During the first battle for Tenochtitlan, the Spaniards had been trapped inside the city, cut off from outside support, and assailed from all sides. Cortés's goal now was to reverse that situation by cutting the Aztecs off from outside support. Well before he marched back into the Valley of Mexico, Cortés had ordered the construction of 13 brigantines in Tlaxcallan. The anchors, sails, and rigging for them were supplied by his scuttled ships from Veracruz, which he had stripped and carried to Tlaxallan. Cortés was joined there by Spanish blacksmiths, more arms, three horses, and 13 additional soldiers from yet another newly arrived ship.

When Cortés began his return march to Tenochtitlan on December 28, 1520, he had eight or nine cannons, 40 horsemen, 550 Spanish soldiers (80 of whom were crossbowmen or harquebusiers), and 10,000 Tlaxcaltec soldiers. Despite meeting, and defeating, an enemy force en route, Cortés reached Coatepec, near Tetzcoco, only two days after leaving Tlaxcallan. The next morning, nobles from Tetzcoco invited the Spaniards into the city in peace.

Tetzcoco was the second most important city in the empire, in whose wealth it jointly, though not dominantly, shared. It should have been a staunch Aztec ally, but the city's failure to oppose Cortés was the legacy of years of political divisions. When Tetzcoco's king Nezahualpilli died in 1515, he left numerous sons who could legitimately have succeeded him, including Coanacoch and Ixtlilxochitl. But Moteuczoma used his enormous influence to place another of Nezahualpilli's sons (and his own nephew), Cacama, on the throne. Ixtlilxochitl rebelled, raised an army, and fought a civil war that resulted in the de facto partition of Tetzcoco's territory, leaving him in control of the north, and Cacama in Tetzcoco ruling the south. When Cacama was killed during Cortés's flight from Tenochtitlan, Coanacoch became king, although the details of his accession are unclear and Tetzcoco remained divided. But Cortés's arrival shifted the balance of power against him, and while Coanacoch welcomed the Spaniards into Tetzcoco, he was merely buying time thereby for himself and his followers to flee by canoe to Tenochtitlan.

After Coanacoch fled, another of King Nezahualpilli's sons, Tecocol, became the new ruler. As the head of the Spanish-backed faction he ordered the city armed and fortified. Despite Cortés's claims that he installed various kings throughout central Mexico, he lacked the knowledge or power to do so. Instead, existing factions seized on the combined Spanish-Tlaxcaltec presence to shift the local political balance and take power for themselves. Ixtlilxochitl, who had accompanied Cortés on his return to the valley, may have been involved in Tecocol's ascent. Whether pro or con, when Tecocol died around the first of February, Ixtlilxochitl ascended to the throne.

The Spaniards built brigantines that played a significant role in the conquest of Tenochtitlan. Here, Cortés directs both the Spanish and Indian workmen constructing the boats.

These political machinations placed Tetzcoco squarely in Spanish hands, giving Cortés a local base of operations and eliminating the logistical problem of supporting his troops locally and for long periods. Now that Tetzcoco was allied with Cortés, the kings of Tetzcoco's dependencies pledged their loyalties as well.

Supported now by more than 7,000 Tlaxcaltecs and 20 nobles from Tetzcoco, Cortés next marched against Ixtlapalapan, but en route he was simultaneously attacked from canoes and on land by Aztecs who assailed him on all sides, though he managed to break through their lines and enter the city. Whether this attack was a Spanish victory or an Aztec feint, Cortés's forces were now vulnerable. Built out into the water, Ixtlapalapan was actually below lake level, protected by dikes. Accordingly, once Cortés's forces were inside, the Aztecs broke the dikes and flooded the city, forcing the Spaniards to flee. Some drowned, but most escaped to higher ground and the Spaniards finally withdrew to Tetzcoco.

When Cortés reached Tetzcoco following this debacle, several Spaniards from Narváez's party allegedly plotted to assassinate Cortés and leave Mexico. Because many important people were implicated, Cortés could not afford to precipitate an open breach, so he seized and hanged only the leader, Antonio de Villafaña.

Unrest continued, but Cortés managed to keep it under control. At the same time, he sought to divide his enemies. The mere presence of a Spanish-Tlaxcaltec force warped local politics. Some kings sought Spanish support to bolster their domestic positions; others resisted. But the latter were often ousted by challengers who did seek Spanish support. The Valley of Mexico was politically fragmented throughout the Conquest, largely by location, into a pair of waxing and waning spheres of influence. But historical affinities and animosities also played a part, as with the Chalca cities.

Aztec imperial troops had kept the Chalcas under control, but they bore the Aztecs no affection and were ready candidates for political realignment. More than simply another group of disaffected tributaries, the Chalcas controlled the best route south and east out of the valley. In a battle at Chalco, 15 to 20 horsemen, 200 Spanish soldiers, and all of the Tlaxcaltecs defeated the Aztecs, upon which the Chalcas switched their support to the Spaniards. Initially, the political circumstances in the Valley of Mexico favored Cortés in that there were many Aztec towns and too few soldiers to defend them all simultaneously from a determined Spanish-Tlaxcaltec assault. But as more towns shifted their allegiance to him, Cortés's success gave rise to the same liabilities among his own allies. The Aztecs could still strike throughout the valley by canoe, and now Cortés could not defend all of his allies simultaneously either. So, like the Aztecs, he kept his forces in one place—Tetzcoco—and dispatched them as needed. But his inherently defensive strategy meant that the response came after the damage had been done. The Aztecs' reprisals were thus eroding the internal political support of the pro-Spanish kings, endangering their positions and the loyalty of their cities.

Cortés therefore realized that he had to take the offensive and strike directly at Tenochtitlan. To this end he fetched timber from Tlaxcallan for the ships. It took four days for the men and material to reach Tetzcoco. Around the first of February, with the construction of the brigantines under way, Cortés undertook the first of two major incursions into solidly Aztec territory.

On February 3, Cortés marched north against the island city of Xaltocan. Although it was reinforced from Tenochtitlan, Xaltocan offered no significant threat to the Spaniards beyond small-scale canoe attacks, which did not depend on the city's continued freedom. Thus, the Spaniards could easily have bypassed it, but Xaltocan offered obstacles like those in Tenochtitlan and may have served as a test of Spanish tactics.

Word came to the Spaniards that the causeway to Xaltocan had been destroyed. They exchanged fire with the Indians' canoes, but these were armored with thick wooden bulwarks that made the Spanish weapons ineffectual against them. The city fell only after enemies of Xaltocan told Cortés that the causeway had not actually been destroyed but had merely been allowed to be covered by water. The Spaniards entered on foot across the causeway and defeated Xaltocan, but the water obstacles had proven effective. Without controlling the lakes, the Spaniards had little hope of conquering Tenochtitlan.

Cortés continued this northern incursion around the lakes to Cuauhtitlan, Tenanyocan (Tenayuca), and Azcapotzalco. Too few in number to fend off the Spaniards, the cities' inhabitants withdrew to Tlacopan. There Cortés was met by a large army and barricades, but he forced the defenders to retreat and sacked the city. When Aztec reinforcements crossed the causeway from Tenochtitlan, Cortés attacked these as well, but once on the causeway the Aztecs counterattacked, supported by canoe-borne troops on both sides. Able to engage only those directly in front of them on the causeway, the Spaniards were forced to retreat, suffering several dead and many wounded. After five or six days under constant attack, Cortés withdrew from Tlacopan, reaching Tetzcoco on February 18.

More towns switched to the Spanish side, but these defections were not effortless. Many, including the Chalca cities, remained under Aztec attack. Political considerations demanded that the Spaniards react, so Cortés sent a force of Spaniards with a few Tlaxcaltecs and a company of Tetzcocas, who had not taken part in the northern campaign, to Chalco. This army, led by Gonzalo de Sandoval, pushed the Aztecs back to Huaxtepec (Oaxtepec), where they were defeated, then marched on and defeated Yacapitztlan (Yecapiztla) before returning to Tetzcoco. The Aztecs then attacked Chalco by canoe once the Spaniards had withdrawn, but the Chalcas, aided by the Huexotzincas, repulsed them.

On February 24, more ships landed at Veracruz and the men and arms made their way to Cortés. The road to Veracruz remained a vital supply line for the Spaniards, so Cortés determined to secure the area by marching to Yauhtepec, which he defeated before moving on to conquer Cuauhnahuac (Cuernavaca) on April 13.

The next day Cortés marched back toward the Valley of Mexico, reaching the city of Xochimilco on April 16. This large city, a major supplier of foodstuffs to Tenochtitlan, anchored the southwest corner of the valley. The Spaniards could have reached Xochimilco overland by going directly west from Chalco, but this would have required marching for miles along the southern lake shore, continuously vulnerable to Aztec canoe assaults long before reaching the city's heavy fortifications. The advance through Yauhtepec and Cuauhnahuac, south of the mountains, shielded the Spaniards from direct Aztec assault until they could reenter the valley at Xochimilco's rear. Nevertheless, Cortés's troops were badly mauled at Xochimilco, and he was finally forced to withdraw.

When Aztec reinforcements arrived on April 15, Cortés marched to Coyohuacan, which was deserted, then toward Tlacopan, passing the deserted cities of Azcapotzalco, Tenanyocan, and Cuauhtitlan under continuous attack from lingering Aztec and allied armies. Retracing the route he had taken during the northern incursion, Cortés reached Tetzcoco on April 22. Despite its significant casualties, this campaign south of the Valley of Mexico created a cordon of towns now loyal to the Spaniards that screened them from possible attack by tributaries farther south.

Because most of the fighting was between Aztec armies and the comparably armed Indian forces allied with the Spaniards, the land battles were largely slugfests, with both sides free to maneuver, engage, disengage, and otherwise control the degree of their own involvement. The balance would have tipped on the water and in confined spaces, however. Control of the lakes was crucial. By the end of February, Cortés's ships had been under construction for several weeks. The assembly site was situated half a league from the lakeshore, which largely thwarted repeated Aztec canoe attacks. Twelve of the one- and two-masted ships were just more than 40 feet long and 8 to 9 feet wide, the 13th being almost 50

Route of Cortés from
Veracruz to Tenochtitlan

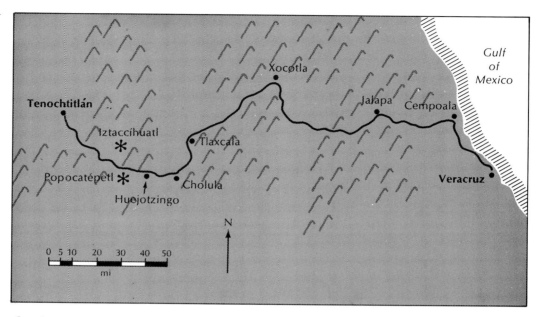

feet long. Each ship held 12 oarsmen, 12 crossbowmen and harquebusiers, and a captain, plus artillerymen for the bow-mounted cannon. The ships were launched on April 28 into a canal dug over a seven-week period by some 40,000 Tetzcocas.

To coordinate this launching with the main offensive, Cortés had sent to Tlaxcallan for 20,000 more warriors and requested soldiers from his allies within the valley. The Tlaxcaltec forces were led to Tetzcoco by Xicotencatl the Younger and Chichimecateuctli, a Tlaxcaltec general allied with Moxixcatl's faction and therefore hostile to the Xicotencatl the Younger. But Xicotencatl left Tetzcoco—in one version because he was in love with a woman in Tlaxcallan—and Cortés then had him seized and hanged for treason. The Spanish explanation for this punishment is weak. Other native leaders left combat, often with their troops, and no action was taken against them, nor were the majority of disaffected Spaniards harshly disciplined. The Spanish account satisfied a certain legalistic reasoning, but the larger context suggests that a political purpose was behind Xicotencatl's execution.

When Cortés had first reached Tlaxcallan, power in the four provinces rested with the rulers of only two, and of those two more rested with Tizatlan, ruled by Xicotencatl the Elder. When his son and heir expectant, Xicotencatl the Younger, led the Tlaxcaltec army against the Spaniards, Maxixcatl, the ruler of the competing province of Ocotelolco, took the counter position, supporting the Spaniards. When they were not quickly dispatched, support shifted to his side and he assumed greater importance in the eventual coalition while the fortunes of Xixotencatl waned. This political situation was upset when Maxixcatl died of smallpox, to be succeeded by a teenage son, and the link he had sought to create with the Spaniards by giving one of his daughters to Juan Velásquez came to naught when they were both killed during the flight from Tenochtitlan.

As a consequence, the fortunes of Xicotencatl the Younger were now significantly improved, with those of Cortés worsened. Had this happened earlier, it could well have proven fatal to the entire Spanish enterprise, but now even though Xicotencatl's domestic position was strengthened, other events—notably Cortés's alliance with the Acolhuas—diminished his external importance. Nevertheless, Xicotencatl the Younger was now a greater threat to Cortés, suggesting that his death was likely a calculated Spanish effort to eliminate a hostile ruler in Tlaxcallan and improve the positions of those with closer ties to Cortés.

Having settled his internal political concerns, Cortés now divided the remaining Spaniards into three armies. Pedro de Alvarado was sent to Tlacopan with 30 horsemen, 18 crossbowmen and harquebusiers, 150 Spanish foot soldiers, and 25,000 Tlaxcaltecs. Cortés sent Cristóbal de Olid to Coyohuacan with 20 crossbowmen and harquebusiers, 175 Spanish foot soldiers, and 20,000 Indian allies. Gonzalo de Sandoval was dispatched to Ixtlapalapan with 24 horsemen, 14 harquebusiers, 13 crossbowmen, 150 Spanish foot soldiers, and more than 30,000 Huexotzincas, Chololtecs, and Chalcas. The Spanish accounts minimize the Indians' participation, but the sheer disparity in numbers makes it clear that they must have played the pivotal role. Moreover, the existing linguistic barriers made the role of the native leaders crucial in commanding these troops and ensuring their cooperation.

The three targets for Alvarado, Olid, and Sandoval were neither the politically most important cities nor the largest, but each was the terminus of one of Tenochtitlan's three major causeways. Severing them would thus constrict the flow of men and material into Tenochtitlan and bottle up the Aztecs inside.

The armies left Tetzcoco on May 22, 1521, with Alvarado and Olid marching north together around the lakes to Tlacopan. They then marched to Chapoltepec (Chapultepec), routed its defenders, and severed the double aqueduct that brought fresh water into Tenochtitlan. As an island city in a brackish lake Tenochtitlan got most of its food and water from outside, and it was these lifelines that Cortés sought to cut. But Tenochtitlan's location did allow it to take advantage of the only truly efficient form of transportation available in Mesoamerica—canoes. Whereas land transportation depended on porters who could carry at most a 50-pound load, a single canoist could easily pole 40 times that weight at the same speed. So while blocking some of the causeways and cutting the aqueduct disrupted those avenues of entry, canoes easily took up the slack.

Sieges were uncommon in Mesoamerica. The lack of wheels and draft animals meant that all supplies had to be carried by porters, so armies could not be sustained in enemy territory for long periods—far shorter than usually required to starve out even the most ill-prepared city. So Cortés's strategy likely caught the Aztecs completely unaware.

Alvarado and Olid returned to Tlacopan and began their assault on the causeway to Tenochtitlan. Normally, in Mesoamerica limiting the battlefront— whether to a causeway or a pass—favored the defenders, because it limited the

These drawings capture the great disparity between the military technology of the Aztecs and the Spaniards. The top image shows the Spaniards advancing on one of the causeways into the city; the bottom picture shows brigantines and barges attacking the Aztec defenders.

number of soldiers who could be brought to bear, minimized the attackers' numerical advantage, prolonged the fight, and meant the attacker would ultimately be forced to withdraw because of logistical constraints. This constriction affected the Spaniards as well, but with different consequences.

For instance, in Alvarado's force there were more than 100 Indian soldiers for every Spaniard, yet the major causeways were approximately 22 feet wide, or enough to accommodate eight horsemen abreast. But in this case the constriction did not simply limit the number of soldiers who could be brought to bear at any one time and allowed a shift in the composition of those forces as well. A much higher proportion of Spaniards, with their far more effective arms, could thus be employed. Even though the Aztecs had a greater depth of combatants, fighting on the causeways prevented them from expanding their front and using their numbers to greatest advantage. Moreover, fighting on the causeways forced the Aztecs to mass their forces, creating ideal targets for Spanish projectiles, even though relatively slow rates of fire meant that most combat was hand to hand. Despite their technological superiority, the Spaniards were nevertheless threatened by their opponent's sheer numbers, a constant Spanish concern thus having been to remain mobile to avoid being trapped and crushed.

The Aztecs were forced to adjust to the more advanced Spanish weaponry. They soon learned that the cannons fired in straight lines and therefore began dodging from side to side instead of marching in straight lines, and started to duck when the cannons fired rather than remaining erect.

The most effective Aztec tactic was the naval assault. In this maneuver canoe-borne soldiers attacked the Spaniards on the causeways, firing arrows, darts, and slinging stones from armored canoes into the Spaniards' flanks while remaining beyond the reach of the Spanish swords and pikes. In this way Olid and Alvarado were repulsed, with heavy losses, and the two armies then separated, with Olid marching south to Coyohuacan and Alvarado remaining on the causeway. Apart, neither army was strong enough to take the offensive, so both remained in their own camps, fighting only to ward off Aztec attacks.

Sandoval began his march on May 30, going south to Ixtlapalapan, which he attacked and burned. At the same time, Cortés launched his brigantines and sailed to Tepepolco, a fortified island near Tenochtitlan. He captured the island but was forced off by an Aztec counterattack.

On the water, the Spanish brigantines proved convincingly superior, sailing through and overturning the Aztec canoes until they fled into canals that were too narrow for the ships to follow. Cortés then sailed his fleet to Coyohuacan, where he landed a small force and seized a portion of the Ixtlapalapan causeway. He reached Coyohuacan the next day, where his ships proved equally effective against the attacking canoes, then breached the causeway and sailed through.

Accompanied by thousands of allied canoes, Cortés's brigantines quickly destroyed or dispersed the Aztec fleet, allowing Sandoval's forces to march on to Mexicatzinco. But an Aztec fleet severed the causeway and prevented him from linking up with Olid. Where the causeways merged, only one force could be used effectively. Accordingly, Sandoval's army was sent to Tepeyacac (Tepeyac) to block the still-open northern causeway.

In response, the Aztecs built traps. They dug pits in the bottoms of the relatively shallow lakes to drown Spaniards who fell or were pushed off the causeway. The Aztecs also planted sharpened stakes in the lake floor to impale Spanish ships.

Protected by their brigantines, the Spaniards advanced along the causeways, but they were unable to consolidate their gains, because the Aztecs reoccupied positions as soon as they were abandoned. Instead of withdrawing for the night, the Spaniards were forced to move their camp along the causeways and post guards to prevent Aztec reoccupation. As the land battles wore on, the Spaniards intensified their efforts to close off Tenochtitlan from all supplies. Shipments of food and water could no longer reach the city by foot, and the naval blockade kept canoe traffic to a minimum during the day. In this the brigantines played the same role for thousands of allied canoes as the few hundred Spanish soldiers did for tens of thousands of Indian allies, serving as an indispensable, though distinctly small, shock element. Without the support of the allied canoes, the brigantines could break up Aztec fleets but could not exploit their gains and risked being overcome by swarms of Aztec canoes when they could not outrun them. With favorable winds the brigantines were faster than the Indian canoes, but Tenochtitlan had too much shoreline to be cordoned off by only 13 of them. Moreover, few brigantines could sail after dark, the ships faced risks from stakes hidden in the water, and they drew too much water to enter many of the shallows, so the allied canoes were crucial to the blockade of Tenochtitlan.

The struggle for the causeways continued, but anyone who charged ahead or became separated from the main force was easily captured. The Aztecs became adept at enticing the Spaniards forward across breaks in the causeways, then turning and pushing them against the breaches, where they were unable to maneuver. So Cortés ordered that all the breaches be filled in before his forces advanced. When the horses were brought forward on the causeways, the Aztecs adapted well by using extra-long lances to spear them before they reached the front lines and by moving the fighting away from open areas to broken terrain where the horses could not charge, as well as by placing barricades and boulders in open plazas.

Nevertheless, the Spaniards and their allies pressed inexorably forward. As went the fortunes of war, so, too, did the allegiances of the surrounding towns. Each Spanish victory shook the loyalty of the Aztec towns. Eventually, Xochimilco and Cuitlahuac turned against the Aztecs, though there were reprisals, and Ixtlapalapan, Huitzilopochco (Churubusco), Colhuacan (Culhuacan), and Mizquic (Mixquic) intercepted supplies bound for Tenochtitlan, provided laborers, and brought food to the Spaniards.

Cuauhtemoc now ordered two simultaneous night attacks on all three Spanish camps. Though a number of Spaniards were killed, they were not dislodged. He then decided to concentrate all his forces against a single camp: Alvarado's at

This image from the *Florentine Codex* illustrates intense fighting for the city of Tenochtitlan. The Spanish lancers have just entered the market-place of Tlatelolco.

Tlacopan. But since this attack occurred during daylight, the Spaniards were able to use their brigantines effectively and repulsed the Aztecs.

Perhaps the worst Spanish setback occurred on June 30. When the Aztecs feigned one withdrawal, Cortés pursued them across an unfilled breach, upon which the Aztecs cut him off by sending war canoes into the breach, catching him between their land and their naval forces. Cortés escaped, wounded, but 68 other Spaniards and eight horses did not. Ten of these soldiers were immediately sacrificed at the Great Temple and their severed heads taken back to the battle and thrown at the Spaniards. The rest of the captives had their hearts cut out and their flayed faces tanned and sent to allied towns as proof of the Spaniards' mortality and as a warning against betrayal.

Buoyed by this success, the Aztecs attacked each of the Spanish camps throughout the next four days. The tide of battle seeming to have turned, many of Cortés's Indian allies deserted. Only token forces remained from Tlaxcallan, Cholollan, Huexotzinco, Tetzcoco, Chalco, and Tlalmanalco as most of the allied fighters returned home. But the Spaniards were not in fact dislodged. With the help of their brigantines they repulsed the Aztecs after two weeks of attacks. When the Aztecs failed to destroy the Spaniards, their allies began returning from Tetzcoco, Tlaxcallan, Huexotzinco, and Cholollan. And the Spanish forces advanced again on the city.

Both sides were being worn down, but Tenochtitlan was now running low on food and water. The Aztecs' combat losses were not being replaced, but more

Spanish ships continued to reach Veracruz and fresh supplies of arms and soldiers again made their way to Tenochtitlan.

When Cortés finally entered Tenochtitlan, he began to raze the city to deprive the Aztecs of cover from which to attack the Spaniards' flanks. As the Spaniards entered the city from the south, the Aztecs withdrew north to Tlatelolco. Nevertheless, the Spanish advance continued, reaching the great market of Tlatelolco around August 1. When Ixtlilxochitl captured his brother, Coanacoch, the Tetzcocas loyal to him switched sides, further depriving the Aztecs of soldiers.

But even at this late date, when famine gripped the city and hope was waning, the Aztecs' superiority over the Indians allied with Cortés was so striking that they were still able to cut off and kill many enemy Indians when they attacked without Spanish support. So the Spaniards sometimes disguised themselves as Indians and marched in the middle of their allies to entice the Aztecs into attacking an apparently all-Indian force.

In a last-ditch effort, Cuauhtemoc dressed the elite warrior who would lead the attack in the attire of King Ahuitzotl, ruler of the Aztec empire from 1486 to 1502 and a great military leader. But the effort ultimately failed, and on August 13 the Spaniards broke through the last Aztec defenses. In the final, decisive act, one Spanish brigantine overtook the canoe containing Cuauhtemoc, and the king surrendered, along with his wife and about 30 nobles, including the king of Tlacopan, and asked to be taken to Cortés.

Tenochtitlan lay in ruins after the three-month siege, yet the Spaniards' allies continued to attack the Aztecs, killing thousands and looting for four more days. The Indian allies were acting as one would expect against a city that had resisted to the end, and Cortés was powerless to stop them. When the killing finally ended, Cortés ordered the aqueduct repaired and the dead removed and buried. He and his surviving Spanish force of 900 men took credit for the Conquest, but the pivotal role had been played by the allied Indians, who had supplied more than 200 men for every Spaniard who participated.

Thus, the conquest of Mexico was not the victory of a Spanish juggernaut. Cortés did supply new and effective military technologies, but what made the conquest of Mexico possible was the hundreds of thousands of Indian allies who exploited the breaches caused by these arms, because it was they who truly made them effective. There would have been no Conquest without the Indians who recognized and seized the opportunity to bring the Aztecs down that was afforded by the Spanish presence.

SECTION II

Crown, Cross, and Lance in New Spain, 1521–1810

✦ ✧ ✦ ✧ ✦ ✧ ✦ ✧ ✦ ✧ ✦ ✧ ✦ ✧ ✦ ✧ ✦ ✧ ✦ ✧ ✦ ✧ ✦ ✧ ✦

Spaniards had established their colonial capital in Mexico City by 1521, nearly a century before English colonists settled a permanent site in Jamestown, Virginia, in 1607. By the time the Puritans had come to Massachusetts Bay in 1620, Spaniards had erected a city of 150,000 with a cathedral, a university, and a print shop producing a local newspaper. The English colonists faced a frontier, but the Spanish colonists lived in a city as modern as any in Europe.

For 300 years, the Spanish monarchs exercised authority over New Spain, an area about double the size of modern-day Mexico. The Spanish rulers insisted on converting the indigenous peoples to Christianity to justify their empire building, directed that the economy be considered the property of Spain to finance European adventures with Mexican silver, and set up a society (a hierarchy, language, customs, and laws) mirroring that of the kingdom of Castile. The Crown insisted on having authority, and attempted to enforce its dictates through, colonial and church agents. But the great distances involved (six to eight weeks by sea from Veracruz to Seville) and marvelous opportunities (the chance for wealth and prestige) served to weaken royal authority. Moreover, many American-born people saw little to be gained from complying with the wishes of a distant European monarch. Just below the surface, old ways and old religious practices continued while human ingenuity found myriad ways to circumvent laws considered onerous or inconvenient.

Nevertheless, the culture that emerged during the three centuries of colonial rule was in its broadest dimensions Spanish. The language of southern Spain, augmented by many Aztec words, to be sure, was the language of the land. The law of Madrid—with local variations, certainly—was the law of the land. And the religion of Rome—admittedly with numerous local adaptations—was the religion of the land.

The Spanish greatly influenced everyday life in colonial Mexico. The daily meal changed with the introduction of European plants and animals, none being more important than pork and chicken as additions to the Mexican diet. But these did not alter the basic staples of corn (as tortillas), beans (now refried with lard), and chiles (the essential spice). This expanded diet, as tacos and enchiladas, now represents Mexico throughout the world. Of the evolving cultural developments, no single event had the enduring influence of the reported appearance of the Virgin to an Indian shepherd boy, Juan Diego. This image, known as the Virgin of Guadalupe, is the best known, most common icon of Mexico. Juan Diego is now the subject of a canonization effort.

4

An Empire Beyond Compare

MARK A. BURKHOLDER *with*
SUZANNE HILES

Three centuries elapsed between Hernan Cortés's destruction of Tenochtitlán and Mexico's political independence. Spain's rapid exploration and conquest of the Aztec empire and beyond led to the creation of Spanish cities, towns, mining camps, and landed estates. Catastrophic losses in the native population, due in large part to the conquerors' introduction of epidemic diseases, shaped the ways in which Spaniards exploited native labor and opened up land for grazing and farming. The introduction of the amalgamation process that employed mercury to separate silver from its ore stimulated mining production, while an increasingly well-organized transatlantic trading system sent Mexican bullion to Spain in exchange for European goods. Coupled with the introduction of European plants and animals, this trade enabled Spanish immigrants and their descendants to live "like Spaniards" despite the distance from their mother country.

As early as the 1570s, the political and administrative stability that would characterize post-Conquest New Spain until the 19th century was firmly established. Evident as well was social stability, based primarily on a racially determined hierarchy. Spaniards from the Iberian Peninsula and their New World descendants (criollos) were at the apex, Indian commoners and black slaves at the base, and a small but growing number of persons of mixed racial background occupied the middle range. The arrival of clergy, the creation of a university in Mexico City to prepare the Spanish youth of the colony for ecclesiastical and civil positions, and the establishment of the tribunal of the Inquisition rounded out a kingdom that half a century after the conquistadores' arrival was in many ways truly a "New Spain."

The consolidation of Spanish rule, the increasing flow of Mexican silver into Spain's royal coffers, and the perfection of a transatlantic trading system based upon the regular sailing of fleets from Seville to Veracruz coincided with the reign

The *Recopilación de leyes de los reynos de las Indias,* a four-volume compilation of basic legislation issued by the Crown for the governance of the Indies, included about 6,500 laws, only a small fraction of those that had been issued. Upon its appearance in 1681, it became the fundamental reference source for colonial law and standard in judges' and attorneys' libraries. The *Recopilación* was subsequently reprinted, but never revised.

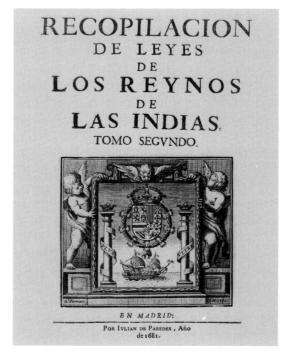

of Philip II (1556–98) and the pinnacle of Spanish power in Europe. However, economic and financial problems in Spain, military defeats with their corresponding loss of Spanish influence, and the progressive collapse of the fleet system from the early 1620s onward soon altered the colonial relationship.

As Spain floundered toward second-power status in Europe, New Spain relinquished its primitive dependence on the mother country. Isolated from military conflict, the colony experienced social tranquility, administrative stability, long-term economic growth, and, after about 1630, an overall increase in population. Although the Crown in Madrid retained administrative oversight, colonial merchants, miners, large landowners, and officeholders forged social, economic, and political relationships and focused their primary attention on personal rather than royal interests. Able to produce everything needed for subsistence and to import luxury items in exchange for bullion, Mexico achieved a measurable degree of economic independence. At the same time, however, the unquestioned legitimacy of Spanish rule provided a solid basis for political stability and, consequently, an undisturbed political environment that encouraged further long-term economic expansion.

In the 1670s, New Spain permanently displaced Peru as the Spanish empire's leading source of registered silver. The northern viceroyalty's emergence as the most important colony until its independence was apparent in other ways as well. Its growing, multiracial population was the largest in the empire, and the viceregal capital outshone all other New World cities. The Crown judiciously selected Mexico's high officials and ended the practice of "promoting" New Spain's viceroys to Peru after 1688. Colonial expansion in its borderlands offered Mexico increased military protection against France and England. When the English capture of Havana in 1762 sent shock waves through the ranks of the king's advisors in Madrid, Mexico was the first mainland target of royal efforts to improve defense, increase revenues, and tighten colonial administration. By 1789, all important reforms, including opening the entire viceroyalty to "free trade within the empire" (*comercio libre*), were in place. However, epidemics, drought, and grain shortages in the 1780s revealed serious problems beneath a surface strewn with silver. Inflation beginning in the 1770s had reduced the real value of the rapidly expanding silver production, while population growth in parts of central Mexico produced serious land hunger and worsening conditions for many Indian and other rural workers. Nonetheless, from Madrid's perspective New Spain was a success story and an indispensable source of royal revenue. In the 1790s, there was no reason to anticipate that Mexico would rebel against colonial rule. After nearly three centuries, New Spain was still the core of an empire beyond compare.

The fall of Tenochtitlán in 1521 whetted Spanish appetites for exploration and wealth. The new territory offered an opportunity to exploit mineral deposits, fertile soils, and dense sedentary populations. Belief in a water passage linking the Atlantic and the Pacific also stimulated exploration. Early explorers frustrated by meager rewards from the conquest of the Aztec empire joined later immigrants eager for adventure and riches. While later conquistadores in New Spain would not match Cortés's achievement, numerous subsequent expeditions quickly expanded the territory under Spanish dominion as well as the supply of geographical knowledge. Settlements and transportation routes soon followed any explorations that revealed potential wealth. Accompanying or quickly trailing the settlers were royal officials and clerics who helped define the major administrative and ecclesiastical jurisdictions of colonial Mexico. Within 50 years Spanish conquerors and settlers had turned the diverse lands and peoples of pre-Conquest Mexico into the colony of New Spain.

Colonial Mexico was the core of the viceroyalty of New Spain established in 1535. The *gobierno* of New Spain, administered directly by the viceroy as governor, was the colony's heartland. East of the Isthmus of Tehuantepec on the Pacific Coast and extending into the Gulf of Mexico was the gobierno of Yucatán. North and west of the gobierno of New Spain lay New Galicia. Further expansion led to the creation of gobiernos of New Vizcaya (1562), New León (1580), and New Mexico (1598). Additional subdivision of frontier regions occurred from the late 17th century until the early 19th century.

The physical size and population of the gobiernos resulted, particularly in New Spain and New Galicia, in their division into the provincial units known most commonly as *alcaldías mayores*. The number of subdivisions peaked in the 1570s, then fell substantially as a result of a declining native population and administrative consolidation, especially in the late 17th century. Within each of these jurisdictions a municipality housed the provincial administrator, or *alcalde mayor*.

Principal Spanish explorations and conquests in the sixteenth century

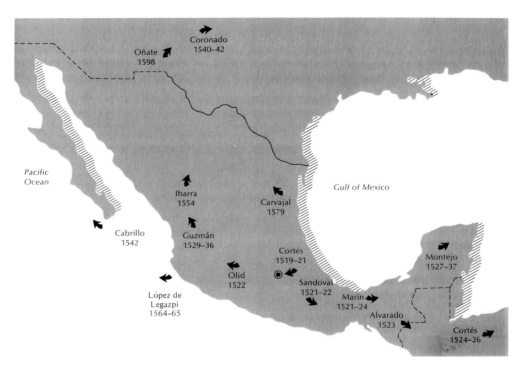

The most numerous territorial units were the municipalities. The Crown confirmed the existence of the native municipalities and their dependent villages (*cabeceras* and *sujetos*) and emphasized their central role. In addition, it required that new municipalities be founded when native villages were consolidated or "congregated." Within the native municipalities, Indian officials handled administrative matters and served as essential links with the Spanish overlords (*encomenderos*) and royal officials.

Emulating the pattern from their homeland, Spaniards made municipalities the focal points in Mexico from the founding of Veracruz in 1519 onward. The jurisdiction of these religious, social, market, and administrative centers originally extended to the boundaries of the adjacent municipality, but the Crown quickly restricted this to a radius of 15 leagues, within which the presence of native municipalities created exempt enclaves. Most Spanish municipalities had modest populations with diverse racial origins. By the early 1550s, all cities that would count 15,000 or more inhabitants in the late 18th century had been established, at least as mining camps. Besides the capital, these included Puebla, Querétaro, Antequera, Guadalajara, Veracruz, Guanajuato, and Zacatecas. There were little more than a dozen Spanish municipalities in the mid–1530s. However, by 1571, New Spain had 35 and by 1624, 82.

Because Mexico lacked navigable rivers and, prior to the arrival of the Spaniards, beasts of burden, developing roads suitable for mule trains if not oxcarts was immediately necessary to facilitate the movement of persons, animals, and goods produced for local and regional consumption, as well as imports and exports. The importance of overland communication between the Gulf Coast city of Veracruz and Mexico City was evident from the time of the Conquest. The "pacification" of the Philippines and the introduction of regular trade with Mexico in the 1560s encouraged improved transportation from Acapulco on the Pacific Coast to Mexico City, although for a long time the road remained suitable only for mule traffic. The discovery of silver at Zacatecas in 1546 quickly led to construction of the Camino Real linking it to Mexico City. This road ultimately passed through numerous northern mining districts before reaching Santa Fe, New Mexico. Lesser roads linked market, mining, and administrative centers. The importance of the landlocked capital as a transportation hub was a striking feature of this communication system that predated the pattern that would be established in Spain after Philip II fixed the capital in Madrid.

Time and distance profoundly affected administration of the colony, by forcing the Crown to delegate more authority to colonial officials than was customary in Spain. Thus, despite institutional checks on their behavior, officeholders in New Spain enjoyed a latitude and flexibility that their Spanish counterparts lacked. An order sent from Madrid in early July typically did not reach Mexico City until late September. The response normally did not leave New Spain until late spring, to arrive in Madrid in the fall. And this lengthy cycle might mark only the first round of communication in resolving an issue. Thus, the distance covered by mounted couriers and sailing ships ensured leisurely communications between Spain and Mexico.

The Crown of Castile fully expected to benefit financially from "the Indies," as the Spaniards termed the New World. The right of conquest, the "legal" title conveyed by Pope Alexander VI in 1493, and the acceptance of absolutist rule in Castile gave the monarchs broad authority to impose, with careful modifications, Castilian administrative institutions on American dominions. By building upon tested institutions and adding to them when necessary, the Crown quickly established its authority in New Spain and created an administrative apparatus there that sustained Spanish rule for three centuries.

The Crown's determination that both its coffers and the Castilian economy should benefit from the Indies took institutional form in 1503 with the creation of the House of Trade in Seville, a wealthy Castilian commercial center with riverine access to the Atlantic. The House of Trade licensed ships and passengers going to the New World, oversaw the loading and unloading of ships, collected duties, mapped contemporary knowledge of coastlines and routes, and handled judicial cases arising from colonial trade disputes or crimes on the high seas.

Cortés's victory underscored the fiscal potential of the rapidly expanding colonies and consequently the need for a permanent body in Spain to oversee their orderly development. Formalized in 1524, the Council of the Indies assumed executive, legislative, and administrative responsibilities for Spain's New World possessions. For nearly two centuries the council formulated policy in an advisory capacity to the monarch, issued legislation in his name, conducted correspondence with officials in Mexico and elsewhere in the New World, and normally participated in selecting administrators of high rank, with the significant exception of the viceroy.

In addition, the Council of the Indies served as an appellate court for major civil cases and oversaw the judicial review of officials (residencia) and the occasional special inspection tours (visitas) initiated in Mexico in the 1540s. The councillors' rare firsthand knowledge of Mexico, the practice of promoting seasoned councillors of the Indies to the Council of Castile (the major governing body and advisor to the monarch), the slowness inherent in administration by committee, and the lengthy time required for communication across the Atlantic reduced the council's effectiveness, and its authority slowly eroded in the 17th century. In the early 18th century a secretary of state for the Indies assumed many of its responsibilities.

The highest-ranking official resident in Mexico was the viceroy of New Spain. To inaugurate the office, Charles I selected Antonio de Mendoza, a younger son of one of Castile's most illustrious noble families and thus someone with the political connections and social rank that would overawe the conquistadores and early settlers. During his unusually long 15-year tenure (1535–50), Mendoza firmly established royal authority in Mexico.

As personal representatives of the monarch, Mendoza and subsequent viceroys lived in a palace located on the central plaza (plaza mayor) of Mexico City, had numerous servants, extended lavish hospitality, and projected an image of royalty. While it encouraged the keeping up of such regal appearance, the Crown simultaneously imposed important restraints on its territorial governors. Among the devices used to curtail viceregal power were limited terms of service, instructions issued by the Council of the Indies, occasional special inspections, prohibitions against establishing local social and economic ties, and a formal judicial review following the viceroys' terms of service. Most important, other colonial institutions and representatives—for example, the *Audiencia* of Mexico, the archbishop of Mexico, treasury officials, and the city council of Mexico City—served as checks on viceregal behavior by virtue of their overlapping responsibilities and their privilege of communicating independently with the king and the Council of the Indies.

As New Spain's chief executive the viceroy had extensive responsibilities, which included preventing "unjust" exploitation of the natives and overseeing defense, exploration, and settlement; the administration of justice, civil administration; and tax collection and disbursement, as well as encouraging economic expansion and remitting surplus revenue to Spain. Above all, the monarch measured his representative's success by that official's ability to remit a sizable amount of surplus revenue to Spain.

As a group, the 44 viceroys between 1535 and 1808—only three of whom were creoles—were capable men with prior military, administrative, or diplomatic experience. Under Habsburg rule (1516–1700), the appointees were noticeably younger. Nine of them advanced to viceroy of Peru. Once New Spain eclipsed Peru as a source of silver and income remission, the Crown ended this pattern with the naming of the Conde de la Monclova as viceroy of Peru in 1688, shortly before the War of Spanish Succession began in 1701. No subsequent pattern of promotion emerged under the new Bourbon dynasty, and death became the most common means of exiting from office; seven Bourbon viceroys died in service, compared with only two Habsburg appointees. Viceroys were invariably of noble birth. Only four Habsburg appointees lacked a title of nobility when entering office, although one received a title during his unique second tenure. In contrast, only 11 Bourbon appointees held titles of nobility when named, although one received a title subsequently. A majority in both the Habsburg and Bourbon eras belonged to a military order.

The broad responsibilities and regal lifestyle of the viceroys gave them a presence that exceeded their actual power. Ranked lower, but at times collectively more important, were the members of the *audiencias* of Mexico and Guadalajara, the high courts and advisory bodies to the viceroy of New Spain and the president of the *Audiencia* of New Galicia. The Crown named viceroys to term appointments, whereas audiencia ministers were appointed for life unless they advanced within a tribunal or to another court. Because ministers on the Audiencia of Mexico rarely moved to Spanish courts or the Council of the Indies and only a few advanced as presidents of other audiencias, the viceregal capital was served by experienced men. Their local ties and appreciation of local agendas gave the audiencias substantial power. Wise chief executives heeded their recommendations.

The Crown established audiencias in Mexico in 1527 and Guadalajara in 1547. Royal legislation specified that all audiencia ministers be men of legitimate birth (all claimed noble status), at least 25 years of age, and recipients of a university degree in law. While the first ministers named were born in Spain, beginning in 1585, a sprinkling of criiollos received appointments.

Most judges named to the Audiencia of Guadalajara during Habsburg rule began their careers on the court, and almost half of them never advanced beyond it. Most who did went to the Audiencia of Mexico. Only 9 of the 64 judges were of American birth. Two were born within the jurisdiction of the Audiencia of Mexico, but none in Guadalajara. With no native sons serving on the court of Guadalajara and only two of the three named to the Audiencia of Mexico before 1700 ever serving in that capacity, local influence on the courts during Habsburg rule was almost exclusively indirect.

The Crown's overriding concern with revenue generated by New Spain led to the immediate appointment of treasury officials and the subsequent creation of treasury offices, beginning with Mexico City in 1521 and Veracruz in 1531. An accounting tribunal created in Mexico City in 1605 signified a further effort by the Crown to control revenues and expenditures and prevent misuse of royal funds by the very treasury officials named to oversee them.

After a period of experimentation, the royal officials of each treasury office finally stabilized at two or three: an accountant and a treasurer, and, in some treasuries, a combination inspector and business manager known as a *veedor* (factor). Of more than 225 identified officials of the treasury offices and accounting office of New Spain named between 1660 and 1780, more than 75 percent were born in Spain, more than 20 percent were from New Spain, and only 4 apointees were from elsewhere in the Indies. While many peninsular Spaniards joined their Mexican-born counterparts by forging local ties through marriage, even single ministers formed part of an integrated social and economic elite whose primary objectives were unrelated to their place of birth.

Provincial officials formed the most numerous category of royal appointees. Originally named to oversee Native Americans previously living in *encomiendas* (grants of Indian labor and tribute) that had reverted to the Crown, these officials also had judicial and military responsibilities. Their number fluctuated considerably, but the pinnacle was more than 270 in the 1570s. Subsequent consolidation reduced this number until on the eve of their replacement by the intendant system in the late 1780s there were 129 alcaldías mayores in the gobierno of New Spain, 62 alcaldías mayores and 7 gobiernos on the northern frontier of the colony, and a few others in the southeastern region.

From Antonio de Mendoza's tenure until the 1670s, the viceroys named most of the provincial officials. The immediate descendants of conquistadores and the early settlers sought these appointments based on their fathers' services; royal legislation issued in 1538 supported their claims. By the end of the 16th century more than 40 percent of such officials were born in New Spain. Viceregal patronage, however, also benefited retainers who accompanied the chief executives to Mexico.

The Crown's decision in the late 1670s to sell appointments to provincial positions profoundly reduced the viceroys' patronage while prompting the purchasers to compensate themselves by milking their positions for all they were worth during a three- to five-year tenure. Typically entering office in debt for the cost of the appointment itself and the performance bonds they had had to post prior to taking office, alcaldes mayores worked hand in glove with their creditors, who were often wholesale merchants in Mexico City, to exploit the natives of their jurisdiction through the notorious system known as the *repartimiento*. For example, in the heavily Indian jurisdictions of Oaxaca, this practice involved the distribution of raw material such as cotton that the natives had to weave into cloths (*mantas*) of a specified size. In return they received a payment substantially below the free market price. The alcalde mayor, either directly or through a lieutenant at times supplied by his creditor, then sold the finished goods at the market price or sent them to the creditor for sale. Although the regular sale of appointments ended in 1750, the corrupt repartimiento system continued unabated.

Beneath these various colonial administrative layers, each municipality, whether of native or Spanish origin, had a local government and local officials. Municipal councils typically had four or more aldermen (*regidores*) and two local judges and councilmen (*alcaldes*). In addition, municipalities had a variety of officials who policed the area; supervised local revenues, expenditures, and retailing; and performed a host of general administrative tasks. Indian municipalities also had responsibility for collecting tribute, maintaining treasuries and communal properties, supporting the local church, adjudicating petty crimes, handling local land and water cases, and litigating to protect local rights and property. Independent Indian villages (head towns) also had local governors. Not surprisingly, the locally born participated extensively at the municipal government level. The largest municipality, Mexico City, had a majority of such aldermen from 1590 on.

Although in its desperate pursuit of revenue to support its military involvement in Europe the Crown authorized the sale of appointments to treasury positions in 1633, provincial administrative posts in 1677, audiencia jobs in 1687, and even the title of viceroy by the end of the 17th century, such sales had temporal limits established by a specified term or, in far fewer cases, the life of the purchaser. The Crown also sold a variety of posts in Spanish municipalities and, after 1606, even permitted (under specified conditions) their resale and inheritance. These sales guaranteed that native-born members of local elites would dominate the formal machinery of local government through direct representation. In contrast, the non-native local elites had to rely largely on indirect means such as social and economic ties to influence treasury and audiencia officials.

In maintaining Spanish rule through recourse to law with only minimal reliance on military force, balancing the conflicting interests of Crown and colonists, conquerors and conquered, and remitting surplus revenues to Spain, the bureaucrats of New Spain were generally quite successful. Although many enriched themselves through illegal means, their involvement in local economic affairs and social ties through marriage, kinship, and as godparents made them sensitive to local interests and thus tempered their implementation of royal dictates. The political stability they helped create and maintain through this balance between royal and colonial interests contrasted sharply with the instability that followed independence.

The Spanish Conquest irrevocably altered the social order of Mexico, by creating broad categories of victors and vanquished identified by race. It also facilitated the mixing of races and provided Spaniards and some natives with opportunities for upward social mobility. While the Crown recognized the distinction made between nobles and commoners among the native population, it nevertheless lumped natives of distinct ethnic and cultural backgrounds into the single category of Indians and subjected most Indian commoners to making tribute payments as a sign of their vassalage. Whites, on the other hand, were exempt from direct taxation, an implicit indication of nobility in Spain.

Encomiendas helped to fulfill the dream of status enhancement that had originally attracted conquistadors and settlers to the Americas. No conquistador in Cortés's entourage came from the upper Castilian nobility, and no more than a fifth of the original *encomenderos* could legitimately claim noble origin. However, because an *encomienda* gave its recipient virtual lordship over tributaries, the institution's very nature implied noble status beyond that suggested by the tax exemptions. Participants in the Conquest who received an encomienda immediately formed the founding apex of the new colonial society. However, recognizing

Two *encomenderos,* probably members of the de Nava family, observe the baptism of leaders from the nearby villages. By observing the baptism, the encomenderos were fulfilling their responsibility to the indigenous people regarded as their tributary wards.

the potential perils of having a bona fide nobility in Mexico, the Crown steadfastly and effectively prevented the emergence of lords with the seigneurial power and jurisdiction enjoyed by the great Castilian noble families.

Beyond the broader delineations of conqueror and conquered, pre-Conquest hierarchies as well as race, gender, and ethnicity played important roles in determining economic and social status. Mixing of the races began in New Spain, no doubt, when Cortés and his men first camped on the Gulf Coast. Cortés's own liaison with the native interpreter Malinche, or Doña Marina as the Spaniards called her, confirmed that sexual encounters would accompany military advances. The arrival of African slaves beginning in the 1520s added further complexity to a society in which ancestral origins were a primary determinant of status.

The Spaniards encountered a series of native social hierarchies descending from chieftains and nobles to slaves. Moctezuma II sat at the pinnacle of pre-Conquest Mexican society and thus at the apex of the most prominent hierarchy. Although the Spaniards' assumption of central authority seriously wounded the native nobility, those nobles who survived retained a degree of social status. Moreover, in the immediate aftermath of the Conquest some daughters of native rulers married Spaniards. In a unique case, Doña Isabel Moctezuma, daughter of Moctezuma II, married three Spaniards in succession after the death of her first husband, the Aztec emperor Cuauhtémoc. Her sister, Leonor, married two Spaniards in succession. In both cases, the women brought encomiendas to their marriages. The initial shortage of Spanish women led some Spaniards to wed native women of less celebrated ancestry. An interpreter for Cortés, for example, married a native woman, by whom he had seven children. Conqueror Gonzalo Rodríguez de la Magdalena also married a native woman, by whom he had eight children. Because of the primacy of the paternal line, these children were considered Spaniards.

Less formal relationships were more common than marriage between Spaniards and Indians. Cortés acknowledged six illegitimate children, including a son with Doña Marina, a daughter with Doña Isabel Moctezuma, and two daughters by other Indian women. Conqueror Alonso González de Portugal formally recognized two *mestiza* (offspring of Spanish and Indian parents) daughters. Early settlers Pedro Núñez and Diego de Ocampo each left three natural daughters, undoubtedly born of Indian mothers. When acknowledged by their fathers and brought up as Spaniards, *mestizo* children became part of Spanish society. A growing number of mestizos of illegitimate birth, however, lacked this parental protection, belonging to neither Spanish nor Indian society. They also suffered overt discrimination and were barred from holding a variety of offices. Typically lacking formal education and opportunities for economic advancement, most mestizo youths appeared to Spanish officials as shiftless troublemakers, vagabonds, and thieves.

The native population thought of the few initial Africans in Mexico as "black whites," indistinguishable from the other conquerors in any way but skin color. The subsequent importation of slaves from Africa quickly increased their number. Predominantly male, the slaves quickly emulated their masters by expanding the genetic pool through sex with native women. Their offspring joined the mestizos of illegitimate birth in the growing population of mixed origins collectively referred to as *castas*. By the middle of the 17th century, offspring of Spaniards, Indians, blacks, and castas in ever more racially complex combinations outnumbered the Spanish population, which was principally comprised of criollos, Spaniards born in Mexico. This numerical predominance would continue beyond the colonial era.

Population figures before 1570 are notoriously unreliable, particularly for the native population, but the overall trends are clear. From the Conquest until the 1620s, the number of natives fell. Meanwhile, whites, blacks, and persons of mixed ancestry increased in number. By 1650, Mexico's total population was about 1.7 million, three-quarters of which (1.3 million) were Indians. In addition, there were approximately 185,000 whites (14,000 Europeans and 171,000 criollos), 225,000 castas (116,000 mulattoes [offspring of black and white parents] and 109,000 mestizos), and 35,000 blacks. With the exception of the black population, each of these categories expanded for the remainder of the colonial era.

The conquistadores had followed Cortés for wealth and a better life and therefore expected to benefit from the labor and tribute of the vanquished. Cortés obliged and, acting initially without royal authorization, applied the precedent established in the conquest of the Caribbean islands of rewarding many of his early supporters with encomiendas. These and subsequent grants of native labor and tribute provided approximately 500 conquistadores and early settlers, about half of whom resided in Mexico City, with the means to support themselves, their families, and retainers without engaging in manual labor. By also exploiting land and, on occasion, mines for profit, they accumulated capital that could be invested in a variety of money-making activities. While encomenderos did have responsibilities—for example, overseeing the Christianization of the natives

Prior to the Spanish Conquest, Indian carriers like the men depicted here transported all goods throughout Mexico, except in the lake region of the Valley of Mexico where canoes could be used. Although the introduction of mules, oxen, and donkeys provided alternative means of transportation, the Spaniards continued to use Indian porters, especially in the first decades after the Conquest.

provided by their grants and supplying military service to the monarch—their principal interest was self-aggrandizement.

Through the encomienda system, and to a much lesser degree native slavery, the Spanish conquistadores and early settlers laid the foundation of colonial rule almost literally on the backs of the native population. The large size of Mexico's sedentary population, coupled with the long-established native tradition of commoners owing their rulers labor and tribute, enabled the conquerors, working through native leaders, initially to impose their demands with remarkable ease.

The encomienda system, however, increased both the components of tribute and the requirements for labor beyond that required by the Aztecs. Pre-Conquest tributaries provided the Aztecs, among other things, corn (maize), tomatoes, beans, cotton cloaks, amber, feathers, baskets, cacao, chiles, salt, and turkeys. Following the introduction of European crops and animals, this list expanded to include wheat and fodder for horses. The increased use of coinage ultimately introduced monetary tribute. Labor demands included those for the human conveyance of goods and materials, the construction of private residences and outbuildings, field work, road building, and mining and domestic service.

Spanish municipalities created during and immediately after the Conquest became market destinations for tribute where encomenderos could sell items that exceeded or were irrelevant to their households' direct needs. These municipalities were also major sites of native exploitation, because the encomenderos demanded residential construction, the clergy supervised the erection of churches, and government officials oversaw the building of city halls, streets, and other public amenities.

Had the native population remained stable, the demands of the small number of Spaniards could have been met for many years. The population, however, was in decline even before the fall of Tenochtitlán in 1521. Its continued descent and the simultaneous growth of the Spanish population prompted the Spaniards to alter their demands for tribute and the ways in which they harnessed native labor.

From a pre-Conquest total of probably 10 to 12 million (one estimate exceeds 25 million), the native population numbered only about 750,000 by the early 1620s. Epidemic disease, exacerbated by the Spaniards' abusive treatment and excessive labor demands, primarily determined the chronology of population decline. Smallpox, the first epidemic, spread from the Greater Antilles to Mexico in 1520, afflicting the Spaniards' native enemies and allies alike. Other widespread epidemics occurred in 1545–48, 1576–81, and 1629–31, with deadly local outbreaks adding to the losses. After stabilizing around 1630, the native population increased, with occasional interruptions and regional variations, for the rest of the colonial era.

The declining native population reduced the value of encomiendas quickly while increasing the burdens on the survivors. At the same time, newly arriving Spanish immigrants expected access to the economic benefits of native labor. Some clergy who witnessed the natives' exploitation outspokenly denounced the encomienda system. More important, the Crown had no interest in turning encomenderos into a full-fledged New World nobility by granting them indefinite hereditary control over their encomiendas. The "New Laws" issued in 1542 reflected both royal and clerical perspectives in their attack on the encomienda system. Although the encomenderos secured repeal of the prohibition of inheritance, demographic losses and the Crown's continued efforts to expand its control over the remaining native population eliminated labor as a form of tribute.

In 1549, royal officials began to distribute compulsory rotating labor drafts to Spaniards for work in agriculture, mining, construction, and other activities allegedly in the public interest. The resulting repartimiento system thus provided more Spaniards with access to labor while exploiting the laborers more efficiently than did the encomiendas. Continued depopulation, however, also affected the repartimiento system. By the early 17th century it, too, proved unable to sustain the loss of labor and the economic demands of Spanish employers.

When employers found the declining number of repartimiento laborers inadequate, they offered villagers willing to engage in seasonal work wages that substantially exceeded those for repartimiento labor. In 1632, the viceroy of New Spain outlawed the use of repartimiento workers for any activities other than the drainage and flood-control project for Mexico City and mining, which was a relatively small-scale project. Henceforth, seasonal and part-time wage laborers and workers resident on rural estates (haciendas) were the principal sources of colonial labor in rural New Spain.

The abrupt population losses resulting from the 16th–century epidemics also stimulated a resettlement program. The comparatively small number of friars in New Spain urged the Crown to "congregate" the survivors from several villages into new settlements known as *congregaciones* in order to make it easier to provide religious services and sacraments. Crown officials, encomenderos, and other Spaniards also realized that consolidating the native population would benefit their interests. Thus they supported royal legislation in the 1550s that ordered the creation of native towns laid out in the typical Spanish grid pattern. By 1560, most of the principal pre-Conquest communities served by Spanish missionaries had been relocated, and many Indians in smaller outlying communities had moved as well. The epidemic of 1576–81 led to a second wave of forced resettlement from 1593 to 1605, which was encouraged by both clerics and Spaniards anxious to gain control of vacated lands.

The population loss sustained by the epidemic of 1576–81 led to an unprecedented expansion of haciendas as a result of there being more land available as well as favorable market conditions and a labor pool attracted by good wages and offers of land use. Although municipal councils and royal officials began issuing land grants immediately after the Conquest and encomenderos routinely employed "their" Indians on these lands, the native population density in central Mexico precluded the early formation of numerous large estates. The introduction of livestock by the conquistadores and other settlers altered the balance between land and labor. In contrast to the comparatively intensive nature of agriculture, pastoral activities required relatively few workers but needed substantial amounts of grazing land. The sizes of the land grants issued for these different purposes varied accordingly. Agricultural grants were typically for amounts from 100 to 400 acres. Pastoral grants, on the other hand, ran to almost 2,000 acres for sheep or goats and nearly 4,500 acres for cattle.

Spaniards settled in locations that offered a labor supply, opportunities to make money, or some combination of the two. Thus, the first Spanish settlements tended to be close to sedentary native populations that could provide labor and tribute through the encomienda system. The richest silver lodes, however, were located far from the native population centers. While this required finding alternative sources of labor, it also meant that unexploited lands near the mines were immediately available for agricultural and especially pastoral activities.

The quest for precious metals quickly expanded territorial exploration beyond central Mexico. Spaniards led by Nuño de Guzmán advanced to the north and west of Mexico City into what became the province of New Galicia. This and the futile expedition led by Francisco Vázquez de Coronado in 1540–42 into the southwestern U.S., and the short-lived Mixtón War (1541–42) marked two decades of failure in the search for precious metals beyond the frontiers of the Aztec empire. Nonetheless, a few friars and cattlemen pushed north and east of the fledgling city of Guadalajara in the aftermath of the war.

The discovery of silver in 1546 near what first became a mining camp and later the city of Zacatecas stimulated movement to the north and led to the creation of numerous agricultural haciendas to supply wheat, meat, and leather to the newly settled region. Indians recruited from the south arrived in the 1550s and 1560s to provide wage labor. In addition, miners developed mining haciendas that included refining mills, processing and storage facilities, stables, a house for the owner, rooms for workers, and a chapel. Nearby lands were used for breeding mules and growing grain. The mining boom in Zacatecas also fueled the quest for additional riches and led to discoveries of silver ore at Guanajuato (1550), Pachuca (1552), Real del Monte (1552), Sombrerete (about 1558), San Luis Potosí (1591–92), and Parral, where there was a major strike in 1631.

Spanish expansion into the Gran Chichimeca, as the unconquered region beyond central Mexico was known, provoked native hostility almost immediately. The ensuing conflict resulted in the creation of fortified towns along the Camino Real linking Zacatecas to central Mexico. After peace was achieved in the 1590s, sedentary natives from central Mexico—notably Mexicans, Tlaxcalans, Tarascans, and Otomíes—migrated northward. Moreover, the end of hostilities freed up capital that Zacatecans had designated for financing the war. Zacatecas itself was no longer a frontier town but, in the eyes of its residents, second in importance only to Mexico City among the municipalities of New Spain. In turn, it served as a base for settling lands still farther north in New Vizcaya, New León, and New Mexico.

Much of the wealth produced by silver mining ultimately passed through Mexico City, the colony's trade and financial center, which in 1560 supported a population of nearly 100,000 and was a substantial market for foodstuffs, fuel, textiles, and luxury goods. It was not only New Spain's largest market center but also the nexus of an imperial trading network that extended from the coast of the Gulf of Mexico to the Pacific Ocean, south to Guatemala, and north to scattered settlements on the distant frontier. Through Manila, starting in the 1560s, came silks, porcelains, and other goods from China. Slaves arrived from Africa and textiles, olive oil, wine, paper, glass, iron, and other merchandise reached the capital from Seville, as well as, illegally, from other European ports.

Most residents of Mexico City, however, were more concerned about access to a ready, affordable supply of locally or regionally produced food and textiles than the availability of olive oil, good wine, fine textiles, hardware, and the many luxury items that arrived by way of the transatlantic or Pacific trading systems. The introduction of sheep, cattle, and pigs soon enabled colonists to add lamb, mutton, beef, and pork to their diet. Wheat quickly took hold, and soon farms in the Valley of Mexico were marketing it. In the latter part of the 16th century, Puebla and its surrounding valleys were selling wheat to buyers in Mexico City and the

Caribbean, as well as provisioning the Atlantic trading fleet at Veracruz. A regulatory system of municipal public granaries and adequate supplies encouraged, with rare but important exceptions in 1624 and 1692, generally stable prices throughout the 17th century. Indeed, after 1600, transportation was normally the most important variable in determining the price of wheat, corn, and barley.

Wheat was a crop of the highlands, whereas the lowlands were known for their production of sugarcane. As early as 1531, the sale of sugar from properties in Morelos was an important source of income to Cortés. Within easy reach of the market and exporters of Mexico City, the sugar industry thrived in Morelos. The region remained the major producer throughout the colonial era and into the 20th century.

Although textiles were New Spain's most valuable import, few people could afford luxury fabrics. The majority of the colony's inhabitants used cloth spun domestically. Vast flocks of sheep supplied the raw wool that workshops (*obrajes*), some employing hundreds of workers in dismal conditions, turned into cheap woolen cloth. Central and southern Mexico emerged as the most important centers of wool production, with Querétaro claiming primacy in the 17th century. While the *obrajes* produced substantial amounts of cloth, individual native weavers continued their domestic textile production.

Throughout the entire colonial era and during most of the 19th century, silver was Mexico's leading export. Registered bullion production, most of it silver, increased rapidly after the Conquest. Stimulated by the introduction of the amalgamation process of separating silver from its ore in the mid–1550s, silver production exceeded 25 million pesos in the decade from 1561 to 1570 and peaked at more than 53 million pesos in the decade of 1611 to 1620 before dropping to a low of 34.6 million pesos from 1641 to 1650. It climbed to just below 60 million pesos between 1681 and 1690, declined to a low of 48.3 million pesos from 1701 to 1710, then expanded in every decade but that of the 1760s through the first decade of the 19th century. The registered total of 216.4 million pesos from 1801 to 1810 was thus about four and a half times what it had been in the first decade of the 18th century.

Because these figures represent only legally registered silver, they understate actual production by an indeterminable amount. It seems clear, however, that from the 1650s through the 1720s more bullion—and in some decades more than 50 percent more—reached Europe than was registered in the Spanish colonies. What is particularly important for Mexican history, however, is that registered Mexican silver production surpassed that of Peru in the decade of 1671 to 1680, at which time the northern viceroyalty emerged as the Spanish empire's most valuable colony.

The spread and expanded production of European plants and animals, the arrival of Spanish artisans to instruct the natives and black slaves in European crafts, the growth of silver production (especially after the introduction of the amalgamation process), and the purchase of contraband imports meant that the colonists were progressively shedding their primitive economic dependence on Spain. Nonetheless, the trading system based primarily on the exchange of silver for imported textiles and other European and East Asian goods remained central to the Mexican economy.

Mexico's silver proved to be an ongoing source of temptation to Spain's enemies. The Crown responded first by forbidding its ships to sail alone and then by employing convoys in the 1530s. Perfected by 1564, the fleet system ideally involved annual sailings of two convoys from an Andalusian port to Veracruz and a Panamanian port, followed by a return voyage from Havana the following year. The fleet bound for New Spain would set sail in April and, after dropping off ships with goods for Central America and the Caribbean islands, reach Veracruz, 4,860 miles from Cádiz, two and a half months later.

The convoy to Veracruz sailed with regularity until the 1620s. Thereafter, the legal Atlantic trade declined until 1660, when the volume and value of the merchandise shipped began to rise. Despite the increasing volume, the number of fleet sailings declined during the second half of the 17th century, to average only five a decade. Although not formally abolished until 1789, fleets sailed irregularly in the 18th century. Mercury ships, mail ships, and individual licensed ships from the time of the War of Jenkins' Ear (1739–48) sustained Spain's trade with Mexico and ensured that silver reached Castile.

Cumbersome and irregular though it was for much of its existence, the fleet system achieved its primary objective. Protected by heavily armed ships of war, merchant vessels reached Veracruz without serious foreign peril. Armed naval ships then carried the bullion on the return trip to Spain. Only once did foreigners capture an entire fleet. Under Piet Heyn, in 1628, the Dutch surprised the silver fleet off the coast of Cuba and seized its entire cargo, worth about 10 million pesos, enough to give stockholders of the Dutch West India Company a hefty dividend and finance an invasion of Brazil in 1630. The success of the English admiral Robert Blake in destroying most of the New Spain fleet in the Canary Islands in 1657 was the only other major disaster inflicted by Spain's maritime enemies.

Regular trade between Manila in the Philippines and Mexico began in 1571 and continued until 1814. The voyage, conducted by large galleons weighing up to 2,000 tons, took only about three months from Acapulco to Manila, but typically six to nine months to return. An entrepot for goods from Asia, Manila became the center of a valuable exchange network. There merchants from New Spain traded silver from the Americas for Chinese silks, damasks, jewelry, and porcelains as well as Indian cottons, Japanese lacquerware, Indonesian spices, and Philippine cinnamon and beeswax. The strong Mexican demand for Asian goods, especially for high-quality, inexpensive silks and other textiles, threatened the previous monopoly of textiles imported from Spain. Alarmed Spanish merchants thus pressured the Crown to prohibit the burgeoning trade between New Spain and Peru, which principally involved Asian goods after the onset of the trade with Manila, and to restrict the volume and value of Mexico's trade with Manila.

Because the trade with Manila in some years equaled or exceeded the registered Atlantic trade, the Crown officially severed the trade links between Peru and Mexico in 1634. Although the prohibition of trade between New Spain and Peru reduced its volume substantially, some contraband continued: Travelers in the mid–18th century noted that residents of Lima were wearing oriental silks.

Such legal prohibitions were most effective, however, when they limited the number of sailings between Acapulco and Manila. But shippers simply laughed at the 500,000-peso restriction on outbound cargo from Acapulco. Fraud almost invariably doubled this amount; at least once in the late 1630s it was exceeded by more than tenfold. So much silver flowed to Asia that the Mexican peso became a common medium of exchange within China.

Public celebrations brought together people of all ages, colors, and occupations. Church and state leaders organized galas that reaffirmed their own status, as well as corporate and racial divisions, within a setting designed to promote social harmony. Spaniards, Indians, castas, and blacks participated in or at least observed events that provided diversion for all segments of colonial society. The wealth, size, heterogeneity, and status of Mexico City enabled it to offer celebrations unparalleled elsewhere in New Spain. The capital hosted an array of festivities in their full glory associated with the arrival of a new viceroy and, because of its many religious bodies, guilds, and other corporate bodies, witnessed the largest number of these spectacles. In addition, as in Spain, every municipality also celebrated its own saint's day and numerous other religious holidays. Moreover, the universal recognition of Corpus Christi and other important holy days provided all of New Spain with a sense of communal experience and reinforced its religious and cultural ties to the mother country.

Throughout the Habsburg era, (1516–1700) the arrival of a new viceroy offered an occasion for festivities along the route from Veracruz to Mexico City, as well as an excuse for celebrations in the capital that might last weeks if not months. Thousands of residents and spectators from beyond the city enjoyed this most pretentious, elaborate, and costly of all civil fiestas. The city council regularly spent well over a year's average income to enhance the image of the state and the king's personal representative. Bullfights, dances, mock battles, jousts, music, oratorical presentations, solemn oaths, floats, literary competitions, and parades were among the scheduled events. Because they assumed the white population's unwavering support of the colonial regime, organizers tried to attract similar allegiance from the rest of the urban population by incorporating them either as participants or active spectators in the viceregal entrance.

In this ceremony each formally dressed group of officeholders proceeded, according to rank and convention, to the city's triumphal arch, some 70 feet high. Symbolic, mythological, and allegorical illustrations on this arch set forth the viceroy's qualifications for office and the city's expectations of its new governor. By passing through the arch the viceroy implicitly supported the aspirations of the people. Accompanying the celebrations were native dances and

Demonstración de la Danza de los Indios

Encouraged by viceroys and city officials, Native Americans took an active role in the celebration of Corpus Christi in Mexico City, providing decorations of flowers and ornamentation and constructing a thatch canopy along the procession's route. They were particularly conspicuous in the performance of music and dance. Official disapproval of these unseemly "excesses" led the city council to end the employment of dancers in the mid-eighteenth century.

music, fireworks over several evenings, and other entertainments. Although in the 18th century the attention paid to the celebrations accompanying the oath of allegiance to the Bourbon monarchs eclipsed the more frequent viceregal receptions, the emphasis in both was on the legitimacy of the state.

Unlike the periodic viceregal receptions and less frequent ceremonies honoring new monarchs, the festival of Corpus Christi was an annual event. Corpus Christi celebrated a nominally shared religion and brought together the total populace under a more homogeneous guise than could the secular fiestas, which emphasized distinct corporate identities. Devotion to the Host formed the essence of this religious communion in which citizens of all ethnicities participated in a procession and provided the accompanying altars, costumes, dances, music, and theatrical presentations. While one's membership in a specific group determined one's position in the procession and thus reinforced the existing social stratification, no one group patronized or dominated the event.

Corpus Christi was a celebration for everyone. In Mexico City, as in the cities of Spain, even councilmen participated equally in an event that symbolically dissolved, however briefly, the social order. The Bourbon reforms in the capital first regulated but then prohibited dancing, drinking, and unacceptable dress during the festival in an effort to prevent unrest such as erupted in 1692. However, although these and other changes altered people's participation in the celebration,

Corpus Christi continued as before to mirror the capital's society and provided many inhabitants with a welcome distraction from the routines of daily life.

Trade, unlike festivals, could not be controlled as easily by the Monarchy. The Spanish Crown considered New Spain its private property and tried to prevent any direct contact between the colony and other European countries. Legally, the colonists could contact other Europeans only through the mother country. However, this restriction failed to keep Mexican products and illustrations of its pre-Conquest inhabitants and Spanish conquerors from spreading throughout the Old World. The treatment of New Spain's native population prompted the Black Legend, detailing unique Spanish cruelty. These stories started to spread in Italy and were subsequently broadcast by Dutch and English authors. Attempts to identify and establish the nature and rights of natives occupied major thinkers in mid–16th–century Spain, a debate whose implications ultimately flowed into the origins of international law. Moreover, manuscripts, artifacts, and exotica from New Spain, especially those produced by the pre-Conquest peoples, entered royal and aristocratic collections in Europe. Although exported silver epitomizes New Spain's material contribution to Europe's economic system, cochineal, indigo, maize, cacao, vanilla, chili peppers, and tomatoes were also important.

Thus, New Spain's entry into European consciousness was conditioned by the New World's riches and Europe's perceptions of Spanish rapacity, abuse, and exploitation of the native peoples. Religious and political conflicts arising from the Reformation added an anti-Catholic element to portrayals by Protestant countries envious of Spain's colonies. Especially in times of international tension, English and Dutch propagandists gleefully seized on Spanish sources documenting mistreatment of the native peoples as incontrovertible proof of Spanish cruelty and confirmation of the ill-gotten nature of its New World wealth. The English translation of Bartolomé de Las Casas's 1552 *Brevísima relación de la destrucción de las Indias* in 1583, for example, highlighted the horrific conditions of the Spanish Conquest and the exploitation of the natives throughout the Indies and reported that the Spaniards had caused more deaths in New Spain than anywhere else in the Indies.

The title of an English translation in 1689 underscored this book's anti-Spanish, anti-Catholic bias: *Popery truly display'd in its bloody colours: or, a faithful narrative of the horrid and unexampled massacres, butcheries and all manner of cruelties, that hell and malice could invent, committed by the popish Spanish party on the inhabitants of West-India.* While English translations of Spanish publications before 1603 had been generally anti-Indian as well as anti-Spanish, subsequent translations sometimes revealed the achievements of native societies. The persistence of an anti-Spanish dimension, however, was evident in the exceedingly popular *The English American*, published in 1648 by Thomas Gage. Based on translations of Spanish sources and the author's own experiences in New Spain and Central America, this work provided an account of Spanish colonial corruption, especially by Catholic clergy, and stressed the ease with which Spain's possessions could, it claimed, be seized. Gage's analysis stimulated Oliver Cromwell's plan known as his Western

Design of 1654, which, following an unsuccessful attack on Hispaniola, led to the English capture of Jamaica.

Knowledge of Cortés's conquest spread quickly both by word of mouth and in print, starting with a Spanish edition of his Second Letter in 1522. By 1532, 18 editions of one or more of his letters in Spanish, German, Latin, Italian, French, and Dutch-Flemish had furnished literate Europeans with the unprecedented drama of New World conquest. As colonization increased and the extent of New Spain's wealth became more apparent, the Crown sought to prevent descriptions of Mexico and the growing empire from circulating among potential rivals and detractors. Accordingly, beginning in 1527, it embarked upon a policy of censorship—prohibiting further Spanish editions of Cortés's letters—to restrict the flow of information about its expanding empire.

Similarly, in 1553, the Crown banned Francisco López de Gómara's history of the conquest of Mexico, published the preceding year. The Franciscan friar Bernardino de Sahagún's great compilation of material on the Mexica's pre-Hispanic beliefs and daily life, now known as the *Florentine Codex,* never appeared in his lifetime. In 1577, the Crown ordered the author's papers confiscated as part of a general suppression of writings on the New World's native civilizations. This official ban on works about pre-Columbian civilizations continued until 1820.

Despite Spain's attempts to control European dissemination of information about the conditions of the Conquest and the wealth of the New World, knowledge of the colonies and their natives' cultural achievements spread increasingly on the continent. In their quest for exotica, wealthy European collectors welcomed the artifacts of pre-Columbian civilizations and actively sought maps, codices, and examples of native art and artisanship. Even before the Conquest, European maps reflected some geographic knowledge of New Spain's Gulf Coast. A published map of Tenochtitlán that appeared in 1524 provided a vision of native urbanization, while a 1536 world map showing the Magellan-El Cano circumnavigation gave Europeans a general view of the Gulf of Mexico along with central and southern Mexico. Maps of North America and the New World in the 1560s clearly, but not precisely, delineated New Spain as a major part of the New World.

Knowledge concerning the native Mexicans and their art and artifacts quickly reached Europe's reading public. In his *Fourth Decade*, published in 1520 in German and Italian and subsequently in numerous other editions, the Italian humanist and councilor of the Indies Peter Martyr described the appearance of six Aztecs and certain items of gold and silver, codices, feather art, weapons, and cotton cloth that were sent by Cortés to Charles I and exhibited in Seville, Valladolid, and Brussels. In the Brussels town hall, the celebrated artist Albrecht Dürer admired the displayed pieces of Moctezuma's treasure, although they did not influence his work. In 1522, Martyr invited the Venetian ambassador and other diplomats to Spain to examine additional articles that Cortés had sent to Charles. The ambassador in turn described them to the senate of the Venetian republic. Pieces of Mexican jade and onyx found their way into Medici collections in Florence and, like other items such as bishops' mitres and ecclesiastical garments made with feathers, into the hands of other collectors, notably in Germany and Italy. The famous *Codex Mendoza,* a 16th–century illustrated Mexican manuscript containing pictographic and glyphic images, was part of the booty seized by French privateers and carried to France, where the royal cosmographer added it to his collection in 1553. Copies of pre-Conquest Aztec manuscripts—no originals are known—made for European viewers in the 16th century remain in European repositories.

Although Indian art served as curiosities for collectors, European artists did not consider it a basis for emulation, and its influence on artists in 16th–century Europe was essentially nil. The Spanish Crown, through suppression of "things pagan" after the Conquest, fed a general European sense of cultural superiority. A German artist's illustrations of natives who had accompanied Cortés to Spain, for example, followed a European style; only the subject matter was Mexican.

However, the cultural and social achievements of Mexico's pre-Conquest peoples attracted the attention of European intellectuals and eventually led to a debate about how the native civilizations should be classified, religiously indoctrinated, and governed. Bartolomé de Las Casas, a Dominican well known for his attacks on the abuses of the conquistadores and the *encomienda* system and his advocacy of conversion through peaceful means alone, pointed to pre-Conquest pyramids in central Mexico as proof of their builders' civilized nature. By contrasting the Aztecs and their achievements with the "rude state" of natives in other locations in the Americas, he contributed to a European conception of social development that was confined, of course, within a Eurocentric view of what constituted development. Thus, even the Aztecs simply confirmed the Europeans' sense of superiority.

Indeed, the Spanish supporters of the Aristotelian doctrine of natural slavery used the Aztecs as support for their argument. For Juan Ginés de Sepúlveda and others, the natives' nature was savage and irrational; thus, they should be under the rule of fully rational beings. At the same time they were, Pope Paul III declared in a 1537 bull, "truly men" and not a subhuman species. In considering Spain's title to dominion in the New World, the Dominican Francisco de Vitoria outlined the property rights and political sovereignty of the natives. The questions raised by Spain's claims in the Indies would later influence Hugo Grotius in his developing of the principles of international law.

Bullion from the Americas had the greatest direct effect on Europe of all the New World's contributions during the colonial era, although historians continue to argue over its relative impact on inflation in 16th–century Europe (what some call the Price Revolution) and on the growth of European capitalism. Mexican bullion contributed to the flow of gold and especially silver. New Spain's cumulative total of these two metals did not exceed Peru's until the 1730s, by which time each viceroyalty had produced approximately a billion pesos worth of registered bullion. Contraband bullion, of course, added an indeterminate amount to these figures.

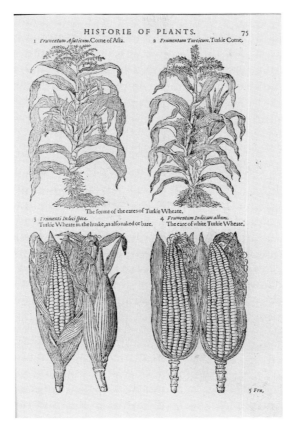

HISTORIE OF PLANTS. 75

The name "turkie wheate" used in these drawings illustrates the early confusion surrounding the actual place of origin of maize. Maize was the most important staple of pre-Conquest Mexico and other New World civilizations. The Spaniards immediately recognized maize as the equivalent of their own wheat, classified it accordingly, and introduced it in Europe.

Funds sent directly by immigrants in Mexico to relatives in Spain or expended on religious buildings, activities, or charity there were also important. In fact, the House of Trade had a special office dedicated to handling probate for peninsular Spaniards who had died in the Indies and left heirs in Spain. Income-yielding assets in Mexico also routed wealth from the colony to the mother country.

Maize, chili peppers, tomatoes, cacao, vanilla, cochineal, and indigo were among Mexico's direct and indirect contributions to Europe. Original to Mexico and Central America and a staple of the Mexican diet, maize may have reached Europe with Columbus's return from his first voyage in 1493. Although maize was being grown in Spain and Portugal by 1525, most Europeans shared an attitude toward it that was expressed succinctly by John Gerard in his 1597 *The Herball or General Historie of Plants* that it "is of hard and evil digestion, a more convenient food for swine than for men." By the late 17th century, however, peasants unable to afford wheat in a number of European regions ate maize in gruels and breads.

A variety of domesticated chili peppers, another staple of the Mexican diet, also quickly reached Europe. By 1565, they were common in the colorful gardens of Spain. Tomatoes soon spread in Europe as well, but the belief that they were poisonous initially limited their dietary significance. By the late 18th century, however, Italians, Spaniards, and Portuguese were using them in numerous dishes.

A cold beverage of cacao mixed with peppers and spices was popular among Aztec nobles. By adding vanilla, sugar, or cinnamon to it, Europeans found the resulting chocolate tasty, and consumption of it spread throughout the continent. Cacao beans, grown primarily in Central America, quickly became another commodity in the transatlantic trade. The heyday of Central American cacao was over by 1600, but other colonial sources supplied a growing European market centered in Amsterdam. By the mid–17th century hot chocolate was the favored beverage of western Europe's aristocracy. In England, Samuel Pepys was using it as a cure for hangovers in 1661. It remained popular among aristocrats and clerics until the French Revolution. Vanilla, then produced primarily in mountainous regions of Veracruz and Oaxaca, reached Spain as an additive for chocolate beverages. After its use spread to the French court in the 17th century, English corsairs considered it a valuable prize. Chocolate drinkers routinely added vanilla to their beverage until the 19th century.

New Spain was home to a variety of products that excited Europeans for their alleged medicinal qualities. A Spanish physician named Nicolas Monardes reported the supposedly therapeutic qualities of sarsaparilla as a cure for syphilis, and shortly thereafter, in 1577, the English merchant John Frampton translated Monardes's work as *Joyfull Newes Out of the New Founde Worlde*. The purgative root of Michoacán also enjoyed favor as a cure for innumerable ailments. Tobacco, too, benefited from early European enthusiasm for its reported curative powers, although New World regions other than Mexico became the major suppliers.

Cochineal, a scarlet dye produced in Oaxaca, quickly became an important export, with shipments first reaching Spain in 1526, Antwerp in 1552, and England no later than 1569. Of the 250,000 to 300,000 pounds per year sent to Spain by 1600, most was reexported to the Netherlands for use in manufacturing textiles. In the 17th and 18th centuries Flemish, Dutch, and English textile weavers constituted the major market for this dye.

Indigo reached Spain, via the fleet that served Mexico, by at least 1576. Although Mexico produced some indigo, Central America dominated the export market, and by 1600 this blue and purple dye had surpassed cacao as its most important export. Legal exports, which made up perhaps less than half of the total production, averaged 240,000 pounds a year in the early 17th century. One hundred years later, about 600,000 pounds a year passed through Veracruz. Production peaked in the second half of the 18th century in response to the expanding textile production of northern Europe.

Although Mexican silver had a direct, immediate impact on European economic life, New Spain's importance in the development of European attitudes toward Spain, which could be summed up by the Black Legend, the spread of new plants, and the introduction of dyes for textiles, had lasting effects on European society. Not surprisingly, the Europeans' sense of cultural superiority persisted

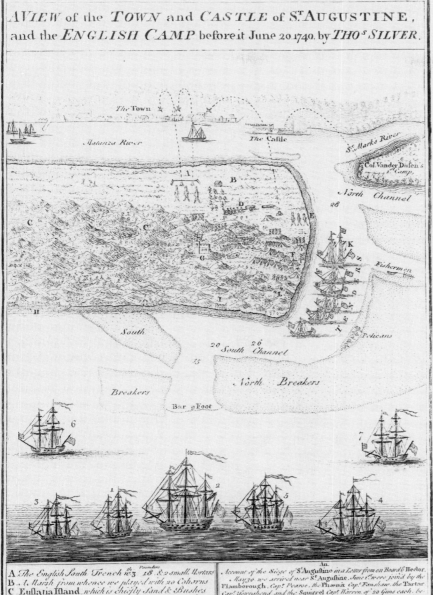

The English navy lay siege to the Spanish colonial town of St. Augustine, Florida, in June 1740. Though the effort failed, the battle is an example of the incessant European challenges to the far-flung Spanish empire. Following defeat in the Seven Years War, the Spanish king had to cede the colony of Florida to England in the Treaty of Paris to recover both Cuba and the Philippines.

society. Not surprisingly, the Europeans' sense of cultural superiority persisted despite New Spain's varied contributions to their daily life.

By the latter 17th century, Spain valued New Spain more than any other colony and, indeed, more than New Spain valued the mother country. No precise date marks this shift, which resulted from New Spain's increased importance because of its territorial, economic, and demographic expansion. Slowly and irregularly at first, the Crown tried to capitalize on this growth. By the 1760s, Spain's efforts left no doubt that it wanted to accelerate New Spain's growth while simultaneously tightening its grip on the colony's ever more valuable resources.

Spain's involvement in European conflicts beginning in 1793 led to increased fiscal pressure on it and a crisis in trade with the colony at a time when Mexico's demographic expansion and inflation were bringing a deterioration of living standards for a growing number of Mexicans. The divergent political and economic interests of Spain and New Spain took on a new and ominous dimension toward the turn of the century. The abdications of Charles IV and Ferdinand VII in 1808 and the consequent political crisis abruptly began a new period in Spanish history. By then, however, New Spain's greatest prosperity was already past and soon the colony would emerge as the independent state of Mexico.

Beginning in the late 17th century, colonial settlement in New Spain spread far into the sparsely populated northern region. There, threats from Indians as well as French and English explorers, traders, and settlers in the borderlands provoked greater defensive efforts involving both missionaries and military garrisons. The Jesuits erected missions as far north as present-day Arizona. New Mexico was resettled in the 1690s following the disastrous Pueblo revolt of 1680 that forced the Spaniards to abandon Santa Fe. French threats brought the creation of a buffer zone of missions and garrisons in Texas starting in the 1710s.

The establishment of Fort San Carlos on Pensacola Bay, Florida, in 1698, despite its French occupation for two and a half years, solidified Spain's presence on the northern Gulf Coast, although French traders remained active in Louisiana. Spain's acquisition of Louisiana from the French by the Peace of Paris of 1763 furthered Spanish interest in this sparsely populated region. Successful defenses of St. Augustine against the English during the wars of the Spanish Succession and Jenkins' Ear underscored the importance of Florida to New Spain's defensive perimeter, although the eastern part of the region fell under English rule from 1763 to 1783. Missions dating from 1697 in Baja California and missions, several garrisons, and towns in Alta California beginning in 1769 extended Spain's presence into what today forms part of the southwestern United States. In short, although its settlements were few and far between in the borderlands, New Spain's territorial spread was significantly greater in the 1790s than it had been a century earlier.

The economy of New Spain expanded substantially, beginning in the 1670s, although this growth was uneven and affected specific areas of production. Figures by John Jay TePaske reveal that registered bullion production emerged from a low plateau, averaging about 3.5 million pesos annually from the 1640s through the 1660s, and rose to an average of more than 5 million pesos a year during the next four decades. The production level of 1701–10 (48.3 million pesos) doubled (to 96.9 million pesos) by 1741–50 and more than doubled again (to 201.7 million pesos) between 1791 and 1800.

In contrast to this dramatic rise in bullion production, commercial textile production grew only modestly as a result of a preponderance of homespun production by a larger Indian population. Nevertheless, the quantity of imported cloth, both legal and illegal, increased substantially, especially as cheaper English cottons were smuggled into the colony late in the 18th century. This expanded cloth importation was but the largest part of an enhanced trade made possible both by greater bullion production and by heightened consumer demand for foreign manufactures.

Despite fluctuations of varying severity and duration, the overall volume and value of trade undoubtedly increased after 1660. However, both the extent of the increase and the exact timing of the trade cycles of expansion and contraction are disputable. Historians have estimated the total (as distinct from the officially registered) bullion production figures as well as the unknown magnitude of contraband trade conducted both within the fleet system and by traders carrying goods directly from foreign ports and entrepôts, notably shippers embarking from Jamaica after its capture by England in 1655, but lack precise figures.

Faced with intermittent wars and an expanded contraband trade, Spain struggled to stabilize its trading system with New Spain and, in the process, ultimately moved away from its reliance on fleets. Although the fleet system functioned more regularly for New Spain after 1650 than for Peru, an average of only five fleets a decade reached Mexico from 1650 to 1699. The War of the Spanish Succession dealt a further blow to the fleet system so that between 1701 and 1707 at least 50 French ships carrying European goods arrived at Veracruz. At the end of the war, the Treaty of Utrecht authorized the English to send one ship per year with the fleet and also to transport slaves to the Indies.

The contraband trade accompanying these legal activities provoked strong Spanish countermeasures in the Caribbean and the Gulf of Mexico that ultimately fed into the outbreak known as the War of Jenkins' Ear (1739–1748). To maintain shipping during this conflict, the Crown used individual, licensed ships instead of the large, militarily vulnerable fleets. Although seven fleets ultimately sailed to Veracruz between 1717 and 1738, individual ships accounted for 80 percent of the sailings from Spain to New Spain. As a final step to opening up the Americas' colonies to free trade (comercio libre), begun in 1765, the Crown in 1789 authorized direct sailings from nearly all the Spanish ports to all of New Spain's. The new policy was in effect only briefly, however, for Spain's involvement in war against Britain in 1796 and the latter's blockade of Cádiz the following year quickly led to the introduction of neutral trade.

Comercio libre further stimulated New Spain's already expanding legal trade. While silver remained the leading export, agricultural and manufactured products complemented the historic reliance on bullion. Cochineal shipments registered

Fitted for war with heavy broadside armament and a larger crew than merchant ships, the Spanish galleons escorted the fleets carrying cargo such as mercury and royal orders on the voyage to Veracruz and silver and official correspondence on the return voyage to Spain. Although smaller galleons were common, by the 1570s some galleons were as large as 750 tons, and most were close to 500 tons.

in Oaxaca fell below 900,000 pesos only once between 1758 and 1791 and exceeded 2 million pesos a dozen times, 3 million pesos three times, and once ran to even 4 million pesos. Although its value was scarcely one-eighth that of New World silver, in 1786 cochineal ranked fourth among the most important American exports to reach Cádiz, surpassing gold pesos. Yucatán unmistakably benefited from comercio libre, with exports through Campeche at least tripling as the new policy enabled traders to send goods other than the traditional cotton cloth to markets outside New Spain. Havana proved a particularly important market for Yucatán's henequen cordage and rigging; maritime provisions such as salted meat, maize, and beans; and hides and dyewood, which it then reexported. The total value of exported agricultural and manufactured products in the late 18th century was about 6 million pesos per year, just more than a quarter of the value of bullion.

The production of food for domestic consumption also expanded after the mid–17th century and, even when bullion production was at its apogee, exceeded the value of mining. Maize remained the most important crop, with New Spain's overall production exceeding its domestic needs in most years. There were significant regional variations, however, and in some areas, such as the Bajío, a fertile region that included the mining center of Guanajuato, agricultural expansion was unable to keep pace with rapid population growth. Bad years, moreover, were fatal. In 1785, an early freeze that severely crippled an already low maize supply was accompanied by an epidemic that resulted in an estimated 300,000 deaths.

Despite crop failures and epidemics, the population expanded by nearly 50 percent between the mid–17th and mid–18th centuries. After reaching a low point of about 750,000 individuals in the 1620s, the Indians—increasingly a social rather than a strictly ethnic category—numbered more than 2.3 million in 1793. By that same year the white population was approximately 685,000, the casta population 788,000, and the black population 6,000, giving New Spain 3.8 million inhabitants. This population growth experienced significant regional variations. The population of the Valley of Oaxaca increased 57 percent between 1740 and the 1790s, while that of the intendancy of Guanajuato increased 155 percent. Some Bajío parishes recorded a quintupling of population between 1700 and 1810. The Mayas of Yucatán expanded from fewer than 130,000 in 1774 to nearly 254,000 some 20 years later.

The Spanish Crown encouraged New Spain's territorial, economic, and demographic expansion. Above all, it implemented policies to limit colonial expenditures and secure the remission to Spain of the largest surpluses possible. Although in its quest for New World wealth the Crown changed its tax regulations on occasion and resorted to means of highly questionable utility, especially the sale of administrative and judicial appointments and positions, it did succeed in extracting a surplus from New Spain that surpassed that of Peru in the 1680s and grew impressively during the 18th century. The process and measures were often ad hoc, but by the 1760s the beginnings of a comprehensive program to improve defense, tighten administrative control, and increase revenues were in place. However, in the 1790s, fiscal expediency began to weaken the reform program.

The Crown's preference for having peninsular Spaniards rather than native sons on the Audiencia of Mexico's demonstrates a desire to control the increasingly wealthy colony. Through restricting sales of audiencia positions and removing a greater number of purchasers from office, the Crown clearly demonstrated that the northern viceroyalty was more important than Peru. From 1740 to the mid–1790s, it normally allowed only one native son on the Audiencia of Mexico; the court in Lima, in marked contrast, had 13 serving in 1750 and subsequently never fewer than 5 until the 1790s.

However, personnel appointments were only one way in which the Crown tried to tighten its hold on New Spain. Another measure was to assume direct administrative control over the collection of revenues. The Habsburg kings had traditionally relied upon tax "farmers" to oversee the collection of specific taxes in return for fixed sums paid according to a regular schedule. The sales tax (*alcabala*), collected in New Spain from 1575; the *cruzada*, or the sale of indulgences begun in New Spain in 1537; and playing cards, a royal monopoly for which the tax farmer in some years paid 100,000 pesos, were all farmed. The mint in Mexico City, which opened in 1536, was long operated under contract. By 1600, its chief officials, mostly merchants or their sons, had purchased their posts from the Crown at very high prices, in one 1629 case for 275,000 pesos.

The Habsburgs' reliance on tax farming more than on direct administration continued into the 18th century but then gradually diminished under Bourbon rule. In 1729, a new building for the mint opened in Mexico City, which was staffed after 1733 by salaried officials, of whom there were perhaps 400 by the end of the century. In 1753, the Crown began the direct administration of the alcabalas, a source of revenue that had yielded a little more than 700,000 pesos in 1746 but, aided by expanded commerce, grew to 2.4 million in 1799 and 3.2 million in 1803.

While Spain's New World revenues increased during the first half of the 18th century and the Crown took limited steps to improve administration and strengthen the royal coffers, the British capture of Havana in 1762 sparked a move from bureaucratic conversations and reform proposals to action. Although the 1763 Treaty of Paris returned Havana to Spanish rule, the port's temporary loss shocked Charles III's advisors, who rapidly developed and implemented plans to protect Cuba, Mexico, and ultimately most of the colonies. The agenda for Mexico included sending in regular troops, revitalizing and expanding the militia, ensuring frequent and regular postal service, increasing revenues through new sources, taxing economic growth so that the colony would pay for its now more formidable military defenses, and tightening administrative control. The Crown initiated military reform in Mexico in 1764. The following year it sent a visitor-general with instructions to improve financial administration in particular as part of a broader investigation of administrative practices.

During his inspection tour of 1765–71, future secretary of state for the Indies (1776–87) José de Gálvez demonstrated that the Crown was serious in its pursuit of reform and seeking increased revenue. Gálvez reorganized the customs houses, staffing them with salaried officials. He placed *pulque*, a popular alcoholic beverage made from the maguey plant, and the royal playing-card monopoly under direct royal supervision. In addition, he replaced the previously farmed-out gunpowder monopoly with a staff of salaried officials.

The most lucrative example of the Crown's taking an active role in economic production and distribution was in the tobacco monopoly, which it instituted specifically to provide revenue for Spain's defenses. Although authorization for this monopoly preceded his arrival in Mexico, it was Gálvez who established it as a fully functioning operation. In 1771, some 5,600 workers labored in the Mexico City tobacco factory, with more than 600 others at a plant in Orizaba. In the mid–1790s, more than 12,000 employees in the tobacco industry worked in six locations. Producers and consumers alike detested the new restrictions on production, the forced-purchase policy, the forced sale of tobacco to the monopoly, and the use of state dispensaries for retail sales. But the monopoly achieved its objective. The royal profits exceeded 800,000 pesos annually starting in 1768 and reached more than 3.5 million pesos in 1789.

Gálvez also turned his attention to the mining industry. Increased mercury production at Almadén, Spain, allowed him to halve the price of quicksilver between 1767 and 1776 and thereby expand silver production. He granted tax exemptions to miners who undertook major renovations in older facilities. After they had paid for the improvements, he granted them an additional exemption of 50 percent for the next 15 years. Exemptions from the sales tax on supplies and raw materials and a 25 percent reduction in the price of gunpowder used in blasting further benefited miners. The result was greatly increased silver production on the one hand and improved government revenues on the other. In 1796, the mint in Mexico City produced more than 24 million silver pesos and more than a million gold pesos, while government revenues related to mining production exceeded 5.5 million pesos.

From the Crown's perspective, the portion of the colonial revenue that was actually received in Spain was far more important than New Spain's total output. The Crown expected Mexico to pay its own expenses, subsidize defensive costs within the viceroyalty, and still transfer a surplus to Spain. In fact, government remissions rose substantially, buoyed by higher tax revenues based on commercial growth, increased Indian tribute reflecting population growth, profits from tobacco and other monopolies, and mining revenue. Between 1761 and 1800, Mexico's treasury sent in excess of 90 million pesos to Spain. As confirmation of New Spain's colonial predominance, Peru's treasury remitted none.

By the 1790s, the racial composition of Mexican society reflected the patterns of demographic and economic expansion it had seen over the previous century. The number of Indians, whites, and castas had increased significantly, that of blacks had declined to 6,000 from possibly 80,000 in the mid–17th century (although the number of mulattoes had more than tripled), and the peninsular Spaniards were perhaps only 60 percent as numerous as in 1646, numbering about 8,000. The growth of the native population to more than 2.3 million had important implications for agricultural production, pressure on farmland, the volume of trade (especially as organized by provincial officials), and tribute payments. An increase in the white population, and to a lesser extent the casta population, stimulated international trade.

Despite the persistent use of racial categories by census takers, priests, government officials, and ordinary residents of New Spain in the late 18th century, occupation, income, and cultural characteristics became more significant indicators of social position. Although there were some wealthy Indian nobles or chieftains and even prosperous castas, wealth, income, and Spanish ancestry correlated highly with status. Indeed, Mexico had the largest and wealthiest aristocracy in the Spanish colonies. Granted, Peru had more titled families, but the number of residents of Mexico who secured titles rose substantially after 1700, and New Spain had more millionaires than any other colony. Mexico City displayed the greatest range of wealth in New Spain.

At the pinnacle of Mexico City's society were about 100 "Great Families," each with accumulated wealth approaching or exceeding 1 million pesos. The remainder of New Spain had only about a dozen such families, including four or five in Guanajuato and two in Guadalajara, with similar resources. These families formed the true elite, and having an occasional Indian or black ancestor within the family tree did not alter their status. Generally, children of these Great Families married within their own ranks, including relatives as close as first cousins. Largely composed of criollos, these extended wealthy families linked themselves with the most successful peninsular Spaniards through marriage. In addition to the careful selection of marital partners, their survival strategy included widely diversified investments in commercial agriculture, overseas trade, mining, business, government offices, and other fields. Honorific trappings—titles of nobility, membership in military or civil orders, acceptance as agents (*familiares*) of the Inquisition, and honorary memberships on the city council—were common, although fewer than half the Great Families actually held noble titles. A luxurious lifestyle typically including residence in a mansion in the capital's center, and often a dozen or more servants enhanced the visibility of these families' wealth and status. However, Spanish ancestry was absolutely no guarantee of great wealth or high status. The success of a small number of peninsular immigrants should not obscure the modest fate of many and the complete obscurity of those who worked as household servants and unskilled laborers.

Nearly 99 percent of all who called themselves Spaniards—peninsular or criollo—were born in New World. Although they were dominant among the Great Families and in the professions, criollos were also well represented in mercantile and agriculture activities and could be found in every walk of life. In the regional center of Antequera, Oaxaca, for example, only 9 percent of the criollos could be considered part of the local elite, while 53 percent were low-status artisans and a small number joined castas as servants and peones. In the mining center of Guanajuato, more than 80 percent of the criollos were engaged in occupations that clearly distinguished them from the upper stratum of society. Criollo carpenters and tailors were at the top end of a workforce that included servants, cobblers, mine workers, and muleteers. Even in the humble position of cigarette roller, criollos—including many females—were predominant, holding 60 percent or more of the positions in the factories of Mexico City, Querétaro, and Orizaba.

Nonwhites rarely achieved elite status in the late 18th century, even at the regional level, and only four did so in Oaxaca, where almost 70 percent of the adult males classified as castas were employed as low-status artisans or muleteers. In Guanajuato, mestizos and mulattoes made up slightly more than two-thirds of the mine workers. The castas had also long displaced the Indian population in the textile manufactories (obrajes). Despite regulations limiting militia service to Spaniards, *castizos* (the offspring of Spanish and mestizos) and mestizos, virtually anyone was enlisted, although in some units whites were the only officers. The underclass of Mexico City, estimated at from 20,000 to 30,000 in the 1790s, included people from all major racial groups. The municipal authorities identified 37 percent of the persons arrested in 1796 as being Indian, 30 percent as mestizos or mulattoes, and 33 percent as whites.

In the late 18th century, many Indians still resided in native villages located primarily in central and southern Mexico. For this largely rural tributary population their identification in terms of occupation was less important than it was to the castas. Their economic life revolved around domestic production for individual or local needs through agriculture, pastoral activities, and specialized trade goods. Although a few native families enjoyed considerable wealth, most lived close to the subsistence level and, particularly in areas of rapidly expanding native population and inadequate village lands such as Guadalajara, found the late 18th century to be a time of heightened economic strain.

By the 1790s, black slavery had all but disappeared in Mexico. Unlike their cohorts in Lima, Caracas, and Havana, wealthy families in Mexico City at this time rarely purchased or retained slaves as signs of conspicuous consumption. Most of the colony's few thousand slaves were employed primarily as laborers in warm regions relatively near the coasts, as for example in sugar production near Veracruz.

In 1793, women outnumbered men in every major racial category in Mexico City. Excluding the ecclesiastical establishment, they constituted 57 percent of the total population. Not surprisingly, they also made up an important part of the workforce, just under one-third in 1753 and only marginally less than that in 1811. Most working women were from the lower class, with casta Indian women being far more likely to work than their Spanish counterparts.

The ratio of females to males was much closer in Antequera than in Mexico City, probably due to more limited migration. Among criollos, there were more females than males, but Indian males were more numerous than Indian females. Criollos and Indians continued to marry predominantly within their own groups, but mulattoes were increasingly joining white society. About 60 percent of the men had criolla, mestiza, or castiza wives. In León, Spaniards married Spaniards at a higher rate than in Antequera, whereas León's Indians engaged in more intermarriage. However, unlike in Antequera, mulattoes in León married more often within their own group. In the late 18th century in the Bajío, the basic racial categories had coalesced into two broad groups: Indians, mulattoes, and a few mestizos in one, Spaniards and the majority of mestizos in the other.

Not surprisingly, the population expansion during the second half of the 18th century was accompanied by downward social mobility. Increased racial intermarriage, a growing underclass most evident in Mexico City, the pain of inflation after 1775 for workers on fixed wages, increased pressure on the land, and escalating viceregal government debt all indicated that, despite rising silver production and trade, New Spain in the 1790s faced serious, growing problems, many resulting from increase in population.

For the German scientist and traveler Alexander von Humboldt, an astute observer of Mexico at the time, the problems were far from insoluble, however. To him Mexico's growing population, numerous natural resources, laudable absence of a large slave population, and educational and cultural institutions forecast a bright future for the colony. One major hindrance was the colonial relationship with Spain, which provided an inadequate administration, restricted trade, prevented foreign immigration, failed to promote a balanced economy, and drained New Spain of specie. The hope embodied in Humboldt's observations was not lost on Mexicans, who perceived in them the potential benefits of greater political autonomy. Although in the 1790s almost no one actively considered taking a course of total independence, the Bourbon reforms to strengthen defense, increase

revenues, and tighten administration—efforts coupled with a pro-peninsular personnel policy that rankled a number of ambitious criollos—laid the groundwork for colonial discontent. The Crown's subsequent involvement in European conflicts exacerbated the situation, sparking a series of events that would ultimately lead to the abdications of Charles IV and Ferdinand VII, French occupation of the Iberian Peninsula, political and fiscal crisis, and the loss of Spain's empire on the mainland of the Americas. In 1821, New Spain, the richest colony in an empire beyond compare, became the independent state of Mexico.

Mexico City's main plaza bustles with commerce. As a consequence of the Bourbon reforms, the city underwent important changes at the end of the eighteenth century. Since Mexico City was both the most important urban center of the viceroyalty and the seat of its highest authorities, a campaign was undertaken to change its appearance and transform it into a city worthy of being the capital of the most important colony of the Spanish crown.

5

Faith and Morals in Colonial Mexico

LINDA A. CURCIO-NAGY

Mesoamerican civilization prior to contact with Europeans was composed of stratified chiefdoms, city-states, and imperial governments, all linked by an overarching worldview, cultural traits, and a religious belief system. More specifically, religion ordered the cosmos, the movement of historical time, and the daily lives of ancient Native Americans. Their daily life revolved around an annual cycle of ceremonies that was of principal concern to the entire society. Native Americans believed that the relationship between human beings and the divine was a filial one. Deities, because they had sacrificed themselves to create humanity, were to be honored, appeased, propitiated, and pleased in order to maintain order or balance in the heavens and ward off cataclysm and natural disaster. All of this was understandably important to an agricultural society at the mercy of the vicissitudes of nature. Consequently, a majority of ceremonies to the gods dealt with agricultural and fertility issues.

The ruling elite, the priestly and aristocratic class, positioned itself as the intermediary between the general population and the supernatural. They acquired astronomical and mathematical expertise and monopolized the art of writing and record keeping. In short, they came to control the knowledge that was deemed sacred, that was instrumental to maintaining the precarious balance of cosmic forces.

In addition, the order of the cosmos was replicated at the societal level. Native societies were defined by strict behavioral codes that delineated their members' duties and responsibilities toward the gods, the elite, and commoners. And one's identity was linked to a lineage that was further attached to the gods, the elite, and sacred history.

Upon encountering the Mesoamerican peoples, the early European missionaries were astonished by the complexity of their political structures and the virtuous nature of their lifestyle, yet horrified by their idolatry and practice of human sacrifice. The regular clergy (members of religious orders), charged with evangelizing the natives for most of the 16th century, viewed these aboriginal peoples and their religion through the filter of European history and experience. This was particularly true of the Franciscans who headed up the Christianization of the natives in the population center of Mexico's central valley.

The Franciscans, especially the first generation of missionaries, were highly educated, endowed with a strong millenarian vision, and possessed of an apocalyptic view of history that posited a leading role for their own order. The vast majority of these early friars came from the provincial house of San Gabriel (Extremadura) founded by Father Juan de Guadalupe in 1496. He emphasized a "living Gospel" of extreme poverty in emulation of both Christ and Saint Francis of Assisi, the founder of the order. Both Saint Francis and Father Guadalupe had been influenced by the writings of Joachim de Fiore, who through dreams and a numerological approach to the Bible discovered three different states of mankind, leading to the second coming of Christ. The first state was the epoch of God the father at the time of the secular church, dating from Adam to Christ; this was followed by the era of God the son and the church of priests, from the birth of Christ to A.D. 1260; and the third age, that of the Holy Spirit, was the period of the rule of the monastic orders and the destruction of the earthly church.

The new Christ described by de Fiore would be a founder of a monastic order. Some Franciscans believed Saint Francis to be this messiah who, once the earthly church was destroyed, would reign for a thousand years. The millennium would be characterized by a world of perfect egalitarian charity inhabited by the poorest and most humble. Although many churchmen thought this interpretation extreme, it nevertheless helps explain the existence of the observant Franciscans and the reform movement under Spain's Cardinal Francisco Jiménez de Cisneros, who closed opulent monasteries and emphasized a life of poverty for regular clergy.

The "discovery" in 1492 of the last gentiles, the Native Americans, was seen as a clear sign of the fulfillment of the prophecy regarding the coming millennium. By evangelizing the natives, the first Franciscans believed that they were playing a decisive role in the creation of the millennial kingdom or the Christian paradise on earth. Reports of the devotion, humility, and obedience of the aboriginal peoples caused many friars to suppose initially that the natives were the prophesied Christians of the third age. This explains why the Franciscan missionaries chose the term "indoctrination" when discussing the Christianization of the natives rather than the term "evangelization." They believed that the natives were already prepared to live as Christians and merely needed to be introduced to or indoctrinated in the passion of Christ.

Therefore, the Franciscans sought to teach an evangelically pure Christianity to the natives and to create a Christian Indian state. Thus, they set for themselves the arduous, and impossible, task of eradicating native religion without eliminating native culture. This objective partially accounts for their insistence on teaching in native languages rather than in Spanish, in direct opposition to Crown directives. The friars also opposed the first attempts to institute and collect church tithes from the natives. Both these phenomena would have hispanicized the native populations and secured the rule of the earthly church that was destined to fall.

Even clergymen who did not share the apocalyptic vision of the early Franciscans were profoundly influenced by the writings of another scholar, Desiderius Erasmus of Rotterdam, whose humanist philosophical and satirical essays calling for church reform claimed that the institution had become too sumptuous, too worldly, too distanced from the original Christian church. This attitude led to a harsh view of ordinary Europeans, especially those who emigrated to the American colonies. Some clergy felt that the Catholicism of the average colonist was decadent and tainted, not suitable for the impending third era. These Spanish emigrants brought with them the beliefs and practices of Iberian popular Catholicism, namely the devotion to the saints and Mary, as well as to holy relics.

Apparitions and miracles punctuated the daily existence of contemporary Catholics, and formal religious practice was dedicated to public displays of worship such as processions and pilgrimages, especially to celebrated shrines. Attendance at mass and confession was small, and general religious education was severely lacking. Furthermore, folk Catholicism, particularly in rural areas, was spontaneous and independent of the official church. Mendicants such as the Franciscans were teaching orders, which formed part of a larger movement to educate the population and reassert church control over religious belief and activity. This movement would culminate, in the late 16th century, in the introduction of reforms called for at the Council of Trent in 1545 and Spanish Inquisition efforts to institute an orthodox church-controlled piety.

Disdain for the Spanish colonists on the part of some churchmen was not solely grounded in these religious and philosophical precepts but was coupled with charges of mistreatment of the natives under the encomienda system. Until 1542, the Crown granted encomienda, the right to collect tribute and extract labor service, to early colonists as a reward for their service during the Conquest in exchange for Christianizing the indigenous population. The encomenderos invited friars into their jurisdictions to evangelize, but even so, many clergymen sought to maintain a clear separation between their Indian charges and decadent Spaniards eager to exploit native labor. Some friars, among them the famous Dominican Bartolomé de las Casas, became vociferous opponents of encomienda, especially the personal labor service clause, which they equated (and rightly so) with native slavery. At the same time other clergy believed that the encomienda system, purged of its outstanding abuses, was a suitable one from which to convert the Native Americans. Furthermore, many priests exploited native labor just as much as the encomenderos did, forcing the construction of monasteries and churches and living off what the natives produced.

In the midst of heated debates regarding the practice of encomienda, central Mexico became home to a number of utopian experiments in evangelization and Christian living. The most famous were the Hospitales de Santa Fe, erected and

An official inspection, called a *visita general*, of local government in and around Mexico City resulted in 1565 following numerous complaints from Indian communities about unjust demands for labor, food, and building materials. The Codex Osuna, a fragment of which is shown here, formed part of the official record. It used the pre-Hispanic pictorial tradition, Nahuatl text with the Spanish alphabet, and Spanish commentary to depict the exploitation of the Indians.

supervised by ex-Audiencia (high court) judge turned Dominican priest and later bishop of Michoacán, Vasco de Quiroga. Quiroga based the *hospitales*, or chartered communities under episcopal authority, upon Sir Thomas More's ideal society depicted in his pivotal work *Utopia* (1516).

The traditional native societies and *Utopia* held basic tenets in common that mixed well with Christianity. In the hospitales, natives worked lands communally, produced goods for market, managed the daily operations of the community, and assessed its future needs. Priests living in the communities instructed children in the fundamentals of the faith and in basic reading and writing. In many respects, life in the hospitales approximated the vision of society so sought by the millenarian clergy.

Quiroga and many of his European contemporaries deemed the hospitales a success, and indeed the natives greatly admired Quiroga, calling him Tata, or father, a term still utilized today. However, even though the hospitales continued in operation after Quiroga's death (some lasting until the early 17th century), this evangelization model was never instituted on a great scale because it required large numbers of sedentary clergy and tremendous institutional support. It also removed natives from the labor pool for encomienda and the subsequent labor draft, *repartimiento*. Nonetheless, there is some suggestion that the later frontier mission system took inspiration from Quiroga's hospitales.

The first three Franciscans arrived in Mexico in 1523 and the following year 12 more, known as the 12 Apostles, arrived, walking barefoot for 200 miles from Veracruz to the capital. Other religious orders such as the Dominicans, who arrived in 1525, the Augustinians (1533), and the Jesuits (1571) also played major roles in the evangelization of the Indians. However, it should be noted that the regular clergy were always limited in number compared to the task at hand. By 1559, approximately 800 friars were working among a native population of 2.65 million. Only 6,000 ordained priests were available to minister to the natives and colonists a century later.

A number of factors, in addition to the small number of Catholic priests, conditioned and limited the evangelization or spiritual conquest of the natives. These considerations included the language barrier, cultural ignorance, disputes among the Spaniards such as the aforementioned rivalry between regular clergy and colonists, and even battles with the Crown and within the church itself, such as doctrinal disputes between the orders.

The initial task of the friars was to learn the native languages. As a consequence, they produced a substantial number of dictionaries and grammar manuals to further the missionary work in the field. The Christianized sons of the conquered nobility, who attended centers of learning founded by the missionaries, made this production possible. Two such schools in Mexico City included San José, under the direction of the Franciscan Pedro de Gante, and the famous Colegio de Santa Cruz de Tlatelolco, founded by Mexico's first viceroy and first bishop, Antonio de Mendoza and Bishop Juan de Zumárraga respectively. Young native scholars, fluent in Spanish, Latin, and their own Nahuatl, translated and wrote prayer and confessional manuals, sermons, histories, and other religious treatises that became indispensable to the Christianization program.

Successful conversion of the native population was predicated not merely upon learning the rudiments of native languages but upon understanding native society. This quest to learn about native cultures in order to eradicate a substantial portion of them led to the great pioneering works of such religious chroniclers as Diego Durán, Bernardino de Sahagún, Andrés de Olmos, Toribio de Benavente (Motolinía), and Diego de Landa. These men, although accomplished linguists in their own right, worked closely with native aids, informants, and translators. The Crown welcomed these investigations, because it too was interested in learning about pre-Columbian political, economic, and tribute practices.

While they were learning the local languages, the friars resorted to alternative teaching tools in an effort to educate and convert the natives to Christianity. They developed visual aids such as murals and religious paintings to depict the passion of Christ and the lives of the saints, and to explain religious allegories to native neophytes. This visual approach turned out to be unexpectedly problematic, because its success depended upon how the natives interpreted the images, which could be different from how they were intended to be by the friars.

For example, the missionaries almost immediately held up the cross and paintings of the Crucifixion to the Maya. To the Maya, however, the symbol of the cross evoked their sacred "first tree." This Tree of Life displayed the conjunction of the heavens, earth, and the underworld. At its axis lay the axis of the universe. In addition, it metaphorically showed the manner by which rulers became deified, and members of the heavens. It celebrated creation, sacrifice, and rebirth and, especially when a corn tree was depicted, made direct reference to the agricultural cycle. It also marked a sacred space at which spiritual beings would arrive to accept offerings. Thus, from the Maya perspective, Christ could be viewed as one ruler of many who had followed the divine path in the cycle of life, not necessarily as the one and only savior from sinfulness.

Public ritual had always been essential to both pre-Columbian religion and Spanish Catholicism. Consequently, priests quickly introduced their aboriginal parishioners to religious plays, music and festivals, especially at Easter and Corpus Christi, both of which celebrated the Holy Eucharist. Additionally, the regular clergy also hoped to inspire religious devotion through their own examples of living devout, humble lives informed by Christian zeal. This approach eventually appeared to make an impression on the native commoners, who had initially been perplexed by the European vow of poverty, because their own precontact priests had dressed luxuriously, befitting their noble status.

The early priests were itinerant, worked in pairs, and entered villages, towns, or urban neighborhoods with the express goal of converting the local leadership. Once the cacique (village chief) or *tlatoani* (ruler) was baptized, the rest of the community quickly followed. The amount of religious instruction provided before baptism was brief and made the baptism of 10,000 natives at one time possible, albeit questionable in that their understanding of Christian doctrine was superficial at best. Then, with the initial conversion completed, the missionaries proceeded to discredit and dislodge the traditional native high priesthood, forcing their activities underground. However, it was more difficult for the missionaries to eliminate the role played by lesser religious representatives such as midwives, healers, diviners, and weather conjurers, because these positions correlated with existing positions in Mediterranean Catholicism. As a result, many of these traditions continue well into the present day.

The friars ordered the destruction of any idols or statues in evidence, but the natives successfully hid some from European view. The priests attacked concubinage (cohabitation without marriage) and polygamy, practiced especially among the nobility. Because the number of clergy was limited and they were itinerant, the newly Christian native elite were responsible for the daily operations of the new native Christian church. The indigenous elite clearly mediated between the Spanish and native worlds, governing, collecting tribute, and providing laborers for work projects. In this respect they continued performing the same functions as they had during the pre-Conquest period.

The same can be said for the newly converted in their religious role in the community. Christianized leaders associated themselves with the new "temple" and operated as intermediaries between their people and the Christian faith. For example, the civil post of governor and the religious position of *fiscal* were usually held by the same individual—if not concurrently, then alternately. The fiscal was the church accountant who maintained the daily operations of the new temple, aided individuals with their wills, gave spiritual solace at the time of death, organized funeral services, and served as catechist, or instructor of religion.

The church choir was actually the parish council. Its members also held positions on the town council. The fiscal and the choir ensured that people attended mass and participated in the new rituals. More importantly, they informed the priests of events and incidents that had occurred in their absence. This partially explains why the friars initially believed that evangelization was such a resounding success. Even though a native Catholic priesthood was prohibited throughout the colonial period, clearly the Christian religion came through a native filter, namely the indigenous elite.

The missionaries taught Christianity in terms of what was already familiar to the indigenous people. In other words, the friars not only allowed but purposely encouraged the correlating of native deities, symbols, and rituals with their European counterparts. This methodological approach, known as guided syncretism (combining of beliefs and practices), made for some complicated, fascinating problems, especially when missionaries sought to align concepts of the native deities with those of the Christian god and Satan. At issue was the fact that the native gods were multifaceted and appeared in various manifestations, possessing both positive and negative attributes.

For example, priests generally selected Tezcatlipoca (accompanied by Quetzalcóatl) as the supreme being, because one of his manifestations was that of Lord Possessor of the Near, Possessor of the Surrounding, Possessor of Heaven and Earth. Although this was a suitable correlation, Tezcatlipoca had no particular moral authority, being considered neither good nor evil. In addition, Tezcatlipoca was also known as the trickster and ruler over chaos. The Franciscans sometimes used this manifestation to express satanic evil. Thus, the friars were continually forced to clarify which Tezcatlipoca they were referring to.

A more common correlation to the devil was the Nahua *tecolotl* or human owl, an apparitional spirit associated with sickness, death, the night, and the underworld. However, the tecolotl was a type of *nahualli*, or spirit, not a *teotl*, or high deity. In effect, representing the devil as tecolotl weakened the concept of evil in the eyes of natives. Thus evil was either chaos, which according to the natives was a positive concept, or was not on a par with other deities that were to be feared.

Continuing with this example from central Mexico, the Nahua did not perceive the universe as a struggle between good and evil (God and Lucifer) but rather as a balance between the forces of chaos and order. In the native world, aligning oneself with good to avoid evil was not the basic problem of human existence. What was at issue for them was the discovery and maintenance (through offerings and rituals) of the proper balance between the two in order to survive. Maintaining this balance was seen as a creative struggle in which chaos, rather than being inherently evil, was actually the source of life.

In addition, the friars placed tremendous emphasis on the passion of Christ and salvation, leaving neophytes with the notion that God was primarily concerned with the afterlife. Satan, on the other hand, constantly tempted humanity and was present in the mundane world of the flesh, the here and now. Some natives viewed Satan and God as one and the same, as a dual deity possessing both negative and positive qualities. Consequently, Satan, as well as God, was deserving of honor and offerings.

Further complicating the process of evangelization was the fact that friars utilized the native language to translate stories, prayers, sermons, and catechisms and therefore had to conceive of unique ways of explaining Christian concepts that were alien to their hearers. At hand was the task of selecting native terms to express Christian concepts that did exist in native culture. For example, although Nahua speakers had the concept of remorse or regret for a specific act, there was no specific term for the European concept of sin. Equally ambiguous was the term selected for the concept of *cualli* (good). Cualli was the passive form of the verb "to eat." Missionaries chose the term *cualli inyollo* to mean "good-hearted" or "pure of heart," but in actuality the phrase meant "hearts are good," possibly an odd reference to previous heart sacrifice. It was hoped that, through increased contact with regular clergy, this initial fusion of portions of the two belief systems would give way to a purely Christian interpretation.

Into this mix of deities and cosmological concepts came the concept of devotion to the saints. Some priests were hesitant to introduce this pivotal part of Catholicism, because they feared that the role of the saints would be misunderstood and the natives would see them as deities in their own right. In addition, the statues of the saints could be misconstrued as idols rather than symbols representing supernatural beings. Nonetheless, given the nature of Spanish folk Catholicism, it was impossible to exclude the devotion to the saints from indigenous Christianity. Many friars encouraged natives to honor the patron saints of their own home village in Spain.

Rather than blindly accepting the friars' choice, the indigenous leadership found a means to assimilate the decision through the revelatory dreams of native elders in much the same way they had selected patron deities during the pre-Columbian period. Elders also chose the patron saints and various Marian images for neighborhoods, kinship groups, and households. Quickly, the *santocalli*, or saint's house, replaced the *teocalli*, or pre-Hispanic gods' house, within the native household compound.

Linked to the proliferation of saintly devotions were the *cofradías* (confraternity or sodality), lay religious organizations dedicated to the devotion of a particular saint or Mary. Although these were traditionally exclusively male organizations, native confraternities appear to have included prominent women. The confraternity was quickly associated with the native elite, who became the officers of the sodality, dedicated to the community's patron, which was usually the most important and wealthiest organization in town.

Confraternities collected funds and provided for funeral services and the surviving families of a deceased member. Members maintained the upkeep and decoration of the chapel and the sacred image. Of particular importance to the community was the feast to the patron saint. Confraternity members, especially the officers, controlled, organized, and funded this seminal event. In this manner the native nobility continued the ancient tradition of feasting as a sign of wealth and prestige and as a gift to their vassals. This custom eventually evolved into the present-day cargo system in which select individuals sponsor a large portion of the patron saint's feast (in many cases to their own financial detriment).

In summation, the friars were forced to accept the creation of a flexible belief system defined by a native interpretation of rituals and doctrine. As time progressed, many missionaries came to realize that evangelization would be a lengthy process requiring constant supervision. Most frairs would not understand that although Christianity was exclusive, the native religions had a long tradition of being inclusive, incorporating new deities and accompanying rituals into their already existing pantheon.

Because of the natives' ability to assimilate external religious concepts, a parallel religious system developed in many native communities. They worshiped their old gods as well as the new Christian deity and the saints. Some friars were furious with this and felt betrayed when it became clear to them that the traditional native religions were continuing. These priests demanded immediate action against such ongoing idolatry and utilized their inquisitorial powers to punish natives found to be practicing their traditional religion clandestinely.

The Franciscans and early bishops were granted inquisitorial authority and exercised that power during the spiritual conquest, although not without royal censure for imposing the death penalty. The Crown and many clergy felt that the natives were too newly Christianized to be judged and punished so harshly. Consequently, there was substantial ambivalence about using inquisitorial powers as an instrument to dominate the natives and ensure orthodoxy. Nonetheless, in 1522 an Indian from Acohuacan, was formally accused of concubinage and became the first person in Mexico to be tried by an agent of the Holy Office. In 1527, Friar Martín de Valencia, believing that native culture was the work of the devil, ordered the execution of four Tlaxcalan leaders as idolators. In central Mexico, events reached a climax in 1539, when Juan de Zumárraga executed Don Carlos Ometochtzin, the native leader of the former city-state of Texcoco.

Under Zumárraga the Inquisition was primarily utilized against upstart Spaniards. From 1536 to 1543, the years of greatest activity, 152 *procesos,* or formal investigations, were conducted, but only 19 of these cases involved Native Americans. The natives who were tried by the Inquisition were treated harshly and tended to be members of the nobility. In this respect, it has been suggested that the native *autos-da-fé* (penitential trials) were show trials to demonstrate Spanish authority and seek revenge against native leaders who were supposed to serve as models to their vassals. The extreme and public nature of the penalties

Charged with ensuring the orthodoxy of the faith, the Holy Office of the Inquisition often undertook general campaigns to institute political and social conformity, depending on who made up the court at any given time. Consequently, the records of the Inquisition form a rich repository of social documents on the daily life in the colony. Here, for example, is a love letter obtained during an investigation of an instance of inappropriate behavior.

did indeed serve as a warning to other idolators, but it probably also caused potential dissidents to move underground. Many natives apparently believed that their leaders were burned to death simply to confiscate their wealth.

The most scandalous inquisitorial episode during the spiritual conquest was the torture and interrogation of large numbers of Mayas by Diego de Landa in the Yucatán Peninsula from 1561 to 1565. His actions against the baptized natives are considered the most extreme and ruthless interrogations and tortures of the colonial era. During or as a result of these interrogations, 158 natives died and 13 committed suicide. Many more were crippled for life. Landa was by and large condemned for his actions and was summoned to Spain to explain and defend his behavior, something that he did successfully. He returned to the Yucatán as bishop, but further interrogations ceased. Ironically, Landa had compiled one of the most complete chronicles of Mayan pre-Columbian society. He then presided over a bonfire in which hundreds of codices, native religious documents, were burned as diabolical religious tracts.

Although the Crown essentially promoted Landa, his actions were pivotal to the monarchy's decision to reform inquisitorial practices regarding the natives. In 1547, inquisitorial authority over the natives had been transferred to the Provisorato del Ordinario, the local office of bishops that dealt with all manner of religious matters. After the Landa interrogations, although the *provisorato* could prosecute and punish natives, it could not execute them or resort to torture to extract illicit information and confessions. The native religious cases housed in the provisoratos throughout the viceroyalty are believed to be relatively small in number, confined to the 16th and 17th centuries, and limited to peripheral areas rather than the central valley of Mexico. More important, when the Holy Office of the Inquisition finally did arrive in Mexico in 1571, it did not have jurisdiction over the natives. The Crown felt that it would be more effective if the natives saw Spaniards being punished for their religious errors. This was an insightful action, given that the aboriginal population greatly outnumbered the Europeans and the "idolatrous" culture was the predominant one.

Some indigenous groups did not incorporate European beliefs into their own but rather resoundly rejected Christianity and Spanish rule. For example, the Chichimec during the Mixton War of 1541–42, which broke out on Christmas Day of 1541, in New Galicia (at the time the northern frontier of the viceroyalty) countered conquest and evangelization with a violent response. Indigenous priests announced the return of Tlatol, their primary deity, who, along with their resurrected ancestors, would bring about a golden age and repudiate the Christian god. These priests directed rituals of penitence and purification in order to eliminate all vestiges of the foreign religion and advocated a direct recourse to violence, especially the killing of Christian missionaries, to bring about the prophesied age.

Regardless of the actions, beliefs, and tribulations of the Spanish clergy, one factor more than any other affected the success of the spiritual conquest: the demographic disaster. The decimation of the Native American population from 25,000,000 to 1,075,000 by the end of the 16th century in the Central Valley of Mexico had a profound effect on native culture and religion. The possibility of divine retribution by either the Christian god or native deities bolstered the necessity of constructing a parallel religious system with offerings and rituals for both Christian and pre-Columbian deities.

Such a population loss eventually eroded the natives' cosmology, because the history of a village was dependent upon what could be remembered and recorded by those who survived. Consequently, the natives incorporated more Christian concepts into their belief system. It is a remarkable testament to the indigenous peoples that they were able to retain so much of their cultural integrity, given the circumstances and the passage of 500 years. Present native communities incorporate many Christian concepts, rituals, and symbols, but the overarching worldview remains a native one in many rural villages.

In addition to the myriad of complex issues connected to the missionary program, the friars had other problems to contend with. For example, as the 16th century progressed, the regular clergy found themselves increasingly at odds with the state, because the Crown actively began to promote the secular clergy (i.e., parish priests) especially after the 1570s. The secular clergy were priests who served under their bishop. Regulars were missionaries under the authority of the superiors of their respective orders such as the Franciscans, Dominicans, Jesuits, Augustinians, and others. Secular clergy neither possessed an apocalyptic vision nor the religious zeal of the first generation of regular clergy. Once the colony was stabilized, the Crown essentially wished to implement and solidify European social and economic patterns there. This program included having a strong presence for the earthly church. Although the process would take years to complete, this increasing preference for the secular clergy altered the trajectory of the evangelization mission. This more lax religious approach facilitated the continuation of parallel religious traditions in native villages.

The case of the celebration of Todos Santos in rural Tlaxcala provides insight into this phenomenon. Todos Santos is essentially a festival of commemoration for the departed by their loved ones. In it the souls of the dead return home to receive homage and offerings of food and drink from their living relatives. Specific days are assigned to different souls based upon how they died, a vestige of pre-Columbian religion. Each is celebrated in turn, November first and second being reserved for adults who died a natural death and young children, respectively.

Furthermore, Todos Santos is also spatially divided, with different rituals and belief systems in operation at different locations. Elaborate home altars are erected and decorated not only with statues of patron saints but the favorite food, drink, and even cigarettes of the deceased. The private aspects of the festival are more closely linked to traditional native views regarding the continuation of kinship relations after death. The natives believe that dead relatives continue to protect them and to serve in essence as intermediaries between the spirit world and the living. The public aspects of the celebration—a night vigil in the cemetery, high mass in the church, and decoration of the grave site to honor the dead—all stem from medieval Mediterranean Catholic tradition. Although the Mexican celebration of Todos Santos is a solemn occasion, music and food are essential components of the night vigil, attesting to the native perception that death and life are intertwined and cyclical. Death is not the end but rather a new beginning that is still linked to life and this world.

The removal of Franciscans from the native *doctrinas* (parishes) of the region and their replacement with diocesan priests may explain the dual (private-public) nature of the ceremonies. The Franciscans, at least initially, tended to be more diligent in their scrutiny of native customs and interpretation of Catholic precepts and were more fervent instructors of religious dogma. Many secular clergy, although equally devoted to their parishoners, generally viewed the natives as Christians and consequently were less likely to scrutinize and criticize native practices, especially when those practices outwardly appeared to conform to early modern Spanish Catholic tradition, such as erecting a temporary home altar for private worship.

By the 1570s, not only the secular clergy but a whole new generation of regular clergy were manning the conversion program, and disillusionment clearly had set in regarding the possibility of creating a Christian utopia. The initial enthusiastic, naive reports of the immediate success of evangelization gave way to a more sophisticated understanding of the complex, slow nature of Christianizing the natives and promoting their acculturation. Other issues would also distract from the conversion process, namely conflicts with the Crown and the secular clergy and among the regular orders themselves as rivalry emerged between those born in Spain and those born in the New World.

Just as European religion influenced native culture and religion, so too did native traditions influence European religious forms and concepts, especially the

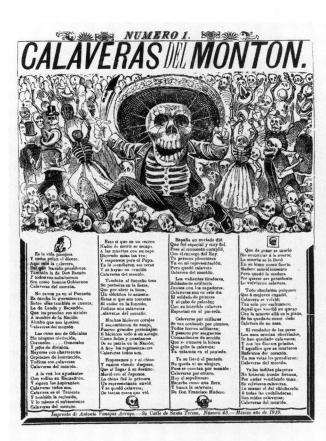

Todos Santos (The Day of the Dead) on November 1 allows for widespread popular celebration of the complementary nature of life and death. As with most Mexican fiestas, the occasion allowed for satire of society. In the last two decades of the 19th century, José Guadalupe Posada drew caricatures of these popular traditions. His skeletons, or *calaveras,* humorously represented social stereotypes. Like most of Posada's work, the broadsheet shown here includes comic doggerel about members of society.

popular religion of the average colonist. For example, it was generally believed that native medicinal and herbal knowledge was more effective in treating New World ailments than conventional European medicine, because it was indigenous to the New World setting. There are numerous examples of Spaniards, mestizos and Africans pressuring Indians to reveal "secret recipes" for curing any type of ailment as well as for procuring physical prowess, the ability to seduce many women, or the ability to change stones into gold bars. There are even cases in which Spaniards and Africans turned to native religion to seek aid or redress for an injustice. Of all the native traditions, the healing arts had the greatest impact on colonial society. Even the Inquisition recognized the validity of indigenous medicine during a time of few European doctors. However, with native healing also came a native worldview, indigenous rituals, and a nativizing of Christian concepts.

This process of cross-cultural assimilation also extended to Africans forceably brought to Mexico. African slaves resided in the Spanish parts of the New World, with the largest percentage living in urban areas. Others could be found on sugar plantations on the Gulf Coast, in textile factories, and in the mining and ranching industries. Africans, mostly from west and central Africa, and mulattoes made up a substantial portion of the population, perhaps as high as 20 percent, especially in Mexico City.

It was generally the obligation of the Spanish master to see to the religious education of Africans who had been baptized before their Atlantic passage. They would have received only minimal instruction in the Catholic faith, because the church did not organize a massive spiritual conquest of Africans as it did with Native Americans. African servants were encouraged to attend religious services, and African and mulatto confraternities hosted festivities for their patron saints and participated in large city festivals such as Corpus Christi. However, during the early 17th century such African groups located at the Church of Santo Domingo in Mexico City were prohibited, because the Crown suspected them of harboring anti-Spanish rebel conspiracies. Even when they were not suspected of subversion, the African religious associations were singled out, because their processions, which included African music and dance, were deemed too scandalous. They did patronize specific parish churches, as the mulattoes did at the Church of San Roque in Mexico City.

Although the slaves brought to Mexico spoke many different languages, hailed from diverse regions of western Africa, and were members of differing nations, they did share important religious concepts, which they brought to Mexico. Traditional African religion entailed a belief in a supreme force, divinities, and ancestors, as well as the practice of magic and healing, each with its attendant devotional practices and rituals. All together, they formed the interrelated fabric of one belief system, a system that allowed many to survive slavery. Africans believed that supernatural forces were omnipresent and consulted and manipulated them in order to ameliorate the slave's life. For example, Afro-Mexicans wore charms and amulets that served as talismans or assisted them in an effort to achieve some desired effect, such as softening the punishments of a cruel master. Africans and mulattoes also carried special earth, usually from cemeteries or human bones, that was probably connected to ancestor worship. Other items, such as ointments and potions rubbed on the body, were designed to calm anxieties and may have formed part of rituals of purification, combined with abstinence from certain foods, to bring about change. Slaves were also preoccupied with using various medicinal herbs to cure illnesses and especially to induce sleep. Slaves surely intended the latter for slave owners, because a sleeping master translated into a measure of freedom of movement for slaves. Other items such as cowrie beads were utilized to foretell future events and predict the behavior of friends, relatives, and, above all, slave owners.

Africans, like the Native Americans, extracted from their new environment the cultural ingredients that were of value to them or were similar to their familiar African traditions. Scholars have long assumed a high degree of cultural interaction between African slaves and the Native Americans. For example, in 1647, a native woman named Petrona hosted a prohibited private ritual to Saint Anthony in her employer's home and invited African and mulatto friends and *comadres* (women who served as godmothers to someone's children) who danced and ate sweets after the ceremony.

The combination of African and native traditions led to interesting religious forms. For instance, in early–18th–century Jalapa an African slave led a series of rituals, again centering around Saint Anthony, in which natives participated by performing traditional dances. The slave, considered the shaman of the group, entered into a trance, consulted with the spirits, and, upon recovering, transmitted the advice received from the supernatural world. Such an interweaving of religious practices eventually led to the creation of completely new belief systems. Although not as widespread in Mexico due to the decline in the slave trade to the colony and the increase in the native population, Afro-Mexican religion shared many of the traits of such religions as *candomblé* in Brazil or Santería in Cuba in which African divinities became linked to Catholic saints and the Trinity and some Indian concepts regarding nature.

As these examples demonstrate, popular religious rituals and beliefs were flexible, spontaneous, and open to other religious traditions present in the colony. These innovations, however, all appeared to take place under a cloak of European Catholic symbols and ritual forms, especially large-scale public worship linked to the widespread devotion of the saints. Every neighborhood, parish, confraternity, guild, institution, village, town, city, and ethnic group maintained its own devotion to a particular saint or manifestation of Mary or Christ. Feast days were celebrated with all the pomp and religious zeal the devout possessed. Such spectacles affirmed identity, were sources of personal and group pride, and could become reasons for great rivalry among different confraternities, as happened in 17th–century Mexico City. In addition to these annual feasts, large processions to specific saints punctuated colonial life, which was constantly threatened by epidemics, drought, famine, and other natural disasters. A prime example for the central valley was the native, Spanish, and *casta* (individuals of mixed racial ancestry) devotion to the Virgin of Remedies, concerning drought and illness, and Saint Gregory, the wonder worker, for floods. Eventually one form of Marian devotion came to dominate in Mexico, that of the Virgin of Guadalupe.

The Virgin of Guadalupe was said to have appeared on December 9, 1531, before a humble native named Juan Diego, asking him to instruct Bishop Juan de Zumárraga to construct a church on the very spot of the apparition on Tepeyac Hill, four miles north of downtown Mexico City. The bishop could not be convinced. Three days later, the Virgin again appeared before Juan and told him to pick some roses and place them in his cloak. Juan carried these flowers to Zumárraga with a second request regarding the construction of a church on the hill. Standing before the bishop, Juan Diego opened his cloak to reveal an image of the Virgin where the roses had been. This sacred image became the focus of veneration. A small church was constructed on the apparition site in 1533. Years later, in 1556, a larger, more ornate structure was built through the efforts of

Archbishop Alonso de Montúfar. By 1622, the shrine was relocated to the bottom of the hill. In 1695, new construction took place at the new location.

Devotion to Guadalupe increased through time until, by the late 17th and early 18th centuries criollo clergy and civil leaders began to see Guadalupe as a uniquely Mexican, as opposed to European, image. Native devotion to the image increased rapidly during the 18th century because of the active promotion of the cult by diocesan, Franciscan, and Jesuit priests. Until that time, natives generally emphasized their various local patron saints or Marian images, including the Virgin of Remedies, who later became associated with royalist forces opposing the Mexican independence movement (1810–1821). On December 12, 1756, the city celebrated a huge festival to Guadalupe in honor of her designation as patroness of the viceroyalty.

Veneration of the saints and Mary dominated private devotional practices. Wealthy criollos maintained private chapels with accompanying libraries filled with prayer books and biographies of the saints, which served to inspire religious contemplation. More modest households erected temporary altars for special occasions such as Todos Santos or private devotional ceremonies. Generally, most houses contained at least one or two statues usually set aside in a *retablo*, a small, brightly colored and decorated wooden cabinet with doors. Retablos were portable and could therefore be carried to mass for blessings or in processions.

Vows made to saints in an effort to secure their divine intercession regarding illness, injury, abandonment, or a spouse were quite common. In return for the desired miracle, the devout would embark on a pilgrimage to a local shrine, donate funds to charity, build a chapel to honor the saint, volunteer to sweep the church, or nurse the sick. In addition, those who had had family members miraculously healed commissioned local artists to paint the main details of the miracle. These paintings, or ex-votos, hung on the walls of chapels and were dedicated to the saints as a testament to their intercessionary powers and as a small measure of thanks to God.

By 1600, popular Catholicism in Mexico was a fascinating combination of African, native, and Spanish traditions. The average citizen believed in miracles and expected to witness divine intervention on a regular basis. Overall, the inhabitants sought to marshal or influence supernatural forces for personal, ethnic, and community gain, whether through the saints, talismans, potions, or rituals. The three overlapping cosmologies—European Catholic, African, and Native American—afforded individuals the opportunity to remedy life's stresses and illnesses. Admittedly, a goodly portion of popular piety relied upon the magical. The Catholic Church itself attested to the miraculous powers of the host, the saints, and Mary, but other popular beliefs smacked of unorthodoxy.

Astrology, the art of foretelling the future with beans, cards, tea, or any other materials and concocting potions and spells to tame a spouse, seek a lover, injure an enemy, or otherwise influence the behavior of another, were part and parcel of popular belief. The church actively sought to eliminate such beliefs, because this magic challenged the doctrine of freedom which stated that individuals have been

From the colonial period onward, the Virgin of Guadalupe has been the single most pervasive symbol of Mexico. As the patron of the colony of New Spain, she was called on in times of community and personal crisis. This 1743 engraving of Our Lady of Guadalupe shows her coming to the aid of the faithful in Mexico City during 1737.

given the right by God to choose between good and evil, thereby stating that nothing was preordained and knowable through magic. The church stated that belief in such magic, known as *hechicería*, was superstition and the work of charlatans intent upon preying upon ignorant, desperate people. Hechicería rarely included supplications to the devil, but many spells and rituals incorporated Catholic symbols and rituals, another attribute of popular magic that found disfavor with the church.

Given this religious and cultural milieu of cross-assimilation, it was only a matter of time before the arrival of the one institution in Spain designed specifically to ferret out unorthodoxy and heresy. On January 25, 1570, Philip II ordered the establishment of the Holy Office of the Inquisition in the Spanish dominions of the Americas. A year later, the first inquisitor, Pedro Moya de Contreras, arrived in Mexico City and set up headquarters on the Plaza de Santo Domingo, near the church of the same name, where the Inquisition would remain until 1819. The primary function of this Mexican tribunal was to preserve the supremacy of the Roman Catholic faith and dogma against individuals who held heretical views or were guilty of actions showing a lack of respect for religious principles. As a result, the Inquisition had the authority to prosecute all perpetrators of religious deviance.

In actuality the ability of the Inquisition to complete its designated tasks was influenced by several mitigating factors. First, Mexico was granted only one tribunal to monitor the religious thoughts and deeds of 1 million people, covering the entire viceroyalty of the Caribbean, Central America, what became the greater Southwest of the United States, Mexico proper, and the Philippines. For comparison, 15 tribunals had been created in Spain for a much smaller territory and population. In addition, the office in Mexico was understaffed for the task at hand. The tribunal consisted of five men: two inquisitors, an accountant, a notary, and an *alcalde*, or jailer. In addition, many of the 17th–century inquisitors were inexperienced, not particularly qualified, and often poorly paid employees, hence they were not always in the office to review testimonies and question individuals who came forward to denounce others.

The Inquisition did attempt to affect the far reaches of the colony by appointing *comisarios*, or representatives, usually parish priests, in Spanish towns. The comisarios were charged with reporting on possible heretical activity in their communities and could hold and interrogate individuals and seek instruction and counsel from headquarters in the capital. The comisarios engaged in a myriad of activities in their communities, only one of which was representing the Holy Office. They were not professionally trained as inquisitors and were not immune to local politics and economic issues. This ensured that the overwhelming majority of denunciations and cases came from Puebla, the second largest "Spanish" city in the colony, and Mexico City.

Most important, the Mexican Holy Office had no official jurisdiction over Native Americans, who constituted about 50 percent of the population during the 17th and 18th centuries. Questions concerning native conversion continued. Early in the 17th century, Catholic priests became acutely aware of the fact that natives were continuing to cling to their old religion. Clerics such as Hernando Ruiz de Alarcón and Jacinto de la Serna published a treatise in which they described, from firsthand experience, the idolatry that continued to plague their native parishes.

Although this first report led to calls for more study, along with increased Inquisition edicts and investigations, there was no widespread campaign launched against the Native Americans. More important, it did not lead to any change in Inquisition authority regarding the indigenous inhabitants. Although there were cases in which natives faced the Inquisitors, in general the accused Indians were referred to the provisorato under episcopal jurisdiction. Although the natives were virtually exempt from the Inquisition, Africans were not, nor were people of mixed ancestry. The reason Africans were not excused from the tribunal's jurisdiction is that the Spaniards believed that the Africans, residing as they had in close proximity to Europeans, should have learned proper orthodox Catholicism.

In addition to these considerations, the inquisitors were frustrated by the fact that heresy, ostensibly the crime the Inquisition was created to eradicate, represented only 15 percent of all the cases brought. Although heresy charges almost

always involved Spaniards, others accused and punished for the offense included
foreigners to the viceroyalty: Protestant pirates, and Dutch, German, and Italian
visitors. The great majority of the heresy cases can be dated almost exactly to
two specific periods in Mexican colonial history: the end of the 16th century and
the years 1640–50. During these eras, the Inquisition prosecuted some 500 cases
in total.

Generally, the Inquisition went after heretics when they came to constitute a
significant group or when an individual's deportment caused a great scandal. Furthermore, studies of the great crypto-Jewish prosecutions show that heretical
inquiries by the Holy Office were clearly linked to local and international political issues. For example, the late–16th–century persecutions were connected to an
overall campaign under Philip II against Moriscos (converts to Catholicism from
Islam), Turks, Englishmen, crypto-Jews, and the Dutch (the Netherlands was
then at war with Spain to gain its independence). The large, dramatic trials of the
17th century were led by a new inquisitor, Juan Sáenz de Mañozca, who had aided
the attack on the Jews in Peru. Many of the accused were prominent members of
society who had the backing of the Count-Duke Olivares. When he fell from
power in 1640, they came under attack by the Inquisition.

By and large, colonial Mexican Jews were *conversos*, forced to convert or flee
Spain, who then settled in Portugal. Later, after 1580, they took advantage of the
union of the two crowns to emigrate to the Americas. Colonial Jews were isolated
from the European Jewish community, making their position more precarious
than that of their brethren in Spain. In Mexico, Jews had to associate with the
dominant class, because they were Europeans and had to live in major Spanish
towns in order to succeed economically (many were prominent businessmen).
However, their black and Indian servants would use the Inquisition to avenge
themselves against Spaniards, especially heretical ones. The greatest threat to
Jews' survival was living in densely populated areas such as the central valley,
which was in close proximity to the Holy Office.

All these factors led to much more pressure for Jews to act as Christians in
public while practicing Judaism at home. Many assimilated and even become
priests; others converted to end the fear of persecution. Marriage, however, was a
complicated matter. Given their social position as prominent Spaniards, they
were pressured to marry outside the Jewish community, although most did not.
Males most consistently had to live a double life. Women, on the other hand,
became the repositories of Jewish culture but could not read or speak Hebrew or
engage in rabbinical studies. Thus, Judaism in colonial Mexico was lacking many
of the nuances of Jewish theology and tended to emphasize customs, rites, fasts,
ritual baths, and funeral rituals.

With few heretics—and even fewer natives—to investigate, the inquisitors
spent their days filing, processing, and reviewing thousands of denunciations
about issues of moral behavior and popular piety. (It is true that some denunciations were politically and economically motivated in an attempt to strike at perceived enemies, a fact that inquisitors were aware of and sought to thwart by

establishing severe punishments for those who gave false testimony against another.) Between 1571 and 1700 there were 12,000 denunciations, but only 2,000 actual procesos led to judgment and punishment. Of this average of 15 procesos per year, 15 percent were never completed and amounted to an acquittal. Others were simply left hanging as a result of poor record keeping.

The inquisitors seem to have been truly overwhelmed by the task of policing orthodoxy in popular Catholicism. However, the basic outline of the Inquisition's denunciations, trials, and edicts over its first 130 years gives us a unique view of the basic program and issues of faith in the colony. For example, clearly one-third of the cases dealt with minor religious infractions, primarily blasphemy. Illicit sexual activity accounted for the second largest group of cases (almost 20 percent) and included charges of bigamy and solicitation in the confessional. Hechicería made up 18 percent of the procesos, but idolatry represented only a small fraction of the cases, understandably, because the natives were not under the institution's jurisdiction. These cases represent those Africans, mestizos, and Spaniards who turned to the pre-Columbian indigenous tradition to improve their status or procure wealth.

Thus, the tribunal sought to educate a heterogeneous population about the evils of blasphemy, magic, and sexual liberty, a task it attempted to complete in a number of ways. For example, the inquisitors regularly issued edicts in which they proscribed, at length and sometimes in great detail, beliefs and actions that were considered heretical or unorthodox. These edicts were read from the pulpit and over time did inform individuals as to what the church considered unacceptable.

It is unclear whether these edicts actually curtailed popular religious activities. In the case of the Jewish community, many became educated in the rituals and customs of their faith from the edicts, thereby undermining the goals of the tribunal. However, the Holy Office had another teaching tool at its disposal that was particularly appropriate for a society so accustomed to spectacle and performance: the great *auto-da-fé*.

These spectacular ceremonies showcased for all the community to see the tried and convicted prisoners, who were intended to serve as examples of what would befall transgressors. The inquisitors announced such an event weeks in advance and ordered preparations to begin immediately. In the case of Mexico, all the large *autos-da-fé* of the Inquisition took place in the main square, or *zócalo*, of the capital. (Smaller events occurred in the Plaza de Santo Domingo, near the institution's headquarters, or in the privacy of the Inquisition offices.) In the square workmen constructed a special stage and bleachers to provide seating for distinguished clergymen, civil servants, the inquisitors, and the guilty prisoners. Generally, the Holy Office waited for a sufficient number of penitents, guilty of particularly egregious crimes, before calling a great *auto*, because they wanted to maximize the impact of the ceremony.

The Inquisition employees overseeing the decoration of the platform paid special attention to the placement of the viceroy's chair, located at the back, center of

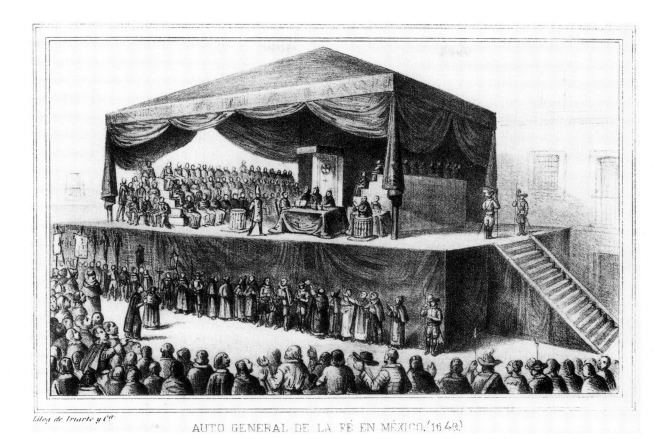

AUTO GENERAL DE LA FÉ EN MÉXICO. (1649.)

Liteg de Iriarte y Cª

the stage. Although the king and governors in Spain rarely attended an *auto-da-fé*, it was the duty of the colonial viceroys to do so, because the placement and role of the governor was quite important to the overall symbolism of the spectacle. The *autos* were designed to represent the final Judgment Day in which Christ would judge all and select those who were to reign with him in Paradise. Those on his right would enter the kingdom, those on his left be condemned for all eternity to the fires of hell. In New Spain, however, the inquisitors judged and selected the punishments for all the prisoners, depending upon whether they had reconciled with the church or not. The guilty sat either to the viceroy's left or his right, making the royal governor, rather than the inquisitors, the symbolic representation of Christ on earth.

Once the viceroy and all the other dignitaries were present, the proceedings began with a sermon in which the evils of heresy and unorthodoxy were emphasized. The prisoners were then called in turn to rise and face the spectators as their names, crimes, state of reconciliation, and punishments were listed. The accused wore the *coroza*, or conical hat decorated with flames and demons, along with a sackcloth garment called a *sambenito*. Different colors of sambenitos indicated different crimes, yellow cloth with red crosses indicating the penitent while black

The Inquisition court held periodic public punishments of those it found guilty of endangering the faith. At these public spectacles (called *autos-da-fé*) the convicted wore colored caps that indicated the general nature of their crime and plaques on their chests that stated their transgressions. Both civil and religious leaders attended the *auto-da-fé* along with crowds of spectators. The punishments ranged from the public humiliation of wearing the special garments to whippings to burning at the stake.

cloth with painted flames marking the impenitent. The vast majority of the accused had reconciled with the church in a triumph for the inquisitors and the mother church, because the goal of the Inquisition was to protect the faith and correct those in error, thereby saving their souls.

But what of the prisoners who refused to recant? Their souls were damned for all eternity, something the inquisitors actively sought to prevent. During the trial, prisoners were always encouraged to recant, confess their guilt, and plead for forgiveness and reincorporation into the orthodox fold. Such confessions mediated the severity of the punishments, which would be much harsher if the individual waited to recant until the last possible moment during an *auto-da-fé*. During the great penitential spectacles, the crowd actively encouraged individuals to recant before it was too late. Those facing the death penalty, who recanted before their sentence was read, received a stay of execution. Priests continued to plead with and cajole those who remained intractable, even as they marched to their doom, the pyre in Alameda Park. Those who had a change of conviction en route or even when tied to the post were garroted so as not to be burned alive.

Unyielding individuals received the full ire of the spectators, who yelled at the victims and demanded that the civil authorities burn them. The great *autos* were popular pastimes much like hangings, and it was felt that those burned at the stake were evil and got their just deserts. Immediately after the autos, the lesser punishments were doled out, to the jeers, taunts, and stares of the city's inhabitants.

The Holy Office meted out penalties and punishments according to the offense or the nature of the infraction, the sex and age of the offender, and his or her comportment before the judges, such as an immediate confession and heart-felt repentance. Approximately 18 percent of penitents reconciled with the Catholic faith, claimed to be truly remorseful, and swore never to commit the transgression again. Penances given under reconciliation included saying specific prayers, attending mass while wearing identifying clothing and holding a candle, or participating in a procession. All the penances were public ones, designed to humiliate the offender and further educate or warn others. In some respect these punishments constituted a social contract, because when they were completed they allowed the offenders to reenter the community of believers. Public whipping was also a common punishment for bigamists, *hechiceros* (individuals who engaged in magical practices), blasphemers, and renouncers of God. The number of lashes varied according to one's crime, sex, and age but began with 50 and could go as high as 400, although the average was 200 lashes.

These lesser punishments could be combined with reclusion, or obligatory service such as working in a hospital or convent, on a state or city project, or on galleys. Reclusion, the alternative to *cárcel perpétua* (life imprisonment), was limited in Mexico to a specific number of years (usually two), because the tribunal in New Spain had neither the infrastructure nor the funds to maintain such a penal system. Consequently, reclusion generally applied to priests who were sentenced to forced conventual life and was designed to keep them from committing further crimes or public scandals.

The galleys, ships propelled by sails and oars, were the punishment for repentant heretics, bigamists, and laypeople who passed themselves off as priests. Sending convicts to serve in the galleys, usually as oarsmen, was costly to the state, because individuals had to be sent either to Spain or the Philippines.

Relajación (relaxing or mitigating a penalty) was for those who were "relaxed" or remanded to the secular arm for the death penalty. Those who underwent this penalty were actually small in number. For example, of the 2,000 procesos between 1571 and 1700, 37 were condemned in person, 107 in effigy. The majority of heretics escaped burning at the stake and received lesser punishments such as exile, which could last between six months and ten years.

Exile was extremely difficult to enforce and supervise, given the nature of colonial society and the Inquisition's lack of resources. Under exile the guilty were escorted to points of embarkation with the expectation that they would leave the colony or city. Of 74 Jews sentenced to exile in Spain during the 17th century, only two actually arrived in Seville, the others having traveled to different parts of the viceroyalty to start their lives anew, and some even returned to the capital. The guilty also had to pay fines, although these were usually in conformity with the economic abilities of the prisoners. Total confiscation of goods was standard procedure until an individual was found innocent, but the severity of this punishment was mitigated by the need to provide for the prisoners' families.

The tribunal's mission was certainly clear to the Inquisitors, who articulated it with sterling clarity, at least in public propaganda, rituals of the *auto-da-fé*, and on the feast day of their patron saint, Peter Martyr. According to official dogma, the inquisitors were empowered by Christ himself and followed in the footsteps of the apostles and the martyrs of the church. Their inquisitorial duties were a heavy burden, a cross to bear, which emphasized their own place as potential martyrs. Additionally, they were charged, as avenging angels, with the responsibility and ability to judge, accuse, and condemn to death. Yet they also recognized that benevolence was a valid way to influence heretics or the misguided and bring them back to the arms of the church.

The popular view of the mission of the Inquisition is more complicated to pinpoint. Average citizens generally accepted and even welcomed the Holy Office's presence in society. They certainly did not hesitate to denounce their fellows. A popular consensus did surround the death of recalcitrant heretics, but it is unclear how the local people felt about the punishments meted out to their neighbors, many of whom were found guilty of holding widespread beliefs or condoning practices such as hechicería and blasphemy. Certainly the citizens of Mexico City must have been aware of the large number of denunciations that were never acted upon in any way, and realized that only the most public, egregious acts brought down the wrath of the Holy Office.

Furthermore, popular satires in the form of broadsides and tavern performances lampooned the inquisitors just as they did other clerics and government officials. People often enough denounced themselves as a measure of safety, before someone else could do so, but others did so out of a clear case of crisis of conscience in which they felt that only the inquisitors could alleviate their fears regarding their immortal soul. And, finally, it is important to remember that the effectiveness of the Holy Office diminished once one left the central valley. We may never know how many individuals emigrated to the farthest reaches of the colony to escape the watchful eyes and ears of the tribunal.

A closer scrutiny of Inquisition cases gives modern scholars a fascinating window through which to view certain aspects of religion in colonial Mexico. As mentioned, the vast majority of cases—72 percent—demonstrate that the tribunal spent almost all its time attempting to change popular beliefs. For example, the charge of blasphemy included such common practices as cursing, taking the name of God or the Virgin Mary in vain, insulting the prerogatives of the Inquisition itself, renouncing God, or committing scandalous deeds such as throwing or stomping upon a crucifix, almost all done under duress or in anger.

Trials regarding sexual notions constituted another major category. These revolved around actions or sayings connected to virginity, fornication, or chastity, including the erroneous but popular notions that sex before marriage and sex with a prostitute were not sins. Also under this last heading are found the cases in which wealthy families sought to marry their prepubescent daughters to older men in an effort to secure familial political and economic alliances. If it was informed of the impending marriage, the Holy Office would aid the young girl and intervene to protect her. The hechicería cases tended to concentrate on individuals, mostly women, who sought to know the future or procure romantic attachments.

One of the most blatant forms of heresy in the minds of the inquisitors was found in this sexual category: solicitation in the confessional. On occasion, priests pressed for, engaged in, or forced sexual relations upon their female parishioners immediately before, after, or during the confession of sins. In order for the Inquisition to investigate such a charge, the allegation had to be connected to the sacrament of confession. Other romantic liaisons or sexual abuses committed by clergymen were the responsibility of local bishops and provincials. The heresy therefore was strictly connected to violating the sanctity and trust necessary for the contemplation and forgiveness of sins. Priests held a special position in society, and it was thought that in the confessional this place should not be abused. After all, they were viewed as mediators between the divine and the devout sinner, and people believed that priests had supernatural powers, especially the ordained ability to administer grace, the accumulation of which limited one's time in purgatory and facilitated one's entrance into heaven.

Of primary concern to most individuals was confessing regularly, in the fear that unexpected or accidental death would befall them, because dying before being absolved jeopardized the immortal soul. Thus, priests could provide spiritual peace and forgiveness. In addition, they held a superior if not dominant position socially in that they were older, presumably wiser, better educated, and Spanish, consequently belonging to the highest social category. Priests were seen as paternal figures who were in many respects the only men that many women encountered who listened intently to what they had to say about all manner of things, including spiritual and theological issues.

Women were encouraged in confession to give their opinions, express their fears, and, ideally, to receive counsel and consolation from their confessor. Confessional discussions were designed to investigate the most intimate thoughts, feelings, and dreams of parishioners. This path led inevitably to sexual matters, because the sins of the flesh were considered the most pervasive in society. Thus, it was possible for these divinely sanctioned confidential discussions to turn into something much more profane. The church tried to regulate confession so as to limit the possibilities for its abuse, which is why it created confessional boxes with walls and screens to guard against impropriety.

It is difficult to determine exactly how New Spain's women responded to such advances or insults to their honor and faith. Recent Spanish studies demonstrate that half the women solicited were so appalled and shocked by what occurred that their faith was momentarily or even permanently shaken. Others furiously, and sometimes violently, condemned the priests. Yet a significant percentage of the women, many of whom were victims of spousal abuse or neglect, apparently truly cared for their confessors and had to be threatened repeatedly to give testimony against them once the Inquisition found out and decided to investigate the case.

Also among the sexual cases came individuals faced with the charge of bigamy, representing a relatively small number of cases but shedding new light on certain aspects of family life and morality. Most bigamists were male Spaniards, but women and castas were also substantially represented, according to contemporary documents. These trials depict a rather mobile society in which individuals emigrated or immigrated in search of economic opportunity, leaving behind a spouse and family, only to marry again before the church. Some men left on military campaigns, exploratory expeditions, or colonization efforts. Others became itinerant merchants or simply relocated to take advantage of silver boomtowns. For a number of reasons, many did not return to their spouses. A majority of the guilty claimed to believe that their first spouse was deceased, although they did little to ascertain the veracity of this information. Others claimed that unusual circumstances in their first marriage, such as being forced to marry against their will, effectively invalidated it and they therefore felt free to marry again.

In many cases, the friendliness so characteristic of colonial Mexican society was responsible for revealing the duplicity of bigamists. Strangers were likely to travel together and chat to pass the time. Conversations usually began with questions about one's birthplace, relatives, and contacts. In the course of these otherwise innocent parlays, a bigamist's secret might well come to light. The general population took a dim view of such dual marriages, and concerned citizens were quick to report possible cases of bigamy or polygamy to Inquisition representatives.

All this is particularly interesting in light of the fact that officially recorded marriages accounted for only about half of all such unions. Common-law marriage, the frequent choice of the popular class, was due to a number of factors. Until the Council of Trent reforms of 1545–63, in which the church emphasized the officiating authority of priests in marriage, many unions were arranged among families, neighbors, and the general community. Historically, public vows were regarded as binding, legitimate, and recognized by all. It was the elite or those with some property who sought the presence of priests and arranged for a church ceremony. Individuals who acquired property while living in a common-law marriage could and did later legitimize their unions before the church in order to clearly establish their children as legitimate heirs to that property. In the case of Mexico, formal marriages before a priest and in church increased through the colonial period, a testament to the slow but inevitable success of the earlier reforms. Clearly, the populace recognized and held officially sanctified marriage as an ideal the value of which was jeopardized when more than one spouse existed.

Family and marriage were overriding concerns to most individuals, but one of the defining characteristics of New Spain's Catholicism was the presence of female religious practitioners. Hundreds of convents were founded in colonial Mexico, especially during the 17th century. However, designation as a daughter of Christ was limited to Spanish women, whether *criolla* or from the Iberian Peninsula, until the establishment of a convent for elite native women in 1723. Young women were attracted to the cloistered life by a number of factors: devotion to God; a desire for a quiet, contemplative life removed from pressures to marry; and the wish to acquire an education or continue one's studies.

Although some women were placed in convents by family members because of a loss of honor, in general most nuns actively sought to enter them voluntarily. Some fought for years against recalcitrant fathers and brothers in order to do so because, although it was an honor to have a sister or a daughter as a bride of Christ, the socioeconomic welfare of the family might be better served by an auspicious marriage.

All convents required a dowry upon entry, which was used to maintain the institution and its religious mission as well as the welfare of the nuns. The most elite establishments required substantial sums that they invested in real estate, especially apartment complexes in urban areas. Convents were generally under the supervision of a particular religious order or bishop, but they did retain considerable financial independence. Although all convents required chastity, obedience, and ostensibly a withdrawal from the mundane world, wealthy institutions bent the rules a bit. In some, women dressed as they pleased, forgoing any requirement to don a habit. They maintained a retinue of servants, developed libraries, and resided in a suite of rooms complete with a small kitchen rather than in bare tiny cells. Some of these convents regularly entertained prominent male ecclesiastics with singing recitals and musical and dramatic performances.

The more financially modest convents had neither the economic resources nor the political clout to live in such a luxurious manner. But they did become famous for charity to the poor and for specific enterprises such as baking pastries and other sweets. Especially during large-scale celebrations such as the inaugural entrance of a new viceroy or bishop, these convents made sizable profits. Nuns also took in foundling girls, ran schools, and worked in hospitals as a means of supporting themselves and as charitable work.

Particular priests were chosen as confessors and spiritual guides and consequently developed close relationships with their religious sisters. Some even crossed the line and entered into sexual relationships. Generally, however, the relationship between confessor and nun was a chaste one, which led sometimes to the publication of a number of fascinating literary works collectively known as spiritual biographies.

The mystical tradition—a purposeful, sought-after ecstatic communion with God—was accepted and encouraged by the church and to a certain extent came to define female conventual spirituality. Women fasted, wore rough clothing, engaged in self-mortification, and prayed for hours at a time. They experienced rapturous visions of Christ or the Virgin Mary, who consoled, challenged, and counseled the nuns, fortifying further their desire to fast, pray, and engage in self-mortification. Male clergy had the unique opportunity to share in these experiences through the confessional. Having a divinely chosen sister confess to one added to the prestige of priests, and some even sought out mystical nuns to take confession from them.

The visionaries were ordered to describe their visions and their lives. This became the basis for the literary genre of the spiritual autobiography, an almost exclusively female writing form. (Nuns also created devotional poetry, prose, and theatrical performances for feast days.) Although these autobiographies were written under the watchful eye of male advisors, the nuns did have the opportunity for self-development and even had a certain degree of autonomy, because in the final analysis they controlled the telling or describing of their mystical experiences and were esteemed for their relationship with God. The final published product was fashioned by a male author who used passages from the nun's account, usually the descriptions of her supernatural experiences. The male author uniformly edited out any difficulties the nun reported encountering in the convent or with particular confessors.

These spiritual biographies in turn became a regular feature of colonial households, at least at the criollo level, as evidenced by the fact that the nuns themselves mention reading such material before entering a convent. Spiritual biographies tended to follow hagiographic guidelines and served as cultural models of piety for other women. Thus, this divinely ordained spirituality became well known outside the convent, influencing popular notions of female piety. The church also published instructions regarding devotional methods or specific prayers received during the divine revelations.

The acceptance of the mystical path as a form of female spirituality can be seen in the long history and sizable proliferation of *beatas*, or holy women, in New Spain's Catholicism. Beatas first appeared there as early as the 1520s, when they were charged with educating young native girls. Ostensibly they sought to duplicate the intense spiritual engagement of the mystical nun, but in fact they retained a tremendous measure of autonomy, because their vows were self-defined. This meant that many beatas did not do penance, engage in fasting, or perform charitable works such as those that nuns undertook. Many were poor and lacked the means to amass a convent dowry but nevertheless lived in houses with other beatas and sought in this manner to duplicate the essence of conventual life.

Financial considerations forced many beatas to work outside the home to support themselves unless they had a patron, a practice that was especially common among those with an ecclesiastical following. Like their officially cloistered sisters, they, too, experienced spells and shaking trances and were said to communicate directly with the supernatural. Yet, unlike nuns, beatas actively engaged with the outside world as healers or seers, either charging or expecting (and receiving) donations of food or money. In effect, many acted as spiritual counselors for their communities and were revered as such. Their neighbors believed that they possessed special gifts from God and that their very presence in the community brought divine favor to it. Because of these more worldly activities and the fact that they were not closely supervised by male clergy, many beatas found themselves targeted by the Inquisition. They were more likely than nuns to be accused of faking revelations and visions to foment superstition and line their own pockets.

As a matter of fact, the first case of the transgression known as *alumbradismo* or (or illumnism, the belief in or proclamation of a special personal enlightenment from God) in New Spain occurred in 1598, revolving around a *beata* named Marina de San Miguel. Alumbradismo was associated during the early 16th century in Spain with a particular sect in Toledo. A small number of its adherents emigrated to Mexico from Córdoba and Seville, thereby transferring this religious movement to the New World. For the Inquisition, alumbradismo always combined sexual license with heretical teachings.

At the center of the movement was a holy hermit, Gregorio López, who lived outside the viceregal capital. He and his followers did not believe in the physical trappings and rituals of Catholicism but rather emphasized personal communion and interior spirituality. They held an apocalyptic view of the world and felt that they were the chosen perfect to inhabit the New Jerusalem. Marina, revered as a saintly woman in her barrio, was the visionary of the group. She granted indulgences and canceled the religious vows of the priests. In doing so she effectively denied the validity of the church as mediator. In addition, she and her fellow sectarians believed that because they were pure they could engage in all manner of sexual activity without fear of perdition.

To be sure, other beatas appear to have been legitimately virtuous and were recognized by the church hierarchy as such, so they had no conflict with the Inquisition. A prime example of such a case is Catarina de San Juan, the famous China Poblana. Originally from India, she was brought to New Spain by Portuguese slave traders and eventually came to live in the city of Puebla. Until her death in 1688 she lived under the protection of the powerful Jesuits. She prayed for the entire Christian community and lived a life of reclusion and penance while experiencing visions. She prophesied regarding the souls of important political and religious figures. Her case attests to the tremendous spontaneous popular devotion that could develop, especially during the 17th century, around the figure of a holy woman. Images of Catarina appeared on home altars, and her house became a shrine and a pilgrimage site. The Jesuits, whom she advised and shared her visions with, actively promoted her canonization, an effort that eventually failed. As part of a larger attack on popularly appointed "saints" her shrine was eventually dismantled and her images confiscated. Yet such popular sanctification movements were numerous and constituted a major characteristic of baroque religiosity in colonial Mexico.

The 18th century brought a wave of reform measures to Mexico that challenged the economic and social position of the church and inevitably affected the practice of Catholicism among the citizens. Not even the Holy Office would be left unscathed by the changing times. As a matter of fact, as the Bourbon century progressed, the inquisitors became less and less successful at accomplishing their stated mission. The battle against heresy became ever more frustrating as Enlightenment thought, published histories, controversial revolutions in the United States and France, and government policies fostered a climate amenable to independence.

The inquisitors attempted to prohibit works of political philosophy and any books that challenged the theoretical existence of the state, lest colonists be tempted to apply general political theories to specific colonial circumstances. Topping the Index of Prohibited Books were tracts about the French Revolution. The Inquisition had always been a political institution and had always equated heresy with treason. But now, more than ever before, heretics were tantamount to social revolutionaries who jeopardized not only the souls of their neighbors but the overall political stability as well. Therefore, it is not surprising that during the Bourbon century of increased Crown control, the tribunal would become a clear tool of regalism, persecuting political reformers and rebels for heresy. However, shifts of diplomatic and military alliances between Spain, France, and England made it difficult to punish foreign heretics and political ideas.

Furthermore, royal and ecclesiastical authorities embraced philosophical eclecticism, making it difficult to keep pace with what was deemed heretical, what acceptable. The defining characteristics of orthodoxy were changing and blurring. The greatest breakdown in Inquisition authority occurred on the frontiers, where it had always been the weakest. As a consequence of their ineffectiveness, the Inquisitors became obsessed to a tedious degree with matters of jurisdiction and with the dignity of their institution. As time progressed, the Inquisition came under heavy attack by more and more enlightened opponents. The Inquisition's ineffectiveness with these larger issues also weakened the institution's ability to affect popular piety.

The Bourbon authorities attacked other ecclesiastical institutions, which also influenced popular culture in a negative manner. In an effort to strengthen and solidify Crown control of the colonies in the political and economic realms, 18th–century reformers attacked the temporal authority of the church. The church not only played a pivotal role as primary mediator between the individual and the divine but also had become one of the most important economic institutions in the colony. For example, since its inception the church had become a major career path for devout, ambitious, politically motivated men seeking social mobility and an education. This was certainly the case for colonial Mexican criollos and mestizos. Eighteenth-century decrees limited the number of ordained clergy and the construction of new convents (for both males and females), thus cutting off one career path. This occurred during a period of population growth, precisely when new priests and convents were most needed.

In addition, two more government measures addressed the privileged social position of the clergy: the elimination of the ecclesiastical *fuero* (a special code of law and court of jurisdiction) and the promulgation of the Real Pragmática de Matrimonios, a decree reinforcing parental rights regarding marriage of adult children. The fuero decree abolished the practice of making clergy immune from secular prosecution for criminal offenses, making priests and citizens at least theoretically equal before the law. Now citizens could watch priests be openly tried and convicted under the civil code. Certainly these proceedings tarnished the clergy's image to some extent, although parishioners were already familiar with priests who gambled, drank to excess, and blatantly disregarded their vows of celibacy.

The Real Pragmática de Matrimonios prohibited church officials from intervening in disputes regarding marriage partners between young lovers and their parents. Under the new law, the state adjudicated all such cases and almost unanimously reaffirmed the concept of *patria potestad*, the rule of parents over their children. By doing so the state downplayed one of the central tenets of the Catholic faith, the doctrine of free will, and limited the clergy's ability to interpret that doctrine in the case of marriages.

Of more ominous consequence to the general population was the large number of decrees promulgated to "clean up" or modernize popular piety. The various religious associations, which were responsible for a majority of local public ritual, came under review. Those confraternities that did not possess proper licenses and charters were officially abolished, although many appealed and attempted to carry on their devotional activities despite royal sanctions. This was especially the case in frontier areas, such as New Mexico, where there existed a shortage of priests to monitor and investigate confraternities and the activities of their members. Processions and religious feast days were now to be celebrated as solemn affairs

GAMBLING IN A CONVENT.

A constant concern among Church officials was the comportment of the clergy. Efforts to regulate behavior included instruction manuals, official directives, and Inquisition investigations. This sketch illustrates a foreign traveler's report of gambling in a Franciscan house in Xalapa, Veracruz. The traveler charged the Franciscans with violating their vows of poverty and both swearing and drinking during the card game.

devoid of popular dancing and entertainments, including bullfights. Spectators were ordered to dress and behave as befitted a religious event. Festivals that were pivotal to the liturgical calendar but appeared too volatile or profane in nature were abolished outright in Spanish urban centers. This was particularly the case with Todos Santos and the Native American carnival in the capital.

In general, indigenous public ritual came under scrutiny and eventual attack in the 18th century. Bourbon officials prohibited native participation in such time-honored events as Mexico City's Corpus Christi *enramada* tradition (the construction and decoration of a thatch arbor). More important, the authorities launched a campaign aimed at eliminating large patron feast-day celebrations in indigenous towns. New royal decrees ordered natives to use the revenue destined for the feast to build a school and hire a teacher to educate native children, with a special emphasis being placed upon Spanish-language instruction. The native leadership viewed this royal intrusion as an assault upon their religiosity, pious traditions, and their very culture. Village priests, instructed to carry out the new orders, faced considerable hostility and even revolt as their indigenous parishioners refused to abide by the new laws.

The Inquisition had sought to monitor internal belief and its external manifestation. But the Bourbons concentrated only upon the latter, attempting to decree the appearance of "modern" piety. Neither completely understood the power of hundreds of years of cultural and religious interaction. Popular religiosity was never effectively or successfully challenged by either. Contemporary

Mexican popular piety is deeply rooted in these traditions developed and refined during the colonial period. The devotion to the saints, feast days, and the very role of the saints as intercessors either for the community or for personal needs is just as strong today as during the late 16th century. On May 15 some villagers still carry statues of San Isidro, the patron of farmers, into their fields so that he may bless their crops, thus ensuring an abundant harvest. On December 12 each year millions walk the Calzada de los Misterios to demonstrate their devotion and fulfill vows made to Our Lady of Guadalupe. Herbs and traditional medicine still flourish, as do love potions. The Mayas in Chamula celebrate carnival with sacred games that retell portions of the creation myth described in the ancient pre-Columbian text the *Popol Vuh*. The celebration includes a procession of Catholic saints linked to pre-Columbian deities. Chamula is the same village where priests, attempting to alter native traditions, were ceremoniously run out of town.

6

Indian Resistance to Colonialism

ROBERT W. PATCH

The indigenous people of Mexico both resisted and accommodated themselves to Spanish colonialism. The forms of accommodation, in fact, affected the nature of resistance, for while the Indians resigned themselves to foreign rule, they learned to use the Spanish legal system against the colonialists. Moreover, the Christian religion they were required to accept included revolutionary ideas that the Indians eventually turned against their foreign oppressor. Resistance, in short, was an ongoing process that changed over time.

Resistance is so general a term that unless we limit its meaning we will end up applying it to a spectrum of behavior that ranges from violent rebellion to snide remarks or dirty looks, thereby making the history of the Indians synonymous with the history of resistance. Our definition of resistance will be somewhat narrower: acts and thoughts—insofar as we can identify them—that were inherently Indian in nature and that constituted an unwillingness to accept colonialism as well as an effort to frustrate the colonialists' goals. This definition excludes behavior that was simply class-based (for example, peasant struggles against landowners, hacienda workers' conflicts with their bosses, and the like), because the conflicts that prompted such acts were not necessarily the result of colonialism.

In practice, Indian anticolonial actions sometimes overlapped with the class-based activities of peasants or workers, and we cannot always easily distinguish resistance from class conflict. One effect of colonialism was to turn an indigenous society, once composed of all social classes, into one big class of peasants. Thus peasant action was frequently the same thing as Indian resistance. Our definition, then, is broad enough to encompass a large part of the history of the indigenous people. Indeed, resistance to colonialism was frequently at the heart of the Indian experience in colonial Mexico.

Mexico is a diverse country, and an awareness of this diversity is crucial to understanding virtually all aspects of its history, including Indian resistance. One distinction is that between northern and southern Mexico, divided by a line that runs slightly north of the twentieth latitude, between 75 and 100 miles north of Mexico City. The southern half of Mexico and the Yucatán peninsula contained the homelands of all the famous Mexican civilizations of the pre-Hispanic era. The northern half, on the other hand, was known even in Aztec times as the "land of the Chichimecs"—that is, the homeland of the "barbarous" and sometimes nomadic peoples who resisted Aztec expansion and even raided the southern societies.

Northern and southern Mexico resisted colonialism in different ways. In the south, the indigenous people were either conquered by or negotiated a surrender to the Spanish conquerors. The Indian economy of the south was highly productive, oriented toward producing a large surplus in the form of foodstuffs (maize, beans, vegetables, turkeys), cacao (the Mesoamerican currency), cotton, and cotton textiles. The Spanish found it essential to preserve a great deal of the indigenous society and political system in order to benefit from this economy. This preservation took three forms.

First, by recognizing the Indian elite as a legitimate nobility in return for its cooperation with the colonial regime, the Spanish helped preserve legitimate authority within Indian society. Because the native people had already developed a strong tradition of powerful local leaders, indigenous society in the south continued to be characterized by what might be called a strong local state: institutions of government that were successful in policing, maintaining order, collecting taxes, and preserving respect for authority. Indians, in short, were used to following their leaders.

Second, the colonial regime took steps to preserve the Indian economy so that the surplus, paid as tribute or informal taxes, continued to be delivered to *encomenderos*, priests, and royal officials. The crown therefore sanctioned the indigenous systems of land tenure, whether private, familial, kin- or lineage-related, or communal. The Indians were recognized as the legitimate owners of the land they used (although what constituted "use" was always debatable), and royal approval was required for the sale of village land to outsiders.

Third, to protect the native people from encroachment and abuse by Spanish, the Crown established the General Indian Court in the late sixteenth century. Paid for by tax revenues, the court gave free legal aid to Indian villagers, thus allowing the native people to sue Spaniards and to defend their interests before the viceregal or *audiencia* courts. Needless to say, these colonial policies did not prevent the Spanish from abusing the indigenous people in the south or from occupying some of their land. They did, however, tend to limit what the colonists could get away with at the Indians' expense. As a result, Indians in southern Mexico continued to own a large part of the agricultural land throughout the colonial period.

The indigenous population cultivated corn, beans, squash, and chiles as dietary staples; these remain the basic ingredients of Mexican food today. This fanciful painting combines the rather savage images of the Indians and the landscape with the orderly image of European architecture.

Social, economic, and political conditions in the south thus ensured the survival of a hierarchically organized indigenous society, with important implications for the nature of Indian resistance to colonialism. On the one hand, the high degree of organization, combined with respect for the authority of the surviving elite, meant that the indigenous people in the south were well-organized for quick action to defend their interests and resist abuse. Thus many rebellions against colonialism took place in the south—hundreds of them, in fact. On the other hand, colonialism had destroyed the large pre-Conquest states, fragmenting their political structure. Each political unit was on its own. A unit usually consisted of a chief village, or *cabecera*, with one or more dependent settlements called *estancias* (ranches) or *auxiliares* (allied settlements). Rebellions, therefore, were almost always local, with local causes. They rarely spread beyond the cabecera and its dependents. Moreover, villages were likely to use the court system in their defense, either before a rebellion could take place or after one had occurred. The courts helped prevent revolts from spreading and provided channels for the termination of an uprising.

The south, therefore, had a large number of small-scale rebellions. Only on a few rare occasions, such as the Tzeltal Maya and Yucatec Maya revolts of 1712 and 1761 respectively, did the Indians of the south call into question the entire colonial system and claim the right to rule themselves. Those events can therefore be termed revolutions.

Conditions in the north were quite different, and so was Indian resistance. Most of the indigenous people had begun practicing agriculture before the

In his "Mapa de Nueva España," Theodoro de Bry included some rather romantic drawings of the peoples and animals of the New Spanish colony.

Spanish arrived, but the economy of the region was never as productive as that of the south. The surplus was smaller, almost nonexistent, and the Indians usually relied on hunting and gathering as crucial supplements to their economy. The continued threat of food shortage helps explain why many of the northern people were drawn to the Spanish missions: The Jesuits and Franciscans came with food to give and the promise of a more secure supply if the Indians cooperated. The missionaries also brought discipline and punishment, however. The Indians would have to get used to whips as well as to catechism.

Although many of the native people of New Galicia and the area north of Mexico City were eventually subject to the *encomienda* system, encomiendas were never as important anywhere in the north as they were in the south, and Indian populations were always much smaller. In places farther north, such as Nueva Vizcaya, the encomienda was a kind of forced labor system—as it was in Colombia, Venezuela, and Chile—precisely because the indigenous economy was so close to subsistence that the Spanish could not extract a surplus in the form of tribute. Some northern Indians were nomadic, but most were somewhat sedentary, living in settlements that the Spaniards called *rancherías*. These were smaller and less densely populated than villages in the south. Because the more dispersed and less productive economy of the north could not support an elaborate political structure, even Indians of the same tribe tended to be fragmented into little political entities in which leaders were selected by the people and lacked the awesome power of the hereditary nobles of the south. In the north, therefore, the local state was quite weak.

A true frontier war was waged in the north. Often it was a war "with fire and sword." The Spaniards destroyed indigenous settlements and enslaved captured Indians; the Indians subjected captured enemies to torture and lingering death. Native people were frequently killed in these conflicts, but they were not always conquered. On the contrary, the colonial viceroys eventually made peace with the northern Indians by buying them off with "gifts" of food, clothing, and other desirable goods. Power relations between the Spaniards and the Indians were not, as in the south, those of the conqueror and the conquered. Although at times the indigenous people were required to allow Christian missionaries into their settlements, at other times the priests entered by invitation. The Indians maintained a great deal of autonomy. The existence of a perpetual frontier in turn meant that they could come and go as they pleased, and many of them stayed in contact with completely independent people farther north. As a result, some Indians in northern Mexico were much less Hispanicized, and thus more Indian, than others. And some belonged to indigenous cultures almost untouched by the conquererors.

Nevertheless, the Spaniards made their mark in the north. The discovery of minerals especially silver, brought a flood of prospectors, mine workers, and adventurers to the vicinities of the strikes. To consolidate their control the Spanish brought with them Indian colonists from the south (usually Aztecs or people from Tlaxcala) to establish agricultural settlements that were intended to enable permanent colonization and spread sedentary civilization through example. In addition, the government set up military colonies, called presidios, to defend the newly occupied territories from Indian attack. The presidios were manned by Spaniards and Mestizos, who received land in return for their military service. Finally, of course, came the missionaries, especially the Franciscans and the Jesuits.

Economy, society, and polity in the north were thus quite different from in the south. Spanish culture affected the indigenous people primarily through interaction rather than force, for the Indians could not easily be kept in permanent settlements. Northern Indians had more control over their culture than those in the south, being less subject to the rule of powerful leaders and to the regimenting nature of colonialism. The extreme political fragmentation, however, made it much more difficult for resistance to spread beyond the individual level. But when it did, the resulting rebellions challenged colonial rule much more effectively than the numerous but minor southern uprisings.

Resistance also differed over time. Rebellions that took place shortly after the Conquest and the imposition of colonialism differed markedly from those that occurred a century or two later. Indians of the early, or Conquest, era were much less affected or influenced by Spanish culture, and most of them who were old enough to participate in a rebellion could remember life before the arrival of the Spanish. Conquest-era uprisings were culturally uncompromising—that is, participants demanded a return to the old ways and a complete rejection and destruction of everything Spanish, from Catholicism to orange trees.

As time went on, cultural interaction between the two groups made a difference. The native people learned things from the colonists. Eventually they retained only distant and distorted memories of a time without the Spaniards. The Indians came to see elements of European culture as desirable; they felt that some things, such as many Catholic practices, were essential to their lives. Rebellions a century or more after the Conquest, therefore, did not attempt to destroy everything Spanish. Instead, these late colonial uprisings frequently combined Spanish and Indian cultural elements into unique mixtures.

Despite the changes that colonialism brought, many significant features of Indian culture survived colonialism. The most important were languages, religions, and concepts of history. Language allowed Indians to live in a world that most Spanish could not enter. Their religion, although changed by Christianity, usually managed to retain certain concepts, such as cosmography—an understanding of the heavens and of the place of human beings in the universe—that colonialism could not destroy. As a result, many Indians continued to believe that history moved not along a continuum but rather in cycles, and that eventually the time would come when Spanish rule would be overthrown and the Spaniards would be subject to the native people. The "good old days" would then return, for if history moved in cycles, then the past was also the future. Beliefs like these had revolutionary potential. They allowed the Indians to accept a painful present because it was understood to be temporary—and because they believed that one day their time would come.

The following survey of Indian resistance to colonialism focuses on some of the more important and revealing colonial rebellions. The indigenous people expressed resistance through certain nonviolent, everyday actions. This of course is to be expected. Given the inequality of power relations between Spanish and the Indians, the latter naturally had to turn to what anthropologist James Scott has called "the weapons of the weak."

Large-scale resistance to colonialism broke out almost immediately after the Conquest, when most Indians could still remember the time before the arrival of the Spanish. The Mixtón War of 1540–42 in New Galicia (specifically in modern-day Jalisco, Nayarit, and southern Zacatecas) and the Cupul Uprising of 1546–47 in eastern Yucatán were grave threats to Spanish rule in Mexico. They were probably the Indians' last, best chance to throw off colonialism before it was too late.

The area that became New Galicia was first brought under control in 1531 by the infamous Nuño de Guzmán, whose atrocities unquestionably filled the indigenous people of the region—the Cazcan, Teul, Tecuex, Tonalá, and others—with passionate hatred of the Spanish. The rebellion of 1540 began against a background of economic extortion and forced labor. The catalyst for large-scale revolt, however, was the arrival of priests from Indian groups farther north, probably the Zacatecos, who were still unconquered. These shamans spread the word that the rule of the old gods should be restored, and that if the people abandoned Christianity they would miraculously receive food without labor, as well as the precious objects, such as turquoises and feathers, that their ancestors had so desired. The old would become young, and no one would have to die. Men would no longer have to remain monogamous, as the Spanish missionaries insisted. Those who remained Christian, however, would never see light again and would be eaten by wild beasts. In short, the shamans declared unrelenting war against Christianity. To maximize their chances of success against the Christians, they chose to begin their rebellion on Christmas Day, 1540, a day when the Spanish would not have their minds on politics and Indians.

The messengers of the traditional religion succeeded in subverting many of the Indians who had been forced to accept Spanish rule and Christianity. It is likely that here, as elsewhere, the Indians found the shamans' promise of a life without death especially appealing because so many had died from epidemic disease during the past two decades. Among those who joined the movement were the leaders of Tlatenango, Juchipila, Xalpa, and many other villages north of Guadalajara. The movement established a stronghold on a fortified mountain peak in Nayarit called Tepestitaque, where a cult dedicated to the old gods emerged. Another stronghold was established on a peak in Zacatecas called Mixtón.

At first the rebellion was not very violent because the shamans acted in secret. Once village leaders went over to the movement, however, adherents began to attack and sometimes kill Spanish people and their black servants, who were unlucky enough to be in unprotected rural areas. Then the colonial regime took action. Captain Miguel de Ibarra assembled a small army composed of seventeen Spanish and more than a thousand Indian auxiliaries. Ibarra marched his force toward Tepestitaque, but most of his allies either deserted or tried to lead him into a trap. The Indians repulsed his attack and forced him to retreat. This victory raised the insurgents' prestige, and their movement spread to even more villages. The great majority of the adherents apparently were Cazcan people, although Tonalás were also said to be sympathetic.

Viceroy Antonio de Mendoza consulted in Guadalajara with local Spanish leaders and decided that a second army should be assembled under the command of Cristóbal de Oñate. This force consisted of more than fifty Spanish horseman, artillery, and many Indian allies. In April 1541, they moved to assault the stronghold of Mixtón. The Indians attacked the Spanish force from both front and rear, inflicting heavy losses and forcing a retreat. This second Spanish defeat encouraged other Indians to rebel. The insurgents set up more fortified strongholds at Nochistlán and Coyna in the mountains of northern Jalisco. The revolt also spread to the area west of Guadalajara, where several Spanish settlements were besieged.

Realizing the seriousness of the situation, Mendoza ordered the mobilization of all available forces. He also asked for help from Pedro de Alvarado—Cortés's right-hand man in the Conquest of Mexico and the conqueror of Guatemala—who happened to be on the west coast with a force organized for a voyage of exploration. The experienced Alvarado commanded an expedition against the rebels at Nochistlán, who turned back Alvarado's attack, again with heavy losses. Alvarado himself perished in the fighting.

The defeat of the famous Alvarado gave still more impetus to the revolt. Many Chichimecs moved south to join the rebels in their strongholds. After driving the Spanish entirely out of Jalisco, a large Indian army assaulted Guadalajara

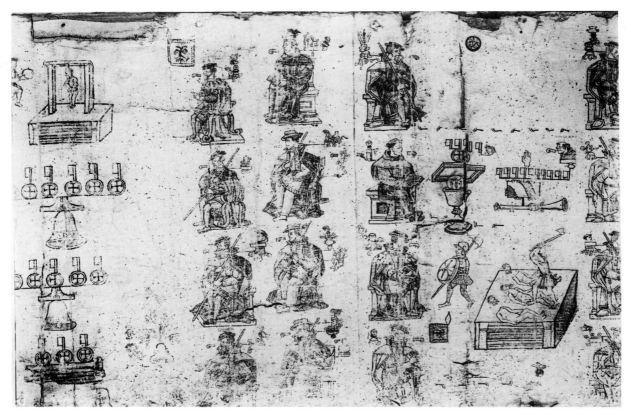

and almost captured the city. The situation was so desperate that Spanish women became combatants. Never was Spanish rule in Mexico more threatened.

In September, Viceroy Mendoza himself took the field, commanding a large force that included siege artillery. He immediately invaded northern Jalisco and besieged the Indian stronghold at Coyna. After unsuccessfully attempting to reach a peaceful solution, Mendoza attacked. Two weeks later he captured the site. Finding evidence of idolatry and human sacrifice, he meted out what the Spanish called "exemplary punishment," executing or selling into slavery many of his captives. This convinced other Indians in the area to surrender when offered amnesty. The Spanish force then moved to Nochistlán, which Mendoza also besieged and eventually captured.

Mendoza's next move was to attack the last great stronghold of the Indians at Mixtón. An Indian army numbering tens of thousands attacked Mendoza's forces from both front and rear, but the Spanish army was too powerful to be overwhelmed; the Indians retreated into their fortress. Once again the viceroy organized a formal siege, supported by his artillery. Eventually some defenders deserted the rebel cause in exchange for amnesty and betrayed their former comrades by showing the Spanish a secret path up the peak. Mixtón fell to Spanish assault. This time Mendoza, realizing that the rebels no longer posed a grave threat to the colonial regime, allowed many Indians to escape, thereby spreading news of invincibility of Spanish arms. After the fall of Mixtón, Mendoza found it relatively easy to force the Indians to submit. By early 1542 the war was over.

But resistance was a wildfire that, stamped out in one place, burst forth anew in another. Four years after the Mixtón War, a large rebellion called the Cupul Uprising seriously threatened the colonial regime. The Cupul Uprising took place in Yucatán, far from northern Mexico, but its causes were similar to those of the Mixtón War.

The Maya of eastern Yucatán, organized into minor states called Cupul, Cochuah, Sotuta, and Uaymil-Chetumal, had successfully resisted Spanish conquest for more than 20 years. They surrendered only after Maya groups in central Yucatán had become Spanish allies. The eastern people thus remembered their past success and, of course, resented the economic burdens of colonialism. Once again the catalysts for rebellion were the native priests, who convinced many people that Christianity, recently introduced, was a threat to the Maya way of life. Epidemics probably also stimulated the desire to return to the past; thousands of Maya had died of disease during the previous two decades.

The outbreak of the rebellion differed in one important way from the Mixtón War. The Cupul Uprising was a conspiracy that was organized, led, and executed most capably. Maya in eastern Yucatán and even some of those in the central part of the region rose up on the night of the first full moon of November (November 8–9, 1546). As had been the case in New Galicia, many Spanish encomenderos and their servants were in the countryside on business, and the Maya easily killed or captured them. The Maya of the Cupul region displayed the most fury and dedication to the cause. They tortured their Spanish captives and killed them in gruesome ways. The rebels also killed hundreds of Indians. Some of these were Maya who refused to abandon Christianity; others were Nahuas from central Mexico who had come to Yucatán as Spanish auxiliaries. The rebels destroyed all things Spanish: people, animals (cats and dogs as well as horses, cattle, and pigs), plants, even the trees planted by the Franciscans. This was a movement that permitted no compromise.

The Cupul people then took their rebellion to the Spanish town of their region, by attacking Valladolid. Only half of the resident conquistadores, about 22 in number, were still alive, the others having already been killed by the rebels. Nevertheless, the Spanish men and women of Valladolid and their Indian allies defended the town with such determination that the attackers were forced to settle into a siege.

Fortunately for the Spanish, the Maya leaders of the Mérida region, which had the largest concentration of resident conquistadores, delayed taking action, waiting to hear how the rebellion fared in the east. This gave the magistrates of Mérida time to arrest the indigenous leaders before they could urge their people into revolt. Without leaders, the Maya of western Yucatán would not participate in the revolt, and the magistrates of Mérida were thus free to organize a relief force for Valladolid, whose inhabitants were near the end of their tether after a siege of several weeks. An army of some 40 mounted Spanish and 500 Indian allies began fighting its way toward Valladolid. Meanwhile the Sotuta Maya continued to defy Spanish authority after a successful uprising in central Yucatán, and on the east coast the small Spanish town of Salamanca de Bacalar was in danger of falling to the Indians of the Uaymil-Chetumal region.

When the Spanish reinforcements from Mérida arrived at Valladolid, the Cupul did not lose heart. They continued to besiege the town, and only after days of fierce combat did the Spanish and their allies succeed in breaking the siege. The Cupul then withdrew to their villages and continued their resistance, forcing the Spanish to reconquer the region village by village. By this time additional Spanish forces, with Indian allies from the Campeche region, had arrived. These troops were commanded by various members of the Montejo family, which had led the Spanish conquest of Yucatán for decades. They finally succeeded in reconquering the Sotuta region, and the people of Uaymil-Chetumal on the southeast coast peacefully submitted to colonial rule. This allowed the Spanish to concentrate their forces on the remaining rebels in the northeast. By March 1547 the fighting was ending.

The Spanish investigated the uprising to determine the identity of the leaders. Eventually they executed a handful of people, mostly Maya priests. In Yucatán, as elsewhere after rebellions, the colonial authorities turned quickly from repression to pacification, for dead Indians could pay no tribute. Nevertheless, the native people in the eastern part of the Yucatán peninsula remained hostile to the Spanish for many generations, a fact that discouraged colonists from emigrating to the region. It was here, almost exactly three centuries later, that the last of the great Maya uprisings—the Caste War of Yucatán—would break out.

The Mixtón War and the Cupul Uprising illustrate three characteristics of resistance and repression during the colonial period. First, in both cases, and in all succeeding rebellions, the Spanish relied on Indian allies to fight and defeat the rebels. Indeed, these auxiliaries always constituted a majority of the repressive forces; colonialism could not have survived without them. It is not surprising that Indians fought Indians. The native people were of different cultures. They had been sharply divided and mutually antagonistic long before the Conquest. It proved simply impossible for them to present a common front against the invaders. Had the indigenous peoples of Mexico not been divided among themselves, with rifts and ruptures that the Spanish could exploit, is is hard to imagine that the Spanish could successfully have dominated such a large population.

Second, both the Mixtón War and the Cupul Uprising produced the typical Spanish reprisals. Colonial policy was to punish the "guilty" in an exemplary fashion, but not to destroy entire villages. Genocide of a population capable of paying tribute did not serve Spain's interests. Rather, the Spanish strove to get the Indian society functioning again, and therefore paying tribute, as soon as possible.

Third, these Conquest-era rebellions demonstrate the importance of religion as the vital motivating force behind violent resistance to colonialism. It was in the interest of the Indian priests to preserve their position in society, a position threatened by Christianity, which all but excluded Indians from the priesthood. Religious motives, however, went much deeper than simply the priests' self-interest. Christianity was not just a new body of rituals or one more god to add to the existing pantheon. It was the culture of a conquering people who would use force to guarantee that the conquered accepted Catholic priests in their midst. In the long run, the greatest threat to the Indians was not extinction or economic exploitation, but rather the cultural change that Christianity and other aspects of colonialism entailed. If the indigenous people lost their culture, they would take on a new Hispanic culture and cease to be Indians. To the Indians who lived in the turbulent years just after the Conquest, native religion represented the best possible reason to resist colonialism. It was one of the few things worth dying for. And when Spain crushed the Conquest-era rebellions, it opened the door to cultural change and transformation.

Once the Conquest was over, Spaniards and Indians settled into a pattern of colonial relationships that subordinated the indigenous people to their conquering masters. This process entailed change—and resistance to change. The survival of indigenous culture hung in the balance. The Indians were able to preserve at least some of their culture only through resistance and frequent resort to Scott's "weapons of the weak," such as "foot dragging, dissimulation, false compliance, pilfering, feigned ignorance, slander, arson, sabotage, and so forth."

Resistance to colonialism, while sometimes violent and even revolutionary, was an everyday process. For that reason, it rarely shows up in documents and is difficult to study. It nevertheless existed, as a priest revealed when he complained that without coercion the Indians would pay nothing to the church. Another sign that resistance was widespread is that fact that the Spanish frequently had to use force to carry out the commercial *repartimiento* system (a commercial exchange in which Spanish government officials either sold goods to or bought goods from the Indians at prices greatly favorable to the Spanish) or to recruit people for labor drafts. Another example of persistent resistance occurred when Indians who had been forcibly relocated to concentrated villages reverted to their original, more dispersed pattern of settlement a few years or decades later. People also just ran away, establishing free clandestine settlements in the thinly populated tropical lowlands of Chiapas and Yucatán. And, of course, the universal reluctance to pay tribute was a form of resistance.

The native people resisted colonialism in other ways, too. They used colonial institutions against the Spanish. The General Indian Court gave villages free legal aid, allowing them to bring lawsuits in the colonial courts. This tactic could be quite effective, as is demonstrated by the huge volume of Spanish complaints from all over Mexico about the litigious nature of the Indians. If these complaints are to be believed, the native people were always taking the Spanish to court, bringing suit at the drop of a hat. The records also reveal that the legal element of resistance helped the indigenous people maintain ownership of their land and water, the resources essential to their very survival as Indians.

The indigenous people also employed the new writing system, another Spanish innovation, to resist colonialism. They wrote down their own history, creating both a record for the future and a pre-Conquest tradition vital to their own identity as people of importance. They also wrote religious texts, dramas, and poetry to prove their equality with the Spanish. They kept track of their village land titles and guarded them like treasure, for these documents were extremely valuable in land disputes with outsiders. Finally, some Indians even wrote their own secret commentaries on the world, criticizing colonialism and in the process preserving their own worldview for future generations. The low literacy rate meant that this activity was not available to most Indians. The commentaries were important, however, because they allowed the Indians to express their own point of view—a point of view that, although not revolutionary, did counteract the ideological hegemony that the colonial regime tried to impose.

Religion was another crucial area of resistance to colonialism. The defense of indigenous religion meant defense of Indian culture. In general, the Indians of Mexico did not actually oppose or resist Christianity (although some groups did so, especially in the north, where many people were unconquered). Most Indians were willing and even eager to embrace the new religion. But they did so on their own terms, as they had done with other, earlier religions; they had a long history of accepting new religions after conquests. In the case of Christianity this meant adapting new concepts to old ways of thinking, rather than the other way around. The Indians became Christians while retaining features of their indigenous religion. Among these beliefs were an understanding of time as cyclical; a sense that an individual is a member of a people and is thus not entirely responsible for personal ethical behavior; a pantheon in which deities were sometimes both good and evil; and animism and pantheism.

Christianity itself contributed to a great deal of theological confusion. Christians did not doubt the real existence of the devil, but for the Indians the presence of a powerful spirit independent from God raised questions about the meaning of monotheism. Similarly, the Catholic doctrine of the Blessed Virgin and the cult of the saints could be equated with indigenous polytheism. Therefore Indians generally interpreted Christian doctrines in their own way. Saints, for example, became the patrons of village people, the equivalents of local gods; the people of one village would have been indignant had anyone told them that their St. Michael the Archangel, for example, was the same saint as the St. Michael the Archangel of many other villages.

The indigenous people not only maintained their own ways of understanding Christianity but also, at times, continued to hold their own non-Christian religious rituals. Throughout the colonial period the colonial authorities investigated numerous cases of "idolatry," often involving shamans and the use of traditional hallucinogenic substances. Such rituals must have been fairly common, as undoubtedly many more took place than are recorded in colonial archives. Indigenous rituals persisted not only because Indians wanted to maintain their traditions but also because traditional medicine, relying on local knowledge of herbs, frequently worked.

Indian resistance to colonialism thus took on numerous forms, some more successful than others. The indigenous people of Mexico were not simply the victims of colonialism. They were also, to a certain extent, agents in history. We should not exaggerate or romanticize their resistance, for in the long run colonialism succeeded in transforming and impoverishing them. Nevertheless, although resistance is sometimes difficult to document, it was real and important. The best-documented and most unambiguous resistance, of course, was violent rebellion.

As the Spanish moved north, beginning in the late 16th century, they continually encountered new groups of indigenous people who for the most part were living so close to the subsistence level that no surplus could be extracted from them. The Spanish colonists raided Indian settlements to loot and capture slaves, but after doing so they generally left the Indians alone—unless and until they discovered silver or gold in the area. When that occurred, the Spanish viewed the native people as obstacles and pushed them aside. Precious metals, however, were not found everywhere. They occurred at widely separated sites, which meant that the Spanish found a great deal of territory in the north unworthy of occupation. Mining towns and presidios, in other words, were like oases in the desert, and the Spanish left the desert to the Indians.

But although the Spanish regarded the northern Indians as economically useless, they did not ignore them. The Crown took its Christianizing mission seriously. Eventually the colonial government sent representatives of the Franciscans and Jesuits to the Indians to arrange for the establishment of missions. The indigenous people agreed, for the most part, to accept the priests, and missionizing got under way in earnest in the late 16th or the 17th century. Soon after the missionaries arrived, rebellions against colonialism broke out. Resistance in the north, then, was similar to the great Conquest-era rebellions of the south. It occurred before the native people were Christianized and when many of them remembered the precolonial age. Still close to their original culture, the northern Indians were sometimes inclined to reject all aspects of Spanish culture and religion in order to revitalize their own.

Although many native peoples tenaciously resisted Spanish expansion from the beginning, the Tepehuanes, who inhabited the Western Sierra Madre in western Durango and southwestern Chihuahua, were the first Indians in the north to rebel after having submitted to colonialism. Jesuits had begun Christianizing the region in the 1590s. Because the missionaries' methods included concentrating the population around missions, it is likely that they contributed to the outbreak or spread of epidemics that killed a large part of the Tepehuán population in the early 17th century.

The Tepehuán Rebellion of 1616–20 took place in the context of cultural shock caused by epidemics, the introduction of a new religion, and perhaps attempts to force the Indians to labor for Spanish encomenderos. The rebellion's leader was a newly Christianized Indian named Quautlatas, who apparently came to doubt the truths of the new religion and began to say so. The Jesuits had him flogged, but this only made him hate them more. Quautlatas began an anti-Christian religious movement aimed at restoring the traditional region to

The Franciscan missionaries arrived first in Mexico and established a reputation for their work among the indigenous people. This anonymous painting from the museum in Querétaro shows two Franciscan martyrs.

dominance in Tepehuán society. He encouraged his people to reject all aspects of Christianity, to recover their faith in their old beliefs, and to drive the invaders out of the land. He traveled from settlement to settlement and even spread his message to some Tarahumara Indians farther north. The rebel ideology included the belief that people who joined the movement and were killed in battle would be resurrected seven days after the final victory. The rebellion, in short, was typical of an age in which the indigenous people were just encountering the European invaders.

The uprising that broke out in November 1616 caught the Jesuits and the colonial authorities completely by surprise. They believed that their evangelization program had been a great success and were unready to admit that it had failed so completely. Within a few weeks the rebels had killed more than four hundred Spaniards, including six of the seven resident Jesuits, a Franciscan, and a Dominican. Also among the victims were more than a hundred settlers who left the safety of their church in the town of Santiago Papasquiaro on the promise of safe passage out of the war zone, only to be slaughtered. The rebels burned churches, careful to destroy all Christian religious images, including statues of the Blessed Virgin. Most of western and central Durango fell to the Tepehuanes, and to the north some Tarahumaras joined the revolt and assaulted Spanish settlements in Chihuahua.

Of course, the Spaniards reacted with force. It took more than two years to defeat the Tepehuán rebels. More than a thousand Indians died in the process, and hundreds more were sold into slavery. The Spanish were ruthless in crushing this

The arduous mining for silver and other precious metals in New Spain relied exclusively on human beings. The miner on the right is extracting ore that must be taken out of the mine by the worker on the left. With the basket on his back, the worker had to climb a series of ladders (usually nothing more than notched logs) to the surface.

uprising—they had nothing to lose because the Tepehuanes, subsistence produc-ers at best, were economically useless to them. Moreover, the Jesuits, like many missionaries before them, were especially outraged that so many of their so-called converts had participated in the revolt. To the missionaries, apostasy was treason. The priests therefore explained the uprising as the work of the devil and declared Quautlatas, who died in the fighting, was the Antichrist. The Spaniards finally succeeded in crushing the rebellion, primarily because the Tepehuanes were few in number. Historians estimate that more than a quarter of the Tepehuán people died or were enslaved because of the uprising. Peace did not fully return to the region until 1623.

North of the Tepehuanes lived the Tarahumaras, whose resistance delayed the Spanish advance for almost a century. Occupying what are now western Chi-huahua and southern Sonora, the Tarahumara people never threatened Spanish control as seriously as the Tepehuán, but they did carry out several important rebellions and sometimes joined those of others. Because the Tarahumaras were politically fragmented, however, their resistance to colonialism was never united.

Except for the southernmost Tarahumaras, who participated in the Tepehuán uprising, colonialism hardly touched the Tarahumaras until the Spanish discov-ered rich silver deposits at Parral in 1631. The Spanish frontier then took a big leap northward, bringing settlers to the eastern edge of the Tarahumara region. The Spanish tried to subject the Indians to forced labor, and at the same time the Jesuits began setting up missions in the southern district that was then called the Lower Tarahumara. By the 1640s—only a decade after the start of substantial contact with the Spanish—the Lower Tarahumara was seething with revolt. More than four thousand Indians had been baptized and were settled around the mis-sions, but they resented the labor requirements and the punishments inflicted by the priests. Like the Tepehuán Quautlatas, many converts became apostates, a process made easy by the close presence of so many unchristianized Indians to the north and west. The first violent resistance broke out in 1648, resulting in the destruction of a Jesuit mission. The Spaniards quickly put down this poorly organized uprising.

Colonial authorities then tried to take advantage of their victory by establishing a new Spanish settlement and several missions to the north, in the area called the Upper Tarahumara. This move almost immediately generated another revolt, led by a Christianized Indian named Tepórame and two others who were either apostates or unchristianized. Once again only part of the Tarahumara people supported the revolt, and once again the Spanish quickly crushed it.

In 1650 Tepórame led another revolt in the Upper Tarahumara. This time the rebels killed a missionary, crucifying him and then mutilating the body. The Spanish abandoned their settlement in the region, and colonial authorities sent in still another military force to fight the rebels. They succeeded in reestablishing the Spanish settlement and several missions in the Upper Tarahumara. The rebels continued to resist, however, and in 1652 they killed not only another missionary but also all the Indian converts in the Upper Tarahumara. Again the Spanish fled from the region. Raiding to the east, the rebel Indians destroyed seven Franciscan missions administering to the Concho Indians, but they failed to get the people of the Lower Tarahumara to join them. Eventually, after more than a year of fighting, the Spanish put down the revolt by offering amnesty to the participants in exchange for their leader. The Indians turned Tepórame over to the Spaniards, who executed him.

But Tepórame's work had been done. The Spaniards chose not to reoccupy the Upper Tarahumara, which remained free from missionaries and settlers for 20 years. Only in the 1670s did the Jesuits dare to enter the region again, and by the 1680s they had established several missions. In 1685, however, the Spanish found silver just east of the Upper Tarahumara. Soon the inevitable miners showed up and began to press the Indians. These new incursions led in 1690 to the fourth Tarahumara uprising, which began, as usual, with the slaughter of the local Jesuits. The Indian leader apparently won support by claiming that those who joined the movement would be resurrected if killed. The Spanish crushed the revolt only to face a new one in 1696.

This fifth uprising of the Tarahumaras proved to be the last but the greatest of all. It was preceded by a wave of epidemics that swept the whole of northern Mexico and New Mexico, stimulating Indian rebellions throughout the entire area. Throughout the land of the Tarahumaras people were discontented with the new religion, which they blamed for the epidemics—and undoubtedly the concentration of people at the missions did contribute to the spread of disease. Shamans, called wizards by the Catholic priests, spread the word that the revival of the old ways would restore health to the people. Recent converts returned to their traditional religion in hopes of a better life.

To discourage the Tarahumaras from rebelling, the colonial authorities resorted to terrorism, killing many hostages and parading their heads throughout the land. But as is frequently the case with terrorism, this simply infuriated the Indians even more, and a large-scale rebellion broke out. Eventually the rebels once more freed the entire Upper Tarahumara from Spanish control. Of course, in the end the Spanish defeated the rebels, and after 1698 they began reestablishing missions in the Upper Tarahumara. New silver discoveries brought more Spaniards to the east, so the Tarahumaras avoided problems by moving west or south, away from the Spanish settlements. Throughout the rest of the colonial period the Tarahumaras were bothered only by the missionaries. Many Tarahumaras managed to avoid even those representatives of colonialism by moving to inaccessible strongholds in the Western Sierra Madres, where their descendants still live today. Many others continued their resistance by joining raiding bands led by Apaches and harassing Spanish colonists throughout northern Mexico.

The most successful uprising in the north during the colonial period was the great Pueblo Revolt in New Mexico. It differed from most other northern rebellions in that it occurred several generations after Spanish colonization began. In 1598 Juan de Oñate led an expedition into the upper Río Grande valley and forced the Indians to submit to colonial rule. Unlike most other northern Indians, the people of the region lived in concentrated, although not very large, settlements; indeed, the Spanish word *pueblo*, "village," became the collective name of these Indians. Here the Spanish could introduce the encomienda system, although it did not work very well because the Indians' tribute capacity was limited. The Pueblos were not a culturally united group, for they spoke several different languages. Like most other northern Indians they were politically fragmented and rarely cooperated with each other.

The Crown entrusted New Mexico not to Jesuits but to Franciscans. Missionary policy at first tolerated many elements of indigenous religion. That began to change significantly in the 1650s, however, for the Franciscans had come to understand that the continuation of native religious ceremonies meant not the survival of "superstition" but rather the existence of a parallel religion. Doubting the Indians' loyalty to Christianity, the Catholic priests took steps to suppress some rituals thought to be too overly idolatrous. The Franciscan campaign to stamp out most indigenous rituals could not help but antagonize the Indians. Meanwhile, the material conditions of the Pueblos began to deteriorate substantially. At the same time, Apache raids grew more intense, and the Spanish failed to stop them. Drought and famine struck in the 1670s. Epidemics followed.

As was frequently the case, belief in the native religion grew stronger in the face of these crises, which Christianity had been unable to halt or avert. Shamans claimed that famine and epidemic were punishments inflicted on the people for abandoning their traditional gods. These native priests, fighting for their existence against Christianity, promised that a return to tradition would mean an end to sickness and death. The chief leader of this religious revival was a man named Popé, who had earlier been arrested and whipped for practicing native rituals. He joined with other shamans and planned an uprising to drive the Spanish from the Río Grande Valley.

The Pueblos had been noted for their lack of political unity, but in 1680 they showed more unity than ever before, for most of them joined in the rebellion. The rebels killed the majority of the Spanish missionaries and many of the colonists, and in August besieged Santa Fe. The Spaniards were forced to abandon their capital to the Pueblos, eventually abandoning the entire valley of the upper Río Grande and retreating all the way to El Paso. There the arrival of refugees, however, put a strain on the local Indian society, and soon more anticolonial revolts were underway. Eventually rebellion spread to practically all the Indians of northern Chihuahua and Sonora, including the Tarahumaras. Indians over a vast area repudiated both Spanish authority and Christianity.

Because New Mexico was far from the sources of Spanish power in Mexico, it took the royal government some time to assemble the people and resources to respond to the Pueblo Revolt on the far northern frontier. Not until 1692 were the Spanish, under their capable leader Diego de Vargas, able to launch a concerted effort to reestablish their rule in New Mexico. The bitter resistance of many Pueblo groups meant that it took a long time for the Spanish to regain control, but the reconquest ultimately succeeded—partly because of factionalism among the Indians. In 1680 the Pueblos had temporarily overcome their old political disunity, but the rifts reappeared, especially after the death of the leader Popé in about 1688, and eventually there was outright war between Pueblo groups. This conflict let the Spanish win the submission of some of the Pueblo people who had quarreled with their former comrades-in-arms. In 1694 Spanish forces retook the colonial capital at Santa Fe and began to reestablish the mission system. The Indians resisted as best they could and killed several more missionaries. However, the Spanish crushed all resistance, including a second significant uprising of the Pueblos in 1696. Many villagers moved west to avoid submitting to colonialism. The valley's population, reduced by death and out-migration, never returned to the pre-Revolt level during the colonial era. The cost of reconquest was high.

The revolt of the Yaqui and Mayo peoples in 1740 stands out from the regular pattern of northern Indian rebellions as well. Religion was not a crucial cause. Jesuits had begun founding missions in the area in 1617; the Yaquis, having learned that priests provided their neophytes not only with desirable trinkets but also with food in times of shortage, probably asked for the missionaries. The presence of the missions, however, did not ensure abundance for the Yaquis. The revolt of 1740 took place during a famine caused by crop failure, and many attacks on Jesuit missionaries and on other Spaniards were uncoordinated acts by unrelated groups of Indians in search of food. The failure of the Jesuits to fulfill their end of the bargain—food in case of famine in return for peaceful submission to Christianization—was undoubtedly a major factor causing the rebellion.

But here, as elsewhere, there were complicating factors. First, Spanish settlement in the region had been on the rise, for the mines in the mountains east of the region needed foodstuffs and workers. This led to the establishment of haciendas, sometimes on lands claimed by the Yaquis and Mayos, and to the introduction of a labor draft for the mines. Needless to say, these innovations greatly disrupted the Indian way of life.

Second, there were abuses by the Jesuits, who tried to make their missions profitable by engaging in commercial agriculture and selling crops to the mining camps. They also sent livestock from the Yaqui area to the missions in Baja California, using the labor of the local Indians to support missionary expansion elsewhere. To accomplish this, the Jesuits made the native people work for them several days of the week, and they sometimes used non-Yaqui Indians and mestizos as foremen, a practice that antagonized the Yaquis. Those Yaquis who showed reluctance to work risked a whipping.

Finally, conflict between the Spanish colonial, civil, and religious authorities allowed the native people to play one group against the other. In 1734 the Crown began introducing civil government into what had been the Jesuits' own private domain. The priests resented this intrusion. By this time, however, the missionary Indians had their own resentments against the Jesuits, and they turned to the civil authorities for redress. In 1736 a Yaqui village head named Muni, who opposed the discipline of the Jesuits and the use of outsiders as foreman, and who had been whipped for his uncooperative attitude, complained to the newly introduced civil authorities about these abuses. The Jesuits, however, sweet-talked the officials into seeing things their way. As a result the officials arrested Muni and Bernabé, his *compadre* (a person linked to another through sponsorship at baptism), as well as several other so-called troublemakers. When word of this got out, a large group of Yaquis marched on the town jail and forced the Spanish to free their leaders. To avoid violence the authorities gave in to Indian demands, demonstrating the power of the people. The offended Jesuits sought revenge, first by forcing Muni and Bernabé to resign their position as village leaders, then, after the Spanish authorities had reinstated them, by concocting a scheme to make it appear that the Yaqui villagers wanted Muni and Bernabé removed.

Muni and Bernabé found an ally in 1737. The Archbishop of Mexico, who wanted to reduce the power of the missionary orders and who had become interim viceroy, invited them to Mexico City to give evidence against the Jesuits. There they complained about the increasing work loads that the missionaries had imposed. Perhaps the Yaqui leaders saw that an appeal to a higher authority outside their region could induce the newly introduced civil powers to diminish the role of the Jesuits. Meanwhile, the priests had already complained that the Indians were becoming more and more uncooperative and hostile.

In January 1740, while Muni and Bernabé were in Mexico City, floods caused severe crop damage in the Yaqui region. The Jesuits failed to supply enough food to the Indians because they were trying to send livestock to Baja California to stock their ranches. Yaquis therefore began raiding Jesuit missions and Spanish-owned ranches to steal cattle and other foodstuffs. By March this activity had developed into conflict between Indians and Spaniards. In one famous case the Yaqui captured a squadron of soldiers and stole all their clothes, forcing the soldiers to retreat stark naked. The Indian attacks, however, do not seem to have been coordinated; it appears that individual groups were acting independently. In May a rumor spread that Muni and Bernabé, still in Mexico City, had been executed. The rumor stimulated more rebel activity, and the Yaquis drove the Spanish out of all the missions and towns between the Yaqui and Mayo Rivers. In a sense, the Indians did better without recognized leaders. Had Muni and Bernabé been present, their power might well have been disputed by the fiercely independent, semi-anarchistic little groups of people who called themselves Yaquis. But the rumor of their death galvanized the Indians more than flesh-and-blood leaders could have done. Among the Yaqui, outrage proved to be a more effective force than leadership.

At first the colonial authorities could do little about the uprising because they lacked soldiers. Eventually the Yaquis lost their enthusiasm for the struggle, and the Spanish governor, Manuel de Huidobro, pacified some of the rebel villages. He was helped by Muni and Bernabé, who returned from Mexico City in August or September and convinced many rebels to return to their normal activities. A new viceroy, however, judged Huidobro inept (or cowardly, which was the Jesuits' accusation) and in 1741 replaced him with the more determined Agustín Vildósola.

Vildósola defeated the last few Yaqui raiding parties, but when he suspected Muni and Bernabé of conspiring to lead another uprising, he had them executed in June 1741. Whether or not the two leaders had been plotting, their execution did provoke the Yaquis to rise again, but with less force than before. By August Vildósola had restored Spanish control over the territory, and by September 1741 the rebellion was all but over. Thereafter the region was quiet, although good relations between the Indians and the Jesuits were never restored.

The major factors in the uprising were the Yaquis' claims to the fruits of their own labor and their desire to retain their autonomy. They had never considered themselves conquered people. When their power relative to Spanish settlers and missionaries deteriorated, they took steps to regain control of the situation. Although they did not defeat and drive out the invaders, they did embarrass the Jesuits; indeed the Yaqui uprising was one more nail in the coffin that the Crown was building for the black-robed missionaries. The Yaquis also succeeded in making their territory less attractive to Spanish colonists—which, in effect, restored a great deal of their autonomy. For this reason it can be said that the Yaquis were more successful than most Mexican Indians in resisting Spanish colonialism. Had large deposits of precious metals been found in their region, however, the Spanish would have had a stronger motive for entering the area and dispossessing or conquering the Yaquis.

Indian resistance to Spanish colonialism in northern Mexico was neither futile nor unsuccessful. In some cases the indigenous people's actions either delayed Spanish expansion or halted it altogether. Most Indian groups survived the colonial era with part of their culture intact. Often the real threat to their existence emerged after independence, when there was little restraint on settlers' activities and when state and federal governments served the interests of the local or national elites who wanted to gain access to Indian land or the minerals it contained.

In addition to the important revolts discussed here, there were many others too numerous to include. Violent resistance, moreover, was by no means limited to rebellions by the conquered. Many unconquered groups such as the Apaches and Comanches resisted the advance of colonialism by raiding the Spanish settlements and missions, killing or enslaving people, and stealing goods and livestock. These activities went on throughout the colonial period and did not end until the 19th century, when the authorities of Mexico and the United States pursued different policies toward the indigenous people and when the technology of warfare gave a decisive advantage to the invader.

Demographic factors shaped northern resistance. Indian groups in the north were small. Epidemics reduced their numbers even more, weakening their long-term capacity to fight back. Yet the continual outbreaks of disease also made many Indians question the validity of the missionaries' new religion; epidemics sometimes strengthened resistance in the short run by giving rise to revitalization movements that frequently served as the ideology of rebellion.

Silver, and to a lesser extent gold, were also of crucial importance in the history of Indian resistance in the north. Wherever the Spanish found major silver deposits, their arms eventually triumphed. The economic motives and concommitant military might of the Spanish in search of wealth were too much for the indigenous people to withstand. Indians in mineral-rich regions were first forcibly recruited as laborers in the mines and then driven off the land. But where there was no silver or gold, the Spanish were less eager to go. Missionaries did try to go everywhere, but they were much fewer in number than the secular settlers who set up the great mining camps and haciendas. As a result, some indigenous groups, in a sense, were lucky. Their poverty helped protect them from intensive Spanish colonization, which was the greatest threat to their existence. Many Indians survived the colonial era because they lived in places of little economic interest to the Spanish—and of all motives behind Spanish expansion in the Americas, the economic had by far the greatest impact on the Indians.

Southern Mexico's Indian population was several times greater than that of the north. It is no surprise to find that there were more revolts in the south—too many to discuss more than a handful here. The great majority of revolts in the south shared certain characteristics. They were almost always local in nature and rarely affected more than one village. Causes of rebellion varied, but the revolts usually followed the same pattern. With little planning but lots of spontaneity, villagers would suddenly vent their anger at the source of their dissatisfaction. These targets were usually agents of the colonial government, priests, Indian village officials, non-Indian residents, or Indians from other villages. The insurgents often assaulted royal government offices, jails, and churches. Many participants—and often the leaders—were women. This is in marked contrast to the revolts in northern Mexico, where traditional values survived and fighting was largely limited to men.

Almost all revolts were violent, but the toll of dead and injured rarely was more than ten and frequently was a good deal less. Indiscriminate looting never occurred. The rebels' weapons reflected the spontaneous nature of the revolts. Rocks were the most common, followed by the usual possessions of a peasant society (machetes, knives, sticks, clubs, axes, hoes, and the like). Firearms were very rarely used, both because they were expensive and because colonial policy restricted their ownership. The targets of the people's anger either died, fled, or hid in a church or convent, leaving the village in the hands of the rebels. The rebels' glee at their success would then quickly turn to fear of reprisal, and the people would either submit peacefully to the colonial authorities or flee their village for a few weeks or months and negotiate an end to the uprising.

The colonial government had several methods of restoring order. Rarely did the authorities need much force to put down rebellions; in any case, for much of the colonial period, the government had few soldiers ready to participate in repressive actions. Normally the local magistrate called up some members of the local militia (to which all able-bodied Spaniards theoretically belonged). Sometimes he asked for the help of Indians from other areas who received special rights and privileges in return for serving as auxiliaries. The colonial regime usually restored order within a few days and then acted quickly to find someone to blame. Within weeks the investigation was all over and a handful of people, at most, had been identified as ringleaders and punished. Punishments usually consisted of flogging, temporary exile, sentence to forced labor.

Hundreds of such events, which in many respects resembled urban riots in rural settings, took place during the colonial era. Full-scale insurrections or revolutions were rare; rebels almost never even considered challenging the legitimacy of authority. In fact, they overwhelmingly accepted that legitimacy, even with respect to their obligation to pay taxes. Those who revolted understood that their actions were aimed at local people who had done them wrong, not at the king, the viceroy, or the colonial system. Moreover, the revolts rarely took on the characteristics of class warfare. The people who rebelled did not have the consciousness necessary to see themselves as a class having something in common with similar people elsewhere.

The seizure of Indian land did not go unchallenged. This image is from the *Codex Osuna,* a legal record of complaints against land loss, labor exploitation, and unjust demands for food. The Spaniards, surrounding an Indian household, are preparing to take the property from the Indian father, mother, and children.

These revolts were not rebellions by landless people against Spanish landowners. The villages in question always owned land, and the villagers who used it had a strong sense of themselves as the collective or familial owners. Only a few of the small, local revolts were caused by Spanish landowners' attempts to seize Indian land. Sometimes, villagers revolted because they feared that the boundary surveys carried out by government officials might result in the loss of village land. The most effective way to resist the expansion of the haciendas was to take the aggressors to court, not to take up arms against them.

If the local revolts were not caused by land grabs or class consciousness, what did precipitate them? The great majority were of two types. First, Indians took the path of violent resistance when government officials or priests tried arbitrarily to change the existing economic relationship between villagers and the outside world, such as by raising taxes, increasing repartimiento allotments or demands for forced labor, augmenting fees for services or sacraments, or interfering with

Como çesan de marbales S. Alvares p̃ darcuẽpã des
porlos reg̃ ruy y aluares de mexicas en t̃ ansi de / Juã de Saldaña
las pãni des

y denluarriba

español qmtlani
tlalli

attoes çelor

regidores

¶ Yeastilteca attiesme y huem regidores ynigmte mamaca tlalli. y mico
mexico. y tocalla. ynigmte tetezonona. estaca. y nituca Juã de Saldaña
y naca y paricac. y mcaltiyin ymtlaltyin ỹ macehualhinthi. y e cuely e
qmtetezozona. ỹ quahniti y Juan de Saldaña. auỹ ỹ ma cehual
hintli. cenca mo choqmilia. y cãpa qm mõ mo hmiqmliz y mpilhuã
yiyin. y cãpa õ niotlalliçã ẽ
luarriba

Indian-controlled production and commerce. The indigenous people recognized their obligations to church and state, even though they may not have liked them, but they also had a clear sense of their rights, and they resisted any attempt to go beyond what was acceptable. English historian E. P. Thompson has called this the moral economy, the understanding between elites and masses regarding acceptable levels of exploitation and acceptable standards of behavior. When the exploiter goes beyond what is regarded as moral, the exploited feel that they have the right to take steps to reestablish the moral balance, and these steps sometimes involve riots and revolt.

The second type of revolt resulted from what might be called the violation of the moral polity of the colonial regime, when Spanish magistrates interfered with indigenous political practices. Sometimes they did so by appointing village leaders or governments without consulting the Indians, or even in deliberate defiance of Indian wishes. By supporting one village faction against another, the magistrate got the colonial government directly involved in village politics. The Spanish also interfered in local political affairs by arresting village officials for failing to carry out the wishes of the colonial rulers. Indians strongly felt, and Spanish law provided, that although the colonial regime had to confirm the election of village officials by the village electors (usually a body of elders or "principal" leaders), the Spanish had no right to make the selection themselves. Whenever magistrates tried to do so, they met with opposition and sometimes rebellion. When Indian leaders were arrested for failing to do the bidding of the colonial rulers, revolts frequently took the form of attacks on the jail to free the prisoners. On the other hand, if the Indian officials had cooperated with 'outsiders' efforts to disturb the moral economy or polity, the people might turn their hostility against their own leaders.

Villagers rose up in defense of their right to perform their established religious ceremonies, usually associated with a particular shrine or brotherhood, in their own way. When bishops or colonial magistrates interfered or tried to "reform" such activities the local people sometimes rebelled violently in support of tradition, frequently led by their own parish priests. On other occasions people revolted to assert their village's religious autonomy—in other words, to be recognized as a parish in order to avoid being subject or subservient to another village.

Uprisings in San Luis Potosí and Michoacán in 1767 are notable as examples of the extreme violence of the colonial response. The expulsion of the Jesuits prompted the rebellions; the people revolted not against the priests but in defense of the existing state of religious affairs. The order of expulsion had been issued by José de Gálvez, a peninsular official whom the Crown had made visitor general to Mexico. Gálvez's mission was to determine what changes in colonial policy were needed, but he had neither understanding of nor respect for the colony's normal ways of solving problems. He ordered newly arrived regiments of regular soldiers from Spain to suppress the revolts with maximum force. The punishment that followed was both cruel and unusual: Eighty-five people were hanged, seventy-three flogged, one hundred and seventeen exiled, and six hundred and seventy-four sentenced to prison. Such repression of behavior that was essentially simple rioting, not revolution, was extraordinary. It was not repeated in the colonial era until the outbreak of the wars of independence.

It would be a mistake to think that the Indians of the south were normally happy and peaceful unless provoked by outside government officials or priests. When revolts occurred, the Indians' words and actions frequently displayed deep-rooted hostility to the Spanish, to outsiders, and to colonialism—a hostility well beyond anger over whatever had caused the uprising. Once rebels took control of their village they often began insulting the non-Indians, frequently using the same insults that the Spanish used for Indians. They also spoke of how good it would be to change the system, and to have Indians ruling over the Spanish.

Such thoughts and actions reveal that although the Indians may not have had class consciousness, they had a clear understanding of injustice and exploitation. They knew, in other words, that in the social order they were the wretched ones. Their actions show that they knew they must resist all new demands for money, goods, and labor or be exploited even further. The large number of revolts over these issues demonstrates that relations between the Spanish and the Indians were dynamic and changing. Officials of the state tried frequently to increase existing levels of exploitation, and just as frequently the indigenous people resisted, but the outcome was never predetermined. In effect, the reality of colonialism was negotiated in a continual process of state formation and popular resistance. The colonial regime was contested, its nature shifting back and forth from place to place, depending on the outcome of the political and social struggle. The Indians had a clear conception of what might be called their constitutional rights—not a written document like the constitution of the United States, but something in the English sense of a constituted political order that could not be changed arbitrarily. The indigenous people recognized their obligations to the state, but not to a capricious state, and they accepted rule by outside kings, viceroys, and magistrates in return for some local political autonomy. This defense of rights is one of the characteristic features of Indian resistance to colonialism.

In the eighteenth century the Maya region of southern Mexico was the center of two movements that were so radical in their attempts to overthrow colonialism that they can be called revolutionary. Several factors may have made the Maya more prone than other Indians to such radicalism. First, although the Maya were by no means isolated from the world economy (in fact, they were linked to it by the export of locally manufactured cotton textiles), they were less affected by Spanish settlement and economic activity than most other people in southern Mexico. Colonialism changed but did not altogether disrupt their basic patterns of living. Second, the Maya managed to retain more of their basic worldview, cosmography, and the religious underpinnings of those cultural patterns, than perhaps any other indigenous people of Mexico. They were affected by Christianity, as they adapted it to their own way of thinking. In many ways, the revolutionary movements were fighting for a Mayanized version of Christianity.

Highland Chiapas (at that time called Chiapa) was populated by many different kinds of Maya people, the most important of whom were the Tzeltal, the Tzotzil, and the Chol. The province became a hotbed of religiosity in the late 17th century. Many Maya witnessed apparitions of God or of the Virgin Mary, participated in unorthodox rituals, and founded religious cults outside the confines of the Catholic Church. The ecclesiastical authorities did their best to suppress such potentially heretical activities. This religious ferment formed the background of the uprising of 1712, for although economic motives contributed to the outbreak of rebellion, religion turned it into a full-scale challenge to colonialism.

The Chiapan Maya, like all Mexican Indians, were exploited by colonialism, but what seems to have broken the camel's back was a particularly rapacious bishop. During an episcopal visitation in 1708, this bishop found that he could extort money from the Indians by requiring them to pay high fees for the sacrament of confirmation and for episcopal approval of their religious brotherhoods. The province took years to recover from his depredations. Then, in August 1712, he announced that it was time for a second visitation.

The bishop could not have found a more inopportune time for such an announcement. A new and powerful cult of the Virgin had just emerged in the Tzeltal village of Cancuc, northeast of modern-day San Cristóbal de las Casas. There in May, a thirteen-year-old girl named María López, the daughter of the village sacristan, had seen a vision of the Blessed Virgin, who ordered the construction of a chapel and the founding of a cult dedicated to her. The village government complied with the Virgin's request, and soon the cult was thriving. In an attempt to suppress it, the local priest had María López and her father whipped, and the Spanish magistrate of Chiapa jailed the village government officials for having sanctioned and supported the movement. The cult nevertheless continued to grow. But then the village officials escaped from jail, just as word arrived of the bishop's dreaded visitation. Upon returning home the leaders of Cancuc proclaimed rebellion against the Spanish and in support of their religion. Those who fought in the movement called themselves "Soldiers of the Virgin."

The Cancuc uprising differed from the great majority of colonial revolts because it spread to other villages and fueled an outbreak of massive violence. The violence was directed against Indians as well as the Spanish, for when villagers refused to join the movement the rebels killed them. The rebels also killed captured non-Indian men, sometimes children as well. They forced creole women to marry Indians, thereby allowing the Maya to change places with their colonial masters. Finally, when rival Maya cults also appeared in the highlands, the "Soldiers of the Virgin" slaughtered their adherents to defend the one true cult. Eventually most of the Tzeltal Maya people, as well as a few Tzotzil and Chol villages, joined the movement, which controlled a large part of the northeastern highlands. Hundreds of people—Maya, Spanish, and mestizo—had been killed. The cult leaders created their own Catholic church in Cancuc by naming one of their members bishop so that he could ordain Maya priests. The rites and sacraments

This carving of a pacified Indian from the *retablo* (or altar screen) of La Caridad Church, San Cristóbal de Las Casas was made shortly after the rebellion of 1712. By associating the image with European products, the Spanish intended to demonstrate the benefits of pacification for the indigenous peoples.

continued to be administered. The Maya, in other words, strove to achieve religious as well as political autonomy.

Before a month passed, the colonial government organized the forces necessary to crush the uprising. By late August the rebels were on the defensive. On November 21, 1712, Cancuc fell to the Spanish. Some fighting continued into the next year, but the movement was by then dead. Most of its leaders had died defending Cancuc. The Spanish executed all prisoners known to have participated in any of the massacres, but they flogged and then freed the great majority of the captured rebels. María López, whose vision had started the revolt, escaped the fighting but died in childbirth shortly thereafter. It is likely that several thousand people died in the most violent uprising in southern Mexico in the entire colonial period.

Religion caused another Maya rebellion, in Yucatán in 1761. Economic factors undoubtedly contributed to the willingness of people to revolt, but there is no indication that they felt themselves more grievously exploited in the middle of the 18th century than previously. The new factor was a man who showed up in the small and unimportant village of Cisteíl, in central Yucatán, in November 1761. He claimed to be at once the messiah, Christ, the king, and Moctezuma. He was Jacinto Uc de los Santos, a wandering shaman who had lived on the wild east coast of the Yucatán peninsula. His startling proclamation was, in a sense, anticipated: A large-king-Christ figure would come to liberate them and overturn existing colonial relationships by establishing Maya domination of the Spanish.

After some discussion the village government of Cisteíl recognized Uc as the hoped-for messiah, and thereafter he called himself King Canek (the name of the last independent Maya monarch) Moctezuma. He established himself in the church, moved the silver crown from the statue of the Virgin to his own head, and conducted religious ceremonies using the vestments and chalice of the Catholic clergy. His followers carried him in procession in the streets, burned incense before him, and revered him as a man-god. People from surrounding villages visited Cisteíl to see the long-expected king, and the movement gathered strength.

Violence first occurred when a traveling Spanish merchant insulted Canek to his face. The king ordered his followers to kill the man. They did so, and thereafter the movement took on a revolutionary character. Canek appointed a government and began to assume the powers of the Spanish governor of Yucatán. He proclaimed that the Spanish must die, but then ordered that Spanish women be spared and forced to intermarry with the Maya. Canek also raised an army, appointed commanders, and appealed to other villages for support. Yet he made no attempt to conquer surrounding people, nor did he try to negotiate with the Spanish government. He was, after all, claiming Maya sovereignty; there was nothing to negotiate.

More violence occurred when a detachment of twenty Spanish soldiers entered Cisteíl to reestablish colonial authority. Canek's followers attacked the soldiers with pikes and machetes, killing all but two of them. The survivors managed to escape and spread the alarm. The Spanish government then called up the militia and organized an expedition of some 500 soldiers to crush the rebellion. As this small army approached Cisteíl it discovered that many local Indians along the route had killed all their pigs, for Canek had said that swine had Spanish souls and that killing pigs would allow the Indians to kill the Spanish. On November 26, 1761, the Spanish force attacked. Canek encouraged his followers by claiming that they would not be killed by Spanish firearms, and he manufactured medicine to cure wounds.

Needless to say, firearms did kill Indians. Canek's movement was crushed. Most of the Maya in Cisteíl died in battle or were summarily executed. Canek and some other leaders escaped, but the Spanish captured them almost immediately and took them to Mérida for trial. Of the two hundred and fifty-four prisoners, nine—including Jacinto Uc de los Santos—received the death penalty. Most of the rest were sentenced to flogging and the loss of an ear, then freed.

The Maya rebellions of 1712 and 1761 were revitalization movements, efforts to recover lost cultural elements and to strengthen the existing ones. They were expressions of the people's desire to create a more satisfying state than the one they inhabited in colonial Mexico. Colonialism had removed Indians from the highest positions of political and religious power. The Cancuc leaders and Canek manifested the Maya's desire to control their political system by assuming the names and full trappings of sovereignty and to control their religion by giving their king or bishop priestly powers to communicate with the supernatural world and appoint clergy. They did succeed briefly in carrying out their religion without Spanish supervision, but the movements did not last long enough to give us much of an idea of what political independence would have meant.

These rebellions differed in important ways from the Conquest-era revolts. After a century and a half of colonialism, indigenous culture was changed. It had incorporated Spanish and Catholic elements which the Maya did not want to reject. In Yucatán some Indians killed pigs, brought originally by the Europeans, but they did not kill horses, cattle, chickens, and other animals of European origin. Most important, in both Chiapa and Yucatán the rebels wanted to preserve basic features of Catholicism, especially the rituals and hierarchy. These had become such an important part of Indian life that they could no longer be abandoned. The rebels wanted not to reject but to control aspects of the foreign culture. But that meant revolution.

The religion of the Spanish contributed to the revolutionary nature of the Maya movements. Judeo-Christian messianism reinforced the traditional Maya understanding of history as a cyclical process; the long-awaited messiah-king would be the person whose coming would signal the end of one cycle and the beginning of the next. The Maya thus borrowed an element of Christianity and used it to resist colonialism. But although the Maya revolutions resulted from cultural imperatives, radical resistance to colonialism also had material roots. The Maya knew that they were the oppressed; they wanted to turn the world on its head by ruling over the Spanish. The reality of the material world—the exploitation and subjugation of the Indians as a result of colonialism—was the sine qua non of their worldview. Without it, there would have been no desire for the return of the past as future. Economic and cultural factors were inextricably linked in the revolutionary challenges to colonialism.

In the Conquest era and the late colonial period, in the north and the south, Indian resistance to colonialism was a long-drawn-out process rather than a series of discrete events. Although most of those who resisted failed to achieve their goals, resistance played an important role in history. It slowed the process by which the Spanish took control of Mexico, not just politically but also economically and culturally. The existence today of a large number of people of indigenous culture—changed, of course, but with many basic concepts intact—is proof of the Indians' commitment to maintaining their way of life and thought. Resistance, in short, made a world of a difference.

7

Disease, Ecology, and the Environment

ELINOR G. K. MELVILLE

In 1576, after years of telling and retelling his story, the conquistador Bernal Díaz del Castillo published his history of the conquest of Mexico. His descriptions of the landscapes the Spaniards passed through on their way to the heartland of the Aztec Empire have such clarity that they can still be used to identify not only natural landforms such as mountains and valleys but also human-made structures such as the huge catch basins built to trap water for villages and towns. But his description of the Valley of Mexico in 1519, when he saw it for the first time, is the most compelling. The soldiers who marched with Cortés to meet the emperor Moctezuma marvelled at the sight of cities, palaces, and gardens seeming to float on water in the clear mountain air. They thought they were seeing fabled lands of myths and legends. The grandeur, strangeness, and beauty of the scene captured Díaz's imagination, and more than 50 years later he had not lost the wonder of it all: "I stood there looking at it," he wrote, "and thought that never in the world would there be discovered other lands such as these, for at that time there was no Peru, nor any thought of it." Then, in a wistful statement resonating with our 20th–century consciousness that by simply entering alien worlds we can change them beyond recall, he wrote: "[o]f all these wonders that I then beheld today all is overthrown and lost, nothing left standing."

The idea that the Spaniards found a strange and powerful empire—a "lost world"—and that they conquered it and in doing so destroyed it has fascinated people since the 16th century. In traditional histories, the story of the conquest of Mexico was told as a tale of Spanish might, of "natural" European superiority. But as a better understanding of indigenous societies developed, historians no longer took Spanish superiority as a given. They began to ask how a tiny group of soldiers managed to conquer highly complex societies and expand into densely settled lands, and in recent years historians have argued that this isolated world held

The Sierra Madre Occidental, the most imposing physical feature of Mexico, serves as the country's north-south spine and continues into the Rocky Mountains of the United States. The Sierra Madre has also played a prominent role in the nation's history as the location of some of the world's richest silver and mineral deposits. These mountains have been home to various indigenous groups and small communities that resisted incorporation into the Mexican nation-state.

the seeds of its own destruction. Because, the argument goes, there had been only irregular contact between the "new" and the "old" worlds before 1492, the indigenous peoples were strangers to the disease organisms introduced by the Europeans and their African slaves, and when these alien disease organisms entered American ecosystems, they brought about catastrophic epidemics. The high mortality rates associated with these epidemics reduced the size of the defending populations, and the collapse of the defenses enabled the Europeans to invade and settle successfully.

Environmental historian Alfred Crosby has gone one step further and proposed that it wasn't just alien diseases that facilitated European invasion into New Spain and the rest of the Americas; it was a combination of the diseases and the plants and animals the invaders brought with them in order to reproduce their previous environments, what he calls their "portmanteau biota." Eurasian and African diseases formed the "shock troops" of the invasion, he writes, but the ecological changes associated with the introduction of all these alien species were what brought about the consolidation of military successes and the development of enduring patterns of conquest of millions of people and domination of great expanses of land. Suggesting that the ecological processes underlying the replacement of the indigenous landscapes by European-like landscapes, as well as the replacement of the indigenous peoples by Europeans and Africans, constituted a biological conquest, he coined the term "ecological imperialism" to describe the process by which Europeans, together with their portmanteau biota, invaded the Americas (and later Australasia and the Pacific islands).

Crosby examined most closely the formation of what he termed "neo-Europes," places such as Canada, the United States, Argentina, Australia, and New Zealand. These are the lands of the "demographic take-over," to use Crosby's term—the places where Europeans and their descendants have succeeded in becoming numerically, as well as economically and politically, dominant; where immense herds of cattle and sheep graze; where prairies and plains are filled with wheat and barley, and great expanses of European fruit trees fill immense orchards. In these cool temperate lands, landscapes reminiscent of European ones obviously reflect the biological success of the invading portmanteau biota.

Mexico presents quite a different scenario. Mexican landscapes have been profoundly influenced by the presence of introduced animals such as cattle, horses, donkeys, sheep, goats, and pigs, and plants such as wheat and fruit trees. But these landscapes also reflect the continued presence of indigenous environments and cultures, as well as the development of new ethnicities and cultures out of a mixing of indigenous and European peoples. Although Spaniards were highly successful in achieving economic and political dominance, they were never numerically superior to the indigenous populations—that is, they did not achieve demographic dominance. The Mexican landscapes also reflect the fact that even though introduced agricultural elements such as wheat and cattle gained importance, indigenous species such as maize remain critical to both the national and subsistence economies. Hence the conquest of Mexico cannot be explained as a straightforward replacement of the indigenous landscapes by European-like ones; it certainly cannot be explained in terms of a demographic takeover. As Crosby notes, Mexico is not a neo-Europe.

Ecological imperialism was played out differently here: Although the Spaniards introduced virtually the same set of plants, animals, pests, weeds, and diseases into New Spain as was introduced into North America—thus initiating the same or similar biological processes—the outcome was very different. In this chapter we examine the impact of Eurasian and African diseases, flora, and fauna on indigenous environments, the influence of Mesoamerican ecologies and societies on the invaders, and the formation and structure of Spanish colonial environments. We will treat the physical environment as taking an active role in social change, rather than seeing the environment as a static backdrop to human affairs—a place of natural resources that attain importance only when used by humans. Because this is a fairly new approach to the history of Mexico, we often have only one half of the equation, or maybe less; what follows is thus a brief and preliminary discussion of the environments after the Spanish invasion.

Before beginning this examination of colonial environments, we need to have some idea of the environmental and social processes that were already in place when the Spaniards arrived.

A story concerning Hernán Cortés has it that when the Spanish king, Charles V, asked him what Mexico was like, Cortés crumpled a piece of parchment, threw it on a table, and said, "Like that." While this is undoubtedly an apocryphal story, it is remarkably evocative of Mexican geography: The highland central plateau stretching from just north of the Valley of Mexico into Texas and the lowlands of the Yucatán Peninsula in the Caribbean Sea are relatively flat (or at least contain quite extensive flat mesas, basins, and valleys), but for the most part Mexico is a highly fractured, mountainous land.

The central plateau rises from near sea level in the north to over 5,000 feet above sea level in the Valley of Mexico. Two long chains of mountains (the Sierra Madre Oriental and the Sierra Madre Occidental) snake down either side of the central plateau—rather like a double backbone—and culminate in mountains rising to over 18,000 feet around the Valley of Mexico. This high point, known as the neovolcanic axis, lies just to the west of the narrowest part of the country, which means that the distance to the coast decreases as the land rises to its highest point. The land drops sharply down to the Caribbean and Pacific coasts from the Valley of Mexico in a series of large steps—the valleys of Puebla-Tlaxcala, Cuautla-Matamoros, and Cuernavaca—and culminates in long stretches of steep-sided hills.

This long, pyramidal-shaped landmass separates two oceans, the Caribbean Sea to the east and the Pacific Ocean to the west. These bodies of water have a marked impact on the Mexican climate: The annual hurricane cycle arising in the Caribbean, for example, brings heavy summer rains to the eastern coast that at times reach far inland; and events arising in the Pacific, such as El Niño, strongly influence the weather during specific years, changing the timing and intensity of the rainy season. Two-thirds of the landmass lies south of the Tropic of Cancer, and hence should be characterized by hot, humid weather. Along the coasts and in the lowlands this is true, but the southern two-thirds of the country also contain the highest mountains and valleys. Altitude thus exerts a strong influence on the climate of any particular region, and folk definitions of the region's climate were (and are still) based on altitude: Areas below 1,000 meters are referred to as *tierra caliente* (hot land), those lying between 1000 and 2000 meters are called *tierra templada* (temperate land), and those above 2000 meters are known as *tierra fría* (cold land). Therefore, despite the fact that they lie well within the subtropics, the basin floor of the Valley of Mexico falls within the category of tierra templada, and the surrounding mountains fall within that of tierra fría.

An annual cycle of warm, wet summer seasons alternating with cool, dry winter seasons is found over most of Mexico—but there is remarkable variation over even short distances. Latitude, altitude, and position relative to mountain chains influence the climate of individual regions (location in a rain shadow, for example, will be reflected in lower annual rainfall). However, the rainfall regimes in the south exhibit a greater abundance of precipitation and little annual variability, while the north is characterized by less abundant rainfall and greater variability. Indigenous settlement patterns have long reflected this rough division of the rainfall regime: Dense populations of sedentary farmers were found in the regions of predictable and abundant rainfall while mobile agriculturalists and hunters were found in the regions of unpredictable and sparse rainfall. Very early in their

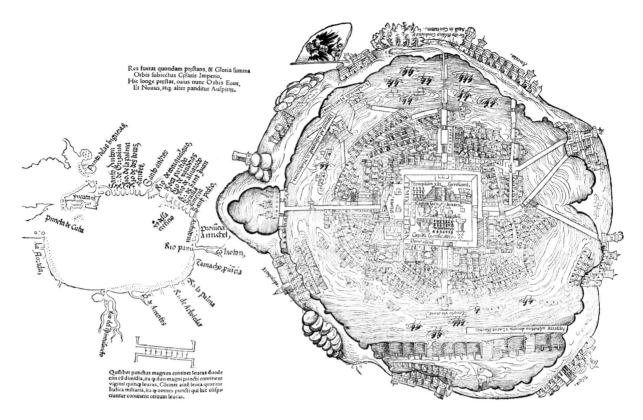

Res fuerat quondam preftans, & Gloria fumma
Orbis fubiecctus Cefaris Imperio,
Hic longe preftat, cuius nunc Orbis Eous,
Et Nouus, atq; alter panditur Aufpicijs.

Quilibet punctus magnus continet leucas duode
cim cū dimidia, ita ꝙ duo magni puncti continent
viginti quinꝗ leucas, Cōtinet autē leuca quatuor
Italica miliaria, ita ꝙ omnes puncti qui hic cōfpi
ciuntur continent centum leucas.

history the indigenous inhabitants took advantage of these differences and specialized in the production and exchange of goods between contrasting ecosystems.

By 1519, extensive systems of local and long-distance trade linked very different regions and served what were, by all accounts, very large populations. For
the most part, these populations were composed of rural agricultural peoples we
can divide into two broad groups on the basis of mobility: The first group were
sedentary peasant farmers who lived in villages and worked the land to produce
raw materials for subsistence, manufacture, and sale, as well as for taxes and tribute payments to elites; the second group were mobile agriculturalists who moved
across the land, shifting their cultivations in accordance with soil fertility and
water resources. There were also large urban populations who lived in quite
densely populated cities and towns; indeed, the city of Tenochtitlan was one of
the largest cities in the world at contact. Some of these groups were organized
into states and empires, others were small independent societies; but all, whatever
their size and their social complexity, altered their landscapes—and hence
influenced the ecological processes that underpinned them.

Sedentary agriculture and the formation of dense populations brought about
some of the more profound landscape changes evident in the pre-Hispanic era.
Associated changes in the physical environment had important consequences for
the human populations themselves—not all of them benign. Perhaps the most
obvious consequence of the development of sedentary agriculture for both landscapes and environments was the transformation of the vegetative cover: Simply

The Aztecs prepared this
map of Tenochtitlan (the
earliest known map of
the city) and presented it
to Cortés. It indicates the
city's dense population by
the representation of
compact dwellings. On
the same sheet is a map
of the Gulf Coast. Cortés
sent the sheet with both
maps to Charles V, the
king of Spain, in his
second letter describing
the expedition.

in order to produce surpluses of staple foodstuffs and the raw materials needed for the manufacture of clothing and other essentials, the indigenous peoples cleared land. And in place of the complex natural ecosystems, they developed simplified agro-ecosystems more suited to the production of large surpluses of certain selected plants. As their populations grew in size and density, the indigenous peoples further modified the physical environment: They intensified agricultural production. When the fertile lands were used up, they put marginal lands into production. Where the water supply was either too little or too much, the timing and amount of rainfall was irregular, or the pressures of increasing populations brought about artificial scarcity of water, the indigenous farmers developed systems of water management, such as canal irrigation.

These modifications had environmental consequences. Deforestation and the cultivation of marginal lands—especially in regions of steep slopes—can lead to problems such as erosion. Simplification of the ground cover, and intensification of the quantity of products that are removed from the immediate ecosystem for use as subsistence, manufacture, and exchange—and hence exportation of nutrients out of the ecosystem—can give rise to soil infertility. Canal irrigation often leads to problems of salinization. There is little doubt that the indigenous farmers faced these problems and more. For example, archaeologists have found extensive evidence of heavy erosion—generally associated with high population densities—at different times in the pre-Hispanic era. These findings confirm the position taken by Sherburne F. Cook, writing in the 1940s, who argued that the growth of huge sedentary populations at various times in the pre-Hispanic era had resulted in severe erosion. Cook's argument has been so persuasive that many archaeologists use a similar argument to explain the collapse of civilizations such as the Maya in the ninth century.

Cook also proposed that the growth of huge populations just prior to the Spanish invasion resulted in such severe erosion that by the time the Spaniards arrived the central highlands were on the verge of an ecological collapse. This thesis is more difficult to prove, primarily because the Spanish did arrive and because their arrival changed the native environments—most spectacularly the density of the indigenous populations. Added to that, there is evidence indicating that the indigenous peoples were quite successful in mitigating the consequences of dense populations and intensive agriculture. They fought erosion, for example, by constructing terraces on hillsides and check dams in gullies, by leaving the stalks from the harvests standing so that the soil was not open to wind erosion, by growing trees and bushes around fields to act as windbreaks and to prevent the rapid flow of surface water. And although it is clear that in some places the terraces were built too quickly and without sufficient care, and that they collapsed carrying the soil that had been packed behind them downslope into the valley; it is also clear that in many places the terraces were successful in preventing, or at least checking the extent of, erosion. The pre-Hispanic farmers had the advantage of not having to deal with the destructive activity of domestic grazing animals, notorious for their propensity to scramble over terraces knocking down retaining walls, and where there are no grazing animals, the soils of abandoned terraces tend to be stabilized by weeds and bushes.

The indigenous agriculturalists also developed practices aimed at maintaining soil fertility, such as resting the land for varying lengths of time, as well as fertilization. Native Americans domesticated few animals—and, outside the Andean region, no grazing animals—hence they lacked the source of fertilizer that has had such a marked impact on the development of Eurasian agriculture. In place of animal manure they used green manure (the weeds and leaves and stalks left after the harvest) and human waste to replenish soil fertility—something that had implications for the disease environments both before and after the arrival of the Europeans. Instead of alternating crops, which is practiced in monocultural systems, the indigenous farmers practiced polyculture: They grew several species of plants together in the same space. Even the simplest of the indigenous agro-ecosystems, the traditional maize field, was polycultural. Beans and squash were grown along with the maize, and as the plants matured, the maize stalks provided support for the beans while the squash functioned as a ground cover that kept the soil moist and retarded the growth of weeds. Maize cultivation draws very heavily on soil nitrogen, while beans are very effective at returning atmospheric nitrogen to the soils. By growing maize and beans together, the indigenous farmers counteracted to some extent the heavy drain on soil fertility of maize cultivation.

In order to keep abreast of the demands of increasing populations for food and raw materials, the indigenous farmers developed ever more intensive methods of agricultural production. Intensification of agricultural production requires not only the maintenance of soil fertility to counteract the heavy drain of soil nutrients but also the development of systems of water management to ensure a steady supply of water. Canal irrigation, floodwater irrigation, drainage, and the management of wetlands were all practiced by the indigenous agriculturalists. Wetlands agriculture is one of the more intriguing systems of intensive agriculture practiced by Native Americans, and has been justly praised as among the most productive systems of land management found anywhere. Perhaps the best-known example of wetlands agriculture is the *chinampas*, the so-called floating gardens of the Valley of Mexico. Chinampas seem to have evolved out of a system of growing plants in swamps on basketlike structures supported by poles above the water. Over time the structures were stabilized, and long, low, narrow planting platforms were formed that extended above the surface of the water. Trees and bushes grew on edges of the platforms and further stabilized them. The narrowness of the chinampa made sure the plants in the center of the planting surface received sufficient water through their roots—thereby avoiding the problems of salinization associated with surface irrigation. If the chinampa was too wide, an island effect occurred and the plants in the center no longer received water by filtration and had to be watered by hand—with attendant problems of salinization. As the number of chinampas increased, an intricate pattern of planting surfaces and canals developed. Canoes moving along the canals carried the products away from the chinampas to the markets and brought seedlings and human waste (used for fertilizer) to the platforms. Regular dredging was necessary to keep the canals free and clear, and this very fertile mud was also used to fertilize the soil of the chinampas, which were thus able to sustain multiple, perhaps even continuous, cropping.

The chinampas are a local example of widespread systems of wetlands management that were developed in the pre-Hispanic era and have been carried up to the present day. These systems are generically termed ridged, or raised, fields and were characterized by raised planting surfaces separated by ditches or canals. The function of the ridging and ditching differed according to local hydrology. In regions of perennial swamps, for example, they acted to provide raised planting surfaces and thus to prevent root rot. In regions of annual flooding the ditches acted either to drain away water or to trap and conserve water for use during the dry season. They ranged from single mounds built and maintained by individuals to the vast expanses of ridged fields found in the lowland Maya region and the Valley of Mexico. By the time the Spaniards arrived in the Valley of Mexico, approximately a third of Lake Xochimilco had been reclaimed and transformed into chinampas. In some places they seem to have acted as a means of augmenting staple crops; in others—the Valley of Mexico, for example—they may have supplied the major percentage of the foodstuffs for the cities and towns.

The indigenous farmers also practiced extensive systems of land management that involved ecosystem management as well as simplified agro-ecosystems. One such system of land management is swidden agriculture. In its contemporary incarnation as slash and burn, swidden agriculture is thought to be simply the rough-and-ready cutting and burning of patches of forest for the cultivation of cultigens such as maize. The idea is that the farmers are compensating for poor soils by cutting and burning trees and bushes, thereby using the fertilizing qualities of wood ash. They are thought to move on when they have exhausted the nutrients of that particular patch; they then repeat the whole process of slash, burn, and cultivation somewhere else. But recent studies of modern swidden agriculturalists have concluded that the goal of swidden farming is not simply the cultivation of crops for a short period of time in a forest opening; rather, it is a system of long-term forest use and management. The Mayas regard the milpa stage (the period when maize is grown in a forest clearing) as only one aspect of a process of successive plant associations that may last a century or more. Swidden agriculturalists utilize the forest after a patch is cleared—returning to the secondary-and tertiary-growth forests for herbs, roots, wood, et cetera. They recognize and name each successive plant association from the tall forest through the milpa and succeeding stages of secondary growth until finally the tall forest returns. And they recognize that human activity may result in the return of a forest different from that which began the succession. (See figure 7.1 for a schematic representation of the forest successions.)

In swidden, as in other systems of land management, the indigenous peoples mimic natural processes. Swidden agriculture closely mimics the effects of hurricanes and fires, which open patches of varying size in the forest canopy, thereby allowing the regeneration of plants requiring sunlight and/or disturbed soils and beginning a process of successive plant associations. House gardens and the artificial forests of the Yucatán Peninsula are other modern agro-ecosystems that mimic vegetation associations. House gardens, for example, contain domesticated and "wild" species planted in a manner that mimics local plant associations. But it is the artificial forests in Yucatán (the *pet kol*) that are particularly interesting. The pet kol were for long thought to be relict forests— until it was realized that some species growing in these small isolated forest patches are from far outside the immediate region, that local farmers regarded the pet kol as sources for the regeneration of forests and useful plant species, and that they consciously protected them by enclosing them with stone fences.

Archaeological evidence suggests that the indigenous peoples have been mimicking and manipulating ecosystems for millennia. Indeed, the fact that undomesticated wild maize and bean species have been found growing together in the same way as domesticated species (with the beans growing up the maize stalks) has been used by some researchers as evidence to suggest that the indigenous farmers consciously imitated the natural ecology in their development of maize and bean domestication and cultivation.

The statement that indigenous farmers manipulate, manage, and mimic ecosystems should not be taken to imply that the indigenous peoples have some secret unknown to modern farmers, not even present-day factory farmers. Modern agricultural fields are so obviously artificial, and we have become so used to thinking of agriculture as an essentially human cultural activity somehow distinct from "natural" process, that we forget that not so many decades ago the grandparents of many modern farmers in the United States and Europe drew on wastelands for medicines, famine foods, wood, and the like, and that they practiced techniques such as pollarding and coppicing useful trees to be sure of a sufficient supply of canes to make baskets, storage bins, furniture, and so on.

What was unusual in the American case was the limited number of animal species that were domesticated by the Native Americans. Drawing on her studies in Central America, Olga Linares has suggested that instead of domesticating specific species of animals, the Native Americans made their living areas attractive to the animals they wished to utilize for food, fur, and skins, by planting certain plants; that they were, in effect, domesticating ecosystems instead of species. The paucity of domesticated animals in the Americans had profound implications for indigenous societies in the pre- and the postcontact eras. The complete lack of animals that could be used for traction and carrying, for example, meant that all these agricultural systems were implemented by human labor only using various tools, including the such as the *coa* (huictli), or foot plow. The lack of herd animals also meant that the indigenous farmers lacked their manure for fertilization. The introduction of pigs, sheep, goats, cattle, and horses thus had the advantage of supplying manure and providing traction; unfortunately, it also brought decided disadvantages.

✦ ✦ ✦

By 1519, the indigenous landscapes of Mexico had been shaped by millennia of human activity: Forests had been cut down and had grown back as the populations rose and fell; ground cover had been simplified, manipulated, and moved from place to place; soil had been built up and had washed away; water had been channeled, drained, and managed according to highly sophisticated technologies of soil-water management. The plants that were cultivated in the milpas, chinampas, raised beds, terraces, and flood plains were species that had been domesticated in this same region; and the farmers who worked the land in 1519 were the descendants of those people who had developed both species and the systems of cultivation.

With the arrival of the Spaniards, not only the landscapes but also the ecological processes that sustained this world of plants and humans were profoundly changed. Domesticated grazing animals were introduced for the first time—with extraordinary consequences for the native vegetation, and for soil and water regimes. Even the addition of new plants and new schedules and approaches to land and water management changed ecological processes in unforeseen ways. The indigenous human communities and the physical environments did not disappear; indeed, they have been highly successful in reproducing themselves up into the late 20th century. But over the centuries since the Spanish arrival, both human societies and ecosystems have been redefined by the addition of new humans, animals, and plants. In their turn, the indigenous worlds have shaped the new arrivals and redefined their ways. So that, in the end, we have Mexican landscapes and Mexican environments that are a synthesis of native and introduced plants, animals, and land management systems.

It is this process of addition, definition, and reproduction that we now take up. The topic of the Spanish impact on the native environments is so large and so complex that we will focus only on a few selected areas: disease, vegetation, animals, and water.

> "... a la sazón de la tierra por todas partes hervía de gente."
> ("at that time [the 1520s] the land everywhere teemed with people.")
>
> FRAY TORIBIO DE BENAVENTE O MOTOLINÌA

Perhaps the most profound consequence of the Spanish invasion for Mexican environments was the introduction of disease organisms that included smallpox, chicken pox, measles, influenza, whooping cough, typhus, typhoid fever, cholera, scarlet fever, malaria, yellow fever, bubonic plague, and diphtheria. The indigenous populations proved to be highly susceptible to these alien diseases. They were struck by epidemics that were shocking in the extent of the infections, their virulence, and the resulting mortality rates; these epidemics were what are called "virgin-soil" epidemics.

As their name suggests, virgin-soil epidemics occur in populations that have had no experience of the alien disease organisms. Virgin-soil epidemics are characterized by global rates of infection and high mortality rates, especially in that section of the population between 15 and 40 years of age—in other words, the primary caregivers and food producers. A modern example is the epidemic caused by the Ebola virus; in this case the population affected by the Ebola virus was "virgin soil" because the disease is new. In the case of the epidemics that afflicted the Native Americans, the indigenous populations were inexperienced because of their long isolation from the populations of the Eurasian and African continents. The indigenous populations of the Americas had never been infected by these organisms and had no acquired immunity to them; as a result the disease organisms spread very quickly.

In New Spain, at least at first, there was no pool of native people with acquired immunity to provide care for those infected with the alien diseases; and although some Spaniards tried to help, they were very few and the numbers of infected people enormous. Therefore, the mortality rates soared far beyond anything that had been seen in Europe, and the populations declined at an alarming rate. In a classic article on virgin-soil epidemics in the Americas, Alfred Crosby (1976) suggests that the problems facing the indigenous communities were exacerbated by a pervasive acceptance of the inevitability of death and hopelessness—especially when it was realized that contemporary medical practices were unable to prevent infection, let alone prevent death. Quarantine was not practiced because no one had any experience with the diseases, and terrified people fled, very often carrying the disease organisms far from the points of initial infection. Crosby also notes that many of the diseases that accompanied the invaders are still potentially fatal in their lands of origin. Measles, whooping cough, and chicken pox are not the harmless childhood diseases that we now (mistakenly) consider them, although mortality rates are far lower. Despite modern medicine, there are no cures for these diseases, and the infection simply runs its course. The only thing that can be done is to make sure the patient is not infected with secondary infections such as pneumonia, and receives needed liquids and foods. In virgin-soil conditions, however, where primary caregivers and food producers are very often the hardest hit of all, people who might otherwise survive the primary infection die of secondary infections or starvation or simple dehydration or all three. The outbreak of the Ebola virus in Zaire in 1995 gives us a very clear idea of the terrors of virgin-soil epidemics: No one seems to be immune from infection, the cause of infection is unknown, nothing appears to help, and death is fearsomely rapid.

The mortality rates experienced by the American indigenes appear to have been excessively high—even given virgin-soil conditions—over both the short and the long term. Over the short term of individual epidemics, for example, the mortality rate in certain epidemics may have reached 75 percent in certain populations. Over the long term, the indigenous populations of New Spain lost around 90 percent of their total population over the first 100 years; a mortality rate that

A smallpox epidemic ravaged the Aztec empire and the city of Tenochtitlan in particular. The disease struck the city between the time the Spaniards fled initially and when they returned to complete their conquest.

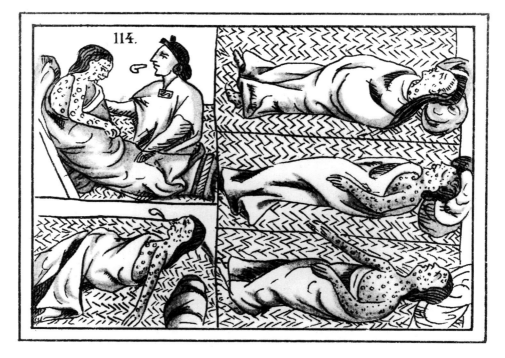

can be compared with the loss of one-third of the European population during the 14th century as a result of the Black Death.

Traditional explanations for the high mortality suffered by the American populations argued that the natives were inherently weak. The fact that the Europeans survived while the American Indians died in great numbers was often seen as yet another indication of the superiority of the Europeans. More recent explanations focus on the population history of the Americas, as we have seen in the explanation for the appearance of virgin-soil epidemics; these focus on the history of the diseases themselves and on environmental factors. Crosby (1976) has suggested, for example, that one contributing factor to the very high mortality rates was undoubtedly the fact that the indigenous communities were not afflicted by just one disease, but were infected with several diseases at once—and these several infections were repeated regularly over a period of about 100 years. And in trying to answer the question Why did so many die? Francis L. Black (1992) has suggested that the relatively high level of genetic homogeneity of the American populations (a result of the limited number of original migrations) could have helped the rapid spread of the diseases and the very high death rates. Black notes that because the genetic structure of the virus becomes adapted to one host and is thus preadapted to a genetically similar host, viruses will become more virulent when they move between hosts that are genetically similar, such as family members. Because the Native American populations were, and are still, remarkably homogeneous genetically, there was an increased chance that viruses would encounter genetically similar hosts outside the immediate family and that the virulence of the infections would increase in American populations. Thus population history—a limited number of migrations and subsequent isolation—helps explain not only the susceptibility of the Indian populations but also the increased virulence of Eurasian diseases in the Americas.

Perhaps the clearest influence of environmental factors on the disease environments of New Spain was the introduction of domestic animals and the development of new systems of resource exploitation such as mining and grazing. Because the Native American societies domesticated relatively few animals, they had not lived in close proximity with many animals and thus were spared many of the diseases that move between animals and humans. This situation changed with the arrival of the Europeans. The Spaniards introduced a variety of animals—such as chickens, ducks, pigs, goats, sheep, cattle, horses, and donkeys—into Mesoamerica, and these animals were incorporated into the villages and households of the indigenous peoples, with extraordinary consequences for indigenous cultures, societies, and disease environments.

The most obvious and immediate impact of the addition of these domestic animals was the pollution of water sources. Indigenous communities reported indignantly to the Spanish officials the contamination of drinking water by animal manure, by mud stirred up by animals walking in the dams and irrigation canals, by offal from slaughterhouses, by the effluent from tanneries and wool manufactories. Not obvious to the naked eye, but far more lethal, was the entry into the disease environment of the microflora and microfauna carried by these animals.

There is no doubt that long before the arrival of the Spaniards the indigenous humans carried a heavy load of intestinal parasites that were spread throughout the population by the use of human manure for fertilizer and by the simple runoff of sewage into watercourses. Indeed, the fact that the indigenes collected and ate the algae growing on ponds and lakes indicates pollution by sewage from human settlements. But the addition of the alien microorganisms carried by the incoming animals, to say nothing of the microbial load carried by the invading humans, undoubtedly increased the disease load in a population unused to sharing its microflora and microfauna with many other domestic animals. The introduction of a large variety of alien animals may also have provided conditions that gave rise to more virulent strains of old diseases, or perhaps to entirely new diseases. Recent studies indicate that living with domestic animals can lead to the diversion of an animal virus into humans (Morse, 1990). The process of diversion involves the reshuffling of genes so that the virus appears as a "new" disease in human populations—one that is particularly virulent, because viruses that are diverted into humans exhibit increased virulence.

The occurrence of several virgin-soil epidemics repeated regularly over a period of decades in a small population can result in the loss of the entire population. However, the occurrence of several repeated virgin-soil epidemics in a large population is not likely to result in the disappearance of the entire population, although it can cause an abrupt decline in population size, so that the density of the population and their presence in the landscape is markedly reduced; that is a demographic collapse can occur. Over the first 100 years of the colony of New Spain, for example, the indigenous populations slowly acquired immunities and the Eurasian and African diseases became endemic, only occasionally flaring up into epidemics; but by the time this happened, the populations had shrunk to possibly one-tenth of their size at contact.

The size of the populations when Cortés arrived in 1519, the rate of their decline, and hence the extent of the collapse of the population are the subjects of intense debate with implications for our understanding not just of the conquest process and the shape of the colonial society that emerged at the end of the 16th century but also for our understanding of the impact of the pre-Hispanic populations on the environment. Estimates of the native population at contact for the area covered by present-day Mexico range from as few as 2 million to as many as 25 million. Given the nature of the documentation of 16th–century populations, the debate between "maximalists," who argue for a large contact population and a truly appalling drop in numbers, and "minimalists," who argue for a smaller population and a less dramatic collapse, probably cannot be resolved. Even when researchers shift their focus from absolute numbers of the magnitude of the decline—whether the demographic collapse was on the order of 90, 80, or 50 percent—there is heated discussion. But regardless of the stand taken by individual researchers on questions of numbers and rate of decline, none question the central fact of a demographic collapse.

The decline of the indigenous populations was reflected in the landscape: Lands under cultivation shrank and fallow expanded; urban centers were depopulated, cities and towns became smaller, and some villages disappeared. At the same time as the indigenous presence in the landscape was reduced, their communities were reorganized according to new systems of administration and production developed by the Spaniards. This, in turn, meant that the Spanish presence in the landscape became more noticeable—even though the invading population remained much smaller than the indigenous one. But whatever their actual numbers at contact, and despite the dramatic decline in their populations and the economic and political domination of the Spaniards after the mid–16th century, the indigenous populations remained numerically in the majority—and this fact shaped Spanish actions and the development of colonial society. After the nadir of the population crash in the early 1600s, the indigenous populations of New Spain began to grow, and by the end of the 18th century, their communities faced problems of overpopulation, land hunger, and water shortages. Indeed, all the ethnic groups making up the population of New Spain grew in numbers over the colonial era. The pressures and problems associated with increasingly dense populations were nowhere more noticeable than in the cities and towns of the viceroyalty. These cities became the sites of epidemics associated with overcrowding and poor hygiene: cholera, for example, and typhoid. And the city fathers began the process of separating purely "urban" from strictly "rural" pursuits.

The absolute decline of the indigenous populations and their spatial reorganization during the 16th century, followed by a steadily increasing population over the 17th and 18th centuries; the rapid increase in the populations of the introduced animals and their subsequent collapse the development of new systems of resource exploitation; and, of course, the addition of many new crops, fruit trees, flowers and weeds—all had consequences for the vegetation of New Spain. The picture is complicated by the fact that nowhere do we find a straightforward replacement of indigenous populations by Spaniards or of indigenous systems of land use and land management by Spanish systems. Neither did indigenous systems of land use persist uncontaminated by the adoption of new plants or animals. To the contrary, the indigenous peoples adopted most of the exotic species (with a couple of important exceptions), even though, as we will see, these species brought with them many—sometimes profound—ecological social, and cultural changes. Current research is beginning to demonstrate patterns in the shifts and changes in the vegetation of New Spain.

As discussed earlier in the chapter, we can state with a fair degree of accuracy that deforestation in the pre-Hispanic era was directly related to the density of human populations. Roughly speaking, deforestation was advanced in regions with large, dense human populations, where land had been cleared to provide space for the intensive agriculture needed to produce food. Deforestation was correspondingly less advanced in regions where small, sparse human populations were scattered across the landscape.

The direct correlation of human populations with deforestation changed as the Spaniards expanded into New Spain. In the era of Spanish settlement there was no longer a direct relationship between deforestation and dense human populations. In fact, the reverse was often true: Deforestation was more likely to occur in regions of low population density. As the Spaniards developed new and different systems of resource exploitation, they often moved into and cleared lands in sparsely settled regions. Silver mining and grazing, two of the most important forms of Spanish resource use, were developed to their greatest extent far from urban centers. The great silver mines of Zacatecas and Guanajuato, for example, were located in the sparsely settled northern lands, hundreds of kilometers from Mexico City. Although grazing was carried out close to the urban centers, the huge grazing haciendas that became such a typical feature of Mexican economic life and culture also developed to their greatest extent in the north.

Mining was associated with extensive tree cutting because silver mining required large amounts of lumber for the construction of mine shafts, as well as wood for fuel to burn the ore and separate out the silver. Miners drew heavily on the forests within an increasing radius around the mining settlements. Future forest regeneration would have been possible, but the areas around the mines generally remained clear of trees because they were used for food production and for ranching. Huge numbers of animals were needed, their skins utilized for the myriad uses leather was put to in the era before plastic; for example, to make the bags

This map on Amate paper pictures the lands within Texcoco around 1540. This kind of pictorial record, done in the pre-Hispanic style, continued to be produced to record land, census, and tribute information well after the Spanish arrived. The map has both Spanish and Nahuatl descriptions, references to seventy-five plots of land, and, in the lower left, depictions of European fruit tree grafts on native trees.

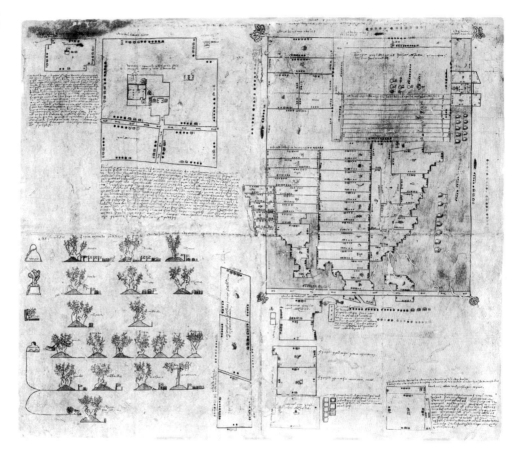

in which the ore was carried out of the mines. Live animals were used to mix the ore and to carry the silver to Mexico City, and, of course, animals provided meat.

Land clearance was still carried out near urban centers in the conquest era. The Spaniards accelerated tree cutting already under way for the production of lime, and most likely also for charcoal manufacture (there is some question as to whether charcoal was produced prior to contact). They cut for lumber to build their cities and towns, including immense numbers of trees for lumber for church roofs. But although tree cutting was still associated with urban areas, it was no longer carried out to clear land for the production of foodstuffs and raw materials for huge rural and urban populations. Indeed, the indigenous communities were reduced by up to 90 percent during the 16th and early 17th centuries, as their populations succumbed to the diseases carried by the invaders. This demographic collapse resulted in the retraction of indigenous agricultural fields, often to the best lands available, the humid bottom lands. There was a corresponding increase in fallow lands, a process that could—and in places did—lead to forest regrowth. But the regeneration of native forests on fallow lands, as on the lands cleared for wood and lumber for mining, was often retarded by Spanish land use and land

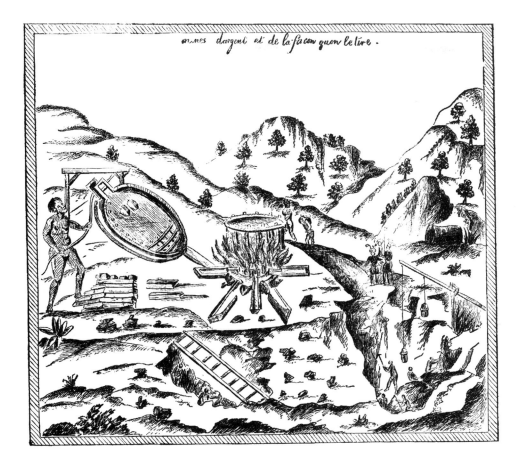

armes d'argent et de la façon quon le tire.

At the beginning of the 17th century, the Spaniards still employed a rudimentary method of reduction to produce silver. In this image of a silver mine in 1599, Indian workers carry leather bags of ore from the mine shaft.

management practices. And again, as in the mining areas, perhaps the most important, and certainly the most extensive, of these new practices was grazing.

Before looking at the impact of grazing on native vegetation and soils, however, we will examine two important new crops that replaced indigenous agriculture in certain parts of New Spain: wheat and sugar. Wheat was one of the most important crops for the Spaniards, and they made efforts to have it grown by the indigenous farmers as part of their tribute payments—with little success. The problem with wheat was that it represented a replacement of the indigenous grain, maize, and as such it faced stiff competition on grounds of custom and preference. It faced competition from maize on religious grounds as well. Maize was more than the staff of life for the Native peoples; it was a critical element of their worldview and their belief systems. Wheat cultivation had other problems. When wheat was sown in the spring and harvested in the fall—at exactly the same time the indigenous farmers were planting and cultivating maize—it competed with maize for labor. Not only that, a spring sowing meant that wheat was coming to maturity during the summer season of heavy rains; and the crops often failed under heavy rains and occasional frosts. Added to these problems, the types of wheat suitable for the production of bread were subject to rust and root rot. When the Spanish agriculturalists realized the disadvantages of a spring sowing, they shifted to sowing in the fall, using irrigation during the dry winter months, with a spring harvest. The schedule change solved a lot of their problems but made it necessary to build huge barns to store the wheat and protect it from early rains. In the case of wheat, then, we find the Spaniards having to adapt their scheduling to indigenous work schedules and climate.

Sugar production, by contrast, appears to have had a greater impact on the environment of New Spain than the reverse. Labor and scheduling problems in the production of sugar were solved by importing African slaves, and climatic conditions were favorable, as hot regions with ample water supplies were exactly what sugar required. But sugar production also required an abundant supply of firewood to cook the crushed cane and extract the sugar, representing a heavy drain on soil nutrients.

Although they were very important to the developing colonial economy, sugar and (especially) wheat cultivation were, relatively speaking, quite restricted in extent. By contrast, grazing animals very quickly spread into virtually every part of the colony, and herding—whether part of household, village, or hacienda economies—was, by the end of the 16th century, a pervasive fact of colonial life. The simple introduction of pigs, goats, sheep, cattle, horses, and donkeys initiated often profound changes in the composition of plant communities.

When ungulates (hard-hoofed grazing animals such as sheep, cattle, pigs, and horses) are introduced into alien ecosystems, they require a period of acclimatization that takes about 11 to 13 years to complete. When they have adjusted to the new climates and vegetation, the animals begin to multiply extremely rapidly. (If they do not acclimate, they die out, and this did occur in some places, especially where temperate-zone animals failed to make the adjustment to hot, humid tropical climates.) The key to the rapid increase in the ungulate populations is the amount of forage available. If there is more than sufficient to enable the animals to replace the population, the ungulate populations enter what is known as an irruptive phase and begin to increase at remarkably rapid rates. With an abundance of food, females begin to reproduce at an earlier age, the percentage of live births increases, and a larger percentage of the young survive. The population grows until it overshoots the food supply, at which time the animals starve and the population crashes. When the population falls to the point at which the remaining vegetation can support it, the population stabilizes. The entire process—increase, overshoot, crash, and finally adjustment—is called an ungulate irruption.

Vegetation communities go through a reciprocal trajectory: They decline in bulk as the animal populations increase, and they recover somewhat as the animal populations crash. Finally, the plant and animal populations accommodate to each other. This accommodation is dynamic, and plant and animal communities continue to oscillate around each other: The animals will begin to increase whenever there is an excess of vegetation and crash when they overshoot the carrying

Indigenous farmers hoeing corn. Civilization came to the region we now call Mexico with the domestication of crops, especially squash, beans, chiles, and above all corn. Throughout the twists and turns of political, economic, and social events, the corn tortilla has remained the staff of life in Mexico.

capacity of the range. The process, from introduction of the alien animals to accommodation between animals and plants, takes between 35 and 40 years and is called an irruptive oscillation.

There is much more going on in the plant communities than shifting quantities of vegetation, however. As the ungulates expand into a new ecosystem, they stimulate quite radical changes in the structure and composition of plant communities. Tall grasses are replaced by shorter grasses and herbs. Bare spaces between plants increase, and hotter, drier microniches form, which are invaded by arid-zone species—cacti, for example. Plants that cannot withstand browsing and trampling are replaced by browse-resistant or unpalatable species that generally have a higher proportion of wood to foliage. Mesquite is a typical invasive woody species in the arid and semi-arid regions of Mexico; ocotillo is a superbly armed species whose woody trunk and branches are covered with hard sharp spines that defy even goats. As the composition and structure of the vegetation changes, so do the associated faunal populations. The end result is a transformed biological regime.

Humans indirectly influence the changes in vegetation because they control the numbers and densities of the animals. When pastoralists hold their animals at very high densities, for example, they amplify the vegetation changes and run the risk of overgrazing—of removing such a high percentage of the vegetative cover that it cannot recover in one growing season. Where overgrazing occurs, the likelihood of forest regeneration is reduced because the animals eat the tree seedlings and ring-bark saplings, and even, in their desperation, dig up the roots. They not only transform the vegetation as they move into the ecosystems of the region but often remove it entirely, with devastating consequences for soil and water supplies. The loss of forage leads the pastoralists to attempt to improve forage for their herds, and their actions can lead to both irreversible changes in vegetation and erosion.

The favored technique for increasing the growth of the vegetative cover in New Spain, as in many parts of the world, was burning, and by the last quarter of the 16th century a pall of smoke hung over the grazing lands of the central highlands in the early spring as the field hands set fires to stimulate the regrowth of grasses. The combination of overgrazing, trampling by hard-hoofed animals, and burning opened the soils to the scouring effects of wind and rain. And in heavily grazed regions such as the Valle del Mezquital, which lies across the northern end of the Valley of Mexico, extensive erosion was reported by the end of the 16th century.

Erosion patterns exhibit clearly the complexity of the environmental changes brought about by the Spanish invasion and settlement. Pre-Hispanic patterns of erosion were associated with dense human populations; as we have already noted, archaeologists have found clear evidence of erosion, particularly where steep slopes were cleared and cultivated without taking sufficient care to prevent slips and washouts. Erosion in the conquest era, by contrast, often occurred in areas that were characterized by very low or falling densities of human populations, where accelerated tree cutting for mining and the manufacture of charcoal and lime, burning, and/or overgrazing put unusual pressure on the soils by removing the vegetative cover and opening the soils to erosion. Grazing animals can put undue pressure on the soils in other ways: Soil is compacted and hardened as cattle move to and from water sources, and the channels thus created act to direct water, often initiating gullying.

The likelihood of erosion also appears to have increased with the change in methods of plowing. The European plow disturbed the soil far more deeply than the indigenous foot plow, thereby loosening the soil and making it more vulnerable to increased wind erosion. Plowing also formed rows that channeled rainwater in ways that the mounds made by the indigenous farmers did not, thereby increasing water erosion. That is, erosion also occurred in agricultural regions near population clusters, as it had in the pre-Hispanic era. But it was no longer associated with land clearance for huge populations of humans; instead, it was more likely to be associated with huge flocks of sheep and goats and herds of cattle.

Students of Mexican landscapes and environments are just beginning to trace the changes in the vegetative cover and soils that were associated with the Spanish invasion and settlement. The picture is complicated by a lack of information about the extent and type of tree cover present before the Spaniards arrived, and our conclusions concerning the impact of the Spaniards and their portmanteau biota are therefore tentative. Nonetheless, we can see a couple of broad patterns. The first is that extensive deforestation associated with Spanish settlement was no longer associated with land clearance for huge populations of humans, as it had been in the pre-Hispanic era; rather, it was very often associated with large populations of grazing animals, as well as mines. The second tentative generalization we can make is that extensive deforestation in the colonial era and associated erosion were increasingly located in sparsely settled places that were very often great distances from the former urban centers. At the same time, however, we must note that because urban centers continued to be associated with often quite intensive agriculture, and because that agriculture now involved domesticated animals such as cattle, pigs, and goats—and the use of the European plow—accelerated deforestation and erosion continued to occur around urban centers in the conquest and colonial eras. Rural regions could see increased tree cover as the indigenous populations, and their cultivated fields, decreased in number and density. Thus, the impact of the Spanish invasion on vegetation and soils did not result in the simple replacement of indigenous patterns by Spanish; on the contrary, we find a far more fluid situation that is not easily predicted by either indigenous or Spanish experience.

Wheat, bread, and milk products such as cheese, meats such as pork and mutton, and fruits such as oranges—to say nothing of wine, olives, and olive oil—were considered essential for the continuation of civilized settled life by the Europeans. And, starting in 1493 with Columbus's second voyage to the New World, the Spaniards began the process by which they, and the other Europeans who followed them, introduced the animals and plants so necessary to their diet into the American environments. These species were first taken to the Caribbean islands and from there introduced into the mainland by conquistadores as well as settlers. In 1519, Cortés and his men went to the mainland with 16 horses and many war dogs, and in 1540 Francisco Vázquez de Coronado took a huge herd of pigs and horses on his journey north into what is now the southwest of the United States. As the Spaniards settled, they bred flocks of sheep and goats, chickens and ducks, herds of pigs, cattle, horses, and donkeys, as well as mules for carriage, plowing, and riding (mules were particularly appreciated for their smooth gait).

The introduced animals did very well in the new lands; indeed, many of the grazing animals escaped their human minders (or were deliberately set free) and became feral, fending for themselves in grasslands and woodlands, and increasing at staggering rates into immense populations. Some, like horses, took longer to adapt to the American environments and to begin to reproduce, but once they had adapted, they also began to multiply, and travelers wrote wonderingly of horses without number on the northern plains. The animal populations that remained under human control in the very densely settled agricultural regions also grew to enormous size and began to compete with the indigenous humans for space and water. The animals invaded the croplands and polluted drinking water; they ate plants the indigenous communities needed for medicine and food and trampled others. As their numbers exceeded the carrying capacity of the land and they starved, the animals dug up roots in their desperation. By the 1540s, the Indians were besieging the Spanish officials with complaints of animals destroying their

This Nahuatl account of the conquest of Mexico depicts Aztecs watching the Cortés expedition disembark. The Spanish have livestock—a novelty in the Americas—and other cargo. In addition to the horses, the crew unloads sheep, pigs, and a plow ox while a Spanish clerk keeps a record of the cargo.

crops—and of shepherds and cowboys ravaging their women. The Spanish government responded by passing laws that attempted to control the movement of livestock: The grazing of Spanish livestock was limited to a minimum distance of 1,000 paces beyond any village, the use of harvest stubble as forage was restricted to a period from January 1 to February 28, *ganado mayor* (cattle and horses) were expelled to regions outside the densely populated central areas, and grants for the right to graze livestock were to be made for lands well away from the villages.

As the human populations collapsed due to death from disease and their agricultural fields shrank, the expanding animal populations caused fewer problems. And, later in the 16th century, the animal populations collapsed in their turn—bringing about a crisis in wool and meat production. But by the time this happened, grazing had become a critical feature of the landscapes of New Spain, and of its economy, society, and culture. Even where dense indigenous settlement could have provided serious obstacles to land takeover, livestock owners had succeeded in acquiring extensive areas of land. A closer examination of the ways in which the introduced grazing animals expanded into the lands of New Spain indicates that they made spaces for the human invaders, which were later transformed into formal title. The expansion of grazing was successful because the grazing animals arrived with conquering humans. But the reverse was also true: The expansion of grazing—and later the acquisition of territory—succeeded because the animals themselves were, in Alfred Crosby's terms, "weedy" opportunistic species that thrived in disturbed conditions. Let us examine how power and biology combined to enable Spanish expansion and conquest.

The first question we have to ask is how the Spaniards were able to introduce their animals into regions that were already densely populated. The question may seem somewhat surprising because conquerors generally get to do as they please, and in any case, not all land was used for agriculture. Surely the conquering Spanish pastoralists could put their animals in those "unused" lands? But recent research has shown us that the Spaniards could not do as they pleased (at least at first) for the simple reason that there were very few of them, while the indigenous populations numbered in the millions, and it has also become clear that the most attractive lands for grazing were precisely the densely populated agricultural lands, where the water sources so necessary for the survival of the animals were well developed.

The Spaniards were successful in introducing their animals into densely populated agricultural lands for two reasons: First, the numbers of these animals, at least initially, were very small; and second, according to medieval Spanish law and custom, livestock could graze on grass wherever it grew, which meant that the livestock owners did not have to have title to a specific piece of land in order to keep grazing animals. As long as the pastoralists did not claim exclusive right to land but continued to graze their animals alongside crop lands and practice a sort of mixed farming, and as long as the numbers of animals remained small and the flocks were well tended so they didn't stray into croplands, there was little cause for complaint, and these odd new creatures were added to the landscape along with their (mostly African) minders with little difficulty. Spanish agriculture, by contrast, needed to have access to a specific area of soil and thus ran up against the millions of indigenous farmers who already owned and used the best arable lands.

The second question we need to address is how the pastoralists were able to develop huge flocks within the settled agricultural regions; that is, how they were able to expand. In 1952, Lesley Byrd Simpson suggested that the animal populations increased to fill the lands left vacant by the demographic collapse of the human populations. But when the introduction of sheep in the 16th century into a region located in the central highlands known as the Valle del Mezquital was examined more closely, it was found that the animal populations grew exponentially and expanded across the land before the human populations collapsed and that the animals competed with the agriculturalists.

It was also found that the animal populations crashed at around the same time as the human populations slid into the nadir of their own collapse. In other words, grazing animals increased and decreased despite dense human populations, and the answer to the problem of their successful expansion did not lie in the removal of the human competitors by disease, as Simpson had suggested. Rather, the reason for their success was to be found in unexpected consequences of the policies aimed at protecting the indigenous communities, and in the transformation of the vegetation that occurred as the animals moved into the American environments. For example, the law keeping the Spaniards out of a league radius around towns and villages actually worked to restrict Indian autonomy to the lands immediately around their villages and gave the Spaniards a freer hand in the considerably larger area outside the village lands. The expansion of Spanish control over how the land was to be used, and the concurrent restriction of Indian control, was increased by the growing numbers of grants for grazing in lands away from the villages, this meant that traditional resource areas like woodlands were under siege as well as the agricultural lands. This, in turn, meant that the changes associated with the expansion of the alien animals into new niches occurred over an ever larger extent of land. Sometimes the transformation of the landscape was so complete that evidence of former systems of land use were completely erased, leaving evidence only of grazing. Such landscape changes were used by the Spanish pastoralists to confirm their title to land: Spanish law gave primacy of ownership to the current user of the land, and pastoralists could argue that because there was no sign of crop cultivation but every sign of the land's having been grazed for years, they had the right to the land itself—and not simply to the grasses and other vegetation growing on it. In this way, pastoralists were able to move considerable areas of land out of the indigenous systems of land holding and into the Spanish system.

But this is not a simple story of the imposition of unwanted cultural items on a hapless colonized peasantry. The "push factors" represented by an "invading force" of humans, and all the environmental changes associated with invasion by alien animals, certainly help to explain how vast territories ended up in the Spanish system of land tenure in a very short space of time. But there were "pull factors" at work here as well. And it is clear that the ultimate success of the alien animals was further aided by the fact that the indigenous peoples adopted them with great enthusiasm once the many advantages of a continuous supply of meat and leather, and the superior warmth and comfort of wool, became clear. They certainly resisted the pressure of the growing Spanish herds on their agricultural lands; but they did not reject animal herding itself. And it is more than likely that a large number of the flocks and herds that brought about the transformation of native vegetation were owned by indigenous communities and individual elites as well. Indeed, we have extensive evidence from regions such as Oaxaca, Tlaxcallan, Meztitlan, and the Valle del Mezquital that indigenous groups and individual pastoralists held title to extensive areas of grazing land. The introduction of the grazing animals into the agricultural lands was somewhat after the manner of introducing a Trojan horse: It was not often the case that huge herds were moved into a region; rather, they expanded and took over space from within. The tiny flocks and herds that were introduced at first had little impact, but then they began to grow, to expand in situ and to change local environments. The indigenous communities became part of a pastoral as well as an agricultural world.

The history of the expansion of grazing confirms Crosby's thesis of the importance of biological factors for the success of European expansion. The introduced grazing animals were successful because they did not come alone—they were an integral part of a much larger "invasion force," if you will—and the invading humans were successful because they came with a portmanteau biota that caused such profound environmental changes that, even though the Europeans were not numerically dominant, they were able to gain control of land and people.

Different forms of agro-pastoralism developed in New Spain, reflecting responses to local environmental conditions, to local cultures, and to local needs. In some cases the systems of range and livestock management that had evolved in Spain were carried to the new lands and set up in similar environments. For example, Spanish cattle herders from the marshlands in the south of Spain, *las marismas*, moved to the swamps in Pánuco on the Gulf Coast and developed similar systems of open-range grazing there. On the highland plains distinctive systems of open-range cattle management developed that became characteristic of American practices: Huge herds of feral cattle were "rounded up" every year and branded or slaughtered principally for their hides. It is intriguing how similar the village household herding practices that developed in New Spain are to peasant practices in other parts of the world, despite the fact that herding was new to the indigenous peoples. Because of the need to control flocks around village lands, for example, peasant herders took their animals out in the day to graze and brought them back at night to corrals next to their houses.

Different breeds evolved in New Spain, as in the rest of the Americas. In fact, variants of the original species developed that were highly adapted to the local environments, the so-called *criollo* breeds. These ecotypes are so important to local economies and environments that it is now often necessary to crossbreed the improved breeds with the criollo breeds so that the newcomers are not rejected by the local ecosystems.

It is hard to imagine the Mexican landscapes without Eurasian grazing animals. A Mexican village without pigs, goats, and possibly some sheep, cattle, donkeys and/or mules, or horses is almost inconceivable. And the northern Mexican landscapes are identified with huge latifundios with thousands of head of livestock. We have examined some of the changes brought about by the introduction of these animals, especially the development of extensive herding. We noted that erosion resulted from accelerated tree cutting and overgrazing. Another environmental impact of the development of huge herds of grazing animals and the changes in vegetation and soils was seen in changes in the water resources of the region.

In the highland central valleys of Mexico, Puebla, and the Mezquital, people complained about increasing dryness during the colonial era. There were reports of fewer rains, of springs that dried out, and of previously perennial rivers and streams that flowed only part of the year. Spanish land management practices may have played a part in the desiccation of the highlands; but the picture is complicated by environmental and social factors. For example, the colonial era (approximately 1580–1810) fell within the so-called Little Ice Age, a period that was characterized by lower than usual rainfall in some areas. It is also clear that much of the water shortage experienced during the colonial era, especially in the 18th century, was artificial, and rather than being entirely a result of absolute decline in the quantity of water available, was a factor of the political economy of New Spain and increasing populations. And, indeed, water management and distribution demonstrates more clearly than any other aspect of colonial life the inequalities and differential access to power of the various groups making up the society and the economy.

That said, however, it should be pointed out that similar processes to those introduced by the Spaniards, such as accelerated tree cutting and deforestation and the initiation of overgrazing and extensive plowing, have resulted in increasing aridity in other parts of the world. All these practices result in the removal of ground cover; in the case of grazing and plowing, they also channel the flow of surface water. Where the ground cover is removed, water flows more freely over the surface and can result in flooding. In an apparent paradox, the same process of clearance retards the amount of water soaked up by the soil—because water is not detained for sufficient time by surface litter and stems and stalks to allow it to soak into the soil; and where livestock have formed paths, or plowing has furrowed the soil, surface waters are channeled and runoff is increased. The result is a drop in the amount of water reaching the water tables, and hence a reduction in spring and stream flow. Whether these practices actually reduced rainfall is unclear. Folk wisdom says that deforestation results in lowered rainfall; scientists are not so sure.

Before we examine more closely the social and economic pressures on water supplies in the late colonial era, let us look briefly at the differences between Indian and Spanish attitudes toward water management. There were many things about indigenous water management, and especially the distribution of irrigation waters, that were familiar to the Spaniards. Where rainfall was abundant, the indigenous farmers grew rain-fed crops. Where rainfall was low and water scarce, they trapped water in dams, changed river courses, and channeled water to their fields through irrigation canals. They also used terraces on steep hillsides and long low slopes to regulate water for their crops and to provide adequate planting surfaces. Where water was too abundant and flooding occurred, they drained the excess away though systems of ditches. All these were familiar systems of land management, and the Spaniards often took them over with little change. They used the indigenous systems of canal irrigation, for example, expanding them in some places and improving them in others.

But there were other indigenous technologies that were not familiar at all; that reflected a very different approach to water and soil management—and to water itself. The major difference lies in the attitudes toward still waters and marshlands. The Spanish perceived still waters as stagnant and unhealthy and marshes as infertile and dangerous; healthy clean water was water that moved. By contrast, Indians viewed marshlands as optimum places for the development of intensive agricultural systems, and where lakes and marshes provided standing water and rich bottom mud, they developed highly productive systems of wetlands management.

The best known example of wetlands agriculture, the chinampa system, was developed in the marshlands ringing the lakes of the Valley of Mexico. Chinampa agriculture exemplifies the differences between Spanish and Indian attitudes to still waters. The genius of chinampa agriculture is its use of marshland edge habitats as a model for the development of intensive agricultural ecosystems. Chinampas reproduce the islands found in marshes, and allow the regulation of soil water so that all manner of grains, fruits, and vegetables can be grown continuously. Rather than draining the marshes, the indigenous farmers developed a system of alternating water and land; and extended agriculture out into the lake so that by 1519 almost a third of Lake Xochimilco was covered in growing surface.

By contrast, the Spaniards used wetlands as dry-season grazing lands or attempted to drain them so that they were suitable for plow agriculture. Their lack of understanding of the principles and techniques involved in chinampa agriculture was reflected in the fact that while they took over and used pre-Hispanic systems of canal irrigation, they left wetlands agriculture in the hands of the indigenous farmers. At the same time, however, they began to drain the Valley of Mexico. The Valley of Mexico lies in an inland basin with no natural external drainage, and up to the end of the 16th century the basin contained extensive lake systems. During the middle decades of the 16th century the Spaniards were plagued by persistent flooding of the city of Mexico Tenochtitlán. The Aztecs before them had faced the same problems, as had all those who had lived on the lakes—although it is possible that the Aztecs and the Spaniards had exacerbated the problem by deforesting the foothills of the surrounding mountains. But whereas the Aztec engineers had worked with the wetlands and had built dikes to regulate the water levels in the lakes, the Spaniards decided to get rid of the water. In this way, they reasoned, they would correct the problem of flooding and gain extensive areas of land for agriculture. And so, rejecting the advice of Aztec engineers and using European technology, they began the ill-fated *desagüe* project and carved a channel from the northwest of the Valley of Mexico to connect with the Tula River system. The consequences for the environment of the Valley of Mexico can be seen to this day: The dry seasons are plagued by dust storms as the fine soils of the former lake beds are blown by the winds of February and March; in the wet seasons the water cannot drain away because the water tables remain very high; and shallow lakes extend across the former lake beds, making agriculture next to impossible. Because the Mexico City sits on water-logged soils, the heavy buildings tilt at precarious angles and the city faces the problem of getting rid of not only the wastewater of nearly 20 million people but also the runoff from the heavy summer rains—due to the high water table, it cannot soak into the soil and must be channeled out of the valley.

As the indigenous populations declined over the 16th century, new systems of land use were implemented. In moving from indigenous systems of land holding to Spanish title, village lands were more and more restricted. As long as their populations remained small, however, the loss of extensive areas of their former agricultural lands does not appear to have caused immediate difficulties. In any case, it appears that the Indians held on to the very fertile humid bottom lands in many places—to the vast irritation of their Spanish neighbors. But as they acquired immunities to the diseases introduced in the 16th century, and these diseases became endemic in the American populations, village populations began to grow and to press on the available land—and on water resources. At the same time, the population of Spaniards and Africans, and mestizos and mulattoes, also expanded, so that by the mid–18th century, the number of people from all ethnic groups in New Spain had grown to about 7 million. All these people needed water, and water supplies became the focus of intense conflict as the colonial era wore on.

As the population grew and the amount of water required for human consumption in villages, towns, and cities increased, the amount available to each individual correspondingly decreased. At the same time, the volume of water decreased in absolute terms: Spring flow declined as the water tables dropped; and while surface water could be trapped in dams, most seemed to have washed away across the land in the violent summer storms. The problems posed by real shortages—of decreasing volumes of available water for more and more people—were amplified by artificial shortages that were the result of the inequitable distribution of water typical of colonial society.

The major contenders in the struggle for water in the Mexican countryside were municipalities (villages, towns, and cities), landowners (large landowners such as hacendados, plantation owners, and monasteries, and smaller landowners such as ranchers and labor owners), and manufacturers (of wheat flour, wool, and leather). Landed estates that specialized in wheat production and plantations growing sugar needed considerable amounts of water. As noted above, wheat was grown in the central highlands in the dry winter months and required irrigation water to germinate the seeds; sugar was another crop requiring irrigation water, especially when it was grown in regions of marked seasonal variation. Streams were dotted with flour mills that also required water power to function.

By the 18th century, complex systems of water distribution linked these units, and there was ample opportunity for conflict. Confrontation between these groups was played out on the ground and in court: It could result from the simple diversion of water from irrigation canals or streams, or it could arise from a disagreement over title to water rights. Conflicts could be resolved without violence, with the parties agreeing to a certain distribution of water, or they could be as threatening as the standoff between a village and a private army. The importance of rural products for the economy of New Spain, and the often considerable resources of landed estates, meant that large landowners held correspondingly greater power in these conflicts. They had the means to hire thugs to defend illegal water diversion or to frighten villagers and small landowners; and they could continue to pursue lawsuits until the other side ran out of money. Villages and smaller landowners were not without resources, however. The most effective was geographical location—location at the head of an irrigation system gave considerable bargaining power. And villagers were not above intimidation and sabotage either: The records of decades-long court cases between villages and landowners (and between villages) extending back to the conquest testify to the importance of water and to the tenacity of the villages in defending their rights. But overall, water was consistently diverted to haciendas and plantations from the other social groups.

The municipalities required more and more water for their growing populations—animal as well as human—and for the increasing number of processing plants, mills, and textile manufactories. As urban areas expanded in the 18th century, they grew around processing installations, such as tanneries, and livestock corrals and slaughterhouses, which were generally located on the edge of town. The inclusion of such places, along with often very large numbers of animals, had consequences for water distribution, as well as for water pollution and disease environments. The city of Puebla provides us with an example of an urban environment in the late 18th century that demonstrates the pressures placed on the volume and cleanliness of the water supplies by the presence of large numbers of domestic animals—in this case, an enormous population of pigs.

Water is critical for life; that much is obvious. What is not so obvious is how very differently people define not just the use of water—whether it is to be used for irrigating maize fields or diverted to flour mills, for example—but also what constitutes the correct place of water in the environment, its very nature. For Europeans the stagnant still waters of the marshlands were unhealthy places to be drained where possible; for the indigenous peoples the marshlands were miracles of richness and productivity. The fact that the Spaniards and their systems of land management came to dominate the colonial landscapes meant that the presence of water in the environment changed in character, moving toward increasing aridity. As a result, the landscapes of conquest and civilization differed markedly from the pre-Hispanic landscapes.

The years following the Spanish entry into the lands that became New Spain were years of rapid and profound change in the structure of indigenous populations and society, landscapes and environments. The transformations that Díaz del Castillo lamented reflected much more than the simple imposition of Spanish social, political, and economic systems on the lands and people they invaded; they also encompassed processes of mutual adjustment between indigenous ecosystems and invading species, and between the invading and the native human populations.

In an outpouring of innovative writing, historians of the Conquest have presented us with descriptions and analyses of the colonial world that have expanded our understanding of conquest and domination (see Chapter 3). These new histories make it clear that the process of conquest was not the simple domination of one group by another; the new American worlds were fluid and extraordinarily complex. The fact of the matter was that the Spaniards were few and the indigenes many—so many, in fact, that despite crippling epidemics and a resulting decline in population size of up to 92 percent over the first 100 years, the indigenous populations still remained demographically in the majority. And because of the large numbers of indigenous peoples, Europeans were not automatically powerful; they were forced to negotiate with indigenous peoples who were not always and everywhere victims. The process of negotiation implies compromise and adaptation by everyone and in all areas of life, and the societies that evolved out of the conquest process were syncretic and hybridized.

The colonial era is often contrasted with the conquest era and pictured as a stagnant and unchanging time, a period when colonial societies and economies became entrenched and underwent little development. But although the colonial era was less spectacular than the conquest era, the status quo was not maintained. The colonial era was a period of increasing complexity as populations grew in size and in ethnic complexity, and these changes had implications for the landscapes and environments of New Spain.

The landscapes of colonial Mexico did not simply reflect the replacement of indigenous cultures by Spanish (or African) cultural elements. Nor did they reflect its obverse—the persistence of indigenous cultures and societies—although the indigenous peoples were remarkably successful in reproducing their societies and cultures despite the often striking environmental changes associated with the introduction of new species directly into their space and the development of entirely new forms of land management. Rather, they reflected choices and negotiation—as well as force.

In the struggle to maintain their individual worlds intact within the context of hybrid colonial societies, the different ethnic and economic groups that made up colonial society shaped and constrained one another, and change occurred as Spaniard and Indian, mestizo and mulatto, struggled to reproduce familiar landscapes, very often in the same space. A key characteristic of hybridized colonial societies is a preoccupation with place and displacement. The indigenous peoples have a sense that their place has been changed (often subtly, more often brutally), that the familiar has made unfamiliar. The incoming peoples, whether they come as administrators, settlers, or slaves, perceive a place for which they don't have words. Perhaps the only groups who are at home in the transformed colonial worlds are the new "ethnicities" that have evolved out of the mixing of invading and native groups: the mulattoes and mestizos. The picture is complicated by the fact that economic groups such as landed estates and municipalities also fought to control access to and use of elements of the landscape such as water and land.

It is not possible to move elements of the landscape around like pieces on a chessboard without affecting environmental processes, however. As we have seen, the addition of alien animals and their population explosion and crash, or the development of new systems of land use such as mining and grazing, brought about often profound changes in the physical environment. We can perceive a situation where multiple landscapes can exist in the same space—a kaleidoscope of landscapes and places that could be perceived as one shifted in and out of the different groups. The landscape from the vantage point of a hacienda was different from the same place viewed from an Indian village, for example. But it is difficult to see how we can have overlapping environments, since the ecological processes underlying the landscapes do not stop at the border—of the village, the hacienda, or what have you. The problem is resolved if we stop thinking of colonial societies and landscapes as collections of discrete elements. Colonial society was syncretic and hybridized, and the different ethnic and social and economic groups were all critical elements to the successful maintenance of colonial society. Colonial environments encompassed the places developed by different ethnic and social groups; they were physical expressions of social and biological syncretism and hybridity.

8

Women in Colonial Mexico

ASUNCIÓN LAVRIN

The encounter of European and indigenous peoples in the land thereafter called New Spain was mediated by an indigenous woman who served as "tongue" or translator to the conquerors. La Malinche or Doña Marina, the Nahua- and Maya-speaking woman who was given to Hernán Cortés by a coastal chief, was an invaluable companion to the conqueror. Without her adept intervention the task of understanding indigenous resources and mentalities would have been difficult for Cortés. Equally, the presence of her and other women in the ranks of the newcomers was more than a symbol of women's objectification in patriarchal societies. Women were the channels of rapprochement between the two cultures, and the beneficiaries, coparticipants, and victims of the process of conquest and settlement.

The conquest period altered significantly the situation of indigenous women, as the terms of understanding among them, the newly arrived Spaniards, and their own male relatives had to be recast in practical as well as religious and moral matters. While indigenous women were directly affected throughout this period as the subject of negotiations between men, when Spanish women began to arrive in significant numbers from the Iberian Peninsula the individual and social relations between men and women increased in complexity. Spanish women brought with them a culture totally European in values and expectations. Their exalted status as the female kin of the conquerors gave them social supremacy over other women that they and their offspring were to retain. Yet, three more groups of women added complexity to the picture. The offspring of Spaniards and Indian women, mestizas, were also joined by the small, albeit increasing, number of African women who began to arrive in the sixteenth century, and the biological products of the mixing of these three races, known as *castas*, were to complete the spectrum of women who populate Mexican colonial history. These three groups could, and did, establish ties at many levels (affective

Marriages between Indians and Spainiards were much more common and important in the 16th than in the 18th century (when this painting was made). By the 18th century men of the elite—such as the one depicted here—rarely married indigenous women, even if the women were cacicas.

and religious) and it is possible to write of circumstances that comprised all women as a gender. Yet, their experience was not homogeneous.

In the early colonial period, until the middle of the 17th century, the two most influential cultural elements were the indigenous and the Spanish, but mestizas and castas were of extraordinary importance from the midcolonial period onward. All racial and ethnic groups of all social classes had a common ground in their understanding that men held power and authority in the arenas of home and community. Men ruled, set the laws, and headed families. The exaltation of martial values among the Mexicas of Tenochtitlán was perhaps stronger than but not alien to that brought by the conquistadores, who had just finished the Reconquest of the peninsula from Islamic rulers. In both societies women received respect mostly for their reproductive and nurturing roles but were firmly kept out of decision making at the highest levels.

Once the conquest of the core region of central Mexico was accomplished, the lives of all men and women, the process of family formation, and the consensus that ruled gender relations would undergo a process of slow transformation in which the indigenous societies preserved some of their most sui generis community and personal practices but had to adapt to the common denominator contained in Spanish legislation, within which all women, regardless of ethnicity or race, were contained. The Siete Partidas, a law code written between 1256 and 1265 under the direction of Alfonso the Learned and promulgated in 1348 as the law of Castile, and the Laws of Toro, enacted in 1505, formulated the rights and duties of men and women as single members of society and as members of the family. These laws established the principle that women were legally subject to men in the family and in civil society. Men exercised *patria potestas*, the undisputed right to dictate their children's behavior and control their property until they became adults by their own marriage or by reaching age 23 for men and age 25 for women. Married women came under the legal jurisdiction of their husbands, so a single woman could only attain complete control over her decisions before age 25 if her father released his patria potestas, a very unlikely event. Husbands exercised nearly complete control over their wives. Complete juridical personhood was acquired as a single adult or as a widow. In that capacity women had the right to buy, sell, and administer property and money, inherit and bequeath, initiate suits in court, and appear as witnesses. Thus, it was a woman's civil status that determined the breadth of her freedom as an individual. As a husband a man had the right to determine who was to have guardianship over his children during their minority in case of his death. A husband could appoint a guardian outside the family or appoint his wife, which entitled her to exercise control over the children until they became of age or married. Children, regardless of sex, received equal shares of their parents' inheritance. The overarching rights of men over women and of husbands over their wives and children established the basis of a patriarchal system that gave men a privileged position.

While the laws put women, especially married women, under rather restrictive circumstances, they attempted to balance their situation with some protective measures, especially in regard to inheritance. The Laws of Toro protected a woman's property by forbidding her husband to dispose of it at will. Furthermore, a widow received half of the communal property acquired after marriage and up to the full value of her dowry, if she had brought one to her marriage. The condition of marriage imposed on a woman a severe compliance with her husband's will and granted him the right to represent her in all legal transactions. A man could and often did renounce his rights, which entitled the married woman to act with complete independence. Many of the woman's rights could be dissolved or placed at risk if her conduct was unbecoming. Thus, a father could disinherit an offspring for a number of reasons valid before the law. A widow could lose her control over her children if she remarried. A married woman involved in questionable sexual behavior lost many of her rights and gave cause to the aggrieved male party to take revenge against her and her lover to the degree that

The family of the Count of Penasco kneels before the Virgin of Guadalupe. This type of family portrait is not common in Mexico, but there were quite a few more in the 18th century than in the preceding century. Even so, most paintings of elite members of society in colonial Mexico are of individuals, not family groups.

he deemed appropriate. However, the exercise of such broad prerogatives was unusual, and it would be inaccurate to envision a society in which these restrictions were everyday practice.

As the Spaniards settled in what they began to call New Spain, they applied the principles of the Partidas to all peoples, regardless of race or class. In theory, all women were bound by the same strictures, but whether or not they were required in full was an issue beyond the scope of the law. Only slaves, as property, were not covered by legislation that applied to free people. Even so, slaves of both sexes had access to ecclesiastical and civil authorities insofar as their humanity was recognized before the law, and they sought recognition of rights under the principles of family, civil, and ecclesiastical law.

Aztec women controlled a number of rituals for worship and oversaw market functions, positions that gave them authority in community activities. Women of the pre-Conquest nobility had political roles to fulfill through arranged marriages, and recent archaeological discoveries point to the fact that as queens, women could exercise political power on behalf of their male sons, in a manner similar to that exercised by their counterparts in Europe. Legally, noble women who were considered adults before the law could inherit the right to land use and

Martin Xuchimitl was accused of having four sisters as his concubines. Missionaries were very concerned about the issue of concubinage. They attempted to uproot the custom from among the indigenous elite, the only social class that was allowed concubinage prior to the conquest.

tribute from vassals. *Cacicas*, or noblewomen (*principales*), in post-Conquest society claimed rights to land and tribute from pre-Hispanic laws as well as from the new peninsular legislation. Moreover, both Spanish and indigenous women simply assumed more responsibilities than the narrowly defined codes would seem to have allowed.

As upper-class indigenous women and subsequently other women of all conditions and ethnicities began to understand the legal system, they appeared as plaintiffs and defendants in a variety of cases. Since social and economic conditions in New Spain were different from those in the peninsula in the 15th and early 16th centuries, ad hoc legislation had to be adopted to fit situations specific to the needs of the viceroyalty. *Derecho Indiano* or law relative to the Indies (a term customarily applied by Spain to its possessions) addressed issues such as whether indigenous women were exempt from tribute, whether women could inherit *encomiendas* (the right to receive taxes from indigenous tributaries as a reward for service to the crown) or whether parents had any legal recourse against the marriage of their underage offspring to persons of recognized lesser social or racial standing. Another important legal and social issue raised by the Conquest was the resolution of polygamy practices among the indigenous nobility, a pre-Conquest right rejected by Christian principles. In fact, the church paid considerable attention to the inculcation of monogamy and the eradication of polygamy as one of its goals in the process of evangelization.

The process of conquest resulted in a meeting of the sexes that broke— temporarily—the established rules of personal conduct in both Spanish and indigenous societies. Each society had a code of behavior that regulated unions and legitimated family life for the sake of social order. Hernán Cortés and his men received women from indigenous chieftains, who hoped to establish kinship and political ties with the newcomers. From voluntary offer to open demand was only a short distance. The degree of abuse of such sexual contacts will remain unmeasurable, but it gave the evangelizers a tough problem to resolve. As they attempted to spread the teaching of the Christian rules of marriage to the Indians, they seemed unable or unwilling to control the behavior of male Spaniards for some time.

As the Spaniards began to procreate with indigenous women, the mestizo (Indian-Spanish) issue became a biological reality that eventually had important demographic as well as political significance. The process of *mestizaje* was carried out mostly between Spanish males and indigenous females. High-status females, such as daughters of chieftains and nobles, were much sought after. The Crown followed a wavering policy in setting a marriage policy for the newly discovered people and the future settlers. In the early stages of the Conquest in the Caribbean islands the Crown's policy was enunciated by men such as Cardinal Francisco Jiménez de Cisneros (archbishop of Toledo, 1495–1517), who in 1516 advised marriage with the daughters of caciques (chieftains). The expectation of the lay and religious authorities was that the children would be Spaniards in culture, and marriage was a policy of assimilation and overlordship. Many fewer indigenous noble males married Spanish women, but this was by no means a rare event. Among the first was Diego Luis Moctezuma, grandson of the emperor, who married a Spanish woman and became the founder of the powerful family of the Counts of Moctezuma.

The conquerors understood the fact that the indigenous nobility "endowed" their daughters in a manner similar to the peninsular practice, a fast method to acquire property and status. Spaniards seeking high-ranking indigenous wives were seeking profitable alliances. Indeed, these men, residing in the indigenous communities, attempted to infiltrate the local government, one of the reasons why the Crown soon tried to ban Spaniards from Indian towns. Indigenous women themselves had something to gain from such unions. Their husbands had access to the dominant society and knew all the legal recourses necessary to afford them protection in case of litigation in the courts of justice. While a legitimate marriage guaranteed a woman and her children access to property, consensual unions were apparently more frequent than legitimate ones, although there are no confirmed numbers for either in the initial stages of colonial settlement. Conquistadores such as Hernán Cortés and Pedro de Alvarado established consensual relationships with Indian women but, having achieved a high rank in Spanish society, sought peninsular women of equal status as their legitimate wives. Cortés, who had affairs with two of Moctezuma's daughters, married them off to well-born Spanish husbands and recognized his son with Malinche, providing for him in his will. Spanish officials everywhere in New Spain could and did maintain consensual relations with high-ranking women for purposes similar to those of the conquistadores. For the most part, such unions yielded more uncertain gains or losses to the parties. If the woman was abandoned, the man lost his contact and influence over the indigenous community.

While the indigenous population declined precipitously during the 16th century, the mixed-ancestry population grew in number and began to take its place in the demographic profile of the colony. By the 17th century mestizos, having reinforced their numbers by biological reproduction and augmented by Indian-Spanish unions, began to constitute the majority of the population of certain urban areas. The additional presence of Africans—who first arrived in New Spain as slaves or, less frequently, as free men—created a special situation of increasing interracial unions. No legislation forbade such unions, and the Catholic Church protected freedom of choice in legitimate marriages. Nevertheless, Spanish and indigenous social practice favored marriage between social and ethnic equals. Ecclesiastical advice leaned in that direction also without breaking the principle of freedom to chose. Those who did not care about social prescriptions lived or married according to their wishes. The resulting variety of racial and ethnic mixtures created a population that, although numerically indigenous in its majority, showed the results of random miscegenation, while peninsulares and their descendants remained a minority. The social result was the adoption of a loose sense of "race" whereby vertical or lateral ascent or passing was possible and where categories were not rigidly marked. This instability in the concept of race led those at the top of society, the descendants of *peninsulares* (peninsular Spaniards), to cling to the concept of racial purity in order to maintain their political control over the rest of the population and their position of power and authority in society. The concept of *limpieza de sangre* (cleanliness of blood) had been used in Spain to establish distinctions among Muslims, Jews, and Christians. Cleanliness of blood signified an ancestry of several generations without Jewish or Muslim input. In New Spain, cleanliness of blood would, in principle, include the original definition. Indeed, recently converted Jews and some Muslims (new Christians) established themselves in New Spain, and some of them were extremely successful explorers and settlers in the 16th century. Not until the late 16th century did the Inquisition begin a broad search for pseudo-Christians who were assumed still to be practicing Judaism under the cover. On the other hand, the infusion of Africans and the increasing multiplicity of mixtures in the population injected a new meaning into the concept of limpieza de sangre, which applied mostly to people with either African and Jewish ancestry.

The social situation of the first mestizos is difficult to ascertain, but it was guided by two factors: equality of class between the parents and legitimacy. Children born of Spanish men of social standing and indigenous women of equal social standing in their community, could reap the benefit of social recognition even if born out of wedlock, if the father took responsibility and the child was educated as a Spaniard. Contrariwise, children born of casual unions or as the result of the sexual exploitation of indigenous women, for whom the father eluded responsibility and who were raised by the mother, often remained "Indian" and suffered the stigma of their racial ambiguity by being excluded by the Spaniards and their descendants from access to higher education or appointment to bureaucratic positions. Their position within the indigenous community varied. By the mid–16th century many indigenous local leaders were biological mestizos and had not lost their social status. It was the poorer offspring of casual unions with *macegual* (commoner) indigenous women who remained in an equivocal and unresolved social situation. In time, this group found its niche in servicing many needs of the urban populations, in long-distance trade and in specialized crafts. The fate of mestizas was tied to their rank in society, since they had few occupational expectations and were assumed to fulfill their destiny as women by marrying and becoming mothers.

In order to establish and maintain social recognition Spanish men, whether conquerors or early or late settlers, would revert to the social notions from the motherland. They sought to reassert the concept of a clear *linaje* (lineage) by marrying peninsular women, who would preserve cleanliness of blood and legitimacy. Indeed, purity of blood was fundamental to those seeking to become members of the judiciary and the royal bureaucracy and those who aspired to ecclesiastical positions. Certificates and witnesses were required to prove limpieza de sangre. Peninsular women thus became an object of social desire, which quickly put them in a privileged situation vis-a-vis indigenous women, even those of Indian social distinction. While some Spaniards continued to marry or live with Indian women throughout the colonial period, it seems that this choice was mostly that of men of lesser social standing and in provincial or rural milieus rather than in important urban sites, let alone in the capital of the viceroyalty. At the highest peak of the immigration movement from Spain to the New World in the 16th century, white women comprised only 28 percent of the total number of peninsular immigrants. This means that their numbers were relatively small and that their stake in the marriage exchange was high. While peninsular women continued to arrive in lesser numbers, their offspring, the women born to peninsulares in New Spain, were classified as *españolas*, meaning of European descent, with its prestigious social and racial connotations. By the beginning of the 17th century the most common type of española was born in New Spain, not the peninsula. It is to them that the privilege of ancestry belonged for the rest of the colonial period.

Racial privilege did not necessarily ensure economic privilege. Spanish women were subject to the same vagaries of economic fate as men, and many who came with high hopes for improving their social position were disappointed. Enticed by male relatives or informed by news and rumors spread in the peninsula, they came seeking not only marriage but property, business, and the service of indigenous women. Men who had earned encomiendas fought arduously to preserve that right and pass it to their legal heirs. Legislation enacted shortly after the mid–16th century stipulated that single or intestate men would lose their encomienda. To retain that privilege they had to marry, and they mostly chose peninsular women for that purpose. Female encomienda holders were few, but they commanded power over an income and a social entitlement not available to the majority of women émigrés.

In their desire to carve a secure future for their daughters, settlers apparently began to endow them with generous dowries that attracted the best men available. Dowries consisted of either goods or properties brought by the women to marriage that the husband could administer during the marriage. A dowry in cash would provide the husband with ready capital to foster his interests. It is difficult to determine the quantity and size of these dowries, but in the last quarter of the 16th century men in positions of authority began to spread the notion that dowries had skyrocketed and were becoming an obstacle to the marriage of otherwise eligible young women with the right racial accreditation. The threatening possibility of having those women choose suitors who did not meet the standards of increasingly self-conscious social elite of the viceroyalty became one of their main preoccupations. Letters addressed to the Crown by bishops and comments elicited by royal officials in communication with Spanish authorities raised the specter of prostitution, a trumped-up explanation for their concern about the possible decline in the number of pure Spaniards.

To preserve and strengthen the social order a number of barriers were raised between women of Spanish descent and other women, and while those barriers were not as high as those raised among men—since women had no access to education or public service, as men did—in time they hardened to create a chasm between white and nonwhite women. Endowment practices initiated by 16th–century men began to separate white and nonwhite women. Endowment for marriage and profession in religious orders were popular forms of social "beneficence" in New Spain. Endowing a poor española to marry or helping her to profess was a way of either raising her above her status or of at least maintaining it. Throughout the colonial period Spaniards and their descendants (later called *criollos* or *españoles americanos*) created numerous endowments for white "orphan" girls for either marriage or profession. Orphan status was satisfied by the loss of one parent. These funds were administered either by confraternities or the episcopate and were not available to those who could not prove legitimacy and cleanliness of blood. The funds were invested to produce a yearly income that provided for 300–peso dowries. Each institution had a list of aspirants and allocated the moneys through a lottery. Three hundred pesos was a small amount, barely enough to rise above one's standing, but enough to attract a "decent" husband who would protect a girl. Besides, some girls were on several lists and gathered several of these dowries. Private endowments to allow a woman to profess were not unusual. Profession in a convent demanded a much higher sum of money (at least 2,000 pesos in the 17th century and 3,000 in the 18th century), and patrons had to be prepared to restrict the number of recipients. Intrafamilial patronage to favor relatives was not unusual and was another means to maintain an endogamious hold on women and to preserve class and racial distinctions.

Social mores privileging women of Spanish descent had tacit support from church and state. Pedagogical and religious educational books always stressed the value of marrying an equal in family background and education, but even though most of these books were written by clerics, the church never adopted any policy barring marriages on account of race or dissimilarities of background. On the other hand, the state did. The Spanish Enlightenment, especially after the advent of King Charles III in 1759, was a peculiar blend of desire for economic advancement and regression to traditional concepts of hegemonic domination of its subjects. The management of racial politics was also contradictory. While it created battalions for blacks and persons of mixed African ancestry, and enacted the Black Code for a more humane and efficient administration of slaves and slavery, it imposed strict control of marriage among army officers beginning in the 1730s. Officers' marriages were closely supervised to avoid this elite's marrying down in race or social standing. In 1776, the Crown enacted a sweeping set of rules to put a stop to "unequal" marriages. This Pragmática was extended to the colonies in 1778, where the issue at stake was racial as well class-based. The Crown sought to end 300 years of miscegenation and loosely held social conventions about marriage among the nonelite. The Pragmática was an ex post facto attempt to codify marriage and curb the social porosity of the racial and class makeup of the colonies. The legislation established that all minors of the white race must request and receive permission to marry from their parents or legal guardians. Elite Indians could also enforce this legislation among themselves. Pointedly excluded was the rest of the population. Lacking cleanliness of blood, they did not merit any special concern from the Crown. The law aimed at giving parents veto power over marriage when they deemed that suitors were of mixed ancestry or too lowly in the social scale. In either case, the purpose was to keep marriage a venue to solidify the racial elite. The juridical problems that the enforcement of this law posed by mixing civil and canon law, and the ambiguity of circumstances surrounding some cases, was not helped by royal legislation enacted in 1803 and 1805. In 1803, the Crown authorized anybody over 25 years of age to marry without parental consent, while in 1805, it established that only in certain instances would it allow such freedom of choice.

The influence of the Pragmática beyond a certain thin layer of people who regarded themselves as the social elite is questionable, since the litigation involved in challenging a child's choice or challenging a parental denial was a long and expensive process. The local courts paid more attention to the merits of each case than to the general principle behind the legislation, and the rulings favoring the choice of the couple was always greater than those giving the parents the right to block the marriage. Given the relatively small number of cases so far traced, we must conclude that this legislation did not affect the majority of the population, which had been its intention. The laws only had an impact on the socio-racial elite, who experienced a negative intrusion into their private lives by a state intent upon strengthening the mechanism that the elite itself had used to build its position of supremacy in society. If the Pragmática caused some members of the elite any legal discomfort, it had little time to disturb patterns already adopted by this group.

Demographic studies of marriage patterns show that the Spanish group was socially quite closed, marrying and reproducing itself through endogamous practices, whether in rural or urban areas. When they married outside their group, Spaniards took mestizos as partners—those closest to them in appearance. In areas where indigenous peoples were a less important element, such as in the northern mines, the rate of exogamy increased in the late 18th century, perhaps as a result of greater population mobility in times of economic boom. The behavior of women within this pattern is unclear, given the number of studies and variances in their conclusions. In general and in comparison to men, women were more conservative in their choices and less inclined than men to marry outside their group. The patterns discerned in recent studies apply to marriage and not to extramarital unions, through which white males continued to beget mestizos and other mixtures and to complicate the genetic pool. Some demographers see a decline in the number of children born out of wedlock toward the end of the 18th century as an indication of a decline in the number of consensual unions among the population at large.

After the Conquest, and throughout the colonial period, Indian women's status depended on that of their family, and whether the latter fared well in the new society or remained at its pre-Conquest level. While during the 16th century many indigenous women either married Spaniards or cohabited with them, as time passed this kind of union declined. Since the children of such unions were mestizos, marriage to a Spaniard could dilute the ties of a woman to her original community (unless the man moved into it) for succeeding generations. In time, the migration of poor women to the large cities of the viceroyalty also accelerated this process. To preserve ties with the indigenous communities, men and women had to reside in them, whether they were racially "pure" or not. The catastrophic demographic effects of the Conquest on the indigenous population created havoc but forced the survivors to regroup under royal orders to come to terms with Spanish rule. The choice of an Indian partner seems to have strengthened the sense of community necessary to overcome demographic decline in the 17th century. By the 18th century the rate of endogamy, or marriage within their own group, was very high in indigenous towns in central and southern New Spain, and the indigenous population was increasing fast. Yet, even indigenous communities experienced an increase in exogamous (outside the group) marriages in the second half of the century. Significantly, this happened more among men than women, which suggests that there was greater family control over women's marriage choices.

Given this internal cohesiveness of the indigenous communities, the issue of class and different forms of interaction with the dominant Spanish culture and its authorities affected women differently. Prior to the Conquest there were clear class differences among most organized indigenous groups. Nobles and commoners were separated by established rules of taxation, obligations within the communities, access to political decision making, education, and even dress. The Conquest upset the hierarchical order and gave many individuals of the lowest ranks of society the opportunity to ascend by utilizing the new legal systems and economic avenues produced by contact with the Spaniards. Those who had been at the top of society struggled to preserve their status by becoming mediators between their people and the Spaniards, reconfirming their privileges through the new legal system. The cacique class continued to have considerable weight in the 17th century, as the Spaniards preferred to deal with them in recognition of their condition as lords. *Principales,* or people of distinction, also retained ascendancy in the community. Both groups used to their advantage the corporate view of social order the Spaniards brought to New Spain. Women of these classes exercised political leverage in the local elections of indigenous cabildos and were not ignorant of the authority tacitly acknowledged to their rank by Spanish and indigenous authorities. Property rights and community affairs sometimes moved these women to become plaintiffs in their own name or in the name of their communities. Conversely, they could become the targets of opposing factions or groups if the latter sought to challenge them on the basis of their gender and its expected social behavior. Thus, many times they acted behind the scenes, although their leadership was known to their contemporaries.

Throughout the colonial period property ownership and traditional rights separated the indigenous elite from those who were bound to serve the community and the Spaniards. High-ranking females were exempted from paying tribute. Women in the indigenous communities were recognized as legal heirs and protectors of their family's properties. Their titles had to come from the male lineage to be recognized as *señoras naturales*. Indigenous peoples, like the Spaniards, held a patriarchal view of society in which women could marry into nobility and maintain it. They claimed nobility was a quality inherited from the fathers, not the mothers. Women who married into cacique families would keep their status as long as they did not remarry, in which case the woman took the status of her second husband. *Cacicazgos,* Indian noble positions, could be inherited by females, and throughout the colonial period women continued to do so. Thus, beginning in the 16th century, female cacicas, like their male counterparts, claimed ownership and renewal of titles of properties as well as services of former subjects. In fact, in the 16th century they went more frequently than men before the courts to engage in litigation. In general, patterns of inheritance gave both male and female children the same rights to a share of the parental properties, but men gave preferential treatment to their male relatives or to their children over their wives. Women could act as custodians if men allowed them to do so, but men more often acted as administrators of family properties in the absence of the father. Consanguineous kin were preferred over affinal or acquired relatives. Marriages among indigenous people of social distinction were endogamous to maintain the political power of families and their position as leaders of their communities. Yet, in areas such as Michoacán, the pre-Conquest nobility was greatly reduced in numbers by the 18th century. It has been argued that while in the 17th century mixed racial heritage did not preclude influence or inheritance of a post of governor within the indigenous towns, a growing awareness of racial purity seemed to have become fashionable and necessary among the indigenous nobility in the 18th century. The convents founded for Indian females in this century never relaxed the

Portraits of indigenous women, even of the cacica or elite class, were unusual in colonial Mexico. The cacica in this portrait is sixteen years old.

cleanliness of blood requirement for those who professed, and rejected attempts to allow white or mestiza women to profess in them, in blatant imitation of Spanish models.

The worst colonial burdens for the non-elite women was the taxation imposed by ecomiendas in the form of goods or labor or both, and the taxation of married couples to raise revenues. Tribute payments put commoners under the obligation to pay taxes to their native lords as well as to the Spanish collectors. In Yucatán, the production of textiles, a female home craft, was the main source of cloth tax payment. Cooking, house chores, and nursing were common tasks demanded as tribute payment, much the same as chickens, beeswax, and cotton cloth. *Macegual* women were the most common and available servants in Spanish and high-class mestizo homes. Single indigenous women residing in their villages remained exempted, as the Crown argued that having to seek money to pay their taxes would put them at risk of losing their virtue. The exemption lasted until 1758, when, presumably, honor lost its persuasion for the tax-collecting mind of imperial reformers. It has been argued that the status women had as healers, teachers of young females, matchmakers, and property owners declined in some areas throughout the colonial period. This conclusion is based on the much smaller number of land titles in women's names, decreasing representation in property litigation, and increasing pressure against unorthodox religious practices. The number of impoverished women in urban centers eking out a living as maids or market sellers also suggests that indigenous women bore a deteriorating economic situation. While such conclusions contain much truth, it should also be remembered that a self-conscious cacique class was still strong in the 18th century and that in certain areas heavily populated by Indians, such as Oaxaca, such a decline may not have taken place.

While specificity is possible and desirable when referring to either Indians or Spaniards, the majority of women of mixed ancestry were marginalized in legal texts. Most legislation was addressed to whites or Indians, and when castas were targeted it was for exclusionary purposes. Mestizas, and other women of various ethnic provenances called coyotas, lobas, and chinas, lived within the boundaries of prescribed norms but without the benefit of full recognition as a category. Their rank in society was determined by their physical closeness to the elite and by the degree of acceptance of the elite's forms of behavior. Their mixed ancestry eliminated the darker and poorer castas from the "desirable" marital choices for biologically unmixed Indians or Spaniards. However, because women of mixed ancestry were increasingly the prototype of several urban areas, their presence in historical records identifies them as engaged in the most varied forms of economic activities. Moreover, they began to challenge social prescriptions from ecclesiastical authorities and to peninsular values. A difficult group to categorize, *castas* had a variety of behavioral practices, whether facing the law or facing the social elite, that reflected different levels of hispanization and social rank. Nonetheless, they lived within the same patrilineal and patriarchal demarcations as Indians and Spaniards, and their gender placed them equally under men's authority.

The interrelation of men and women in such a complex society as colonial Mexico was perforce intricate and sometimes perplexing. The clear-cut boundaries established by Spanish legislation on marriage were not followed to the letter by all. The ecclesiastic and civil records show that the response to legislation was as varied as the problems of the people responding to them. Upper-class or elite behavior was close to prescriptive norms because such people reinforced their status by proper behavior. Among the poor there was less pressure to conform to the letter of all laws.

In their social intercourse, men and women were guided by Spanish and indigenous codes of behavior that were heavily colored by religious values. The Spanish concept of appropriate and expected behavior in public and private, broadly called honor, had its counterpart in well-known pre-Conquest indigenous formulations that demanded restraint and composure from men and women. Gender relations began with the informal education imparted at home in childhood. It was based on the assumption that men and women should be educated differently for their different roles and kept separate while that process was taking place. Masculinity and femininity resulted from strong demarcations between male and female. Such gendered education inculcated passivity, obedience, religiosity, and submissive behavior among girls. Reading and writing were deemed superfluous for poor women, whether Indian, white, or casta. When a formal primary education was available, it was provided by self-taught women or by nuns in convents, and it benefitted mostly white girls. Womanly occupations, such as sewing and embroidering, or cooking for the poor, were sufficient for the formation of most women.

Boys were expected to lead, guide, and dominate. As soon as they could be trained in an occupation for men, poor boys began the arduous road to earning a living, on the assumption that they would be the providers of the family. Social hierarchy did not diminish that expectation, but for boys of the ruling elite, a formal education broadened the scope of their power. Forming a man to lead was an implicit recognition of their right to be the wielders of power undisputed by either females or lower-class males. The separation of the sexes from childhood reaffirmed gender-defined behavior by the time of courtship and family formation. Women were expected to follow feminine rules of comportment, and men assumed that masculinity was, in part, the exercise of authority over women.

Civil and canon law established clear patterns to direct the process of engagement and marriage that applied to all colonial peoples. The initial stage was a word of promise (*palabra de casamiento*) whereby men and women pledged to marry each other. There is little historical knowledge on how this process took place in the earlier years of the colony. Either publicly or secretly expressed, with or without the exchange of gifts, this formal pledge was understood as having a religious base and serving as a binding word of marriage in the future. The validity of that word could only be challenged by some impediment acceptable to the ecclesiastical authorities. Among them were a forbidden degree of kin affinity up to the fourth degree. Previous engagement to somebody else, lying about one's social circumstances or race, imprisonment, contagious disease, or proven impotency were other important impediments. Both sexes were liable for an engagement promise, although suits for breach by men against women were very unusual.

Once the marriage was concerted the groom could formally accept a dowry from the bride's family, while he offered an *arras* (money pledge). The dowry was a Roman institution that had evolved and changed throughout the Middle Ages. While in late medieval Italy, for example, almost all women had a dowry recorded in the notarial records, this was not the situation in Spain or in New Spain. In the latter it was less frequent than in the peninsula and seemed to have been a sign of status among those women of Spanish descent. Few indigenous women (except perhaps the elite) and even fewer women of casta descent had notarized dowries, let alone arras. Comprising money, portable goods, and maybe real estate and slaves, the dowry was notarized and charged to the care of the husband as a substantial part or share of the bride's parental inheritance. The dowry was not a gift to the husband, and while he was legally in charge of administering it, he was also bound to return its value to the wife at his death. Usually, the first item in a married man's testament was the disposition to put aside the value of the dowry to return it to his wife, or to her family or children if she had died. The Arras, a sum of money not larger than 10 percent of the husband's assets, was pledged by him to his bride as a reward for or homage to her virtue, virginity, and clean lineage.

This page is from the record of the dowry of Getrudis de Anguiano, of Mexico City.

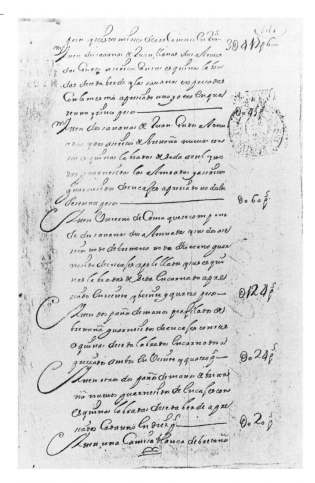

The future husband did not have to show the money in cash at that point. At his death the value of the arras was also removed from his estate and given to the widow. Since husbands administered the dowries, they could, of course, mismanage them and lose the cash or properties. In such cases, there was little a wife could do. However, if she feared that such an eventuality could occur, she could make a legal demand that her dowry be ensured. It was a difficult decision that few wives resorted to, since it was bound to create enormous tensions in the marriage. Even so, desperate cases are recorded as examples of women's agency.

As stated, dowries were already becoming an inflated instrument for the pursuit of good matches in the 16th century, but it was during the 17th and early 18th centuries in the colonial period that dowries were most frequent. Very rich brides brought with them dowries consisting of large quantities of clothes and furniture meticulously described and assessed. Cash in the amount of several thousand pesos, and properties such as houses and slaves were the most durable items in any dowry, since clothes and furniture could deteriorate. Loss or deterioration in no way altered the value of the dowry. The issue of timing in the award of the dowry was crucial. Cash and properties at the time of the marriage could buttress the husband's rise into business, for example. A decade or two later it was hoped that his assets had increased as a result of the original value of the dowry that he had enjoyed. A dowry statement was issued a few days before the wedding, but it could also be withheld for years before it was formalized, and many times there was no legal instrument but a simple oral understanding.

Marriage was not formalized until the marriage ceremony took place before a priest and consummated with sexual relations. However, many couples engaged in sexual relations before the final ceremony took place, under the promise of marriage given by the man. Courtship and promise of marriage opened the gate of sexual activity for couples who were willing to transgress the spiritual penalties prescribed by the church and the potential social damage to a woman's honor. Virginity was represented as the most desirable possession in a woman prior to marriage, the guarantee for a groom that the offspring of the marriage were his. For women the loss of virginity had a personal meaning relative to her own moral understanding of its value. Yet, social acknowledgment of the loss of virginity had personal and family consequences that could be exacerbated by pregnancy. In such cases the family was implicated insofar as its members had failed to protect the woman, and the whole family's reputation was "stained" by her fall. There were many forms of resolving loss of honor. Marriage was the most appropriate one and the only one wholly acceptable to the church. If the suitor was reluctant to follow that path, the men in the woman's family could put personal pressure on him to force the marriage that would restore her honor and the family's honor. The woman or a member of her family could sue the man before the authorities, demanding either marriage or monetary compensation.

Public dishonoring by loss of virginity applied only to women. Because of double standards of morality, men were expected to be sexually active and aggressive, and lost no sexual honor in the short run. It could be that later in life they would try to restore their own sense of honor by doing the "right" thing and legitimizing or acknowledging children born out of wedlock, but that option was entirely personal. To avoid compromising situations, single pregnant women who cared about their reputation and their family's hid their pregnancies and left their children in charge of relatives or simply at the mercy of private charity. The presence of many "orphans" in birth registries or in the wills or the marriage certificates of many persons indicates irregular births. The legal system reflected the modes of conception. A child born to a couple who was free to marry but chose not to do so was called a "natural" child (*hijo natural*). A child born to a married man or woman and a person other than the spouse was illegitimate and adulterous. The difference between these two categories had social significance. In the first case the stigma was less and the possibility of legal "recognition" or "acknowledgment," or even a legitimation by the father— albeit remote—existed. In the second case the child had no legal rights to any inheritance—which belonged only to legitimate children born within wedlock—and the chances of legitimation were practically nil. In all cases, men were the only ones entitled to establish or to acknowledge paternity. It was very difficult, although not impossible, for a woman to prove legally that a given man was the father of her child. This did not discourage many women of various backgrounds to sue men who had abandoned them, seeking monetary compensation from the fathers of their children.

The degree of honor lost by a pregnancy without the benefit of marriage was determined by the social class of the woman's family and by a more personal assessment that escapes neat definition. Women of all racial categories and economic situations sought redress for loss of virginity and male abandonment. Most suits were established by women, but it was not unusual for men to come forward to seek marriage with the women they had deflowered, pressed by personal, family, or religious concerns. The outcome of suits initiated by women is often missing, and it is risky to establish any conclusion on their effectiveness. Some historians see shifts in the receptivity of ecclesiastic and civil authorities to women's suits and a decline in their chances to obtain redress as the 18th century advanced. Such a conclusion is not sustained by a broad sampling in different areas in the viceroyalty. The increasing interest of the state in separating spiritual cares from more tangible social issues, in order to place such issues under its jurisdiction, affected gender relations in subtle ways. Mandating more parental power in the process of marriage and trying to take over the process of divorce from the church, the state began to erode the ethical and religious understanding of betrothal prevalent in the 17th century. It seems that a new understanding of gender relations was in the making at the end of the colonial period whereby women were assigned more responsibility for their actions, especially if they were not part of the group legally protected by the expanded parental restraints imposed by the 1776 royal edict on marriages.

Irregularities in the prescribed forms of sexual behavior have been detected more frequently among the non-elite because their actions were more "public" than those of the elite. While not all those who were poor or of mixed ethnic backgrounds were liable to have a looser sense of the timing and conditions of sexual relations, the formal channel of marriage was not the only venue for them. At some point in their lives many of these men and women formed consensual unions and begot children later recorded as naturales, orphans, or lacking a known mother or a known father. The last two options were devices to shelter the reputation of men and women of all social classes who for social reasons could not or would not disclose their parenthood. The rate of children born out of wedlock was very high in the 17th century in those areas so far checked by historical research. It could be as high as two-thirds of the births among castas, and one-third among the descendants of Spaniards. A detectable decline in this rate in the late colonial period suggests better ecclesiastical surveillance, changing sexual and social mores, or, more likely, a recognition of the social and legal benefits of wedlock among a larger sector of the population.

Consensual unions (*amancebamientos*) were far from unusual, although the rate and duration of such unions is difficult to discern. All races and ethnic groups engaged in the practice, although it must be noted that the indigenous groups living in the core areas of New Spain, perhaps as a result of being under more attentive religious supervision and living under a different set of community pressures, had a lower rate of such unions. Even so, in the 17th century, high-ranking indigenous men in remote areas engaged in polygamous relations, which had been common to their culture prior to the Conquest. The higher the social rank of the individual, the more likely marriage was the only honorable venue to form a family. The rate of marriage and legitimacy was higher among whites and lowest among castas.

In general "bad friendships," "lewd relationship," and "shameful" cohabitations were not unusual in New Spain. While men saw a satisfaction of their sexual prowess in such relationships, women who willingly entered into such relations had something to gain. They were usually women of low social extraction—either in class or ethnicity—and they or their children could hope to climb socially or even secure income or property. The relatively lax attitudes of people at their social level toward such unions and the inability of the church to eradicate those customs gave them the margin of freedom necessary to successfully carry out their lives beyond the parameters of legislation and religious rules. Since virginity was the crucial asset in a woman with honor, there was an obvious tension between the model prescribed by social mores and the church, and the reality of many women. Virginity was desirable but not always maintained or cared about. Its loss was only to be regretted if the promised marriage failed to materialize. Since virginity was lost outside of marriage most frequently among poorer and darker women, its relevance as a sign of social status was useful for members of the upper classes to reinforce their difference in the same vein that marriage defined respectability.

Marriage was a lasting bond between man and woman recognized by the church and state as the venue for legitimate sexual relations and procreation. The Council of Trent (1545–63) established that marriage had to be performed by the church before a priest and witnesses to be legal. In New Spain the practice was adopted without trouble by most of the marrying population by the last quarter of the 16th century. Marriage determined the legal status of the family members and established hierarchies of power between male and female, parents and children, that had the weight of law and custom. The family, conceived as a miniature state, had its head in the father, who as paterfamilias exercised complete authority over his subjects: wife and offspring. The parameters of such power were broad. A man was legally entitled to physically punish or chastise his wife and children, as long as he did not endanger their lives. His own sexual transgressions had to be public and scandalous to warrant recrimination and correction from either civil or ecclesiastic authorities. A wife had to demonstrate pervasive and morally detrimental abuse of a man's prerogatives to obtain the redress of her situation through exemption of her duties or separation from her husband. Expressed as separation of table and bed, this form of "divorce" was the only one possible to women in colonial Mexico. Husband and wife could live under the same roof or discreetly apart, and the degree of financial responsibility that the man had to assume under such circumstances was determined by his earnings and his disposition to pay. Many men evaded such responsibilities by simply walking away from them.

A man who abandoned his wife could seek elusive happiness by living in consensual union or could even attempt to "remarry." In either case he committed bigamy, a transgression under the purview of the Inquisition. Those who appeared before a priest to get married—providing witnesses to their faked "singleness" and willingness to marry, and going through the ceremony—left legal tracks that helped to capture and try them. Bigamy and polygamy were punished with a period of incarceration and the ultimate return of the erring parties to their original homes. The second party, who was frequently an innocent victim, had nothing to gain, since compensation for damages was an unknown concept.

Whether a woman was willing to push her quest for marital peace or justice to divorce depended on her ability to survive with little or no assistance from her ex-husband, usually by relying on the support of her own family. Unfortunately, most women were financially dependent on their husbands and were unlikely to fend for themselves. Thus, they endured what has been called *la mala vida*, or the bad life. Physical abuse characterized the bad life for ill-married women. Canon and civil law allowed a husband to chastise his wife and children in a moderate manner. Judges had to determine when the husband had reached the justifiable limits of punishment, the fine line between wise chastisement and endangerment of life due to violence. If the wife felt that her husband's mistreatment was putting her life at risk, she could resort to the civil or ecclesiastical authorities, either to obtain his restraint or a separation from marital life. This process was in itself a challenge for the woman, since it followed strict legal procedures. The intervention of witnesses and lawyers exposed the intimacies of the home in public, inviting rebuttals from the husband, whose authority and masculine ego were challenged.

Violence directed at women was sometimes publically displayed. On occasion male violence found acceptance within the community and even within the family as a form of personal and social "release." Yet, there was a general consensus that a man dishonored himself if he did not know the boundaries of his power. While control over the household was expected, abusing a female was not held as honorable among the upper classes, who took the protection of the women of their family as a sign of their own honor. Most physically abused women resorted to the protection of their families, but familial intervention offered at most a temporary respite. Only the intervention of a lawyer and a royal official promised more lasting and effective relief.

Love and a stable marital life leave fewer tracks than violence and mistreatment. Doubtless, the bonding that some theologians suggested as the base of marriage existed, although its special form of expression must be understood. Christianity contained a strong misogynist strain that placed marital love as second best when compared to divine love. Sex was assumed to be an intimate experience with a higher purpose: reproduction of the species. It was assumed to be a dangerous sentiment that needed to be harnessed and properly channeled. Those who erred and indulged in improper relations did so at the risk of their souls. After the Council of Trent ecclesiastical sources imposed a heavy layer of restraint over the public expression of sensual love even within the permitted boundaries of matrimony. Marital love was understood to be the foundation of the relations between husband and wife if they were cojoined in a Christian marriage. Testaments, the ultimate expression of a person's will, often contain the brief expressions of love, trust, and companionship that members of the family had felt for each other. On the other hand, enough love letters have been unearthed from public archives to document the passions that moved men and women to marry or engage in pleasurable relationships and illicit bondings. Many marriages among the elite or families climbing the social ladder were arranged by the parents, who had much to say in the choice of a partner. If love or passion was lacking in such cases, affection was expected to grow with time or to be transferred to the children as the objects of a selfless and rewarding experience for the woman. In most marriages the true boundaries of intimacy, love, and endearment are less easy to detect than the violence of the cases of marital dysfunction, but neither the hierarchical subordination to their husbands that women accepted as a natural situation nor the lack of public displays of love or affection should leads us to conclude that all marriages were pacts of convenience.

The hierarchical authority of men over women had considerable flexibility in daily life. Legal constrictions were circumvented by the margins provided by the laws themselves and by the power of customs and understandings evolved from the acquiescence of husbands and male relatives. Widowhood, unmarried cohabitation, and poverty forced women to become heads of household and their own agents of survival. Judging by some area studies, such as that of late–18th–century Antequera (Oaxaca), in urban areas households headed by white women could be as high as one-fifth among women age 23 to 27. Among women age 60 or older, the incidence of heads of household was about 50 percent. On the other hand, the percentage of Indian women who were heads of household was much smaller than that of white women. In the same period, in some parishes of Mexico City, women of all ethnic provenance were roughly 25 percent of all heads of household.

Whether living on inherited properties or on their own means, women of all racial groups and social classes developed a multiplicity of activities, which challenges the notion of complete submission and subjugation. It is clear that non-white women of the lower classes endured tremendous challenges when they found themselves without a consort or a male supporter and were forced to rely on their own means for survival. Even when married, women were forced by the limited resources of their husbands to find ways to make a living. Indian women provided poultry, vegetables, and textiles to the local markets and brought their wares to the traditional *tianguis* (weekly market), which had its roots in pre-Columbian times. Poor Spanish and mestiza women were most often seamstresses or sold alcoholic beverages, cigars, sweets, candles, and trinkets from small stalls.

At a middle level of entrepreneurship, widows or married women with independent means entered into partnerships with traders by providing the capital that they needed to operate and collecting 50 percent of the profits.

Women showed the same ability and fallibility as men in the exercise of their administrative duties, except that their activities demanded a strong dosage of self-assertion and, at times, the knowledge that delegation of certain tasks to men was absolutely essential. Male overseers, lawyers, and agents had to perform operations that convention limited to men, such as traveling with merchandise or managing rural properties. Litigation over land, whether among cacicas, castas, or white women, was not unusual and was expected in a period in which land ownership was a yardstick of social status as well as a means of survival. Whether as large or small landowners and managers, female agency in the countryside was exercised more frequently than assumed, even if we admit that women acted as caretakers between generations of patriarchal rule. The ability of women to fit into physical and cultural spaces related to management is best illustrated by the ability of 16th century Mixtec cacicas to learn the Spanish legal system of property inheritance and rise to and maintain a privileged status. Exempted from taxes and enjoying the service of common Indians in their properties, they owned vast amounts of land, reaching what has been termed a golden age of power between 1550 and 1600. Ana de Sosa, cacica of Tutupec, had holdings more valuable than those of some rich encomenderos, and her estate was considered second only to the estate of the conquistador Hernán Cortés. While in general cacicazgos lost power and wealth throughout the colonial period, they still played a role in the local economies, and women were not marginal to the efforts spent in maintaining their viability.

In urban areas women owned textile sweatshops known as *obrajes*, as well as bakeries and printing shops, businesses often inherited from a deceased husband. There was a guild of women silk weavers, but most women weavers carried out this occupation as a home craft. Women were missing, however, in wholesale and long-distance trade. At the end of the colonial period the opening of the Royal Tobacco manufacturing plant began the industrial employment of women in New Spain. Half of its 7,000 employees were women who earned regular wages in a presage of the opening of salaried occupations for women in the 19th century. In the second half of the 18th century and the Bourbon dynasty, inspired in part by the philosophical influence of the Enlightenment, advisors to the Crown began to popularize the concept that women could and should be part of the economic development of Spain and its colonies. By the 1760s, the state had begun to advocate the adoption of primary education for women and their training in any skill that would permit them, especially those of the lower strata, to serve in state-promoted industries such as tobacco factories, or to earn an independent income if widowed or single. Several important schools were founded in the city of Mexico: Las Vizcaínas, for girls of Basque descent, and La Enseñanza, of the Order of Mary. The latter took boarders from the best families but, moved by social concerns, opened a public schools for girls of all ethnic and economic backgrounds. Other schools founded in provincial cities adopted similar patterns of service to the public as well as to the rich. In the last years of the 18th century there were more urban schools for girls than ever before, and attendance was high. And yet, they were insufficient to meet the needs of most of the female population and remained institutions of little use to the large number of rural women of New Spain. Illiteracy among women remained high for the next century.

While the world of petty and small businesses, personal service, and wage earners was the appropriate realm of non-elite women, elite agency had a different meaning. If the male line of authority in the administration of large family affairs had a temporary hiatus, some women stepped in to govern until a younger man became of age to take over. Exceptional cases of extraordinarily rich women, such as the marchionesses of Selva-Nevada, indicate that given the opportunity, women managed the fate of the family resources with abilities similar to those of men. The original holder of this title, Antonia Gómez Rodríguez de Pedroso, was endowed with an entail that would only be inherited by the female line of the family, which it was for four generations. Awarded a noble title in 1778, the first marchioness took pains in planning the marriage and life of every one of her surviving children, and as a widow she used a great deal of her well-tended and enormous wealth to found two nunneries. Equally interesting is the case of the heiresses to the Count of Santiago and Marquisate of Salvatierra, María Isabel de Velasco Altamirano y Ovando, who as an unmarried holder of two titles and three entails managed the entire family business. Together she and her younger sister, María Josefa, ran the family affairs between 1797 and 1809.

There is no better example of upper-class women's ability to fill spaces of self-rule and authority than that offered by the administration of nunneries. These institutions had a double administrative tier. Inside the convent nuns took charge of every detail in the daily running of the institution, including the management of loans, liens, and properties. The second tier was external and represented by a majordomo or administrators and the bishopric's officers in charge of all conventual affairs. The majordomo and the nuns kept separate sets of books, where they recorded every entry and debit. The books had to be reconciled regularly, and the majordomo was liable for debits or maladministration. The episcopal officers kept a final supervisory eye over all convents in their jurisdiction and had the power to approve or veto all loans, liens, purchases, and sales of properties.

Nuns rarely had any previous preparation for the accounting tasks and simply had to learn them. Failures were to be expected. Some convents had, from time to time, problems with their administration, while others excelled at the task of improving their finances. External problems, such as the flood of Mexico City in 1629, bad crops, or slow trading trends, affected institutions that had varied economic interests. However, the role of the nuns as administrators never changed. It was a rotational duty that enabled them to control their own moneys and pursue their own interests. Their feminine condition did not impair their abilities to meet the challenge. When circumstances were propitious, other women performed similar administrative or decision-making tasks. There was no ethnic, racial, or color barrier to women's agency.

Agency was not simply an economic issue. Religious patronage—the endowment of masses for the dead, the celebration of religious feasts, or the creation of a fund to support the profession of a priest or a nun—was a responsibility dear to women of means. Such acts of charity were undertaken either by wives in agreement with their husbands or mostly by widows, who had complete control over their assets. Thousands of these endowments were created beginning in the early 17th century. Sixteen out of the 30 convents founded in New Spain between 1600 and the end of the colonial period were the work of women. These pious deeds enhanced the social rank of the family and gained the donor's confidence that the good deed would help to save their souls. In several cases, patronage provisions made places within the convents for female relatives of the founder, thus providing support for kin who either showed religious vocation or were in need of a safe place or retreat. Wealthy childless women also exercised their charity through the adoption of children, whom they raised and provided for until they married. Given the fact that out-of-wedlock births increased significantly in the 17th century and that many of the children were of Spanish descent, informal adoptions were relatively frequent, even among castas and people of limited means. The adoptees were known as "orphans," and they could be the out-of-wedlock babies of well-born women or simply the offspring of women who were unprepared to confess publicly their transgressions or who lacked support from the father of the child. Adoption was commonly exercised among people of the same race or ethnic group, and among the elite this was a mechanism that provided social redress for a select number of children of their own class.

Life as a religious was an option to women in the same manner that taking the vows as a priest or friar was an alternative way of life for men. Indeed, the only identifiable corporate group of women in New Spain was that formed by the thousands of women professed as nuns. There was one significant difference between men and women when it came to living a life within the church. While men made vows of poverty, chastity, and obedience, women had to add the vow of enclosure, which meant that once they took the final vow, they never, under any circumstance, left the premises of the convent. Men had the freedom to move about, and their life was understood as one of service to the community, for which mobility was essential. On the contrary, female enclosure was regarded as the optimum state to fulfill the goals of female religious life. As she took her vows, the nun became the bride of Christ. In the convent she served him, for the sake of her own salvation, and served the community as a model of piety and spirituality, interceding for others with her prayers. Like a wife in her house, a nun was protected from the potential risks of the world by enclosure: Cloistered life was perceived as a privileged state and received strong social endorsement.

Conventual life was also a social mechanism to shelter women of the elite who either found themselves in adverse circumstances or were seen as in need of protection from the possibility of undesirable unions with social inferiors. The service of God and the fulfillment of a vocation were conflated with socioeconomic reasons. Sixteenth-century founders argued for a place of shelter where daughters and descendants of conquistadores and early settlers who had experienced bad economic times could live a life of dignity appropriate to their rank in society. In later periods the social need remained in the wording of foundations even though women seeking profession had to meet stiff economic demands.

The rules governing the admission to conventual life speak of the directness of their intentions: Only descendants of Spanish settlers could profess. Limpieza de sangre and legitimacy of birth had to be proven to take the veil. While the legitimacy requirement was occasionally wavered for the hija natural of a man of social distinction, a clean peninsular lineage was not. The first convent of Mexico, Our Lady of the Conception, sheltered some descendants of Moctezuma, but this was due to their exceptionality, and the situation was never repeated. It was not until the 18th century that indigenous women had some convents where they too could profess. Castas never had access to religious life, and their presence in the convents as maids or even slaves made evident the social chasm between them and the professed nuns. The first convent for Indian women was founded in 1724 as the result of the patronage of Baltasar de Zúñiga, Marquis of Valero, and Viceroy of New Spain (1716–22). Only cacicas or elite full-blooded Indians would be allowed to profess in it, thus maintaining the concept of cleanliness of blood that applied to the convents reserved for women of Spanish descent. Daughters of men engaged in "vile" or lowly occupations were also forbidden from entering, reducing the candidates to a narrow fringe of the indigenous population. Cacique and elite families had no objection to this precondition. Two other convents for Indians were founded in the 18th century: Our Lady of the Purest Conception of Cosamaloapan in Valladolid, approved in 1734, and Our Lady of the Angels in Oaxaca, in 1774. All of them upheld the racial and social exclusion of lower-class women. Corpus Christi and Our Lady of Cosamaloapan experienced disrupting internal troubles due to the admission of white nuns by Franciscan provincial. As the nuns and their protectors and friends feared that the nature of the convent could change if this process was not stopped, Corpus Christi resorted to the Council of the Indies to obtain a royal ruling forbidding the admission of white novices in 1745. By the end of the century these convents were regarded highly by public opinion as places of observance and discipline in no way less exemplary than those of white nuns.

Convents flourished in colonial Mexico, with nearly 60 of them founded between 1550 and 1811. They became symbols of urban status: All urban settlements that aspired to gain in rank also aspired to have a nunnery within its midst. The far north never achieved that distinction, but Mérida in Yucatán, and Oaxaca and Chiapas, the farthest boundaries to the south, succeeded in having their convents, as did minor places such a San Miguel el Grande and the small town of Atlixco, near Puebla. The number of religious varied according to the economic capacity of each institution and was in some cases predetermined by the founders. But some large convents, such as those of Our Lady of the Incarnation and Jesús

This book details the rules for the sisters of the convent of San Bernardo, in Mexico City. Very ornate conventual books were often commissioned to professional artists. This particular rulebook was painted by an untrained hand.

María, both in Mexico City, sheltered hundreds of nuns and thousands of servants throughout the centuries. Aside from their spiritual symbolism and the elliptical social service of removing white women from the feared fate of uneven social matches, convents had important economic meaning. They were sources of labor while under construction and an outlet for artists and craftsmen afterward. More important, they owned real estate in the cities and, less often, land in rural areas. By the end of the 18th century the nunneries of Mexico City, for example, were among the strongest urban landlords. Although many of them spent their founding capital on the construction of cloisters and churches that demanded renovation periodically, convents slowly became key sources of credit in New Spain. Dowries, donations, and the increase of capital accruing from the interest of mortgages made on their behalf gave most of them a surplus of capital that was lent to willing landowners, merchants, and even the royal coffers. By the end of the colonial period nunneries had become lending institutions of stature, a role never matched by any of their male counterparts.

Since all professed nuns were required to be literate, and since some of them were highly educated women, nunneries were the only places where a female culture can be detected and studied. The nature of that culture was exclusively religious, and its expression was carefully overseen by male ecclesiastical authorities. Many nuns wrote of their own accord; others at the instigation of their confessors, who examined the orthodoxy of their beliefs and encouraged some of them to create what turned out to be an intimate record of their spiritual experiences. In the 17th century nuns often wrote biographes of their sisters and chronicles of their convents, but most of these works remained anonymous. Male biographers and historians of the orders recast their information and published it under their own name. Female writing had not yet gained enough authority to stand by itself and circulate outside the walls of the convent. This situation changed in the 18th century, when several nuns published under their own names. The best-known spiritual writer of that century was Sor María Anna Agueda de San Ignacio (1695–756), a nun from Puebla whose works were encouraged and published by her bishop. Despite such support, neither the nature of nuns' writing nor the general tendency to write for their sisters without pursuing publication changed much. Since laywomen were not encouraged to write or publish, the writing of nuns, published or unpublished, stands out as the largest body of female writing in colonial Mexico.

The opportunity and privilege of education and the possibility of writing nurtured the genius of one exceptional nun, who confessed in her mature years that she had professed because she lacked interest in marriage and, although aware of the problems implied in cloistered life, it would allow her to enjoy the freedom she wished for learning and writing. This exceptional woman was Sor Juana Inés de la Cruz, who professed in the Hieronymite convent of San Gerónimo in 1669 and died in April 1695. Sor Juana was born out of wedlock to a mother who had three other children without the benefit of marriage and who remained illiterate all her life. Yet, proving that a formal education was not required to manage home and real estate, she ran a rural property and succeeded in placing her daughters in social positions above her own. Sor Juana spent some time in the viceregal palace as an exceptional child, but perhaps owing to her birth and her admitted vocation for studying, she chose to profess. Although a faithful and practicing Catholic nun, Sor Juana was not interested in writing religious works but in exploring all the possibilities of formal learning and writing. She wrote religious and secular plays, sonnets and poems for innumerable social occasions, songs for religious offices, and even a lost textbook on music.

The unusually high quality of her baroque writing gained her a reputation beyond New Spain. A friend of the vicereines and the literati of her time, she eventually ran into trouble with two ecclesiastical authorities: the bishop of Puebla, Manuel Fernández de Santa Cruz, and the archbishop of Mexico, Francisco de Aguiar y Seijas. Encouraged by the former to write a critique of Jesuit spirituality and venturing to offer her own theological interpretations, she ran into trouble when the bishop published her essay under the title *Carta atenagórica*. The newly arrived and stern archbishop of Mexico, exercising his episcopal authority, threatened the nun with an inquisitorial investigation of the concepts expressed in the *Carta* and demanded she stop publishing and sell her books. Under the vow of obedience Sor Juana did so, but only after writing a tour de force in her own defense known as *La respuesta*. Although now we know that she continued writing and reading in secret, she was pushed by the circumstances to demonstrate her religiosity and became mortally ill while tending her sick sisters during an epidemic. Although Sor Juana Inés de la Cruz was not the only nun or

Sor Juana Ines de la Cruz, a nun in the convent of San Gerónimo, wrote many plays, sonnets, and songs. Although the painting states that it was made after a copy of a self-portrait by the nun herself, this story is now considered apocryphal.

female writer in New Spain, the complexity, power, and perfection of her writing, especially her poems, have earned her the title of the Tenth Muse. She is regarded as one of the best colonial writers and has become a popular cultural icon among literary critics and the public in general. The irony of her life consists in having had to adjust her genius to living in total enclosure, subjected to the codes imposed on women by a religious patriarchy, while exercising intellectual attributes not recognized in her gender.

As indigenous women lacked convents of their own until the 18th century, they channeled their religiosity through local confraternities. Beginning in the early 16th century women had a definite role in many rural indigenous confraternities as active members and sometime officials. A few female-only confraternities have been spotted in colonial records. On the fringes of acceptable religious orthodoxy, women engaged in shamanistic practices for curing, casting spells and controlling other people's behavior for their clients. Networks of indigenous, casta, and Spanish women shared their practices, which existed at the local level as underground activities. From time to time they were unearthed and condemned by the ecclesiastic authorities, but such practices never disappeared.

At the close of the colonial period the legal status of women remained unaltered, but the winds of change had begun to spell new roles for them. The diversity of female experiences in colonial Mexico reflects the complexity of a multiethnic and hierarchical society dominated by a patriarchal social system. While these three factors enclosed women's lives in a defined framework, there was room within for a negotiation of situations in gender relations with many regional and chronological nuances. Breaking through the limits of the framework was a possible choice at the personal level, as the individual lives of many men and women indicate. Between the 16th and the late 18th century the contact among the different racial and ethnic groups in New Spain was established on the basis of a constantly changing terrain of human relations that gave each group and its women a different experience. Yet, for women, the bonds of gender established certain commonalities, such as the submission to parental authority, the imbalances of double standards of sexual behavior that restrained the sexuality of most women, and the restrictions implied by the authority of the husband. While there remains much to be learned about women in colonial Mexico, the general picture we can draw at this time is a source of considerable historical excitement that enriches significantly our view of society in the period.

Collapse, Regeneration, and Challenge, 1810–1910

+ ❖ + ❖ + ❖ + ❖ + ❖ + ❖ + ❖ + ❖ + ❖ + ❖ + ❖ + ❖ + ❖ + ❖ + ❖ + ❖ + ❖ + ✛

Independent Mexico sputtered into existence in 1821 with a confused effort to bring a European monarch to Mexico, followed by the tentative ten-month-long empire of Agustín de Iturbide, ending in the creation of a republic in 1824 with the inauguration of President Guadalupe Victoria. His four-year term offered only a brief respite as republican leaders battled each other as well as those who still desired a monarchy. These political struggles, which erupted during much of the 19th century, took place within the context of three wars that shaped the politics and the politicians of the nation.

Three particular military campaigns served as defining moments for the Mexican leaders of the 19th century. The veterans of the independence struggle—men who had fought on both sides—dominated Mexico until 1850. Then a second generation of political leaders came of age during the disastrous United States-Mexican War of 1846–48. Finally, the generals who constituted the Porfirian regime, including the dictator Porfirio Díaz himself, had as their reference point their resistance to the French occupation of 1862–67. These veterans of course found in their wartime experiences self-fulfilling and self-justifying lessons.

For the survivors of the wars of independence, the victory carried two sentiments. The first was opposition to King Ferdinand VII of Spain personally and, for most but not all, to the monarchy as well. Secondly, the veterans generally supported the Constitution of 1812, which had been formulated by delegates from Spain and the empire, including Mexico. This document attempted to invigorate local municipal regimes. Solving the problem of how to divide and distribute authority between the central and local governments remained the critical issue for much of the century.

The men who experienced the United States-Mexican War of 1848 also found in it at least two lessons that shaped their politics, especially that of liberalism, for a generation. Those who survived the war and its loss of territory blamed the intense political divisions that had been rife within the political elites for Mexico's defeat. And, dismal as the war was, these men found only inspiration in the valor of the hastily organized militias. For these men, epitomized by Benito Juárez, the civilian soldier became the model. Juárez's admirable attempt to move to civilian rule as president after 1861 was counterbalanced by his disrespect for the service of loyal regular army officers, many of whom became his peacetime opponents.

The men who first defeated the French legions on May 5, 1862, a day since celebrated as Cinco de Mayo, had to endure five years of occupation before finally driving the French from Mexico. These men had honed a sharp-edged patriotism in war, part of which was a determination to make Mexico secure by making it modern. They concluded that it was better to have foreign businessmen in the country than foreign garrisons, better to induce self-discipline through authoritarian rule than to have it imposed by foreign legions invited in by constant political warfare.

Of course, not everyone in 19th-century Mexico shared these interpretations of the wars or the political solutions their veterans suggested. The church, for example, was represented by its highest authorities, whose first loyalty went to Rome. And isolated, often Indian, villagers, whose political point of reference was their pueblo and who did not distinguish between foreigners from France and those from Mexico City, had very different views of Mexican life. The churchmen tried to protect their own religious prerogatives, and the villagers strained to defend their community lands against policies established by Mexico City politicians who saw both religious practices and communal property as obstacles to the creation of a modern society.

9

The Old Colonialism Ends, the New Colonialism Begins

VIRGINIA GUEDEA

The rise of the House of Bourbon to the Spanish throne in 1700 involved something more than a simple dynastic succession. At the beginning of the 18th century, a reorganization of the whole Spanish state was put into effect, in a shift largely driven by the urgent need Spain felt to meet the growing rivalry posed by other European countries, particularly France and England. The main goals of this reorganization were to strengthen the royal administration, finance operations, and build an able imperial defense.

The reform plans that first got under way in Spain took more than 50 years to reach the Spanish American colonies. Moreover, the plans were introduced into New Spain and the other Spanish colonial territories in a somewhat uneven, incomplete way. Yet the changes they brought were deep enough to produce a crisis in the viceregal government, as they transformed its structure and functions. The resulting crisis was also stirred up by the propagation of concepts of rationalism and natural philosophy which led the criollos to embrace the new approach to reasoning that has since been described as the Enlightenment. These new ideas strengthened the colonists' feelings of being Americans, of identifying with the land in which they were born. The two major 18th–century revolutions, the U.S. revolutionary war and the French Revolution, played an influential role too, though more by the way of example than through the direct influence of political ideas.

About the middle of the 18th century, the idea of modernizing the Spanish empire to enable it to face the challenges posed by new European industrial powers ruled by centralized, authoritarian, more-efficient regimes became compelling. King Charles III and his government (1759–88) were responsible for organizing and executing these reformation plans, which became known as the Bourbon reforms.

Carlos II, the Spanish monarch who embodied the Enlightenment, decreed the application of the Bourbon reforms in his American colonies. He intended to instate a more rational and efficient administration, including the introduction of tax collection, in his empire. The reforms achieved their goal but created hostility among most of the colonial population and eroded loyalty to the Spanish crown.

According to the Bourbon reforms, New Spain, "the richest jewel of the Spanish crown," was to become a truly modern colony. The first task was to overhaul its economy to make it wholly independent from peninsular Spain—but more productive nonetheless—to increase its contributions to the royal treasury. On the other hand, the Crown felt that the viceroyalty should be held under the firm control of royal authority. This meant reducing the degree of autonomy and self-government that increasingly self-confident New Spaniards had already attained while limiting as well the influence of native oligarchies and local institutions. "Once and for all, subjects must know that they have been born to obey, not to discuss lofty governmental designs," emphatically stated the royal decree banishing the Jesuit order from all Spanish territories, including New Spain.

In order to achieve their reformist, modernizing goals, the Bourbon ministers found themselves compelled to build up a wholly new, extensive bureaucratic machine with no links to local power groups, made up of Spaniards brought from the Iberian peninsula expressly for this purpose. This proved to be the only way to collect more taxes while at the same time imposing harsher controls over the political life of the viceroyalty.

The Crown also found it necessary to build up a strong military apparatus. The fall of the strategic seaport of Havana to Britain in 1762 made it abundantly clear that the colonial military system was indeed vulnerable. To furnish New Spain with an adequate defense system, Juan de Villalba was appointed inspector general in 1764 to organize a professional army and create a new militia. Villalba executed his mission well, but his course of action stirred up discord among the

D. JOSÉ DE GALVEZ

Marques de la Sonora

Visitador de la Nueva España y despues Ministro Universal de Indias.

Named *visitador general* (general inspector) of New Spain by Carlos III, José de Gálvez instituted the Bourbon reforms in Mexico. In 1784, he created new administrative units, dividing Mexico into twelve intendancies and establishing a northern frontier zone under military direction called the Internal Provinces. Galveston, Texas, was named for him.

population by ignoring or disdaining local customs and political realities; the troops he brought from Spain behaved abusively and with an arrogant awareness of their own power toward the Americans.

The following year José de Gálvez was appointed inspector general of all the Tribunals and Royal *Cajas* (Coffers) of New Spain and quartermaster general of the armies, offices he held from 1765 to 1771. Invested with ample authority, Gálvez appeared to personify the Bourbons' reformist ideas in New Spain. Supported by his brother Matías, his nephew Bernardo, and other peninsular functionaries, he put into effect a metropolitan policy aimed at alienating the criollo elite from the viceregal administration. Thus he reinstated the Spaniards' supremacy in the *audiencias* (high courts) and tried to control the *ayuntamientos* (municipal governments) by introducing two new public officers, the *regidor* (honorary alderman) and the *corregidor* (magistrates). He also tried to cut back the extensive power in New Spain of the consulado of Mexico by promoting its counterpart, the consulado of Cádiz. Increased military spending by both New Spain and the main military posts on the North American continent led Gálvez to reinforce tax collection and administration. In fact, the fiscal overhauling he undertook became the economic basis of the Bourbon reforms in New Spain.

In this way the *alcabala*, a sales tax collected by individual entrepreneurs because of the lack of an adequate fiscal officers, was transferred to the colonial government. Seeing that this policy had been successfully carried out in Mexico City since 1754, Gálvez resolved to extend it to the rest of the viceroyalty. An adequate tax policy for the Indians was another of his concerns. He undertook the task of revising and standardizing tax collection in this area, even to the extent of revoking old tax exemptions the natives had long held in mines and many Indian towns. Blacks and mulattoes were given the same treatment. Especially important was the establishment of the tobacco monopoly, which eventually came to be the biggest revenue source for the treasury of New Spain.

New Spain's tax collections substantially increased under Gálvez's administration, and his policies stirred up almost general unrest in response to the severity of its application and the economic impact it had in most sectors of the population. Rising alcabalas jacked up prices, especially for food and household goods. The tobacco monopoly decreased the quality of its products while increasing their price. The tax reform was, so efficient that, according to Carlos Marichal, at the end of the 18th century New Spain's taxpayers were yielding 70 percent more than their counterparts on the Iberian peninsula.

One of the main objectives of the newly created bureaucratic and military apparatus was to shackle the Catholic church, the main pillar of the colonial regime and a major factor in the social and political stability of the viceroyalty. A first step in this direction was to reassert the *real patronato* (royal patronage) while reducing the resources and privileges of the clergy. To achieve this, the Crown diminished the influence of the regular clergy by secularizing parishes, a decision that provoked much annoyance among the population. A major part of the policy carried out by Charles III toward the church was its expulsion of the Jesuit order from all the Spanish territories in 1767. This decree was motivated in part by the notable successes the Jesuits had achieved all over the Spanish empire as well as their total obedience to the papacy. This decision would bring severe consequences, however, because of the opposition it provoked in New Spain's society.

Gálvez's reformist, modernizing measures were not endorsed by the different sectors of the population in the viceroyalty. Indeed, by following an increasingly authoritarian policy and by exhibiting a voracious appetite for taxes, Gálvez's administration caused the colonial regime to lose acceptance among its subjects. The expulsion of the Jesuits therefore became the spark that ignited rebellion in several regions.

The provinces of Michoacán, Guanajuato, and San Luis Potosí—the future theatre of a violent and bloody insurgent war during the subsequent generation—were shaken up by several popular movements of both local and colonial origin. As Felipe Castro has shown, the opposition to reformist measures didn't emerge only as rejection of definite actions, such as the expulsion of the Jesuits or the imposition of a harsh new tax policy. It also unfolded against an expansionist policy led by a state that was deliberately trying to change the traditional relationships between the government and its subjects.

Gálvez immediately devoted himself, with great rigor, to subduing the insubordinations by means of a punitive expedition. He ruthlessly punished the rebels and their towns. An equally harsh treatment was meted out to rebellious Indians in the northern region of Sonora. Gálvez used this opportunity to assert unequivocally the power of the state he personified, to reorganize the relationships between the Spanish monarchy and the population of New Spain, and to terminate the resistance against reform once and for all.

The colonial reorganization gained momentum once Gálvez was appointed Minister of the Indies in January 1776. The reform plans entered then into their most radical phase. Yet this time, the Spanish state offered its subjects in the Americas something in exchange for its demands, certain inducements to achieve political support both for the reform plans and the Spanish Crown.

In 1777 the *Tribunal de Minería* (Mining Tribunal) was created to regulate and increase mining activities. The Crown also dispatched technical missions to New Spain's mining districts, and, in 1792, created the *Escuela de Minas* (Mining School). These measures were useful and well received, even though the mining activity in New Spain was by then already on the road to recovery.

The crown also endeavored to modernize and make functional the main urban centers of the viceroyalty, particularly Mexico City, the major metropolis of the North America. The ordering of its suburbs, improvement of its sanitary and traffic conditions, restoration of its older buildings and construction of new ones were measures undertaken at that time by the viceroys, particularly by the second count of Revillagigedo. The arts and sciences were also fostered by creating new institutions like the San Carlos Art Academy and the Botanical Garden, both in Mexico City.

Foreign trade was a critically important area, to be reformed by removing trade barriers. This process began in 1778 when the Ordinance for Free Trade was proclaimed to break down the monopoly held by the port of Cádiz on commerce in the Americas. The trade benefits for New Spain lagged behind because some restrictions remained on its commerce and ports. In fact, the viceroyalty experienced free trade during only two years, 1788 and 1789. An additional incentive to free trade was the war then going on in Europe, with Spain campaigning against France first, then later against England. These campaigns encouraged neutral commercial exchanges. A further move by the Spanish Crown to diminish the power of the consulado of Mexico by creating two new competing consulados in Veracruz and Guadalajara turned out to be a further stimulus for trade, bringing new power groups on the scene in spite of rivalries among different consulados.

The *Comandancia General de Provincias Internas* (General Commandancy of the Internal Provinces) a body not subject to the authority of the viceroy, was created in 1776 to cope with growing troubles in northern New Spain and guard its frontiers in the face of a growing menace from several foreign powers. Yet the territorial reorganization of the viceroyalty would not be fully carried out until eight years later, when the intendancy system was established.

By following an early model originating in Spain in 1749, the introduction of the intendancy system into New Spain in 1784 meant the complete reorganization of public administration at its three levels: local, provincial, and viceregal. By introducing this system and creating new provinces, the Crown intended to organize and simplify the viceregal administration in a rational way.

The viceroyalty was then divided into 12 intendancies whose intendants, or heads, were empowered with functions that had previously been under the control of the viceroy. These new officials were responsible for administering the provinces in four areas: government, justice, mining revenues, and war. The introduction of this system, rather than being a unifying move, turned out to be a decentralizing one. Horst Pietchmann has argued that the weakening of the central government resulted from the delegation of royal authority to the provincial and local constituencies. Nevertheless, by creating a wholly new and able administrative hierarchy for the provinces, the Spanish state made the representative's presence felt in regions and among groups that would otherwise have remained beyond the Crown's reach.

By introducing all these reformist measures Spain intended to diminish the viceregal authority, strengthen local finances, and forbid the monopolistic distribution of goods by the alcaldes mayores. Yet the introduction of the intendancy system did not in fact contribute to reinforcing the monarch's authority in regard to local and provincial interests. Instead, the ayuntamiento became the institution representing the interests of the local and regional oligarchical groups then setting deep roots into their territories. So the intendancy system did not accomplish its aim of eliminating political autonomy at the provincial level. On the contrary, local and regional groups became even stronger. In the end, the intendancy system did not attain centralized authority for the monarchy at either the viceroyalty level or the imperial one. This failure came as a result of the fact that the new officials, if willing to exercise their new responsibilities, were nevertheless forced to bargain with local groups. Likewise, the aim of having an efficient, honest government was not achieved either, because the intendants often adopted the alcaldes mayores' old cunning habits, especially the practice of controlling distribution of goods, which yielded substantial profits.

One form of revenue enhancement was loans, both voluntary and compulsory, that the central government requested on numerous occasions to feed its military spending in the European wars. These loans became an important part of the Crown's income. The loans and the pressure of growing taxes had an effect on—and indeed impoverished—all the socioeconomic strata of New Spain, thus weakening the colonial credit system and reducing the amount of currency in the market as well.

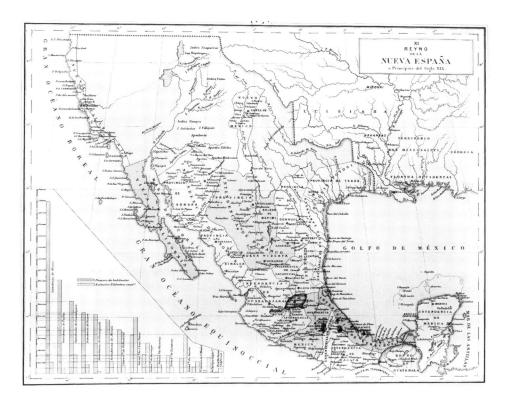

The intendancies formed the administrative expression of the Bourbon reforms. Created in 1784 under the orders of Inspector General José de Gálvez, they delegated royal authority to the intendants in an effort to increase Spanish control of the colonies. Nevertheless, the reform failed to achieve its goal. Instead it strengthened local and regional elites.

The severest of the exactions was yet to come. It occurred when the *Real Orden de Consolidación de Vales Reales* (Royal Order Consolidating Royal Bonds) was proclaimed by Charles IV in December 1804. Resolutely driven by its inveterate, distressing requirement to collect money to pay for European military adventures (as a French ally against England at that time), the Spanish Crown decided to extend to its American dominions a royal decree ordering them to sell off any assets belonging to *capellanías* (chaplaincies) and *obras pías* (pious works). The products of these sales should then be given to the state in return for 3 percent annual interest. Because more than half of New Spain's available capital was at that time engaged in loans made by the church from these two sources, the viceroyalty's credit system was seriously threatened by this royal order. The church was New Spain's main creditor, through mortgages and other financial instruments.

This measure was ruthlessly implemented by Viceroy José de Iturrigaray (1803–08), who, not so incidentally, had the authority to take a good sum for himself. The church was not alone in feeling the new order's impact. Miners, merchants, farmers and even Indian communities, which lost the funds of their cajas de comunidad (community savings), were severely affected by it. Moreover, the Consolidación worsened the relationships between the Spanish state and the church. The Church stirred up discontent against home-office policies among the population of New Spain. The loyalty that New Spain had professed to the Crown for almost three centuries began to erode.

At the time of Gálvez's death in 1787 and Charles III's a year later, the pace of reform began to moderate. Several measures were reversed, and subsequent viceroys devoted themselves to regaining their lost power. Veteran public officials eagerly defended their acquired positions, while merchants succeeded in transforming the mechanisms of economic control to preserve their own power. The ayuntamientos resisted the corregidors' interference and went so far as to express their disagreement to the Crown, while local oligarchies took refuge in them, strengthening their position.

The political success of the Bourbon reforms was uneven at best. For the central administration it was certainly profitable, because the royal income increased fourfold. For New Spain, though, the story seems to have been a different one. Production did not increase, monetary inflation grew out of hand, and a modern capitalist economic structure was not achieved. And despite the fact that free trade helped increase revenues considerably, this growth was offset in the end by military spending.

The Bourbon reforms produced economic success, according to Pedro Pérez Herrero, but also represented a political failure for the Crown. For New Spain, on the contrary, it meant political success mixed with economic failure. As David Brading rightly asserts, these reforms turned out to be a true revolution within the government, which caused the colonial regime to lose control of the political processes of New Spain.

Like other emancipation processes in Spanish America, New Spain's move toward independence was also ignited by the political crisis of 1808, which broke out at the very center of the empire, and soon reached all over the Spanish dominions. This event was indeed a turning point for subsequent changes which, like the one that originated them, were at their beginning of a political nature.

To understand New Spain's emancipation process, it is essential to recognize that political changes are as significant as military events. One reason for this is that while war occurred as a chain of events that remained regionally circumscribed, the political changes affected the whole of the viceroyalty. The political evolution, which began with the Napoleonic imperial crisis of 1808, was a process in which political activity became intense, engendering new ways of political thinking and acting. This shift led to the formation and development of a new political culture, with which the new country started its independent life. On the military side, the armed struggle that began in 1810 opened the way to a process of militarization that also continued once political independence had been achieved.

The imperial crisis of 1808 actually began a year earlier, when Napoleon Bonaparte sent troops through Spanish territory without the consent of the Crown to punish the Portuguese for supporting England. In the process, the French army took control of the main peninsular strongholds. Napoleon took advantage of the discord then rampant among the Spanish royal family, which had led Charles IV to abdicate in favor of his son, Ferdinand VII, in March 1808. Napoleon induced both father and son to go to France, where he forced them to abdicate in his favor the crown of Spain and its possessions in the West Indies, which he immediately conferred upon his brother Joseph.

The overthrow of the Spanish monarchy swept away the legitimate ground upon which the entire Spanish political organization rested. Then something happened in the peninsula which had a great influence upon everything thereafter. A new political actor stepped forward—the people. Indeed, it was the anonymous, undifferentiated mass of the people who, in view of the submission of the Spanish monarchs and many governmental authorities to the French, took the lead. In doing so, they fully embraced resistance against the French invaders.

The military and political methods used by the people of the Iberian peninsula would exert a decisive influence on coming events abroad. In the first place, the guerrilla warfare that had been reinvented by the Spaniards themselves, became the model for ensuing revolts in the Americas against colonial military forces. And politically the Spanish people decided—by defending their king, country, and religion—to take the government into their own hands. Since then, in one way or another common people participated in the newly created institutions, mainly through governing juntas. The impulse to create these juntas was peripheral at its onset but quickly became provincial, later trying to include all the Spanish dominions.

In most of the Spanish American colonies we find at the beginning a similar response in that their inhabitants also resolved to defend their king, country, and religion by creating governing juntas. Such a corresponding political attitude was the result of their similar circumstances vis-à-vis the metropolis and their colonial situation, which implied their having similar feelings and grievances. Yet the very driving force that conditioned their response was that of the many autonomous and regional interests that had grown out of, or had become stronger, because of the Bourbon reforms. The final outcome was a wide range of experiences obviously mirroring the diversity of local conditions.

The case presenting the most diversity was that of New Spain, where the social pact was broken by a crisis that began in the center of the viceregal regime—that is, Mexico City—and at the very top, at the highest political levels. This affected the whole of colonial society. The imperial crisis seemed to allow for an expression of individual interests. It offered an opportunity to reverse some of the Bourbon reforms, which in an attempt to achieve better, more efficient exploitation of the viceroyalty had alienated the native-born from the colonial government, and advanced egalitarian claims in respect to the Spanish.

The ayuntamiento of Mexico City took the lead in asserting the interests of the autonomists, or those who wanted home rule. In support of its proposal to create a governing junta, the ayuntamiento of Mexico City employed the same arguments used in Spain against the French, points that other ayuntamientos all over the Spanish empire also used against the home government. The ayuntamientos contended that, because New Spain was a kingdom constituent of the crown of Castilla by right of conquest, as long as the monarch was absent, sovereignty became an attribute of the whole kingdom, particularly of its ruling institutions like the higher tribunals and the ayuntamientos. This reasoning rested on laws then in force, yet had not applied for many years, and appeared as a threat to the viceregal authorities.

As a reaction against the movement in the Americas for home rule, the imperial interests took the stage, sustained by European Spaniards who were closely related to the metropolis. Their leading voice, the Audiencia of Mexico, openly justified colonialism in the Spanish dominions and argued for their total submission to Spain. This emerging confrontation brought to an end the alliance between criollo and peninsular elites that the Real Orden de Consolidación de Vales Reales had provoked, thus sowing dissension in the whole of colonial society.

In an attempt to take advantage of the current political momentum to shore up his own power, which had been weakened by the events taking place in Spain, Viceroy Iturrigaray convened several meetings to discuss the proposals of the ayuntamientos. While these debates were discussing such questions as what role New Spain should now play within the empire, they were suddenly and violently interrupted on the night of September 15, 1808, when defenders of the empire used force to put the viceroy and the principal supporters of New World interests in jail.

This coup radicalized the confrontation in a definitive way. The events that took place in Mexico City during the summer of 1808 made possible the definition first and the polarization later of the different stances held by the inhabitants of New Spain regarding the new circumstances that the Spanish empire, particularly New Spain, had to face. The differences between these two postures arose from how their interests were oriented—the peninsulares or Europeans toward the metropolis, the creoles or Americans toward the colony. The common people also burst onto the political stage at this point, both in discourse and in action.

The new political circumstances opened the way to possibilities for action. Some of these developed within the system through the new procedures introduced by the reforms already instituted in Spain, where the liberal forces took the lead in the reorganizing process that came to encompass the whole political system of the Spanish empire. This process led to establishing the Cortes Generales y Extraordinarias (Parliament), which represented the whole of the Spanish nation, including the colonies, and later led to the writing of a new political charter, the Political Constitution of the Spanish Monarchy, which stated that sovereignty resided essentially in the nation rather than the monarchy and that the nation was the only entity with powers to establish its own fundamental laws.

The first chance New Spain had to engage in this process came about in 1809 when a representative from New Spain was elected to the *Suprema Junta Central Gubernativa del Reino* (Supreme Governing Central Junta) instituted in Spain. Because the organizing role in this election was played by the ayuntamientos, this institution regained the power it had apparently lost with the events of 1808. The representation of the Americas in the highest echelons of the metropolitan government—by itself an endorsement of the criollo claim that the viceroyalty was a constituent of the Spanish monarchy—once more opened the way to the interests seeking home rule that the coup had apparently closed. A second chance came in 1810, when the Cortes Generales y Extraordinarias were convened. Once more elections were held, with the ayuntamientos again playing their organizing role.

Chances for political action developed outside the system, too. The use of violence became a viable alternative for the discontented as a result of the example given by the defenders of the colonial regime. After the coup of 1808, almost all the uprisings against the colonial regime emerged from secrecy and conspiracy. A number of anonymous pamphlets displayed the general uneasiness of the populace. Going further, conspiracies were organized to plot the overthrow of the colonial regime. Most of these appeared in urban centers with their members being individuals from very diverse social origins, including many Indians. Because many of these conspiracies failed, many of them reemerged as secret groups under the protection of *tertulias* (social gatherings) and other social events that arose in the relative anonymity offered by cities and towns. In such situations the initiative was taken by urban groups, a case in point being the conspiracy of Valladolid, Michoacán, which was uncovered in 1809.

The colonial authorities reacted with alacrity. Understandably, fear of escalating discontent drove them to crush every sign of disaffection. As a consequence, both sides—the defenders of colonialism and the advocates for home rule—became polarized and took more radical positions.

It was an urban conspiracy, this time in Querétaro and other places in the Bajío region, which on being uncovered by the colonial regime opened the door to the famous movement that emerged on September 16, 1810, exactly two years after the coup. In spite of its lack of definite plans that could offer New Spaniards viable alternatives of action the insurrection led by Father Miguel Hidalgo (1752–1811) got a quick response from certain groups, many of whom belonged to the lower social strata.

This speedy response gave rise to important contradictions within the insurgency. The leaders initially argued that they were fighting against bad government, defending the kingdom, king, and religion, as well as opening spaces for political action and taking part in the decision-making process. These were home-rule demands deeply rooted in the purest criollo tradition. One of these points was to establish an alternative government, a governing junta, which had been longed for by discontented New Spaniards since 1808. Besides the claims held by the insurgent leaders, there were also demands brandished by other social sectors—for the most part peasants and workers, many of them Indians—who made up the majority of the insurgent forces. Their claims were of a different nature, such as land ownership and working conditions, and had more to do with the agricultural crisis and demographic growth, which had not been accompanied

The insurrection led by Padre Miguel Hidalgo mobilized *campesinos* (peasants) and workers who saw the rebellion as a means to redress their grievances about the loss of land and poor working conditions. This uprising of people from the bottom of society alienated New Spain's *criollos* (descendants of Spaniards born in New Spain).

D. Miguel Hidalgo y Costilla y Gallaga; nació el 8 de Mayo de 1753. Primer Gobernante de México por la voluntad nacional.

by corresponding growth in production, than with the political crisis then affecting the whole of the Spanish empire. The insurgent forces were also made up of many of those lacking a place in the social structure of the viceroyalty, those living on its fringes, and individuals of all sorts who imposed on the armed movement their own peculiar disorder and anarchy.

Regional differences also emerged within the insurgent movement, which sprang up in several regions of the viceroyalty but in a rather isolated, idiosyncratic way. That is, the insurrection was in most the cases an answer to the particular local and provincial promblems rather than to general conditions prevalent colony-wide. In fact, several insurgencies sprang up. Moreover, leaders who tried to unify the movement and give it cohesion, like Ignacio Rayón (1773–1832) and José María Morelos (1765–1815), eventually slipped into a provincial perspective. And the second-rank commanding officers took hardly any interest in the movement as a whole. These local interests accounted for much of the difficulty in developing an all-inclusive insurgent leadership.

In spite of the efforts of its principal leaders, the insurgent movement caused violence, disorder, and ruptures at all levels, especially at the beginning. This had the effect of alienating many of those who were discontented with the colonial regime (in particular those belonging to the uppermost social and economic strata) and was thus beneficial to the Spanish authorities.

On the other hand, the response the colonial regime gave to the insurgent movement was, in fact, single-minded. It quickly organized its armed forces to crush the uprisings. It devoted itself to suffocating every sign of discontent, convinced—not without reason—that grievances could escalate or, worse, the discontented among the colonial regime would join the armed rebels. To oppose the insurgent movement, the colonial authorities relied on well-organized troops— the professional army created by the Bourbons during the second half of the 18th century—plus expeditionary forces later sent from Spain. The insurgents' armed forces, however, were disorganized and ill equipped in spite of having some well trained and able commanding officers. Additionally, threatened by simultaneous uprisings in several regions, the colonial authorities and their supporters, especially Brigadier Félix María Calleja del Rey, the most distinguished officer in the royalist army, understood the need to create local forces to oppose insurgency. Accordingly, they restored to the pre-Bourbon system of local militias. The well-organized royalist troops defeated the undisciplined insurgent forces on several occasions—in San Jerónimo Aculco, Valladolid, Guanajuato, and, conclusively, in Puente de Calderón—pushing them northward and finally apprehending the insurgent leaders on March 21, 1811, just six months after hostilities had begun. All of them were put to death shortly thereafter. Father Hidalgo suffered the added punishment of being defrocked, that is, stripped of his priestly duties.

It was a bloody and destructive war. Because of a firearms shortage, both sides fought with lances, knives, slings, and clubs in hand-to-hand combat. In addition to the great expense of the war and the resulting erosion of the economy, already affected by the constant drain of money to Spain, both sides contributed to the declining economy even more by razing cultivated fields and burning down haciendas and towns. The commercial infrastructure was severely damaged, compelling insurgents and royalists alike to create a new one and engage in new ways of trading.

As if all of this were not enough, the war was also fought on the front of religion. In alliance with the colonial regime, the higher levels of the clergy hurled anathemas and excommunications upon the insurgents, raising fears among the general population. On the other hand, the potential impact of these steps was partly lost when some of the lower clergy supported the insurgent movement.

For many of the insurgent leaders, the problems affecting the rebellion became abundantly clear from the beginning. So, in an effort to achieve better results, they decided to transform the movement into a well-organized, integrated one. All of the principal leaders took part in this undertaking, particularly Rayón and Morelos. In the process they attracted growing support from the disaffected in regions controlled by the colonial regime. The material support included one or two printing presses, which helped the insurgent movement make known its demands and proposals and to defend itself from the charges of a government that had been until then in control of the press. Numerous, if ephemeral, newspapers speaking for the rebellion began to appear. Skilled professionals, including many lawyers like Carlos María de Bustamante and Andrés Quintana Roo, joined the movement and cooperated in its political organization. Their advocacy had important repercussions, as it improved the public image of the insurgency by making it appear to be a well-organized movement politically and militarily.

Shortly after the disastrous capture and execution of the first insurgent leaders, Rayón decided to establish a governing junta that would among other things coordinate the military activities of the insurgent movement. He announced his intentions to Viceroy Francisco Xavier Venegas in April 1811 and carried them out the following August.

The ensuing *Suprema Junta Nacional Americana* or Junta of Zitácuaro, even though it assumed national representation, did not formally withdraw from the Spanish empire and continued to recognize as king Fernando VII (1808–33), imprisoned at the time in France. The junta should have been comprised of five members appointed by provincial representatives according to its founder's intentions, but the pressures of time allowed for only three to be elected: Rayón himself, José Sixto Berdusco, and José María Liceaga. Moreover, only 13 insurgent commanding officers took part in the electoral process. Yet intensive consultations were made to carry out the election, including in regions then under the control of the colonial authorities.

The Suprema Junta did not achieve the success it might have been expected to reach and that the founders and supporters had hoped for. This failure was due not to the efforts of the colonial regime but to inner discord among the junta's members themselves. Because the war was being fought on many fronts, the leaders had to separate. The resulting differences of opinion fueled by distance and lack of communication ended in open confrontation. The rebellion therefore drifted toward fragmentation, having lost its core of authority, and split into four large zones commanded by as many captains-general, who disagreed most of the time. Morelos, appointed the fourth representative and overall captain-general because of the distinguished military and political activities that made him the most important insurgent leader of his time, tried to make his fellow representatives and captains-general come to terms, but to no avail. When this effort failed, he decided to replace the junta with a more representative congress composed of delegates elected by the inhabitants of the provinces controlled by the insurgents. He hoped the congress would be a body powerful enough to end the division among the insurgent leaders.

Consequently, as Morelos laid siege to the fortress of San Diego in Acapulco, New Spain's chief seaport had on the Pacific Coast, he initiated electoral processes in the territories then under his control: Tecpan (in what now is the state of Guerrero), Veracruz, Puebla, Mexico, and Michoacán. In Oaxaca the fifth and final representative to the Suprema Junta elected by that province became the first representative to the new congress. Some of these electoral processes were carried out following the model established by the liberals in the Spanish Constitution of 1812. In spite of the differences in the two constitutions and the unevenness of

Andrés Quintana Roo, from Yucatán, was one of the group of lawyers who dominated the Supremo Congreso Nacional Americano, the insurgent government created in opposition to the colonial administration.

the successes in the new electoral processes, they nevertheless fostered ample popular participation.

Established in Chilpancingo, Guerrero, in September 1813, the *Supremo Congreso Nacional Americano*—in whose structure constituted a true alternative government. Composed of representatives of several provinces encompassing a vast territory, the Congress was designed to concentrate all that government's powers and coordinate the exercising of them throughout its territory. One of the congressional functions was to ratify both the executive and judicial branches of government after their election, in which individuals and corporate entities from several regions took part. Morelos, once duly elected as the head of the executive branch, was appointed generalissimo to coordinate the military activities of the insurgent movement. On November 6, 1813, Congress passed an act finally declaring independence from Spain.

Then, to establish a foundation for the new nation, Congress approved a constitution in October of the next year, after consulting with different sectors of the viceroyalty's population. But replacing the junta with the Congress not only could not put an end to dissension among the insurgent leaders, but rather multiplied the possibilities of confrontation among them, especially between the lawyers and the military.

One critical issue of the revolutionary executive body was to establish relations with other countries. In spite of sustained efforts, the new government was unsuccessful at gaining substantial foreign support. The exception was the northeastern portion of the viceroyalty, where the support obtained by Bernardo Gutiérrez de Lara, a criollo insurgent from Mexico City, from the United States materialized in an expeditionary army, composed for the most part of Anglo-Americans (as the inhabitants of the United States were then commonly called). An aftermath of this expedition was the setting up of a governing junta in San Antonio de Béjar that proclaimed the independence of the province of Texas in April 1813 in a declaration very much resembling the Declaration of Independence of the United States.

While the insurgent movement gained momentum, new alternatives for political action arose within the colonial system, as the result of the emergence of new institutions and a new political order in Spain itself. The new legal order was of paramount importance, because it allowed the participation of formerly disenfranchised large sectors of the population in the political life of the viceroyalty. This new-found political voice also had the effect of lessening the appeal the insurgent movement had achieved for those who were discontented with the colonial regime.

The September 1812 promulgation in New Spain of the liberal Spanish Constitution of Cádiz opened the way for those in the independence movement not only to make themselves known but also to satisfy their goals of freedom. This new stature was achieved on three levels: local, provincial, and imperial. Furthermore, the freedom of the press that had been declared by the Spanish Cortes fostered open criticism of the colonial regime.

At the local level, the process of establishing constitutional *ayuntamientos* encouraged the promotion of autonomous political entities and the strengthening of local groups. According to the constitution, *ayuntamientos* were to be established in towns having more than 1,000 inhabitants, by means of long, complicated electoral processes in which large groups of the population were supposed to take part in the first stage.

Although the constitution gave citizenship only to Spaniards and Indians, excluding those of African origin and, with them, all the different *castas*, political participation in New Spain was in fact widespread and varied, among other reasons because by then it had become increasingly difficult to identify who was of African descent and who was not. An example of how varied popular participation could be was the elections held November 29, 1812, for the new constitutional ayuntamiento of Mexico City. Large sectors of the population took part in this process, including the inhabitants of the two Indian *parcialidades* (districts) of the capital and many castas as well. And if this were not enough, all those who became elected were Americans, many of them known for opposing the colonial regime if not openly favoring, the insurgent movement. These results were happily celebrated by the majority of the residents of the capital over the better part of two days. But despite the novelty, everything did not go according to plan for the colonial regime. The viceroy ordered the electoral process suspended and abolished freedom of the press. The electoral process did resume in Mexico City, in April 1813, but only after Félix María Calleja had relieved Venegas as viceroy. However, the electoral events of Mexico City, important though they were, did not hinder the elections in the many other cities, towns, and villas of New Spain.

The provincial or regional interests were articulated in the Provincial Deputations. This institution was promoted by several representatives from New Spain to the Cortes of Cádiz, particularly Miguel Ramos Arizpe and José Miguel Guridi y Alcocer. To establish these new bodies, the territory of New Spain was divided into six regions. This scheme was not always implemented, and even in those regions in which the provincial deputations were actually established they did not last, due to the shortness of the first constitutional period (1812–14). Yet electoral processes were needed to establish them, which in their first stage allowed the effective political participation of large sectors of the population.

At the imperial level, similar events occurred. The election of deputies to the Spanish Cortes, which would represent New Spain, in the first stage—popular participation—the electoral process coincided with the election of the provincial deputations.

Because the elections made abundantly clear the extent of the popular uneasiness with the colonial regime, the authorities sought to reverse their results. Besides suspending some of these processes, electoral supporters of the rebellion, well-known independents, and those who had expressed discontent with the royalist regime were persecuted. The punitive program came about as many individuals took advantage of the political options opened by both the insurgent movement and the constitutional regime. These two avenues also led to the joining of efforts between those fighting within the system and those on the outside.

One of the ways the insurgents found to unite their efforts was the secret political organizations that began to emerge, demonstrating in the process that a new political culture was on the make. Organizing secret societies was not an easy task for the inhabitants of New Spain. On the one hand, they had no previous experience with such matters. On the other hand, they did not know how to keep a secret. The carelessness they showed led on several occasions to their discovery by the authorities, as occurred in Mexico City, where two conspiracies were uncovered in 1811. The first, denounced in April of that year, attempted to establish a governing junta, maintaining the tradition of home rule. The second, discovered the following August, had intended to support Rayón and the Junta de Zitácuaro.

The secret society known as the Guadalupes was organized around a small nucleus that included several well-known residents of the capital, many of whom were lawyers. The Guadalupes articulated the interests of many (including several Indian functionaries) who were discontented with the colonial regime. They formed primarily to support the insurgent leaders in organizing their movement politically by establishing an alternative government. Their help was very useful to the insurgents, because the Guadalupes succeeded in dispatching money, arms, men, and information to Rayón and later to Morelos and Mariano Matamoros. At the same time, the Guadalupes fostered their own interests within the system and some took part, with great success, in the electoral processes then being held in Mexico City. The group remained active until 1814, when the defeats suffered by the insurgent leaders they were in contact with allowed the colonial government's authorities to proceed against them.

Another secret group emerged in 1812 in the city of Jalapa, Veracruz, as a branch of the *Sociedad de Caballeros Racionales* (Society of the Rational Knights) that had been established the previous year in Cádiz by several delegates to the Cortes from the Americas. Like the Guadalupes, the Jalapa group supported the insurgent movement by supplying money, men, arms, and information. It was also closely linked with an alternative government, the *Junta Provisional Gubernativa* (Provisional Governing Junta) established in the town of Naolingo. Unlike the Guadalupes, this secret society did not last long, just three months. When its existence was revealed many of its members were imprisoned, while others fled the city and joined the insurgent Junta Provisional Gubernativa.

Unfortunately, a real conjunction of interests among the rebels and the discontented could not be reached. This failure weakened the uprising and strengthened the colonial regime. On the other hand, the division and confrontation between the lawyers and the military, and between the men of letters and the men of arms then going on in the Supreme Congress led to the predominance of the former in each case. Henceforth, the direction and control of the armed struggle ceased to be exclusively in the hands of the military, which led to severe defeats and finally the collapse of the insurgent movement.

In obeying marching orders issued by the Supreme Congress, both Rayón and Morelos suffered terrible defeats. Morelos's defeats had serious consequences, because he lost his able seconds in command Mariano Matamoros and Hermenegildo Galeana. He also lost many of his men in the battle of Tlacotepec in February 1814, which allowed the colonial authorities to find out who his supporters and contacts were and to proceed against them. Several members of the Guadalupes were then prosecuted. As a consequence of this chain of defeats, Morelos was stripped of his executive power by Congress. No longer in command of an important army, he became a mere adjunct to the legislative power.

The year 1814 saw many insurgent defeats. It was also the year of the return of Ferdinand VII to the Spanish throne, of the abolition of the constitutional order, and of the restoration of the ancien regime. These events would have serious consequences for New Spain, because the colonial authorities, once freed of the fetters imposed on them by the liberal dispositions of the Cortes, could proceed against the independence seekers and the discontented.

Morelos's imprisonment and ensuing death at the end of 1815 signaled the beginning of the end for the organized insurgent movement, especially after the

dissolution of the Congress by insurgent commanding officer Manuel Mier y
Terán in Tehuacán, Puebla that December. The movement lost its offensive impetus and finally fell to pieces.

According to Christon I. Archer, the dissolution of the organized forces of
rebellion did not imply the end of the insurgent movement, nor even its diminu-
tion. Archer argues that the dissolution of a never fully united movement meant
an increase in military activities, which had a negative impact on the colonial
regime, because the regime had to invest more men and money to keep up with
this increase. From 1815 on the insurgency almost ceased to exist as a political
movement by losing its coordinating and organizing core, and became almost
exclusively a military one.

In spite of this dispersion and disintegration, efforts to organize the insurgency endured. Once the Congress was dissolved, the *Junta Gubernativa de las
Provincias de Occidente* (Governing Junta of the Western Provinces) and *Junta Sub-
alterna de Taretan* (Subaltern Junta of Taretan) emerged. Shortly after, the Junta of
Taretan was followed by the Junta of Jaujilla, which lasted until 1818. Although
this junta was not acknowledged by Rayón, it carried out several actions, among
them the organizing of insurgent troops. Furthermore, its legitimacy was
acknowledged by other insurgent leaders like Vicente Guerrero (1783–1831).
Xavier Mina (1789–1817) asked for and received support from the Junta of Jaujilla to undertake various military actions, but in the end the junta had a fate similar to that of its predecessors. It capitulated after being pursued and attacked by
the royalists and its members were taken prisoner, thus ending its activities. Its
successor, a junta established in Las Balsas by Guerrero, did not last long either.

The lack of cohesion of the insurgent movement clearly appeared during
Xavier Mina's expedition to New Spain in 1817, which aroused terror among the
colonial authorities and ended in failure. The presence of professional foreign
troops commanded by such an excellent officer as Mina and accompanied by such
a well-known personage discontented with the colonial regime as Father Ser-
vando Teresa de Mier (1765–1827) should have given a great impulse to the
insurgent movement, but this was not the case. Mina not only failed to obtain
insurgent support for his expedition but found himself harassed by the very commanding officers who should have helped him but refused, because they saw him
as a threat to their acquired positions.

In order to meet the new demands posed by this regionalized and fragmented
insurgency, besides sending troops to fight it, the colonial authorities extended
indultos (royal pardons), thus persuading many insurgents to lay down their arms.
In this way the insurgent movement lost not only its military momentum but its
political impulse as well. As a result, by 1820 New Spain was almost entirely
pacified.

Because of the colonial condition of New Spain, the end of its emancipation
process, like its beginning, ran parallel to the events then taking place in Spain,
where the struggle between constitutionalist and absolutist forces led to the triumph of the former and to the restoration of the constitutional order in 1820.

Secret societies that developed in the Iberian peninsula around that time in connection with the constitutionalist forces paid a key role in this process. These societies also started to proliferate in New Spain. It should be said that, with the exception of the secret society known as the Guadalupes and that of Jalapa the rest of the secret societies established in New Spain had no direct links to the insurgent movement. This was true even though masonic groups had already began to organize in urban centers like Mexico City as early as 1813, and later in Campeche and Mérida around 1818, encouraged by the commanding officers of the expeditionary troops sent from Spain. In the capital, secret societies had much to do with the restoration of the constitutional order in 1820 and with overthrowing Viceroy Juan Ruiz de Apodaca (1816–21) a year later. Those of the Yucatán Peninsula succeeded in recruiting both the former members of the liberal and constitutional-oriented Society of San Juan and its former rivals, the staunch defenders of absolutism known as the *rutineros*. They also promoted the restoration of the constitutional order and overthrew the governor and captain-general of the Yucatán peninsula.

The restoration in 1820 of the constitutional order in New Spain, and the numerous electoral processes that came with it, allowed many New Spaniards to promote their own interests. Local and regional power groups were strengthened by the establishment of constitutional ayuntamientos and provincial deputations. Nevertheless, this restoration convinced the majority of the inhabitants of New Spain that in order to achieve the changes they desired it was going to be necessary to free themselves from Spain's political vacillations. So the separatists as well as the discontented and disaffected of all kinds once more engaged in plotting. Like the armed uprising of 1810, an urban conspiracy, this time in Mexico City, opened the way to a new rebellion. The similarities stop here, however, because the independence movement of 1821 was of a very different nature than the insurgency of 1810.

In the first place, the new rebels were former royalist troops led by distinguished officers commanded by Colonel Agustín de Iturbide. Iturbide was sent by Viceroy Apodaca to fight against the insurgent forces that remained in the south, but instead of fighting them he decided to make a deal with their leaders, especially Vicente Guerrero, to proclaim independence. So the new rebels were professional soldiers, well disciplined, well armed, and organized.

Secondly, only a few battles were fought. Towns and cities adhered to the Plan of Iguala proclaimed by Iturbide on February 24, 1821. There was very little bloodshed or destruction. On the other hand, almost all the insurgents joined Iturbide's movement. This insurgency received the name *Trigarante* because it stood for three guarantees—religion, independence, and unity—even if these guarantees were less important than the royalist officers who joined its ranks.

The consensus achieved by Iturbide's movement was based upon a simple, concrete goal: to become independent from Spain. This agreement, which started with his Plan of Iguala and progressed further with the Treaty of Córdoba, was also the product of fatigue: Everybody was exhausted by 11 years of war.

El general don Ignacio Rayón

Because of his military and political abilities, José María Morelos y Pavón became the most important leader of the insurgent movement. His well-organized and disciplined troops achieved major military victories over the royalist forces. He also made possible the establishment of the alternative government, the Supremo Congreso Nacional Americano. He was captured in 1815 by royalists while defending the congress and was executed.

A *criollo* from Michoacán, Anastasio Bustamante relocated early in his career to San Luis Potosí, where he fought against the Spanish loyalists in the struggle for independence. Bustamante supported Augustín de Iturbide's Plan of Iguala, which created the consensus that led to independence.

Agustín de Iturbide and his Army of Three Guarantees entered Mexico City on September 27, 1821, achieving independence for Mexico. He and his troops entered the capital peacefully, amid the cheers of the residents. Iturbide's plan for independence had obtained the support of the majority of the population of New Spain.

The Plan of Iguala argued for the adoption of a constitutional monarchy with Ferdinant VII or some other member of the Bourbon family on the Mexican throne. It began with a summons to all the inhabitants of New Spain to join in a union that would be the solid basis for common happiness. Yet it addressed only Spaniards and citizens of the Americas who could prove descent from Spaniards, leaving out Indians, blacks, and Castas. Moreover, the plan left the clergy, government structure, bureaucracy, and justice administration intact while organizing a new army upon the basis of the old.

Among the many interesting proposals contained in the Plan of Iguala we find one for establishing a governing junta that would rule the country while the Mexican congress met to write the constitution of the Mexican empire. With this plan reappeared the old desire for autonomy that had moved numerous individuals on all levels and in all circumstances since 1808: the establishment of a governing junta. The Treaty of Córdoba, which repeated the plan's proposals, were signed by Iturbide and O'Donojú on July 30, 1821. They specify the provisions for setting up the *Suprema Junta Provisional Gubernativa* (Supreme Provisional Governing Junta), which was to be composed of the "most conspicuous and renowned men" of New Spain. The Treaty also established that the executive power should be exercised by a regency, with the legislative authority residing in the junta until the Mexican congress could be convened.

The Declaration of Independence of the Mexican Empire was promulgated on September 28, 1821, one day after Iturbide and the Army of the Three

Vicente Guerrero, a hero of independence, collaborated with Iturbide to achieve the break with Spain in 1821. In 1828, he was chosen the second president of Mexico. He served until 1830, when his government was overthrown, and shortly afterward he was shot to death by his opponents.

Guarantees had made their triumphal entrance into Mexico City. As interesting as the political ideas contained in the declaration are the names of those who subscribed to it. They include the most distinguished personages of New Spain's elite, including old home-rule proponents and prominent royalist officers, but none of the old insurgent leaders. Many of the signers of the Declaration of Independence would become members of the Suprema Junta Provisional Gubernativa.

To convince New Spaniards to support his independence movement, Iturbide relied on persuasion rather than force. By doing so he articulated the varied interests of the autonomists, the discontented, and even the insurgents, besides the great majority of the royalist troops and a considerable portion of the clergy and the nobility. After all, the Plan of Iguala offered something to every one of the society's sectors, including those who wanted a Bourbon king on the Mexican throne. The ease of creating consensus, which in a few months allowed the takeover of the until then unattainable capital city, and the establishment of a very much desired governing junta, proved misleading. Consensus had been reached for the sole purpose of becoming independent, but once this goal was achieved, discord about how to build the new nation broke out. There were to be serious consequences as Mexico set out to fashion the contours of a new nation.

10

Fashioning a New Nation

CHRISTON I. ARCHER

On September 27, 1821, Agustín de Iturbide, liberator of Mexico under the Plan of Iguala, entered Mexico City in triumph. Soon prisoners held in the infamous presidio prison—some of them criminals, others army deserters or civilians held on suspicion that they were enemies of the now defunct regime—received their freedom and three pesos in cash with which to support themselves as they commenced new lives. They emerged from prison into a shaken nation.

A decade of bloody warfare had fragmented the Viceroyalty of New Spain, divided the population into hostile factions of patriots and royalists, and intensified old hatreds among peninsular or European-born Spaniards (*gachupines*), American-born *criollos*, the complex racially mixed groups, and the indigenous population. In many regions, the native villagers were angry, resentful, and politically mobilized. The war had taught different segments of the population that mobilization and the effective use of political action—even violence—could address their political demands, their interminable grievances concerning landholding, and their chronic disputes over taxation.

These peasant insurgent and guerrilla fighters, many of whom knew little Spanish, fought tenaciously and often successfully for different factions and regions. Although some sought to escape combat and brutal suppression by fleeing into rugged mountains or posing as neutral noncombatants, guerrilla warfare, endemic banditry, and pervasive violence changed the lives of village people. Many Indians and racially mixed people first served under the banners of Fathers Miguel Hidalgo and José María Morelos. Later they hardened their attitudes—and their affinity for violence—in the multitude of guerrilla-bandit gangs that became ubiquitous in Mexico. Part-time bandits raided businesses and elite-owned haciendas, prospering during wartime's anarchy by occupying the agricultural and grazing lands that lay beyond the command of hacendados and government authorities. In the cities, large floating populations of vagabonds, gamblers, and petty criminals frequented cockfights, bullfights, and other popular entertainments; loitering in parks and public markets, they made the night extremely dangerous for respectable urban residents. Nevertheless, as indigenous and mixed-blood people suffered from the dislocations of rebellion, war, domination, arbitrary military duty, heavy taxation, imposed schedules, and narrow paternalism that reinforced low esteem, some also developed feelings of pride and empowerment that would find new expression in the post independence decades.

Although the decade of war affected the Mexican regions unevenly, an entire generation grew up questioning old certainties and learning to live with chronic insurgency, counterinsurgency, and political disorders. Whether royalist or patriot, urban resident or rural campesino, rich or poor, everyone had to deal with interdicted commerce and communications, banditry and other criminal activities, arbitrary demands for recruits to serve the different military factions, and oppressive taxation levied by both sides in support of the war effort.

The crushing authoritarianism of the military-dominated regime in Mexico City was both repressive and reactionary. The regime's leaders—supported by senior army officers, much of the urban elite, and segments of the old landowning, administrative, clerical, and merchant classes—reflected a strong centralism based upon concepts that would be retooled for the future. But this politico-military authoritarianism emanating from Mexico City and from regional capitals such as Puebla, Valladolid (now Morelia), Querétaro, San Luis Potosí, and Guadalajara had lost ground when the imperial government implemented the liberal Spanish Constitution of 1812. In many far-flung regions, particularly where rugged geography, sparse population, and endemic tropical diseases made military operations extremely hazardous, centralized power never gained effective control.

Even when the combatants in Mexico's struggle had worked out actual programs in advance, during the disruptions of warfare most participants lost track of the theoretical principles of liberty and reformed governance. Slogans such as "Death to bad government and the gachupines," "Long live religion," "Long live the Virgin of Guadelupe," "Long live America," and "Long live the king," lost impact, having been repeated for so many years. Royalists wondered if *la causa buena* (the good cause) were any better than *la causa mala* (the bad cause) of the insurgents. Sometimes there seemed little difference between the two: Insurgents and bandits tracked down by royalist military detachments could petition for amnesty if they agreed to change sides, although often they rebelled again once the army was no longer present to enforce compliance. The people of rural Mexico, confronted by regulations and sometimes quite brutal counterinsurgency, strengthened their resolve to control their own destinies. The precipitous collapse of the royalist armies and of the Spanish colonial regime in 1821 opened a future obscured by competing visions.

The Mexican Republic in 1824. This first republic comprised nineteen states and four territories.

	States			Territories	
1.	Chiapas	11.	Querétaro	20.	New Mexico
2.	Chihuahua	12.	San Luis Potosi	21.	Old California
3.	Coahuila y Texas	13.	Sonora y Sinaloa	22.	New California
4.	Durango	14.	Tabasco	23.	Tlaxcala
5.	Guanajuato	15.	Tamaulipas		
6.	México	16.	Veracruz		
7.	Michoacán	17.	Jalisco		
8.	Nuevo León	18.	Yucatán		
9.	Oaxaca	19.	Zacatecas		
10.	Puebla				

Adapted from Romeo Flores Caballero, *Counterrevolution: The Role of the Spaniards in the Independence of Mexico* (Lincoln: University of Nebraska Press, 1974), p. 85.

In many respects, Iturbide's victory was the product of universal war fatigue rather than of a clear decision in favor of a particular plan or new direction. The Plan of Iguala with its three pillars—independence, religion, and union—offered a healing process or a timely compromise program rather than a detailed plan for the creation of a new nation. The 1820 liberal revolt in Spain that restored the Constitution of 1812 throughout the empire presented a model for the reform of colonial governance and an alternative to the highly centralized and authoritarian Bourbon regime that had ruled New Spain. Throughout Mexico in 1820 and 1821 the document was read clause by clause to the assembled populace. Attentive listeners realized immediately that the liberal charter opposed the local military taxation that had been crucial to royalist counterinsurgency programs and that it transferred significant powers away from major centers to towns and villages. Cities, towns, and villages embraced the constitution with unbridled enthusiasm, although many demonstrations surrounding its reception were carefully choreographed, not spontaneous. Such celebrations usually included a high mass in the main district or town church, profuse decoration of the streets with garlands of flowers and banners, evening fireworks and orchestral performances, artillery salvoes, several days of fiestas, and the liberation of prisoners from local jails. Clearly, the organizers and the populace recognized the occasion as an important turning point.

In the city of Zacatecas, the formal meetings organized to celebrate the constitution soon drifted out of control and fueled the rising expectations of the newly empowered classes. When urban authorities suspended popular assemblies, spontaneous informal mass meetings took place outside the city. Municipal leaders and elites feared that such gatherings would incite violence and possibly spark a popular uprising; for example, soldiers of the Zacatecas Mixed Provincial Battalion, known locally as the Pelones (the Dull Ones or Baldies) joined civilians in subversive talk about the outright independence. Elsewhere, lawyers, priests, merchants, and minor criollo bureaucrats in many towns and cities participated in informal political clubs and discussion groups. In addition to examining autonomy or independence, they supported the growth of regional political power against the old central regime and underscored their arguments with agitated calls for the "total destruction of the evil gachupines."

By granting absolute liberty of movement, the new constitution abolished many of the restrictive controls of the militarized regime. It terminated the policy of regulating travel through a system of passports and checkpoints that had helped to maintain wartime order. Then and for decades to come, the escorts of civilian travelers and commercial caravans carried an arsenal of weapons, from muskets and pistols to swords, machetes, and knives, for defense against bandits. Without documents to identify individuals, the authorities could no longer know whether they were dealing with honest merchants and travelers, with rebels, or with bandits. Vagabonds—including escaped criminals, army deserters, and other unsavory elements—mocked police and judicial officers, often addressing each other by the revolutionary term *ciudadano* (citizen) and rejecting the jurisdiction and legal powers of all officials.

In promulgating new guidelines for governing Mexico, Iturbide went beyond the model proposed in the Spanish constitution. His suggestion in the Plan of Iguala that King Ferdinand VII or some other member of the Spanish Bourbon dynasty might come to govern an autonomous and monarchist Mexico made some form of home rule or even outright independence more palatable to former royalists. In addition, the new government would protect the Catholic religion, which was popular with almost everyone. Everyone, regardless of race, was a citizen of the empire, and in theory all had equal access to employment according to their individual merits. Many people of European Spanish origin, who had much to fear from the mass of the population, joined Iturbide with almost indecent haste.

Iturbide pressed the view that the Plan of Iguala was for the general good of a nation threatened by domination and internal collapse. He played upon old xenophobia and upon the fear of invasion by a foreign power that had long been directed against Protestant England and atheist revolutionary France. Such fears, although quite illusory, remained a popular rallying theme and the subject for Sunday sermons by village priests. The elites were more interested in Iturbide's declaration that the government would protect the property of all citizens. Word of the Iguala guarantees spread like wildfire until people of the smallest towns and villages spoke of the program as if it had been accepted by everyone. Even the most implacable of the remaining insurgents—"El Indio" Pedro Ascencio, known for his sanguinary ways—was said to have been so swayed by Iturbide's project that he discontinued raiding and began returning goods and property stolen from his opponents.

The immense popularity of Iturbide and the Plan of Iguala temporarily obscured deep divisions that were to make the new nation almost ungovernable. Throughout 1821, most European and criollo Spanish royalist commanders of the highest and intermediate ranks rushed to place their swords at Iturbide's service. Unreconstructed in their political and social thinking, they made the transition from colony to empire and then to republic as opportunists who clung tenaciously to rank, status, and power. Ramón Dominguez, one European Spanish officer who remained loyal to the royalist cause, observed with dismay in 1821 that "the evil [of the Plan of Iguala] has progressed colossally to compromise the commanders of the different garrisons." Army officers and many civilian leaders accepted Iturbide's warning that his approach was the only means to avoid the danger of catastrophic social violence in all of the provinces of New Spain. Although some senior former royalist army officers were later expelled from Mexico under anti-Spanish laws, many others who had once upheld the Spanish cause with vigor made the transitions necessary to rule Mexico and its regions until the 1850s.

The Constitution of 1812 and the Plan of Iguala reflected underlying forces that in the aftermath of war helped to mold a complex new civic culture. After years of centralism dictated by wartime conditions and militarization, the regions, towns, and district populations reached out to grasp a much larger share of power. While the army officers were deciding to support Iturbide, many towns held elections to form *ayuntamientos constitucionales* (constitutional town councils). They then refused to pay taxes or to heed any directives from the central government. Their representatives endlessly quoted articles of the Spanish constitution in support of their position that Mexico City, the provincial authorities, and any other level of government must find funds elsewhere. Hundreds of municipal governments disbanded local defense forces and abolished military support taxes that had funded and maintained the royalist militias.

The councils of small, mostly native, communities such as Miacatlán complained that the abusive system of military taxation had been a terrible burden upon the common people. Men who lacked funds had been stripped naked by tax collectors who sometimes seized their few "miserable rags" of clothing. Some who resisted suffered beatings and such cruel tortures that there had been suicides. In the city of Puebla, a *cabildo extraordinario* (an extraordinary city council meeting) met to discuss reestablishing militias but soon turned instead to condemning the central government in Mexico City that had sanctioned the free import of foreign manufactured goods at Veracruz—a policy that had damaged Puebla's industry and eroded its tax base. In May of 1821, the commander of the province,

Brigadier Ciriaco de Llano, went to the municipal governments and regional hacendados seeking permission to recruit militia forces and levy taxes to combat Iturbide's rebellion. Local authorities shielded themselves from having to comply by reciting clauses of the constitution. Llano was not the only one to find his constituents refractory. From the village of Santa Ana on the outskirts of Mexico City, Subdelegate Joseph María Torres complained that the townspeople in his jurisdiction believed that the constitution "is some printed patent that authorizes them to evade the recognition of any authority." Torres lacked police officers or soldiers to maintain order. Especially on fiesta days, when drunken quarrels and fights broke out, the villages of his district became almost ungovernable. Churches stood nearly empty, schoolmasters suffered insults from Indian pupils who had lost respect for authority, and vendors sold *pulque* (maguey liquor) openly in the markets before mass on Sundays.

Once the Spanish constitution had decentralized political power even to indigenous towns; much of the elite believed that anarchy had taken its throne, and many of those who opposed decentralization would later reject the federalist Constitution of 1824 and support centralism and conservatism in the 1830s and 1840s. Within rural communities, villagers developed their own politics to resist large landowners, outside tenants, and servile supporters of the state administrators. With quite broad male suffrage through the 1820s and early 1830s, peasants not only managed to control many communities but could delay, ignore, or reinterpret laws passed by other levels of government. Little wonder that frustrated elites in district towns, state capitals, and Mexico City would come to despise unbridled federalism and to view centralism as essential for national progress.

The last days of New Spain saw the disintegration of the royalist army, with the flight of officers and troops to join Iturbide's army, and the total collapse of the royalist central regime. Viceroy Juan Ruiz de Apodaca suffered humiliation after humiliation as his forces deserted to join Iturbide and previously loyal officers reassessed their immediate futures. Earlier the Viceroy had hardly been able to believe the news that Iturbide, his own hand-picked commander, had joined forces with the insurgent chief Vicente Guerrero at Tlacotepec near Iguala "in the motherland of rebellion" and that together the two had robbed the Manila convoy for funds to finance their future operations. Apodaca described Iturbide as "a perfidious and ungrateful chief who has forgotten his duties and abused the extraordinary confidence that I placed in him." Other European Spanish commanders such as the military governor of Querétaro and the former intendant-governor of Oaxaca also expressed horror at the news. Later they would forsake their own roots and careers to join Iturbide.

Unlike many other senior army officers who had come to New Spain with the Spanish expeditionary regiments to crush insurgency, Iturbide was an *hijo del país*, a son of the country. Apodaca knew that Iturbide possessed a complete knowledge of the country—particularly his home territories of Michoacán and Guanajuato—and experience with military tactics and strategies that dated back to the beginning of the Hidalgo revolt. More than any other threat to date, Iturbide was

Don Anastasio Bustamante

Anastasio Bustamante eventually supported Agustín de Iturbide's Plan of Iguala. Later chosen vice president to Vicente Guerrero, Bustamante overthrew the government and ruled as a dictator from 1830 to 1832. He held the office of president from 1837 to 1839.

un enemigo temible (a fearful enemy) who, with the Plan of Iguala, had a popular program. Of even greater concern, Apodaca recognized that Iturbide possessed the raw energy and charisma of the caudillo—the capacity to seduce the gullible and to flatter the interests and ambitions of many who desire the emancipation of these provinces.

He was a dangerous prototype for successive caudillos. As though the blow of Iturbide's defection were not enough, a few days later Apodaca received word that Brigadier Pedro Celestino Negrete, one of the most highly respected royalist commanders in New Spain and second in command of Nueva Galicia, had joined Iturbide. Before long, Negrete grew rich selling exit passports to anxious peninsulares who wished to abandon the country.

The rest was a story of falling dominoes. Each dispatch brought word of new desertions by military, civil, and religious leaders. Before the end of March, troops of Valle de Santiago and Pénjamo under Colonel Anastasio Bustamante (later to serve as president of Mexico, 1830–32, 1837–39, and 1842) accepted the Plan of Iguala and occupied Guanajuato without firing a single shot. Lieutenant Colonel Luis Cortázar, the commander of the Salvatierra garrison, withdrew detachments from the towns of Apasco, Tenería, Amoles, and Sarabia, confiscated funds from local treasuries, and issued receipts that he signed as commander of the Second Section, Army of the South for Independence. With this force Cortázar marched to join the new command headed by Bustamante. Only 257 troops showed up for duty out of a garrison of 2,225 royalist soldiers and officers in New Galicia. The captain-general of New Galicia, Field Marshal José de la Cruz, angrily resisted the sweet blandishments of Iturbide and remained loyal to Spain, but he recognized that revolutionary and separatist thinking infected the city of Guadalajara.

The viceroy ordered the few remaining regular royalist army units to fall back upon the capital, where plotting and recriminations made reorganization impossible. In the abandoned garrisons, small detachments of local soldiers—many of whom were amnestied former insurgents—were quick to join Iturbide's rebellion. An incident in the local garrison at Zacatecas showed the high potential for danger. Two soldiers, one European and the other Mexican, fought with bayonets and knives after they spotted a coin on the ground. Although military police arrested both men before they could do much more than inflict minor cuts, a patrol of the Mexican soldiers commanded by a very inebriated sublieutenant appeared at the scene. Employing the foulest of language imaginable, the sublieutenant told his men that they should not allow gachupines to get away with wounding one of their comrades. He encouraged his men to open fire, pointing out that if the Spanish were killed he could become commander of Zacatecas. The shouting and commotion attracted a crowd, who began throwing stones at some men of the European soldier's regiment who guarded a nearby fort. In response, they fixed bayonets and opened fire, driving the civilians and the provincial troops up the slopes of a nearby mountain. After much firing and many exchanges of volleys of stones, the Zacatecas commander managed to get the troops back to their respective barracks; he then reinforced patrols and doubled the guards at local jails. The incident, unimportant in itself, illustrated how a spark could blow up into a conflagration.

In Puebla, a large mob gathered when the local newspaper reported—wrongly—that an independent government had been proclaimed in Mexico City. The news provoked a spontaneous celebration in which church bells were rung and rockets fired. The governor and military commander, Brigadier Ciriaco de Llano, was under intense pressure to order his soldiers to fire salutes. Fearing violence, he authorized several celebratory cannonades and called out the town musicians for concerts. It took days for local officials to restore calm and to explain that there had been no proclamation of independence.

The confusion at Puebla continued to boil. By the beginning of April, rebels who now supported Iturbide occupied Atlixco, Izúcar de Matamoros, Tepeaca, Huamantla, and many nearby districts surrounding Puebla. Among them were Nicolás Bravo (later vice president of Mexico, 1825–29), José Joaquín de Herrera (president of Mexico in 1844, 1845, and 1848–51), and José Francisco Osorno (an old insurgent chief). Llano's agents reported the devastating failures of royalist garrisons that had simply gone over to Iturbide's force, the Army of the Three Guarantees. A Carmelite friar sent as a spy interviewed some peninsulares fleeing to Veracruz who spoke in awe of the Army of the Three Guarantees and reported that the entire country had embraced Iturbide.

In late April, Lieutenant Colonel Antonio López de Santa Anna, formerly a scourge of rebel leaders in Veracruz province, joined Iturbide. The rapidly eroding royalist regime had few supporters left among the officers. Each night 30 or 40 cavalrymen and dragoons of the Puebla garrison armed themselves with the best weapons available, emptied their company treasuries, and rode out of the city to join the rebels. One group of officers stationed guards on rooftops and armed local residents to protect their escape from Puebla with 60 dragoons. Even more scandalous, a captain deserted with almost his entire regiment. In most cases, these men left their wives and dependents behind to serve as spies who informed the insurgents of every move made by the royalists. By the time Brigadier Llano ordered a captain and another officer to sleep in the barracks to prevent further desertions, only the most useless soldiers remained. Viceroy Apodaca's harsh orders that deserters be condemned by summary trials and executed by firing squads were not only ineffective but ridiculous: Officers with whole garrisons, detachments, and companies were simply changing sides.

In many towns, wealthy residents who had hoped to protect their assets during a smooth transition lost control to radical popular elements. One evening in Puebla about 200 men, women, and children assembled in front of the bishop's palace shouting, "Long live religion, long live the bishop, and death to those who want to take him from us." Fearing that their controversial bishop, Antonio Pérez Martínez, might have been arrested and deposed on orders of the viceroy because he had written in favor of the Spanish constitution and made positive remarks about the Iturbide uprising, the crowd yelled for him to appear on his balcony. People tried to break into his palace to conduct a search and beat upon the cathedral doors, intending to ring the bells and arouse the entire city. Brigadier Llano strengthened army patrols and alerted the artillery. While the populace was kept out of the palace and cathedral, an angry crowd of more than 4,000 people gathered in front of the bishop's palace. There were scattered shouts of "Viva la independencia: Muere el gobierno y los gachupines" (Long live independence: Death to the government and the spaniards).

Llano tried to control the mob, and ecclesiastics and members of the city government attempted to explain that there was no order to arrest Bishop Pérez Martínez or anyone else, but to no avail. After demonstrating their feverish support for the bishop, large bands of men left the main demonstration for other points in the city. Some went to the barracks of the Urban Regiment of Commerce and tried to force their way into the barracks to distribute arms or to mobilize the troops. Unable to resist the pressure of so many people, the commander of the barracks agreed to dispatch 25 soldiers to the bishop's palace. By 11:00 P.M. there was still no sign of the bishop, but a great crowd of men was now armed with shotguns, pistols, swords, machetes, and lances consisting of knives tied to long staves. Tension built until someone in the crowd fired a shot. Without apparent orders, soldiers stationed on the roof of the nearby jail opened fire. Two men fell mortally wounded, and eight suffered lesser wounds. Although the mob dispersed almost instantly, Llano commented that some troops of the Battalion of

Commerce appeared to have joined the rioters rather than trying to restore order. At 11:15 P.M., Llano convoked the municipal council to consider steps to prevent further outbreaks of violence. Bishop Pérez Martínez emerged from a hiding place when he was certain that there was no viceregal order for his apprehension. By midnight the city was calm, except for a few errant shots fired at the army barracks. Llano expressed confidence in his remaining men, who had generally acted with moderation and prudence, but he knew that the situation would have been much more serious if insurgent forces outside the city had intervened. He warned that Puebla had old traditions of popular ferment, as well as a significant number of people predisposed toward revolution.

Viceroy Apodaca dispatched a division of loyal troops to suppress insurgents around Puebla and reopen communications with Veracruz. Senior commanders— including Francisco Novella, who would soon overthrow Apodaca as Iturbide's insurgents swept toward Mexico City—argued that it was foolish to concentrate artillery and munitions in Puebla, where the party of revolution was so strong. By mid-May Puebla was entirely cut off by insurgent forces. Irregular units, described by the royalists as bandits, occupied the roads and threatened the remaining royalist towns. The commander of the royalist expeditionary force died in combat when his troops were defeated at Córdoba. At Puebla, Llano surrendered on July 28 after a short siege and an hour of resistance that claimed the lives of four soldiers. A relief force dispatched from Mexico City with orders to take any risks necessary to save Puebla bogged down in rainy weather at Texcoco and was recalled without achieving success.

To the west, during March and April, Colonel Jose Joaquín Márquez y Donallo led one last expedition in a futile attempt to overwhelm rebel forces on the road to Acapulco. He left Mexico City for Cuernavaca with 600 troops, but many men deserted each day. Overexertion of the horses and lack of good feed left the road scattered with dead and dying cavalry animals. When Márquez went to the barracks at Cuernavaca to ask his men why they were deserting, they responded that many of them had not been paid for months. Some lacked even a single shirt. Many soldiers were weak from dysentery; some officers were unable to mount their horses. Loyal Spanish officers and bureaucrats everywhere looked on dumbfounded at the similar erosion of their forces. At Guadalajara, Field Marshal José de la Cruz corresponded with Iturbide but refused to break his oath to defend the Spanish king and constitution. He informed Viceroy Apodaca that he could not compromise his reputation and honor, which he valued more than life itself.

When Guadalajara collapsed in May, Cruz fled on foot, making his way to Zacatecas, then north into exile. Other loyal officers were not so fortunate. The commander of Guanajuato province, Colonel Antonio Linares, escaped to Celaya when his troops joined Bustamante and Cortázar and then tried to capture him. Linares started fortifying Celaya, but one night young men of the city opened the gates and, with the compliance of the garrison officers and troops, assumed control. A small loyal force of 23 men and one officer from Querétaro refused to surrender the barracks, but Linares ordered them to lay down their arms; he did not want these valiant men slaughtered uselessly by the mob of insurgents. Remarkably, Linares was left alone in his house under loose observation, and he was able to continue sending dispatches from Celaya to the viceroy in Mexico City. He reported that the young officers were the most committed to Iturbide's insurrection; he doubted that without their enthusiasm the common soldiers would have joined the uprising. On March 25, Linares reported the fall of Guanajuato without a single shot fired. San Miguel and other towns in the Bajío provinces changed sides simply because no one remained to defend the Spanish cause.

The sudden collapse of the regime and its army severely damaged commerce, mining, and agricultural production. Subdelegates, town administrators, magistrates, militia commanders, tax collectors, and other officials—particularly those of Spanish origin—often found their lives endangered. In March, Manuel de la Hoz, subdelegate at Huichapan, learned of a conspiracy to declare independence that was to be launched on Sunday during mass, when the militiamen on duty would be at prayer without their weapons. The plan was to capture the militiamen, to rob the customs house and other government offices that held tax funds, and to loot the houses of Spaniards. Hoz was petrified by the threat. He remembered an incident in 1817 when rebels had not only captured him for a short time but dragged him to the same gallows where he had displayed the severed heads of a powerful rebel clan. Gathering up government funds and his archive, Hoz fled to Jilotepec, closer to the capital.

On the roads, gangs of robbers and army deserters took advantage of the growing state of anarchy to attack merchant convoys and rob any traveler who appeared to have money. Town treasuries lost income, which compounded other financial difficulties. At Pachuca, silver mining came to a standstill. As the provinces went over to Iturbide, the capital was seen as the only possible safe destination for senior administrative officials, clergymen, loyal army officers, and even some troops.

As the royalist system collapsed, Apodaca drew increasingly sharp criticism from loyal senior army officers and officials, who also blamed the constitution and new freedoms for giving rise to Iturbide and regenerating revolution. Some arrogant peninsular Spaniards were certain that a few battalions of disciplined European troops and some exemplary punishments would be sufficient to restore peace. The pressures upon the capital increased with the failure to open communications with either coast or with the north and south, and finally with the disastrous defeat of the expeditionary column at Córdoba.

The intendant of Valladolid, Manuel Merino, reported that he had always feared the prospect of rebel forces recruiting the small garrisons of royalist troops stationed in outpost towns and isolated detachments scattered throughout his province. Through April and May, troops and officers under Merino's command abandoned their posts and joined the rebels until the garrison of Valladolid was reduced from 3,500 to fewer than 1,500 men. Merino was anxious to send a cavalry force to Zamora and Jiquilpan to rescue government funds deposited in the district treasuries. He discovered to his horror that he could not trust any of his

General Miguel Barragán, from San Luis Potosí, was a member of Agustín de Iturbide's army that took the capital city in 1821. He opposed Iturbide's coronation as Emperor. As commander in Veracruz, he forced the Spaniards to surrender Fort San Juan de Ulúa in 1825. He later served in the cabinet of President Antonio López de Santa Anna, and was named the interim president in 1835.

General don Miguel Barragán

commanders or those of neighboring jurisdictions. When Merino ordered Colonel Miguel Barragán's column of 600 troops from Pátzcuaro to help defend the city of Valladolid, he received an outright refusal. Barragán (who would later serve as minister of war, 1833–34, and president, 1835–36) responded that Valladolid should take the oath for independence under the Plan of Iguala as he and the people of Pátzcuaro already had done. Merino's other senior commander, Colonel Luis Quintanar, sent his son-in-law to convince Barragán to return to loyalty. This produced no result; in fact, Quintanar proclaimed for Iturbide, confirming Merino's opinion that he was "a man of little talent, lacking energy, and without resolution." Merino knew that there was a dangerous split within his declining garrison between those who were loyal and those who wished to join the rebels. He begged the viceroy to send a loyal force of 800 cavalry and 500 infantry so that he could drive Barragán, Negrete, and Iturbide back to being mere vagabonds.

On April 25, Barragán and 800 or 900 troops appeared on a hill less than a league from Valladolid. Several officers went out to parley; as a result, the insurgent force moved off to join Iturbide. Inside the city, loyal officers and troops chafed at the inaction and demanded permission to go out and fight Barragán's column. Merino, who also continued to negotiate with Negrete, stated that he simply could not understand why no loyal force could be sent to smash the rebels who toured the country with apparent impunity. What the intendant neglected to consider was the fact that officers and soldiers of both sides knew each other well and had no real appetite for combat against former and possibly future comrades. As would become evident during the instability of the next decades, even with the emergence of caudillos, caciques, and factions, most soldiers seldom wished to settle their differences in combat to the death. Together with young, better-educated civilian political leaders who reflected local and regional issues, army officers and soldiers were to play significant roles in the emergence of the new civic culture.

With the old edifice of New Spain collapsing around him, Apodaca had no idea what to do or whom to trust for sage advice. By the end of May, Mexico City was a defended island of Spanish rule surrounded by a sea of insurgency. Many provinces had declared for Iturbide, and the desertion of troops and civilian administrators left even defended places ripe for capitulation with the slightest push. Apodaca recognized that the insurgents had achieved such strength that it was only a matter of time before they succeeded in isolating and besieging Mexico City. By June, Apodaca's remaining army numbered only about 6,000 troops—mostly Spanish expeditionary soldiers. In addition, there was a heterogeneous force of Mexican regular and provincial militia troops—infantry, dragoons, and cavalry from all units—some of whom were loyal to Spain, others of whom were caught in the capital and biding their time until they could defect to the insurgents. Apodaca also enlisted urban militia companies and volunteer groups and mobilized the old merchant Urban Regiment of Commerce.

Until the very end, Apodaca maintained a brave countenance and claimed optimism that the insurgency could be crushed. He took steps to make certain that the troops were paid their normal wages, field rations, and wartime bonuses. During June, garrisons at Chapultepec and Guadalupe protected access to the city, and civilian laborers constructed a new system of trenches, parapets, and barricades. A mobile division of more than a thousand troops observed enemy movements. Dragoon forces protected outlying posts at Chalco and Texcoco, San Agustín de las Cuevas to Huichilango, and Cuernavaca. When the subinspector general of the army and military governor of Mexico resigned his post, Apodaca appointed the subinspector general of artillery, Field Marshal Francisco Novella, to replace him. The viceroy worked day and night with a junta of his senior officers to work out strategies.

Apodaca was hopelessly trapped between hard-line European Spanish officers who demanded the restoration of the absolutist regime and others, including Mexicans, who wanted more moderate solutions. His position soon became untenable. By the end of June, Iturbide's forces had so successfully blocked communications that Apodaca had to write dispatches destined for Spain on tiny pieces of paper that could be smuggled out of the country by couriers. In one, he begged the Spanish government to send 8,000 to 10,000 troops, concluding that the situation was extremely critical and the Spanish cause was "within an inch of total loss." In near desperation, on June 28, Apodaca informed the imperial government that he was sending his own personal agent, Colonel José Joaquín Márquez y Donallo, commander of the Infantry Regiment of El Infante

Don Carlos and the most senior leader of the Spanish expeditionary forces, to present a full situation report and to strengthen his requests for fresh European reinforcements. Ironically, this letter did not arrive in Spain until March 28, 1822—well after Mexican independence. Neither did Márquez y Donallo appear to make the final appeal for assistance. Only a week later after Apodaca wrote the letter, officers and troops of the Regiments of El Infante Don Carlos, Castilla, and Ordenes Militares surrounded the viceregal palace, blocked nearby streets, and threatened to open fire on Apodaca's loyal guards. The viceroy, who was in a meeting with his senior commanders, met with rebel officers, who demanded that he resign in favor of Novella. Apodaca conversed with the troops and begged them to desist from a plan that would undermine public order, but they responded with "a profound silence." Without any alternative, the viceroy signed a letter handing over military and political command of New Spain to Novella. He stated that he had done so voluntarily after what was termed a respectful petition made by the Spanish expeditionary officers and troops. Apodaca requested that the security of his family members be guaranteed and that he be escorted to Veracruz for the voyage back to Spain.

Apodaca arrived in Havana on November 11, 1821, suffering from illness and exhaustion. Later he admitted that he had seen trouble coming after the proclamation of the constitution in 1820. Squeezed between, on one side, the politics of the Mexican people demanding autonomy or independence and much more regional and local authority, and, on the other, the intransigence of European Spanish army officers backed by supporters of the old regime, he had lacked room for negotiated settlements or half measures. As the new Mexican nation would illustrate time and again, polarization between mutually hostile factions over intractable issues produced *golpes de estado* (coups d'état) and *pronunciamientos* (military coups d'état), with officers and soldiers playing major roles in support of civilian leaders.

The imperial government appointed General Juan O'Donojú captain-general of New Spain. His arrival in Veracruz from Spain provided the framework for the definitive surrender of the remaining Spanish forces. The Treaty of Córdoba that O'Donojú and Iturbide signed recognized the independence of what had been the Viceroyalty of New Spain as a new entity called the Mexican Empire. O'Donojú accepted the mission of withdrawing the Mexico City garrison. Although Novella and his hard-line supporters in the capital had played no part in the negotiations, the settlement was inevitable. The fall of Puebla, Veracruz, and other strategic points, along with the tightening siege of the capital, had created a near frenzy among both those who wished to join Iturbide and those who wanted to flee the country. Novella said later that he knew that the end was in sight when O'Donojú arrived without a Spanish army. He also noted that judges of the Audiencia, senior tax administrators, public officials, and all classes had joined what he described as the general "treachery." Those who were Mexican-born wanted to blur their Spanish connections and establish new credentials. Among them were

Juan O'Donojú, the last of the viceroys of New Spain, played an important role in the way the colony achieved its independence. Possessing liberal ideas, he understood that New Spain did not want to remain within the Spanish empire, so he signed the Treaty of Córdoba, ending Spanish rule.

army officers and soldiers, government bureaucrats, wealthy priests and friars, and women of all classes.

O'Donojú met with Novella at Guadalupe, outside Mexico City, and told him that New Spain had fallen and that Spain would not raise a finger to assist any remaining loyalists. He went on to point out that any further resistance or clash of arms would serve only to make life impossible in the future for the European Spanish in Mexico. Novella agreed to surrender only when O'Donojú threatened either to return to Spain or to ask Iturbide to use force against the capital. Novella then gave interim command to another officer and went to Veracruz, where he discovered that the remnant of Spanish forces had retired to the offshore fortress of San Juan de Ulúa, swearing to continue the struggle. Proceeding to Havana, Novella met with the captain-general of Cuba, who had no forces available to support the vestiges of the Spanish cause in Mexico. O'Donojú fell ill and died—which saved him from facing Spain's renunciation of the Treaty of Córdoba. Novella's interim commander oversaw the withdrawal of the 492 expeditionary officers and the 3,699 noncommissioned officers and soldiers who had petitioned to return to Spain.

Iturbide's successful campaign of six or seven months had been remarkable for its political simplicity and for its capacity to enlist support from the military and all other sectors. War weariness, new optimism about a better future, and the message of the Plan of Iguala had made Iturbide the right man in the right place at the right time. Victory was thrilling. Nevertheless, Mexico's new rulers—a provisional governing junta and five-man regency—soon confronted the staggering problems of governing the new nation. A congress convoked from the intendancies, provinces, and certain professions dominated by conservative urban leaders grappled with a host of questions: What sort of nation should Mexico be, monarchy or republic? What sort of government should it have, centralized or decentralized? What to do with the bloated but victorious army led mostly by unreconstructed royalists and many peninsulares? How to rebuild an economy and society fragmented by 11 years of war? Where to find a balance in the developing struggle between executive power and legislative supremacy? How to respond to the different expectations of people from all classes who united temporarily against Spain under the Three Guarantees?

Even the borders of the country were fluid. When Iturbide sent an army to Guatemala in December 1821, a Central American congress that had been meeting to discuss the future agreed to join with Mexico. Until Central America declared its independence in July of 1823, the fragile empire of Mexico extended from California, Colorado, and Texas in the north to Costa Rica in the south. For a time, ambitious Mexican leaders even contemplated a plan to reclaim the North American Pacific Ocean littoral as far north as Russian Alaska.

Although the Treaty of Córdoba provided for a European monarch to rule Mexico, it left open the possibility that the Mexican congress might choose an American-born candidate. Taking full advantage of his popularity, Iturbide surrendered to his ambitions and accepted the crown. His ten-month reign—from May of 1822 until his abdication in March of 1823—compounded the divisions within Mexico and underscored the fact that fragmentation would make nation-building almost impossible. Equally ambitious army officers supported by civilian leaders—many of them former royalists like Iturbide himself—repeated the process Iturbide had begun, issuing their own plans and rebelling against the government. Brigadier Santa Anna at Veracruz, supported by former insurgents Vicente Guerrero and Nicolás Bravo, issued the divisive Plan of Veracruz to oppose Iturbide and to reiterate the guarantees enshrined in the Plan of Iguala. Besieged at Veracruz and accused of conniving with the Spanish who controlled the fortress of San Juan de Ulúa there, Santa Anna faced a bleak future. But the imperial officers sent to destroy him joined him in proclaiming the Plan of Casa Mata, which reiterated the view that arbitrary centralism enforced by a Mexico City regime was unacceptable to people of the regions. In the provinces, local authorities abolished central government taxes, rejected paper money, and refused where possible to contribute to forced loans. Clearly, some form of decentralized government or federalism was essential to satisfy the needs of the Mexican provinces.

Throughout 1823, the provinces of Oaxaca, Yucatán, Jalisco, and Zacatecas declared themselves sovereign states and raised militia forces for defense, if necessary, against the regular army. A constituent congress convened to draft a new national constitution had to recognize that most provinces now described themselves as states. A small minority, including Carlos Maria de Bustamante, opposed federalism. Yet those who believed that Mexico required a strong centralized government—including many church leaders, wealthy merchants, and senior army officers—could not stand in the way of a charter that would grant considerable sovereignty to the states. Others advocated moderation, pointing out that Mexico was still technically at war with Spain and that the national government needed to be strong enough to deal with internal social and economic dislocations. In the end, the moderate delegates' concept of shared sovereignty won approval.

The Constitution of 1824 incorporated many principles of the Spanish Constitution of 1812, with modifications to reflect federalism and republicanism. Despite strong reservations about dangers inherent in establishing a powerful executive, for the sake of efficiency the idea of a controllable executive committee was dropped in favor of a single president of the nation. In many respects, the constitution dealt with realistic demands and the unique circumstances of molding a Mexican nation. Unfortunately, internal chaos, violence, and external forces would erode the effectiveness of the First Federal Republic.

Unfortunately for the infant Mexican nation, the Spanish imperial government angrily rejected O'Donojú's Treaty of Córdoba and refused to recognize Mexican independence. Adopting an intransigent position, Spain set a disastrous course that was to make life hell for many peninsular Spaniards who remained in Mexico; at least part of the powerful thrust to expel the Spanish during the 1820s and 1830s might have been avoided had Spain recognized the new nation. And because Spain posed a clear danger to Mexican independence, the army and defense remained major priorities despite their high cost. Indeed, an abortive attack on Tampico in 1829 by an expeditionary force from Cuba proved to Mexicans that military preparedness was essential. This need accentuated the importance of martial institutions and of individual army commanders such as Antonio López de Santa Anna, who, as the hero of Tampico, strengthened his already powerful support in the province of Veracruz. His ability to capture political power as the foremost national caudillo of the coming period would owe much to his reputation for having defeated the Spanish.

Many peninsular officers abandoned their Spanish army careers to embrace the Plan of Iguala and remain in Mexico with high military and civil posts—a fact that made many Mexican-born officers jealous. With Spain continuing to threaten Mexican independence, ambitious Mexicans did not have far to look when they wished to attack the Spanish as disloyal, dangerous, and evil. After 11 years of war, the militarization of society, and the fostering of deeply entrenched guerrilla and bandit traditions, Mexico needed a long stretch of peace in which to settle divisions, establish institutions, and make fundamental assessments directed toward the formulation of the nation. Sadly, Mexico did not get peace. But if the fashioning of democratic institutions was a messy, complex, time-consuming process, there were those who believed that they could short-circuit gradual evolutionary processes and impose more immediate arbitrary solutions.

The presence of external enemies such as Spain (and later France and the United States) created an ideal atmosphere for the rise of individual caudillos and caciques. Critics then and today of military men and of martial institutions have failed to recognize that army commanders often believed sincerely that they alone could end disorder and anarchy. The regular army and provincial civic militias became the tools of ambitious politician-commanders who took on dual roles, defending both the new nation and their individual regional fiefdoms. Politics and attitudes would be hardened by unwavering principles, narrow philosophies, stubborn regional interests, and a palpable unwillingness by Mexicans of different views to make the concessions necessary for national consensus.

Spain's corrosive role in all of this commenced with Iturbide's victory and rested upon the mistaken belief that a powerful expeditionary force could restore Spanish rule and that the insurgents had failed to deliver on their promises to produce a better nation. In this vein, a Veracruz resident named Aryoso Garrido reported at length in December of 1821 that Mexican towns suffered heavy unpopular taxation, that former soldiers of European birth labored at trivial tasks for pay below subsistence levels, and that there was an air of general insubordination in the country. In Madrid, Ministry of War officials developed plans to retake the Americas, with Mexico as their principal target. Although the Spanish liberal regime decided that it could not order army units to Cuba as a staging area for an invasion at Veracruz, in September of 1821 the Ministry War authorized the the creation of a volunteer force that would enroll soldiers from existing regiments. By December, despite an effort to advertise for volunteers, only four lieutenants and 837 noncommissioned officers and soldiers had come forward from the Spanish army.

In the meantime, exiled Spanish officers such as Apodaca, Novella, and many others, with their families, arrived at the port of La Coruña in Spain. Brigadier Ciriaco de Llano, former governor and commander of Puebla, wrote from Havana in January of 1822 offering his services for the reconquest of New Spain. He had arrived in Cuba with 126 soldiers and some officers of his old unit. The officer who had remained behind in Mexico City to assist the transport of departing royalist soldiers arrived at La Coruña on June 1, having been expelled from Jalapa with only 24 hours' notice to assemble the ragtag band of Spanish expeditionaries.

The Spanish fifth column in Mexico centered upon the fortress of San Juan de Ulúa in Veracruz until 1825; later a succession of agents would travel in Mexico covertly to observe the political situation, to meet disaffected supporters, and to collect a broad range of published data. As might be expected, relations between Mexican authorities in the port of Veracruz and Spanish defenders of the offshore fortress often flared into conflict. Episodes of random shelling back and forth or mere threats of destruction interrupted the normal commerce through Veracruz, which continued to be Mexico's main port of import and export. In 1822, Brigadier Domingo Luaces, who had surrendered Querétaro to join Iturbide, took charge of negotiations at Veracruz. His intention was to get the old and highly eccentric Field Marshal José Dávila at San Juan de Ulúa to give up the spoiler's role in a lost cause. As might be expected, Dávila would have nothing to do with Luaces's request; he refused even to consider a withdrawal of Spanish forces from

San Juan de Ulúa. Responding to critical remarks by Luaces, Dávila answered in a similar vein and rubbed in the element of treason to belittle his adversary. He informed Luaces: "I am neither stubborn nor insubordinate. I am a Spaniard, a soldier, and believer in my views. Do not think that you could make me a criminal against my government and my nation." Members of Veracruz's merchant guild complained bitterly that Dávila had locked himself up in San Juan de Ulúa, from whence he interfered with the flow of commerce. The merchants appealed directly to the minister of overseas affairs in Madrid, arguing that they wanted open trade with Spain and the removal of Dávila to prevent rivalries and "a horrible effusion of blood."

Although such a peaceful solution would have been wise, the Spanish government vacillated between planning military reconquest and seeking other means to achieve a negotiated return of Mexican dependency. Dávila's successor at San Juan de Ulúa, interim captain general of New Spain, Francisco Limaur, would observe the uprising of Santa Anna against Iturbide and later the overthrow of the Mexican Empire. Although the fortress capitulated in 1825, Spanish archives for the 1820s contain many reports by spies and plans to retake Mexico. For many Spaniards, the loss of Mexico was a mortal blow that simply could not be accepted. Spanish observers misunderstood Mexican internal instability and believed erroneously that Spain alone could restore Mexican peace and good government—although such a conclusion required the Spanish to forget 11 years of bloody conflict and all of the reports by knowledgeable observers that the vast majority of Mexicans wanted to control their own affairs. Spanish observers were gleeful at the 1822 uprising of Santa Anna and the 1823 overthrow of Iturbide, who abdicated after military revolts by Santa Anna, Guadalupe Victoria, Vicente Guerrero, Nicolás Bravo, and other officers.

The animosity was not all on one side. In Mexico, fear of European Spaniards—especially those who had served in the royalist army—led to restrictive decrees that foreshadowed the 1827 laws expelling the gachupines. While the disaster of Colonel Barradas's 1829 expedition from Cuba to Tampico ended all belief in widespread residual support for Spanish rule in Mexico, oppressive patriarchal pressures from Spain had served to wreck the lives of many Spaniards still resident in Mexico and made those who governed the new nation maintain wartime military footing in anticipation of an expedition of reconquest from Cuba.

The independence war left the new nation prostrate and for a time almost unable to restore basic communications and commerce. Foreign travelers described the perils, miseries, and deprivations encountered as they attempted to move about the country. Customs officials fell upon them and caused excessive delays during surprise inspections and at the numerous internal customs posts situated at the entrances to cities. These officers examined passports, searched baggage carefully, and collected inflated taxes on commercial goods—although the payment of bribes sped the process. Inns were dirty, food and drink (including dried beef and pulque) made many foreign travelers suffer diarrhea, dysentery,

Following the ten years of fighting for independence, banditry became endemic throughout Mexico. Often travelers from Veracruz to Mexico City would be robbed two or three times before reaching their destination.

and stomach cramps. And there were the ubiquitous bandits, robbers, and pickpockets waiting to remove possessions and threaten lives. Even in Mexico City, the American minister Joel Poinsett and other visitors noted that despite good lighting and patrols, robberies, murders, and assassinations were so frequent that everyone of substance went about heavily armed. Lieutenant Robert Hardy reported violent crimes in districts of the capital involving *léperos* (vagabonds and homeless paupers) who engaged in gang attacks, assaults, and stabbings. When one visitor reported to a magistrate that he had run through an attacker with his sword and wounded others, he was told that the best advice was to keep quiet about the incident. In the countryside, muleteers hired guards and armed themselves and their employees with machetes and firearms to protect their caravans against bandit attacks. As late as the early 1840s, Frances Calderón de la Barca described a "pestilence of robbers" throughout the country. Cloaking themselves as insurgents, these robbers were able to remain active because of civil conflicts and political instability. She noted, as did other travelers, that murderous bandit gangs infested the road between the capital and Veracruz—ruining commerce and paying no attention to political opinions.

Wartime damage to towns, burned-down villages, destroyed haciendas, ruined bridges, and impassable roads made travel in many parts of Mexico both difficult and dangerous. In 1832, British traveler H. G. Ward reported that Veracruz presented a "mournful sight" with houses riddled by shot, ruined churches, and rotting carcasses of animals lying in the streets. The small towns just inland from the coast were ruined, and even Mexico City showed the ravages of the long war. Dark streets, broken pavement, abandoned houses, and obvious poverty were signs of a country that required peace to restore the economy and society. It is often said that half a million people were killed during the independence war; that figure seems highly inflated, but epidemics, population dislocations, and disruptions of agriculture took a heavy toll in human lives. In mining districts, the abandonment of drainage systems and public works and the dispersal of skilled workers slowed economic recovery.

From independence to the mid–1850s Mexico and its states were governed by military leaders who had developed their careers on both sides during the war and were now backed by powerful civilian politicians. Former insurgents Guadalupe Victoria (1824–1829), Vicente Guerrero (1829), Nicolás Bravo (on various occasions, 1839–46), and Juan Alvarez (1855) became president. Famous former royalists who served as chief executive included Anastasio Bustamante (1830–32, 1837–39, and 1842), Manuel Gómez Pedraza (1832), Antonio López de Santa Anna (who became president 11 times), Miguel Barragán (1835–36) José Joaquínde Herrera (1844, 1845, and 1848–51), and Mariano Arista (1851–53). Many others served as cabinet ministers, governors, military region commandants, generals, and diplomats. Former soldiers such as Santa Anna and Alvarez not only attained national prominence but also dominated their regional strongholds. Santa Anna operated from his estates between Jalapa and Veracruz, while former insurgent commander Alvarez made the enormous territory that became the state of Guerrero in 1849 almost his personal fiefdom.

Given the level of political, regional, and local instability in postindependence Mexico, the emergence of ambitious caudillos (political leaders backed by military force) should not come as a great surprise. From the interior to the borderlands and within each sector of the population, the independence wars had left the new nation driven by violence, political clashes between those who supported centralized or decentralized forms of government, and incessant controversies over the power to hold the land, tax the people, and wield district or regional command. In the absence of any other arbiter, those who possessed armed power intervened at every level to force solutions favorable to their views. Army officers backed by civilian factions launched pronunciamientos in which they attempted to apply their own favored solutions and to expel or to intimidate opponents. Some military commanders who became regional caudillos benefited from the disorder, acquiring significant fortunes and vast landed estates. Nevertheless, despite the proliferation of these leaders, no one possessed sufficient power to unravel the national political conundrum, to solve social and economic crises, or to craft solutions acceptable to the central and peripheral regions of the new nation. The loss of the frontier province of Texas and the persistence of chronic separatist movements in the Yucatán were symptomatic of the deep fissures that divided Mexicans. In later life, when he came to write his autobiography, Santa Anna described his own desire to achieve success for his "magnificent country" and his frustration at the "constant upheavals and surges of revolution that opposed me." While he was most certainly self-serving in his analysis, Santa Anna, like other Mexican leaders, failed to discover the key to stability.

Many of the military caudillos of the postindependence epoch found it most difficult to make the transition from powerful regional army commander to political leader constrained by laws and constitutions. These men were accustomed to employing force and often to winning significant rewards through confiscations, control of commerce, and quite arbitrary use of martial law. European Spanish officers who supported Mexican independence often possessed unsavory records that made them the special targets of the state and federal anti-Spanish expulsion laws of the 1820s and 1830s. Even criollo officers such as Agustín de Iturbide faced criticism for his wartime record and his continuing tendency to use force when other means of persuasion failed. Iturbide was well known for his abuses as commander at Guanajuato during the war years; there were so many complaints that in 1816 he was ordered to Mexico City for investigation. For four years, Iturbide complained that he suffered "the degrading metamorphosis from warrior to litigant." He knew very well that his career as a Spanish officer had been damaged beyond repair, and when the opportunity arose he joined the side of independence. Many of the ideas attributed to Iturbide were those of his contacts in Mexico City and elsewhere who were more sophisticated in their thinking. In assessing Iturbide, Joel Poinsett concluded: "I do not think him a man of talents. He is prompt, bold, and decisive, and not scrupulous about the means he employs to obtain his ends." Although some historians have attempted to rehabilitate Iturbide, his support for monarchy and centralism and his inability to tolerate opposition during his brief period as emperor led inevitably to his exile and execution when in 1824 he returned to Mexico from Europe.

Much more important than Iturbide, Antonio López de Santa Anna, a product of the independence wars, is perhaps the principal inhabitant even today of Mexico's black pantheon of those who failed the nation. Lucas Alamán, historian, senior bureaucrat, and leading conservative thinker, characterized the postindependence period as the history of Santa Anna's revolutions. Many textbook writers agreed and called the period before the Revolution of Ayutla in the early 1850s "the Age of Santa Anna." Santa Anna aroused strong emotions. His supporters glorified him as "Defender of the Homeland," "Illustrious Hero of Tampico against the Spaniards," and "Intrepid Son of Mars," while his detractors called him "Traitor to the Homeland," "devious," "overambitious," "vulgar," and "corrupt." Like Iturbide and many other postindependence leaders, Santa Anna commenced his career as a zealous royalist army officer. So anxious was he to stamp out insurgency that he sometimes exceeded his orders to produce an enemy body count. As a young acting captain, Santa Anna soon won the attention of senior officers, who described him as "active, gallant, zealous, indefatigable in the royal service, and of a fairly good level of education." Disgusted by the lack of initiative on the part of timid royalist commanders in Veracruz province, Santa Anna chased rebel bands, hounded Guadalupe Victoria, and executed rebel gang leaders in direct contravention of orders. Commanded to resettle tropical lowland towns and villages such as Medellín, Xamapa, and Santa María, Santa Anna used his knowledge of the region to redistribute land to former rebels, gain the confidence of the populace, and establish the foundation of a permanent regional base. Upon independence, Santa Anna first supported Iturbide. Then, like many other army commanders, he was pushed back and forth in the turbulence of the

Santa Anna represents the stereotypical caudillo in Mexican history. At times a hero and others a villain in the public view, he served courageously in Mexico's struggles against foreign invaders, battling the Spanish, Texans, French, and Americans. His opportunistic politics made him a Liberal, Conservative, and uncrowned king.

The conscience of early conservatives, Lucas Alamán (1792–1853) believed he could guide Santa Anna as president and restore Mexico's national stature following the disastrous U.S.–Mexican War. His sudden death left Santa Anna to his own schemes, including selling the Mesilla Valley to the United States.

1820s, courted by civilian politicians of different factions and driven by his own ambitions. Although he succeeded in achieving high military command in Veracruz, had he not defeated the Spanish at Tampico in 1829, Santa Anna might not have emerged as an enduring figure on the national scene.

The politics of the 1820s and 1830s reflected the division of views and the personalities that emerged from the independence period. In the 1820s, previously clandestine groups in Mexico City and other urban centers formed factions centered about Masonic lodges. They supported leaders such as Santa Anna, Vicente Guerrero, Manuel Gómez Pedraza, and other regional caudillos and army chiefs who made good figureheads because of their powerful regional bases, recognition, and capacity to raise armed forces. The secret conspiracies and earlier political groups coalesced into two major Masonic lodges, first the *escoceses* (the Scottish rite) and a little later the *yorkinos* (the York rite). The escoceses attracted conservatives and moderates, including many former aristocratic royalist leaders who advanced the view that Mexico should adopt a centralized system that would re-create some elements of the old viceroyalty. The yorkinos included liberals and radicals who advocated federalism and nationalism and who resented the European Spaniards who had remained in Mexico and were fearful of Spain's projects to regain control of the country. Radicals who supported the decentralization of power to the regions or states especially resented former royalists who had enjoyed relatively smooth transitions to high positions in the army, church, and civil bureaucracy as well as in mining, manufacturing, and commerce. In some respects, the winners of the war of independence felt themselves losers of the peace.

Even within the church, independence brought deep divisions that were difficult to heal. The Mexican clergy reflected broader society: Many rural village priests and friars supported indigenous peoples and regional issues, while others held more centralist, urban, criollo views. Some clergy believed that by supporting independence they opposed earlier Spanish Bourbon efforts to reduce clerical privileges and to seize church assets to redeem war debts. Traditionally the church had played an enormous role in the daily life of Mexico. It kept registries of births, baptisms, marriages, and deaths and dominated education, hospitals, orphanages, pension funds, and other charitable institutions. Mexicans of liberal views, however, criticized ecclesiastical privileges and immunities, attacked the church's role in education, and demanded the secularization of schools up to and including the University of Mexico. Liberals argued that with independence the old power to appoint officials *patronato real* that had permitted the Spanish state to control church appointments had transferred to the new Mexican national government. Peninsular Spanish priests and friars left the country after independence; the archbishop of Mexico was gone by 1827, leaving only three bishops in the country. They could look for little help from Pope Leo XII, who opposed the rebellion and supported a return of Spanish colonial rule. The Mexican clergy had good reason to fear that the impecunious new government would pursue church wealth and property. Although the Mexican government negotiated an agreement with Rome in 1832 to replace clerical appointments, church leaders felt threatened by increased criticism and projects designed to transfer wealth into the civil sector. A national law in 1833 that abolished legal enforcement of tithing interfered with efforts to rebuild the church's economic position.

In the presidential elections of 1824, former insurgent General Nicolás Bravo, grand master of the escoceses, competed with General Guadalupe Victoria. Bravo, who had accepted amnesty from the royalist regime during the war, was considered the more sympathetic to conservative centralists and to European Spaniards. When Victoria won the presidency, the constitution made Bravo, who came second, his vice president. Victoria's administration stood out for decades, if only because the first republican executive managed to complete his term in office. His successors who held the presidency from the 1820s to the 1840s exercised insufficient power to overcome opposition forces arrayed against them, partly because the Constitution of 1824 had been designed to restrict the powers of the executive branch.

To confuse matters further, regional yorkino factions based in the states emerged to defend radical federalism and regional autonomy. While the escoceses attracted men of position and authority, the yorkinos drew upon the large numbers of aggressive and ambitious individuals from less affluent segments of the population such as government civil servants and clerks, artisans, and noncommissioned officers, many of whom organized lodges. By the late 1820s, populist yorkino lodges could be found in many cities and towns from California and Texas in the north to Chiapas and Yucatán in the south. Their campaigns and virulent attacks, conducted in the press and through pamphlets, broadsheets, and slogans, disseminated their political views. Some yorkinos supported radical state legislatures that passed laws to enlist state civic militias for self-defense and to enshrine regional power against the centralism of Mexico City. For example, in Zacatecas Governor Francisco García raised a militia force that totaled almost 17,000 men. Often, state and local militias represented opposition to the federal army and to the *fuero militar*, which gave the military special legal exemptions and privileges—such as soldiers' right to have their legal cases tried by courts martial rather than by the ordinary criminal and civil courts of the nation. In states such as Michoacán, Oaxaca, and Mexico, legislatures anxious to defend regional interests ensured that recruits for the regular national army came from jails and included those men considered useless to society—unemployed drunks, gamblers, beggars, petty criminals, chronic social misfits, and other unproductive delinquents. In general, Mexicans had a tradition of disliking military service beyond the defense of their home provinces and communities, and that feeling remained strong after independence. With the deepening financial crises of the republican regimes, unpaid soldiers often deserted, sold their uniforms, and carried off any military equipment that they could steal.

Political and economic tensions were inevitable as Mexicans debated how to arrange new institutions of governance and to reorder civil society. Foreign loans negotiated with British banks by the minister of the interior and foreign affairs,

Lucas Alamán, helped restore part of the mining industry and kept the administrative bureaucracy afloat, but Mexico was left with a growing burden of unemployment and debt. And other stresses were tearing at postindependence society. The gachupines became the focus of resentment that gave rise to riots, demands for their removal from public office, and calls for their expulsion. With Spain at war with Mexico and hispanophobia still strong, anti-gachupín campaigns were to be expected. In 1827, concerns about conspiracies involving European Spaniards, invasion scares, and the machinations of some former royalist soldiers led to the arrests of prominent gachupín leaders, including Generals Negrete and José Antonio Echávarri. After being jailed for a year, the two generals were exonerated from treason charges and abruptly expelled from the country. In some states general expulsion laws directed against the Spanish produced violence and divided families. Mexican women married to former Spanish soldiers often could not obtain permission for themselves and their children to leave Mexico with their husbands.

Many of the anti-Spanish political initiatives of these years originated as state movements, particularly in Zacatecas, Jalisco, Oaxaca, Mexico, and Yucatán. By the end of 1827, pressure upon the central government compelled the national Congress to pass an expulsion law directed against surrendered Spanish soldiers and members of the regular clergy. There were special exemptions for the aged, the disabled, and those who had demonstrated their loyalty in the service of Mexico, and many state governors used these loopholes to protect at least part of their resident Spanish minority. Nevertheless, the expulsion laws significantly reduced the Spanish population and removed many productive people. The torrent of emotional, nationalistic, anti-Spanish rhetoric and the expulsion laws underscored invasion fears, concerns about economic failures, and ongoing disputes between centralists and federalists.

As Jaime Rodriguez, the leading historian of this period today has pointed out, the complex events surrounding the presidential election of 1828 set the scene for the economic crises and political chaos of the 1830s. With the escoceses discredited, the victorious yorkinos now split into moderate and more radical factions. The moderates nominated the minister of war, General Manuel Gómez Pedraza, while the more radical elements led by Lorenzo de Zavala and other leaders supported former insurgent chief and popular hero General Vicente Guerrero. Gómez Pedraza, with moderate and conservative support, won more states than Guerrero, whereupon Santa Anna declared himself in revolt. While he occupied the fortress of Perote inland from Jalapa, Zavala organized an uprising called the Acordada Revolt in Mexico City. Incapable of exerting leadership at the end of his mandate, President Victoria failed to suppress violent outbreaks that included skirmishes between soldiers of the different parties and desultory artillery bombardments across sections of the city between the national palace and the Ciudadela arsenal. When Guerrero joined the revolt, Gómez Pedraza gave up and fled into exile. As a direct result of these events, a mob of more than 5,000 people pillaged shops in the market located in the Zócalo, the central square of the city.

In January 1829, Congress accepted the victory of violence over constitutionalism, annulling the election of Gómez Pedraza and recognizing Guerrero as president and General Anastasio Bustamante, who had come third in the election, as vice president. While Guerrero represented federalist and populist views, Bustamante emerged as the leader of the conservatives and centralists. Confronted by government bankruptcy, continued uprisings, disorders resulting from new expulsion laws, and the long-anticipated Spanish invasion of reconquest in July 1829, Guerrero not surprisingly failed to restore stability. Desperate to raise funds, the president introduced unpopular new taxes and attempted to nationalize church properties—initiatives that made him extremely unpopular with many moderates and the conservative propertied classes. When a revolt broke out against Guerrero, the vice president, along with Nicolás Bravo (recently returned from exile) and many others, joined it, although Santa Anna remained loyal to the president. Guerrero retired to his home base in the south. In 1830, with his comrade from the independence war, Juan Alvarez, he organized guerrilla fighters against Bustamante. In January 1831, he was captured through treachery at Acapulco and executed by order of the central government.

Bustamante assumed the presidency at the end of 1829 and immediately appointed the conservative politician Lucas Alamán to the most powerful post in his cabinet. Like previous and future military presidents, Bustamante depended upon a group of civilian leaders to develop policy, to grapple with the shortage of funds needed to operate the central government, and to search for means to repay Mexico's foreign debt. Alamán had no faith whatsoever in the anarchic and effervescent political scene that emerged with the yorkino factions. He opposed the proliferation of bellicose bombast in newspapers and pamphlets, and he disapproved of the states' jealous guardianship of their rights. He admired some aspects of the earlier Bourbon viceregal administrations of the late eighteenth century, especially their orderly administration and enlightened authoritarianism. Led by Alamán, Bustamante's government purged state legislatures, governors, and opposition elements. To further these goals, the government sent former royalist commanders to disband the civic militias in states such as Zacatecas and Yucatán that had backed radical federalist aspirations.

Despite some successes in the economic sector, the repressive policies of the central government brought increased opposition from the states and regions. By early 1832, several states were again striving to blunt the initiatives of the central government. In radical Zacatecas the president of the legislature, Valentín Gómez Farías, supported a petition demanding that President Bustamante replace his cabinet. Jalisco and Tamaulipas echoed this view. In Veracruz, Santa Anna established his headquarters in the walled port city further made impregnable by the mortifying climate, yellow fever, and malaria—a successful siege by troops from the interior was most unlikely. Santa Anna confiscated government funds from the customs house and prepared his troops for combat. Although central government forces defeated the Veracruz rebels on the open battlefield, they did not assault the port city. An expert in irregular warfare within his home region, Santa

Anna organized guerrilla attacks and allowed yellow fever to do its terrible work on soldiers from the interior highlands. Even before government troops pulled back from the tropical lowlands, civil war in other states and promises of aid to Santa Anna made Bustamante's presidency tenuous. Confronting many uprisings—despite a number of victories in bloody skirmishes that defeated state civic militia forces—by December the government was overwhelmed and compelled to surrender. In a peace agreement heavy with irony, Gómez Pedraza returned from exile to complete the presidential term that he had lost in 1828 to Guerrero. Santa Anna rode in triumph with his old enemy Gómez Pedraza as they entered Mexico City to claim victory. Lorenzo de Zavala and other radicals demanded without result that Bustamante's cabinet members, including Alamán, suffer severe punishment for complicity in the murder of Guerrero.

During the 1830s and 1840s, Mexicans struggled over two broad approaches to governance—federalism and centralism—that in some respects were not as distinctive and unremittingly opposed as some historians have suggested. Many federalists who sought to protect the autonomy of their states and regions recognized that centrifugal forces could cause states such as Yucatán, Coahuila and Texas, Zacatecas, Jalisco, and Oaxaca either to separate or to embrace quite radical forms of decentralization. Taken to extremes, federalism could make any form of central government so weak that the nation might fly apart. The goal of caudillos such as Santa Anna in Veracruz, Juan Alvarez in Guerrero (carved from the state of Mexico in 1849), and many other former royalist and insurgent military politicians was to protect the people of their regions, restore economic health, and stimulate agriculture, pastoral industries, mining, and manufacturing. Depending upon the nature of their regions resources and economies, some regional leaders attempted to protect textile production and other industries with tariffs, while others advocated free trade.

Although many Mexicans viewed extreme centralism as a plot to restore control to the discredited system of the Spanish and other reactionaries, within many regions a backlash developed against the extremely narrow localism caused by the proliferation of autonomous municipal councils. Small towns of a thousand people used their powers to resist taxation and other intrusions from larger district towns (the *cabeceras*), state capitals, and the central government in Mexico City. Local officials blocked the implementation of laws and prevented encroachments by elite hacendados, merchants, and miners. In some cases, the local people frustrated good governance, prevented economic recovery, and withheld desperately needed tax funds. Forces unleashed in the independence period continued to produce peasant mobilizations, armed resistance, and separatism at the peripheries of Mexico's regions.

Jurisdictions that had controlled the districts and provinces under the colony often longed for the reestablishment of a more orderly economic and political system. Sometimes the interests of moderate federalists and centralists coincided, and they agreed that too much decentralization of political, power was dangerous. Many leaders blamed the economic malaise, instability, and obvious weakness of

The caudillo of southern Mexico ruled the area that today represents the state of Guerrero. Juan Alvarez fought in the wars of independence on the patriotic side and remained a committed Liberal in the 1850s. He became the titular head of the revolution of Ayutla that overthrew Santa Anna for the last time and brought the Liberals to power. Serving briefly as president, Alvarez ushered Mexico into the liberal reform period.

the nation upon the Constitution of 1824 and recommended replacing it with a national charter that would reduce regional powers. Under the centralist Constitutions of 1836 the *Siete Leyes* (the seven laws) and 1843 the *Bases Orgánicas*, (the organic bases) the states lost power and became administrative departments. As might be expected, more radical federalists—including peasant villagers in regions such as Guerrero—viewed these attacks upon state and district autonomy as absolute anathema.

Compounding the tendency toward a more centralist outlook was the fact that of 19 army division generals before 1847, 13 were former royalists and only 6 had been insurgents. Of 20 brigade generals, 16 had served as royalists and only 4 as insurgents. Many former royalists—including Santa Anna, Anastasio Bustamante, José Joaquín de Herrera, and Manuel Gómez Pedraza—occupied the presidency; others were interim executives, influential cabinet ministers, state and department governors, and leading political figures. Even among the younger generals who came of military age during the independence decade, most who developed successful careers were of urban backgrounds and from families that had sided with the royalists against the insurgency. Many men born in the 1780s and 1790s were still active in politics and the military at mid century. Of the smaller number of former insurgents, Guadalupe Victoria, Vicente Guerrero, Nicolás Bravo, José Maria Tornel y Mendivil, and at times even the more radical Juan Alvarez supported moderate federalism, while others became centralist in their political views. As presidents, cabinet ministers, regional bosses, even as former rebels with regional allegiances, they sought solutions designed to keep the nation together.

In the national elections of 1833, the state legislatures elected the Hero of Tampico, General Santa Anna, as president. Valentín Gómez Farías became vice president. Having won power with a broad coalition of liberal support, Santa Anna showed no interest in actually serving his term in the chief executive office. As he would on many future occasions, he remained in the capital for a short while and then, claiming illness, abandoned Mexico City for his Veracruz hacienda Manga de Clavo.

Vice President Gómez Farías stepped forward to fill the breach. Supported by influential liberals such as José María Luis Mora, he introduced the first radical liberal reform program. In Mexico City as well as in state capitals, governments authorized the removal of centralist bureaucrats, attacked church properties and privileges, appropriated some estates that had belonged to members of the old elite, secularized education, and debated the expulsion of all Spaniards, without exception. Making the church a major reform target, the Gómez Farías government moved to control clerical appointments, canceled civil obligations to pay tithes, eliminated the enforcement of monastic vows upon friars and nuns, and began to disentail church estates and other properties. Gómez Farías also sought to reduce the size of the regular army and to eliminate the special privileges of the fuero militar. Conservatives reacted with inflammatory pamphlets and newspaper articles describing the radicals as dangerous revolutionaries and the incarnation of evil. Fueled by such reports, rumors spread that the government contemplated a program to suppress monasteries and convents, confiscate their wealth, and turn church buildings into stables, dance halls, and theaters. Alamán described Gómez Farías as playing the part of Robespierre in a revolution that now careened out of control.

The radical liberal program united the clergy, the military, and the elite classes in a general cry of "religión y fueros." Numerous delegations went to Manga de Clavo to demand an end to radical reform, and in April 1834, Santa Anna returned to the capital. Accepting the argument that the liberals had tilted the balance so far that general civil war might result, the president now took up his mandate. He silenced Congress by locking the legislative chambers, overturned radical laws, repatriated exiles, and sent a new batch of exiles abroad, including Gómez Farías and other leading liberals. Convinced that the Constitution of 1824 had made the nation ungovernable, Santa Anna and his supporters sought other approaches. In January 1835, a new Congress took office. It was composed of centralists and moderate federalists, including many clerics and

Don Valentín Gómez Farías

One of the outstanding early Liberals, Gómez Farías remained committed to federalism (which meant that the states, rather than the central government, exercised a great deal of authority), anti-clericalism, and a broad-based suffrage for Mexican males. Some of his ideas came to fruition during the reform era of Benito Juárez.

army officers who were Santanistas, personal supporters of the president. This Congress tore up the liberal laws of the federalists and accepted Santa Anna's view that the undisciplined and regionalist state civic militias were both inefficient and a chronic danger to the nation. Restating an old debate about the relative merits of regular and militia forms that had originated in the late 18th century, Santa Anna passed legislation to establish a professional regular army enlisted from the Mexican population. The continuing repugnance of young men toward military service, however, made any form of draft or levy extremely unpopular. Desertion became the escape of choice for those who could not evade enlistment.

Santa Anna once again claimed illness and retired temporarily to the tranquillity of his Veracruz hacienda. But the federalist states refused to surrender their freedom and autonomy without a major fight. The redoubtable Juan Alvarez, federalist to the core, organized guerrilla forces and pronounced a revolt against Santa Anna, claiming that the president had replaced the federation with a dictatorship. In Oaxaca and other states, supporters of the Constitution of 1824 condemned the new direction of centralism and contemplated military uprisings. Governor Francisco García of Zacatecas mobilized his civic militias and ordered his people to construct fortifications. The government of Miguel Barragán (1835–36) recalled Santa Anna to lead a full military expedition to suppress the federalists. Santa Anna's army defeated the poorly armed and almost untrained militiamen of Zacatecas with relatively few casualties on either side. His troops proceeded to loot much of the city, attacking the populace, destroying commercial houses, and damaging the properties of foreign mining investors. Santa Anna followed up this military victory with triumphal visits to Aguascalientes, Guadalajara, Morelia, and Querétaro. Even before his return to the capital, his name was inscribed once again on a column for his heroic service to the nation. Santa Anna received adulation from his supporters and was awarded a grand celebration that included special music composed in honor of the victory, displays of fireworks, and the illumination of the main square.

By this point Santa Anna agreed that centralism was necessary to end the disorder and regional uprisings that blocked economic, political, and social progress. Many Santanistas viewed the state civic militias, radical liberal factions, and politicians who supported dangerous popular movements as principal barriers to national progress. By the end of 1835, the traditional elites, the upper clergy, and powerful army officers of royalist and colonial antecedents were taking action to reestablish the nation on centralist-conservative foundations. The Constitution of the Siete Leyes reduced the autonomous states with their elected legislatures and governors to departments with central regime-appointed governors and councils. The president was to be elected indirectly to an eight-year term, with consultation from the departments. To avoid dissension, there would be no vice president. Furthermore, many assertive small-town municipal governments lost their status and the ability to speak for people of the surrounding districts when the centralists returned power to larger towns and cities that had ruled their regions before independence. By restricting suffrage to men who earned at least 100 pesos annually, the centralists believed that they had eliminated many of the weaknesses of federalism and radical democracy.

Unfortunately for the centralists and for Santa Anna, the temporary impotence of federalists in the populated core of Mexico did not extend to the peripheries of the nation. In February 1836, Santa Anna headed north with his army in an exhausting march into Texas, where pro-slavery Anglo-American settlers had taken advantage of Mexico's political turmoil to declare independence. Santa Anna captured the Alamo at San Antonio in March 1836, only to suffer a humiliating defeat at the Battle of San Jacinto. With Santa Anna imprisoned by the Texans and discredited in Mexico for his acceptance of Texas independence, the conservatives chose General Anastasio Bustamante as his successor. When Santa Anna returned to Mexico in 1837 following his visit to Washington, he retired to Manga de Clavo, apparently discredited and unpopular with the nation that had granted him so many laurels, yet his supporters in Mexico City and elsewhere refused to hold him responsible for the Texas debacle. Continued turbulence in the nation and the threat of complete national bankruptcy kept Bustamante busy negotiating loans from the church and seeking new ways to raise capital. In many regions, small federalist uprisings against centralism and the new constitution frustrated the centralist efforts to solidify their system. Bustamante wavered and even seemed to favor federalist efforts to restore the Constitution of 1824.

Mexico was beset by crises. A pervasive spirit of depression affected many Mexican leaders, who were already at their wits' end about how to drag the nation out of anarchy. Then, in March 1838, a French naval squadron arrived to blockade Veracruz. The French demanded the payment of claims for financial and property losses suffered by French residents in Mexico since independence, including a claim from a pastry chef that gave its name to the improbable conflict—the Pastry War. When negotiations failed, French warships bombarded the fortress of San Juan de Ulúa and the city of Veracruz. Santa Anna went to Veracruz, and when the Mexican commanders decided to surrender the ill-equipped castle and city, the government ordered him to take command. On December 5, French marines raided the city—and in an instant restored the luster of Santa Anna's fame. Santa Anna managed to organize some troops and attack the French as they withdrew to their boats. Several Mexican soldiers were killed outright by a blast of grapeshot from a French cannon. Santa Anna's horse was shot from under him, and he suffered wounds in the left leg and arm. The surgeons decided that his severely injured leg would have to be amputated below the knee. Santa Anna dictated a farewell message to the Mexican nation. He soon recovered from the wound, however, and returned once again a resurrected national hero to the center of the Mexican political stage. The severed limb was buried at Manga de Clavo and disinterred in 1842 for a ceremonial funeral in a luxurious cenotaph in Mexico City. Santa Anna's enemies now referred to him as "the Cripple," and historians ever since have relished stories about the leg and its retrieval by an angry mob that dragged it through the streets in 1844.

At the end of the 1830s Mexico appeared no closer than at the moment of independence to working out a system of governance and a social contract that would bind together the diverse regions and populations. The possible annexation of Texas by the United States was only one of many areas of national concern. In 1839, elite groups in Yucatán deposed the centralist government and severed all ties with Mexico, and until an expeditionary force from Mexico arrived in 1842 to recover the peninsula, it appeared that the Texas secession would be repeated in the distant southeast. During the interregnum Yucatecan liberals privatized lands controlled by peasant communities and set the scene for violent insurgency during the Caste War (1847–1854). In Guerrero peasants led by Juan Alvarez rose up against the centralists. Conflicts over disputed lands, high taxes, suffrage restrictions, and the removal of local municipal governments produced a resurgence of guerrilla warfare and rebellion that continued through the 1840s. Although the peasant ideology was difficult to define, it is clear that the village populations identified their own demands for local autonomy with the broader federalist movement and the Constitution of 1824. These uprisings and many other regional outbreaks illustrated that no central government possessed sufficient military power to restore peace.

In the summer of 1840, the violence spilled from the regions into Mexico City when federalists, led by Gómez Farías and General José Urrea (who had been jailed in the capital for leading a federalist uprising in Tampico), took on the Bustamante regime. Artillery bombardments and heavy musket fire in the downtown area produced many civilian and military casualties. The federalists

U.S. troops under the command of General Winfield Scott enter Mexico City. After defeating the Mexican military at Cerro Gordo and Molina del Rey, Scott's troops occupied the capital until peace agreements were negotiated and signed.

captured the national palace, temporarily arrested President Bustamante, and demanded the restoration of the 1824 Constitution. Frances Calderón de la Barca, wife of the Spanish ambassador, watched the battles from her rooftop and reported: "All the streets are planted with cannon, and it is pretended that the revolutionary party are giving arms to the léperos. The cannon are roaring now. All along the street people are standing on the balconies, looking anxiously in the direction of the palace, or collected in groups before the doors, and the *azoteas* (rooftops), which are out of the line of fire are covered with men. They are ringing the tocsin—things seem to be getting serious." The urban bombardments went on for 12 days and ruined many public and private buildings, including the National Palace. Criminal gangs used the cover of general anarchy to loot abandoned property and to rob anyone who dared move through the streets. The wealthy classes thought that the much-feared social revolution—and the inhuman violence associated with radical liberalism—had arrived. Desperate for a solution, some conservatives concluded that monarchy, dictatorship, or a combination of the two was the only answer.

The 1840s underscored the deep divisions within Mexican society. Within the regions, continued anarchy and minor pronunciamientos (uprisings) damaged the economy and weakened society. Still much feared by young men, the army lost prestige in the Texas debacle, at Veracruz against the French, and in the seemingly mindless combat that ripped apart sections of Zacatecas and Mexico City. The country's very borders were in peril: Texas and the Yucatán remained burning issues, and there were increasing foreign encroachments on the coasts of the Californias. Santa Anna became interim president again in 1841,

Troops prepare to defend the National Palace during the struggle for independence. The activity in the courtyard reveals a good deal about weaponry, uniforms, and preparations during the years of the insurgency.

more convinced than ever that strong centralism and near-dictatorial control were needed to bring peace to the nation. Army intervention banished an elected liberal Congress in 1842, paving the way for a revision of the Constitution of 1836 in favor of the Bases Orgánicas of 1843, which further strengthened the presidency. Property and income qualifications for voters rose dramatically to ensure that the conservative and centralist elite would dominate.

After introducing a new round of forced loans upon the church, Santa Anna again claimed illness and returned temporarily to his estates in Veracruz. By 1844, news that the United States planned to admit Texas into the Union led to efforts to raise forces through conscription and to levy new taxes upon a virtually bankrupt nation. This time, Santa Anna lacked sufficient support or reputation to protect his presidency. In December 1844, General José Joaquín de Herrera led a coup accompanied by mob actions in Mexico City and other major centers. Rioters tore down Santa Anna's portraits and statues; in the capital, they broke into the mausoleum that housed his amputated leg. Santa Anna tried to fight, but his forces deserted and he was jailed in Jalapa. In 1845, the Herrera regime exiled Santa Anna for life and faced the imminent outbreak of hostilities with the United States.

For modern historians, as well as for his contemporaries, Santa Anna has always been an enigma defying easy analysis. He was cunning, devious, likely corrupt, yet also a magnetic personality who attracted the loyalty of highly intelligent individuals such as Lucas Alamán. Like many other leaders of the period, he was a blend of military leader and regional political boss, capable of inspiring intense loyalty from the Veracruz population. He was not a dictator who grabbed and maintained power in the capital; indeed, he preferred to live a country life at Manga de Clavo and his other haciendas. Because of the violently conflictive nature of Mexican politics, his own well-developed ambitions, and his longevity through many decades, Santa Anna was hated with great passion by many enemies. Santa Anna could be blamed for the loss of Texas, for the even worse loss of almost half the national territory in the war that was to come with the United States, and for his inability to control the boisterous new nation. His shifts from royalist to monarchist, liberal, federalist, centralist, conservative, and authoritarian dictator enraged many ideologues. The fact that despite all of these shifts he remained popular and powerful through victories and defeats and the tempestuous disorders of the period makes some modern Mexicans question their ancestors' judgment. Yet although Santa Anna was an ambitious rogue in some respects, he was also a patriotic Mexican and a reflection of the turmoil of a newborn nation and a society grappling for identity and direction. His long career did not end with his 1845 disgrace. Many twists and turns would come during the war with the United States, the subsequent turbulence of the Reforma, and the French intervention.

Mexico's process of state building was shaped in part by ideological themes traceable to the late 18th century that hardened into the politics of liberalism and conservatism after 1821. The church was involved in these developments. During the first years of independence, clergy participated actively in state and national government. Like the former royalist and insurgent army commanders who emerged as soldier-politicians throughout the country, leading prelates served in the first regency and promoted their conceptions of the new nation; for example, the dean of the Cathedral Chapter of Puebla was also a member of the national Congress as well as being the minister of justice and of the treasury. Although there were some restrictions upon high-ranking clerics, the Constitution of 1824 and most state constitutions allowed curates and parish priests to serve in state and national offices; the prohibitions were aimed mainly at the friars of the regular clergy. Especially during the centralist regimes of the 1830s, clerical politicians played significant roles in protecting church interests and opposing liberal designs to reduce church wealth and attack other privileged corporations. José Maria Luis Mora was an exception. A cleric who was also a great scholar and doctrinaire liberal, he advised Gómez Farias to eliminate tithes and to separate the church from the education of Mexico's youth. He praised the concept of the proprietary farmer, attacked the great landed estates, and opposed the system of indigenous communal land tenure. Although truly radical approaches were not attempted until the 1850s, many liberal reformers became convinced that church, army, and communal indigenous communities must lose their corporate powers if the new nation was to prosper. With clashes of righteous ideologies, different realities from region to region, fears of domination by one class and population segment over others, and the aggressive ambitions of those who sought to guide the nation, the dynamic process of nation building continued.

At the outbreak of the war with the United States, Mexico was ill-equipped and unprepared to defend its territory. Its economy was in ruins, its army lacked modern weapons and training, and many of its citizens were unwilling to engage in the defense of a nation that occupied a continental expanse that they did not fully comprehend. On the positive side, through the tortuous first decades the Mexican nation had achieved success in framing basic questions about the future, and had there not been an aggressive, expansionist nation on its northern border hungry to absorb the almost empty expanses Mexico had inherited from Spain, the nation might have avoided the loss of territory and some other disasters. But that neighbor, the United States, indubitably existed, and conflict loomed. In 1846, Santa Anna returned from his "lifetime exile" to lead the republic in its heroic but impossible defense.

11

War and Peace with the United States

JOSEFINA ZORAIDA VÁZQUEZ

Translated by Michael M. Brescia

The United States Army started invading Mexican territory in May 1846 and by September 1847 had occupied its capital. Completely defeated, Mexico had to sign the Treaty of Guadalupe Hidalgo in February 1848, losing a great part of its territory. Mexico's defeat marked the end of the grand dream that had encouraged the 18th–century prosperity of New Spain. This defeat deserves explanation in light of the contrast between the 13 English colonies at the time of their independence and the viceroyalty of New Spain. While the English colonies of North America were less important than the West Indies to the mother country, New Spain was generally considered "the most precious jewel of the Spanish Crown." New Spain had attained dynamic growth in all sectors of its economy, with mining its essential pillar. Vital for financial transactions, European wars, and trade, silver had been key to incorporating the colony into the Atlantic world. The principal contenders in the Napoleonic Wars of 1804–15 found Mexican silver indispensable, thus further expanding New Spain's role in the global economy. However, the commercial appetite for Mexican silver would make the colony vulnerable to European ambitions after New Spain achieved independence. How, then, did the role reversal occur between these two countries of North America by the 1840s, when Mexico's stagnant economy and unstable society came to contrast sharply with that of the more dynamic United States, which became a nation capable of seizing a large part of Mexico's north?

The Treaty of Paris, which ended the Seven Years' War of 1756–63, proved decisive not only for the not yet independent United States but also for New Spain. As a result of this war the victor, Great Britain, as well as the losers, France and Spain, went bankrupt. All three powers resorted to similar measures to solve their problem: new fiscal and administrative reforms that modernized the state but at the same time generated unrest that fostered independence in the colonies.

New Spain's more intimate links with the mother country, and the prosperity it enjoyed, delayed its separation.

A series of circumstances, as well as the importance of independence favored the 13 English colonies; within the framework of the 18th–century Enlightenment, their struggle awakened sympathy in Europe at a time when continental rivalries were making it easier to forge alliances to challenge Britain. France decided to recognize the United States of America. Spain did not sign a treaty but, interested in weakening Britain, supported the struggle. The invaluable alliance isolated Britain at a time when it was coping with a ministerial crisis prompted by George III's accession to the throne in 1760. The American struggle for independence was thus short and relatively bloodless. The British decision to recognize the independence of its former colonies in 1783 bestowed full membership for the United States in the world community.

The political experience of its founding politicians allowed the United States to overcome problems by negotiating the creation of a federal republic. This happened alongside another favorable event: the beginning of the French Revolution in 1789, which initiated a quarter century of European wars. This distraction provided breathing space for the United States to experiment with its form of government without interference, to increase its commerce through neutrality, to purchase the Louisiana Territory from France in 1803, and to force Spain to cede Florida to it in 1819. The Florida cession defined the boundary between the United States and New Spain. Thus, while Mexico was fighting for its independence for 11 years (1810–21), the United States was doubling both its territory and population, as well as enjoying a thriving economy.

The history of its southern neighbor was not as fortunate. With the Bourbon reforms of 1765–1804, the Crown tried to take advantage of New Spain's prosperity. The Crown reorganized the colony's government and economy to obtain the necessary resources called for by its European wars and resulting bankruptcy. The reforms disrupted the older, developed colonial structures to integrate the markets of an immense empire that had been poorly linked. The reforms bolstered the cause of New Spain's provincial merchants at the expense of Mexico City's powerful merchants guild, thus laying the foundation for future conflicts between regional elites and those in the capital. Moreover, the Bourbon reforms weakened the one institution that had served as an important instrument of social control for more than 250 years, the church.

The reforms also sought to bolster New Spain's links to the Atlantic world and strengthen royal power. The reorganization of the colony into intendancies, headed by efficient royal administrators, led to tensions within the highest levels of the colonial administration on the eve of a Spanish crisis in 1808. New fiscal structures, as well as voluntary and forced loans, affected everyone, fostering discontent in the colony. The issuing of the Consolidation of Royal Vouchers in 1804, which called for the confiscatation of the church's liquid capital, served only to increase tensions, especially since the merchant class had been using these church funds as a bank. Thus, at the start of the 19th century a discontented New Spain was decapitalized and bankrupt.

In this context, the abdication of the Spanish monarchy in 1808 became a critical turning point that allowed New Spain to achieve autonomy legally. But Gabriel de Xermo's coup d'état on September 15, in which the viceroy was taken prisoner, unleashed an armed struggle. Several factors contributed to the long, violent duration of the Mexican wars for independence: the importance of the colony for the mother country, Mexico's lack of foreign allies, and the deep social divisions that existed within the viceroyalty. By 1821, the entire population was tired of the chaos, the Spanish Crown was discredited, and independence was achieved through an alliance between the two groups—the insurgents and the royalists—that had previously fought each other.

The Mexican Empire was established with the acknowledgment of independence by the last Spanish official in New Spain. But the mother country refused to accept independence, thus resulting in the arrival of Agustín de Iturbide (1783–1824), who served as emperor from 1822 to 1823. After its long struggle, Mexico inherited a precarious situation marked by disorder, a lack of resources and international recognition, and little political experience. In 1823, it fell victim to the dissolution of the alliance that had sponsored independence.

The collapse of the empire brought Mexico to the verge of losing its territorial integrity. The establishment of a federal republican government managed to maintain the union, but an inherited regionalism ensured that the Constitution of 1824 would embrace a radical form of federalism, with a weak national government fiscally dependent upon the states. Under these circumstances, the new government lacked the financial means to confront efficiently the great challenges ahead.

The weak foundations of the new nation-state were evident: It was bankrupt and decapitalized, with a disorganized economy and a divided multiethnic society of great contrasts that had lost half its labor force in the violent struggle for independence. The new government did score some important diplomatic victories, however, such as securing recognition from Britain in 1824 and expelling the occupying Spanish army from Veracruz a year later. Mexico nevertheless needed two British loans to reach the threshold of economic growth. The harsh bankers' terms were impossible to comply with, and the country lost its credit, making the functions of the government difficult.

The Constitution of 1824 conferred upon the legislature a preponderance of authority, so it trampled on the powers of the states and the judiciary. The election system chosen was quite democratic, without the literacy and poll tax requirements, which were a common practice of the age, so the constitution granted extensive voter participation, which ultimately fueled demagoguery and factionalism. This impeded a peaceful transition of power from the first to the second presidential administration in 1828. Having the army interfere in the electoral process undercut the federal system. This system was hence discredited, and by 1835, most politicians favored a change in system.

After the Spanish Crown acquired Louisiana from France in 1763, it relaxed its prohibition against foreign immigration. The urgent need to populate the far northern frontier of New Spain pushed the Spanish monarchy in 1786 to permit the settlement of French Canadians, Irish Catholics, and even such Protestant groups as Anglo-American Tories, Prussians, and Dutch. Napoleon Bonaparte forced the Spanish to return Louisiana in 1800. Then, in 1803, following the expansionist policy of Thomas Jefferson, the United States bought Spanish Louisiana, claiming that the purchase included Texas. The Spanish responded by closing the border, which many Anglo-American mercenaries had penetrated by the start of the wars for independence. Spain's attempts to colonize Texas failed, and it was scarcely populated. Miguel Ramos Arizpe, New Spain's representative to the Spanish Cortes in Cádiz in 1810–14, stressed in his report the need for settlements, a port, and relief from the military government.

Despite the ratification of the Adams-Onís Treaty in 1819, which defined the boundaries of New Spain, North American expansion became more evident each day, prompting a renewed effort at colonization. Once again, the Spanish Crown gave permission to former residents of Spanish Louisiana and Florida to settle in Texas. This ruling prompted Moses Austin (1761–1821), a former subject of the Spanish Crown as resident of Missouri, to request a concession to colonize Texas with 300 families. The town council of San Antonio de Béja (now San Antonio, Texas) worried about Indian attacks, supported Austin's project in 1819. With a certain reticence Governor Antonio María de Martínez (1760–1823) sent the petition to the general commandant of the interior provinces.

Commandant Joaquín de Arredondo (1778–1837) consulted the provincial deputation and approved the request on January 17, 1821. Moses Austin died, but his son, Stephen (1793–1836), decided to make use of the concession. He and the first 16 colonists arrived in San Antonio on August 12. The governor approved Austin's plan and granted 640 acres of land (called a section) to each colonist, but required the 300 families had to be Roman Catholics from Louisiana, of good reputation, who swore allegiance to the constitution of the Spanish monarchy, Article 12 of which declared that its religion was and would perpetually be that of the one, true Roman Catholic Apostolic Church. This requirement undercut later protests of religious intolerance and the abolition of federalism in 1835, because Austin and his colonists had taken the same oath under a centralist, intolerant Spanish monarchy.

On June 28, 1821, the Spanish Cortes issued a colonization law that remained in effect until 1824, when it was replaced by a Mexican law. And once again the colonists swore allegiance to a new law, Article 28 of which prohibited the introduction of slavery and declared free all slaves who had been brought into Spanish territory. Stephen Austin had lived in Louisiana and assumed that in Texas the French system applied, so he authorized the importing of slaves.

After inspecting the appropriate land, Austin left for Louisiana, and in early 1822, he returned to Texas with several families. Governor Martínez advised him that, given the success of the independence movement, it was necessary to

In his settlements Stephen Austin attempted to abide by his contract with the Mexican government, but many other colonists and new arrivals from the United States ignored Mexican laws and customs.

reconfirm his concession with the new government in Mexico City. Accordingly, Austin arrived in the capital at the end of April, where he met with other petitioners, among them Benjamin Milam, James Wilkinson, José Trespalacios, John Austin, and various Europeans. But several factors kept Stephen Austin apart from the rest: his prior concession, his education, his knowledge of the terrain, and his projects for improving conditions in Texas.

The colonization commission of the first Mexican congress did no more than to collect the petitions and introduce legislative drafts in August 1822; all of the petitions limited the concessions to Catholics, with preference given to Mexicans, soldiers, and nomadic Texas tribes. They prohibited slave trafficking and freed slaves' children at 14 years of age. By January 1823, after replacing the old congress, the National Legislative Junta approved the new law and ratified Austin's contract, which was clearly limited to Catholics, on March 10.

Because the empire collapsed in March 1823, Stephen Austin needed a new ratification. His membership in the Masonic lodge facilitated the ratification process, so while the other petitioners had to wait until 1825 and negotiate their concessions in Saltillo instead of Mexico City, Austin and a Mexican, Martín de

The constitution of the state of Coahuila and Texas established the Roman Catholic Church as the sole religion in the state. Another provision expressly stated that no one could be born a slave in the state and that six months after the promulgation of the document no slaves could be imported. Some colonists from the United States routinely ignored both constitutional tenets.

THE EAGLE OF LIBERTY.

THE FREE EAGLE OF MEXICO GRAPPLING THE COLD BLOODED VIPER, TYRANNY OR TEXAS.

AMERICAN ANTI-SLAVERY SOCIETY.

Resolved:—That we regard the project of annexing Texas to these United States, as designed for the extension and perpetuation of slavery, the slave trade, and slaveholding tyranny and extortion throughout the land; as unjust and perfidious to Mexico and to this country, and equivalent, if accomplished, to a dissolution of the Union.—*Decennial meeting at Phil., Dec.* 7, 1843.

León, were the only ones to get the contracts ratified in 1823. Being first clearly proved advantageous for Austin.

Texas attempted Mexican statehood in 1824, but its small population would have allowed it to pursue two other alternatives: to seek status as a federal territory or to become part of the state of Coahuila. Ultimately, Mexico's Congress approved the second option, but its drawbacks were felt immediately when Texas lost the representation that it had enjoyed under the empire. Texas was made one of the districts of Coahuila, with a governor who supervised the town councils and its own district administrators. Militarily, Coahuila, Texas, Nuevo León, and Tamaulipas formed a single jurisdiction.

Unfortunately, the Constituent Congress of 1824 did not abolish slavery entirely, which could have avoided future problems. The congress delayed a decision as it debated whether or not to consult a wealthy colonist named Jared E. Groce to determine if emancipation would affect the 100 slaves he had brought with him to Texas. The congressmen could not resolve the issue of whether the right of freedom superseded the right of property, so they left the issue of abolition pending. Their indecisiveness would prove costly.

In Mexico, colonization was a mirage in the quest to achieve the same material progress as in the United States. The interior minister Lucas Alamán insisted that vacant lands belonged to the nation and ought to be controlled by the federal government. The congress, however, put the colonization issue in the hands of the states with an August 24, 1824, law. Only lands 20 leagues (approximately 52 miles) from the border and 10 leagues (approximately 26 miles) from the coast remained under federal control. The law also gave preference to Mexicans and sedentary Indians "from all towns that border the state, as well as the nomadic tribes that are found within the borders." Moreover, the law prohibited the sale of grant lands and subjected the introduction of slaves to laws currently in effect. (A July 13, 1824, decree prohibited the introduction of slaves.)

Coahuila's state legislature rushed to enact the colonization law of March 24, 1825. Austin lobbied actively to change the religious requirement from "Catholic" to "Christian," but the change was irrelevant because the supreme law of the land, the Constitution of 1824, had declared Roman Catholicism to be the official and only tolerated religion. Despite the predominance of antislavery opinion, the Anglo-American petitioners succeeded in confining the abolition debate to the convention drafting the state constitution. Austin also promoted the signing of a memorial stating that slaves introduced during the empire were not African but domestic servants raised from infancy and thus were exempt from any emancipation law, and if one were approved, the colonists would need authorization to remove them from Texas. Austin was convinced that he could preserve the slaves that were already there and, with luck, their children until they reached the age of 14. Unyielding in his fight to maintain the institution of slavery, Austin even proposed extending the introduction of new slaves until 1840, at which time the male grandchildren of slaves would be freed upon their 25th birthday and the female grandchildren on their 15th birthday.

Mexico's antislavery stance did not hinder future migration, because a profound economic crisis in the United States had made the Mexican offer of land there quite attractive. In Austin's 1823 concession the land was free. The state of Coahuila and Texas set a nominal price of 30 pesos for grazing plots of 4,428.4 acres (generally termed *sitios de ganado mayor*); the price of unirrigated land (*tierra de temporal*) was 2.5 pesos for a plot of 177.1 acres; and an irrigated plot of the same size (*tierra de labor*) cost 3.5 pesos. (The peso and dollar were equivalent until 1895.) Typically, the head of a household received both a *sitio* of grazing land as well as additional cropland. In addition to the payment of 30 pesos to the state, the head of a household also had to pay 60 pesos to the *empresario* under whose grant he entered and 27 pesos in fees for surveys and title registration. These additional costs included 2 pesos for the official papers, 15 pesos to the state land commissioner, and 10 pesos for a notary. The total price for the generous allotment of land, including all fees, was 117 pesos. The state's portion (30 pesos) could be paid over a four-year period. The empresario also obtained five sitios (23,025 acres) for every 100 families he brought with him. Because land was much more expensive and had to be paid in cash in the United States, the colonists grew to 1,800 by 1825.

Settled in between missions and garrisons, the original colonists in Texas developed social and military solidarity as a result of resisting Indian attacks. In 1823, the provincial diputation commissioned Austin as a lieutenant colonel in the local militia and outlined his authority and responsibilities. His broad powers lasted until the issuing of the state constitution in 1827. Austin delegated some of his responsibilities by drafting instructions and regulations for the use of the mayors (*alcaldes*) of each settlement.

Austin obtained further contracts by winning the political favor of various federal and state officials. In 1825, he received a contract for 300 families; in 1827, another for 600 families to settle near Galveston Bay; in 1828, yet another for 300 families. The Galveston contract, located in federal territory, was Austin's reward for quelling a rebellion in Haden Edwards's colony near Nacogdoches, Texas, in 1826.

With the exception of colonies contracted for by Stephen Austin, Martín de León, and Green De Witt, all the others remained practically illegal. Often, the settlements were irregular and the land was at times even nonexistent. The majority of the colonists were non-Catholics who imported slaves. In the region adjacent to Louisiana, the lack of surveillance encouraged illegal settlers: fugitives from justice and adventurers.

The majority of disputes derived from overlapping boundaries between the empresario grants and from the character of the frontier people. Haden Edwards serves as a good example. In 1826, he obtained a contract to settle 800 families in Nacogdoches, ensuring future conflict, because the territory already had Mexican colonists. Edwards, the typical misinformed adventurer, overestimated his authority and confused his post as commander of the militia with that of a military commander. He demanded that the Mexicans exhibit their land titles, and committed electoral fraud to ensure the victory of an Anglo-American as mayor of Nacogdoches. When the Mexicans lost patience and complained to the state legislature, Edwards's grant was canceled. Although Austin counseled reconciliation, Edwards preferred to travel to Louisiana to "sell" his concession. His brother, Benjamin, who had been left in charge of the colony in the interim, decided to convert it into what he named the Republic of Fredonia. His revolt was put down by the army and Austin's militia after Benjamin rejected the governor's offer of amnesty. The incident is noteworthy because it alerted the Mexican government to the dangers of the Anglo-American presence in Texas and sent General Manuel Mier y Terán to draw up the boundary.

The Mexican government's distrust of the United States dated from the first contact between the two nations. President James Monroe extended diplomatic recognition to the empire in December 1822, but he failed to appoint an ambassador. In 1825, Joel Poinsett was finally appointed minister plenipotenciary. Poinsett's instructions included the purchase of Texas and moving the boundary to the Rio Grande, but the Mexican government insisted that the United States respect the boundary that had been established in the Adams-Onís Treaty of 1819. Poinsett developed close ties to radical Mexican congressmen, exerting much influence over them through their membership in the Masonic lodge. His indiscreet participation in Mexican domestic politics even made his friend Vicente Guerrero, president of the Mexican Republic, ask for his recall in 1829. In spite of his efforts, Poinsett failed to negotiate a treaty of friendship and commerce with Mexico because of his insistence that Mexico guarantee the return of fugitive slaves.

Andrew Jackson appointed Anthony Butler, a Texas land speculator, to replace Poinsett. By dropping the article that demanded the return of slaves, Butler succeeded in negotiating a treaty of commerce. He initiated the indiscriminate gathering up of North American claims against the Mexican government, which would later prove a useful instrument in pressuring Mexican officials.

The hostility of Anglo-Texans toward Mexicans has been attributed to a cultural clash and a supposed military dictatorship. Although it was not easy for people of two different cultures and value systems to coexist, and the Mexicans did resent the privileges afforded to the foreigners, frontier life favored cooperation. Moreover, there was no military dictatorship before 1841. The military commanders of the northeast were honorable officers such as Anastasio Bustamante, twice president of Mexico in the 1830s, and Mier y Terán, who deserved the admiration of the colonists. It was Texas's dependence on Coahuila that created problems, especially after the issuing of the state constitution of 1827, which moved many proceedings to the seat of the state government in Saltillo.

The major sources of Texan discontent could be found in Mexican antislavery attitudes and the establishment of a customs house, which ended years of tax exemption for imported goods. The majority of the colonists were recalcitrant slave owners who rejected Hispanic traditions that, as Hans Baade has argued, permitted "the master . . . [to] manumit his slaves without official or judicial license. The slave, if cruelly treated, could institute judicial proceedings for sale to another master." Ever since the debates over the state constitution, the issue of slavery had aggravated the profound differences between Mexicans and colonists. In 1827, legislators decided to abolish the institution but soon backed away when Stephen Austin injected the question of compensation to slave owners. Due to a lack of funds, the legislators tempered their stance in the Coahuila y Texas Constitution of 1827: "No one is born a slave in the state from the time this Constitution is published in the seat of each district; and after six months the introduction of slaves is prohibited under any pretext."

The colonists were not long in violating the law, negotiating contracts with their slaves upon entering Texas. In them slaves declared that they had received their freedom by promising to work for their masters to pay off their debts. Slaves could collect their minimal salaries after they reached 18 years of age, and since the master deducted room and board, such an arrangement assured them of perpetual servitude. Austin succeeded in obtaining legal confirmation for this contract. On September 15, 1829, President Vicente Guerrero decreed the emancipation of slaves throughout Mexico and, although he granted Texas an exemption, fear spread among the Anglo-American colonists, who were certain the institution was destined to disappear.

Before Mier y Terán's report of November 14, 1829, arrived, the Mexican government had only vague ideas about Texas. Accompanied by three scientists, Mier y Terán's mission was to draw the boundary line according to the

Adams-Onís Treaty of 1819, establish garrisons and other defensive measures, and report on general conditions. The disproportionate lot of Mexicans and foreigners stunned him. He classified the Anglo-American colonists as "poor laborers, who have not had four or five thousand dollars to buy a plot of land in the north [United States] . . . and quite often are hard-working and honorable," as compared to the "fugitives, thieves, and criminals" he found in the Nacogdoches area. In his report, Mier y Terán advised the government to promote Mexican and European colonization and to install a governor in Nacogdoches to supervise the region more closely.

If Mier y Terán had witnessed the wave of immigrants that arrived in 1829, which included wealthy colonists from Alabama and a few whose goal was to promote annexation, perhaps he could have prevented future problems. But he had to leave for Tampico to confront the Spanish expedition attempting to reconquer Mexico and was thus distracted from Texan affairs. At that time Sam Houston arrived, who later wrote to his friend Andrew Jackson: "I am in possession of information that will doubtless be interesting [to] you; and may be calculated to forward your views if you should entertain any: touching upon the acquisition of Texas, by the Government of the United States." Jackson had already instructed Minister Butler to purchase Texas, and the latter spread rumors that its acquisition was imminent. In his correspondence Austin expressed opposition to such a transfer.

Foreign Relations Minister Lucas Alamán, at the beginning of 1830, after receiving the Mier y Terán report, hurried to draft a colonization law that was approved by the Congress and enacted on April 6. The law placed colonization in the hands of the federation, supervised by a commissioner. Its two principal articles follow:

> Article 10. No change shall be made with respect to the colonies already established, nor with respect to the slaves which they contain—but the general government and that of each particular state, shall exact, under the strictest responsibilities, the observance of the colonization laws and the prevention of further introduction of slaves.
>
> Article 11. In the exercise of the right reserved to the general Congress by the 7th article of the law of 18th August, 1824, the citizens of foreign countries lying adjacent to the Mexican territory are prohibited from settling as colonists in the states or territories of the republic, adjoining such countries. Those contracts of colonization, the terms in which are opposed to the present article, and which are not yet complied with, shall consequently be suspended.

The law offered land and support to poor Mexican families who would move to Texas. It created eight garrisons headed by Mier y Terán and christened these new outposts with indigenous names to Mexicanize the region. The law fostered both ill will between the colonists and tensions between the federal and state governments, especially as the latter began to lose control over unsurveyed lands.

Mier y Terán sent the federal government comments on the law on June 6, 1830. He found that some of the provisions of the law were politically naive and ineffectual: The colonists would find new ways to evade the prohibition against slavery; for example, "with false certificates of freedom." He feared that the law might encourage the Anglos-American to embrace "the interests of the north, of which until now they hesitated to do. . . . Like all Mexicans, I loathe slavery, but this sentiment will only mislead the government and the nation in its best interests." He believed it expedient temporarily to tolerate the introduction of slaves. This would, he argued, guarantee the cotton trade and facilitate the passage of a law for the administration of justice, "the most reasonable complaint that the Texas colonists have."

Mier y Terán and Vice President Bustamante informed Austin of the impending legislation. Although the Mexican minister in Washington, José María Tornel, publicized the prohibition, Mier y Terán tried to ensure that the law would not harm those Anglo-Americans already in the process of moving and ordered the consul in New Orleans to expedite passports for Green De Witt's and Stephen Austin's colonies. He even authorized Austin to extend border-crossing permits.

With scant resources Mier y Terán organized Texas's military garrison for defense against the Indians, but he failed to attract Mexican colonists. Only a few pacified Indians acquiesced. Mier y Terán proceeded to terminate all the colonies that did not have at least 150 inhabitants. This affected Sterling G. Robertson, who hurried to bring in 15 families in October. Robertson's grant was suspended, and he and his companions lacked permits, so they were detained at the border. They were authorized to continue to Austin's colony. By the time Austin had been elected a deputy to the state legislature in Saltillo, Robertson asked him to carry through the ratification of his own contract. Upon his arrival, Austin was informed that the Robertson contract had been awarded to a Frenchman, Gabriel Laisné, who had decided to secure it for himself and his business associate.

While Mier y Terán did succeed in blunting the effects of the April 6 law, latent discontent remained, especially after a new law limited work contracts to 10 years. Moreover, two events—the suspension of state land titles to squatters, and the opening of the customs house in 1832—acted together to produce the first outbreak of open hostilities. Mier y Terán favored recognizing squatters' rights, regardless of the fact that these lands were located in prohibited areas (the coast and the border). Even though the law of 1830 stated that land titles had to be issued by the federal government, state officials still tried to issue them. The commander of Anáhuac (Galveston), the Anglo-American-born colonel, David Bradburn, obstructed their attempts to do so. Bradburn was already unpopular because he had refused, in conformity with the law, to return two fugitive slaves from Louisiana to their owner, who entrusted the case to William B. Travis. Unable to solve the problem legally, Travis threatened to organize a rescue attack from Louisiana. Because this act of rebellion against the government occurred on federal lands under his jurisdiction, Bradburn jailed Travis to be tried by a court-martial, but the colonists revolted and Bradburn had to flee.

Mier y Terán had favored the appointment of foreigners to foster better communication between the colonists, and therefore made George Fisher, a former U.S. citizen, chief of the customs house at Anáhuac. It was difficult to establish a customs house after many years of tax exemption, and Fisher was not the right person. When the first North American vessel was stopped to pay duties, the crew responded with gunfire, and the colonists supported the aggression. Mier y Terán dismissed Fisher but also lost patience when Austin protested, answering in an angry tone:

> So many favors that you owe the Mexican government . . . they have not produced more than a readiness to form erroneous judgments and unjust complaints. . . . The payment of custom duties is the obligation of all colonists of Texas, the same as Mexicans everywhere, and only in Brazoria [the port where the customs house was installed] does this cause an uproar. . . . You say that the towns in Texas have valid complaints . . . because nobody knows where the laws governing the Texas towns have been violated or how they are different from the rest of the Mexican Republic. . . . look at the entire east coast of the American continent, from the Hudson Bay to Cape Horn. In what nation, in what port, are taxes for commerce not paid. Where do you not find a customs house?

Meanwhile, Santa Anna revolted against the Bustamante government in January 1832. Mier y Terán tried to mitigate the effects of the revolt in his jurisdiction, but news of a rebel landing in Texas on June 26, headed by José Antonio Mexía, caused him despair. He had informed Austin of an extension of the colonists' tax-exempt status for two more years; nevertheless, Austin continued to complain that the Mexican government was jeopardizing Texas by allowing it "to be filled with Indians and bad people." Ill, depressed, and convinced of his failure, Mier y Terán committed suicide on July 3, thereby destroying perhaps Mexico's last opportunity to keep Texas.

The rebel leader Mexía left Texas with the Mexican troops from Nacogdoches, leaving the border defenseless. In San Felipe the colonists signed a petition in support of Santa Anna, using the document to attack the "military tyranny of Bustamante" and "the arbitrary acts of Commander Mier y Terán." Anglo-Americans convened in October to request that the prohibition against migration from the United States be rescinded, to ask that titles be granted to squatters, and to seek separation from Coahuila. A second convention decided to draft a constitution for the state of Texas and sent Austin to Mexico City to seek approval for these requests. The town council of San Antonio de Béjar objected that the colonists had not followed the Mexican methods of protest and drew up their own document.

In Mexico City, Santa Anna's movement had triumphed. Elections were held that placed the radicals in congress and Antonio López de Santa Anna and Valentín Gómez de Farías in the executive branch. Austin arrived on July 18 at the most inopportune time, because the government was confronting a military rebellion, a cholera epidemic, and general discontent over a decree that exiled enemies of the regime. Congress postponed the Texas question after receiving contradictory reports. An impatient Austin sent a letter to San Antonio de Béjar's town council on October 2 advising that they should proceed to organize a state government without waiting for the Mexican government's response. But soon after the Congress agreed to rescind the prohibition against Anglo-American migration and granted a deferment on paying taxes. Santa Anna explained to Austin that the question of Texas separation was inopportune but he would see to it that the state of Coahuila and Texas enacted reforms.

In December, a satisfied Austin departed Mexico City. But his letter to the San Antonio de Béjar town council had already been forwarded to the federal government. Gómez Farías was furious with Austin and, considering him a traitor, ordered his detention in Saltillo. Impudently, Austin had written letters to Coahuila politicians, commenting that it was best that Mexico sell Texas "before losing it." These letters aggravated the situation.

The Coahuila and Texas government proceeded to enact Santa Anna's promised reforms—an increase in the number of town councils in Texas, the creation of a new department in Brazos, trial by jury, the use of English in legal and administrative matters—and even appointed Jefferson Chambers, an Anglo-American, as superior court judge. Gómez Farías worried about the Texans' reaction to Austin's detention and sent General Juan N. Almonte to Texas to reassure the colonists.

Stephen Austin arrived in Mexico for a trial but was later released from jail by Santa Anna, although he had to remain in the capital. After years in Texas, he enjoyed the delights of urban life and published his *Exposition to the Public about Texas Affairs* (1835), in which he explained that Texans only desired separation from Coahuila. Free to depart, Austin arrived in Texas by way of New Orleans in July 1835 only to find that the province had changed. Rampant speculation and the faction that favored the annexation of Texas to the United States dominated the scene.

In 1835, as it had in 1832, the reinstatement of the Anáhuac customs house triggered discontent, but this time the politically complex situations at the national and state levels favored the separatist Texans. In the national context, the radical federalists had been discredited by their intransigence with their opponents and their determination to exercise control over the Catholic Church. (The Pope had granted the Spanish Crown privileges, specifically the rights to propose candidates for ecclesiastical office and to inspect papal documents destined for the New World.) The radicals lost the elections of 1834, and the Congress and cabinet became dominated by moderate federalists. Blaming instability on the civic militia, the moderates sought to weaken it, but some states considered the militia their best guarantee of autonomy and opposed the measure. Despite the constitutionality of the new decree approved on March 31 by the National Congress, Zacatecas and Coahuila-Texas refused to obey it. Conciliation attempts by the federal government failed when Zacatecas defied the national government, which had to then mobilize the army. Although a direct confrontation did not take place because the state's governor and its military commander fled, the national army occupied the state capital.

In the case of Coahuila-Texas, the politicians were divided. The factions from the cities of Saltillo and Monclova fought to control the state government, offering a propitious opportunity for the Texans. Fearing that the army would now proceed against Coahuila-Texas, the legislature in Monclova authorized the governor to transfer the capital to any part of the state. But the governor was imprisoned for various unlawful acts, and the Texans used his imprisonment as a pretext for rebellion. When the governor arrived in Texas after fleeing prison, the Texas colonists disregarded his authority.

Within Texas, division also prevailed. Speculation divided the various land contractors, and the colonists themselves held different points of view. Some preferred union with Mexico, others autonomy; a third group favored annexation by the United States. Travis belonged to this latter group. Learning about the imprisoned governor, he organized the eviction of the remaining Mexican troops from Texas. Colonists from west Texas refused to follow Travis, but in Nacogdoches, where the annexationists dominated, local authorities formed a corps of volunteers on July 8, 1835, and began the struggle.

The Mexican government acted slowly. Commander Martín Perfecto de Cos was ordered to avoid provoking the Texans and concentrate his troops in San Antonio de Béjar. But his incompetence, and the spreading rumor that the Mexican army was preparing to free the slaves, aroused the Texans. The rebellion escalated when Austin gave his support to the cause and Lorenzo de Zavala (1788–1836) arrived. Besides being Santa Anna's staunch enemy, Zavala had his own vested interests in the province. "Texan Committees" sprang up throughout the United States, offering volunteers, arms, and money to the cause in exchange for an offer of free land. Sam Houston was put in charge of organizing the volunteers while Austin led the militias.

In Mexico's capital, the news of the events in Texas strengthened the centralist faction, which favored a stronger national government that would control public revenue and convert the states into departments with limited autonomy. Arguing that federalism was leading to the disintegration of the nation, they contended that only a change to the centralist system could prevent it. After long hesitation, the moderate federalists, worried by the events, finally agreed to change the system on October 6, 1835. This change provided an ideal pretext for the Texas convention to organize a provisional government by declaring that Mexico had broken the pact with Texas on November 3. The convention did not go so far as to declare independence, so as not to alienate the support of the radical Mexican federalists who were convinced that the Texans shared their objectives.

While a Texas mission departed for the United States seeking loans and support, besieged Mexican troops surrendered at San Antonio de Béjar on December 14, giving up their arms and abandoning the fortified Alamo. These events

accelerated Santa Anna's military expedition to Texas with expeditionary forces who were in great part untrained soldiers. The first Mexican troops entered Texas in January, followed by Santa Anna's men in February. These troops captured the Alamo on March 6.

On March 2, the convention had declared independence and elected David G. Burnet president and Lorenzo de Zavala vice president. The Texas declaration of independence, written to gain U.S. support, echoed the declaration of 1776. It argued that Mexico's "military" tyranny justified separation because Mexico had violated its guarantee of "republican federal institutions" that it had offered the settlers so that they might colonize "the deserts of this country." Among the other offenses cited in the Texas declaration of independence were the denial of statehood, Stephen Austin's imprisonment, the lack of jury trials, the absence of an educational system, religious intolerance, and "the arrival of government-paid emissaries to incite the savages [Indians] to murder the inhabitants." The majority of these charges were false, failing to acknowledge the scheming of local contractors through free concessions made under the centralist governments of the Spanish and Mexican monarchies, the violation of the Catholic requirement, and the breaking of various Mexican laws. Despite being alien to Hispanic tradition, in 1834 trial by jury had in fact been instituted in Coahuila y Texas. Andreas Reich has argued that 90 percent of the Texans' complaints had been resolved by 1834. The Texans made no reference to slavery in the declaration for fear of alienating support in the United States, but its importance there is evident, because

Santa Anna used the battle of the Alamo as an object lesson about the high cost of secession from the Mexican union. Although many folk tales and romantic stories have obscured the actual events of this battle, Santa Anna's decision to take no prisoners came back to haunt him.

the Texas constitution declared it legal: "Congress [of Texas] shall pass no law that inhibits the importation of slaves into the Republic [of Texas] . . . nor shall Congress have the power to emancipate slaves, nor shall any slave holder be allowed to emancipate his or her slaves without the consent of Congress, unless he or she sends his or her slave or slaves outside the limits of the Republic."

President Andrew Jackson declared U.S. neutrality in an "internal" Mexican affair, but he did not enforce it, because local authorities openly supported the Texans. The rush of armed volunteers to Mexican territory forced the Mexican Congress to issue a decree declaring them pirates. But this measure did not justify the cruel application that Santa Anna gave it when he ordered the killing of the Texans who surrendered at Goliad. This act outraged many Mexicans and especially colonists, since war regulations anticipated a "surrender . . . will be religiously observed in conformity with the law of nations."

It is possible that the loss of Texas was inevitable. Certainly, Mexico did not have a good start in its independent life. Spain had left it financially devastated, and radical federalism had weakened the national government, which was unable to respond to foreign threats. The Mexican setback suffered at San Jacinto on April 21, when Santa Anna was defeated and imprisoned, became a total disaster with the absurd obedience of Vicente Filisola, who, upon receiving an order from the imprisoned general, withdrew beyond the Rio Grande. His action sealed the loss of Texas because Mexico lacked the resources to dispatch another expedition.

While Santa Anna undertook his doomed expedition to Texas, the Mexican Congress determined to avoid the errors made during the drafting of the Constitution of 1824. Thus began the long process of drafting what was known as the seven laws, or the Constitution of 1836, which instituted a complicated system of government inspired by European liberalism. The states were transformed into departments, to eliminate competing national and state sovereignty that had impeded the smooth functioning of the federal republic. Popular representation was limited by instituting property qualifications for voting, and town councils were restricted, but the separation of powers was maintained, and a degree of political and administrative autonomy was granted to the departments. A fourth branch of government, the Conservador, was created, designed to check the executive, judicial, and legislative branches and to protect individuals from abuses of power. The seven laws also included a bill of rights. Although the vice presidency was eliminated and the presidential term of office was lengthened to eight years, the executive branch was still weak, subject to the power and authority of the Conservador, Congress, and a Council of Government.

The seven laws took effect on January 1, 1837. Perhaps because of an excess of checks and balances in the executive branch, the seven laws became unworkable and left the government paralyzed. In the popular mind they also were linked to the loss of Texas, as well as to secession movements in Yucatán and California.

Santa Anna remained a prisoner in Texas, but after Houston's electoral triumph he was sent home by way of Washington. There Santa Anna met with Jackson, who expressed his interest in purchasing Upper California. Finding himself totally discredited at home for having signed the 1836 Treaty of Velasco that recognized Texan independence, Santa Anna withdrew from politics. He did not return to the national scene until 1838, when the French invaded Mexico and Santa Anna lost a leg fighting them.

Amid a federalist revival in San Luis Potosí, Anastasio Bustamante won the presidential election, but a delicate situation soon enveloped him. Without resources and with northern Mexico up in arms, Bustamante faced threats from France and the United States. Both pressed for a payment of claims to their citizens in Mexico, who reported losses in revolts, abuses of power, and forced loans. Most of these complaints were either groundless or exaggerated. France presented an ultimatum in March, but the United States was suffering a deep economic recession and decided to accept the Mexican offer to assign the claims to international arbitration directed by the king of Prussia.

France lacked what it needed to maintain an effective blockade of the Mexican ports but left its fleet anchored in Veracruz. Britain, the nation most affected by the maritime blockade, displayed a great show of force in the port city to pressure France to negotiate peace. Mexico was forced to borrow more money to pay the unjust claims, fueling financial speculation.

The centralist experiment proved no solution to Mexico's problems, but the unpopular Conservador branch of government blocked Bustamante's efforts to promote reforms of the seven laws. In 1840, when it seemed that the reform process would in fact start, a federalist uprising occurred in the capital, provoking general indignation and discrediting the government. The perception that centralism had failed prompted voices to advocate other solutions: a military dictatorship or a monarchy with a European prince. José María Gutiérrez de Estrada, in a letter to Bustamante, proposed a monarchy with a European prince. His suggestion caused a huge scandal that forced him into exile.

British recognition of the Texas Republic ruined the Bustamante regime. Mexico's politicians were convinced that Texas had been lost, but the topic had become a hot political issue. Mexican recognition of Texas was made more difficult by the Texans' insistence on the Rio Grande as the western border although it had always been at the Nueces River, with its mouth near Corpus Christi. In 1840, the minister of foreign relations, Juan de Dios Cañedo, discussed the topic with the Council of Government. The council named a commission, headed by Lucas Alamán, to render an opinion. The commission recommended that Mexico recognize Texas if it agreed not to annex to any more territory, pay an indemnity to Mexico, and act with France and Britain as guarantors of the treaty. The discussions of the commission were leaked, and public scandal ended the attempt, forcing Cañedo to resign.

Scarce funds pushed Congress to approve a 15 percent import duty to help pay salaries. This measure prompted a business collapse and fanned discontent. In this context, the situation fostered a military movement for a dictatorship, instigated by foreign businessmen. A Veracruz merchant met in turn with the principal army leadership: Santa Anna in Veracruz; Mariano Paredes y Arrillaga in Guadalajara and Gabriel Valencia in Mexico City. On August 8, 1841, General Paredes rebelled against the Bustamante government and called for a meeting of the constituent congress and the abrogation of the import tax. When both Valencia and Santa Anna supported Paredes's move, the main units of the army converged on the capital. In Tacubaya, on the outskirts of Mexico City, they suspended the constitutional order. The army proceeded to install a dictatorial regime with Santa Anna serving as provisional president until a constitutional congress could issue a new constitution.

After the failure, in succession, of monarchy, federalism, and centralism, many believed that only dictatorship was capable of restoring order and solving Mexico's financial problems. The moderates cooperated with Santa Anna in the beginning, but it did not take long for them to become disillusioned. They accepted dictatorship with the hope that the constituent Congress would restore the federal system. With that goal they concentrated their efforts on winning elections. Meanwhile, the architects of the movement enjoyed their rewards: The military received promotions, and foreign businessmen earned tax cuts, the right to acquire property, and a generous policy regarding mine exploitation. The honeymoon with the dictatorship faded quickly, when in March 1842, Santa Anna had to impose new taxes, among them an infamous annual head tax every citizen was obliged to pay.

The military leadership hoped to control the upcoming elections. The federalists won a majority, thus sealing the fate of Congress, because its federalism would be unacceptable to the dictator. Under the pretext of poor health, Santa Anna left the executive and named Nicolás Bravo president. Soon after, the army organized protests against Congress and on December 19, 1842, Bravo dissolved the legislature and chose a Council of Notables to draft a new constitution.

The three most active congressmen were imprisoned during the debates over the new centralist constitution called the organic bases. The bases corrected some of the errors found in the seven laws, eliminated the tyrannical Conservador, strengthened the executive branch, and increased the representation in the legislative branch of the departments. The bases maintained a centralized control of revenues while also increasing the departments' budgets. The moderate federalists did not approve of the bases but, preferring legal order to dictatorship, breathed a sigh of relief when Santa Anna swore allegiance to them on June 12, 1843.

After manipulating his popularity to win the presidency, Santa Anna turned his attention to Yucatán and Texas. From the moment it had recognized Texas's independence, Britain had been pressing Mexico to do the same to avoid losing California. Santa Anna believed, on the other hand, that many Texans remained loyal to Mexico and he was confident of his northern army's strength after it successfully stopped Texan attacks in 1841 and 1842. He therefore developed an unrealistic plan to reannex Texas and defend California in exchange for increased autonomy in the two provinces. Meanwhile, President Sam Houston

The inauguration of Santa Anna as president in 1844. Despite Santa Anna's humiliation at the hands of Sam Houston and his concession of Texas independence under duress, he successfully regained some of his national stature during the so-called Pastry War against the French. In the fighting that followed the French occupation of Veracruz in 1838, Santa Anna received a cannon wound that cost him his right leg below the knee. His fight against the French and his wound once again gave him political prominence that led to his election.

was negotiating Texas's annexation with the United States. Yucatán, after long negotiations, accepted a special status and temporarily rejoined Mexico.

Santa Anna, confident that he would be elected president, abandoned the capital to return to his estate, with Valentín Canalizo remaining behind as interim president. Santa Anna won the elections of January 1844, but he did not return to the capital until June 4. An agent of U.S. Secretary of State John C. Calhoun visited Santa Anna at his hacienda in May and informed him of the U.S. annexation of Texas. In fact, the treaty between the governments of the Texas Republic and the United States had already been signed, on April 12, 1844.

In Washington, Juan N. Almonte, the Mexican minister to the United States, had lodged a protest with Calhoun, forcing him to send an agent to explain that the annexation of Texas was necessary to deter British ambitions in the region. Almonte expressed confidence to his government that the U.S. Senate would not approve the treaty. The minister of foreign relations, José María Bocanegra, instructed Almonte, however, to advise the U.S. government that Mexico would consider annexation an act of war.

Upon his June 4 arrival in the capital, Santa Anna took the oath of office as president and requested funds for an expedition to Texas. But he encountered a congress dominated by federalists convinced that Texas was lost forever and more concerned about getting him to abide by the law. However, despite their lack of trust in Santa Anna and even though they considered the expedition useless, they felt obliged to approve the funds. When news that the U.S. Senate had rejected the treaty reached Mexico, Santa Anna postponed the expedition, causing alarm in Congress, which soon demanded a full accounting of the funds.

General Mariano Paredes y Arrillaga, military commander of Guadalajara, took advantage of the general uneasiness to revolt against the Santa Anna government in November. Santa Anna raised an army to subdue him while interim president

The Mexican army on the march near Río Frío. This lithograph shows the grave condition of the Mexican forces, who had only a few horses and a cannon. Still, the bravery of these men remained unquestioned.

Canalizo and his cabinet decided to suspend the constitution and dissolve Congress. This time, Congress refused to back down and organized a civic movement to resist the unconstitutional measure. On December 6, with the participation of the judiciary, the city council, the military garrison at the capital, and the inhabitants, Canalizo and two of his ministers were imprisoned to shouts of "Constitution and Congress." In accordance with the bases, Congress proceeded to recognize the head of the Council of Government, José Joaquín de Herrera, as provisional president of the country. This step caused jubilation and raised hope. Santa Anna was jailed in Veracruz. Shortly, the new government exiled him to Havana, Cuba.

Herrera's government found itself in a delicate situation. Without resources, and facing an extensive group of federalists who wanted immediate restoration of the Constitution of 1824, Mexico had to deal with two threats: U.S. expansionism and a monarchical conspiracy orchestrated by the Spanish government. Britain had continued to insist that Mexico recognize Texas to avoid losing California and in 1844 even offered a French-British guarantee of the border in exchange for Mexican recognition of Texas, but Santa Anna did not accept until it was too late. Before Santa Anna lost power in November 1844, British Minister Charles Bankhead in Mexico had convinced him to recognize Texas independence.

Meanwhile, in the United States the successful presidential campaign of James Knox Polk exploited expansionist sentiment. This prompted his predecessor, John Tyler, to gain approval of the Texas annexation as a domestic affair through a joint resolution of the U.S. Congress on March 1, 1845.

Herrera's government, wanting to avoid war with the United States, had accepted the French-British initiative to open negotiations for the recognition of Texas when the news of U.S. congressional approval of the annexation arrived. The Mexican government immediately broke off relations with the United States and attempted to follow British advice to avoid all provocations so that the United States would have no pretext for invading Mexican territory, while offering conditions for negotiating with Texas. The Mexican offer was untimely. In July 1845, a Texas convention approved annexation to the United States.

Herrera was elected president of Mexico, but he promoted only the reforms of the organic bases that expanded regional autonomy and increased the departments' budgets. Herrera believed that a change of governmental systems was dangerous in the face of war. His decisions, though reasonable, cost him the support of the federalists, who demanded the immediate restoration of the Constitution of 1824.

President Polk, for his part, was ready to risk war with Mexico to obtain California, but he preferred to negotiate the acquisition, fearing that a war would increase tensions and intensify U.S. sectional politics. He therefore decided to send an agent to Havana, Cuba, where Santa Anna was exiled. Polk had reports that the federalists were conspiring to bring Santa Anna back, so his agent tried to convince him to support the cession of California. Polk also tried to convince the Mexican government to receive a commissioner. Conscious of its own weakness, the Mexican government's minister of foreign relations accepted, on the condition that the United States send a "special commissioner to resolve the pending issues," meaning the annexation of Texas. Ever the instigator, President Polk appointed John Slidell to serve as minister plenipotentiary with instructions to press for the payment of claims and to make several proposals for purchasing Mexican territory. The assignment was a provocation. In the first place, although the government was in arrears, Mexico had been paying the arbitrated claims. Moreover, the proposals overlooked the fact that Mexico had broken off relations with the United States.

News that the Herrera administration had agreed to receive a U.S. envoy sparked rumors that Herrera was planning to sell Texas and California. Federalists, monarchists, and General Paredes alike took advantage of the uneasiness these rumors caused to conspire against the government. Paredes proved the most dangerous enemy because he commanded the most important army division and was working in concert with the monarchists. On December 14, 1845, instead of obeying orders to march toward the Rio Grande, Paredes revolted against the Herrera administration and marched toward Mexico City. By the end of the month, General Gabriel Valencia, who was based in Mexico City, joined the movement, and Herrera had no other recourse than to leave office. Accordingly, on January 2, 1846, Paredes entered Mexico City. Two days later the Council of Representatives elected him interim president.

Without the support of the legislative assemblies, Paredes ruled by sheer force. Employing a mix of legal tricks and coercion, he dismissed those who expressed opinions contrary to his own. After he announced elections for a new congress that would choose the next regime, Lucas Alamán, a monarchist, drafted the conditions for the elections. As had the Congress of 1822, his document restricted eligibility for office to the principal groups of the elite: miners, landowners, merchants, military officers, clergy, and other professionals.

The Spanish minister in Mexico, Salvador Bermúdez de Castro, financed newspapers furthering the monarchist platform. This propaganda campaign was attacked violently in pamphlets, newspapers, and even in letters to Paredes himself. Although Paredes used his claim that Herrera had failed to mount an efficient defense as a pretext in order to seize power, he found himself focused on domestic politics, which weakened Mexico's position. Despite his reputation for honesty and efficiency, Paredes could not solve the financial problems that continued to plague Mexico.

Meanwhile, the threat from the United States continued along Polk's course. Relying on a new government that he hoped would be more receptive to his proposals toward granting of territory, John Slidell remained in Mexico, but Paredes would not meet with him. With news that Herrera had not received Slidell, Polk had then ordered General Zachary Taylor, who was in Corpus Christi, to march toward the Rio Grande, invading Mexican territory. Paredes was confident that the dispute between the United States and Britain over Oregon would provoke a war that would weaken the American menace to Mexico. He was counting on support from Europe, especially because a monarchist project enjoyed both French and British approval.

Taylor arrived at the Rio Grande in March 1846 and began to construct a fort near Matamoros. At the same time, Paredes was facing a political crisis brought on by the monarchist propaganda. He was forced to declare republican principles and assume that the forthcoming Congress, not the president, would decide the system of government.

Paredes's declaration failed to reassure anyone, and on April 15 the federalists started a movement in Acapulco that spread to Mazatlán and Guadalajara, insisting on the illegitimacy of the Paredes government and demanding the return of Santa Anna and the Constitution of 1824. Failing to quell the rebellion in Guadalajara, Paredes weakened the northern defense. His errors had multiplied. In January, Paredes had removed Mariano Arista from his command of the Army of the North, only to reappoint him after making two other changes in the command structure. These rapid changes provoked divisions among the principal military leadership just when war was imminent.

After an incident between the two armies on the Rio Grande, General Taylor sent a short message to President Polk on April 25 to inform him that "hostilities may now be considered as commenced." Immediately, he had requested 5,000 men from the governors of Texas and Louisiana to continue the campaign toward the interior of Mexico.

As Polk prepared for war with Mexico, he was seeking to negotiate the Oregon dispute with Britain. The British did not want war, so this made possible an agreement in May that established the Oregon boundary at the 49th parallel, the present U.S.-Canadian border, despite expansionist cries for a boundary farther north, at the 52nd parallel.

Successful negotiations with Britain allowed Polk greater freedom to attack his southern neighbor. Upon receiving the message from Taylor on May 6, Polk discussed the situation with his cabinet and started to draft a declaration of war. He sent this message to Congress on May 11. It justified Taylor's presence on the Rio Grande as being in compliance with a U.S. obligation to defend a threatened Texas border. Polk also accused Mexico of being the aggressor and of committing multiple offenses against the United States: "The cup of forbearance had been exhausted even before the recent information . . . But now, after reiterated menaces, Mexico has passed the boundary of the United States, has invaded our territory and shed American blood on American soil."

Polk further alleged that Mexico's refusal to receive Plenipotenciary Minister Slidell left the United States no alternative but war, for which he was requesting resources. The House of Representatives quickly approved the request. But in the Senate, John C. Calhoun's faction sought to distinguish between war and defensive measures, and the Whigs objected to the concept of Mexican culpability. Nevertheless, the war was popular and Polk ultimately secured his war bill.

In the far west, the invasion had already started as well. Since December 1845 John Fremont had been in California with Mexican permission for a supposed scientific expedition, but soon he gave signs of his real intentions to promote the independence of California. Mexican authorities threatened to expel him, but with Commodore Sloat's fleet off the coast, Fremont felt confident in declaring California's independence on July 4, 1846. Sloat ignored the state of war, but assuming that Fremont was following instructions he had received, he occupied Monterey on July 7 and two days later took San Francisco. Thus, when Robert Stockton assumed command of the U.S. forces in California, he was able to march to Los Angeles. There, upon hearing news of the war between the United States and Mexico, he annexed California, although he would later face a revolt of the Californios, the Spanish colonists of California.

Threatened on all fronts, Mexico failed to unite. News of the first defeats caused astonishment, discrediting both the army and the government. Bermúdez de Castro hurried to suspend the propaganda newspapers, and when Congress reconvened on July 6, nobody dared mention the monarchist project. The deputies in Congress ratified Paredes as provisional president and debated the state of war. A decree on July 6 declared that "the government, in the natural defense of the nation, shall repel the aggression which the United States has initiated and sustained against the Mexican Republic, having invaded it."

Paredes's failure to defend the nation and subdue the federalists left him without supporters. He felt forced to assume military command, conscious that at any moment his government could fall. After delaying his departure until August 4, Paredes set off, only to find that the garrison at the national armory had rebelled in support of the Constitution of 1824 and the return of Santa Anna. Soon after, Paredes was captured and exiled.

The movement for the restoration of the Constitution of 1824 put General Mariano Sala and Gómez de Farías in charge of the interim government and new congressional elections were called.

Santa Anna was ready to return from exile in Cuba. He knew that his agreement with Polk's agent would allow him to cross through the Gulf of Mexico blockade. Although his conduct ruled out charging him with treason, Mexican politicians were highly suspicious of their supreme military and political leader, especially since the visit of the U.S. agent in Havana had leaked to the press. These suspicions weakened the military front.

Internally, the struggle between the radical and the moderate federalists was paralyzing the government. The profound changes that had accompanied the return of federalism distracted attention from the war. The confusion between old and new government practices and the renewed state and municipal autonomy hindered the cooperation needed to wage the war. The national government found itself with full responsibility for the war effort at a time when its revenues were reduced to state quotas and customs duties. The impoverished states rarely paid their share, and both the blockading of the ports and the federalist program of reducing taxes limited the collection of duties.

The United-States-Mexican War had begun. Considering the marked asymmetry between the two nations, the conclusion was predictable. The two countries had a similar amount of territory, but the United States had already reached a population of 20 million inhabitants, whereas Mexico had only recently exceeded the 7 million mark. Mexico's bankruptcy and stagnant marketplace contrasted with its neighbor's dynamic economy. While both nations suffered from political divisions and factionalism, expansionism tended to neutralize these divisions in the United States but crippled Mexico.

The contrast between the two armies was even more pronounced. Small for the size of its country, the Mexican military lacked both a professional officer corps and discipline in the ranks. The army was also much in need of resources, provisions, arms, medicines, and horses. Lacking proper quartermaster and health services, the soldiers were fed and cared for by their women who followed the troops, often with their children, limiting the troops' mobility. The army had to cope with antiquated short-range artillery and limited ammunition that did not always match the weapons. There was a chronic shortage of volunteers, especially in the north, where men preferred to stay home and protect their families from Indian attacks. Because of the shortage of ammunition, the volunteers available often fired a rifle for the first time when in battle. The lack of services led the wounded to be abandoned, and facing defeat after defeat caused depression to set in among the troops.

The U.S. troops, in contrast, relied upon a professional officer corps and thousands of volunteers. They had abundant resources, modern weaponry, and the most advanced artillery. The commanders could order various armies and fleets to attack simultaneously. Moreover, volunteers were trained and replaced constantly. Victory on the battlefield and the booty that followed promoted their enthusiasm.

Toward the end of August 1846, at a time when General Taylor was approaching Monterrey and Colonel Stephen Kearny was occupying Santa Fe, Santa Anna arrived in Veracruz from Cuba. By September 14, he entered Mexico City but left immediately for San Luis Potosí to organize an army. On the way he received word that Monterrey had fallen on September 23 after a five-day siege.

In San Luis Potosí, Santa Anna was kept busy trying to secure funding, fortifying the city, and training volunteers. The press attacked him for not fighting, which forced him to march north to face General Taylor. Given his lack of supplies and shelter and the prevailing bad weather, Santa Anna would have been better off waiting for Taylor to emerge from the long desert march between San Luis Potosí and Saltillo. Santa Anna lost many troops to an intense winter weather. In Saltillo, Taylor and General John E. Wool had plenty of time to choose an adequate place to defend themselves, and Santa Anna failed to sever Taylor's lines of communication with Saltillo. On February 22 and 23, the Mexican army faced its toughest battle of the war so far, at Buena Vista. Even the superiority of the U.S. artillery failed to prevent the Mexicans from pushing back the U.S. army on several occasions. It appears that it could have been a Mexican victory, but the command staff decided that, because of a lack of water and other supplies, it was best to retreat to a better location. The following morning Taylor no doubt sighed with relief upon seeing the Mexican army withdraw. He did not even attempt a pursuit. The Mexicans suffered considerable losses in the countermarch.

Meanwhile, in Mexico City the power struggle between the radicals and moderates had intensified after Gómez Farías had been elected for the presidency. Gómez Farías was distrusted by the moderates, especially after he tried to enforce the January 15, 1847, decree authorizing the sale of church property in the amount of 15 million pesos. The church had been contributing to the war effort with loans and guarantees for private credit, so the moderates became convinced that the biggest obstacle for an efficient defense was Gómez Farías. This pushed the moderates to organize a rebellion in the capital with some elite militias, but the unfortunate movement took place at a point when Santa Anna was fighting Taylor in Buena Vista and Scott was preparing to land in Veracruz.

By that time, Mexico suffered from invasion on multiple fronts. The blockaded ports were occupied and remained so until mid–1848; the north was also occupied. Yucatán, still separate from the rest of Mexico, declared itself neutral to avoid U.S. occupation of its own ports in Campeche and Sisal. In 1848, when Yucatán fell victim to a brutal indigenous uprising, fearful criolos considered annexation to either the United States or Spain to save themselves.

Simultaneously, the expedition in the western United States showed clearly that this war was a matter of conquest. Colonel Kearny and Colonel Alexander W. Doniphan and their forces had departed from Missouri for Santa Fe on July 5, 1846. New Mexico lacked an adequate defense and its governor, Manuel Armijo, actually hindered the implementation of defensive measures. Thus, Kearny's troops encountered little resistance to occupying the principal towns. On August

President James K. Polk made clear during his 1844 presidential campaign that he intended to make the United States a transcontinental nation by settling the Oregon question with Great Britain, which he bellicosely expressed as "54' 40" or Fight," and by annexing Texas and obtaining ports in California from Mexico, which he explained as the "Re-annexation of Texas."

18, after capturing Santa Fe, Kearny declared New Mexico to be annexed to the United States. Not every New Mexican accepted the occupation and rebellions broke out, but they were harshly put down.

On September 25, after a new U.S. government was organized in New Mexico, Kearny left for California; Doniphan, with 924 men, ultimately left for Chihuahua. Governor Angel Trías organized the Chihuahua defense effort but was defeated in December at Tesmacalitos. In February 1847, with a Mexican defeat at Sacramento, the U.S. occupation of Chihuahua was assured.

In December, Kearny arrived in southern California at a time when the U.S. invaders were facing difficult times with the rebellion of Californios, so his arrival seemed almost providential. His forces reinforced the U.S. troops already there and enabled them to recapture Los Angeles on January 10, 1847. This victory assured California's annexation to the United States.

In light of such promising news, President Polk concentrated on capturing Mexico City, which he entrusted to General Winfield Scott. On March 7, 1847, a force of 70 troopships approached Veracruz and two days later began to bombard the port city. A landing was postponed because of bad weather, but on the 23rd the bombing resumed. Four days later the civilian population fell victim to artillery, fire, and a lack of food. The resistance had faded by the 26th, and the surrender of Vercruz was negotiated the following day. Scott established his

As President Polk's representative, Nicolas Trist negotiated the end of the United States–Mexican War. Trist did not obtain all the territories expected by the president, but Polk decided to push the agreement through Congress. It stands as the Treaty of Guadalupe Hidalgo.

headquarters there at Santa Anna's old estate while his troops advanced inland toward Jalapa, en route to Mexico City.

After his defeat at Buena Vista, Santa Anna returned to the capital to assume the presidency, restore order, rescind the January 15, 1847 decree authorizing the 15 million peso sale of church property, and negotiate a church loan. The moderates ensured the exclusion of Gómez Farías by including among some of the ammendments to the constitution the elimination of the vice presidency. The Congress named an interim president while Santa Anna departed with his troops toward Veracruz to deter the U.S. advance, but he chose an unsuitable mountain pass called Cerro Gordo to defend. By contrast, Scott's officers were able to control the flanks and close all the avenues of escape. On April 18, Scott inflicted a rapid defeat on Santa Anna. He tried to rejoin his troops in Orizaba but, lacking supplies, headed for Puebla and then for Mexico City. Santa Anna had failed to stop the U.S. advance and so, together with his generals, decided that he had no other alternative but to concentrate his efforts on defending Mexico City. His retreat in that direction allowed General William Worth, now under the orders of Scott, to occupy Puebla on May 15, 1847. On the 28th, Scott arrived in Puebla. The U.S. peace commissioner, Nicholas P. Trist, also arrived a few days later.

Mexican troops now considered defeat inevitable and were totally demoralized. The Congress, which distrusted Santa Anna, annulled the executive branch's constitutional authority to negotiate a peace. A weakened Santa Anna then proceeded to try to fortify the capital. Again he ignored more experienced voices arguing in favor of defending the southern part of the city, in case Scott avoided the direct routes.

Meanwhile, Scott kept low, waiting for reinforcements, and it was not until August 7 that he began his march. By the 16th, part of his army was located south of the capital. Four days later, General Gabriel Valencia failed in a desperate attempt to halt a U.S. advance on Padierna, on the outskirts of Mexico City. On the same day, another army attacked the Convent of Churubusco, which was defended by troops under generals Pedro María Anaya and Manuel Rincón as well as by the St. Patrick Battalion of U.S. deserters of mostly Irish descent. Although the defenders resisted until their last cartridge was fired, the plaza ultimately surrendered and the deserters were court-martialed. Those who avoided hanging were branded with the letter *D* on their cheeks for "deserter."

An armistice, which turned out to be a temporary one, was reached after the Mexican defeat at Churubusco. The U.S. peace envoy, Nicholas Trist, took advantage of the armistice to present the conditions for peace to Santa Anna's commissioners. Given that the executive branch of the Mexican government lacked the authority to sign any sort of peace treaty and the territorial demands of the United States were considered by Mexico to be exorbitant, the cease-fire ended on September 6.

Hostilities resumed on September 8 with the battles of Casa Mata and Molino del Rey. On the 13th, the last battle of the campaign took place at Chapultepec Castle. By nightfall of that day an advance on Mexico City's center began. The U.S. army forced its way through the city's entrances so that the general staff, deciding it was impossible to defend the city further, ordered the army's withdrawal to avoid more bloodshed.

The city council negotiated guarantees for the safety of the general population with General Scott. But once the mob was made aware of the U.S. advance, they launched an attempt to defend the city. The marked inequality between the unarmed inhabitants and the well-equipped invaders resulted in a two-day bloody struggle. Scott had to announce that any resident who attacked his army would be shot on the spot. Slowly, calm was restored. On the evening of the 15th, with the invader's flag fluttering over the national palace, the U.S. army celebrated victory with music and alcohol. Meanwhile, the civilian population tended to their dead, and Santa Anna resigned the presidency.

The United States forces under the command of General Winfield Scott landed at Veracruz and moved inland, defeating the Mexican forces at major battles at Cerro Gordo and Molina del Rey and in other engagements. Scott's troops entered Mexico City and occupied the capital for the next ten months, until peace agreements were negotiated and signed.

A few days later, the occupying army substituted leisure for marching. Theaters, dance halls, and gambling and pool halls opened their doors. Coffee shops, bars, and *pulquerías* served their new customers. Photography studios were set up so that soldiers could buy sketches of themselves and Mexican landscapes as souvenirs. Gradually, the soldiers' money revived the local economy, and English-language newspapers even appeared.

With a certain reticence, in accordance with the Constitution, Manuel de la Peña, the chief justice of the Supreme Court, assumed the presidency in Toluca on September 27. With a few soldiers and government officials, he moved the government to Querétaro. Soon military men, public officials, and politicians arrived. It was not easy for the government to function under these conditions, but the moderates concentrated on reconvening Congress and the governors of the states, some of whom had withdrawn their support for the provisional government. In November, a few governors had arrived in Querétaro and the Congress. Having obtained a quorum, the government gained legitimacy and could start to move toward establishing peace. The Congress then adjourned in December and would not meet again until the newly elected one convened in May to ratify the peace treaty.

The country's situation was depressing. A large part of its territory was under occupation, its sources of income in the hands of an invader. Several states experienced insurrections or indigenous revolts. The radicals and monarchists favored fighting until the last man and were conspiring. Part of the bourgeoisie supported General Scott's dictatorship, and a few radicals favored outright annexation. In this context, the moderates' efforts to preserve the nation's existence were admirable.

While the Mexican government's weakness foretold the loss of some of its territory, news of the U.S. victory aroused President Polk's ambitions for a bigger slice of the country and even saw a movement initiated to absorb all of Mexico. As a result, Polk recalled his envoy Trist to Washington.

Unaware of Polk's decision, Trist had rushed to communicate through the offices of the British minister his readiness to negotiate peace with the provisional government of Mexico. The minister responded that he would appoint commissioners for the purpose. Accordingly, Bernardo Couto, Luis G. Cuevas, and Miguel Atristáin were chosen just as Trist received orders from Washington to return home. Both the Mexican government and the British minister pressed Trist to remain, given the delicate situation. Trist, harboring serious doubts, but convinced that Washington was interested in peace and ignorant of the difficult situation in Mexico, decided to stay.

In January 1848, the difficult process of treaty negotiation began. The British consul, a merchant who had recently bought a concession for a railroad to cross the Isthmus of Tehuantepec, tried to intervene in the negotiations, but Trist managed to circumvent him. The Mexicans employed international law to defend Mexican rights. Trist, in a difficult position, considered Polk's demands unjust but stuck to his original instructions. He refused to accept Nueces as the border and did not agree that San Diego should remain in Mexican hands. He even reduced the indemnification from $30 million to $15 million. It is important to realize that this sum was not a payment for conquered territory; rather, it covered damages and the proration of Mexico's foreign debt as a whole. Mexico managed to keep Baja California. Moreover, the treaty guaranteed the rights of the Mexican residents of the lost territories, the only provision favorable for Mexico, Article 11, which committed the United States to defend the northern border from Indian attacks, was never honored, the rights of the Mexican residents of the lost territories were often violated, and many lost their property.

On February 2, 1848, the treaty was signed in the town of Guadalupe Hidalgo. Trist's wife recorded the scene of the ceremony:

Don Bernardo Couto remarked to him [Trist], "This must be a proud moment for you; no less proud for you than it is humiliating for us." To this Mr. Trist replied, "We are making peace, let that be our only thought." But he said to us in relating it, could those Mexicans have seen in my heart at that moment, they would have known my feeling of shame as an American was far stronger than theirs could be as Mexicans. For though it would not have done for me to say so there, that was a thing for every right-minded American to be ashamed of, and I was ashamed of it, most cordially and intensely ashamed of it. This has been my feeling at all our conferences, and especially at moments when I had felt it necessary to insist upon things which they were averse to. . . . I should have yielded in every instance. Nothing prevented my doing so but the conviction that the treaty would then be one which there would be no chance for the acceptance [of] by our government. My objective throughout was not to obtain all I could, but on the contrary to make the treaty as little exacting as possible for Mexico, as was compatible with its being accepted at home. In this I was governed by two considerations: one was the iniquity of the war, as an abuse of power on our part; the other was that the more disadvantageous the treaty was made for Mexico, the stronger would be the ground of opposition to it in the Mexican Congress.

President Polk received the treaty on February 19. He despised Trist's audacity, but since he followed Polk's initial instructions and a presidential campaign was approaching, Polk forwarded the treaty to the Senate. The Senate omitted Article 10, which dealt with Texas lands, and approved the rest of the treaty on March 10.

Because the Mexican government was sharply divided, it decided to accept the omission of Article 10 from the treaty. The signing of the treaty allowed the states under U.S. occupation to hold elections. The situation was ticklish, however, because the Congress of 1847 was divided and had to approve a treaty signed under a dubious executive authority. The government avoided making the contents of the treaty known until the Congress reconvened, but radicals and monarchists attacked the treaty in any case.

During his May 7 inauguration, Manuel de la Peña presented the treaty to the new Congress. In his speech he recalled the terrible circumstances in which he had been entrusted with the government. Despite some fears, common sense prevailed, and the Mexican Congress ratified the treaty. On May 30, U.S. Senator Ambrose H. Sevier and Attorney General Nathan Clifford arrived in Querétaro to exchange the ratified copies of the treaty with Minister Luis de la Rosa. The presidential election favored José Joaquín de Herrera, who by the middle of June could re-instate his government in Mexico City once the occupying army left.

The consequences of this war were important for both countries. The United States consolidated its continental dominance, and Mexico's destiny was linked to its northern neighbor. But the war's violence and the unjust nature of it left a deep wound in the Mexican soul. At the same time, the conflict also stirred the national conscience and paved the way for a clearer definition of national policy. The French would encounter a more united Mexico when they invaded in the 1860s.

Mexico was later the object of several individual military adventurers' agressions and pressures from Washington that forced the signing of the so-called Gadsden Purchase. This 1853 treaty redefined the Mexican border along Arizona and New Mexico and abrogated Article 11 of the Treaty of Guadalupe Hidalgo, which had in intention but not in effect held the United States responsible for keeping peace with the Indians along the border.

12

Betterment for Whom? The Reform Period: 1855-75

PAUL VANDERWOOD

The outcome of the U.S.-Mexican War of 1846–48—the loss of half of Mexico's national territory—both traumatized and energized Mexicans. It laid bare the weaknesses of the country's economy and its political system, highlighted the flaws in its social fabric, and raised the specter of further United States territorial aggression. At the same time, it emboldened the leaders who aimed to modernize Mexico, as well as a number of ordinary folk demanding a say in their country's future.

Those hoping to calm the turbulence of the early independence period and to drive Mexico down the alluring pathways offered by the West were called liberals. The political orientation of these liberals ranged from truly radical to extremely moderate, differences that were bound to create controversy within their ranks. But in a broad overview, the liberals yearned to democratize and secularize the country, stimulate capitalist ventures, protect human rights and private property, guarantee equality under the law, and forge a nation out of all the disparate regions whose disunity had led to the just completed military disaster. And they meant to do all this quickly, come what may.

Their opponents, called conservatives, also believed in their own principles with different degrees of radicalism, endorsing many of the ideas of their adversaries but advocating a much slower pace. They feared that the liberal program would hurl the country into social chaos, stimulating peasant movements like those that had occurred in the 1840s, perhaps including a race war by Indian campesinos (small-scale farmers). Thus they demanded that the time-tested pillars of order—the army and the church—be retained intact and that efforts to increase the participation of ordinary people in government be restrained. For a short period these points of view were vociferously debated in the public forum. But ultimately the contenders, claiming irreconcilable differences, plunged the country into civil war.

The catalyst for the renewed strife was none other than the previously seen, widely known national figure Antonio López de Santa Anna, nearing age 60, who was returned to the presidency by a military coup in 1852. General Santa Anna, who demanded that he be addressed as His Most Serene Highness, moved rapidly to fix himself in power, assuming imperial pretensions and demanding military recruits, additional taxes, and obedience from the provinces. The general and his conservative supporters meant to create a highly centralized order in Mexico, devoid of the local elections and popular choice that had been at work for decades now in Mexico's federalist system. However, the provinces were not about to give up their freedoms, where many *caudillos* (regional strongmen) and common folk were seething with ambition, fueled by the liberals' declarations.

Resistance to Santa Anna's audacities erupted most forcefully in the southern state of Guerrero, where longtime regional strong man Juan Alvarez enjoyed widespread popular support. Alvarez had helped the local commoners receive land and garner overall better treatment from the area's officialdom, including a reduction in taxes. He had also insisted on recognizing their rights as citizens of the nation-state, among them a meaningful vote in elections, as well as a significant say in how governance should take place. So when in early 1854 Alvarez openly declared himself against the new regime usurping power in the capital, he received the enthusiastic endorsement of the peasantry.

Nineteen months of unfettered guerrilla warfare against the central powers and their allies ensued. As the forces of Alvarez enjoyed success, Mexicans in the neighboring states of Michoacán, then Mexico, Morelos, and Oaxaca, joined the revolt. Many of the paramilitary units entering the struggle had been organized in the waning months of the U.S.-Mexican War, when the beleaguered Mexican government ordered the mobilization of a state militia, which was really a national guard, to defend the country's honor. A few contingents did so heroically in Mexico City itself, but most saw little action against the invaders. Yet when peace came, the militia units remained intact, battalions of volunteers, largely peasants, who elected their own officers and were imbued with an esprit de corps that made them not only fierce defenders of territory but also of their rights as people in a larger cause.

Finally, the flames of revolt spread north to Nuevo León. Army garrisons in Zacatecas, San Luis Potosí, and the nation's capital then denounced Santa Anna, who fled into exile in August 1855. Three months later Alvarez rode triumphantly into Mexico City with a brigade of his rugged rustics called Pintos (ferocious warriors so called because, in earlier times, they wore face paint) at his side. The period of Mexican history known as the reform period had begun.

Almost as soon as it took power in the capital with Alvarez at the helm, the liberal coalition began to fall apart. Social liberals such as Ponciano Arriaga emphasized significant land reform, while others such as Benito Juárez aimed to reduce the power of the Roman Catholic Church. Ignacio Comonfort was a through-and-through moderate on all issues, whereas Alvarez himself was most interested in protecting his enclave in Guerrero along with his support group of

Lázaro de la Garza, the Archbishop of Mexico, threatened to excommunicate any public official who supported the liberal constitution of 1857. Pope Leo XIII later issued a simpler declaration in an effort to overthrow the government of Benito Juárez and the liberals.

campesinos. Alvarez tried to balance the various interests among the cabinet members he selected, but to no avail. He gave up, named Comonfort his successor, and went home with his troops, whose tough, somewhat ragged appearance had begun to unnerve the socially conscious elites of the capital city. These traditional moderates soon had much more to worry about.

Even before summoning a congress to write a new national constitution meant to legitimize their political takeover, the reformers began to hammer against the old order. First Juárez, as minister of justice and ecclesiastical affairs (initially acting with the executive authority of Alvarez), issued a law depriving the army and the church of their customary cherished special privileges, called *fueros*, such as the right to maintain their own, self-interested court systems outside the system of civil law. The ideal of equality under the law was to become a hallmark of the reform movement. Then the finance minister, Miguel Lerdo de Tejada, declared it law that corporate entities such as the church could no longer hold land. Church real estate would henceforth have to be broken up and sold off into private hands as part of the liberal attempt both to diminish the overall power of the church and to put ecclesiastical holdings to productive use. The state intended to tax such sales to benefit the national treasury.

The communal holdings of native groups were also declared corporate property that were to be divided up and parceled out to individuals. In this way the liberals hoped to create a political constituency of hardworking, reasonably substantial, independent farmers dedicated to protecting their family interests and with loyalties to the state. Seen another way, this stunning law was meant to change the way of life as well as the belief systems of Mexico's indigenous peoples. Of course, there was nothing entirely new in this project. Ever since late colonial times the government, even if with considerable ambivalence, had been interested in incorporating its Indians into the larger body politic. And following independence many states had promulgated laws toward that end, but with only limited success. Now the reformers meant to bring that vision to reality.

Defenders of the church, the army, the Indians, and the status quo naturally railed against the effect of these new laws. But for the conservatives something more ominous seemed to have been unleashed by the reform trend: Agrarian movements had broken out in broad areas of Puebla, Morelos, the state of Mexico, and Jalisco. Driven by the promises and disruptions of reform, peasants were taking over estates owned by the wealthy, stalking foreign businesses and their administrators, striking out against their bosses, demanding higher wages, and evincing racial concerns, all of which could be construed as insisting upon the right to participate in the affairs of state.

Much of the turmoil roiling the country involved settling old scores and traditional feuds and defending traditional rights against the appeal of new opportunity. While the material demands of these country people often involved land claimed to have been taken illegally from individuals and villages, their outcries also carried a clear and strident ideological strain—give us popular representative government and state sovereignty (meaning federalism) as promised by the reformers. There was not often solidarity between one pueblo and another or even within the villages themselves over these issues, and the national guard units raised locally to protect a locale's interests could be unpredictable. In order to pursue their own personal ambitions or whims, the guardsmen might suddenly switch their allegiance from one leader to another, and any number of the contingents remained staunchly conservative, which naturally intensified the struggles. But by late 1856 the federal army, though itself prone to defection, coupled with state forces and personal troops raised by property owners, managed to instill an uneasy (but certainly not total) peace over the countryside as delegates gathered in Mexico City to write a new constitution.

Some 155 delegates to the 1856 constitutional convention, mostly professional middle-class men such as lawyers, doctors, engineers, and notaries, modeled their work after the renowned liberal constitutions of the United States and Spain. These constitutions guaranteed basic human freedoms, protected private property, and preserved a largely federalist system with its power in a legislature. The Mexican version also incorporated the attacks against special privilege and corporate property that had been encompassed in the laws propagated by Juárez and Lerdo de Tejada, limited presidents to one four-year term, and guaranteed universal adult male suffrage. Basically, the constitution was a negative document in that it outlined what the government could not do and reflected a fear of autocratic centralism. It granted the national government only limited power to legislate and enforce social change. At the same time, the federal deputies meant to fetter popular sovereignty, so as to keep it within bounds that the various elites could live with. For example, they rejected the notions of trial by jury and religious freedom. Therefore, Mexico retained a judicial system of magistrates, Napoleonic-style, and remained essentially, although not officially, Catholic.

No one was much satisfied with this new constitution. The church, the army, and their conservative supporters ranted against it. The archbishop in Mexico City pledged to excommunicate any public servant who swore to uphold it. The liberals themselves were split over its specific provisions, and some state governors suspected that it encroached on their powers. Radicals thought the document lacked immediate effectiveness and soon found its implementation ploddingly slow. Centers of popular Catholicism in Jalisco and Michoacán thought their religion threatened and rebelled. Ignacio Comonfort, who had been elected president in the summer of 1857, could not hold the center together. In December of that year he allied himself with a military coup headed by the conservative general Félix María Zuloaga. Comonfort had his own cabinet members arrested, dismissed congress, ruled by executive decree, and determined to cast the constitution into a more workable form. But within a month he had had misgivings about his turnabout and become disenchanted with his new, conservative partners, so General Zuloaga sent him packing into exile and assumed the presidency for himself.

Meanwhile, the liberals began to rally under Benito Juárez, president of the Supreme Court and therefore, in accordance with the constitution, next in line for the presidency. With Comonfort cashiered, Juárez automatically became the country's chief executive, at least in the eyes of the liberals. So Mexico, which now had two competing presidents, plunged into a raging civil war.

General Zuloaga, age 45, was a military man through and through. He had fought Apaches in Chihuahua as a teenager, defended Monterey against the U.S. invaders, fought the Mayas in Yucatán, and supported Santa Anna's imperial designs in the 1850s. Now he relentlessly defended the country against the anarchy he saw as being unleashed by liberalism. He did so with the support of some state governors, the church, and financiers, whose loans were secured by church property. Now he pursued his fleeing rival president to the north. In February 1858, a resident of Guanajuato wrote a friend in the capital that "an Indian by the name of Juárez, who calls himself President of the republic, has arrived in this city," a rather dismissive evaluation of the man who would come to head the pantheon of Mexican heroes.

Benito Juárez was indeed an Indian, a full-blooded Zapotec born in 1806 in the state of Oaxaca. After a brief stint of seminary training, Juárez enrolled in Oaxaca's Institute of Science and Arts, where he studied under a politically active, moderate liberal, Miguel Méndez, a professor of logic, mathematics, and ethics. Méndez set Juárez's political sails and advancement quickly followed: Oaxaca city council, state legislature. After receiving his law degree with distinction in 1834, he became a magistrate on the state court at a time when long-held prerogatives of the church were coming under scrutiny and attack. Even when conservatives came to power during the next decade, Juárez served the state's court system.

During the U.S.-Mexican War he became a federal deputy from Oaxaca and then the state's governor, where he revealed his preferences for individual enterprise and village autonomy, strict adherence to the law and Indian advancement—potentially contradictory positions that could lead only to social conflict.

When Santa Anna resumed power for the short period in the mid–1850s, he scattered the Liberal Party's leadership and exiled Juárez and others to New Orleans in the United States. While he was abroad, however, the liberals sharpened their political consciences, and when Juan Alvarez ignited his revolution in 1855, they were ready to join it and take power, although they were hardly of one mind. Now, in 1858, the conservatives were once again threatening to submerge the liberal cause, but this time their enemy could not be so easily cornered and defeated. Powerful state governors—all lawyers, none of them soldiers—from Guanajuato, Jalisco, Michoacán, Veracruz, and other states ordered their militia units to go to the defense of the liberal cause. Then the potent, if avariciously opportunistic, governor of Coahuila-Nuevo León, Santiago Vidaurri, who controlled the northeast and its lucrative commerce with the United States, also cast his lot with the liberals and their ideal of free trade. He helped Juárez establish a power base at the vital port of Veracruz from which an attack on the capital could be launched. But first the liberals sought to broaden their base of common support by strengthening their statement of purpose. The church caught the brunt of the barrage that followed.

The radical liberals supporting Juárez had pressed for more stringent measures against the church since the outbreak of the latest phase of civil war. By mid–1859, the more moderate Juárez could no longer hold them off. The church, they felt, should be punished for its support of the conservatives. Furthermore, confiscated church property, signaling a move toward purchasable real estate, might well secure loans from the United States government that were needed to replenish the depleted liberal war chest. The radicals also argued that the liberals should make clear their aim to separate church and state in a new secularized republic. The political blows began to strike on July 12, 1859, when all church property (except the church buildings themselves) was nationalized—in other words, confiscated—to be sold at auction, with the proceeds accruing to the national treasury. Naturally, the law could be implemented only in liberal-held territory, but denunciations of property in enemy domain were also encouraged, with the actual sales to follow the liberals' victory.

The new law separating church and state also guaranteed religious freedom. Henceforth, the government would protect the public practice of all religions. In addition, monasteries would be closed; that sort of male religious life ended now. Nunneries were prohibited from recruiting novices, which would lead such institutions to die off. On July 28, a civil registry system was established, meaning that births, marriages, and deaths would hereafter be registered by the state. In this way the government gained control of a person's most sensitive passages through life. In short, the state became the watchdog of the country's demography.

Two weeks later the Juárez group announced a calendar of official celebrations for the populace, mixing religious and civil observances. This law forbade civil officials' attendance at religious functions: Public servants could go to mass as individuals but not as representatives of the state. Religious ceremonies such as processions were prohibited outside of church buildings. Clergymen could not even appear in religious dress beyond their churches proper. Police regulations severely limited the time for church-bell ringing, and the clergy were to be taxed like all other individuals. Finally, on December 4, the liberals guaranteed the liberty of religious belief for the first time in Mexico. Freedom of conscience was to reign throughout the country.

To proclaim such radical laws was one thing; to enforce them, another. People do not change their traditional beliefs, their morals and ethics, especially ones tied to their spirituality, overnight. (Witness the recent struggles over desegregation, affirmative action, and abortion in the United States.) Therefore, these so called Reform Laws should be seen more as the start of a process than an accomplished task—a process that would be spotty, incomplete, and resisted by many for a very long time. Even today, much of the program is hardly realized and likely never will be. However, these laws did open the way for religious diversity—for Protestantism, Mormonism, spiritism, and other spiritual innovations—to enter the Mexican mind. And these new creeds, attractive or not, must have encouraged believers to examine and perhaps to challenge the dogma of the official church as well as ways in which the servants of the church—its bishops and priests—practiced their duties. The laws nourished popular religiosity. Thenceforward, people could practice their spirituality as they saw fit and as served their needs, regardless of official sanction from either church or state.

Of course, the church did not take this fusillade sitting down. Its prelates protested openly, and its priests designed ingenious ways to get around the new laws. What was a priest to do when a parishioner dying at home requested last rites? The law dictated that there were to be no religious ceremonies outside the church itself. So a priest dressed in common street clothes might hide the Holy Eucharist in his clothing and wander nonchalantly to the home of the stricken parishioner to administer the sacrament. Or priests prohibited by law from collecting tithes might assign that task to loyal parishioners organized into a lay brotherhood.

Religious processions customarily twisted through the pueblos and towns and out into the surrounding countryside. How could the law now successfully proscribe the traditional ceremonies at which drought-stricken peasants prayed for rain or, conversely, thanked the divinity for a good harvest? These were, and are, people in touch with the Lord in a way they always have been, and no governmental edict could sever that connection. So compromise and accommodation occurred. Civic officials looked the other way when a religious procession came in their direction. Or they allowed the procession to take place, then fined the practitioners a nominal fee for breaking the law. In this way the officials did their duty.

However, such agreements were not always possible. Occasionally a *presidente municipal* (mayor) or a police chief might dig in his heels and prohibit a procession from advancing. After all, such religious manifestations are not only representations of religious needs but demonstrations of power. Processions display—often fervently—whom the marchers intend to obey and whose justice they will seek, and in these moments God stands far above the reach of civil authority. Representatives of government might balk at such challenges to their authority, and bloody confrontations could follow. In Mexico they did, and often continued to fester for a long time.

Likewise, the new civil registry frequently became a source of contention. First of all, while people had often grumbled about paying fees for priestly services, they had still attached a spiritual significance to the act. If nothing else, the fees had kept a priest in town. Second, local power was at stake, raising the question of whom the people would literally pay allegiance to, the church or the state. Those appointed registrars by the state were usually politically favored, middle-income (but still only moderately wealthy) people in search of additional prestige and resources. They could be arbitrary and mean-spirited in pursuit of their duties. What was a truly poor woman who had just lost her months-old infant to dysentery to think of a new registrar who was hounding her for a burial fee? Or the impoverished father who secretly had buried the body of his disease-ridden child in his cornfield, then was denounced to the registrar by a longtime personal rival and fined for a violation of the civil code? Or the wealthy hacendado, accustomed to burying family in or near the private chapel on his estate, now forced to report and pay for the burial to a money-grubbing civil servant? Under such circumstances people simply ignored the new edicts, but the registrar had the law on his side and could be demanding, and conflicts flared. The liberals in charge of the government may have had their ideals and goals, but people everywhere still made their own choices about how they intended to live their lives.

Nor did the new laws produce much income for the liberal cause. Loans backed by church property did not, after all, much interest U.S. officialdom. The potential foreign lenders from both the public and private sectors did not want church lands. They had their eyes on bigger stakes, such as the entire territory of Baja California or transit rights across the Isthmus of Tehuantepec, connecting the Gulf of Mexico with the Pacific. In 1859, the financially desperate liberals considered making such formidable concessions, but the issue became moot as the United States increasingly focused on the uncertainties of its own civil war.

As for the conservatives, they also were in financial straits but had managed to secure usurious loans guaranteed by church property from the house of Rothschild, and later from Swiss and Spanish sources, which financed military offensives on the enemy at Veracruz. The first push, in February–March 1859, had failed, but a year later the conservatives were again on the march, only to be turned back by the liberals' determination a second time. Conservative general Miguel Miramón now assumed the (conservative) presidency from Félix Zuloaga and beat a retreat for Mexico City, where with the archbishop's consent he ordered articles of silver to be taken from churches and melted down for coinage, also pawning off precious jewels and gold from the same source. Then in desperation he confiscated from the British legation certain interest payments that were owed to English lenders. But the conservatives' fortunes were running as dry as their financial coffers, and the liberal armies tightened the noose around the capital.

The two military forces collided on the outskirts of the city on December 22, 1860. Three days later—on Christmas Day—General Jesús González Ortega, a journalist by profession, led the victorious liberals into Mexico City proper. Three weeks later Benito Juárez was seated in the president's chair, but his position was hardly secure. Conservative guerrillas, unbowed and viciously revengeful, remained in the field, while on the political front Juárez had powerful challengers for the presidency with protracted, indirect elections set to begin in early 1861.

The rivals for the office of chief executive included General González Ortega, now a national hero for his role in the civil war; Miguel Lerdo de Tejada, a brilliant radical liberal and author of the Ley Lerdo, the body of law laying out attacks against corporate property. He was an experienced finance minister at a time when Mexico's money problems threatened to drive the country into bankruptcy and political ruin. And of course there was the moderate Juárez, with his proven leadership, political, and diplomatic skills but also a vulnerability to charges of illegal incumbency. The race for the single four-year term ran neck and neck in the spring, but when Lerdo died on March 22, his backers turned to Juárez, whom Congress declared president in June 1861.

The tasks facing Juárez were daunting. Constitutionally, the presidency was still a weak institution, and Juárez therefore sought to shore up his government's centralized power by authorizing the creation of a federal constabulary, a rural police force that in time matured into the famous Rurales. It would take years, however, to move that force from paper to the field. More pressing at the moment was the question of foreign loans. French, British, and Spanish lenders backed by their respective governments agitated for repayment, and Mexico's treasury was close to bone dry. What was to be done?

Juárez and his government had few options. Under different circumstances the United States probably would have given or loaned money—even manpower—to assist the republicans in their battles with the European monarchies, but on the eve of its own civil war it could offer only sympathy and moral support to its neighbor. Up to this point, Mexico had done reasonably well in servicing its international debt obligations, most of them owed to Britain. In fact, the Juárez government, using customs revenue from the port of Veracruz, had just paid off some 24 million pesos (about the same in U.S. dollars) of its indebtedness. Nonetheless, it still owed more than 80 million pesos, with 64 million of them to the British. Moreover, debts piled up by the conservatives worsened the crisis. President Miramón had borrowed heavily from the famous Jecker bank in Switzerland, which had as a heavy investor the Duc de Morny, the half-brother of the French emperor. Juárez repudiated the conservatives' indebtedness, but this hardly satisfied the powerful Duc, who agitated in high places for relief. He

Although the U.S. Civil War prevented the government of President Abraham Lincoln from doing more than protest the French intervention, there was widespread sympathy in the Union states for Benito Juárez and Mexico. This support found in expression in numerous newspaper editorials and magazine cartoons such as this one, which mocks both France (represented by Napoleon III, in the front) and Great Britain (represented by Mrs. Bull, running away).

FRANK LESLIE'S ILLUSTRATED NEWSPAPER.

A GENTLEMAN IN A FIX—AN UNNATURAL PARENT.

An old woman by the name of Bull recently played a most cruel hoax upon a gentleman, one Mr. Napoleon, of France. It appear that the woman Bull, by means of her tears and lamentations, induced Mr. Napoleon to aid her in carrying her baby Intervention. No sooner, however, had the gentleman taken up the infant than the unprincipled parent ran away, at the same time denying any relationship to her offspring. She is an old offender.

demanded that the irresponsible Mexicans be forced to pay their debts and be punished for their delinquencies.

Thus, with no alternative in view, on July 17, 1861, the Juárez administration suspended payment on its foreign debt for two years. How he and his advisors intended to bleed revenue from their virtually bankrupt country was not made clear, but they needed time to devise a strategy. Three months later Britain, France, and Spain made a pact to seize the port of Veracruz and enforce payment of the debt. But France's impatient emperor, Napoleon III (Louis Napoleon Bonaparte), had more grandiose visions than debt collection. Urged on by the ambitions of his Spanish wife, Eugénie, he was determined to spread French influence in this age of empire. Specifically, he dreamed (as in fact others had before him) of building a canal and railway across the Isthmus of Tehuantepec to complement the Suez Canal on routes to the East.

To promote his scheme Napoleon III needed a puppet figure to govern Mexico, to which end he convinced the Austrian archduke Maximilian von Habsburg

124   HARPER'S WEEKLY.   [FEBRUARY 22, 1862.

BATTLE BETWEEN THE MEXICANS AND THE ALLIED INVADERS, AT THE NATIONAL BRIDGE, NEAR VERA CRUZ.—[SEE PAGE 114.]

that the people of Mexico would welcome him eagerly as their king. At another time, the United States would certainly have vigorously protested the establishment of a monarchy in the Western Hemisphere, but the Civil War was then consuming all of the nation's energies. Napoleon III, understanding that his time to act was now, ordered a French expeditionary force of 27,000 troops drawn from what was said to be the best army in the world to set Maximilian on the throne of Mexico.

When they learned of Napoleon's intentions, the British and Spanish withdrew from the outrageous venture, but the confident French marched on, banners waving, toward their goal of Mexico City. The French commander, Charles Ferdinand Latrille, the Count de Lorencez, a vain and pompous aristocrat, wrote to his minister of war on April 25: "We are so superior to the Mexicans in race, organization, morality, and devoted sentiments that I beg your excellency to inform the Emperor that as the head of 6,000 soldiers I am already master of Mexico."

French troops invaded Mexico in 1862, winning easy victories at the national bridge (depicted here) and elsewhere on their march toward the capital city. At Puebla, on May 5, 1862, the overconfident French suffered a stunning defeat that sent them back to Veracruz and delayed the occupation of Mexico City for a year. The Mexican victory is celebrated each year on Cinco de Mayo (the fifth of May).

Such puffery did not impress the Mexicans, who did not intend to give up without a fight and had dug in under General Ignacio Zaragoza at the city of Puebla. There the battle was joined on May 5, 1862. When the smoke and smell of black powder had cleared from the battlefield, the defenders had achieved the improbable: They had thoroughly defeated the glorious French army, sent it scuttling back toward Veracruz in disarray, and given all Mexicans an annual national holiday to be everlastingly celebrated: Cinco de Mayo.

Winning the battle hardly ended the war, however. In just over a year a reinforced and much chastened French army under Marshal Elie Forey captured the capital and sent the Juaristas fleeing north. The renewed offensive also gave the French foreign legion its moment of glory. Assigned as scouts and pickets on convoy duty, a company of some 60 legionnaires had on April 30, 1863, run into more than a thousand Mexican guerrillas outside the tiny pueblo of Camarón in the state of Veracruz. Inspired by their commander, Captain Jean Danjou, who labored with a wooden left hand due to an earlier musket accident, the beleaguered soldiers put up a heroic resistance for about ten hours. Then, with Danjou dead and only five men (said to be of differing nationalities) still on their feet, they surrendered, later to be freed through a prisoner exchange. This brave stand at what the French termed Camerone immediately became Legion lore. Since then, annually on April 30, legion units stationed everywhere—including on the disastrous Dien Bien Phu battleground of Vietnam in 1954—have "stood down" to hear an officer narrate the events of "Camerone." Danjou's wooden hand is still revered as the most sacred relic of the corps.

Nonetheless, despite the historical footnote engraved at Camerone, the delay in taking Mexico City cost the interventionists dearly, for it gave the Juaristas time to mobilize resistance in various parts of the country. It also meant that Maximilian did not ascend the throne until May 1864, almost one year after Vicksburg had fallen to the Union and the battle at Gettysburg had been decided. Napoleon knew he had to have his foreign enterprise deeply rooted before that conflict ended, especially now that it looked like the North would prevail.

French soldiers under the capable marshal François Achille Bazaine steadily pushed Benito Juárez and his coterie of government officials toward the northern frontier. Bazaine, who had replaced Marshal Forey in July 1863, had risen through the ranks from simple legionnaire in the Algeria of the 1830s to brigadier general during the Crimean War. He spoke Spanish as well as Arabic, and the counterguerrilla tactics that he had learned in Africa served him well in Mexico. Reinforced with North African Zouaves (colorfully dressed Algerian infantrymen) plus some Egyptians (supposedly more adaptable to Mexico's hot regions), he headed nearly 40,000 troops, including legionnaires and Mexican conservatives, in his attempt to pacify the country and bring Maximilian to the throne.

But the task was not easy. Mexican loyalists of various stamps—militiamen, bandits turned patriots, regular soldiers under determined generals such as Mariano Escobedo and Porfirio Díaz—contested every drive. Towns taken by the

French had to be occupied and held. From the start of this tortuous struggle it was a no-holds-barred contest. The Mexican combatants were considered bandits by the French, and were court-martialed and shot. Those who gave aid to the juaristas—money, matériel, lodging, food—were harshly punished, along with anyone who spread stories of republican successes or failed to report their activities. Finally, towns and villages held by the imperialists were ordered to organize their own self-defense brigades, with a refusal to serve carrying stern, even vengeful, penalties.

The republicans under Juárez were equally tough minded. Decrees in January and October 1862 declared allies of the invaders to be outlaws and traitors, the penalty for collaboration being death. But even with this Damoclean sword hanging over their heads, a good many Mexicans wavered between allegiance to the French and loyalty to the republic. Among the undecided were governors such as Luis Terrazas of Chihuahua and Santiago Vidaurri of Nuevo León, who wondered if their futures might not lie with the monarchy. Nor did Juárez trust all his generals, with good reason. Powerful landowners such as the Sánchez Navarros in Coahuila cast their fortunes with the French, and any number of factions in regional and local disputes thought they could better their lot by siding with the empire.

A national crisis like this often encourages power blocs in communities and regions to link themselves to outside causes in hopes of bettering their own local fortunes. Of course, this worked both ways. In this case, the French fighting through areas holding republican sympathies urged the area's dissidents to join the intervention, making promises of relief and offering rewards from the new regime. Local groups, attracted by such offers and eyeing any opportunity for advancement over their rivals, weighed the latest proposition against the risk. Often enough the fit was a good one, and old, still-smoldering rifts in the region again became activated. None of this interplay had much to do with ideology or patriotism, and even less with nationalism. It was merely a case of opportunists and pragmatists weighing their chances.

In the spring of 1865, for example, with the French closing in on the state capital at Chihuahua City, a call went out to citizens of the state to defend the republic with money, weapons, and personnel. Some quickly responded with assistance, but others grumbled about forced loans and cited a need to retain one's rifles to fend off bandits and the like. Drought, explained some of those hesitating, had caused hardship everywhere. Under the circumstances, they would rather not contribute to any political cause right now.

Then in August certain towns along the lower Papigochic River, in the western side of the state, dramatically declared for the imperialists. These pueblos, located up against the first upward thrusts of the Sierra Madre, had names like Temósachic, Mátachic, Namiquipa, Yepómera, and Santo Tomás and had long craved autonomy from the bigger, richer, snobbish, politically domineering population centers upriver such as Guerrero City. They called themselves the Coalition of the Pueblos.

Once French troops had occupied Mexico City, Napoleon III arranged for his puppet emperor and empress, Maximilian and Carlota, to go to Mexico to rule. The French commander staged this reception for the new royal couple, although large numbers of the Mexican people opposed the rule of European monarchs.

The advancing French forced the state governor, Miguel Ojinaga, to flee the state capital and seek refuge among backers in Guerrero City. Meanwhile, the self-proclaimed imperialists downriver defeated the military unit sent to suppress them. Now the pro-French rebels marched on Guerrero City itself. The harried governor retreated into the safety of the rugged Sierra, but French sympathizers caught him at a Tarahumara Indian village called Arisiachic and killed him in a brief firefight.

During these tumultuous times Benito Juárez did what he could to keep his regime viable. He confiscated the property of his opponents and deeded land to those who joined him, even if such grants overlapped the legal holdings of others. He declared territories that balked at his presidency to be under a state of siege, which called for federal government control and martial law. President Juárez stood firm: "This is the way the world is—and the Mexican world in particular, which is capable of startling Louis Napoleon himself, should he ever trouble himself to come and live here for a few days. The Mexicans are quite unique: Anyone who does not know them and is at the same time conceited, allowing their praises and adulations to intoxicate him, will be cast aside by them and ruined." These were brave words to be sure, but the outcome of the intervention in Mexico was far from decided.

The emperor Maximilian arrived in Veracruz with Princess Carlota to claim the throne of Mexico on June 10, 1864. The populace hardly rendered the couple the promised royal welcome. In fact, people gave the interlopers the cold shoulder. Aides to the royal couple apologetically explained that disease had broken out in the port city, confining the residents to their homes. Napoleon III had agreed by treaty to secure Maximilian's kingdom with French troops until 1873, when the army would be returned home. By then Maximilian was expected to have the monarchy politically anchored.

From the start the new emperor made it clear that his regime would be more liberal than the conservative Mexicans promoting the monarchy had envisioned. Indeed, Napoleon himself favored a tolerant dictatorship for Mexico. As for Maximilian, he settled for a constitutional monarchy and at one point thought that his rival, Benito Juárez, would make a fine prime minister. The archduke completely misunderstood his subjects. Still, he remained determined to win them over to his point of view. Was he a hopeless romantic, pitifully ignorant, or just plain obtuse? History still has not rendered a final judgment on Maximilian the man.

Maximilian incorporated moderate liberals into his cabinet. To let the rancor unleashed by the earlier civil war settle, he assigned his two most prominent conservative military commanders, former president Miguel Miramón and General Leonardo Márquez, to insignificant positions in Europe, just to get them out of the country. To the chagrin of the church, he declined to return church property confiscated by the reform laws and indicated that such lands should be divided up and sold—for extremely modest amounts—only to the poor. The emperor decreed that Indian villages could own communal lands, and those that had none should receive property grants. The religious orders were not restored, and schools did not revert to their original ecclesiastical supervision, for Maximilian hoped to enlist the clergy as servants of his government, paying them state salaries so as to obviate ecclesiastical tithing and fees.

The emperor also drafted a remarkable new constitution that approached many of the liberals' ideals. It provided for both a moderate hereditary monarchy, headed by a Catholic prince, and religious toleration. The document guaranteed equality under the law to all Mexicans and mandated the freedom of labor. Debt peonage and corporal punishment of workers were prohibited, child labor and working hours restricted. Debts of more than ten pesos were canceled, and monopolistic company stores were opened to outside competition. Certainly, Maximilian was playing politics with these provisions, hoping to attract moderates of whatever political persuasion to his regime. He was searching for some sort of national consensus. But staunch conservatives detested him even as a good many ordinary Mexicans came to venerate him.

There stood the archduke, Ferdinand Maximilian Joseph, the Order of the Golden Fleece pinned to his full-dress uniform of the Austrian navy. Blue-eyed, of fair complexion, now in his early thirties, he was distinguished by a long golden beard parted in the middle. When his older brother Franz Joseph I was crowned Habsburg emperor in 1848, Maximilian was second in line for the title. But when his brother married and had a son (Rudolf, who died mysteriously at Mayerling in 1889), Maximilian fell in the order of succession. Then, in a secret agreement with his brother, when Maximilian accepted his Mexican mission he renounced all claims to the Austrian throne.

His marriage, with his six–year–older wife Carlota (Charlotte), the comely daughter of King Leopold of Belgium, was a strained one. Maximilian consorted with prostitutes, and Carlota feared that he already had, or soon would, infect her with the syphilis he had contracted, so after 1860 the couple did not sleep together. In Mexico, Maximilian's extramarital flirtations persisted, to the disgust of some of his closest supporters. Carlota's refusal to have sexual intercourse with Maximilian cost the couple an heir to the Mexican throne and thus created a serious succession issue. Maximilian resolved it by adopting as his son the grandson of Mexico's first emperor (or rather the pretender to that position), Agustín de Iturbide, and proclaiming the boy his successor, a move that appeased few, and certainly not the lad's mother.

The French presence in their land angered many Mexicans. "It is true that no one finds a welcome here," an Austrian interventionist wrote home to his mother. "The French here are hated like the devil and we too are not regarded with much friendliness. Altogether one has no idea of the ignorance of the middle class. I even heard more respectable people ask whether Maximilian was also the emperor of Austria or whether he was the son of the Austrian emperor. In a word, they know nothing and also do not care about anything; altogether they seem to regard the whole government as only a short, unsustainable interregnum." Indeed, more and more Mexicans began to think of the entire intervention as "a short, unsustainable interregnum."

Despite the cold shoulder turned to the imperialists, French influences crept into Mexican society, especially in the capital. Hoop skirts, the Eugénie hat (named for the empress of Napoleon III), and the décolletage (low neckline) became fashionable among elite women. Some bare-armed ladies even appeared, as if strolling along the Champs-Elysées. French literature, pianos and other musical instruments, and paintings and drawings made their appearance, along with private schools at which French was taught. The interventionists also imported European opera, including the star soprano Angela Peralta and the leading conductor Cenobio Paniagua. Meanwhile, French engineers constructed roads and stretched telegraph lines across the countryside. With new culverts and drainpipes they alleviated the capital's perennial drainage problem. Finally, they brought ideas, such as scientific positivism, and endorsed Freemasonry, which was to have a lasting influence on Mexican thought. So while the Mexicans might not have been especially good hosts, they tasted the culture and fashions of the interventionists.

While the emperor strove to woo moderate Mexicans to his regime, to renovate his stately residence at Chapultepec, and to pursue his curiosity about Mexico's indigenous botany and butterflies, Marshal Bazaine sought to pacify the country. Because Maximilian attempted (largely unsuccessfully) to restrain the commander's heavy hand, the two men did not get along well. Their arguments fueled debate about the intentions and course of the entire intervention. Then in July 1864, the marshal turned his army south to confront Porfirio Díaz in Oaxaca City. It took a siege of more than six months to bring the city down, but when it fell, in February 1865, it left the republicans in control of only four states: Guerrero in the center, and Chihuahua, Sonora, and Baja California in the north.

President Juárez was by now hanging on only by his fingernails, aided by the audacity of guerrilla loyalists, many of whom were proud—even legendary— bandits, principally in Tamaulipas and Michoacán. But the interventionists struck back against these marauding extramilitary forces with counterguerrilla drives of their own, and for both sides rank terrorism ruled the day. The infamous colonel Jean-Charles Dupin, recalled to France to account for his conduct of the war, insisted to Napoleon III that he had been quite merciful toward the Mexicans he had hanged by the neck until dead. His adversaries, he explained, typically strung up their captives by their feet, upside down and facing the sun, where they were left to die of thirst. He labeled these Mexican warriors uncivilized.

The tough, even cruel, tactics employed by the Mexicans were perhaps uncivilized to some, but they proved effective on the battlefield. In a letter written to his Austrian mother on March 13, 1866, a French officer admitted as much: "The enemy here has a peculiar and, for him, very practical method of fighting. Large units of from 400 to 500 men can hardly ever expect to encounter these fellows in the open, even if they are four times as strong. But, hidden behind all kinds of objects, they will discharge several vigorous salvos, which cost us many men, and then run away as fast as they can. If, on the other hand, a small unit—for example a company or half a company—is somewhere on its own, we can be sure that there will be an alarm almost every night. This is tiring and causes many casualties—since someone or other always cops it—and achieves nothing. In these circumstances the most effective system is to leave the fellows undisturbed so long that they feel safe in some place or the other and then to surround them completely, catch them and string them up. In this way one rids oneself of this rabble most easily and with the least bloodshed."

Thus the battle raged, but time was running out on the French. Two months after Díaz capitulated to Bazaine, Robert E. Lee surrendered his sword to Ulysses S. Grant at Appomattox and the U.S. Civil War was over. Soon afterward, the U.S. military maneuvered so as to increase pressure on the French imperialists. On the pretext of having to mop up some stubborn Confederates, General Grant ordered Major General Philip H. Sheridan, a keen liberal like himself, to the border with 42,000 men. The majority of these troops camped at Brownsville, eyeball to eyeball with interventionists under Tomás Mejía dug in at Matamoros. For a time it seemed that the U.S. Army might invade Mexico on behalf of that country's republicans. A flurry of diplomatic exchanges followed in which the United States officially denied having any military invasion plans, but the threat remained.

Napoleon III, who for more than a year now had been privately expressing misgivings about his exasperating Mexican involvement, had made three miscalculations. First, he had not anticipated the tenaciousness of the Mexican guerrilla resistance. Second, he had not expected Maximilian's failures to consolidate his regime and regulate its finances nor his inability to work through his publicly aired differences with Marshal Bazaine and to ease unsettling frictions with his older brother, the emperor Franz Joseph. Finally, he had thought the South would win the Civil War. Now the French emperor faced the increasing unpopularity of the Mexican war at home, the prospect of getting into a serious scrap with the United States, and sword rattling echoing from Germany's Otto von Bismarck to the east. This was no time to be mired down in a failed intervention.

Maximilian knew of the emperor's growing reservations and was impatient with the progress of pacification in his own kingdom. Why would his subjects not recognize his largesse and goodwill? Why would they not come around to his liberal point of view? But the Mexicans would not, which led the frustrated young monarch to issue his notorious Black Decree, on October 3, 1865: Anyone captured with arms or associated with an armed band would be summarily put to death, even if they claimed patriotic or political motives. (Normally such punishment was reserved for brigands rather than political adversaries.) Furthermore, prisoners taken in military engagements would be executed by the French commander-in-charge. There would be no courts-martial, no pleas for clemency, no pardons by the emperor. All this from an emperor trying to win the admiration and loyalty of his people. The Black Decree damned Maximilian in the eyes of many Mexicans, both liberals and conservatives, who now claimed to know the man for what he was.

A week later a furious Marshal Bazaine, reacting to guerrilla atrocities in which the irregulars had mutilated the bodies of French soldiers they had killed, extended the meaning of the Black Decree: "I direct you [his field commanders] to inform the troops under your command that I will not permit them to take prisoners. There will be no exchange of prisoners in the future. Our soldiers must realize that they must not lay down their arms to adversaries of this kind. What is now taking place is a war to the death, a struggle to the finish between barbarism and civilization. On both sides it is necessary to kill and be killed." For the first time, Bazaine and the emperor were in accord about how to handle their adversaries. The bloodbath deepened.

It was in the midst of this savage ferocity, on January 15, 1866, that Napoleon III informed Maximilian that he intended to withdraw French troops from Mexico. Nine thousand were to be brought home that October, another 9,000 the following March, and the remaining 11,300 in October 1867. Accordingly, in concert with these withdrawal plans, Marshal Bazaine began to pull back his forces from outlying districts toward Mexico City. Liberal forces quickly filled the gaps and kept the pressure on the retreating French. After the marshal evacuated Chihuahua City in the summer of 1866, Benito Juárez, long pinned against the border to the north, expeditiously moved his government to that state's capital. As more republicans (and unabashed opportunists) caught the scent of victory, patriotism billowed and the Juarista armies grew. Maximilian must have been alarmed, but he did not despair. Carlota stood by him, even more as the deluge approached. Frustrated and increasingly angered by the turn of events, the empress was determined to save the royal regime.

The middle of July 1866 found Carlota at the court of Napoleon in Paris, where she demanded in no uncertain terms that the emperor fulfill his promise, confirmed by the Treaty of Miramar, to leave French troops in Mexico until Maximilian's regime was secured in place. But Napoleon refused to budge on his timetable for withdrawal. Carlota wrote her husband that Napoleon was "quite the devil in person." After a brief rest at their still-unfinished castle at Miramar, outside Trieste, Italy, Carlota traveled to Rome to seek the pope's intercession on behalf of her husband. Nothing is known of his response, if there was one, but the news from Rome was that Carlota had became irrational and was slipping into insanity. Her brother, now Belgium's King Leopold II, insisted that Carlota be brought for care to the castle of Tervuren near Brussels. From there her doctors wrote to Maximilian only that his wife was ill, but he soon learned the truth.

Maximilian knew that his wife did not wish him to abdicate the throne of Mexico, but then Napoleon accelerated the schedule for withdrawing his troops: Now all would be home by March 1867. This date meant that the departure of the first contingent would be delayed by five months but all the troops would be returned to France seven months earlier than anticipated. Rumors that Maximilian intended to abdicate circulated in Europe and the United States, but he could not make up his mind. In late November 1866, he summoned his council of ministers to seek their recommendation. By a close vote of ten to eight his councillors urged him to stand firm and not abdicate. Despite the narrow margin, Maximilian prepared to fight the republicans with the assistance of the Mexicans still loyal to the monarchy.

The French departed Mexico City on February 5, 1867. Marshal Bazaine urged Maximilian to join them, but to no avail. A week later the emperor left for Querétaro to establish headquarters for a showdown with the Juaristas. He knew he could rely on the support of steadfast conservative generals such as Mejía and Miramón, returned from his overseas assignment, but their armies were far outnumbered by those of the enemy—some 21,700 royalists against 69,700 republicans—and munitions and money were running short. A month later, 35,000 Juaristas under generals Mariano Escobedo and Ramón Corona held Querétaro and its 7,000 defenders under siege. The last French soldiers left Veracruz on March 16. The Mexican empire was suffering its final agony.

Meanwhile, Porfirio Díaz, who had escaped his captors and taken command of the Army of the East, stormed over Orizaba and Córdoba. On April 2, he captured Puebla and placed a final exclamation point on the campaign by condemning the commander of the conservative forces and 74 of his officers as traitors, ordering them executed. In early April, Porfirio Díaz defeated another conservative army outside Mexico City and put the capital under siege. Capturing Chapultepec Castle, he established headquarters there to await developments in the north. At Querétaro the beleaguered defenders planned to surge out of their fortifications and cut through the siege on May 15, but a commander of the emperor's household cavalry betrayed his ruler's trust and opened a gate to the

Maximilian and his two principal generals, Tomás Mejía and Miguel Miramón, were captured at the battle of Querétaro and sentenced to death. Despite pleas from across Europe, President Benito Juárez refused to pardon the emperor. Liberal troops executed the three on the Hills of the Bells outside Querétaro in 1867.

besiegers, who promptly imprisoned Maximilian in a local convent. Now Juárez had only to decide His Majesty's fate, along with the likes of Miramón and Mejía.

At the end of May 1867, Maximilian learned that he was to be tried for treason under the Juárez decree of January 25, 1862, because he had waged war against the republic. He had further taken the title Emperor of Mexico, intending to set aside the country's republican institutions. Miramón and Mejía were also charged with treason. The court-martial of the three defendants began on June 13 before seven officers. It lasted two days, after which the verdict came quickly: guilty. The sentence was to be execution by firing squad on Sunday, June 16, at 3:00 P.M. only some 42 hours away.

Capable, respected defense lawyers sought clemency for their clients from Benito Juárez himself. The president refused, although he extended the execution date three days to ensure that the contending legal forces and foreign diplomatic observers had their say. Prosecutors argued that the people of Mexico, especially the army, would not tolerate leaders who allowed the crimes and cruelties of their adversaries to go unpunished. They asserted that a pardon to Maximilian would be seen by others, including foreign governments, as a weakness of will among the Juaristas and added that if freed, Maximilian might plot to return someday. They found none of this politically acceptable and none of the charges pardonable.

Foreign governments and dignitaries—Austrians, Prussians, British, Spanish—urged Juárez to reconsider. Two of the president's greatest international admirers, Victor Hugo and Giuseppe Garibaldi, pleaded for clemency. Queen Victoria's private secretary predicted that "lawless as these Mexicans are, even they will pause before they outrage every European feeling by the murder of the Emperor." The U.S. government dodged the issue, trying to offend neither Juárez nor the Europeans. When the attorneys for the condemned made a final personal plea to President Juárez, he responded: "Today you are unable to understand the necessity for this severity, or the motives of justice on which it is based. Only time will enable you to appreciate this measure. The law and the sentence are inexorable now because public safety requires it, and this will enable us later on to be sparing of the blood of those who have been led astray, which will be for me the greatest happiness of my life." To the wife of a German prince who had allied himself with Maximilian and now begged for the emperor's life, Juárez responded: "If all the kings and queens of Europe were in your place, I could not spare that life. It is not I who take it but the people and the law, and if I should not do its will the people would take it and mine also."

The executions took place early on the morning of June 19, 1867, on the Cerro de las Campanas (the Hill of the Bells) outside Querétaro. However, Maximilian was not buried until mid–January 1868, because Juárez would not release his body to the Austrian officials. Mexican physicians embalmed the corpse in closed quarters guarded by the military for fear that masses of Mexicans would display strong devotion, and perhaps even reverence, toward the fallen emperor. The government must have recognized a certain popularity for Maximilian that it did not care to admit and that the emperor himself did not suspect during his lifetime. But then veneration is just one short step from adoration in a religious sense, and the faithful are certain that even in death the Lord may choose to grant special powers to those who have suffered an injustice. Mexico's republicans did not relish having a martyr on their hands, even less so one thought to possess a divine presence.

Faced by a storm of worldwide criticism and diplomatic exclusion from many countries, Juárez validated the execution of Maximilian as "just, necessary, urgent, and inevitable." He continued: "We inherit the indigenous nationality of the Aztecs, and in full enjoyment of it, we recognize no foreign sovereigns, no judges, and no arbiters." Strange as it may seem for this full-blooded Zapotec to be lauding the Aztecs, his declaration was consistent with the liberal intention to construct a nation, a representative republic, out of the regional and racial diversity that characterized the country. That arduous task began immediately.

Porfirio Díaz captured Mexico City two days after the executions on the Hill of the Bells. Juárez returned on July 15 to the jubilation of the people, but storm clouds were overhead. The Liberal Party remained splintered about its goals and the timetable for fulfilling them. Regional and local strife, stirred both by long-held traditions and more than a decade of devastating civil war and foreign invasion, raged at various levels of intensity throughout much of the country. The peasants wanted land. The pueblos wanted the autonomy they thought had been promised by reform. Thousands of republican soldiers (many of whom had only recently joined up) agitated for rewards for their military service. Banditry was rife. Foreign powers generally shunned the country, although the United States remained friendly. The national treasury, supported by a rickety tax system, lay stricken.

General Porfirio Díaz had a brilliant military career against the French, including a leading role in the Cinco de Mayo victory at Puebla. He felt his contributions to the struggle against the French entitled him to some reward from the Liberal party, but President Juárez believed the nation needed to return to civilian rule. The one-time allies soon became political rivals.

Moreover, Juárez's right to the presidency was under challenge. After all, the 1857 constitution limited presidential terms to four years and did not permit reelection. At the time, Juárez had been president for almost a decade, albeit in an emergency situation recognized by the Congress. But now it was time to adhere to the letter of the law, a constitutional issue at the service of partisan politics.

Based on his past experience as president, in fact Juárez now thought the office itself ought to be strengthened and thus proposed constitutional amendments toward that end. This line was a dangerous political position to take when confronted by a unicameral national legislature that by and large defended states' rights and a populace that could become emotional about dictatorship.

Benito Juárez, the consummate liberal, became the embodiment of Mexican resistance to foreign invaders and influence. His commitment to liberal political programs continued after the expulsion of Maximilian and during the restored republic (1867–76) his policies helped create a modern nation.

Recognizing that he could never push such changes through a combative Congress, Juárez went straight to the people with a plebiscite that would have created a second legislative body to balance the first, increased presidential veto powers, and determined the order of the presidential succession beyond president of the Supreme Court, among other things. Then, in a blatant attempt to broaden his constituency, he decreed that the clergy held the right to vote, gave federal employees the right to sit in Congress, and eliminated the requirement for congressional deputies to reside in their home districts. Clearly, this chief executive wanted substantially more power to direct the affairs of state.

Juárez's controversial constitutional changes were linked to the national elections of August 1867, in which he handily defended his candidacy against his longtime political adversary and relentless critic General Jesús González Ortega and a relative newcomer to the national political scene, General Porfirio Díaz, a war hero extremely popular with the military rank and file. As for the constitutional amendments, the administration saw them headed for an embarrassing defeat at the polls and decided to withdraw them from the balloting. But all this political maneuvering for the most part occupied only political activists in the capital and settled nothing outside it, where local and regional strongmen struggled to retain or gain supremacy.

In Puebla, for example, successive governors could not rein in the power of liberal chieftains in the Sierra, nor did the imposition of a governor in Guerrero quiet the state's powerful feuding factions. Juárez lost political control of his own state, Oaxaca, to the brother of Porfirio Díaz, and agrarian unrest that saw the campesinos at odds with the government's land measures swept the central part of the republic. At the same time, the "Tiger of Nayarit" (a small state in western Mexico), Manuel Lozada, and his rural followers took up arms in the name of their agrarian rights. Mexico seethed as its politicians and populace pressured the government to fulfill the promise of the reform movement.

The precise nature of the reform promise, of course, rested in the eyes of the beholder. The liberals had long draped their banner loosely so that its position could be adjusted to their myriad ends—differences and contradictions be damned. While any number of factions, pueblos, and even entire states and larger regions agitated for autonomy from the federal government, Juárez and his supporters aspired to increase central control. It was not necessarily that they sought to establish a dictatorship or anything near it, but they believed that if Mexico was to modernize it needed order and strong leadership from the capital. They wanted to build a nation from all its disparate parts. As one step in that direction they began to organize and put into service the rural police force, the rurales. To accomplish this, they did what other rulers before them had done: They took bandits and enrolled them as policemen, which allowed the brigands to work both sides of the law. Regardless, the rurales were to gain an international reputation as a tough, always-get-their-man constabulary, even if their image far outstripped the reality.

The government also took tentative measures toward building the infrastructure necessary to attract foreign capital investment. Roads were improved, telegraph lines went up, and railroad building moved from the drawing board to the craggy, challenging terrain. Nor did these reformers neglect the cultural side of their program. They began to establish secular primary schools and developed a curriculum outlining what they thought children should learn in school. Mexicans must learn to discipline themselves, to work hard, be responsible, control bad habits such as drunkenness, and even save for a rainy day. They must devote their allegiance to the nation as a whole rather than to just their traditional communities and the church. Old superstitions must be discarded; only science defined and explained the truth. They said women should be moral, dedicated domestics, the guardians of family life, and patient sufferers, much as in the past. Even the duties of children to family, community, and country were carefully spelled out as the socialization process fell into place.

In a striking way these secular and liberal principles were painted on the walls of the school buildings themselves, thus giving birth to Mexico's rightfully heralded muralist movement. Juan Cordero first decorated the walls of the National Preparatory School in Mexico City, at whose inauguration the minister of education proclaimed that "the Preparatoria has had the honor of opening a new field to Mexican art. . . . The painter is one of the benefactors of the school; he will make his contribution to the general spread of knowledge with his brush, as we are making ours with our work and our writing. . . . He will share our struggles and triumphs." Unfortunately, Cordero's painting was replaced by a tasteless stained-glass window during the succeeding epoch of Porfirio Díaz, but since the Revolution of 1910 such renowned Mexican muralists as José Clemente Orozco, David Alfaro Siqueiros, Diego Rivera, Fermín Revueltas, Jean Charlot, and Fernando Leal have all left remarkable paintings on the walls of the prep school, which stand as masterpieces of our times.

Much of the high-level theorizing about the future of Mexican society was reflected in the evolutionary ideas that were au courant at the time. It was argued that countries, like civilizations and people, passed through stages of evolution from the primitive through the metaphysical and on to the scientific and rationalist level of development that promised material gain. Such doctrines borrowed much from the ideas of Auguste Comte, the father of sociology; Charles Darwin, the patriarch of natural selection; and Herbert Spencer, an evolutionist influenced by earlier strains of pragmatism and utilitarianism. Catchphrases such as "the greatest good for the greatest number" and "the survival of the fittest" abounded, all in the name of progress, but said little of justice. "Being modern" effectively meant being more like the United States and western Europe regardless of the social cost.

The heady message concerning the route to progress delivered from above was not always (or even often) well received at the lower social echelons. You cannot change people's belief systems overnight, nor is the process ever complete. Despite the revelations of science about the ways in which the world worked, most Mexicans continued to inhabit the cosmos with which they felt most familiar and comfortable. They may have flirted with, or even adopted, some of the new ideas and practices swirling around them, but at the same time they continued to believe in miracles and to believe that their God could get angry, that he touched certain people, that not everything in the world can be known.

They believed in spirits, both good and evil, and even in witchcraft, which explained behavior to them. They continued to consider and to treat the lovely and original (if crudely carved) santos, customarily wooden or plaster statues of saints in their homes and churches, as family. They prayed to their icons for favors—and railed at them when the Divine seemed not to respond. In this atmosphere Benito Juárez and his fellow moderates reached an accommodation with the official Catholic Church: They eased up on enforcing the reform laws, while in return the prelates spoke less harshly of the government's overall civil and secular program for the country. Meanwhile, most ordinary people charted their lives by the rules they thought best for themselves. As individuals, families, cliques, and organizations, they agreed here, adjusted there, and when something chafed too badly, protested and occasionally went into rebellion.

Still, as the country edged into the 1870s it was evident that the reform movement had wrought great changes—imperfect, never all-inclusive, still in the process of being debated, negotiated, and worked out—but impressive, challenging, even intimidating alterations. Just as many of the strands of modernity that twisted their way into the patterns of the reform program had been spun in earlier times, reform did not (and could not) eradicate all the old colonial ways of thinking and doing things. Political cultures do not adjust to new regimens quickly. But the reformers did discredit the Conservative Party and relegated the monarchists to parlor-room nostalgia, albeit monarchism was still in evidence, thanks to oral tradition and memory.

The reform movement also reaffirmed the liberals' ideas of representative government, even as a stronger state emerged. It endorsed equality under the law and a country of citizens making their own decisions on how to live their lives, albeit with the guidance of an educational curriculum. It questioned the place of the church in Mexican society, and in its whirl of innovations, ideals, programs, and activities it awakened ambitions and expanded the outlook of a good many Mexicans. Some latter-day observers also suspect that the reform—especially the fight against the French—sowed seeds of nationalism, meaning that the people began to think of themselves as a nation of patriotic Mexicans as opposed to identifying more with their pueblo, a cacique (local powerbroker), a district, or some other traditional locale. Today others identify the period with the emergence of mestizo (mixed-bloods) dominance where once criollos (American-born whites) had ruled. In other words, it represented the dawning of today's Mexico.

Whatever alterations developed during this period, most did not penetrate very deeply or carry very far. They did not patch over ethnic conflict in any meaningful way, nor did they lessen differences of class. The reform movement vigorously stirred up the society in substantial and even profound ways, but regardless of the intentions of its notably divided leadership, it did not revolutionize it. The Mexico that emerged from reform was different, yet the same. The sorting out continued, as it does today. For his role in so steadfastly defending the fatherland against foreign intervention (but less so for his Indianness and stand against the conservatives), Benito Juárez now stands as a magnificent amalgam of myth, actuality, and wishful thinking in the rotunda of Mexican heroes. Elected president for yet another term in 1871, he died of a heart attack the following year. In the ensuing melee for succession, Porfirio Díaz emerged the victor, shaky at the start to be sure, but on his way toward advancing (yet also undermining and perverting) the programs proffered to Mexicans by the reform movement.

13

The Culture
of Modernity

ROBERT M. BUFFINGTON *and*

WILLIAM E. FRENCH

The revolution of Tuxtepec, the 1876 coup d'état that raised General Porfirio Díaz to the Mexican presidency, brought to a climax the nation's seemingly interminable courtship of modernity. After more than a century of frustrated intentions that began with the late 18th–century reform efforts of enlightened Bourbon autocrats in Mexico's last period of prolonged stability, many Mexicans plighted their troth to the new regime in eager, if wary, anticipation of a protracted honeymoon. The bride might be a bit tattered but she was lovely still, and if the groom's blood wasn't exactly blue (thanks, some said, to a Mixtec Indian grandmother), he was certainly dashing— and liberal—enough. The marriage was about to be consummated. Or so it seemed. Seizing the moment, propagandists heralded the beginning of a new era of "order and progress" that would finally end decades of political instability, economic depression, and social degeneration. "The country was a wreck," one commentator observed, but "seldom in history has there been a people with a more unanimous, more anguished, more determined aspiration" for peace. And indeed the Mexican cult of modernity found its purest expression during the 35–year pax porfiriana.

Surprising perhaps in a country that German scientist Alexander von Humboldt, the most respected of Mexico's many 19th–century visitors, had called the "land of inequality," the dream of modernity was widely shared (albeit in different guises) by Mexicans from all walks of life. In a typically florid paean to modern technology delivered in 1886 at Mexico City's prestigious National Preparatory School, Díaz's influential education minister Justo Sierra encouraged students to "study [electricity] with profound passion, extract its secrets, and reveal them to us converted into mechanical forces that will renew our riches, and entering them into world circulation, resolve the problem of our destiny." Meanwhile, on the northern frontier, with little pomp and less circumstance, balladeers

General Porfirio Díaz, seen here in an ostentatious motorcade, personified modern Mexico during his regime. With the exception of the four years between 1880 and 1884, Díaz served as president from 1876 to 1911.

sang longingly about the fabled city of Jauja, where "no one . . . wears sandals nor *güichol* (straw hats) because there everything is inexpensive and of the best quality." To a still-fragmented nation-state about to cross the threshold, the often ambivalent and always ambiguous notions that comprised modernity exuded an irresistible, seductive power.

Not that modernity's ambivalences and ambiguities were immediately obvious or openly acknowledged. On the contrary, inspired by the "scientific" sociologies of European positivist gurus Auguste Comte and Herbert Spencer, ideologues like Justo Sierra and his fellow *científicos*—"men of science," as Díaz's technocratic advisors were generally known—downplayed such potential incongruities as longstanding inequalities of race and class. Instead, they crafted national redemption narratives that spared Mexico the supreme indignity of losing out in the international "struggle for life." In his contribution to the aptly titled *Mexico: Its Social Evolution*, Sierra warned that

> Science . . . has accelerated a hundredfold the evolution of certain peoples. The other human groups either become subordinate and lose self-awareness and personality or else, finding strength in ideals, in moral forces . . . tend to absorb every foreign element, in the process of rounding out their own personality, thus quickening the pace of their evolution.

Confronted with the possibility that "the formidable Yankee locomotive" would once again crush the fledgling national spirit as it had most recently in 1848,

Mexican positivists like Sierra welcomed General Díaz's firm hand and his "will to unify our moral forces and transmute them into normal progress."

The científicos' argument was logical, nationalistic yet cosmopolitan, Darwinian enough to appear "scientific"—perfectly suited to its self-consciously modern audience. Political stability, they argued, was the crucial first stage in Mexico's social evolution. By stressing "metaphysical" notions of human rights and imposing "foreign" political structures like federalism, the constitutionalist liberals of the early republic and the reform movement had attempted too radical a break with the past. The resulting political struggles had devastated the economy and undermined social harmony. The redemptive discipline of General Díaz was thus a historically necessary corrective to more than half a century of political indulgence and social anarchy. This period of unrest had followed hard on three centuries of colonial degeneration "whose destructive breath," as one commentator put it, "poured out men's lives in rivers of blood [and] killed the source of vigor and idealized love in the pollen of flowers." More to the point, political stability would create the necessary conditions for economic development: reliable markets, stable currency, protection from unreasonable demands such as land seizures and taxes, and the right to secure property, the absence of which had thus far discouraged trade and investment.

Buttressed by the Porfirian peace, economic development, driven at least in its initial phase by increased foreign investment, would revive the moribund Mexican economy. In the short term, having more investment capital in such crucial industries as mining, export agriculture, and manufacturing, as well as increased government revenues to fund infrastructure improvements like railroads, roads, harbors, docks, and public works projects promised a secure economic foundation for further development. In the long term, a strong economy would bring social benefits as well: an expanding middle class ("the class that progresses," as Sierra called it) and funding for public education, the great liberal panacea for social inequality. Increased upward mobility would expand internal markets, which would then accelerate economic development, thus furthering even more upward mobility, and so on, in ascending spirals of economic and social progress. Once set in motion, modernity would reproduce itself effortlessly, even mechanistically, into the foreseeable future.

Mature modernity was barely visible on the Mexican horizon and, as a consequence, more difficult to imagine. Enthusiastic Mexican elites flocked to foreign universities from the Sorbonne to Berkeley and took the obligatory grand tour through western Europe and the United States. But these suggestive glimpses required blinders and the willing suspension of disbelief. After all, even Paris, the cultural capital of the 19th century, had its "apaches" (although they transgressed urban rather than international borders).

Of one thing, the científicos were sure: from economic development would flow a dizzying array of possible futures. These would be constructed variously from a combination of advanced technologies, capitalist economics, modern social relations (a well-educated elite directorate, an entrepreneurial bourgeoisie, and

patriotic proletarians, all grounded in strong nuclear families), and, ultimately—
but only when Mexico was ready—democratic politics. The last characteristic
was a particularly important reaffirmation of liberal principles, still the touch-
stone of political legitimacy. "Mexican social evolution," Sierra insisted, "will
have been wholly abortive and futile unless it attains its final goal: liberty." Nevertheless, for all its nationalistic optimism, scientific pretensions, and liberal tele-
ology, this gradualist approach to social Darwinism boded ill for the 90 percent of
the nation's population ("infamous plebes" was the elites' epithet of choice) who
were unlikely to enjoy the immediate fruits of Porfirian modernization.

Further ambivalences and ambiguities, many inherent to modernity itself,
lurked just below the surface of científico ideology. Some were painfully obvious.
Ironic commentaries from Mexico City's vibrant penny press routinely excoriated
the Porfirian cult of modernity. *El Chango*'s 1904 cartoon article "Death in Electric Form," for example, condemned the new streetcars and their "daily heaps of
mutilated victims" as symbols of the impersonal cruelty of modern technologies
that crushed "the crippled and beaten down" under relentless steel wheels.

Nor were modern social practices spared the satirical lash. Broadsides with
engravings by popular artist José Guadalupe Posada alerted working-class readers
to the sexual dangers of "feminism" and a Porfirian "chic" that allegedly tolerated
the mixing of tuxedoed *lindos* (pretty boys) and male transvestites in public
dances. Moreover, elite social reformers, whether scientifically inclined or not,
were hardly promoting a city of Jauja where "they give a beating to anyone who
wants to work": a worker's paradise predicated on the pursuit of happiness rather
than industrial production might just subvert the *perpetuum mobile* of modernity
altogether. And these deliberately contrarian positions represented just the tip of
the iceberg that loomed ahead for turn-of-the-century social engineers (and not,
incidentally, just in Mexico).

At its most basic level, structural contradictions in the Porfirian model of
export-driven development guaranteed that Mexico's voyage into modernity
would encounter stormy seas. Foreigners did in fact invest heavily, and the
gross national product grew at a phenomenal 8 percent between 1884 and
1900, the halcyon days of the Porfirian experiment. But this growth only exacerbated the traditional incongruities in Mexico's economic and social structures. Not surprisingly, the rich got richer and spent much of their new
wealth on imported luxuries—indoor plumbing, electric lights, motorcars,
Parisian-style mansions—that reflected both their traditional status and a
modernist persuasion.

Some of this wealth certainly trickled down to the middle classes in the form
of government jobs and business opportunities in the export economy. But the
"infamous plebes" benefited only occasionally, conditionally, and selectively. It
was a rare soul who managed to cross permanently the boundaries that separated
the *peónes* or *pelados* (pejorative terms for Mexico's rural and urban underclasses,
respectively) from the "progressive" classes. A century later, Humboldt's
unflattering characterization still rang true. And while these social inequalities

rarely produced class struggles in the classic Marxist sense, their disruptive potential was nonetheless considerable.

Nor were class inequalities the only, or even the most disruptive, of Porfirian Mexico's structural contradictions. Uneven development threatened to fragment the country even further at a crucial juncture in the process of national consolidation. On the one hand, economic sectors geared toward exports—henequen, sugar, coffee, textiles, mining, steel production—attracted foreign and domestic capital, which encouraged (sometimes successfully) the modernization of everything from technology and finances to work rhythms and labor relations (with significant regional variations). On the other hand, sectors geared to local and regional markets, like corn and wheat production in particular, resisted innovation.

Uneven development inevitably took on a regional dimension. The traditional grain-producing haciendas of central Mexico contrasted sharply with the booming peripheral economies of northern and southeastern Mexico. Even within the modern sectors, the more diversified northern economies bore little resemblance to the single-crop plantation economies in the south. To further complicate matters, Mexico's eager embrace of foreign investment and external markets increased economic opportunity but deepened economic dependence on, and thus vulnerability to, global economic forces just as it strengthened the financial and technological power of the centralizing Mexican state, but weakened its ability to respond to specifically national needs and concerns. The prophets of modernity had promised material wealth and security. The former was misdistributed and conditional; the latter was a lie.

Wrenching changes in traditional social relations—some produced by economic modernization and globalization, others driven by cultural forces (including Sierra's "foreign elements") which proponents hoped would forge a Mexican national culture—often worked at cross-purposes. Begun in the late 18th century with the Bourbon reformers, attacks by liberals on corporate structures, especially the church, the army, and autonomous Indian communities, sought to undermine traditional colonial social relations that had been based on group identity and networks of reciprocal obligation. After nearly a century of liberal legal reform and civil war, the corporate structures themselves had indeed been shorn of most of their temporal authority. But corporate identities continued to play an influential role in public affairs.

To counteract this influence, modernizers operating within and through the increasingly powerful Porfirian state expanded their assault on corporate society to include all manner of traditional social relations. Their goal was to replace a traditional society based on local loyalties and forms of knowledge with a modern one grounded in universal, abstract notions of time and space shared by all its members. They saw such a perceptual conformity as crucial to a unified nation-state. Even the grand patrón himself, Porfirio Díaz, argued that "all citizens of a republic should receive the same training, so that their ideals and methods may be harmonized and the national identity intensified." To this end, women of the "progressive" classes (along with their religious tendencies) were to be pushed firmly into the private sphere of the family to perform the crucial task of forming future (male) citizens while their plebeian counterparts received the vocational training that would prepare them for factory work. And Mexico's still-substantial Native American population would be transformed by secular, public education from superstition-ridden savages into social assets. Earlier in the 19th century, liberals had attempted a legal revolution that they assumed would transform Mexican society from the top down. Their positivist successors retained the end but reversed the means. For them the cultural formation of citizens would henceforth take precedence over legal enfranchisement.

This Porfirian cultural revolution was not without consequences. For one thing, the culture of modernity was based first on giving privileged status to rational (defined as scientific) and, in particular, reflexive knowledge—knowledge that not only accumulated but constantly revised itself in the process. Thus, reflexive knowledge rationally applied to the human condition supplied the driving force behind the limitless spirals of economic and social progress made possible by political stability and economic modernization.

In practice, however, reflexive knowledge often subverted what it was supposed to revise. For example, newly collected Porfirian crime statistics demonstrated that crime had increased dramatically under a regime whose "order and progress" mantra suggested quite the contrary. The unintended consequences of reflexive knowledge could sometimes shake the confidence of the most avid modernist.

This unsettling effect went even deeper, however, to subvert the glue of a modern society, which was the new notions of trust—in abstract systems rather than personal honor, in scientific principles instead of local knowledge—that united a people no longer bound from birth to the society and life rhythms of their *patria chica* (little fatherland). In this newly imagined national community, the corruption of local *jefes políticos* (political bosses) or even the adulteration of pulque, for example, took on a much larger significance, because such problems symbolized not just a violation of local moral economies but of the national trust. By the same token, the clientage networks and political dealmaking that Porfirio Díaz managed so adroitly for much of his tenure, and that were so crucial to the political stability required for economic development, ultimately delegitimized his regime and undercut the project they were intended to foster. Modernity might promise security, but in practice it resulted in the most ambivalent and ambiguous of all historical events: social revolution.

Porfirian Mexico is too often portrayed as having been a staging ground for the great Revolution. This interpretation, predicated on positivist notions of inevitable social progress, both distorts and oversimplifies the historical field. The Revolution that ended the Porfiriato was not an inevitable product of incomplete, insincere, or failed modernization, even though the modernization efforts of that period were indeed incomplete, often insincere, and sometimes failed altogether. Nor was it an unavoidable consequence of dependent capitalism, although dependency grossly distorted the development process and thus contributed greatly to internal stresses. Rather it emerged from the ambivalences and ambiguities inherent in modernity itself, grown perhaps to monstrous proportions on the dynamic periphery of a new global society. Any number of historical twists— Don Porfirio's early death, an acceptable successor, dumb luck even—might have forestalled the violent political and social struggles that surrounded Díaz's ouster. Regardless, the Mexican Revolution was already well under way. Porfirio Díaz, as he left Mexico for exile in Paris, is reported to have said of his successor, "Francisco Madero has unleashed a tiger; now let's see if he can tame it." This comment might just as well have served as his own epitaph.

Order was the raison d'être of the Porfirian regime. In the 1876 Plan of Tuxtepec that justified his revolt against an elected government, General Díaz complained vociferously that President Sebastián Lerdo de Tejada's refusal to abide by constitutional provisions against reelection, his repeated interference in state and municipal politics, and his heavy-handed violence against "worthy citizens" had made a "farce" of political suffrage, a "cruel joke" of democracy, and a "prostitute" of justice. In light of his own later reelections, interventions, and repressions, these early complaints became a source of some embarrassment and much irony: penny press editors in particular mocked the hypocrisies of the "Indispensable Caudillo." The subversive potential of these attacks was kept at bay only insofar as Díaz could deliver on his promise to restore order to a violent and divided country. "We adopted a patriarchal policy," he reflected in the last years of his presidency, "with full faith that an enforced peace would allow education, industry, and commerce to develop elements of stability and unity in a naturally intelligent, gentle and affectionate people." Whether for legitimation or national development, the regime's obsession with order reflected the high stakes involved.

Not surprisingly, then, the regime deployed a broad range of techniques— some traditional, some modern; some overt demonstrations of state power, some more subtly coercive—to discipline Mexico's heterogeneous and too often recalcitrant peoples. As elite reformers saw it, the goal was to forge, in Justo Sierra's words, "a national soul." The official line had it that Mexicans lacked the self-restraint necessary for democratic government and productive labor, and a panoply of corrective and preventive measures promised to overcome this perennial obstacle to development. All in all, these techniques were remarkably successful—at least for a while.

At the base of this complex disciplinary apparatus was the not-so-hidden threat of state violence. "There are times," Don Porfirio once told a U.S. reporter, "when a little cannon smoke is not such a bad thing." In his first term, there was more than a little.

The first order of business was dealing with the political opposition. Díaz was not the only prominent political figure disturbed by the illegalities of Lerdo's 1876 reelection. Chief Justice of the Supreme Court José María Iglesias refused to ratify the results and declared against the government as well, delivering a fatal blow to the incumbent, who until then had successfully kept the rebellion at bay.

José Iglesias, longstanding liberal politician and rival of Porfirio Díaz, was forced out of the presidential office by Díaz's revolution of Tuxtepec in 1876.

With Lerdo on his way into exile, Díaz sought a deal with Iglesias, president by constitutional order of succession. When he refused to cooperate, Díaz made short work of his rapidly dissolving army. Ever respectful of democratic conventions, Díaz was formally elected president in 1877.

If many Mexicans welcomed the onset of peace, Díaz's political opponents did their best to undermine it. A series of uprisings by Lerdo supporters over the course of his first four-year term, several launched from the relative safety of the United States border, were easily and often brutally suppressed either by Díaz's army or the forces of powerful allies like the Nuevo León *cacique* (strongman) Jerónimo Treviño. Disgruntled generals, some displeased with the division of spoils, others resistant to the growing power of the Porfirian state apparatus met a similar fate. So did less prominent opponents, whether dispossessed *campesinos* (peasants) or alienated *puro* (radical) liberals. When asked by Veracruz governor Luis Mier y Terán to decide the fate of nine local businessmen accused of sedition, Díaz reputedly telegraphed back "kill them at once." True or not, this often-repeated anecdote demonstrated the president's resolve to his potential opponents. It also highlighted the benefits of a rapidly growing infrastructure of telegraph lines, highways, and railroads that considerably improved the regime's ability to deal with internal threats to public order.

Political theater and the practical virtues of modernization also took center stage in the regime's escalating attack on bandits, the scourge of the Mexican countryside. Judging from published accounts by travelers, Mexico's bandits were a constant source of worry and conversation. At midcentury, Fanny Calderón de la Barca, the Scottish-American wife of the first Spanish ambassador to Mexico, graphically depicted an infamous "robber-capitán" clothed in a "dark-coloured

President Díaz initiated a series of reforms intended both to modernize and professionalize the national military. The reforms included providing the most modern equipment available.

blanket, and a black hat, the broad leaf of which was slouched over his face, which was the colour of death, while his eyes seemed to belong to a tiger or other beast of prey." And the French ambassador of the time remarked sarcastically that bandit gangs were the only Mexican institution that functioned "with perfect regularity." Such comments, ubiquitous in the mid–19th–century travel literature, may have titillated or amused their international audience but would have hardly inspired the confidence of foreign investors, the one group that Mexican policy makers were counting on to fund economic development.

To make matters worse, marauding Indians, including the Apache leaders Geronimo and Victorio, frequently crossed the international border into Mexico, raiding small villages, waylaying travelers, and disrupting commerce. Histrionic accounts of their plunder, especially in the North American press, fueled concerns about the safety of investments in Mexico. The Porfirian solution to both problems was, in the words of historian Luis González, the "sanitary rifle."

To wield that sanitary rifle, General Díaz and his ministers turned not to the army (always a potential threat to state security) but to a national police force created by Benito Juárez in 1861: the *rurales*. In the chaotic political climate that preceded the Tuxtepec revolt, the poorly trained and organized rurales had created nearly as many public order problems as they had solved. But by 1880, when Díaz temporarily relinquished the Presidency to his army crony Manuel González, a 90 percent increase in personnel (to 1,767 men) and a 400 percent increase in funding had transformed the rurales into a loyal cornerstone of the Porfirian disciplinary apparatus.

Aided by the expansion of the railroads, telegraphs, and roads, the rurales extended the increasingly long arm of the state into the Mexican countryside. The publicity generated by daring pursuits and dramatic shootouts with bandits like Veracruz's elusive Santanón and Heraclio Bernal, "the Thunderbolt of Sinaloa," enhanced the corps's reputation for tenacity and rough justice (even though army units actually killed both bandits and rurales and spent more time assaulting striking workers and repressing rebellious campesinos than in pursuing "robber-capitans"). Nevertheless, banditry and other rural disorders persisted throughout the period. Santanón, for example, was not caught until 1910, and some of the most dangerous workers' strikes and campesino revolts occurred in the regime's last years.

The facts were of little consequence. Given the regime's preoccupation with reassuring foreign and domestic investors, image—in this case the appearance of order—came first. In this endeavor, the rurales demonstrated their true worth. Clad in the traditional *charro* garb of Mexican cowboys and portrayed as tough quasibandits themselves (a false image propagated by regime publicists), they became staples in public parades and rodeos throughout Mexico. And, following in the wake of Buffalo Bill's internationally acclaimed Wild West show, the rurales traveled abroad to entertain and instruct appreciative foreign audiences with inscrutable visages, exotic outfits, and flashy horsemanship. At home and abroad, this dashing image had a practical side as the rurales brought a semblance of order to areas of heavy foreign investment, often supporting foreign owners and supervisors in their efforts to control unruly Mexican workers. The rurales may not always have restored order to the Mexican countryside, but they were effective enough.

Although it was less romantic, the apparent professionalization à la française of the Mexico City police and the strategic positioning of gendarmes in the capital's better neighborhoods also contributed to the illusion of stability. The Porfirian científicos were much chagrined when their vaunted efforts to collect "scientific" statistics revealed that Mexico City had a higher annual murder rate (1 in 1,000) than Calcutta, but in an 1897 speech the científico jurist Miguel Macedo reminded an audience of lawyers that "among the middle and upper classes there exists a firmly rooted sense of personal security that manifests itself in an extraordinary liberty of action." There was plenty of plebeian violence in Porfirian Mexico, but it posed little threat to the progressive classes and their foreign counterparts.

Moreover, statistics aside, the illusion of stability made a real difference. As the new century began, foreign travelers remarked on the folkloric, quaint, and above all orderly aspects of Mexican society. In the aptly titled *Viva Mexico!*, for example, U.S. travel writer Charles Flandrau reported that "besides the small but businesslike policemen with large, visible revolvers who seem to be on every corner and who materialize at the slightest infringement of the code, the highways are patrolled by that picturesque body of men known as the rurales, of whom there are between four and five thousand."

For this remarkable turnaround, U.S. secretary of state, Elihu Root, credited the Indispensable Caudillo himself. "If I were a Mexican," he remarked, "I should feel that the steadfast loyalty of a lifetime could not be too much in return for the blessings that he had brought to my country." These well-publicized impressions earned Díaz the sobriquet Master of Mexico and an international reputation that returned to Mexico as dollars, pounds, francs, marks, and pesetas. "A little cannon smoke" (with a pinch of publicity) was indeed "not such a bad thing."

But as Don Porfirio was the first to admit, modern societies, especially modern ones with liberal aspirations, are not disciplined by cannon smoke alone. Since before independence, Mexican social reformers of all stripes—Bourbon administrators, enlightened conservatives, and liberals—had, like their European counterparts, espoused a modern carceral system grounded in the schoolhouse, army barracks, and penitentiary. Colonial subjects might have been disciplined by arbitrary decree and terrorized by gruesome exemplary punishments when they resisted, but modern citizens exercised inalienable rights and learned to discipline themselves. The visible threat of state violence might placate foreign investors, but generations of Mexican social reformers realized that the holy grail of modernity could be attained only by the pure of heart: the virtuous citizen.

The prospects for reaching a comprehensive citizenship were daunting. Although Mexico's citizens were born and nurtured in the bosom of the nuclear family, their civic virtues might well be subverted by a mother's love and religion. Thus the nation-state had a compelling interest in the formation of its citizenry. To this end, Mexican policy makers turned to the modern technologies of social control pioneered by their western European and North American counterparts: compulsory secular public education, professional military training, and rehabilitative penitentiary regimens. Some strides had already been made. Juárez's positivist guru Gabino Barreda founded the National Preparatory School in 1867 to train a new generation of policy makers and educators in "scientific politics." His justice minister Antonio Martínez de Castro drafted and promulgated a liberal penal code in 1871. But these were just preliminary steps; the real work lay ahead. If the social reformers understood that discipline and trust formed the double helix of modernity, the pax porfiriana provided the first real opportunity to bring these modern disciplinary technologies to Mexico.

Public education, with its potential to reach all Mexican children, was the regime's top priority. Mexico's strong federalist tradition (especially with regard to states' and municipal rights) posed difficulties, but in 1888, with Díaz's blessing, education minister Joaquín Baranda pushed legislation through Congress that extended the Federal District's obligatory free public education program to the entire nation. Two years later his successor, Justo Sierra, warned a national educational congress that "our life is linked with iron chains to the industrial and economic life of the world. . . . Centrifugal force in the heterogeneity of habits, languages and needs must be transformed into cohesion thanks to the sovereign action of the public school." At the grass roots, treatises on moral education admonished primary school teachers "to inspire a love for work, for the nation, for

Joaquín Baranda, who belonged to President Díaz's inner circle of advisers, formed part of the group of positivists, known in Mexico as the Científicos. They advocated opening Mexico to foreign investors to bring about the kind of economic growth they identified with modernization.

Justo Sierra remains one of the outstanding ministers of education in Mexico City. He also formed part of the circle of positivists who dominated politics during these years, taking a leading role in creating the national educational system.

other people, for justice and truth, and for respect for the law and constituted authorities." With so much at stake, Porfirian educators engaged in heated debates over issues such as the proper role of science in the school curriculum and whether or not public education could transform Indians into "social assets." Education was much in the air.

There were notable successes. The percentage of federal and state budgets allocated to education more than doubled from 1877 to 1910, and primary school enrollments tripled. Literacy rates went from less than 15 percent to nearly 20 percent in same period. More than half the Federal District's residents could read and write by 1910. To ensure a steady supply of trained teachers, normal schools opened all over the country. Between 1895 and 1910 the number of teachers increased from 12,748 to 21,017, from just over 10 teachers to almost 14 per 10,000 students, the fastest growth rate of any profession in Porfirian Mexico.

Not all schools were secular or public. Taking advantage of the regime's unofficial tolerance, the number of Catholic schools increased from 4 percent to almost 5 percent of the nation's total. Even Protestant missionary schools got in on the act, quadrupling their enrollments to nearly 12,000 by the end of the period. To oversee this expansion, a national secretariat of education was created in 1905 under Justo Sierra's leadership. At the state level, education-conscious governors like Chihuahua's Enrique Creel, Nuevo León's Bernardo Reyes, and Yucatán's Olegario Molino spoke out in favor of education, as did Sonora's Ramón Corral, Díaz's last and most controversial vice-president. The more conscientious, like Creel, personally funded new schools.

The culmination of the Porfirian regime's education efforts came, fittingly enough, in 1910 when education minister Sierra inaugurated the National University as the designated training ground for the next generation of leaders. Things looked rosy indeed, and educators publicly proclaimed their pride and confidence in the nation's schools. On the eve of Revolution, for example, school authorities in Puebla were assuring delegates to a national education congress that, thanks to the public schools, "the people of Puebla . . . are losing their prejudices, errors, and rudeness and acquiring habits of morality, economy, and order." (Little did they suspect that their city would supply the revolution's first martyr, shoemaker Aquiles Serdán, the president of the local Light and Progress Club, a local liberal club with no particular political affiliation.)

Nor did Porfirian policy makers ignore the barracks, another potent venue for the formation of citizens. As a former rebel general himself, President Díaz knew well enough the dangers of a politicized army. After receiving pro forma congressional permission in 1878, he began a massive reorganization of the military's command structure. This reorganization, carried out mostly during the four-year Presidential interregnum of loyal Porfirista general Manuel González (1880–84), divided Mexico into a flexible grid of zones, commands, and *jefaturas de armas* (subdivisions of a command) whose actual shape, command structure, and troop allocations were all to be determined by the President or his war minister.

The pax porfiriana also encouraged demilitarization. The number of troops dwindled from 30,000 to some 14,000 by 1910, and the number of generals was reduced by an astonishing 25 percent. Higher budgets; European munitions; Prussian-style uniforms; a modern military academy to train officers in the latest European military techniques; and higher pay for the troops demonstrated the regime's commitment to a modern, professional army. The president even recalled another army crony, the "progressive," efficient governor of Nuevo León, General Bernardo Reyes, to oversee the modernization of the military. While he was at it, Reyes created a nationwide volunteer civilian militia, the Second Reserve, to further defuse the power of the reformed army. The once notoriously fickle Mexican military was thus carefully crafted into an apparently well-behaved, efficient, peacetime army.

For those unresponsive to education or military training, there remained a final possibility for redemption and citizenship: the penitentiary. Mexico's social critics had long lamented the deplorable condition of the nation's prison system which, as Sierra put it, "actually encourages crime [by] providing the criminal with everything he needs to complete his education [in crime]." The regime's leading penologist, Miguel Macedo, went further. "The punitive function of the state," he insisted, "which can do so much for social morality when directed with knowledge, conscience, and rectitude . . . is surely one of the principal elements of social order." In response, Federal District Governor Ramón Fernández appointed a blue-ribbon commission in 1881, including Macedo and future finance minister José Limantour, to formulate plans for a modern penitentiary. The following year the commission presented an elaborate proposal that boasted an innovative French-inspired radial design, a carefully calibrated behaviorist regimen of rewards and punishments, and corresponding modifications of the 1871 penal code.

After several construction delays—the massive prison walls kept sinking into Mexico City's unstable soil—the national penitentiary finally opened in the first year of the new century. At the opening, attended by General Díaz and the cream of the Porfirian elite, one official welcomed "a new era in the evolution of repressive systems in Mexico." As the commission report had noted, the penitentiary provided a new paradigm for a society whose members recognized that "the means of obtaining health and happiness is honesty and that vice always leads to pain and ends in misfortune." Penologist Miguel Macedo was even more expansive. The new penitentiary, he declared, was just the latest addition to "the already fecund fields of our efforts and ingenuity, whose fruits . . . mark a new era in the annals of national progress." His enthusiasm was contagious, and progressive state governments followed suit with model penitentiaries of their own. (Some facilities, like Puebla's, were finished earlier.) The national government opened a penal colony in 1908 on the Islas Marías off the Pacific coast of Nayarit state, which was designed specifically to rid Mexico City of "the habitual criminals . . . who comprise the daily clientele of our jails." Less numerous and less immediately threatening, the insane had to wait until the 1910 centennial of independence for their first modern facility.

As with more traditional means of social control like the rurales, the Mexican carceral system was more image than substance. Reflecting its own economic development patterns, Porfirian education reforms were uneven. Urban areas fared much better than rural ones, rich states were better served than poor ones, and the best-trained teachers gravitated toward the more prosperous regions. Moreover, chronically underpaid teachers often became vocal, influential opponents of the regime. Similarly, as the regime's quick collapse in 1910 would illustrate, although Díaz's "professional" army was eminently suited to such peacetime requirements as parades, maneuvers, and quelling minor disturbances, it lacked the combat training, patriotism (troops were still forcibly conscripted through the dreaded *leva*, or draft), leadership (by 1910 all the division generals were older than 70), and sheer numbers to handle a large-scale uprising on several fronts.

The new penal facilities served an essentially ideological function that made little impression on the nation's criminal population. Most of these members of society, according to a prison inspector, continued to "pass the time lying around, smoking marijuana and tobacco" and otherwise corrupting each other in the notoriously promiscuous galleries of overcrowded local prisons. Further, jailed political prisoners mercilessly exposed the many practical failings and fundamental hypocrisy of the regime's reformist discourse.

Despite these failures, the Porfirian obsession with its own public image was more than just rhetorical. As the Mexican elite knew from pilgrimages to western Europe and the United States, the voyage to modernity began with isolated acts of faith—a modern school curriculum, a Prussian drill instructor, daily showers for prisoners. But the tangible results it produced, such as a generation of scientifically trained technocrats, impressed foreign investors. And the regime's demonstrable commitment to the creation of a modern citizenry initiated the ascending spirals of economic and social progress that would guarantee the national future. The unintended consequences of the Porfirian efforts to construct a modern carceral system, which resulted in teachers and literate shoemakers as political opponents, an inadequate army, and a subverted reformist discourse, would become apparent only later.

Convinced of the transformative power of public image, the Porfirian intelligentsia displayed a fondness for positivist slogans, for just the right mot d'ordre: Thus, "Order and Progress" expressed the regime's program, "Less Politics, More Administration" its strategy. After years of internecine struggle, this advice seemed sound enough. According to Díaz's social engineers, bureaucrats, not generals, and technocrats, not politicians, were the logical architects of a modern nation-state. Colonial subjects had been bound together by personal relations (to family, community, patron, church, and sovereign), disciplined by notions of honor, and characterized by loyalty to the patria chica. Modern citizens, on the other hand, would trust in impersonal bureaucratic systems (state-sponsored education, public administration, and railroads), defer to the rule of law, and direct their loyalties toward the nation-state.

In Mexico, as elsewhere, this realignment of affinities was easier said than done. In Porfirian Mexico, the slogans revealed a fundamental contradiction. There the commitment to order meant less violence perhaps and more administration certainly, but it also meant more politics (and more personalized politics) rather than less. In fact, Díaz's remarkable ability to manipulate the traditional social relations of patronage, clientage, and even godparentage was the keystone in the arch of order. Without politics, and traditional politics at that, the regime stood little chance of success. So the Indispensable Caudillo proceeded to play politics with a vengeance.

To the intelligentsia, Porfirio Díaz was the quintessential Mexican politician. Sociologist Andrés Molina Enríquez, for example, remarked on "the mutual comprehension and confidence" that Díaz shared even with ignorant *indios*, a trait he ascribed to the general's mestizo heritage. "Physically and morally," he concluded, "General Díaz [is] a wonderful example of the national mestizo racial type that has begun to be, and plainly will be in the future, the true national type." For francophiles like novelist Federico Gamboa, his very Mexicanness made Díaz something of an enigma. After years of observation, the era's foremost chronicler of the human condition could only conclude that "he is the Sphinx, even by his color and by his origin, he is the Sphinx!"

More analytical than most (although just as condescending), Justo Sierra commented on Díaz's "inverted" mental pattern in which "deliberation follows the act of will . . . and modifies or even nullifies the original decision." This typically mestizo mental pattern, Sierra added, "has given rise to imputations of political perfidy (deceiving in order to persuade, dividing in order to rule)" even if these traditional political vices are "contradicted by the qualities that we all recognize in the private man." Don Porfirio's political gifts clearly disturbed his científicos, but they nevertheless admired his more than oriental splendor. They calculated that Díaz's inscrutability in the service of modernity just might unlock the door to a glorious national future. As was so often the case, Sierra had it exactly right: "Deceiving in order to persuade, dividing in order to rule" (mitigated somewhat by the president's reputation for personal integrity) precisely described the Porfirian modus operandi.

Díaz's most significant deception, his legal subversion of democratic institutions, was widely recognized. Even Sierra averred that Díaz had established a "social dictatorship" (although "without breaking a single law"), but he insisted nonetheless that "while our government is eminently authoritarian, it can never, at the risk of perishing, refuse to abide by the Constitution." And if the much-beloved Constitution of 1857 performed an essential legitimizing function in liberal Mexico, it could always be (and was) amended at Díaz's request, as for example to permit the reelection of the President and extend the term from four to six years. Presidential control of congress, the federal judiciary, and the national bureaucracy, with Díaz often selecting the candidates himself, ensured the desired result.

Control of the press, while by no means absolute (in the 1880s, opposition journalists openly announced the formation of a Jailed Journalists' Club, and the penny press continued to satirize, albeit haphazardly, the administration's foibles), helped mute public criticism. By 1910, the hypocrisies of Díaz's "social dictatorship" would prompt the legitimacy crisis that precipitated his downfall. But for 35 years, perfidious or not, the constitutional farce was deceptive and persuasive enough to assuage the consciences of regime loyalists and meet the ritual requirements of Mexico's assortment of local liberal groups.

Real political power was invested not in constitutional forms or conventional political parties but in national and state-level *camarillas* (political interest groups) and in local *jefes políticos* (political bosses). Just as Sierra described, Díaz managed the real power by "dividing in order to rule."

At the national level there were two major camarillas: the científicos and the *reyistas*, supporters of Nuevo León's governor Bernardo Reyes. Both groups maintained political and personal links to the President. The científicos were related to Díaz through his 1881 marriage to an 18-year-old Mexico City socialite, Carmen Romero Rubio. Not only did Doña Carmen get credit for teaching the crude Oaxaqueño the social graces—not to spit on the carpet, not to walk through mirrors—she also bound him to the capital's liberal, civilian elite as represented by her father, Manuel Romero Rubio, a cabinet minister under Lerdo and founder of the científicos.

This camarilla provided Díaz with his most important ideologues and technocrats. In exchange he provided them opportunities for intellectual glory (Justo Sierra, Miguel Macedo, Emilio Rabasa, Francisco Bulnes), personal enrichment (José Yves Limantour, Pablo Macedo), and political advancement (Olegario Molina, Enrique Creel, Ramón Corral). But there were limits to their influence. Prophets of modernity though they were, the científicos never transcended the traditional patron-client relations that brought them to prominence, as is witnessed by their repeated failure to create a viable political party and initiate the much-ballyhooed transition to democracy. The great man brushed aside any attempt to institutionalize politics. And the científicos, their venality under constant attack in the opposition press, lacked the popular (and military) support for even token resistance.

On the other hand, their rival camarilla, the reyistas, who boasted a war hero, liberal credentials, and a reputation for efficient administration, drew on broad support from a nationwide network of political clubs and, more importantly, from within the military. Yet its fate was no different. When Díaz's old army crony and protégé Bernardo Reyes grew too popular in the wake of científico Ramón Corral's unpopular 1904 selection as vice-president, Don Porfirio shipped him off to Europe on a military study mission. Ever the loyal client, Reyes, went peacefully.

State and local politics followed a similar pattern of clientage and camarilla politics. Male heads of powerful families manipulated their followers in true presidential fashion. (Masculine prowess was reflected in the popular nickname *el gallo*, the rooster.) At its most extreme their power, along with the nepotism and corruption that seemed its inevitable corollary, rivaled that of the great landed aristocrats of the colonial era. The Yucatán governor, Olegario Molina, for example, headed a "divine caste" of prominent *henequeneros* (henequen planters) that oversaw the state's political, economic, and social life. And as '*El Constructor*' (the builder) it was only fitting that his construction outfit, O. Molina y Compañía, receive lucrative state contracts to build everything from schools to sewers. He did, however, with proper noblesse oblige and considerable fanfare, donate significant sums, including a year's salary as governor, to help build a modern penitentiary, an asylum, a hospital, and a first-class theater.

Like all successful gallos, El Constructor maintained direct links to national camarillas—he was a prominent científico—and thus to the Indispensable Caudillo. The rewards were tangible. Molina not only served as Díaz's minister of development and facilitated (for a fee) the transportation of rebellious Yaqui Indians from Sonora to the labor-hungry henequen plantations of the Yucatán Peninsula but also, in honor of his accomplishments, Yucatán received its first-ever presidential visit, an event Mexico's fledgling filmmakers recorded and screened throughout the country. On Mexico's periphery with its jarring juxtapositions— debt peonage and penitentiary, blatant nepotism and new sewers, extreme poverty and modern cinema—the ambivalences at the heart of the Mexican modernity project and the personalist political networks that exacerbated them were glaring indeed.

Moreover, this incongruous combination of traditional politics with a modernist style was cropping up throughout Mexico. In Chihuahua, the Terrazas-Creel clan, after some initial difficulties with the President, amassed huge haciendas (7 million acres' worth, worked by thousands of resident peones), dominated state politics, operated the region's largest bank, and invested heavily in everything from modern steel foundries to breweries. In Morelos, sugar planters like the elegant Escandón family, whose Mexico City mansion was the envy of their peers, modernized their processing equipment and turned independent local campesinos into hacienda peones.

Strategic marriages and carefully selected careers for sons or sons-in-law ensured families' prosperity and influence. Pablo Escandón ("the most Parisian of Mexicans") and Enrique "Ricky" Creel (son of Chihuahua's U.S. consul and a Terrazas relative) both served as state governors, moved in científico circles, and maintained close personal ties to the president. Escandón served as Don Porfirio's chief of staff, Creel as Mexico's ambassador to the United States. The trade-off was clear: the President's solicitous concern, and considerable local autonomy, in exchange for loyalty and a commitment to order. (Not coincidentally, Francisco Madero, Díaz's *bête noire*, was the son of a prominent Coahuila family excluded from the president's inner circle.)

Still, powerful *caciques* (chiefs) could, and in the early years often did, resist the expanding influence, if not actual power, of the Porfirian state. When they grew too strong—Luis Terrazas in Chihuahua, Ignacio Pesquera in Sonora—the President replaced them with loyalists, while still allowing them to exercise their economic muscle—at least for a while. (Luis's son-in-law Enrique Creel helped restore the Terrazas's political influence.) To balance this potential threat, Díaz relied heavily on over 300 local jefes políticos whose appointments he indirectly controlled. Governors demonstrated their loyalty by appointing acceptable candidates but risked intervention if they did not cooperate. A former jefe político himself, Díaz understood the position's potential as a guarantor of order and therefore expanded its control over municipal affairs, including police and the local militias. For political opponents the jefes políticos represented a repressive, extra-legal tool of the Porfirian state. Certainly these officials created client networks of their own, undermined municipal governments, and favored the interests of state and national elites. At the same time, the successful jefe struggled mightily to mediate among national, state, local, and family interests, although usually to his own profit. As the central government began to escalate its demands on the jefes toward the end of the Porfiriato, that juggling act would become increasingly difficult to sustain.

Although the Indispensable Caudillo sat at the center of complex webs of political, economic, and social relationships, the Porfirian regime was hardly a dictatorship. For one thing, Díaz lacked the centralized power necessary to impose his will, especially outside Mexico City. And even there, rule by decree threatened to shatter the pretense of constitutional government, the foundation of the regime's legitimacy. For another, Díaz's usually adroit manipulation of clients and camarillas, which derived from his role as gatekeeper to power, proved quite effective in controlling (but not diminishing) politics at all levels. Científicos and reyistas and their local counterparts vied for Presidential attention and its attendant benefits—political preference, economic advantages, and social status—but not at the expense of order. For Sierra, "the political evolution of Mexico [had] been sacrificed to other phases of her social evolution." But only temporarily, for modernity or, more precisely, the public representation of modernity promised among many miracles the eventual transformation of traditional politics. And when those politics unraveled in the first decade of the new century, when state and local authorities began to protest the increasingly heavy hand of the central government, when even patrons' children called for an end to favoritism and a return to democracy, when the ambivalences embedded in Porfirian modernity became blatant hypocrisies, the Porfirian regime finally collided with the submerged mass of its own contradictions.

On September 15, 1899, a procession of allegorical floats, sponsored by railway companies, breweries, insurance companies, bed manufacturers, and electrical companies among others passed under Porfirio Díaz's gaze as he stood on the balcony of the National Palace. On the float designed by the Federal District Railway Company, described as a representation of the volcano Popocatépetl, a train of two electrical cars propelled by a trolley system complete with motormen and passengers continually circled a track and disappeared into a semicircular tunnel bored into the volcano, only to reappear again with its gong sounding. An insurance company float portrayed a figure in scarlet and silver, standing protectingly over a widow deep in mourning with a baby on her lap, as a child in pink and silver with silver wings (an allegorical representation of Fame) floated behind the widow. And on the rear of the float sponsored by the electrical companies stood a female impersonation of "Electricity" controlling the terrestrial globe.

While the date, September 15, seemingly marked this as a celebration of Mexican independence, it was not. Rather, in an attempt to insinuate himself into Mexico's pantheon of national heroes, Díaz now celebrated his saint's day on this date, redefining tradition in order to link himself more closely with the myths sacralizing the founding of the Mexican nation. Nor was this the extent of the ceremonies honoring the president. Whereas companies and business groups organized the procession, the different Mexican states built a series of triumphal arches for the president and other notables to pass under in their carriages while being showered with flowers, confetti, and "Viva!"s. At the first arch, contributed by his own state, Oaxaca, an orator praised Díaz for his supposedly great contribution to improving the conditions of the working class: "At present, when the workman returns to his home at night, he finds his supper ready and his wife and children greet him with gladness, and for each moment of happiness they enjoy they call down blessings on your head."

The day's events reveal many of the main tenets that characterized the dominant vision of progress as well as the common belief that it was Porfirio Díaz who had made its achievement possible. While all agreed that progress was meant to be measured in material terms, as by the number of kilometers of railroad track laid and the extent of electrification, it also required, as the orator above intimated, the inculcation of specific cultural values and the bolstering of traditional gender roles. Moreover, as many members of the Porfirian ruling elite viewed society as an organism—a living being that grew, developed, or weakened, depending on the ability of those within it to react to external elements or stimuli—the perfection of the organism (in other words progress) was also linked to the evolution of the nation and people in clearly racial terms. In Justo Sierra's opinion, for example, the trouble with Mexico was that it was "anemic," carrying an "impoverished blood" in its veins that produced skepticism, lack of energy, resistance to what was useful, and premature aging. He argued that "the condition could only be corrected by great quantities of iron, supplied in the form of railroads, and large doses of strong blood, supplied in the form of immigration."

Although immigrants never materialized in any numbers, great quantities of iron did. Beginning with major projects in the early 1880s, some 19,000 kilometers (about 12,000 miles) of railway track were laid during the Porfiriato. This was possible only with extensive foreign investment, because progress had to be brought about through the infusion of foreign capital into the economy. Much of this investment, which grew more than thirtyfold during the Díaz period (estimated at $1.2 billion up to 1900 and more than $3 billion between 1900 and 1910) was from the United States, with one-third of it invested in railways.

The Porfirian development program included railroad expansion, new foreign-financed factories, and improved ports. Tampico, a longtime port, underwent expansion during the Porfirian years that resulted in the scheduling of regular steamers to New York, New Orleans, and Havana. Shortly after 1900, Tampico underwent a boom with the rise of the oil industry.

Referred to as the agents of progress who would enable Mexicans to "go ahead" (as many *norteños* stated in English), American agents received concessions on extremely favorable terms to build trunk lines from Mexico City to the U.S. border as well as regional routes. So strong was the view that having railroads meant getting ahead that, by the late 1870s, the dominant and unmistakable symbol of progress in Mexican landscape painting was a railroad seen crossing wild, untamed nature.

The impact of railroad construction—some intended, some not—was breathtaking, however much it might differ by region. The Gulf of Mexico port of Tampico, for example, which had been only a marginal town before the 1890 arrival of the Mexican Central Railroad, rapidly grew into an important port city. The railroad's arrival, along with the upgrading of the port's infrastructure and the dredging of a sandbar, prompted an economic boom and population growth. On the Yucatán Peninsula, a new port, appropriately named Progreso, rose to prominence after being founded in 1870. Elsewhere, in the Laguna region of north-central Mexico, the arrival of the "machines of progress" triggered such economic development that the results became known as "the Miracle of Laguna" and the region was regarded as a showcase of Porfirian development. From a small, cotton-cultivating region, the Laguna became one of Mexico's most important agricultural, commercial, and industrial regions, linked with local, national, and global economies. The rural population of Laguna increased tenfold between 1880 and 1910, growing even larger during peak times in the agricultural cycle. This development was the result of an influx of an ever-larger floating population (*población flotante*), another consequence of modernity, which combined wage labor in various parts of Mexico and the United States with subsistence agriculture. Torreón, described as Mexico's first planned city, quickly grew to 40,000 inhabitants, many of them foreigners. The urban space itself—paved streets, sewers, the telephone system, streetcars, and public buildings—became the venue within which the city's inhabitants situated themselves within the constant change that was modernity.

In the far north of the country, in Sonora, the railroad was the catalyst for the emergence of a newly imagined border region. By the 1880s, Sonorans could travel on the Mexican Central Railway through the United States to El Paso, Texas, cross to Ciudad Juárez in the neighboring state of Chihuahua, and then continue on to Mexico City. As the trip, which had previously taken 30 days, could now be done in less than 4, the railroad also allowed the central Mexican governing authorities to exert more control on their formerly distant frontier. By the same token, Sonorans could be in San Francisco in about the same amount of time and in New York in less than a week. Once Sonora's port, Guaymas, on the Gulf of California, was connected to the U.S. border by rail, a spectacular land grab ensued as well as a sweeping realignment of power and politics in Sonora. Yet, by increasing travel within the state itself, the railroad also brought Sonorans face to face with each other and thus helped forge a unique regional culture.

Throughout Mexico, as in Sonora, a land grab of unprecedented proportions took place in the 1880s and 1890s. As land became a commodity to be bought and sold, villagers who had managed to hold on to their lands through 300 years of colonial rule and 50 years of independence now lost them to *hacendados* (large landowners), speculators, wealthier members of their own communities, and survey companies spurred on by a new law passed in 1883. From all corners of the country, rural residents petitioned local, state, and national officials, pleading that they were "under invasion" and on the verge of being thrown out of their homes. While some responded by throwing rocks at land surveyors to drive them off, others protested even more violently: 55 serious conflicts between villages and haciendas broke out during the early railway boom, with the majority occurring within 20 kilometers (12 miles) of existing or projected railway lines. Overall, the wave of commercialization that the railroads helped usher in concentrated landholdings into fewer and fewer hands, leaving the great majority landless. By 1910, nearly half the rural population in Mexico lived within the boundaries of a hacienda.

A major consequence of this concentration of landholding was the spectacular growth of export agriculture combined with the stagnation of staple crop production. Rubber, chicle, chickpea, tropical fruit, cochineal, and livestock production grew to supplement the exporting of established commodities, including henequen, coffee, vanilla, and hides. In the Yucatán, for example, the state with the most extensive rail lines in the country, whose economy depended almost completely on exporting the raw henequen fiber (known locally as "green gold"), exports rose from slightly less than 40,000 bales of henequen in 1875 to more than 600,000 bales by the end of the Porfiriato in 1910. By that time some 20 or

30 families, the *Caste Divina* (Divine Caste), led by the "great modernizer," Governor Olegario Molina, came to control between 80 and 90 percent of the henequen produced. And, once self-sufficient in corn, the state now found it necessary to import increasing quantities of foodstuffs. Other regions also became dependent on one or two export crops. South of Mexico City, the state of Morelos was virtually turned into a giant sugar hacienda while in the Soconusco region of the southern state of Chiapas some 26 large commercial coffee plantations had come into existence by 1892. Both areas, as well as many others, experienced the stagnation of corn, bean, and chile production while the population continued to grow. And although a much more diversified economy developed in northern Mexico, concentration was the rule there as well. In Chihuahua, for example, the Terrazas clan, in addition to its textile factories, flour mills, mines, and banks, managed to accumulate some 15 million acres of the state's most fertile, best-watered land while building their economic and political empire.

While the extension of the hacienda pattern did lead to increased exports, the ambiguities and even contradictions of pursuing modernity through this means quickly became apparent. In addition to the stagnation of staple crop production, which led to rising food prices, the land concentration combined with population growth meant an abundant supply of cheap labor, ruling out much technological innovation. Even in the Yucatán, the area ironically reputed to have the most technologically advanced agricultural plantations, the basic techniques of cultivation and harvesting were thousands of years old. Agricultural laborers worked in what critics described as a "slave mode of production." Although labor conditions varied greatly throughout Mexico, it was overwhelmingly the case that workers were now spending an increasing percentage of their shrinking wages on food, leaving little to contribute to forming a domestic market, thus limiting Mexico's industrialization as well. With rural residents spending as much as half to three-quarters of their income on basic staples after the turn of the century, few of the commodities that were increasingly being advertised as essential to modern life were within their reach.

As well as leading to concentrated land holding, the growth of the railroads also inaugurated a mining boom, especially in the north, where nonprecious industrial metals like lead, copper, and zinc were now increasingly mined and exported in addition to the traditional silver and gold. Of the estimated 44 railroads in operation in Mexico by 1910, nearly half served to link mineral-producing regions with metropolitan markets. In contrast to that of export agriculture, the mining industry was predominantly foreign owned, with U.S. companies controlling nearly three-quarters of the active mining companies and 70 percent of the metallurgy industry by the end of the Porfiriato. Especially between 1900 and 1910, when metals production almost doubled, the northern states of Baja California, Chihuahua, Coahuila, Nuevo León, Sinaloa, Sonora, and Zacatecas were incorporated into the world economy as metals producers. As one foreign observer stated about the Parral, Chihuahua, mining zone, only four years after the railroad had been built: "Parral is over 300 years old, yet it is not exaggeration

El Buen Tono cigarette factory became an emblem of Porfirian Mexico. Foreign dignitaries visiting Mexico always received a tour of the plant owned by Frenchman Ernest Pugibet. In the course of developing a near-national monopoly in the cigarette market, Pugibet pioneered the creation of a consumer society through, for instance, innovative advertising.

(sic) to say that more ore has been mined since the arrival of the railroad than during the whole previous time."

In addition to the expansion of mining, the railroads (along with electrification) helped prompt a considerable degree of import-substitution industrialization. In Puebla and Veracruz (which some foresaw developing into Mexico's Manchester), French capitalists known as the *barcelonnettes* (immigrants from Barcelonnette, in the south of France, who arrived in Mexico over the course of the 19th century) helped finance the creation of a modern textile industry the crowning glory of which was the Santa Rosa factory in the Orizaba Valley, opened by Díaz himself in 1899. As one visiting economist described the mills in 1903, "The machines are completely modern. . . . They have been made in Alsace." All told, 90 factories employed some 30,000 workers in this region.

Light industrial plants for the production of paper, glass, shoes, beer, tobacco, and food processing also appeared, especially in the growing cities in the north and in the capital. Monterrey, touted locally as the Mexican Chicago because of its industrial development, boasted a completely modern brewery, ancillary industries that included a major glass manufacturer, a totally integrated steel works (the second-largest manufacturing enterprise in Mexico in terms of capitalization), one lawyer for every 500 inhabitants, and a thousand commercial houses by 1909.

Mexico City also experienced industrial development, especially in textiles and tobacco. So impressive was the new factory of El Buen Tono tobacco company and so successfully had its owners associated their industry with technological innovation through promotions such as bringing a dirigible to the capital and showing free films to workers that the President's son used it, instead of the National Palace, to impress visiting dignitaries with Mexico's progress.

Nevertheless, the Porfirian model of industrialization meant that large, vertically integrated firms employing the most up-to-date technology replaced artisanal producers. Protected by tariffs and benefiting from a drop in the value of silver that made imports more expensive, textile factory owners imposed a new, strict industrial discipline on the thousands of transitory workers who had come seeking wage labor, while their operations displaced village artisans, one of the major casualties of Porfirian progress. In all branches of manufacturing, oligopoly and monopoly production came to be the rule as a few firms cornered the market in any single product. In mining as well, foreign investment meant the concentration of mine ownership and the introduction of capital-intensive methods of production. Increasingly, mineworkers labored in extracting facilities or operations in which a single company controlled the smelters, concentrators (used to prepare ore for smelting), stamp mills, railroads, blacksmith facilities, and electrical generators as well as the mines themselves. In the words of one U.S. mine manager, "gophering," the disparaging term he used to describe traditional Mexican mining methods, was being replaced with rational, systematic mine development. For the owners of a modern bakery in Mexico City who described their bread as "mechanically produced, absolutely clean" the advantages of progress were clear: "In a few days the unskilled worker can know as much as the long-serving craftsman."

While much of this rhetoric was self-serving, it does point out that increasingly, in the mines, textiles mills, and factories a new type of worker was needed: one not so intelligent and self-reliant, perhaps, but more obedient, industrious, and attuned to the new rhythms of work. At the mine as well as the factory, managers used both incentives and force in their struggle to mold suitably motivated and subordinated workers who wouldn't simply leave the work site once they had saved enough to buy "a bag of beans and a pot of corn meal." When higher pay, bonuses for steady work, schools, hospitals, and company stores where workers might be convinced to develop new wants and eventually discard sandals and wear shoes didn't work, repression was applied. Mining companies funded newly created municipal and district surveillance agents to escort pay shipments, maintain order during paydays, attempt to control vice, and, generally, keep tabs on workers. In the textile mills, managers used an extensive system of fines to impose their brand of order and progress. For many of those affected by changing work regimes and the mania for economic development, even those accepting the rhetoric of "progress," the Porfirian model represented a forced rather than a true expression of the concept. According to one mine worker, local officials were corrupting true progress by imposing arbitrary, tyrannical rule and exploiting

Despite intense modernization campaigns, Mexico still continued numerous traditions of a rural, Catholic country. Here a woman and her children visit the Alameda to see the construction of temporary booths for the Holy Week celebration. The men at the right are dressed in modern, store-bought clothing, but the woman, her children, and the man behind her wear traditional clothes, including the woman's *rebezo* (scarf) and the man's traditional wide sombrero.

resources until they became exhausted. In contrast, he envisioned a kind of progress that placed the greatest possible sum of goods with the greatest possible number of individuals.

This attempt to dispel local knowledge and replace it with new, abstract notions of time and space was not limited to foreign managers. Within some sectors of Mexican society a vigorous developmentalist ethos that stressed thrift, hard work, hygiene, entrepreneurialism, and moral reform took hold, providing an ideological underpinning for capitalism as well as the ethic most suited to those desperately seeking to be modern. The middle classes, self-defined as members of decent or cultured society, in other words the self-proclaimed *gente decente*, sought to set themselves apart from hard-drinking, supposedly uncultured workers while at the same time striving to transform those who refused to share in Mexico's progress into patriotic citizens as a peaceful working people. Three-story clock towers boasting four-sided clocks sprang up in remote municipalities and work sites, reminding workers that time was indeed money. In some schools banks were introduced. Typically, every Monday, in front of their classmates each student handed in a deposit to the teacher. All were expected to participate, even if they could bring in only a few *centavos*. According to government officials, the mission of the educator was to make people realize that the school led directly to the workshop and from there to the home.

The Porfirian home was meant to be ruled over by a guardian angel. In short, women's domestication seemed to promise an ordered society, as Julio Guerrero made apparent in his 1901 study of crime in Mexico. Guerrero divided society in central Mexico into six groups: (1) a large and growing group of street people, including beggars, rag pickers, and others; (2) the rank and file of the military; (3) workers without skills or trades; (4) male and female servants; (5) artisans, policemen, and lower-level public and commercial employees; and (6) those dedicated to intellectual work, including lawyers, doctors, engineers, artists, professors, merchants, military men, and high governmental officials.

Rather than wealth or occupation, each group's defining characteristic for Guerrero was the "moral" behavior of its women. As one moved from "lowest" to "highest," women "progressed" from promiscuous to polygamous to monogamous, eventually becoming at the end of his evolutionary scale *señoras decentes*. Only in her home, which Guerrero likened to being encased in a glass jar (a positive image, for him), could the best qualities of the Mexican woman evolve into a señora decente. The qualities of economy, charity, modesty, motherhood, devotion to family, patriotism, and punctuality, which all went together, were to be practiced in "pure homes" (*hogares blancos*) and then publicly modeled by society women, including Díaz's wife, Carmen Romero Rubio. On occasions such as the celebration of Mexican independence they distributed gifts of clothing and toys to the "more industrious and deserving" pupils in the public schools.

The increased emphasis on domesticity was also seen as a means of forcing workers off the streets and into the safety of the home. Indeed, urban space itself was greatly contested as adherents to the developmentalist ethos came to view the city through the lens of a moral geography of vice. To control drinking, prostitution, and gambling—the "vile trinity of vice"—new legislation was passed to limit the hours of operation of establishments where alcohol was served, while specific urban zones known as *zonas de tolerancia* were set aside to house brothels. City centers especially were to be reserved for the gente decente so they need not observe scandalous behavior or rub shoulders with prostitutes, conceptualized as at the opposite pole from the señora decente. In towns large and small, authorities moved to restrict circuses, dramatic functions, concerts, magicians, somersaulters, and amusements like gambling that were associated with national holidays.

This spirit of moral reform, a process described by some as dullification, was viewed as essential to progress in two ways. On the one hand, newspapers of different ideological stripes increasingly lamented the fact that material progress did not seem to be accompanied by progress in the moral realm. Such measures were designed to correct that situation. On the other hand, indulgence in vice was seen as leading to "degeneration," progress's opposite, often conceptualized in starkly racial terms. As *El Correo*, a northern newspaper, argued, alcohol abuse (associated with the laboring classes in the elites' rhetoric) would lead to the extinction of the Mexican "race" within four generations. Such "racial poisons" seemed to them capable of affecting entire populations and threatening the viability of the nation itself.

As "progress" could be measured in material, moral, social, and racial terms, so could it also be measured politically. In fact, a "scientific politics" that promised the end of ideology and squabbling and the triumph of administration was seen as both the great accomplishment and the prime symbol of Porfirian progress, however flawed it might have been. There was much to point to in support of this claim. In the 1880s, Treasury Secretary Manuel Dublán restructured Mexico's foreign debt, enabling the nation to overcome its bad credit rating and establishing the conditions necessary to attract foreign investment. Likewise, export-led growth enabled José Yves Limantour, finance minister after 1893, to balance the budget, reform the treasury, abolish internal tariffs, place the nation's financial system on an orderly footing, and switch Mexico from the silver to the gold standard, further encouraging foreign investors. Along with sound credit and a healthy budget, new penal and civil codes in 1871 and 1884 respectively, the growth of a technocracy, and a growing emphasis on the collection of statistics allowed Mexico to claim its place as a practitioner of the science of modern administration. As Zayas Enríquez, newspaperman, literary figure, and member of the Centenary Commission, boasted at the time, modern administration was enabling Mexico to solve all its problems with "tact, honesty, and good faith, with a clear direction, with no political parties but only one national party scientifically ruled."

The country's rulers put forth this claim most emphatically in various international world's fairs, especially at the Paris Universal Exposition in 1889. In fact, progress in all its manifestations—material, moral, scientific, racial, political—was the central theme around which Mexico's (as other countries') participation revolved at this exhibition. As Mauricio Tenorio-Trillo has shown, Mexico's contribution—an Aztec palace at the foot of the Eiffel Tower—was designed to further the desires of the elite for European immigration, foreign investment, international recognition, and to illustrate its hegemony within the country. The exhibits it housed were visual representations of progress as well as forms or symbols chosen to present Mexico as a unique manifestation of universal principles or concepts. These exhibits included machines, books, paintings, and other displays highlighting the importance of science—especially hygiene, medicine, sanitation, criminology, anthropology, statistics, and public administration—as well as the design of the building itself. Its façade bore witness to the beginning and especially the end of "ancient Mexican civilization." While Mexico's past and history might be unique and even exotic, the country itself was evolving, as the Mexican fair site's organizers insisted, within modern, progressive, evolutionary patterns easily recognizable to Europeans.

While Mexico's exposition organizers were busy crafting the modern image of the nation abroad, nationally it was above all Mexico's cities, and especially the capital, that served as monuments to progress. Between 1877 and 1910, Chihuahua City's population grew from 12,000 to 30,000, Monterrey's from 14,000 to 79,000. The Federal District more than doubled, to house in excess of 700,000 people, with nearly half its 1910 population originating from elsewhere in Mexico. Accompanying urban growth was a quickening and diversification of economic life and an increase in mobility as electrified tram lines created a rapid-transit spine running north-south in the city by 1898.

A new consumerism emerged, which was most evident in the escalating promotional campaigns of the tobacco companies. Money, a new French car, a house, and once even a crocodile was given away in hopes of capturing the imagination and brand loyalty of the urban smoker. That such campaigns sometimes set off newspaper advertising wars offers testimony to the proliferation of the print media and the growth of a reading public in the urban environment. Such publications also helped guide consumers into purchasing the right items, which is to say those that would enhance their "modern" image, while manufacturers linked such products to nationalism, progress, and modernity. The illusion of a consumer paradise was yet another aspect of modernity in which all could participate as long as they had the money.

Urban space itself was also transformed, with cities now sporting new business houses and department stores complete with food, cosmetics, silk, women's fashions, sporting goods, men's attire, and other sections. There were now theaters, movie houses, public buildings, parks, and gardens. Reformed streets boasted elegant carriages, bicycles, and, by the end of the era, automobiles, at least in the urban center and new upper-class neighborhoods. While the elite in Mexico City moved to new suburban *colonias* southwest of the old city, many of whose houses were now illuminated by electric lights, workers congregated in their own colonias to the northeast, with the middle classes to the west. And, in keeping with Guerrero's moral geography of vice, there was a concerted attempted to rid the center city of the poor and Indians, or at least cover up their presence by dressing them "properly" for events including independence day celebrations.

In the "ideal city" that took shape during the Porfiriato, the Paseo de la Reforma became the corridor of power, the path along which official Mexico paraded and the text upon which the national epic of progress was inscribed. At its beginning was a monument to Charles IV, a tribute to Mexico's Spanish past, followed in the next *glorieta* (traffic circle) by a monument to Columbus, symbolizing the New World's discovery. Next came a monument to Cuauhtémoc, a glorification of Mexico's Indian past, culminating with the building in 1910 of a monument to independence in the last glorieta before arriving at Chapultepec, the presidential residence. Bronze statues of the two greatest heroes of each state lined the street. This was the route followed by Díaz as he passed under the arches constructed in honor of his birthday in 1899. The "ideal city" was also the setting for the most spectacular episode in the extensive process of inventing tradition that so engaged the Porfirian elite: the 1910 centennial celebration of the beginnings of independence.

During September 1910, the month that had seen the start of Mexico's war of independence a hundred years earlier, residents of Mexico City struggled to keep pace with their incredibly full ritual calendars. The first two weeks alone saw the inauguration of a new, modern mental hospital; a hygiene exhibition; an art and industry exhibit; a monument to Alexander von Humboldt; a seismological station; a new theater; two primary schools; a new ministry of foreign affairs building; new schools for teachers, one for women and another for men; a new building for the ministry of defense; and the laying of foundation stones for a new national penitentiary.

The last two weeks were equally busy. Inaugurated then were a public park, a monument to Benito Juárez, a statue of San Jorge (a saint called upon to protect against disease and pestilence), a gunpowder factory, hydraulic works, the National University, a livestock exhibition, and a great drainage canal. A giant altar was also constructed at the National Palace to honor the heroes of the wars of independence, and numerous celebrations involving the diplomatic corps were held. All these inaugurations and ceremonies served as a backdrop to the climax of the celebrations, which occurred in the middle of the month when a series of parades took place. These began on September 14 with a great civic procession and ended on September 16, the official day of the commemoration of independence, with a military parade and the inauguration of the monument to independence in the Paseo de la Reforma.

Although these events testify to the central role of monuments (including buildings) and civic ritual in the imagining and constructing of the modern, progressive Mexican nation that its elites desired, it is the parade on September 15 (described by newspapers at the time as the centennial historical pageant) that most clearly reveals the use of history both to invent tradition to teach nationalistic values and to portray the Porfiriato as the culmination of tradition—the end point of progress and the herald of modernity. In the parade, which was divided into three parts to correspond with the three great eras of Mexican history—Conquest, Spanish rule, and independence—Mexico's history literally came alive on the street for all to see.

Using allegory in the same manner as in the floats celebrating Díaz's birthday, the parade's organizers selected the meeting between Moctezuma and Cortés to represent the Conquest, the colonial ceremony that commemorated Conquest to stand for Spanish rule, and the entrance of the Army of the Three Guarantees, headed by Agustín de Iturbide, into Mexico City for independence. As represented in the parade, Mexicans of all "races" came together to form a unified nation under Porfirio Díaz as the logical end point of all that had come before it and the only possible path to progress. While the parades' organizers stressed historical accuracy in all its details, mere historical facts were not always allowed to get in the way of the didactic process of nation building. As one of Díaz's former ministers of development put it, "Oblivion, and I would say that even historical falsity, are essential factors in the formation of a nation."

Yet, despite the fact that many thousands turned out to witness the spectacle ("Nowhere," one paper reported, "was there an available inch of space which was not filled by spectators all eager to view the pageant"), it would be wrong to conclude that this meant that all who attended the pageant were marching in the official parade of the nation. A few months earlier that same year, the symbolic space associated with independence had been a site contested between artisans and police in the north. When artisans in Chihuahua attempted to honor Miguel Hidalgo y Costilla (the Mexican priest generally identified as the initiator of Mexican independence) by placing a wreath at his statue in the Plaza de le Independencia on the anniversary of his death, they were roughed up and arrested. The governing authorities were adamant that the artisans, members of anti-reelectionist parties that were springing up in the north, not be able to portray themselves as Hidalgo's heirs in the current struggle for political freedom.

Still others throughout Mexico had learned the official history lessons only too well, finding that many Porfirian officials were sorely lacking when compared to the heroes of the country honored in the official celebrations and that the current authorities seemed to have forgotten the liberal values they represented. Such views constituted a popular or folk liberalism and an alternative nationalism, with the campesinos and workers drawing their own lessons from the official past. They revered Benito Juárez, the president constantly invoked by Díaz and recognized by the inauguration of a monument during the September centennial; honored the liberal Constitution of 1857; and celebrated victory against the French and the conservatives in the 1860s, both the Constitution and the victory also being honored with major Porfirian official celebrations. These events and figures both inspired and justified resistance against abusive governmental authority. That such groups premised their critique of society on the same events that the elites glorified and idealized in civic ritual confirms that the dominant discourse often provides the symbolic tools from which resistance can be fashioned.

Nor did popular social groups partake in what has been called the Porfirian persuasion, the elite penchant for European—especially French—food, fashion, and *fêtes*. During the Porfiriato the elites, along with turning up their noses at *esquimoles* (ant eggs) in favor of *escargot*, began to absent themselves from celebrations reaffirming the values of the community and, in their place, adopted rituals associated with the life cycle that allowed them to display their prominence in Mexican society as well as their tight grip on modern values. Births, saints' days (like the celebration of Díaz's described above), weddings, and even funerals (celebrated by the family but with the general population as witness from a discreet distance), became occasions for proclaiming their own and, by extension, Mexico's wealth and status through conspicuous consumption, increasingly recorded in photographs for posterity. At some dinners marking life cycle rituals, like that honoring Díaz in 1891, wives and daughters provided the appreciative audience for husbands and fathers, who alone had dining privileges at the Porfirian head table. In these celebrations, as in the historical parade just described, workaday Mexican men and women (and even elite women) were turned from participants into spectators.

So, too, were public holidays reshaped to reflect and teach modern values. Mock battles with blossoms, celebrations in which the elite paraded in decorated carriages and young members of the gente decente pelted each other with flowers, and bicycle parades featuring flower-laced cycles were all the rage for the progressive Porfirian by the 1890s. Military displays emphasizing order, hierarchy, stability, and progress replaced traditional celebrations that had been associated in the minds of elite Porfirians with disorder and its potential to overturn the social hierarchy. In Chihuahua, for example, during the last decade of the Porfiriato, the Santa Rita festival, which had traditionally been a celebration of the state's patron saint, became a carnival of consumerism, an occasion for the public expression of the gente decente package of values that together came to constitute modernity. To begin with, the focus of the celebration was no longer local but regional and even international as organizers subsidized railroad fares to entice people from distant locales to come in and spend their money in the city. It was clear what they should and should not spend it on. The products of Chihuahua's new industries were featured in a parade of floats (one brewery even constructed an Eiffel Tower on its float, thus linking its product to a potent symbol of modernity) while the drinking of mescal and games of chance traditionally associated with holidays were expelled in accordance with the effort to reform vice and the use of city space then under way.

The sporting events associated with the Santa Rita festival were transformed as well. While horse racing still took place, it now featured riders from the ranks of business, high society, the military, and the rurales rather than the countryside. Automobile races and shooting events were also added to the celebrations, not only allowing participants to identify themselves with modern forms of recreation but also reflecting a new interest in sport and "scientific" exercise that, those of the persuasion felt, would help transform cultural values.

In Chihuahua, as in Mexico City and Monterrey, the YMCA, with the encouragement and support of high society, opened branches catering mainly to urban *empleados* (white-collar workers) who found in the institution a way to claim respectability and differentiate themselves from those occupying lower rungs on the social ladder. Association members moved to create a new tradition of their own on national holidays, the holding of athletic meets, including gymnastics, track, and other sports. Such activities enabled Mexican males to measure themselves not only in accordance with international standards and timekeeping, but also in their proximity to an idealized manhood. These events stressed masculine virtues such as self-discipline, the attainment of which promised business success and even national greatness. So identified was the YMCA with these modern values that, as part of the 1910 centennial celebrations, Porfirio Díaz himself presided over the opening of its new building in Mexico City.

The masculine virtue hogging center stage at association competitions and other sporting events left little room, except in the wings, for women, whose main role was to hand out the prizes. Even the women bowlers of the association in Mexico City found their weekly tallies of spares and strikes ignored in the press, which chose instead to focus on their role as men's auxiliaries, more in keeping with the dominant discourse of domesticity. Yet women found some room to maneuver, especially given their increased importance as consumers both of new leisure activities and other goods. When the roller-skating craze hit Mexico City in the 1870s, for example, owners of the newly opened rink, which featured orchestra music and the latest wooden-wheeled skates, encouraged women to participate by charging them 10 centavos an hour less than men to skate, much to the consternation of "respectable" families. Likewise, the new department stores drew women into public space, again giving rise to virulent tirades in the press against "luxury," a vice to which women were thought to be particularly susceptible. For some elite women, like those writing in journals such as *El Album de la Mujer*, the discourse of domesticity provided the rhetorical ammunition that enabled them to stake a claim for women on the nation's public space.

Nor were women's periodicals the only ones to take issue with the social norms envisioned by high society. At the turn of the century, a scathing, satirical penny press, catering to workers and independent artisans, emerged to reject the dominant perception of workers as vice-ridden and indecent. Papers like *La Araña* (the Spider), with its logo featuring the police, the clergy, and tram conductors enmeshed in its web of satire and frock-coated (that is, upper-class) individuals soon to be its prey, turned the tables on the elite by pointing out their foibles. In one illustration the wretched on earth raise their arms to Don Porfirio, seated in the clouds on bags of money, while an angel (Uncle Sam) hands him yet another bag. Such wealth, the paper insisted, was premised on the impoverishment of working Mexicans.

The penny press consistently asserted the respectability of the working class. In fact, the themes of the papers and the actions of organized workers illustrate that, to a large extent, workers constructed their view of the world and of themselves in response to the disparaging view of the gente decente. In 1908, for example, the president of the Union of Mexican Mechanics, defending the idea of celebrating a labor day, pointed to the role his union had already played in limiting the "innumerable days of fiestas." He stressed that such a holiday had the potential to educate, moralize, and elevate the working class, which were concepts dear to the hearts of those comprising "decent" society.

Others, however, rejected moralizing discourse outright. *La Guacamaya*, another satirical newspaper, taunted Guillermo de Landa y Escandón, governor of the Federal District, about the actual impact of the moral reform measures his administration had succeeded in enacting: "With his fine manners he made sure that the children did not learn to drink pulque. Nor should they enter cantinas. But his divine laws, although those of an honorable and sincere man, were laws of

Bullfighting caused widespread debate during the era of of Porfirio Díaz and was banned in the national capital at various times. Carmen Romero Rubio, the president's wife and first lady of the country, was honorary chair of the antibullfighting society. Nevertheless, many people rejected claims that bullfighting was a barbaric act of cruelty to animals, claiming instead that it represented an artistic spectacle of life, danger, and, ultimately, death.

Escandón alone." In Mexico City, as elsewhere in the nation, not-so-modern Mexicans, who comprised the great majority, continued to gather in *pulquerías* (one author has estimated that there was one alcohol outlet for every 149 inhabitants in the Federal District), billiard halls, brothels, and similar establishments, where, among other things, they continued to set their own rules and mores. Likewise, bullfights and cockfighting continued to be among the favored pastimes, and not only of the lower classes. Bullfighting, prohibited in Díaz's first term, returned to Mexico City by the end of the century to cater even to fashionable society, while one newspaper reported that gente decente patrons were pedaling their bicycles out to cockfights on the city's outskirts. Other popular entertainments included various genres of theater, circuses, and puppet shows where, as in traditional popular celebrations such as Judas burnings (in which effigies of Judas, often filled with surprises, were exploded), laughter, language games, and carnivalesque inversions of social and sexual roles teased out official values for inspection and provided a means to deflate the pretentious airs of the gente decente. In puppet shows that traveled throughout the country, characters like Vale Coyote, the "halfbreed bubba," helped unpersuaded Porfirians negotiate the perils of modernity or, at least, provided a good laugh.

During the Porfiriato, the gente decente sought to remake themselves and their urban environment as a means of both demonstrating and attaining modernity for themselves and Mexico. Not just as examples of Mexico's modernization, but as telltale signs that the country had indeed been blessed by the onset of modernity, they pointed to the social and economic changes that had resulted

Workers in factories such as this carpet factory in Santa Gertrudes trusted the national government to protect their rights against foreign owners and managers. They organized mutual societies, unions, and anarchist groups to make their voices heard. The failure of Porfirio Díaz to protect their interests became one of the major causes of the Mexican revolution.

from the Porfirian version of order and progress: the arrival of railroads, department stores, and movie theatres; the transformation of Mexico City's Paseo de la Reforma and urban space in general; the new ritual and festive calendar in which gymnastic routines, elegant private dinners, and allegorical floats trumpeting new consumer products marked stages in the life cycle of both the individual and the nation; and the 6,000 bicycles in circulation in the Federal District.

While the gente decente were willing to cultivate their appearances, feelings, and bodies as testimony to this modernity, the same could not be said for the rest of their countrymen and women. They would need, first, to be identified and defined through statistically measuring the body politic, a task energetically taken up by Porfirian social engineers (although the results were not always to their liking); second, to be disciplined by means of the rurales and a modern carceral system that included public education, military training, and the penitentiary; and, third, to be transformed into peaceful working people and virtuous citizens by being led away from vice and toward the traditional family, the consumption of new goods, and the passive act of observing the national allegory constantly paraded in front of them. That much of the emphasis of this parade and of the trappings of the gente decente itself was on façade and style, like the Aztec palace at the Paris exhibition, testifies to the importance of representation and illusion in becoming modern. Even then, the ways that most Mexicans plotted themselves within modernity were, if at all, not exactly what those orchestrating the performance had in mind.

That becoming modern also seemed to require a stronger dose of traditional gender roles—for both the working class and the gente decente—was only one of the many contradictions characterizing this process. Another was that the famed Porfirian public administration, with its goal of "more administration," was actually driven by the politics of clientage and the camarillas, the dirty secret behind Porfirian order and progress. A third contradiction was that the old oligarchy in Mexico was strengthened rather than weakened by Porfirian progress, its goal being, as one observer has aptly put it, to become "as modern as possible while remaining as traditional as ever." For this group modernity clearly meant maximizing its own interests and portraying them as identical to those of the nation. Thus, while Porfirian publicists could point proudly to railroads, docks, modern city spaces, and the beginnings of industry, much of this growth was premised on foreign investment and the external control that implied. Other contradictions abounded: while the rich got richer, the poor got poorer; while exports boomed, food production stagnated and land ownership became concentrated, even though population continued to grow; and while industries produced new consumer goods, wages remained so low and the cost of food so high that few could afford to purchase it, thus limiting the industrialization process.

Yet the greatest contradiction of all, one that is perhaps inherent in all efforts to embrace modernity, was exemplified in the ambiguous, even contradictory, slogan of "Order and Progress," the defining cliché of the Porfirian regime. To preserve old privileges, hierarchies, and values while hoping to mold citizens and suitably motivated workers around new notions of time, space, abstract knowledge and the nation-state, and to seek a rupture with the past while in fact preserving much of it was an impossible task. It not only left the regime open to harsh criticism for its failure to achieve both goals, but also produced unintended consequences: new teachers as political opponents, an inadequate army, and a reformist rhetoric that could be taken up by others to criticize the regime itself. By 1910, for most Mexicans the honeymoon with the Porfirian version of modernity was over, if it had ever begun at all.

SECTION IV

The Mexican
Revolution, 1910-1940

✦ ✦

After 1910, a generation of generals, this time amateur rather than professional, once again dominated Mexico. Unlike the military officers including Porfirio Díaz and Manuel González, who earned their stars by surviving the war against the French occupation, the revolutionaries were not for the most part trained soldiers. Some rebels, such as Alvaro Obregón, had a talent for war; others, such as Pancho Villa, were adept at leading men; and still others, such as Emiliano Zapata, were able to inspire followers with a just cause. As Mexicans fought for these and other leaders, they experienced the first, and most enigmatic, of the great 20th–century social revolutions like those that occurred later in Russia, China, and Cuba. The Mexican Revolution remains one of a kind in a century of social upheaval and anticolonial struggle perhaps because the monumental Mexican struggle contained elements such as local grievances and antiforeign campaigns against political and economic subjugation that appeared in all the other great social revolutions. In addition, its patterns have become familiar now as the wars of national liberation (dramatically with Vietnam, but also in Angola and Afghanistan). Moreover, the Mexican revolutionaries had the opportunity to experiment with social and economic programs because they lacked the theoretical straitjacket that has limited other revolutionaries in this century. The Soviet Union has collapsed, but Mexico endures.

Only on the question of the church did the revolutionaries (especially during the presidency of Plutarco Elías Calles) adopt such strident programs in the name of the Revolution that they led to a renewal of the bloodshed. The Cristero War of 1926–29 was a popular response to the Revolutionary government's failure to recognize the power of faith among village peoples and to celebrate the achievement of the church's reformers, who were carrying out social action policies parallel to the Revolution's social programs.

In recent biographies of Revolutionary leaders and scholarly monographs that examine the competing movements for land, labor, community self-rule, equality of wages and treatment of foreigners, and provision of food, housing, and education, historians have portrayed the revolutionaries as more human, persons of both greatness and great flaws. Making them more human does not diminish the Revolution (1910–20), its effort to remake society through an equitable distribution of goods and justice (1920–38), and its campaign to create a just society by increasing available income and goods through economic development (1938–45). The revolutionary period represents a heroic age. Moreover, this era overlapped that of the golden age of popular culture, c. 1940–70, in part as a result of the rise of the mass media that captured the spirit of the new Mexico in movies, music, radio, and the arts.

14

The Mexican Revolution, 1910–1920

JOHN MASON HART

Global crises and the awakening of national consciousness in the early 20th century produced violent political revolutions in Russia, China, Iran, and other countries—especially Mexico. Western European and American economic expansion into these exceptionally strong indigenous cultures dramatically affected their polities, production, and cultural practices. By 1910, the benefits of increasing economic prosperity and the movement toward political power sharing had given way to concern about the concentration of wealth and power in the hands of metropolitan elites and foreigners and the eroding status of provincial and local elites, artisans, industrial workers, small farmers, and agrarian workers.

Mexico's was the first successful revolution. Its revolutionaries came from all levels of society: Dissident elites joined the masses in a violent and prolonged civil war. The insurrectionists were strong enough to succeed where their Iranian counterparts failed, and they did so without the crushing defeats in foreign wars that weakened the ancien régimes in Russia and China. The revolutions in these four countries sprang from similar conditions. Governments had tried to modernize each country through economic expansion fueled by foreign capital, the privatization or commercialization of agriculture, and centralized dictatorships. In each case, these programs produced demands for broader political participation, land reform, and national control over resources and the means of production. In Mexico, the stagnation of political, economic, and cultural life, together with the omnipotence of foreigners and the weakness of the Mexican government, gave birth to a popular uprising unprecedented in the West.

Many factors that contributed to the Mexican Revolution fell into place during the Porfiriato, the long rule of General Porfirio Díaz that began in 1876. Díaz seized power with the intention of emulating the spectacular economic and political successes of the United States. He established his regime through means that offered early successes but ultimately led to disaster. In his first 15 years of power Díaz removed restraints on trade, privatized rural community landholding, brought independent and often radical unions under government control, recruited foreign investment to improve industry and technology, and encouraged immigration to develop the countryside.

The land privatization program quickly relocated great numbers of the agrarian workers who accounted for more than half the country's population. During the Porfiriato their community landholdings shrank from 25 percent to 2 percent of the nation's land. During the Porfiriato most agrarian laborers found work on emergent ranching and agricultural estates, and many urban artisans, unable to compete with the economies of large-scale manufacturing and imported goods, joined migrants from the rural population in seeking employment in the new factories.

Foreign capital provided the impetus for growth. By 1900, foreign investors held some 90 percent of the incorporated value of Mexican industry; Americans alone held 70 percent. Foreigners also held 150 million of Mexico's 485 million acres. Again, the Americans had the largest share among foreigners, with 130 million acres. In the early years of the 20th century, however, economic instability led to protests against the granting of "privileges" to non-Mexicans and helped undermine confidence in the regime.

In the last years of the regime the economy suffered a serious contraction, and real wages declined significantly. Agriculture, the most important sector of the economy, suffered disastrous setbacks after 1907. So did the textile industry: Between 1895 and 1910, the number of workers in the economically crucial textile industry dropped by a third. In 1908 and 1909, the failures of the corn and cotton crops in Chihuahua, Coahuila, Durango, Zacatecas, and other states north of Mexico City led to famine and food riots in several northern cities. Mining, the linchpin of attempts to modernize industry, collapsed when the bottom fell out of the world silver market. Adverse market conditions also struck the timber industry, forcing companies to close. Unemployed mine, timber, and ranch workers crowded the towns of the near and far north.

At the same time sugar producers and workers in Morelos, south of Mexico City, saw the U.S. market dry up as the result of a new American tariff designed to protect American sugar producers in Cuba. Mexican sugar growers had to cut production by 7 percent and increase sales to domestic markets at reduced prices. A comparison illustrates the magnitude of the debacle in Morelos: In the early 1980s, a contraction of .5 percent in the U.S. economy produced unemployment rates in excess of 20 percent in the Great Lakes states. The crisis in Morelos meant that many field and mill workers—who had only grudgingly given up their village properties in return for jobs during the previous 65 years of privatization programs and court actions by some of Mexico's most powerful landowners—found themselves out of work. The towns of Ayala and Cuautla teemed with displaced workers, future recruits to the revolution.

Reduced railroad and port activity reflected the overall decline of the mining, timber, agricultural, and ranching industries. Famine stalked dispossessed peasants

and workers north and south of Mexico City. The Mexican economy was traumatized, but Díaz and his advisors feared state indebtedness and believed that the
workings of the marketplace would restore prosperity. They refused to commit
funds for the relief of the now virtually landless rural working classes, or to help
urban workers and the small businessmen who suffered incalculable losses. The
dictatorial state that had earned plaudits during the prosperous years from 1876
until 1899 became, after 1900, the object of a crescendo of criticism. The economically vulnerable regional elites were becoming fed up with Díaz and were
chafing at their lack of political influence.

Even during the prosperous years, some Mexicans had criticized Díaz's
regime. During the 1890s the charismatic Ricardo Flores Magón led a pro-
democracy movement among students at the law school of the National
Autonomous University. This movement anticipated a similar body of demands
that emanated from the intellectual community between the late 1890s and 1910
as writers and poets produced a strong body of protest literature. By 1901,
reformers and radicals had formed more than fifty "liberal" clubs; their national
association was headed by Camilo Arriaga, the scion of one of the leading families
in the state of San Luis Potosí.

That year, at the national liberal convention, Flores Magón delivered a
scathing attack on Díaz as a dictator before police broke up the gathering. His
speech made him the most prominent member of the movement. His group in
Mexico city—which included anarchists, socialists, radical lawyers, writers, and
other professionals—published a series of underground newspapers that became a
staple of political dialogue. Harried by the police, the leaders of the Mexico City
club fled across the U.S. border, eventually establishing headquarters in Los
Angeles. From there they published *Regeneración*, which became the principal
source of written protest in Mexico. In 1906, they announced the formation of the
Partido Liberal Mexicano (PLM) with Flores Magón as its leader.

The PLM was linked to labor actions in 1906 and 1907 that foreshadowed the
violence to come. Strikes at the American-owned Cananea Copper Company in
Sonora and the French-owned Río Blanco textile factory at Orizaba in the state of
Veracruz turned into armed battles. At Río Blanco the workers seized the town of
several thousand inhabitants and held it until the army defeated them the next
day. Strike leaders and rank-and-file workers as well were PLM supporters, and
police and soldiers took to raiding workers' settlements around factories in search
of PLM literature. They evicted anyone found in possession of it. In 1906 and
1910, PLM rebels advocating the breakup of large estates won support from peasants in Chihuahua and Veracruz. By 1910, more than 100 PLM clubs nationwide
were preparing for more armed insurrections.

Mexico had reached a crossroads. Díaz's strategy of economic development
based on dictatorial control, a continuing flow of foreign capital, foreign colonization, and ever growing export market demand had proved unrealistic in the
face of growing pluralism, the rise of nationalism, a global contraction, and a
market downturn in the United States, Mexico's principal trade partner. In the

Francisco I. Madero in Ciudad Juárez, Chihuahua, across the Rio Grande from El Paso, Texas in May 1911. Following the victory of Madero's troops over the federal army at Ciudad Juárez in April 1911, and the eruption of rebellion across the nation, President Porfirio Díaz had his representatives negotiate a peace treaty that ended his thirty-five-year regime and handed power to Madero and the revolutionaries.

northwestern commercial economy, with agriculture in the countryside and industrial life on the edges of the cities, clashed with basic elements of Mexican culture, such as community life and artisanal and local elite individualism. Between 1910 and 1917, this broad-based conflict became a crisis in which opposing segments of the elites turned on each other while mass movements sought to embroil the general population in revolt. The revolutionary movements that swept across Mexico in those years laid bare the conflicts between rich and poor, rural and urban.

The revolution began in the spring of 1910 when the presidential candidacy of Francisco Madero, a Coahuilan provincial elite landowner, industrialist, and banker, galvanized political opposition to Díaz. Madero's supporters—or Díaz's opponents—came from every part of Mexican society, but the most important group was the PLM. Díaz, fearing defeat, disrupted the electoral process by arresting Madero and some of his supporters. While crowds protested the fraudulent results, Madero escaped house arrest and fled to San Antonio, Texas. From there he promulgated the Plan of San Luis Potosí, a document that promised democracy, federalism, workers' rights to collective bargaining, and agrarian reform. These promises mobilized peasants throughout Mexico, and some workers and middle-class supporters as well. Sizable guerilla groups began fighting in Chihuahua, Durango, and Morelos; smaller groups of Maderistas operated elsewhere.

During the spring of 1911, the government lost control of some states. In Chihuahua a mixed force of cowboys, miners, timbermen, farmers, and farmworkers followed Pascual Orozco, the head of the local Maderistas. In the north-

western portion of the state PLM radicals led rebels under Orozco's command, and in the southwest Francisco (Pancho) Villa fought under Orozco's leadership. In a brilliant maneuver the rebels seized Juárez, the city opposite El Paso, Texas, on the southern transcontinental railroad of the United States. The rebels would now have access to vast quantities of arms from American arms dealers. Under Emiliano Zapata rebels in Morelos, south of Mexico City, seized estates and began dividing them among local campesinos as preparation for creating cooperatives and communes. In the midst of this turmoil, Madero ceremoniously crossed the border with what his father called "our eighteen millionaire backers" to negotiate a peace with emissaries from Díaz. The dictator, recognizing the danger from the rising tide of working-class violence, quickly reached an accord with Madero that provided for a peaceful transition of government through elections and an interim government.

Madero was elected and took office in the fall of 1911. He immediately violated some basic tenets of successful governance. Unlike Díaz, who had rewarded and enriched his most powerful supporters, Madero marginalized Orozco, Villa, Zapata, and the PLM leaders in northern Chihuahua, giving prized government positions instead to bureaucrats in Mexico City, regular army officers, and regional elites, many of whom had sat on the sidelines and some of whom had even served the ancien régime during the conflict. Yet the new president did

The clothing, especially the hats, of this rebel cannon squad, photographed in late 1911, reveals their northern origin. Although Francisco Madero had claimed victory in May 1911, men such as these joined sporadic insurrections that disrupted his short-lived regime.

realize the importance of making his government popular through attention to the issues of agrarian reform and democracy. Unfortunately, Madero's agrarian provisions were too weak, and he never had time to institutionalize such democratic reforms as honest elections.

Madero's secretary of development, Alberto Robles Gil, initiated the agrarian reforms, announcing that "in view of the profoundly agrarian nature of the political movement of last year, the federal government is preoccupied deeply with the need for agrarian reform and the breakup of large properties." But Madero's first actions furthered the privatization of properties across the nation, provoking local disturbances in the process. He announced that the government would lend money for the purchase of lands suitable for colonization, identified 25 million acres of publically owned land to be granted to those who wanted it, and amassed a stockpile of seeds to be distributed. The people who needed land were too poor to assume mortgages, and the land he offered was largely sterile and arid. Madero's proposal, in short, looked like something designed to serve the interests of provincial elites and speculators. The largest tracts sold, totalling 105,000 of the 165,000 acres dispersed, went to the Bank of Durango and Ed Hartman, an American real estate promoter and operator of a large timber company in Durango. Few, if any, campesinos benefited. The president also promised to enforce court decisions about land seized illegally during the Porfiriato. Zapata and others criticized Madero's continuance of privatization and viewed his offer of legal redress as a farce because there had in fact been little fraud under the land laws. The legal issue was compounded, in the eyes of Madero's critics, by the fact that the overwhelming majority of serving judges had gained office under the Díaz administration.

Less than three weeks after Madero took office an enraged Zapata and his agrarian supporters in Morelos promulgated the Plan of Ayala, accusing Madero of "bloody treason" and ineptitude. Otilio Montano, a revolutionary anarchist who had learned his politics from like-minded rural teachers at the public school of Ajusco, wrote much of the plan, which advocated municipal autonomy, land redistribution into communes and cooperatives, democracy, and bargaining rights for the working class. The plan legitimized the revolution by giving it definition. It galvanized rural working-class sympathy across rural Mexico. Soon those who joined Zapata in opposition to Madero were calling themselves Zapatistas.

Law and order continued to break down during late 1911 and 1912. Strikes flared among workers on the American-owned plantations of Campeche, while two noted leaders, General Bernardo Reyes and former official Emilio Vázquez Gómez, attempted separate and abortive revolts in the north. Vázquez Gómez, a highly intelligent and ambitious leader, agreed with leftist Maderistas who felt that the president had gone over to the Porfiristas. His revolt began spectacularly when his forces seized Ciudad Juárez. But then all similarity to Madero's earlier success ended.

Orozco, still loyal to Madero although he held only the minor position of commander of Chihuahua's rural police, was strongly supported by the popular

The followers of Emiliano Zapata represented Mexico's agrarian revolution, determined to reclaim the lands that they worked. This painting by José Clemente Orozco depicts the Zapatistas preparing for battle.

classes, who viewed him as a heroic field commander and patriot. He took command of the federal forces and quickly defeated Vázquez Gómez. Reyes, less ideological and more ambitious, surrendered on Christmas Day, 1 9 1 1, after two weeks of fighting. Reyes and Vázquez Gómez had failed because they challenged Madero too early, before his lack of decisive action had demoralized his supporters, and because they attacked him at his strongest point, the northern states where Maderista provincial and local elites now enjoyed power. The most important Maderista of the region was Venustiano Carranza, governor of Coahuila; he had joined Madero in San Antonio when the outcome of the Revolution was still in doubt and followed him to the negotiations with Díaz in Ciudad Juárez. A resolute supporter of Madero, Carranza tolerated no opposition in Coahuila. The equally capable Abraham González administered the even more troublesome state of Chihuahua, backed by Orozco and Silvestre Terrazas, a prodigal son of the oligarchy.

Madero's supporters may have defeated Reyes and Vázquez Gómez, but the Zapatista rebellion was a deeper challenge—an unsolvable one. The president shrank from the long and bloody counterinsurgency campaign that would be needed to subdue the southerners, many of whom had once been his supporters. Soon, Orozco accepted the leadership of similarly discontented popular elements in Chihuahua, and the war had two fronts, in the north and in the south.

The Zapatistas recognized Orozco, the principal hero of the first phase of the Revolution, as the leader in a new search for social justice. Although militarily limited by its lack of artillery, Zapatismo represented a grassroots peasant war that found adherents far beyond its area of control in Morelos. In a broader context, during 1912, rural working-class people calling themselves Zapatistas attacked haciendas, plantations, and mines across the nation. Beginning in 1913, other groups calling themselves Villistas—after Pancho Villa— would carry out similar actions as far south as Chiapas.

The Orozco uprising was centered in Chihuahua and was made up of PLM radicals from the northwest and cowboys from everywhere. Orozco's diverse following in the north also included Yaqui Indians in Sonora, who began raiding rural estates and outlying settlements. Furthermore, reactionary members of the Terrazas clan among the Chihuahua elite, who hated Madero for advocating democracy, seized upon the chance to weaken the president. They quietly supported Orozco despite his populist and sometimes dangerous following.

The Orozquistas promulgated the Pacto de la Empacadora, a far-reaching reform package built on the 1906 PLM social program. It incorporated much of the Plans of San Luis Potosí and Ayala and decried Madero's betrayal of his own declaration. The Zapatistas and the more extreme among Orozco's self-described Red Flaggers sought to depose Madero and bring about a new agrarian order. PLM radicals in northern Chihuahua quickly gained control of a sizable area around Janos and Casas Grandes, driving out several thousand American colonists who lived in settlements there.

No evidence exists that Orozco endorsed the actions of his supporters who attacked the lands of the oligarchy in Sonora and the large Mexican- and American-owned ranches near the Chihuahua border but, like Zapata, he had little control over his supporters in the outlying areas. The Orozquistas of Sonora and northern Chihuahua acted with little outside direction. At the same time, small bands of Zapatistas began to raid great estates and American colonies as far north as Sinaloa and Tamaulipas. During 1912, rural insurgents across Mexico attacked the institutions that they perceived as threats to their way of life. Most of these were Mexican-owned haciendas, but the 35,000 to 50,000 Americans in the country became enmeshed in the struggle because their landholdings constituted some 27 percent of the nation's area. As the rural unrest grew, American refugees straggled across the border. U.S. president William Howard Taft's administration sent the USS *Buford* along the Pacific Coast to pick up desperate Americans. At Salina Cruz, on the Isthmus of Tehuantepec, 130 fleeing U.S. citizens took refuge on the ship, which brought a total of 364 refugees to San Diego, California.

In October 1912, after an arms embargo ordered by President Taft had crippled the Orozquista main forces and enabled the army under General Victoriano Huerta to force them into retreat, another rebellion broke out. Led by the reactionary Félix Díaz, a nephew of the former dictator, this revolt posed a threat because Díaz appealed to the disenchanted officers of the still-intact Porfirian army. Government forces, however, made short work of Díaz's supporters and arrested and court-martialed Díaz, who was sentenced to prison in the Federal District.

At this time the Madero government seemed to be gaining the upper hand over the rural rebellion. In reality, the regime was unravelling from within. From the start Madero had run into problems with the industrial and urban working class of Mexico City and its environs. The majority of industrial workers had rallied to Madero's electoral promises of democracy and labor rights, but they were quickly disillusioned when police used force against strikers. The well-organized anarchists from the Typographic Union of Mexico City began their attack on Madero. They published political polemics and challenged the pro-Madero union, the Gran Liga Obrera, which the Department of Labor sponsored. The Maderistas attempted to stall workers' demands for change. Workers were concerned with wages, hours, and working conditions; with the right to form independent cooperatives and mutualist societies that could provide them with disability, life, and survivors insurance; with protection for women and children in the often dangerous industrial environment; and with the right to create independent unions and to strike without government interference. Some of these concerns grew out of long experience with the government-controlled unions of the Díaz era, when strikes were forbidden and union leaders disciplined. While Madero could not accede to their demands, he did try to compete with the anarchists through the Gran Liga. Madero's idealistic sympathy for the workers infuriated the American ambassador Henry Lane Wilson, foreign industrialists, and domestic elites, all of whom believed that the president's "weakness" was allowing the labor rebellion to spread during 1912.

Industrial working-class groups continued to multiply. In September 1912, they formed the Casa del Obrero, a workers' council for Mexico City. It published a newspaper critical of Madero and began to branch out into neighboring cities. In January 1913, the Casa won a series of violent strikes in and around Mexico City by employing the tactic of "direct action," which included sabotage, attacks on strikebreakers, and resistance to the police. The street battles brought a sharp drop in the prestige of the police, whom the workers began calling Cossacks. Meanwhile, Madero's Gran Liga was a miserable failure. The left ridiculed it as a government ploy, while the right angrily condemned it as an example of how weakness could unleash chaos. Madero's idea of American-style democracy failed to grasp the realities of class confrontation in the Mexico of 1911–13.

The large landowners concentrated in Mexico City, seeking relief from the strife in the countryside. Newspaper publishers denounced the Zapatistas and striking workers as "communistic." Madero made both sides angry by declaring that he had never intended to "despoil" the great estate owners but did want to create small properties through resales. By 1913, the reformers who supported him had diminished in both numbers and enthusiasm, and the countryside had become a mosaic of conflict. The basic antagonism was between village communalists, agricultural workers, and cowboys on one side and hacendados and foreigners on the other. Growing numbers of American landowners, company managers, and settlers protested to their government in amazement and disgust as local campesinos drove them off their properties. The pro-Díaz Mexican elites had opposed Madero from the beginning. Now many foreign investors agreed with them. At the other end of the political spectrum, Madero faced opposition from a growing array of liberals, workers, and agrarians.

Félix Díaz and Bernardo Reyes, held in separate prisons in the Mexico City area, had not given up hope of seizing control of the government. They conspired with General Manuel Mondragón, who released them from prison on February 9 1913. They then marched on the National Palace with 2,000 troops. The presidential guards proved loyal to Madero and killed Reyes in an exchange of gunfire. Díaz led the surviving rebels to the Ciudadela, an obsolete fortress about three miles south of the center of government. The ensuing battle between the besieged rebels and federal troops is known as the *decena trágica*, or ten tragic days. It sealed the fate of the president.

When the rebels wounded Madero's loyal commander Lauro Villar, the president overrode the objections of his supporters and selected the capable but hostile Victoriano Huerta to command the federal assault. Félix Díaz and Huerta arrived at a tacit agreement in which the two sides fired artillery shells around the city for ten days. In this general destruction shells fell near the British embassy, but both sides made sure that the American embassy was never threatened. The people of Mexico City became desperate for a solution to the crisis. Alarmed by Huerta's failure to attack the weak rebel position, Madero ordered the loyal troops of Felipe Angeles brought from Morelos to the Ciudadela.

Huerta now moved to seize power. He neutralized the effectiveness of Angeles's men by ordering them forward into an established field of fire in front of the fortress without artillery or other support. The rebels cut them down. The federal troops who remained were loyal to Huerta. The general then met with American ambassador Henry Lane Wilson, who rationalized his actions as "protecting American interests" and arranged the Pacto de la Embajada, the provisions of which Félix Díaz accepted. Wilson conceived of Mexicans in terms of sterotypes: an "immature" people of the "emotional Latin race." He expected Félix Díaz to step forward and lend his prestigious name to a new government, but Huerta out-maneuvered them both. On February 18, with shells still falling seemingly at random around the city, he ordered General Aureliano Blanquet to lead an assault force against the National Palace. Acting on intelligence reports, the soldiers went to a nearby restaurant and killed Gustavo Madero, the president's brother and closest advisor, while he ate lunch. Huerta eliminated Gustavo Madero, thought to be the most dynamic figure in the government, so that he could not mount resistance to a *golpe de estado* (coup d'état). The troops then took President Madero, Vice President José María Pino Suárez, and numerous government officers into custody. The conspirators, Díaz and Huerta, then announced the Pacto de la Embajada, asserting that President Madero was incompetent and justifying their takeover as an effort to end violence.

The following day Pedro Lascurain, the secretary of foreign relations and a member of the conspiracy, succeeded to the presidency when Madero and Pino Suárez renounced their positions from their jail cells. Lascurain then appointed Huerta secretary of the interior, the next office in line for the responsibility of chief executive. After 24 hours Lascurain resigned, and Huerta became president. Madero and Pino Suárez had renounced their offices in the hope of obtaining exile; without doubt they wanted the chance to organize a new revolution. But they underestimated the ruthlessness of their adversaries. By giving up their positions they made Huerta's accesssion to the presidency technically legal. And by giving up the protection, however feeble, of office, they also made their own assassinations more likely. Sensing the danger, Madero's wife pleaded with Ambassador Wilson, who now took a new tone and told her that he could not intercede in the affairs of a sovereign nation. On February 21, soldiers murdered Madero and Pino Suárez while escorting them to another confinement. Some interpretations of the assassination point to Huerta's direct involvement, while others assert that the troops may have followed orders of Félix Díaz. Regardless of who authorized the murders, General Victoriano Huerta held the presidency.

Earlier the elite had been divided, with some supporting Porfirio Díaz and others, largely provincial leaders, believing in the liberal movement of Camilo Arriaga and the electoral democracy of Madero. This split continued after Huerta seized power, when a new revolution broke out against the new dictator. Some members of the elite would back Huerta, while others would declare themselves leaders of the opposition.

Huerta knew that he had to neutralize the Zapatistas in the south as quickly as possible. They held Morelos, the center of national sugar production and the richest state in the union. The wealth generated by sugar was concentrated in the area that the Zapatistas now controlled. They survived on contraband sugar sales while allowing a limited amount of commercial production. Huerta offered several Zapatista leaders amnesty and land. This stratagem allowed the new president to reestablish order in eastern Puebla, Veracruz, and Tabasco. But in Morelos the Zapatistas coalesced further, tightening their control over far-flung local municipal leaders scattered by almost impassable rugged terrain. This consoldiation prepared them well for the onslaught that followed.

With the Gulf Coast secured and the rebellion confined to the periphery of the nation except in Morelos, Huerta decided to smash the Zapatistas. After eliminating the reform-leaning state government in Cuernavaca, he sent forward General Jovencio Robles at the head of a well-equipped invasion force. Robles employed a scorched-earth campaign, and although the insurgents eluded decisive combat, the largely innocent villagers paid the highest price. In many places local people rallied to the Zapatistas despite the odds against them. At Puente de Ixtla, for example, a tortilla maker named La China led women and children in support of the Zapatistas and in rioting against the army.

As the Robles campaign in the south floundered, an even greater problem for Huerta was brewing in the north. Huerta gained some ground there when he enlisted the support of Pascual Orozco, who aligned with Huerta for reasons beyond personal advantage; Huerta's humble origins and offers of agrarian reform attracted some rural rebels. But he could not count on the support of the provinical elite. Governor Venustiano Carranza of Coahuila and José Maytorena, his less courageous counterpart in Sonora, rejected Huerta and joined together in revolution against him. At first, as Carranza assumed command of rebel forces, Maytorena declared his support, but he soon slipped across the border into the United States. In Chihuahua, an even more dangerous rebel force of mine and timber workers, cowboys, and sharecroppers was coalescing under popular leadership.

The assassination of Abraham González, the Maderista governor of Chihuahua, coincided with the president's murder and eliminated that state's elite revolutionary leadership. That event, combined with Orozco's decision to support Huerta, made the rise of Pancho Villa possible. Like Orozco, Villa ran a transportation enterprise that supplied several thousand miners and their families in the Sierra Madre of Chihuahua. His property included mule teams, wagons, and warehouses, and he employed dozens of drivers at a time. His mule skinners accepted him as a sophisticated and intelligent leader who was also a hardworking, tough man like them. Villa knew every nook and cranny in the rugged Chihuahua countryside. He and his lieutenants—committed to a better life for working people, including equitable wages and land reform—had an agenda far more radical that that of the hacienda-owning elite rebel leaders in Sonora and Coahuila. In a matter of months Villa had rallied many of the cowboys, sharecroppers, miners, and lumberjacks of rural Chihuahua and Durango to his cause. Under Villa's leadership the lower classes of the rural north used the experience they had gained in the fight against Porfirio Díaz to organize a strong military formation. They exploited the cattle markets of El Paso and other border points and used the proceeds to buy arms from sales agents representing manufacturers such as Remington, Colt, and DuPont. Many dealers were ready to sell guns to cash buyers.

Huerta, nevertheless, was not without significant support in his effort to hold power in Mexico City. First he consolidated his backing among the Mexico City elite and the British by issuing oil exploration permits in Tehuantepec and the Gulf Coast to prominent Mexican businessmen and to Weetman Pearson, a powerful British tycoon whose El Aguila company dominated the oil industry in southern Mexico; Huerta also attempted to defend American properties whenever possible. Huerta enjoyed the confidence of most army officers because they knew him to be a talented and decisive leader. The church hierarchy supported him as well. In the north he had the capable Orozco. But Huerta could not bring the countryside rebels under control, and it did not take American president Woodrow Wilson's administration long to recognize that he could not maintain peace and stability. The Americans stopped supplying him with arms in September 1913.

Generals Victoriano Huerta, E. Z. Steever, and Joaquín Tellez photographed on February 18, 1913, during the ruthless fighting in downtown Mexico City known as the Ten Tragic Days. Finally, Huerta betrayed President Francisco Madero and claimed the presidency for himself.

In the north, Villa was on the rise. By supporting Huerta, Orozco had lost the respect of many northern revolutionaries who had backed him against Porfirio Díaz and even Madero. They now turned to Villa as their leader. The Zapatistas, at war with Huerta, denounced Orozco as a traitor. They arrested and executed his father.

The changing alliances of the northern revolutionary leaders may appear chaotic, but the choices of these men made sense to them. For example, in 1911 General Máximo Castillo mobilized a following and supported Madero because he promised land reform and democracy. Castillo was a man of some wealth and did not need land for himself, but he believed that the rural poor needed community lands and smallholdings in order to regain their lost well-being and dignity. He had launched the agrarian reform program in Chihuahua by seizing six of Luis Terrazas' haciendas in the Galeano district and distributing them to local campesinos and cowboys. Madero had infuriated Castillo and Orozco when he refused to provide the 6–million–peso loan requested by Governor González to satisfy the needs of the state agrarian program. At that point Castillo joined Orozco in rebellion, saying, "I saw the system of debt peonage, stronger than ever, tightening its hold on my people. Disillusioned, I regrouped my old veterans in arms." But Castillo rejected Orozco when the latter joined Huerta, and when Villa gained the upper hand in Chihuahua, Castillo fled the country because "Villa" was socially unacceptable. Political, economic, social, and cultural factors determined revolutionary allegiances.

Villa's officers and their soldiers rode back and forth across the steppes of north-central Mexico, surprising federal garrisons with lightning raids and recruiting an ever larger following. Some women and even children joined the men fighters. As these separate but coordinated forces coalesced into larger units, more of them came under Villa's direct command. By February 1913, the Villista forces numbered 3,000. In July the Dorados, the elite Villista cavalry, emerged.

The first official land distribution of the Revolution, near Matamoros, Nuevo Leon, August 30, 1913. Here General Lucio Blanco, whose staff had just surveyed the lands, presents parcels of land to eleven campesinos. The land had been part of Los Borregos Hacienda, owned by Félix Díaz.

In November Villa's forces attacked Chihuahua City, the state capital. Repulsed by the army, they turned suddenly and overran Ciudad Juárez, the crucial center for livestock exports and military imports. After that the Villistas consolidated their victory by fanning out across the state, driving away the federal garrisons. On December 8, 1913, Villa became the provisional governor of Chihuahua.

Villa seized many properties of the state elites and those who had supported Huerta. He created the Bank of Chihuahua with 10 million pesos dedicated to the execution of an agrarian reform program and the creation of urban cooperative stores. He issued currency and authorized the first agricultural *ejidos*, or community landholdings, of the Revolution. But it was his troops, not his governance, that made the news. By early 1914, the main Villista forces had become known as the División del Norte, the largest and by far the most powerful rebel force in the Revolution. The main units now traveled by train, and nothing in Mexico could stop them. They conquered Saltillo, the capital of Coahuila, and Torreón and Paredón. In April Felipe Angeles, a well-educated soldier and Christian socialist, left the less radical Constitutionalist forces in Sonora and joined Villa as his commander of artillery. Other leftists such as Durango's Calixto Contreras joined Villa as well. Contreras brought an army of three thousand *agraristas* to the División del Norte. These men were fighting primarily for the restoration of their municipal ejidos and for *municipio libre*, or political autonomy for their communities.

The Villistas laid siege to Zacatecas and in June crushed the concentration of federal army forces that had turned the city into a fortress. This was the Villistas' greatest victory. It opened central Mexico to rebel invasion. Venustiano Carranza, who had named himself First Chief of the Revolution, ordered the Villistas to

Pancho Villa's army swooped south toward the national capital. Villa's men pushed south along the Mexican Central Railroad line, winning battle after battle against the federal army that supported Victoriano Huerta.

stop their advance, but they moved forward to Aguascalientes, a crucial rail junction halfway between San Luis Potosí and Guadalajara. The Villistas now controlled north-central Mexico.

Like the masses that had followed Padre Hidalgo during the Independence Revolution of 1810, the main body of the Villistas were rural folk. The División del Norte secured its base in the hinterlands before it began to march on Mexico City. Behind it local groups of rebels—and some bandits—attacked Mexican- and American-owned haciendas in the name of the Villistas. Some of the Villistas committed notorious war crimes; General Rodolfo Fierro, a dynamic but brutal railroad worker from Sinaloa, became infamous for the murder of helpless prisoners of war. Villa tried to reassure representatives sent by President Woodrow Wilson that the American owners of land, mines, timber companies, and other businesses were not in danger. He even provided protection to some Americans, but to no avail. Although Villa saw the Americans as essential to the development of enterprise, he insisted on a strong Mexican government and regulatory power, and the Americans could not accept this. American authorities in El Paso cut off the fuel supplies for the trains that moved Villa's army. The amalgam of Villa's humble origins and his roughneck past (which included banditry), his populism, his attacks on the elites, and the war crimes of some of his men created an image of chaos and disorder that would haunt his movement until the end.

Huerta's position continued to deteriorate. The rebels were receiving a flow of military supplies from arms dealers. Then, on April 21, 1914, the United States intervened militarily with the goal of guiding the course of the Revolution. The U.S. Navy initiated a massive attack on Veracruz with 15 ships of the line and 38 more in reserve. Its pretext was absurd but effective: Rather than stopping a vessel called *Ypiranga* on the high seas and determining that it was loaded with arms, the Americans attacked its destination port, Veracruz. An agreement with Mexican army officers seemed to ensure easy occupation of the city, but when the first U.S. marines and sailors landed, they came under fire from local citizens and the cadets of the Mexican Navy Maritime School. The Americans retreated and began a naval bombardment that inflicted heavy casualties on the resisters as well as on the innocent civilians who were caught in the awesome firepower of modern ships. The U.S. Navy then secured the city, and the U.S. Army, under General Frederick Funston, began a fateful occupation. The *Ypiranga*'s cargo was eventually unloaded at Puerto Mexico, south of Veracruz, but the ship and the arms it carried were inconsequential—merely pretext for the Wilson administration to influence events in Mexico. The Americans consolidated their position in Veracruz and from there observed the escalating conflict between Huerta and the revolutionaries.

As Huerta's position deteriorated, rivalries between the insurgent groups came to the forefront. The Zapatistas, peasant and industrial workers who had labored on the sugar plantations of Morelos, allied themselves with the Villistas, who were mule skinners, miners, railroad workers, cowboys, sharecroppers, and lumberjacks from Chihuahua and Durango. This alliance of popular forces from the rural south and north confronted an equally populist and nationalist Constitutionalist movement. Virtually all of the Constitutionalist leaders came from the provincial and local elites in the north and the landowner class in the south. Among these were Venustiano Carranza, his son-in-law Cándido Aguilar, and Pablo González, all well-born, highly able leaders from Coahuila. They were nationalists who appealed to the masses in the name of federalism, democratic rights, and Mexican control of the national resources. The Constitutionalists, although they opposed socialism, supported the right of miners in Coahuila to strike against companies controlled by the Maderos and by Americans.

Their counterparts in Sonora were Plutarco Elías Calles, Alvaro Obregón, Roberto Pesqueira, and Benjamin Hill. The first two men were marginal members of the oligarchy, who passed themselves off as middle class. They did favor a more open, mobile society than the Coahuilans. Like the Coahuilans, they had the ability to lead men, but they combined that strength with a strong appeal to the public for the liberalization of politics, agrarian reform, far-reaching industrial reforms (including the rights of working people to unionize and strike, salary guarantees, improved working conditions, and job security), educational rights, and a host of other improvements. Ultimately, the greatest strength of the Sonorans was their broad political appeal, which would win them the support even of urban workers.

During the spring of 1914, Villa's forces crushed the major army units aligned against him at the battle of Torreón. Then, in June, his army crushed the core of the federal forces at the battle of Zacatecas in the middle of the country. When Zacatecas fell, the federal army began to disintegrate. At that point the U.S.

Once Victoriano Huerta was forced out of the capital in 1914, Mexico City changed hands numerous times during the civil war between the troops of the Constitutionalists and the Conventionists. The Convention leaders were Emiliano Zapata and Pancho Villa.

customs authorities along the border blocked further supplies from reaching Villa. Zach Cobb, the chief of American customs at El Paso, reflected the general attitude that Villa was a "bandit, hypocrite, thief and murderer." With fuel deliveries for Villa's trains halted, the Villistas could not move farther south, and alternate supplies were long in arriving. Meanwhile, rebel forces under Obregón moved forward along the Pacific Coast in the wake of the Villista victories and occupied Guadalajara. Then they moved east toward Mexico City, passing just south of the stalled trains of the División del Norte. Villa's men watched in frustration as Obregón's forces occupied Querétaro, just north of Mexico City. In the summer of 1914, a defeated Huerta stepped down from the presidency and fled the country. Ten days later the interim government under Vice President Francisco S. Carbajal arranged the surrender of its troops to Obregón's men in return for guarantees for the safety of private property and of the affluent people of Mexico City.

At that point, the military position of Carranza and Obregón was weaker than that of Villa and his ally Zapata. The Constitutionalist leaders needed to buy time and find additional support if they were going to compete successfully with the rural working-class appeal of the Villistas and Zapatistas. The two sides began propaganda campaigns designed to solidify their followings and attract wider support. Obregón did not have much time before the much stronger Villistas would be able to move, but he made the best of it. He went to the capital and successfully courted the anarchists and radicals of the Casa del Obrero Mundial, calling the Mexican Revolution the first stage in the world revolution. Claiming a membership of more than 50,000, the Casa provided the basis of working-class support for Obregón's army in return for the right to organize the workers in

The Constitutionalist
leaders included First
Chief Venustiano
Carranza (center),
General Álvaro Obregón
(on far left), who lost his
arm in battle, and
General Pablo González
(between the other two).

whatever cities his forces entered. After Obregón moved toward Veracruz, the
Casa leaders signed a pact aligning their movement with his revolution.

In September 1914, while Obregón courted the Casa and urban intellectuals,
Villa and Zapata launched an all-out appeal to the rural masses. The Zapatistas
demanded that the Constitutionalists accept a barely modified Plan of Ayala with
its aggressive program of land redistribution, while Villa called for Carranza to
approve any agrarian reform program in which land would be redistributed. Carranza, not realizing how desperate the situation he faced was, replied that the
hacendados had property rights that must be respected. He could not violate
those rights simply "to give land to those who had no rights." Villista and Zapatista leaders quickly, but separately, denounced Carranza for betraying the needs
of the people. Obregón saved the situation. He personally hated Villa and
opposed Zapata's radicalism, but he recognized that in the short run Villa's forces
would win a confrontation of arms. He offered to negotiate by bringing the two
sides together at Aguascalientes in order to settle their differences. The historic
meeting of the deeply divided revolutionaries convened on October 10, 1914.

At that moment John Lind, President Wilson's emissary to Mexico and a
Carranza supporter, turned against Villa and called him a traitor. The timing
was important: Carranza's persistent nationalism and his rejection of American
demands for special protection of their oil and other properties had angered the
American leadership, which was trying to play Villa and Carranza against each
other. As the Americans watched, the Villistas and Zapatistas came together as a
voting bloc at the Aguascalientes meeting. They demanded the immediate

redistribution of the land, of which more than one-fourth was owned by American interests, and the creation of self-governing working-class agricultural communities. The Carrancistas did not accede to this demand.

The Americans had been stunned by the lower-class radicalism that had spread across the country in the wake of their invasion of Veracruz. Crowds threatened and attacked American civilians in all parts of the country, and local events sometimes got out of control. In August American forces shipped arms to the constabulary of Campeche to suppress rioting in the capital city of the same name. They reported that neighboring Yucatán was in a state of peasant and urban rebellion.

In October the cautious American administration made the fateful but final decision to support Carranza, Obregón, and their leadership, consisting of Sonoran elites and a wide array of *petit bourgeois* businessmen, professionals, and middle-level functionaries. These men supported radical reforms but were more flexible than the Villistas and Zapatistas. They wanted reforms that respected private property and were controlled by the central government. President Wilson regarded Obregón as a loyal subordinate. During the first three weeks of November, American ships unloaded military supplies at Veracruz. These, combined with those already impounded by the occupation authorities, constituted an enormous stockpile of arms capable of equipping an entire army. The Americans' strategy duplicated that which Wilson ordered General William Graves to carry out during the American occupation of Vladivostok during the Russian Revolution: to provide the White armies with arms while avoiding conflict with the Reds. In Veracruz the strategy worked to perfection. American forces withdrew on November 23, turning over to Constitutionalist troops stationed in the harbor area 12,000 rifles and carbines, 3,375,000 rounds of ammunition (including dumdum bullets), artillery, machine guns, 632 rolls of barbed wire, armorers' tables, cars, trucks, shortwave radios, sabers, uniforms, and 1,250 boxes of sodium cyanide (which forms a poison gas when combined with nitric or sulfuric acid). The Constitutionalist commander in Veracruz was Cándido Aguilar, Carranza's son-in-law.

In December the Villistas and Zapatistas entered Mexico City with only a few violent incidents in the elite suburb of Chapultepec Heights. At a famous meeting at Xochimilco, Villa and Zapata underscored the divisions that had driven their movement apart from the Constitutionalists. Villa described their enemies as "men who have always slept on soft pillows" and added that "we are not going to put those in charge who do not know what to do." The more cynical Zapata summed up the elites and *petit bourgeois* around Obregón and Carranza, declaring that "they have always been the scourge of the people. Those *cabrones*, as soon as they see a little chance, well, they want to take advantage of it and line their pockets!" He added that the revolutionaries should not trust their rivals because if they did, "they would be cut down."

Villa and Zapata were wise, but they grossly underestimated their adversaries. The Constitutionalist leaders knew exactly what to do—and they did it.

By January 1915, Carranza promulgated a special agrarian reform law and immediately began carrying it out. In areas of Veracruz under Constitutionalist control, officials—with great fanfare—announced immediate land grants to defrauded and needy campesinos. Virtually everyone was eligible to receive land. Zapata and Villa denounced the program as a fraud, but it was too late. The great moral difference between the two sides had been blurred, and the Constitutionalists were demonstrating practical results.

The Convention forces, defined as such because they followed the leadership derived from the Convention of Aguascalientes, suffered a loss of unity because of Zapata's distrust of the petit bourgeois and government functionaries. That division hurt them as much as their underestimation of the Constitutionalists. Within the Convention the social types Villa and Zapata feared—the government functionaries and the *petit bourgeois*—undermined the effort to coordinate northern and southern forces. The civilians in the Convention government failed to forward badly needed supplies from Villa's trains to Zapatistas who were undergoing an American naval blockade and unable to receive sophisticated weaponry. One of the bureaucrats cited the "bestiality" and "savagery" of the campesino revolutionaries as the reason for his failure to act. Many officials of the Convention government feared the generals and soldiers of their own army.

Meanwhile, 5,000 workers from the Casa del Obrero Mundial answered the call of their leaders and gathered at Orizaba in Veracruz, where Constitutionalist officers organized them into military units and trained them. These units were known as the Red Battalions. Members professed the anarcho-syndicalist goals of a society run by industrial and urban workers. They had their own field-grade and lower officers, but they accepted the ultimate authority of the Constitutionalist generals in military affairs, presaging the future. John Murray, an observer for President Wilson, posed as a newspaper reporter and approvingly noted the Red Battalions' progress. A contingent of 1,500 largely industrial working-class women—including some 500 who called themselves *acratas,* "those opposed to all authority"—formed a formidable medical corps for the Red Battalions. By December 1914, the reorganized and equipped Constitutionalist army, under Obregón's command, marched forward to face the Villistas in battles that would determine the winners of the Revolution.

Convention armies sent by Villa failed to capture the oil fields around Tampico, the northeast, and the port cities of the Pacific Coast. Meanwhile, the main Constitutionalist forces prepared to face the División del Norte in the Bajío, a strategic valley 250 miles long that runs from Querétaro, north of Mexico City, to Guadalajara in the west. From April to June 1915, Obregón's armies defeated the Villistas in a series of protracted battles at Celaya, León, and Aguascalientes. At Celaya, Obregón employed the same combination of barbed wire and strategically placed machine guns to create crossed fields of fire and stall the Villista infantry and cavalry charges that the Germans were using to decimate British armies at Flanders and Picardy. He also employed indirect artillery fire from behind a range of hills behind the city.

General Álvaro Obregón emerged as the most popular man in Mexico in 1920 and won a nearly unanimous election to the presidency. Here he addresses his supporters in Mexico City in early 1920.

Obregón's tactics were remarkably successful. Yet American military intelligence had reported that Obregón was "a former small farmer and storekeeper of common school education, without technical military training." Both sides in the conflict made use of German military advisors. Obregón also had the advantage of the modern artillery provided by the Americans in Veracruz—an advantage that proved strategically important. Following his stunning defeat at Celaya, Villa retreated to León to await reinforcements and additional artillery headed by Felipe Angeles, his best field commander. After a lengthy buildup of Villa's forces and a tentative beginning, a protracted and vicious battle took place. Obregón's men, including the Red Battalions, once again emerged victorious. When John R. Silliman, President Wilson's special envoy to the Constitutionalists, received the news of Obregón's victory, he informed the German consul, "We have taken León, we have defeated Villa, and we will soon occupy the City of Mexico."

The Villistas suffered tremendous casualties. Some units had been virtually wiped out. Their leader tried to maintain a foothold in central Mexico at Aguascalientes, but he was driven back, and most of the Villista forces dispersed and returned to their home territories. From then on the armed struggle was in the north, mostly in Durango, Chihuahua, and Sonora. Waged by local men on a small scale, it would turn into a vicious guerrilla war.

But as revolution changed to reaction in many parts of the north, it became more radical in the south and in the cities of central Mexico. In October 1915, Manuel Palafox, one of the leading agraristas in Zapata's cadre, issued a new edict: Everything was to be taken from the hacendados, and there would be no compensation. Palafox asserted the "right of all Mexicans to possess and cultivate a piece of land, the products of which permit him to meet his needs and those of his family." The Zapatistas had raised the stakes in the countryside by identifying themselves as the deliverers of the peasantry. Constitutionalist forces, meanwhile, also had radical elements. The Red Battalions and labor organizers moved into states such as Michoacán, Jalisco, and San Luis Potosi, and labor radicals in their midst began organizing the industrial and urban working class of central Mexico en masse. The Constitutionalist leaders had little time to enjoy their military victories.

By mid–1915, the military outcome of the Revolution was no longer in doubt. Political and social results had become the core issues. The Constitutionalists, who had been united against the military prowess of the Villistas and the ideological force of the Zapatistas, disagreed about the degree of democracy Mexico could realistically achieve, the pace of agrarian reform, and the amount of power and independence that the anarcho-syndicalists of the labor movement should be given. That labor movement was growing rapidly under radical leadership; about 100,000 industrial and urban workers now belonged to syndicates affiliated with the Casa del Obrero Mundial. Like the campesinos and artisans, and in the anarchist tradition, the Casa leadership embraced the idea of worker self-management in all spheres of production. This vision of the future had carried over from the 19th century because Mexico's transitional working classes were still preoccupied with the loss of artisan freedoms and community cohesion, rather than with the achievement of state power. It was a vision that threatened domestic and American capitalists.

Some leaders of the Casa envisioned a new industrial order in which working-class youth would attend schools known as Escuelas Racionalistas established by the syndicates. In addition to reading, writing, and arithmetic, they would learn the values and practice of worker self-management, a method of preparation rooted in age-old community practices of local self-government, artisan workshops, and mutual aid. This education would prepare young workers to enter industry committed to community service and prepared to take part in management. In this way the working class could keep its cultural practices intact as it entered the industrial age. Some Casa leaders, consistent with their heritage, saw the future in terms of Christian socialism. Others expected a more violent path of struggle against capitalism; they gathered arms in armories, formed militias, and prepared for confrontations with the government.

During the summer of 1915, the Casa leaders established their headquarters in the House of Tiles, near Alameda Park and the Palace of Fine Arts in downtown Mexico City. In meeting rooms decorated with red and black (*rojinegra*) flags, workers gathered daily for rousing speeches and strategy sessions. On October 13, 1915, they inaugurated what they hoped would be a full-fledged Escuela Racionalista. They also began publishing a Casa newspaper, *Ariete*, which circulated anarchist ideology and called for the reorganization of the economy and polity around workers' syndicates. By that fall many veterans of the Red Battalions had returned to the city as civilians ready to claim their "rights." Meanwhile, a growing wave of Casa-led strikes spread across central Mexico.

Successful strikes in late 1915 and early 1916 caused the Casa's membership to grow by 50,000, at the same time that food shortages in the urban areas lent a sense of urgency to the strategies of the labor movement. Unions began to demand pay in silver-based currency rather than script moneys that devalued quickly when used away from company stores. They also made political demands, calling on the Constitutionalist government to punish food distributors who hoarded staples and to prevent gouging by establishing fixed prices. Carranza and his advisors did not believe in government control of the marketplace, but they recognized the popularity of wage and price controls in the face of food shortages, which had reached the point of famine and rioting in some areas.

Thus working-class radicalism joined Zapatismo in threatening the economic elites of Mexico City and the Constitutionalist political leaders. The elites and the political leaders had significant differences, but their interests were united against workers who were demanding economic and political power. Believing in their own revolutionary commitments and remembering that Obregón, the most powerful man in Mexico, had recruited the Casa to their cause in the darkest days of the Villista threat, the men around Carranza hesitated to act against the workers. But they also failed to constrain the abuses of the economic elites, who continued using script and manipulating food shortages to their advantage. In October 1915, petroleum workers shut down Weetman, Pearson's El Aguila petroleum company in a violent strike. In October and November textile workers closed clothing factories in central Mexico and won a 100 percent wage hike, an eight-hour workday, and a six-day workweek. Although foreigners controlled the oil and textile industries, these strikes cost the government considerable revenues. Then, in December, carpenters struck and paralyzed the construction industry; they won a 150 percent wage increase. And a strike at the mining camp of El Oro in the state of Mexico, again aimed at foreign owners, cost the Constitutionalist regime additional income.

In the winter of 1916, the crisis between the Constitutionalist government and the Casa came to a head. First, the Carrancista leadership sent the remaining Red Battalion members home. This eliminated the Casa's military presence but increased the size and the militancy of the working-class crowds in Mexico City, Tampico, and Veracruz. Impoverished veterans marched in the streets demanding jobs, the nationalization of industries, and compensation for their military service. General Pablo González, a conservative and one of Carranza's most loyal officers, ordered his troops to raid the headquarters of the Casa in Mexico City, where they arrested several members. In protest, Casa leaders organized a general strike under the aegis of the Federation of Federal District Syndicates, a formidable group that claimed some 90,000 members in the greater Mexico City area. On May 22, 1916, the strikers paralyzed transportation and most services and industries in the capital; meanwhile, Villista and Zapatista forces continued their resistance in northern and southern Mexico. To control the situation in Veracruz, Governor Heriberto Jara declared martial law.

President Carranza ordered General Benjamin Hill, his military commander of the Federal District, to negotiate a settlement with the Casa unions. His choice of men could not have been better: Hill had gained experience in labor negotiations while successfully disciplining pro-Villista workers at the mining town of Cananea, Sonora, during Villa's rise to national leadership. He ordered Mexico City's leading industrialists to attend a public meeting during which the workers voiced their complaints regarding working conditions, salaries, and food distribution. The dialogue did not touch on political power or on the release of prisoners taken by the troops under Pablo González. At the close of the meeting Hill ordered the end of unfair working conditions, script currencies, and food hoarding. The Casa leaders wanted to believe him and returned to work. But within a few weeks it became obvious to everyone that, nothing had changed.

The paper-currency pesos promised by General Hill and issued by the government had devalued and were not much better than script moneys. By July the bankers had reduced them to an exchange rate equal to only two gold centavos. Industrialists continued to pay their workers in script money good only in company stores. Meanwhile, the "reds" of the Casa planned another strike to force the concessions they thought had been won earlier. On July 31, the unions of the Federation of Syndicates once again struck, but this time the government was prepared for them. Military intelligence had watched the Casa leadership carefully. Troops moved into the city during the predawn darkness and took strategic positions. They attacked when workers tried to form crowds, scattering them. The soldiers also seized the House of Tiles.

Noted artist Gerardo Murillo, known as Dr. Atl, served as President Carranza's emissary to a workers' meeting held in a downtown theater. Murillo invited the strike leaders to the National Palace to discuss their problems with the president. When Carranza confronted the Casa strike committee, he ordered them arrested for treason, a capital offense. Soldiers aimed their guns at an electricians' union leader and forced him to restore power to the city. When the leaders of some of the nation's largest syndicates appealed to their former ally General Obregón, he surprised them by suggesting that they disband the Casa. Meanwhile, troops raided Casa armories and meeting halls in outlying cities, arresting members, and seizing the weapons and facilities.

The defeat of the anarcho-syndicalist unions was easy for a government and its army that had beaten the forces of Villa and Zapata both militarily and politically. But the rural revolution was not over. In Morelos, the Zapatistas still held what had been and could again become the richest state in the union. They had already divided the land and were prepared to fight indefinitely. Elsewhere the Constitutionalist land reform program had languished except in politically restless areas, and even there local landowning elites had slowed the process or blocked it altogether. Around Canatlan in Durango, the pro-Villista forces of Calixto Contreras

Despite the defeat of the Conventionists and the assassination of Emiliano Zapata, the revolutionaries included a provision for land reform in the Constitution of 1917. President Obregón and other presidents before 1940 made the implementation of land reform a priority during their terms in office.

had returned to farm and ranch. They seized land by force of arms but found that the new Constitutionalist authorities consistently sided with the former landowners in the ensuing disputes. Despite their defeats of 1915, the Villistas were still capable of choosing the time and place of battle across the far reaches of northern Durango, Chihuahua, Coahuila, and northeastern Sonora.

In November 1915, they had chosen the border town of Agua Prieta in Sonora near the Chihuahua border for a showdown with the Carrancistas. After a rapid forced march over difficult terrain, the Villistas sent 6,500 men into battle against a distinctly outgunned garrison. But President Wilson would not tolerate a Villista victory on the American border, especially one that could reopen the flow of arms to a group he had effectively embargoed. The United States moved Constitutionalist troops and artillery west by railroad across New Mexico and delivered them to Agua Prieta. The surprise arrival of these reinforcements turned the battle into a rout of the Villistas, who had to leave their baggage in the field. Following an unsuccessful attack on Hermosillo, the División del Norte ceased to exist.

The embittered Villa then attempted to impose his authority on American mine operators in the Sierra Madre Occidental. At San Dimas, Durango, he executed an American mine owner for bringing in new workers and equipment and for shipping out ore without clearing it with him beforehand. To Villa, Americans who attempted to run their mines without paying taxes to him and recognizing his authority were collaborators with the Constitutionalists. In January 1916, a Villista unit stopped a train at Santa Isabel, Chihuahua. Aboard the train were 16 American mine workers and engineers who carried safe-conduct passes from the Constitutionalists but had not received permission from the Villistas to travel. The Villistas took them from the train and killed them.

Two months later Villa took the war to the Americans. The largest Villista force assembled since Agua Prieta attacked Columbus, New Mexico. The U.S. Army garrison there exacted a heavy casualty toll on the Villistas, but the raiders gained two objectives, one basic and the other strategic. First, they took revenge on two American arms dealers who had accepted money from Villista representatives but not delivered the goods. Second, they goaded President Wilson into an invasion of Mexico. This pitted the U.S. Army against Villa, enhancing his stature as a national hero while the Constitutionalist government watched. To capture and punish Villa, the United States sent 12,000 soldiers headed by General John J. Pershing. The Punitive Expedition drove deep into Mexico. Maps carried by the Americans indicated that the United States had plans for a zone of occupation that included all of Chihuahua and a southern boundary that extended from Tampico in the east to Mazatlán in the west. But the expeditionary force floundered for months in its attempt to smash the Villistas and capture their leader. Meanwhile, the Mexican people saw their government vacillate in the face of a foreign invasion.

Important elements of the peasantry, industrial working class, and local, regional, and metropolitan elites agreed on national sovereignty despite vast differences of opinion about what constituted appropriate Mexican attire, cuisine, pastimes, and distribution of political power and wealth. All of these groups were outraged at the American invasion. The Villistas reaped great political benefits by confronting the invaders. Embarrassed, Carranza publicized his creation of a defensive line south of Pershing's advanced positions. In June the Americans inadvertently helped the Mexican president by blundering into—and losing— a skirmish with Constitutionalist forces at Carrizal. The delight of the Mexican public, however, was shortlived.

Villista forces multiplied and Mexican public sentiment shifted toward the guerrilla leader as he eluded the Punitive Expedition. Villa became an almost mythic figure, presenting the image of a powerful, wily fighter who could be everywhere at once. The last and greatest political setback for the invaders came when U.S. troops violated an agreement and entered the city of Parral in southern Chihuahua. Anti-American and pro-Villa rioting broke out. Then, in the fall of 1916, the resurgent Villistas seized Chihuahua City. The Americans looked hapless. President Carranza could stand no more. He issued a public warning to Pershing, and it was clear to the U.S. officials that they were politically beaten. They announced that they had finished "cleaning up" the border region and withdrew.

While Villa made military and political gains in the north, 5,000 Zapatista troops outmaneuvered and outfought 30,000 less-inspired government troops

United States President Woodrow Wilson, in an effort to impose his political views on Mexico, interfered repeatedly during the Mexican revolution. The result of his efforts was to bolster Mexican nationalism, including hostility toward the United States government.

and put them on the defensive in the south. But the Constitutionalist leaders once again more than met the challenge. They convened a broad cross-section of loyal revolutionaries and produced a new constitution written boldly enough to satisfy everyone's aspirations. The end product revealed the hand of Obregón and his supporters in its emphasis on democratic and progressive reforms tempered by centralized authority.

Articles asserted a strong nationalism defined by the unchallengeable ownership of the nation's shorelines, frontiers, and subsoil resources by the people as personified by the government—provisions that challenged the Americans in Mexico. Other articles provided the legal basis for the reorganization of the country. Among them were the right of all rural community residents to land, the separation of church and state, the inalienable right to universal education through public schools, the regulation of working conditions, and the right of workers to form unions and strike. Agrarians, workers, nationalists, and politicians all rejoiced. The ambitious agenda of the Constitution of 1917 has still not been realized, but like Madero's call for democracy, it stands as a beacon to the Mexican people. It was the greatest achievement of the aptly named Constitutionalist regime.

The Constitutionalists had defeated the Villista-Zapatista effort and the Casa, but their struggles were not over. The Villistas and Zapatistas still had strong support in their home states of Chihuahua and Morelos, and working-class leaders still sought their own labor movement separate from state control.

In addition, recalcitrant provincial elites, such as those in Yucatán, still held out against the progressive reforms and more open society advocated by Obregón and his experienced, but still young, supporters.

In Morelos the fight against Zapatismo had become more difficult because the Zapatistas had reorganized into local Associations for the Defense of Revolutionary Principles. This strategy of decentralization accomplished two major objectives. First, it adjusted to the decentralized military realities of Morelos, where the revolutionaries lacked the resources for formal armies and the broken topography was a barrier to large-scale movements of men and supplies. Second, it centered decision making on the self-interest of pueblos that already had been allocated land. Thus when Constitutionalist armies led by Pablo González entered the state in 1916, they were hindered by the need to create garrisons across a hostile countryside and were routed by lightning-quick attacks by larger Zapatista units. An effective counterinsurgency effort meant losing the support of the rural people for whom the government had designed new agrarian reform provisions. As a result, the struggle for power in Morelos became a stalemate, an intolerable situation for some of the wealthiest landowners in the nation.

The Villistas in the north enjoyed more military success than the Zapatistas in the south, but they lost the political battle nonetheless. Provincial and local elites in Chihuahua, Durango, and Sonora carried out just enough reform to pacify significant zones in these states. The people, weary of war, did not refuse official recognition of the landholdings they had occupied during the fighting. Furthermore, the flight of the American landowners who had held large portions of the states facilitated land redistribution even without the agrarian reform ordinances. Seizures of land for unpaid taxes provided the basis for reorganizing properties and pacifying the countryside from central Durango through Casas Grandes and Janos in Chihuahua and in wide areas of Sonora. Villa's guerrilla war continued seemingly without end, but as time went on his former supporters saw him as a threat to stability and the well-being of their families.

Their urban location made labor leaders much easier to defeat than rural revolutionaries. After the dissolution of the Casa, pro-government leaders confronted the radicals at a series of meetings. The radicals dominated the first two meetings, frustrating their competitors, but in 1918 the pro-government group, headed by the corrupt Luis Morones, created the Mexican Regional Workers Confederation (*Confederación Regional Obrera Mexicana* or CROM). Morones, who wore diamonds on each finger and engaged in notorious orgies with pubescent girls, established a nationwide organization that gradually marginalized the anarchists and radicals. Government approval of their strikes emboldened CROM workers, who fought strikebreakers and radicals alike. Local police often helped them. Sometimes, when CROM members fought the anarchist unions at the oldest textile factories, they received help from the army.

By 1920, CROM had become the fastest-growing labor organization in the nation. It had competition, however. During the early 1920s the former Casa leaders reorganized into the General Confederation of Workers (*Confederación*

General de Trabajadores or CGT) with 40,000 to 80,000 members. They fought hard on picket lines and in basic organizing, and they did a remarkable job of surviving a difficult period in which they faced every conceivable disadvantage. In 1928, CROM virtually disintegrated, losing more than 80 percent of its members when Morones lost favor in the government and resigned from the cabinet. An influx of workers and leaders uncommitted to anarchism flooded the CGT, watering it down. In 1931, the CGT leadership yielded and accepted the heavy hand of government control through the Ley del Trabajo, a law that gave the government the power to authorize unions, strikes, and contracts.

In Morelos and Chihuahua the Zapatistas and Villistas were declining in numbers and influence. The Constitutionalists, who had successfully reorganized the polity, enjoyed similar success with the economy. The restoration of oil and mineral exports diminished hardship and famine, and the public expected a return to normalcy in daily life.

Then, on April 10, 1919, Carranza committed a major error. Constitutionalist colonel Jesús Guajardo arranged the assassination of Emiliano Zapata. In military terms the act cut off the head of the southern rural revolution, but it elevated Zapata to martyrdom and greatly lowered Carranza in public esteem. Even loyal generals such as Lázaro Cárdenas registered their shock and dismay. Obregón, Carranza's secretary of war, had already resigned his job and distanced himself from any connection with the assassination.

In 1920, with Zapata assassinated, the Casa disbanded, and Villa reduced to the status of an annoying guerrilla, Mexico suffered its last governmental overthrow through violence. President Carranza had won victories over the agrarian and working-class revolutionary leaders, but he recognized their popularity and did not have confidence in a broader, more democratic polity. Perhaps Carranza could have used his continued defense of national interests in the face of pressure from powerful American financiers, industrialists, and political leaders to develop nationalistic public support; from 1917 to 1920, he repeatedly rebuffed the demands of American businessmen to back down on the constitutional assertions of national sovereignty over subsoil resources, seashores, and borderlands. But he did so without public displays in order to encourage continued American business activity and Mexico's economic recovery.

It became clear that Carranza intended to handpick his former emissary to the United States, Vice President Ignacio Bonilla, as his successor. This would mean a narrowly defined political regime and continued confrontations with labor, the agrarians, and the Americans—a prospect unwelcome to many. Carranza's failure to carry through on agrarian reform, his hostility to unions and strikes, and the Americans' distrust of him helped bring about his downfall in a strangely quiet but fatal revolution that Obregón led. First, Obregón announced the Plan of Agua Prieta. In its definition of agrarian reform, this plan provided the land demanded by the agrarians but ultimately protected the interests of private landholders; it created a system of communal, cooperative, and private holdings. Obregón explained the program to leading Zapatistas, who joined him in a massive march on Mexico City that drove out Carranza. The president had little support in the capital. He had alienated the working class, while the middle class had no reason to oppose Obregón and his plan for broader political participation. As the principal commander of the Constitutionalist armies during the fighting with the Villistas, Obregon enjoyed the support of most of the army.

Meanwhile, in the north, Felipe Angeles returned to the Villistas and attempted to lead yet another Villista offensive in 1919. The Chihuahua revolutionaries, however, had been worn down and suffered enormous losses in several encounters, including a battle at Ciudad Juárez, the site of so many important turning points. After one battle in which the federal army drove the Villistas from Chihuahua City, federal troops hanged dozens of Villistas as bandits. Embargoed by the United States, on the run, the Villistas were now feared and hated even by many rural people. The citizens of formerly pro-Villa pueblos such as Namiquipa and Casas Grandes formed community-based militias called Guardias Blancas to defend themselves from the seemingly endless requisitions demanded by the guerrillas. Still, rural resistance remained important and Chihuahua governor Ignacio C. Enríquez combated it by maintaining an active land-reform program, distributing many properties after seizing them for tax arrears or idleness. In Durango the agrarian struggles continued in the form of local violence as veterans such as those who had fought under Calixto Contreras used their experience and courage to demand and receive ejidos in the face of considerable opposition from land owners. The administration of President Obregón (1920–24) must bear responsibility for the assassination of Villa in 1923, when he no longer represented a serious threat to political stability.

The Mexican Revolution was part of a global economic and political crisis but followed its own unique path. It was a struggle that united Chihuahuan industrial workers, cowboys, miners, and lumberjacks under leaders from humble backgrounds with Sonoran and Coahuilan counterparts under the direction of local and provincial elites. In Morelos the industrial laborers of the sugar mills who lived on plantations joined sugar-field workers who still lived in ostensibly free villages in a struggle to rectify their powerlessness when massive layoffs left them without the material base to survive. Demands for cooperative ownership of the land were rooted in the age-old rights of the pueblos.

In making their demands all of these groups called for full political participation. They rejected the narrowly based polity of the ancien régime, controlled by metropolitan elites. Leaders of the Porfiriato had successfully expanded economic participation, transforming Mexico from a predominantly peasant nation to a commercial one, but they had failed to provide a broader base of political participation for a newly articulate and demanding public. During the height of the Revolution, Emiliano Zapata wrote to President Woodrow Wilson and explained his movement's demand for full political participation. He wanted a safeguard against the abuses of the powerful. The government would have to deal not just with individual voters but with a public organized into municipios libres, free villages with enough economic and political staying power to withstand the ill-formed policies of those who lost contact with the people.

Like the northern working-class revolutionaries, the Zapatistas wanted modernity, better schools, roads, and health care. Zapata once complained that the horses in the stables of the elite where he worked were given better care than the people. The rural working-class movements sought modernity and inclusion, not antiquity and peasantlike isolation. The Villistas and Zapatistas stepped toward a modern future with one foot while trying to keep the other foot in touch with past tradition. They proposed politically and economically autonomous municipalities as the vehicle for change. Industrial and urban workers sought much the same thing, but within the context of the factories that they hoped to control. What separated the rural groups from their urban and industrial counterparts was the degree to which the latter had been Europeanized, in language, clothing, foods, and political attitudes. They had "voted with their feet" during bygone generations, leaving the rural homes of their families and joining urban life with its lighting, running water, street cars, neckties, polished shoes, parks, opera houses, professional entertainment, and a wide range of government services. When their radical leaders lost to the Constitutionalists, the majority of workers accepted employment and relative powerlessness in the new order with only moderate resistance.

The provincial and local elites who gained control after the violent confrontations of 1915 also wanted a broader polity, but under their control. They used their experience to seek alliances, first obtaining American support by opening the border for supplies, then wooing the urban workers and intellectuals by equating themselves with democracy and progress and labeling their rural working-class rivals as reactionary cultural atavists. In this way the Constitutionalists convinced the metropolitan elites and the Americans that they were the only option. Finally, after obtaining arms from the Americans at Veracruz, they defeated their rural rivals and marginalized the anarcho-syndicalist leaders of the labor movement. In 1917, they successfully completed the first modern constitution, addressing not only the formal structure of government but also the unresolved social issues that had started the Revolution.

The Revolution broadened political participation on a grand scale. It also ushered in agrarian reforms that gave the rural working classes time to cope with full-scale commercialism, abolished the caste system that still plagues those areas of Latin America where large Native American populations survive, and preserved control of the nation's natural resources. In 1920, Mexicans began the reconstruction of their nation under the Constitution of 1917, the crowning achievement of the Revolution.

15

Rebuilding the Nation

THOMAS BENJAMIN

The idealistic and the hardheaded revolutionaries in power during the 1920s and 1930s worked with multitudes of everyday Mexicans to rebuild the country. Their objective was not simply to repair the damage left from nearly ten years of political upheaval and civil war but to reconstruct the nation on a new basis, to regenerate Mexico and its people. Their many and varied efforts to rebuild Mexico constitute one of the most extraordinary episodes not only in that nation's history but also in the world upheavals of the 20th century. A nation organized for the benefit of peasants and workers was under construction; a fundamental change in spirit and structure was taking place. Then, in the 1940s, Mexicans chose a different course and abandoned their remarkable experiment in social democracy.

The very fluidity of the power and interests that existed at every political level in the 1920s and 1930s made the reform process uncertain and imperfect, conflicted and often violent, uneven across the country, and subject to slowdowns. In retrospect we can detect an unfolding process. At the state and local levels, revolutionary leaders nurtured radicalism, encouraged popular mobilization, attacked the Catholic Church, built schools, and redistributed land. In the 1920s, national leaders too were pushed into reform by popular politics more than they wished. During the early 1930s, under the pressure of the Great Depression a revolutionary momentum seeking radical reconstruction emerged from localities, the provinces, and mass organizations and captured the leadership of the ruling "revolutionary family," a fractious coalition of self-made generals, provincial strongmen, and agrarian and labor leaders. With strong presidential leadership supported by a new official revolutionary party from above, and mass mobilization from below, reformers sought to consummate the Mexican Revolution.

In the 1930s, several strands of revolutionary thought and action converged at the national level. Learning from, and building on, nearly two decades of land and

This drawing from the cover of *Economic and Social Program of Mexico: A Controversy (Programa y Social de Mexico: Una Controversia)* sums up the "rebuilding the nation" theme. It displays an active, modern Mexico: industry, schools, agriculture, and land reform (represented by a surveyor).

labor reform, economic nationalism, anticlericalism, and cultural renewal, revolutionaries took dramatic actions to create a new Mexico. This country was designed to be a predominantly agricultural nation composed of democratic landowning peasant communities called *ejidos* (from the Spanish term for village commons). Most ejidos would be divided into parcels worked by individual families. In areas of commercial agriculture once dominated by plantations that grew such crops as cotton, sugar, henequen, and coffee, undivided collective ejidos would be managed and worked by all their members as one enterprise. Consumer and producer cooperatives, aided by government credit agencies and regional agricultural colleges, would help raise peasant productivity and income. Beyond agriculture, an extensive system of rural primary schools would transform peones into modern farmers, informed citizens, and patriotic Mexicans.

This nation of ejidos would be assisted and supplied by a small industrial sector managed and owned by a combination of Mexican businessmen, worker cooperatives, and—for key industries—the state. Sectors of the economy long dominated by foreign interests would be nationalized and operated for the benefit of all Mexicans. The few foreign enterprises remaining would operate strictly according to Mexican law. Powerful labor unions would protect the rights of workers and help raise their standard of living. Night classes and trade schools, along with sports and recreational centers, would transform those who had been exploited wage slaves into happy, productive citizens.

This new society and economy would be guaranteed by a new system of mass politics. All ejidos and unions, as well as the army and the state bureaucracy, would join an official revolutionary party. Through it the peasant and labor sectors would advance their interests, negotiate their differences, and choose their state governors and their representatives for Congress, and the various government departments. Every six years they would choose a national president.

Mexico reasonably approached this revolutionary vision on the eve of World War II. However, powerful forces within the country and without were already at work undermining the ideal scenario as well as what had actually been accomplished. A new generation of politicians who came to power in the 1940s, the "cubs" of the Revolution, were entranced by a different—modern, urban, industrial—vision of Mexico. Subsequent regimes were committed to rapid industrialization and the development of commercial agriculture. Stagnation of the ejido-based economy fueled urbanization, which only further marginalized the countryside. The militancy of the labor unions would be broken by the national government and the harnessing of workers to accumulate capital on behalf of private industry. This new direction was made possible because the institutions of mass politics—the agrarian and labor organizations as well as the party itself—were too centralized to begin with and were therefore subject to subversion by careerists and political hacks on behalf of a new governing and business class.

This turn toward the right did not mean counterrevolution. Granted, the unions had been domesticated, but they remained in place and had their rank-and-file constituency to satisfy or appease. And a revolutionary tradition had developed over the past three decades that obstructed any wholesale reversal of revolutionary reforms, even now and then encouraging populist state action. This more conservative Mexico was still far different from the oligarchic or frankly reactionary regimes of many other Latin American countries. In the 1960s and 1970s, when many of the countries of South America suffered under repressive military regimes that waged "dirty wars" against their own people, Mexico resisted such an authoritarian temptation and instead opened its doors to thousands of political refugees.

Nevertheless, the progressive intellectuals who denounced the "death" of the Mexican Revolution in the 1940s essentially had it right. Every revolution is transitory, of course, and the Mexican Revolution could not be expected to continue without end, despite official rhetoric to the contrary. Thus, while the rebuilding of Mexico proceeded and even accelerated during the postwar era, its revolutionary design dating from the 1920s and 1930s was scrapped. In its place an older, prerevolutionary pattern of social and economic development, one committed to energetic growth without widespread distribution of the fruits of that development, was resumed in the 1940s in the name of the Mexican Revolution. Mexicans thereafter became more focused on achieving apparent economic miracles and political stability than on upholding revolutionary hopes and dreams. A new age of order and progress was in the works.

For the ten years from 1910 to 1920, Mexicans devoted most of their energy to war and destruction. When the officially proclaimed era of peace and reconstruction began in 1920, the nation's population was smaller and poorer. By any measure the cost of those ten years was enormous. The 1921 census counted more than 800,000 fewer people than the country had had 11 years before. Most of the missing, however, were émigrés in the United States, whose number would increase during the 1920s as well. The largest number of deaths came as the result of two epidemics. Famine also took many lives during the worst mid-decade years. The decline in population naturally reduced the working population, perhaps by as much as half a million farmworkers, factory workers, and miners.

The national system of railroads, the proudest accomplishment of those known as *científicos*, supporters of the dictator Porfirio Díaz, was bankrupt and in ruins. More than a thousand miles of telegraph lines were destroyed out of a total of only some 20,000 miles in a nation more than twice as large as Texas. It would take more than a decade to repair the damages and losses, especially since military uprisings in the 1920s only added to the problem.

During the decade, agricultural and mining production had fallen by half. The hacienda system, an economic sector composed of agricultural estates, survived the armed revolution, but thousands of estates were destroyed or simply disappeared. The only sector of the economy to experience growth in this decade was petroleum, which had succeeded to the degree that by the early 1920s Mexico was one of the largest producers in the world. The foreign debt was an astonishing $1 billion, and interest payments were overdue. Foreign governments, the United States in particular, were demanding compensation for damages incurred by their citizens. However, the bloated revolutionary army took more than 60 percent of the national budget. As a result of all these factors, Mexico's economy did not experience sustained growth until the 1940s.

National reconstruction, to say nothing of meaningful reform, would require an enormous investment and years of effort under the best of conditions. Yet favorable conditions were hard to find in the 1920s and 1930s. Nationally, military rebellions and popular uprisings consumed scarce resources. Violence persisted at the local level throughout the country for the entire period. The world economic depression of the 1930s hit Mexico hard and was compounded by the forced repatriation of 300,000 to 400,000 migrant workers from the United States.

These tremendous costs of revolution were the price the nation paid for the Constitution of 1917, arguably the most progressive charter in the world. This document provided the basic plan for the rebuilding project. Its designated articles became revolutionary symbols. Yet in 1920, the provisions of the constitution were, with only a few exceptions, little more than promises on paper. No enabling legislation had been passed by Congress. It seemed that the cost had been great, the result pitifully small.

The constitution nevertheless proved to be a powerful goal and instrument. It was the bridge between the popular mobilization of the decade after 1910 and the revolutionary reforms of the 1920s and 1930s. The victorious revolutionary generals used it to justify a new political order that included organized peasants and workers. Ordinary people allied with populist political leaders used the constitution to rebuild the nation. It was the Revolution in law, but it meant little until the Revolution became government.

The armed struggle of the second decade of the century progressively destroyed the national state. Congress was dissolved by General Victoriano Huerta in 1913, the federal army was defeated and extinguished by the summer of 1914, the courts of law simply disappeared as revolutionary justice was dispensed by new generals, and the various states and localities became the fiefdoms of strongmen. President Venustiano Carranza (1917–20), the first president elected under the new Constitution of 1917, attempted to restore order, recentralize authority and rebuild the state. But his regime practically ignored the constitution and the new political reality of postrevolutionary Mexico: the entry of peasants and workers into local and regional politics. When most of the revolutionary army rebelled in 1920 in support of General Alvaro Obregón (president, 1920–24), Carranza had no popular support to draw upon. Future leaders learned this lesson, for Carranza's government was the last government to fall to armed rebellion in the 20th century.

The men from Sonora who came to power in Mexico City with Obregón had considerable administrative experience and political savvy. Adolfo de la Huerta and Plutarco Elías Calles had been governors. The triumvirate's dominant member, Obregón, had practiced his political skills at the state and national levels as a political broker, conciliating factions and forming populist coalitions. In their years in state government the Sonorans had formed their own professional army, patronized and allied themselves with labor unions, and expanded the government's authority to promote economic development. Now these hardheaded realists were ready and eager to do the same thing on a national scale.

The first task at hand was reconciliation. Although the era of vast armies clashing in great battles was over, Mexico remained at war. Regional rebellions in Chihuahua, Morelos, Chiapas, and elsewhere still were being fought against the national government. In localities and communities too numerous to mention, village fought hacienda and faction struggled against faction. Adolfo de la Huerta, selected interim president until Obregón was elected to a four-year term in November 1920, negotiated the retirement of Pancho Villa (Chihuahua rebel) and the pacification of the Zapatistas (agrarian revolutionaries of Morelos). Other regional rebellions came to an end and jumped on the new bandwagon. The enemies of Carranza, many of them former Maderistas—followers of Francisco Madero in his successful campaign to defeat Porfirio Díaz in 1910–11—such as José Vasconcelos, were welcomed back to Mexico and into the revolutionary family.

The Sonorans claimed to be the rightful successors to Madero, the genuine constitutionalists, and the radicals who had given the Constitution of 1917 its advanced social and economic provisions. They saw themselves as the true representatives of the Mexican Revolution. Now that the violent stage of the revolution was concluded, they would convert the Revolution into government. "The Revolution transformed into government" ("*La Revolución hecha gobierno*") was the phrase that justified the reestablishment of order.

The new president was the undisputed caudillo (political boss) of the Revolution. He was undefeated in battle, fiercely anticlerical, and a friend of peasants and workers. Obregón's reputation was formidable, untainted as he was by the mistakes and corruption of the last years of the Carranza regime. He was, in fact, more the pragmatic politician and capitalist than the social revolutionary. He did recognize the need for redistribution of land here and there in order to pacify those in the countryside. And he made an alliance with organized labor to offset the political power of ambitious generals. Yet beneath these poses Obregón was nothing if not practical. He believed that Mexico desperately needed economic recovery and growth, to be based on commercial agriculture and a small industrial sector. Government's role, for Obregón, was important. But what was central, he believed, was the conciliation of class interests that would bring peace and progress.

The prospects for political stability in 1920 were, at best, uncertain and precarious. Obregón inherited a bloated revolutionary army of more than 100,000 soldiers and thousands of generals and would-be generals. Regional strongmen and factions—some radical, some conservative, many simply committed to power—dominated the provinces and tolerated varying degrees of central government interference. In a move to negotiate better terms for its petroleum companies and citizens seeking compensation for damages, the United States had recalled its ambassador when Carranza was overthrown and withheld recognition of the new regime. Without this crucial blessing Obregón could not obtain foreign financing, but his potential enemies could purchase arms and ammunition at the border.

To offset such problems, the new regime improvised a new kind of mass politics. The revolutionary struggle had provided abundant opportunities for popular alliances. In 1913, Obregón had recruited native Yaquis with the promise of land, and during the civil war with Pancho Villa in 1914–15 he negotiated an agreement with Mexico City's dominant labor syndicate for armed workers organized in "Red Battalions" to serve on the front. As a presidential candidate in 1919, he

President Álvaro Obregón, seated here in the presidential chair, receives the Chinese ambassador, the first diplomatic representative to present his credentials to the new government. The president and his associates, Plutarco Elías Calles and Adolfo de la Huerta, were known as the Sonoran triangle. After driving Venustiano Carranza from office, they initiated the era of reconstruction following the decade of revolution from 1910 to 1920.

reforged that alliance with the new and rising Regional Confederation of Mexican Workers (CROM), headed by Luis Napoleón Morones, a former electrician.

As a result, Obregón received the substantial backing in Congress of Morones's new Mexican Labor Party. The president also solidified his support in rural Mexico. Land redistribution proceeded in the regions where the peasants had mobilized most intensely and fought in the Revolution and where radical state governors encouraged peasant organization into agrarian leagues. In turn, agrarian leaders formed the National Agrarian Party and pledged its support to the president. These broad-based organizations provided a political counter-weight to the unpredictable army, profusion of independent political parties, and "enemies" of the Revolution.

During the 1920s, the most fertile political experimentation took place in the states. With Carranza out of the way, reformers and, in a few states, determined radicals ascended to the governor's palace. The president needed their political support, and they needed his. These governors began to create agrarian and labor organizations (in some states arming them) and to form mass-based political parties. With this backing they started to implement reforms and further encourage and consolidate popular mobilization. In 1923, the American journalist Carleton Beals praised these "experimental laboratories" where "for the first time in Mexican history, a fundamentally new method of social control has been evolved."

Governor Adalberto Tejeda of Veracruz encouraged the organization of labor unions, agrarian leagues, and socialist parties. He made an alliance with the local Communist Party to establish the League of Agrarian Communities and Peasant Syndicates of the State of Veracruz. Similar official agrarian leagues were organized in Michoacán, Aguascalientes, Chiapas, and many other states. The Veracruz league provided the nucleus of the National Peasant League, which was formed in 1926 with a membership of 300,000. In the southeastern state of Yucatán, Governor Felipe Carrillo Puerto took office in 1922, proclaiming the "first socialist government in the Americas." His Leagues of Resistance recruited and organized Maya peasants to advance land reform and the unionization of agricultural workers. In Yucatán and neighboring Campeche these leagues were then organized as the Socialist Party of the Southeast. Carrillo Puerto also organized Feminist Leagues, which energized the nascent Mexican women's movement. In Yucatán he legalized divorce, introduced woman suffrage, and encouraged the election of women to political office.

Governor Tomás Garrido Canabal in the state of Tabasco organized a labor-peasant federation that provided a mass base for his radical Socialist Party of Tabasco. Garrido's radicalism leaned more in the direction of cultural than economic restructuring. In particular, his government sought to break the hold of the Catholic Church on the minds and souls of Tabascans. In the northeastern state of Tamaulipas, Governor Emilio Portes Gil built his Border Socialist Party on a foundation of local agrarian leagues and labor unions. Like many official revolutionaries at the state level, Portes Gil pursued a moral offensive to mold a new Mexican citizen. Through prohibitions and regulations this governor attempted to reduce gambling, blood sports, drinking and drunkenness, prostitution, and other "counterrevolutionary" vices.

Of course, not all provincial regimes were revolutionary. Power in postrevolutionary Mexico was up for grabs, the rules of the game complicated and subject to change without notice. In the state of Chiapas, on the border with Guatemala, conservative rebels endorsed Obregón in 1920 and took office. A landowners' government sought to restore the badly shaken old order. This regime survived during Obregón's term but eventually suffered the same fate as Carranza's government, and for the same reason. The new political factors in Chiapas—organized villagers and farm workers—joined forces with populist politicians allied to powerful political figures in Mexico City. This new system of practicing politics became the wave of the future, as demonstrated by the triumph of the Socialist Party of Chiapas in its takeover of the governor's palace and state congress in

1925. Neither at the provincial nor national levels was there restoration of a reconstituted old regime, nor was such a thing possible. The emergence of mass politics was one of the permanent revolutionary consequences of the Revolution.

Alvaro Obregón, as the self-proclaimed heir to Francisco Madero (who campaigned and ultimately rebelled for "Effective suffrage and no reelection"), and because of the constitutional restriction against it, could not stand for reelection in 1924. An election, however, as 1920 had certainly revealed, was an invitation for political intrigue leading to a military uprising. Although the caudillo was prepared, conflict was unavoidable. The Sonorans patched up relations with the United States during the Bucareli Conference, so named after a street in Mexico City, in the spring of 1923. Then in July the unpredictable Pancho Villa was gunned down near his hacienda in Parral, Chihuahua, which prevented any rebellion or interference on his part. The United States extended formal diplomatic recognition in August. Within days, Plutarco Elías Calles, the minister of the interior, declared his candidacy for the presidency. Obregón had chosen his successor, but it remained to be seen if he could impose him.

The former president, Adolfo de la Huerta, then became a magnet for those who distrusted, feared, and opposed Calles. Pushed and pulled by various constituencies, de la Huerta became the figurehead of a massive rebellion that began in December 1923. More than half the army, dozens of generals, and not a few provincial governors and strongmen joined this movement. The government (that is, Obregón and Calles) asked for and received the support of organized labor and the peasants. Demonstrably revolutionary governors such as Adalberto Tejeda and Tomás Garrido Canabal, as well as more traditional regional strongmen such as Saturnino Cedillo of San Luis Potosí mobilized agrarian forces in defense of the regime. In central Mexico some 120,000 armed farmworkers were raised to fight the rebel Delahuertistas.

Once the rebellion was crushed, by March 1924, there were some 50 fewer generals and a smaller, tamer army. In July the 47–year–old Calles, reputedly more radical and nationalist than Obregón, was elected president for the term 1924–28. He traveled to Europe before his inauguration to study industry and cooperatives in social democratic Germany. Obregón returned to his farm in Sonora, declaring proudly, "I am going to leave by the front door of the National Palace, bathed in the esteem and affection of my people." One did not have to be a historian to recall another general's "retirement" after one term to be followed by seven successive reelections.

New president Calles built upon the accomplishments of his predecessor. His regime's alliance with labor was solidified by the appointment of CROM boss Luis Morones as minister of industry, commerce, and labor. Under him, land redistribution was accelerated, more rural schools built, the railroad system aggressively expanded. Reflecting the temper of the times, Calles expanded the economic role of the national state. A central bank, the Bank of Mexico, was created in 1925. The following year a new National Bank of Agricultural Credit began to finance local and regional cooperative societies. The government built irrigation projects around the country, a new system of highways, and agricultural colleges to modernize that sector.

Presidential power under Calles expanded at the expense of a more profeessionalized military and increasingly dependent state governments. During Calles's term the army was reduced to 40,000 soldiers, and 25 governors were deposed in 15 different states. There were also fewer radical leaders at the state and local level, although by now all the state governments practiced some form of mass politics through labor and agrarian alliances.

Two powers, the United States and the Catholic Church, resisted the expansion of the revolutionary state. Washington began to see the Calles regime as Bolshevik, to the degree that hysteria over "Soviet Mexico" produced a war scare in 1927. As before, the real issue was oil regulation. The church suspended the hearing of mass in 1926 when provocative anticlerical laws were enacted. As a result, militant Catholics rose in The Cristero rebellion in west-central Mexico. By 1927, a savage war was under way that would kill tens of thousands of Mexicans before it ended in 1929.

The return of the caudillo was predictable, though controversial. No revolutionary principle was more sacred than *no reelección*. Supporters argued, however, that the choice was between "Obregón or chaos." In 1927, the constitution was amended to permit one nonconsecutive reelection, and in early 1928 the presidential term was extended to six years. Obregón began his campaign with the support of the National Agrarian Party but without the backing of the CROM and its disappointed boss, who had been a presidential aspirant. Two opposing candidates, both generals, rebelled in the fall of 1927 and were shot to death. The uprising provided an excuse for a murderous purge of political enemies, from Sonora to Chiapas. Obregón survived two attempts on his life before being reelected president in July 1928. "I have proved," he told Calles, tempting fate, "that the presidential palace is not necessarily the antechamber to the tomb." A little more than two weeks later this "indispensable man" was assassinated by a religious zealot during an open-air banquet.

Obregón, as had Porfirio Díaz decades before, knew how to play politics: how to balance interests and rivalries, and how to conciliate and intimidate regional and national political factions. His abrupt disappearance from the scene led to the sharpening of knives. Supporters of Obregón suspected Calles and his closest ally, Morones. Another revolutionary schism of historic proportions, in the midst of the continuing Cristero rebellion, threatened to erupt. To try to head off disaster, President Calles attempted to unite all the revolutionaries in one common political front: a national revolutionary party.

The most immediate concern was presidential succession. In what would be his last annual Informe, or address to Congress, in September 1928, President Calles declared the end of personalist rule in Mexico and the creation of a "nation of institutions and laws." He prudently resisted the temptation of reelection, stepped down at the end of his term of office in December, and handed the presidency to a politician acceptable to both Obregonistas and Callistas, Emilio Portes Gil. The following year both factions created a federation of all the revolutionary parties, the National Revolutionary Party (PNR), and nominated the rather obscure ambassador to Brazil, Pascual Ortiz Rubio to be its presidential candidate. His opponent, the Maderista true believer José Vasconcelos, may have actually garnered the most votes. Nevertheless, Ortiz Rubio was the winner and occupied the presidential office. But Calles, now the Jefe Máximo (Supreme Chief) of the Revolution, exercised the greater power and authority.

During the period from 1928 to 1934, known as the Maximato, the country saw three presidents wrestle politically with the strongman Calles. Mexico City's residents sometimes wisecracked, when they passed Chapultepec Castle, the president's residence, that "the president lives here, but the man who gives the orders lives across the street." Emilio Portes Gil (1928–30) negotiated an end to the Cristero rebellion, improved relations with the United States, and repressed the last serious military revolt against the national government. Pascual Ortiz Rubio (1930–32) got off to a bad start when he was wounded in an assassination attempt on his inaugural day. He had difficulty accepting the political direction of the Jefe Máximo's men and finally was forced to resign. His successor, Abelardo Rodríguez (1932–34), "the Country Club President," served the remaining two years of Obregón's term and knew how to take orders, even if he did not like it.

During the period of the Maximato, during the Great Depression, Calles became increasingly conservative, while the nation's peasants and workers became more radical and assertive. In 1930, in the midst of growing economic crisis, the Jefe Máximo declared agrarian reform a failure and ordered it terminated. Certain governors, Lázaro Cárdenas of Michoacán being one, continued to distribute land and keep the dream alive. But elsewhere the agrarian slowdown and hard times in the countryside produced more militant agrarian leagues and parties.

A revitalized agrarian movement from the states grew to become particularly influential within the new revolutionary party. The PNR was formed of state and regional revolutionary parties that were largely agrarian in their makeup. CROM was not invited into the party (because of Morones's close alliance with Calles and his opposition to Obregón's reelection), so Calles had no counterweight to the agrarian influence within the PNR. In the spring of 1933, the agrarian forces from the provinces and within the party made their move. Led by Portes Gil, they established the National Peasant Confederation and issued a manifesto calling for the renewal of agrarian reform and the nomination of their own Lázaro Cárdenas as the party's candidate for president in the 1934 election. The Jefe Máximo chose not to oppose public opinion and the party he'd created, reversed his position on agrarian reform, and went along with the nomination of Cárdenas—his friend and loyal supporter—during the party convention in December 1933.

Although Cárdenas as the official party candidate faced no opposition, he campaigned across the length and breadth of Mexico with an intensity not seen since Madero's aborted campaign in 1909–10. Cárdenas sought more than votes: He wanted a popular mandate for revolution. In July 1934, "the Boy Scout"—so nicknamed by political insiders because of his personal honesty and austerity— was elected president. He took office in December and set about to advance the rebuilding of Mexico.

First, however, there was the problem of the Jefe Máximo. The new president had witnessed firsthand the frustration and humiliation of his immediate predecessor. Cárdenas thus made prudent political alliances and appointments, and engineered the retirement or replacement of many army generals and state governors, to increase his political support. The new government's acceleration of land reform and toleration of strikes won Cárdenas the backing of agrarian and labor organizations as well as of important elements in the official party. Thus, when Calles began to criticize agrarian and labor agitation and pressure the government to moderate its policies in mid–1935, Cárdenas purged his cabinet of Calles's most loyal supporters. This action demonstrated that the power of the Jefe Máximo was more apparent than real. In its wake, Cardenistas took over the PNR, Congress, and the governments of 14 states.

Calles announced his retirement "forever" from politics and went to the United States, but he could not stay away for long. At the end of 1935, he returned to defend his reputation and, he said, the Mexican Revolution. Confrontation was unavoidable. Over the next four months, tension turned to violence between Callistas and Cardenistas. In April 1936, the president had Calles put on a plane and flown to the United States. "I was exiled," Calles told a reporter, "because I opposed the attempts to implant a dictatorship of the proletariat." Unlike Madero, Zapata, Carranza, Villa, and Obregón, Plutarco Elías Calles was not murdered. The Maximato was terminated without bloodshed.

Thereafter President Cárdenas and his successors would fully control the official party and the government. Cárdenas was brought to office by party leaders but confirmed in power by populist politics. "The Revolution in power" was for the people not simply a figure of speech. It was "a new democracy," as a PNR manifesto stated in 1937, "one in which organized laborers and peasants shall exert a growing influence of political and economic leadership upon the country."

"The Revolution in power" also represented a new kind of government action. Cárdenas argued that since the government was supported by the working classes, improvement of those groups was its "most pressing obligation." Two currents of reform arose in the 1920s. One stream was social and economic, the effort to create a nation of prosperous peasants and workers, one that controlled its resources and destiny. The other current was cultural, the effort to create the new Mexican man and woman. "To save Mexico for the Mexicans and to save the Mexicans for Mexico," Moisés Sáenz stated in 1926, "is, in synthesis, the Mexican Revolution." These two currents of reform, the cultural revolution and the social and economic one, were in fact two revolutions within the Revolution.

Rebuilding the nation meant, before anything else, "saving" Mexicans: reforming, improving, and liberating men and women, peasants and workers, families and communities, native peoples, and—above all—children, the future of the nation. The revolutionaries of the 1920s and 1930s were the faithful heirs of their liberal grandfathers of the reform era. The nation both generations envisioned was republican, secular, and enlightened. The greatest obstacle to and enemy of this modern Mexico for both remained the country's heterogeneity and the Catholic Church. The revolutionaries embraced the new goal of Mexicanizing the nation. They scorned the Porfirian imitation of European high culture and sought to develop a new respect and pride in Mexican ways. They wanted to blend the disparate ethnic and regional elements of the country into one Mexicanized *patria*.

The cultural revolution, like everything else in Mexico during the 1920s and 1930s, was full of contradictions. The national leadership and certain state regimes often followed different—even opposing—agendas. National policy regarding education and the church evolved and changed course as leaders and regimes changed. Moderate reformers often placed their programs, unknowingly, in the hands of radical administrators and teachers, while radicals were just as often frustrated by conservatives entrenched in local and provincial posts. Ordinary Mexicans themselves frequently opposed the blandishments, prohibitions, and intrusions of the state. Mexico nevertheless experienced a genuine cultural revolution. There were too many devout revolutionaries at every level throughout the country committed to small acts of transformation as well as reform on a broader and deeper scale for it not to happen. The cultural crusaders of the 20th century, like the missionary friars of the 16th, were extraordinary in their ambition, efforts, and achievements.

The new Mexican citizen would be formed in the government school. "To educate is to redeem," a slogan of the time stated. Educators sought to redeem the child, the adult, the Indian, the woman, the peasant and the worker, the nation. The program of redemption included not only the three Rs but also hygiene and nutrition, sports and physical fitness, morality and self-control, the fine arts and useful crafts. Agricultural and industrial knowledge and skills, community activism, patriotism, and citizenship were also stressed. This program was called integral or functional education (creating "Action Schools") by its original proponent, the progressive U.S. reformer John Dewey.

Mexico's educational renaissance was due at first to one remarkable charismatic man who made education the central issue of reform in the 1920s, José Vasconcelos. At the age of 39 he returned to Mexico in 1920 with the triumph of the Sonorans and was appointed director of the National University. From that post he initiated a national literacy campaign, "Each One, Teach One," which recruited volunteer teachers and sparked the imagination of the nation. The following year he wrote legislation that gave the national government the authority to establish, staff, and maintain schools and created the Ministry of Public Education (SEP) to administer the new system. Vasconcelos, naturally, received the appointment as minister of public education and became the cultural commissar and social engineer of the Revolution.

Vasconcelos attacked the greatest problem head-on. With generous appropriations in the national budget for two years, SEP began to create a nationwide

On November 1, 1934, congressional deputies led by Carlos Riva Palacio, the president of the National Revolutionary Party (the PNR), marched in support of the cultural revolution expressed in the government's anticlerical and educational policies. These revolutionary campaigns deeply divided the Mexican people.

system of rural primary schools. Mobile teacher-training institutes called cultural missions traveled to villages, built schoolhouses, established libraries, and organized school and community improvement committees. Teachers were trained in academic subjects, teaching methods, health and nutrition, sports, music, agriculture, the mechanical arts, and more. For the longer term SEP established a system of rural secondary schools that provided room and board, education, and training free of cost. SEP also published cheap editions of the great books of Western civilization and placed them in thousands of small libraries in villages and towns.

Here is how the assistant minister of SEP described to a U.S. audience in 1926 the role of the rural school and its teachers, the new "soldiers" of the Revolution: "To integrate Mexico through the rural school—that is, to teach the people of the mountains and of the faraway valleys, the millions of people that are Mexicans but are not yet Mexican, to teach them the love of Mexico and the meaning of Mexico." He continued, "Our little rural school stands for Mexico and represents Mexico in those far-off corners— so many of them that belong to Mexico but are not yet Mexican."

The results were impressive yet frustrating. Before 1920, the education of peasant children was the responsibility either of the states, with most states doing next to nothing, or the church, which in the opinion of revolutionaries did it badly. By the end of Obregón's term, in late 1925, there were nearly 2,000 federal rural primary schools and more than 3,000 libraries. Building more of these remained a priority for subsequent governments; accordingly, the system expanded. By 1936, there were more than 11,000 rural schools, with 14,000 teachers giving instruction to more than 700,000 children. These schools did more than educate: They inoculated children against disease and often fed hungry students a nutritious breakfast.

These schools also welcomed girls, who before had always been secluded at home. During the 1920s and 1930s, the enrollment of girls increased to nearly reach that of boys. The dignity of women was not simply an empty phrase in the official discourse of the period.

The state-level radical governments also expanded the education program. The new regime of the Chiapas Socialist Party, in power from 1925 to 1927, increased the number of state-funded rural primary schools. The poverty of the states' education budgets and the zeal of the national effort are demonstrated by the fact that by 1927 there were nearly twice as many federal as state primary schools in Chiapas. The state also required landowners to provide schools and teachers for the children of their workers. (It was not until 1931 that national legislation required employers to establish similar "Article 123" schools.)

A significant factor in the expansion of rural education in the 1920s was public demand for and support of them. Village leaders, local agrarian movements, and ad hoc school committees petitioned their state and national governments, demanding schools for their children. Localities generally subsidized their schools by building classrooms and supplying furniture. They donated land, animals, tools, and books, and sometimes cultivated a communal plot of land to contribute the proceeds to the public school fund. Schools became important centers of village life as teachers became involved in agrarian petitions, sponsored theater presentations, and organized patriotic ceremonies on national holidays.

Despite these enormous efforts, however, Mexico's illiteracy rate declined only a little in the 1920s and 1930s. In 1937, the Ministry of Public Education estimated that the country required double the number of rural primary teachers currently at work. Yet a high teacher dropout rate and rapid population growth in what remained a predominantly rural society made the situation harder to beat. Part of the problem was political. Idealistic teachers in rural villages often had to face the violent opposition of local landowners and political bosses who did not want their workforces to be educated, literate, and knowledgeable about the new revolutionary laws and constitution. Teachers became caught up in the agrarian movement and often assisted villages in their petitions to the government for land. As a result, teachers were assaulted, driven away, and even assassinated.

Many of the rural schools were located in indigenous communities where the primary goals were teaching the national language and incorporating Indians into the national culture. Dr. Manuel Puig Casauranc, President Calles's minister of public education, established a residential school in Mexico City for indigenous students from every state. He wanted to educate leaders and train teachers who would return to their communities and build schools. Unfortunately, few graduates wished to give up city life. Native culture was celebrated in public art in the 1920s, but any significant national effort benefiting Mexico's indigenous population would have to wait for the 1930s.

Vasconcelos and his successors created other important educational opportunities and expanded the existing ones. A kindergarten system was established in towns and cities to help care for the children of working mothers. In 1925, a system of public secondary schools was set up. The ministry also opened night schools, prevocational schools for young adults, technical and vocational schools, and rural agricultural schools for young peasant farmers.

In 1921, Vasconcelos established a department of fine arts within SEP to encourage and support the plastic arts, music, and literature. At the same time, he commissioned artists to paint public walls to reflect his philosophical idealism and refine the public's aesthetic appreciation. However, the mural painters had a different agenda. In 1922, David Alfaro Siqueiros drew up a "Social, Political, and Aesthetic Declaration" for the Syndicate of Technical Workers, Painters, and Sculptors to guide the new work. "We proclaim," the declaration read, "that this being the moment of social transition from a decrepit to a new order, the makers of beauty must invest their greatest efforts in the aim of materializing an art valuable to the people."

José Clemente Orozco and Diego Rivera produced the most well known and didactic murals. Rivera's work particularly glorified and romanticized the Revolution as a peasants' and workers' movement. His biographer, Bertram D. Wolfe, observed that Rivera "painted what the Revolution should be, what it should become." Orozco, on the other hand, Wolfe noted in *The Fabulous Life of Diego Rivera*, "has painted what the Revolution had been, its brutality, its senseless pattern of demagogy and betrayal." Both these painters and the many others who participated had one thing in common, however: the glorification of Mexico, its people, customs, and history. The Mexican mural renaissance continued through the 1920s and 1930s, covering walls in many of Mexico's most important buildings—the National Palace, the Ministry of Public Education building, the Palace of Fine Arts. These powerful images of a revolutionary people were reproduced and disseminated throughout the nation, creating a powerful cultural nationalism that resonates still, as discussed further in Chapter 17.

The muralists often portrayed the Catholic Church and its clergy as one of the reactionary forces blocking progress generation after generation. Revolutionaries had blamed the church for siding with General Victoriano Huerta against Madero in 1913 and further restricted the institution and clergy in the Constitution of 1917. They sought once and for all to break up the religious monopoly held by the Catholic Church and to lead the Mexican people away from conservatism, bigotry, intolerance, superstition, and fanaticism.

Article 130 of the revolutionary charter sought to remove any remaining religious influence in politics but said nothing about labor organization. This oversight made it possible for a number of Catholic labor unions to arise, which united in the National Catholic Confederation of Labor in 1922. This backdoor entrance of the church into populist politics was unacceptable to the Sonorans, though, and especially to CROM. The church also became involved in agrarian disputes and conflicts, with priests often backing landowners and counseling vil-

José Clemente Orozco, Diego Rivera, and David Alfredo Siqueiros painted the history of the Revolution and of the Mexican people in brilliant murals on public buildings in the 1920s. With their striking, powerful portrayal of insurgent Mexico, the muralists defined the Revolution for many who could not read. This detail comes from Orozco's mural "A Return to the Battlefields," which is painted on the walls of the National Preparatory School in Mexico City.

lagers to join various leagues and petition for land. In many communities the church and state confronted each other in the guise of priest and teacher. Conflict between the "two majesties" therefore became nearly inevitable.

As is often the case in conflicts between powerful forces, each side believed it was being provoked by the other. CROM thugs attacked Catholic unions and dynamited churches while the government turned a blind eye. In 1923, a massive pilgrimage was organized to Guanajuato to crown Jesus Christ the king of Mexico. The government responded by expelling the papal ambassador, who was present at the ceremony. Catholic militancy grew with the formation of the Catholic Association of Mexican Youth (ACJM). In the first year of Calles's term CROM leader Luis Morones instigated the formation of a rival church, the Mexican National Orthodox Apostolic Catholic Church, whose first patriarch, Joaquín Pérez, was a married man and a Mason.

Revolutionary anticlericalism became most severe and systematic in certain states. There governors appropriated church buildings and converted them into libraries, schools, and union halls. They often closed church schools, expelling priests and bishops who protested. Socialist symbols were put up in place of traditional Catholic icons, sometimes even on church buildings. The most radically liberal and anticlerical Jacobin regime was Tomás Garrido Canabal's, in Tabasco, where anticlerical laws prohibited the exhibition of any religious image, required the marriage of every priest, and ultimately closed every church in the state.

Catholic residents of Orizaba, Veracruz on February 15, 1937, protest the death of a girl killed in a police raid on a clandestine Roman Catholic service. Some of the banners call for a reopening of the churches. Even though the Cristero Rebellion by Catholic stalwarts had ended in 1929, in some states, including Veracruz, the bitter struggle between anticlericals and Catholics continued.

At the national level, church-state relations came to an impasse in 1926. When the archbishop of Guadalajara publicly condemned the Constitution of 1917, during a building crisis, President Calles expelled 200 foreign priests as well as the new papal envoy and pushed through Congress a new penal code for "religious crimes." The National League for Religious Defense, a new lay organization, organized an economic boycott to pressure the government to revoke the anticlerical laws. In the end, the church hierarchy suspended all religious services. The Catholic Church went on strike.

Even before this showdown, peasant rebels in the mountains of Jalisco and neighboring states in west-central Mexico began making war on the government in the name of "Christ the King." These Cristero rebels joined the now underground National League for Religious Defense and, by 1927, had organized a massive peasant uprising. The Cristero rebellion lasted three years, consumed nearly half the federal budget, and claimed perhaps 70,000 lives. One repercussion was the assassination of president-elect Obregón in 1928. When the government concluded that military repression was not succeeding, President Portes Gil negotiated a settlement in 1929 that opened the churches in exchange for nonenforcement of the offending laws.

The Cristero rebellion turned out to be only one battle in a longer war. When the National Revolutionary Party was organized in 1929, this made a new vehicle available for waging cultural revolution. During his tenure as party chief, Portes Gil instituted a "cultural hour" every Sunday when revolutionaries in every village, ejido, and union hall would gather to enjoy and learn from cultural programs. These included folk music, patriotic stories, presentations on child care, and other topics of interest to the community. These Sunday programs and others throughout the week would be broadcast by radio to the entire country by new PNR-owned stations. The party was in effect unwilling to concede any ground to the church even on Sunday.

Like many other revolutionaries of his generation, Lázaro Cárdenas was a moralist who detested what he considered the bad and corrupt habits of his people. As president he conducted an anti-alcohol campaign and wanted to institute national prohibition, which had recently been tried in the United States. He prevented the manufacture and sale of dice and playing cards and banned gambling. During his term the casinos on the northern border and the red-light districts of Mexico City were put out of business.

The cultural revolution begun in the 1920s shifted into high gear in the 1930s. In 1934, the Jefe Máximo, Plutarco Calles, proclaimed in a widely publicized speech given in Guadalajara that "we must enter and conquer the minds of the children, the minds of the young, because they do and they must belong to the Revolution." The official party followed his lead later that year with its Six-Year Plan, which stated that primary and secondary education should be based "in the orientations and postulates of the socialist doctrine that the Mexican Revolution supports." This plan sought the elimination of all private schools by the end of the six-year period.

This socialist education program was the brainchild of Narciso Bassols, the SEP minister from 1931 to 1934 and the first Marxist appointed to a cabinet post. Bassols was encouraged and supported by radical teachers' unions, some radical state governments, and the revitalized agrarian movement. He wanted Mexican education to provide a rational explanation of the world and thus combat religious obscurantism and fanaticism but also instill in children a collectivist ethic and thereby bring an end to the exploitation of man by man.

Congress amended the constitution to include socialist education in December 1934. President Cárdenas gave the job of implementing it to Ignacio García Téllez, the new SEP minister. The new so-called socialist schools were in fact the old Action Schools, but now with an ideological mission. "Our socialistic education attempts to inculcate in our children a true sympathy for the working classes and for the ideals of the Revolution," Ramón Beteta wrote in 1937. "We want to convince them of the benefits of land distribution and the protection of labor; we want them to realize the necessity of protecting the country's natural resources and to appreciate the dignity of work." New textbooks emphasized agrarianism and the dignity of labor, a materialist approach to history, and the new Mexicanized national identity. Building on the efforts of the 1920s, teachers put particular emphasis on replacing the traditional religious calendar with a new patriotic and revolutionary calendar of national holidays celebrating the great men and women—revolutionaries all—of Mexican history.

The very word *socialist*, when applied to education, provoked considerable protest and opposition on the part of social conservatives, whether upper-class or peasant, new fascist groups, and, of course, the church and clergy. Prominent clerics characterized socialist education as a "Jewish-Masonic plan." Archbishop Leopoldo Ruiz y Flores stated that no Catholic could be a member of the National Revolutionary Party. Parents who sent their children to socialist schools, the church threatened, could be excommunicated. In 1935, the hierarchy issued a pastoral letter declaring that the church should "organize and direct the integral life of man by means of its moral doctrines in all spheres of human life." Laymen of the church were encouraged to form and did form associations of Catholic action such as the Union of Mexican Catholics, the Catholic Association of Mexican Youth, and others and created a united front to oppose "atheistic laicism and absurd positivism." The ultimate objective, church leaders declared, was "the conquest of [the nation's] legitimate liberties."

In several states, anticlericalism reached a fever pitch. The governor of Chiapas closed every church in the state, expelled the bishop and every priest, and organized public bonfires to destroy religious objects. A new state law there prohibited the inclusion of the names of saints in place-names, which meant that the town of San Bartolomé de los Llanos, as only one example of many, became Venustiano Carranza. In 17 states there were no priests at all. The militant anticlericalism of Garrido Canabal's state of Tabasco shifted to Mexico City in 1935 as the governor joined the cabinet of the new president. "Red Shirts," members of the radical group *Bloque de Jóvenes Revolucionarios*, from Tabasco set up headquarters in the capital and attacked, and in one incident killed, Catholics coming out of church.

Mexico was close to having another Cristero war. But President Cárdenas, though anticlerical himself, had no intention, he stated, "of falling into the error of previous administrations." He took forceful action against the Red Shirts in Mexico City and Tabasco. In 1936, within the hotbed of Cristero militancy, the state of Jalisco, Cárdenas declared that the "fundamental aspects" of the program of the Mexican Revolution were social and economic in character. He argued that "it is no concern of the government to undertake antireligious campaigns." When the government's policy of conciliation was matched by the church, tensions subsided. In 1938, the nation celebrated the 400th anniversary of the apparition of the Virgin of Guadalupe as thousands of pilgrims gathered in Mexico City.

The deep and apparent religiosity of Mexican women convinced many male revolutionaries in the 1920s and 1930s that instituting woman suffrage would advance "reactionary" interests. A small but persistent women's movement that had emerged from the Revolution was campaigning for the right to vote. However, from 1920 to 1934, only four states granted women the vote—Yucatán in 1922, San Luis Potosí in 1923, Chiapas in 1925, and Tabasco in 1934—two of which later revoked it.

"Women must organize," Lázaro Cárdenas stated in a campaign speech, "so that the home shall cease to be looked upon as a prison for them." And organize they did. In 1934, the Revolutionary Feminist Party supported Cárdenas; a year later the new president incorporated the party into the PNR. This step started things moving. Several states then granted woman suffrage, and the PNR granted women full membership as well as the vote in party primaries.

Pressured by a hunger strike staged outside his home, Cárdenas agreed in 1937 to send an amendment to Congress providing women the vote. The amendment passed both chambers in 1938 and was sent to the states for ratification. After all 28 states approved it late in the year, the constitutional amendment and a new national election law were placed before Congress for final approval in 1939. But there the initiative languished. By 1939, a growing conservative opposition to the government and the official party, and the start of the next presidential campaign, combined to produce second thoughts within the ranks of the revolutionaries. The influence of President Cárdenas, now a lame duck, was fading fast. The old concern about Mexican women's supposed innate conservatism in the middle of a crucial tight election led to legislative inaction.

Less controversial than socialist education and woman suffrage was the Cárdenista policy and ideology regarding Indians called *indigenismo*, or indigenism. The folk and cultural nationalism that became more influential in the 1920s flew in the face of the earlier Mexican objective of "civilizing" the Indians and turning them into Mexicans. "Revolutionary Mexico," Moisés Sáenz noted, "has developed a new conscience about the Indian." Yet old prejudices faded slowly. In Chiapas, one of the states with the largest native populations, the state Department of Indigenous Protection initiated in 1934 a "pants campaign" to force the Indians to abandon their traditional costume and wear trousers. Despite regional holdouts such as Chiapas, by the 1930s revolutionary intellectuals believed that government policy should promote the social, economic, and spiritual emancipation of the Indians while preserving the best characteristics and habits of native culture.

Although the Cárdenas administration created a new national Department of Indian Affairs in December 1935 to advance the new policy of indigenism, most action to support that goal came from other agencies. Land reform benefiting Indian regions, for instance, did not begin until Cárdenas ordered it. In the new Cardenista state government of Chiapas, Indian policy was revolutionized. The state department organized the region's migrant coffee workers into the Syndicate of Indigenous Workers, which ended labor abuses and raised wages. In the Yaqui region Cárdenas and the state of Sonora recognized the authority of native governors, thus ending colonial rule by the army.

Indigenous education programs remained with the Ministry of Public Education. In the early 1930s, SEP established regional Centers of Indigenous Education, in effect residential colleges, to educate boys and girls in the mid- to late-teen years. In 1937, the ministry created the Department of Indigenous Education, which supervised 33 regional centers. As in the rural primary schools, integral education—learning by doing—was the preferred method in these centers. There students built their own houses, tended a garden, formed cooperatives, learned different arts and crafts, dances, songs, and games, and used machinery and modern tools. Graduates were expected to return to their villages and put in practice the lessons learned.

Mexico's cultural revolution of two decades, its experiment in social engineering, outraged a significant segment of society, while many of its most committed proponents were disappointed by the survival of the church and capitalism. And yet a new Mexico emerged. By the 1940s, most young people had learned or were learning how to read and write. For the first time, reading was no longer the privilege of just a tiny elite or even the small middle class. Mexicans gained a new understanding and appreciation of their country. The Frenchified Mexico of the earlier Porfiriato, a shallow imitation that rejected its own people and traditions, was Mexicanized. Great murals now portrayed and gloried in a multiethnic nation. Mexican arts and crafts, dance and music were discovered, appreciated, and shared with the rest of the world. In many respects the goal of forging the nation that had long antedated the Revolution was largely achieved as a result of the cultural revolution.

Rebuilding the nation also meant raising the standard of living of ordinary Mexicans and giving them a real stake in their own country. In the 1920s and 1930s, however, revolutionaries were less in agreement about the means and ends of the social revolution than about those of the cultural revolution. The Constitution of 1917, itself a compromise, inspired different visions. As a result, two rather different social revolutions competed for ascendancy in the states and the capital.

In the 1920s, policy at the national level was directed by men from northern Mexico. Their attitudes reflected their region's understanding of Mexico's problems and the Revolution's promises. The northern frontier was a land of hardy individualists, colonists and frontiersmen, and small ranchers who admired and aspired to become *hacendados*, not a land of dense peasant communities. For northerners the goal of the Revolution was conciliation of class interests, balancing the rights and interests of peasants and landowners, villages and haciendas, workers and employers. To the Sonorans, Mexico's "land problem" was agriculture (concerned with productivity) more than agrarian (concerned with land tenure and equality). The goal for them was to modernize agriculture and raise productivity, and in this way better the lives of farmers and farmworkers. Land reform was seen as a way to correct past injustices or simply as a political necessity in regions where the peasants were militant and mobilized.

By the 1930s, the national leadership had passed to men from central Mexico who had a quite different understanding of the nation and its revolution. Their Mexico was what has often been called the "old Mexico" of high plateaus and mountain valleys populated by peasant and Indian villages often under the domination of, or in conflict with, haciendas. Here the means and ends of the Revolution were more radical: The well-being of villages required the reduction, and many argued the destruction, of the hacienda system. Land reform therefore was central to the revolutionary project, with the *ejido* seen as the future of agriculture and rural society.

On one issue the two different regional perspectives tended to converge. Mexico should be master in its own house and economically independent, they agreed. Mexico's workers, employed largely by foreign-owned enterprises, should also be secure in their rights and free from exploitation. Thus, obtaining the government's backing for labor rights and organization was part and parcel of the nation's struggle for independence. In this respect the constitution was perfectly clear: The nation would own and control its resources and require that foreign enterprises strictly adhere to Mexican law. Workers possessed the right to organize and strike, to earn a minimum wage and work an eight-hour day, to receive a share of profits, and much more. The objective was clear—but so was the obstacle. The United States and Britain both opposed the revolutionary constitution's redefinition of property and labor rights, and pressured the Mexican government not to enforce them.

Carranza's agrarian law of January 6, 1915 (later incorporated into the Constitution of 1917), set the basic guidelines for land reform. Free villages could seek restitution of lands that had been taken from them in the past. Villages with insufficient land could apply for a land grant, while those that had received land but still did not have enough could petition for more. Within these guidelines, however, in the 1920s, the various state laws and governors often controlled the speed and extent of land reform, because the process began with the state agrarian commissions. The more conservative state congresses and governors wrote agrarian laws that protected all but the most gigantic estates and exempted lands devoted to export crops.

In areas of intense Catholicism, priests actively opposed agrarian organization and reform. The more radical state governments pushed the process to the limits of the law and redistributed the greatest part of the land. The landowners resisted land reform by all manner of imaginative methods such as obtaining stop orders from judges, controlling village leadership, dividing properties among family members, and preempting reform by giving local peasants unneeded acreage.

Agrarian reform depended on pressure from below as well as leadership from above. In regions where peasants had organized and fought during the armed revolution, primarily in central Mexico, agrarian activism continued; local politicians had to react or face considerable opposition. On the other hand, where peasants were loyal clients of a hacienda, reform could likely be sidelined. The considerable regional variations of reform during the 1920s are revealed by the 1930 census. Extensive agrarian reform is found in states with peasant activism and radical governors (Morelos, Tlaxcala, Guerrero, Aguascalientes, Hidalgo, Mexico, San Luis Potosí, Puebla, and Yucatán), while there was virtually no reform in the states lacking these conditions (Coahuila, Nuevo León, Oaxaca, Tabasco, and Baja California).

Agrarian reform was not simply a legal, bureaucratic, and political process but a violent struggle that continued in many localities for years on end. In the 1920s and 1930s, rural society remained a battlefield of the Mexican Revolution. Landowners in defense of the "sacred" principle of private property frequently had

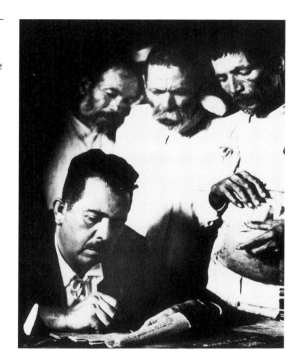

President Lázaro Cárdenas, who held office from 1934 to 1940, became the symbol of the Revolution, especially its program of land reform. This propaganda image implies that Cárdenas is redeeming the Revolution's debt to Zapata. The three agrarians, with bushy moustaches and muslin agrarian clothing, are supposed to be followers of Emiliano Zapata.

agrarian leaders murdered. Haciendas organized armed "white guards" in the name of defense, and peasants involved in agrarian organizations were sometimes hanged from roadside trees as a warning. The peasants fought back, burning haciendas and killing landowners. In several states radical governors armed peasant militias. The opposing forces often met at election time to fight for control of local voting stations.

Presidential leadership was important to land reform, because a national agrarian commission had to approve grants provisionally extended by state commissions. Obregón made sure that the Zapatista movement, a peasant insurgency led by Emiliano Zapata, would not rise again by distributing one-quarter of the land in Morelos to its villages. The agrarian reform process viewed by each presidential administration from 1915 to 1934 demonstrates just how important national leadership was. Interim president de la Huerta, for instance, distributed almost as much land in six months as President Carranza did in five years.

"A new Mexico is being built and the redistribution of land is the foundation stone of [it]," Ramón P. de Negri wrote in 1924. "We are laying it with bleeding hands and in great stress, but we are laying it, and digging it so deep into the hearts of the nation that this work of the revolution will endure forever." By 1934, after nearly two decades of land reform, the state and national governments had redistributed approximately 18 million acres to 800,000 peasants and 4,000 ejidos. When this record is compared to the overall need of the peasantry, however, it reveals how much remained to be done. Only about 10 percent of the cultivated land had been distributed to the new ejido sector. More than 2 million peasants—villagers and resident farmworkers—remained without land. Approximately two-thirds of the great estates and plantations, the latifundios, were undisturbed. This seemingly modest accomplishment nevertheless was radical in the eyes of landowners, as demonstrated by the considerable bloodshed that accompanied it. The once powerful hacienda system was no longer functioning in some regions and localities, and was threatened or in decline nearly everywhere. Where it did take place, successful reform inspired villagers elsewhere to organize and petition. Thus, the dramatic expansion of land reform by Cárdenas after 1934 would not have been possible without the struggles and achievements that had come before.

Although the Sonorans did redistribute land, they placed most of their faith and effort in assisting privately owned agriculture. Calles established the National Agricultural Credit Bank in 1926, most of whose funds were absorbed by large landowners in the north. (In 1926, the largest recipient of credit was the Sonoran chickpea farmer Alvaro Obregón.) The Calles regime was particularly energetic in building dams and irrigation works that almost exclusively benefited large-scale commercial agriculture in northern Mexico. Other public works projects such as road building and railroad repair and extension were also intended to promote commercial agriculture and increase exports.

The economic crisis produced by the Great Depression, combined with Calles's order to terminate agrarian reform and President Ortiz Rubio's slowdown of it, provoked a revitalized agrarian movement in the early 1930s. Pressure from below began to produce modifications at the top. In 1931, the National Agricultural Credit Bank was reorganized to assist cooperative societies made up of ejidos and small farmers. Credit was extended to cooperatives for seed, fertilizer, and farm machinery. In some states, contrary to national policy, agrarian reform was stepped up, but overall the pace of reform in 1933 reached the lowest level since 1922. At this point the agrarian forces went into action.

Several prominent agrarians and leading figures in the official party—Emilio Portes Gil, Graciano Sánchez, Enrique Flores Magón, Saturnino Cedillo, and Marte Gómez among them—came together. With the agrarian leagues of Tamaulipas, San Luis Potosí, Michoacán, Chihuahua, Tlaxcala, and other states, they organized the Mexican Peasant Confederation (CCM) in the spring of 1933. The CCM pushed the presidential candidacy of Cárdenas and intervened in the discussions just beginning for a Six–Year Plan to be presented at the PNR's national convention in December. It also began to organize at the same time a Cardenista "peasant bloc" in Congress.

The effort paid off. Even Calles came to see which way the wind was blowing and declared the need to resume agrarian reform, in 1933. At the party convention Cárdenas was nominated. The Six–Year Plan agreed upon included a call for more land redistribution under greater national supervision. Even before the end of 1933, Congress amended Article 27 of the constitution to remove any judicial interference in the agrarian reform process. In early 1934, President Abelardo Rodríguez created a new, autonomous Agrarian Department, which immediately accelerated land distribution. In March a new agrarian code was approved that revolutionized the reform process. For the first time, resident hacienda workers were given the right to petition for land, while lands producing export crops were brought under the purview of agrarian reform. Reform was simplified and centralized as well, giving the president new powers to push reform. Two years later Congress gave the president the authority to expropriate private property and enterprises.

During 1935, Cárdenas's first year in office, land grants quadrupled. His most dramatic agrarian actions came after the termination of the Maximato in 1936. Starting with the Laguna region in northern Mexico, an area of large cotton estates, the president began to expropriate the richest zones of commercial agriculture in the country. Three hundred communal ejidos, on 600,000 acres were established in the Laguna, benefiting 30,000 peasants. Once they had organized cooperative societies, the new National Ejidal Credit Bank extended financing for hundreds of tractors and other farm implements. Similar actions followed in the henequen plantation zone of Yucatán (August 1937), in the Yaqui Valley in the state of Sonora (December 1937), on the Cusi family haciendas in Michoacán and the sugar plantations of Sinaloa (1938), and in the coffee plantation zone of Chiapas (April 1940).

"We have chosen the ejido," Ramón Beteta, one of Cárdenas's ideologues, stated in 1935, "as the center of our rural economy." During the course of the Cárdenas administration some 50 million acres were distributed to nearly 800,000 peasants. More than 11,000 new ejidos came into being. Land grants were accompanied by the formation of producers' and consumers' cooperatives and the extension of agricultural credit. By 1940, nearly half of Mexico's cultivated land was held by 20,000 ejidos, the number of whose peasant members exceeded 1.6 million. Nine hundred of these were communal ejidos. The great hacienda, an institution that had evolved over four centuries, no longer existed. The basis of a new rural economy was in place, with a new ethic: "We must always keep in mind," wrote Beteta, "that it is people and their happiness and not the production of wealth that matters."

Agrarian reform attacked what was largely a Mexican institution owned by Mexican citizens. On the other hand, the revolutionary constitution's provisions regarding industrial capital and labor for the most part targeted foreign-owned enterprises, which until then in Mexico and elsewhere in Latin America had enjoyed privileged access and treatment. Mexico's mining, petroleum, and textile industries, as well as its roads and public utilities, were all foreign owned and managed, the workers, of course, being Mexican.

The rather weak and precarious government of the Sonoran state postponed real enforcement of the constitution's provisions regarding subsoil rights so as to avoid conflict with the United States. Nationalists throughout the country dearly wished to apply Article 27 retroactively to the U.S. and British petroleum companies and thus transform those oil wells from company property to temporary

This cover of the *Revista de Revistas* illustrates campesinos working their lands. For many Mexicans the Revolution, above all, meant receiving the title to the land they worked. Much of this land was distributed in the form of *ejidos,* that is, land owned by the community but worked individually. The distribution of ejidos was at the core of the Cárdenas revolutionary program.

concessions granted by the state. A 1925 petroleum law threatening such action led the U.S. government first to declare a crisis and talk of intervention, then to negotiate a Mexican retreat.

Empowering workers through unionization and putting the state on the side of labor provided nationalists with a less directly confrontational—and therefore less dangerous—approach to undermining the power of foreign enterprise. Thus, in a country that had had only a small working class and an even smaller labor movement in 1917, the position of labor in politics and the economy would change dramatically. But not immediately. Carranza undermined his alliance with urban labor, an alliance founded solely on political expediency, which prompted CROM to support Obregón's candidacy in 1920. The Sonorans found this new alliance quite useful and backed labor once they were in power.

During the 1920s, unions became free to organize and strike without government opposition or repression for the first time. With government backing and favorable appointments in relevant offices, CROM's membership rapidly expanded. Pro-labor conciliation and arbitration boards helped solidify the position of CROM unions by favorable settlements with employers and let them thereby raise wages. In 1925, CROM obtained the first collective labor contract in Mexican history. By 1926, the zenith of its influence, more than 2,000 individual unions and 75 labor federations (representing two-thirds of Mexican workers) were following Luis Morones and his "official" labor movement. No labor movement in any other country, noted Samuel Gompers, head of the American

Federation of Labor, has been able to strike an equilibrium between capital and labor as quickly as in Mexico.

Nevertheless, CROM never succeeded in unifying the labor movement, despite great effort. Morones's philosophy of class conciliation under state supervision and his policies of support for the government and participation in party politics were contrary to the prominent anarcho-syndicalist tradition of Mexican labor. In 1921, the General Confederation of Labor (CGT) assumed that mantle, having considerable strength among textile and petroleum workers. There were also Catholic and Communist, along with independent, unions scattered across the country. All of these felt CROM's pressure tactics—including violence as well as official disapproval and sometimes repression—and thus paid a price for their independence. In the 1920s, the violence of rival mobsters in America's streets had a Mexican counterpart in union gangsterism.

Despite considerable government support for labor and the CROM, Morones soon came to feel that Obregón had not kept his side of the bargain to earn CROM's election support. Congress neither approved a comprehensive federal labor code nor created an independent ministry of labor. Legislation implementing the guarantees of the constitution was left to the states, which produced a considerable variation. By 1924, Obregón and Morones were publicly trading insults, but the state-labor alliance survived and even thrived. In that year CROM and Morones jumped on the Calles presidential bandwagon and became the greatest supporters of the new president, who returned the favor.

Calles's term, from 1924 to 1928, was CROM's golden age. Morones was appointed minister of industry, commerce, and labor and became the second most powerful man in Mexico. His influence could be seen in the 1925 petroleum law as well as in anticlerical legislation that was passed in 1926. He called in federal troops in 1926–27 to repress a strike by railroad workers, who belonged to the country's largest independent union. Morones made many powerful enemies, sowing the seeds of his own downfall and CROM's. No doubt wanting to succeed Calles himself, he opposed the reelection of Obregón. When the caudillo was assassinated in 1928, most Obregonistas believed Morones to be the intellectual author of the act. For self-preservation Calles distanced himself from Morones.

The period of the Maximato witnessed not only the decline of CROM but a rupture of the alliance between the state and organized labor. CROM and its affiliated political party, the Mexican Labor Party (PLM), did not join the new official revolutionary party, the PNR. President Portes Gil, a noted enemy of CROM, shifted government's favor to the independent unions. Meanwhile, the depression wiped out the wage gains of the 1920s and increased unemployment. It was in this unpropitious period that Congress finally passed a comprehensive labor code regulating Article 123 of the constitution.

Article 123 provides for the balancing of labor and business rights and responsibilities, and the federal labor law of 1931 was faithful to its provisions. In nearly 700 specific articles this law superseded all state labor laws. It confirmed

After serving as president from 1924 to 1928, Plutarco Elías Calles remained the most powerful man in Mexico. He was eventually forced into exile in the United States in 1936, but until then he was the the *Jefe Máximo* (Maximum Leader), overshadowing the men in the presidential chair.

the constitutional principles of compulsory trade unionism, collective bargaining, the right to strike, and the prohibition of child labor. It also provided for accident compensation, the minimum wage, and much more. It created a central board of conciliation and arbitration and 15 regional federal boards to settle disputes between employers and laborers. The Department of Labor was made an independent agency two years later.

Although the 1931 law proved to be one of the most advanced labor codes in the world, it was passed against the wishes of the labor movement, as well as Mexico's business establishment. For one thing, the federal law was not as favorable to labor as were many state laws. It also confirmed the 1920s trend of giving the national government tremendous power over unions, strikes, and settlements. Because the governments of the Maximato period were more conservative, so were its settlements. The manager of an important U.S. company in Mexico City summed up the problem for labor in 1932: "We don't worry much about the boards of conciliation and arbitration, as long as we stand with the government." (There were, however, exceptions. When workers were fired without compensation by the British-owned Tolteca Cement Company in 1931, the state of Hidalgo expropriated the factory and compensated the company. A few years later ownership was transferred to a workers' cooperative.)

In general, however, labor lost ground during the Maximato. As CROM declined and new rivals appeared, the movement fragmented further. A new labor central governing body emerged in 1933, the General Confederation of Workers and Peasants of Mexico (CGOCM), under the leadership of a former CROM official and Marxist intellectual, Vicente Lombardo Toledano. The new labor movement that was evolving in the 1930s was, with only a few exceptions, more combative and politically independent. Any renewed alliance between the state and labor appeared unlikely, however, because neither CROM, the CGT, nor the CGOCM supported the candidacy of Cárdenas in 1934.

Conditions favoring a new alliance were nonetheless developing. The PNR's Six–Year Plan, employing the language of class conflict, called for greater state intervention and national control of the economy. When Cárdenas took office he gave labor free rein, after which a wave of officially approved strikes hit the foreign-owned basic industries. From 15 strikes in 1933 the number increased to 202 in 1934 and to more than 600 by 1935. It was this "unnecessary agitation" and "marathon of radicalism," as Jefe Máximo Calles phrased it, that led him to challenge Cárdenas in mid–1935.

At this point the electricians' union began to organize a united labor front in support of the government. By February 1936, the participating unions, which now included Lombardo Toledano's CGOCM and numerous independent as well as Communist unions, created the Confederation of Mexican Workers (CTM). Under Lombardo Toledano's leadership, the CTM endorsed the policies of the Cárdenas government and soon began to participate with the PNR in electoral politics. The government for its part favored the CTM with important appointments, subsidies, and support for wage demands. A new alliance was forged.

With a nearly united labor movement and a supportive government, labor activism began to show real gains after 1936. Wages rose as new contracts were signed and the government implemented the constitutional guarantee of a mandatory Sunday wage. Strikes became the wedge for Cárdenas to undermine foreign economic power. A general strike of farmworkers and employer obstinacy in the Laguna region gave him an opportunity to expropriate the lands of the three large foreign companies dominating the region. The same thing took place later in the U.S.-dominated Mexicali Valley of Baja California. Then labor problems led to the nationalization of the railroads in 1937 and, nearly a year after that, the establishment of worker management. In other cases around the country, whether in sugar mills, mines, or factories, the government instituted worker control through cooperatives.

The most momentous labor dispute occurred in 1938 in the petroleum industry. Repeated strikes in that sector put the issue in the hands of a local federal arbitration board, which ruled in favor of a significant raise in wages and improved social benefits. But the oil companies refused to pay the increased wages and appealed to the Federal Conciliation and Arbitration Board. When that board ruled in favor of the workers and the companies still balked, Cárdenas acted. The president announced to the nation on March 18, 1938, the expropriation of the single most powerful and valuable foreign sector in Mexico. The oil properties were turned over to worker control. At a mass rally in Mexico City placards hailed "the economic independence of Mexico." This moment was, unquestionably, the high point of the Mexican Revolution.

"And so Mexico is giving the world its great lesson!" a popular ballad about the expropriation proclaimed. "History is being redeemed through our Revolution!" By the late 1930s, Mexico's "great lesson" included not only the reappropriation of the nation's land and resources but the realization of a new kind of economy, "a more humane and just system of economic relations," as Ramón Beteta put it, "by means of the intelligent intervention of a government with working-class interests."

To consolidate his reforms and permanently empower the peasants and workers, Cárdenas reorganized the PNR. He transformed Calles's party of regional factions and ideological currents into an organization that fully incorporated the populist masses. The Confederation of Mexican Workers would form the foundation of the labor sector. To incorporate the peasants into this movement, Cárdenas established the National Peasant Confederation (CNC) out of the older CCM. Party membership was collective: All members of affiliated ejidos and unions automatically became members of the new official party. In addition to its labor and peasant sectors, the party included the military and a popular unit composed largely of state employees. The 1938 party convention formalized these changes and decided upon a new name: the Party of the Mexican Revolution (PRM). With 4 million members the PRM was a genuine mass party.

In 1938, the political nation began to look toward the 1940 election. The power of lame-duck president Cárdenas was slowly dissolving. He did not help himself by declaring that he would not intervene in the electoral process. His opponents started to organize, politics took center stage, and the reform momentum slowed. By the late 1930s, Mexicans realized that the nation was coming to a critical juncture.

Cardenismo revived the Revolution and, in so doing, activated its enemies. To conservative leader and former revolutionary intellectual Manuel Gómez Morín, "the situation in Mexico by 1938 had become intolerable." It was also intolerable to a growing right wing supported by many fervent Catholics and powerful business interests. In 1937, the National Sinarquista Union (UNS), a mass-based Catholic movement and an offshoot of the Cristero rebellion that admired Spanish fascism, was created to reverse the Mexican Revolution. Two years later, more-moderate Catholic activists with support from big business formed the National Action Party (PAN) under the leadership of Gómez Morín. The right wing also included an anti-Semitic fascist movement known as the Anti-Communist Revolutionary Party, which was led by a former PNR chief and one of the country's most decorated generals. There were also the Mexican Falange, Gold Shirts, Brown Shirts, and "fifth column" German-dominated Mexican National Socialist Party. José Vasconcelos, still one of Mexico's best-known intellectuals, wanted Mexico to get in step with the "direction of history," which he believed was indicated by Germany's Adolf Hitler.

In the late 1930s, the world witnessed a revolution that had been destroyed by a mobilized right. The Spanish Civil War of 1936–39 had been a confrontation between social and cultural revolution on the one side and uncompromising counterrevolution supported by the Spanish Catholic church and Europe's fascist dictatorships on the other. The revolution was defeated by a right-wing coalition of monarchists, militarists, and fascists named the Spanish Traditionalist Falange, led by General Francisco Franco. Cárdenas had given material support to the revolutionary republic. When it was defeated, he welcomed to Mexico thousands of Spanish refugees. The triumph of Franco's nationalists was, however, applauded in conservative Mexican circles and even viewed there as a precursor to what was seen as the inevitable defeat of Cárdenas. If ever there was an example of extreme ideological polarization and the violence it can generate, the Spanish Civil War was it, and Cárdenas knew that.

In the last two years of his term, during the slow death of the Spanish republic, Cárdenas moderated his course. The pace of land reform slowed. His administration created the Office of Small Property to protect small landowners. In the wake of the March 1938 petroleum expropriation Cárdenas asked labor to reduce strike activity in order not to further disrupt production. Militant anticlericalism came to an end and socialist education was put on hold, although it remained official policy. Moderation did not mean abandonment of the Revolution, though. Cárdenas believed that the PRM would continue the course of reform favoring peasants and workers. He left in place, he would write, "a revolutionary instrument," a powerful one indeed, "with which Mexico could continue its liberation."

True to his word, in the 1940 race President Cárdenas stayed out of electoral politics. Center-right politicians in the PRM organized the candidacy of Cárdenas's defense minister, General Manuel Avila Camacho, and expertly gained the support of the CTM and the CNC. The party thus bypassed the genuine Cardenista candidate, the radical Francisco Múgica, and backed the candidate of moderation, conciliation, and national unity. Avila Camacho campaigned on a promise "to consolidate the gains of the Cárdenas regime."

General Juan Andreu Almazán, another military man who represented, as best he could, the diverse interests of the conservative opposition to Cárdenas, opposed the official party candidate. His Revolutionary Party of National Unification received the support of Catholics, small landowners, the urban middle class, peasants unhappy with official agrarianism, and more than a few labor unions and workers. Because of Almazán's substantial popularity with peasants and workers, the PRM conducted an intense—and dirty—campaign. There were violent clashes between followers of the two candidates that continued even on election day in July 1940. Cárdenas never campaigned for Avila Camacho. He wanted the election to be free and democratic, but of course every department head, governor, and local official was behind the formal candidate. The revolutionary family would not give up power. Avila Camacho was declared the winner by an overwhelming majority, although it is possible that Almazán actually won more votes.

Manuel Ávila Camacho was often called the Unknown Soldier because so little was know about him. He was overshadowed by his flamboyant, playboy brother, General Maximino Ávila Camacho, who ran the state of Puebla. Nevertheless, President Cárdenas tapped Manuel as the official revolutionary party candidate to succeed him. The presidential campaign was bitterly fought between Ávila Camacho and conservative General Juan Almazán. Widespread voter fraud marred the election won by Ávila Camacho.

The Avila Camacho government (1940–46), though publicly committed to consolidating the gains of the Cárdenas regime, in fact guided Mexico in a different direction. "The Gentleman President," so called because he was courteous and well dressed, in the name of national unity and class conciliation, ended "rational education" and the socialist schools where it was practiced, looked the other way as church schools multiplied, and shifted school construction to the cities. In 1943, however, Jaime Torres Bodet took over as education minister and embarked upon a new literacy campaign that included bilingual education in Indian learning centers, funding for state instruction centers, and new cultural missions to remote villages. By 1946, the nation's commitment to the principle of education for all Mexicans was undisputed.

On the other hand, the nation's commitment to landless peasants wavered. By 1943, the distribution of land was reduced by 50 percent; by 1945, it was reduced by more than 90 percent, compared with Cárdenas's last year in office. The collective ejidos were starved of necessary financing, and wherever possible, the land was divided into individual parcels. Public policy, investment needs, and changing technology all favored private farms and commercial agriculture.

In 1943, the Rockefeller Foundation and the Mexican Ministry of Agriculture established the Mexican Agricultural Project, which promoted hybrid grains and modern technology. The resulting "Green Revolution" dramatically favored commercial farmers (whose wheat yields, in time, became the highest in Latin America), but the project essentially bypassed Mexico's peasant farmers (whose average corn yields remained the lowest).

The Cardenista vision of a rural Mexico of prosperous ejidos was replaced by a new government policy favoring industrialization. The entry of the United States into World War II in late 1941, followed by Mexico's entry in 1942, greatly stimulated Mexican industry and expanded the industrial labor force. Lombardo Toledano and other labor leaders who were behind the push for industry suspended strike activity during the war. Mexico's industrialists organized powerful business associations to represent their interests and shape official economic policy. The U.S. government helped with an Export-Import Bank loan to develop a steel- and tinplate rolling mill. Mexico's industrial sector grew on average 10 percent a year from 1940 to 1945.

Mexico's large industrial unions had watched inflation eat up wages during the war and with the coming of peace wanted a fair share of the national income. Government and business, on the other hand, feared that strikes and higher wages would slow capital accumulation, discourage foreign investment, and thus undermine industrialization. The CTM, after 1941 in the hands of Fidel Velázquez and other fervent collaborationists (Lombardo Toledano had been pushed aside), was willing to go along with government priorities. Its change of motto in 1947, from "For a society without classes" to "For the emancipation of Mexico," signaled this tendency. The CTM emerged from the war weaker and more dependent on government. It would fall to Avila Camacho's successor, President Miguel Alemán (1946–52), to discipline the labor movement, strengthen the CTM, and keep wages low. As he told a CTM conference in 1947, Mexico needed "a policy of order and progress."

Cárdenas's "revolutionary instrument," the PRM, failed to stop this right turn. Avila Camacho removed the military sector from the PRM in 1941 and strengthened the popular sector in 1943, creating in the National Confederation of Popular Organizations a powerful conservative counterweight to the labor and peasant sectors. The dissolution of the PRM in early 1946 and its reconstitution as the Party of the Institutional Revolution (PRI) was accompanied by "reforms" that increased the authority of the top leadership. Cárdenas's "revolutionary instrument" was by these steps transformed and downgraded into the electoral apparatus of the state.

At the end of Avila Camacho's term in late 1946, the noted economist Daniel Cosío Villegas wrote an article called "The Crisis of Mexico," published the following year in Mexico's most prestigious intellectual review, announcing the "death" of the Mexican Revolution. Cosío Villegas maintained in it that the great principles of the Revolution had been corrupted or abandoned. In *Mexico: The Struggle for Peace and Bread*, published in Spanish translation four years later, the U.S. historian Frank Tannenbaum agreed. This history of the Revolution criticized Alemán's policy of industrialization, because it benefited a few narrow groups at the expense of most Mexicans. Many Mexicans were outraged by this foreigner's "attack" on their Revolution, but Cosío Villegas defended Tannenbaum and his conclusions.

Despite the apparent reconciliation in this *abrazo* (embrace) between Vincente Lombardo Toledano (left), the leader of the Socialist Party, and Fidel Velásquez, new leader of the Confederation of Mexican Workers (CTM), after their bitter struggle for leadership of the labor movement, the two remained deeply opposed to each other. Lombardo Toledano became increasingly radical as Velásquez became increasingly entrenched in the official bureaucracy, where he dominated the official labor movement for the next fifty years.

As the decades passed, Cosío Villegas and Tannenbaum were in fact shown to be right. The "death" of the Revolution did not mean the undoing of mass politics, the closure of rural schools, the return of the hacienda system, or the abolition of the labor unions. It meant rather the abandonment of a humane vision of society that emphasized "people and their happiness and not the production of wealth" (Ramón Beteta). This vision had decried the "evils of the machine age" and celebrated the agrarian ideal of the prosperous peasant working his own land. It included an expectation that, in time, people would migrate from the city to the countryside. This vision condemned, in a PNR manifesto, "those forms of concentration of capital" that were destructive to the common good. It promised that "if anything like prosperity should ever come to Mexico it should be based on a growing acquisitive power of the workers" (Ramón Beteta). The abandonment of this vision required corrupting and weakening the institutions that had begun to create this new and better society.

Beginning in the 1940s, a different Mexico was envisioned—and created. The ejidos became increasingly marginal in national agriculture, and growing rural poverty pushed the peasants into shantytowns. A relatively small number of business groups came to own and control industry, commerce, communications, and finance. An increasing portion of the national economy was owned by foreign companies and investors, mainly with U.S. capital. Private farmlands became concentrated in the hands of a few landowners and agricultural companies. Wages for most workers lagged behind inflation. From the 1940s to the present, decade by decade, as the publication of each succeeding census demonstrated, income inequality increased, with the rich becoming richer and the poor poorer.

Revolution comes about when an alternative version of society is envisioned and destructive violence and constructive action are taken to create it. In the 1910s, Mexican revolutionaries fought for a better Mexico. During the 1920s and 1930s, they implemented significant reforms, which began to rebuild the nation. The Revolution was, therefore, revolutionary. This was made even clearer by the right turn made in the 1940s. But official Mexico's continued attachment to revolutionary rhetoric and symbols after 1940 could not disguise the fact that the Revolution had ended. It was replaced, as one critic noted, by "old, senseless words."

16

Mexico and the Outside World

FRIEDRICH E. SCHULER

All Mexican governments after the end of the 19th–century French occupation and Maximilian's ill-conceived liberal monarchy had tried to bring about national economic development through foreign involvement. This meant enduring the consequences that came with the importing of foreign know-how, technology, and investment. Foreign pressures came in the form of arrogant, demanding French creditors, political pressures from the U.S. State Department and manipulations by recently knighted British oil barons. Mexican governmental planners also dealt with merchants and financiers from the recently unified Germany, which they esteemed as less imperialistic than their counterparts in London and Paris. However, Mexican planners also discussed rumors and stories arriving from Venezuela and the Caribbean, where German gunboat incidents suggested that the Germans, too, continued to nurture the hope of a Latin American sphere of influence into the new 20th century. Privately, high-level officials in the Porfirio Díaz administration admitted a certain sympathy for such aggressive foreign impulses. After all, for decades Mexicans had affirmed a distinct Mexican sphere of influence over Guatemala and other smaller Central American countries. It seemed that hegemonic designs were not limited to Europe or the United States and were as much fueled by the simple human impulse of wanting control as they were part of white Western "civilization" politics.

Foreign cultural influences shaped Mexican attitudes as much as capitalistic economic constraints and diplomatic pressures from London, Paris, or Washington. Mexico's Catholic church, dominated as it was by Spanish clergy, preached its mantra of a revival of European piety based on the iron dogmas of the Counter-Reformation. With it came an insistence on the preservation of Spanish social, racial, and gender hierarchies as well as the unfounded, but inspiring and romantic, ideals of Hispanidad; that is, that groups of Spanish speakers form an almost biologically separate ethnic group in the world. Mexico was included in 19th–century global efforts by the Catholic Church to deter believers from falling under the influence of new and attractive ideologies such as the natural sciences and Marxism. Indirectly, this papal support for a new, more radical Catholic labor policy was also addressing the inhumane working conditions of industrial workers in cities such as Puebla and Monterrey.

In the few large urban centers, upper-class Mexicans continued efforts to impose one national culture based on European mores on the rest of Mexico. Sometimes this meant promoting Italian opera and imitating Parisian dress codes. At other times it appeared in the form of promoting new behavioral norms at small industrial shops and, on occasion, as a frontal attack against Catholic holidays by less pious but more entrepreneurial modernizers. The Porfirian government backed this battle for the hearts and minds of Mexico's mestizos with architecture competitions for federal buildings and designs for historical monuments and stamps. Even the national archaeology and international fairs were employed for this purpose. The elites expected that these new cultural rituals and their accompanying blatant government symbolism would transform Mexico from a composite of many diverse geographical areas, dominated by Mexico City, into one nation that had left its Native American legacy behind and functioned increasingly according to European positivist standards.

Mexican rural folk stubbornly undermined these high-class flirtations with foreign ideas by creatively disregarding them culturally, as well as by staging the occasional riot. The majority of the rural population did not want to become modern, rejected the emotional adjustments that came with the industrial lifestyle, and laughed at French aesthetic ideals. All the tensions created by the contradictions of the last 34 years of Porfirian developmental policies connected more and more Mexicans through an increasing number of frustrating experiences. By 1910, Mexicans from all classes were voicing the idea that the government and its president had to change.

Most contemporary foreign observers did not understand the profound depth of Mexico's contradictions. Whatever political tensions and accompanying rebellions occurred during the electoral game in 1910–11 between Porfirio Díaz, Bernardo Reyes, and Francisco Madero, foreign observers interpreted them as something that could be expected in a cultural and political setting they considered deeply "uncivilized." They noticed the more than usual number of local rebellions in the north, Zapatista fights against sugar plantation owners in Morelos, and the suppression of urban revolutionary conspiratory cells in Mexican cities. But they consoled themselves with the cliché that these, too, were just another "Latin American uprising." Owners and managers of foreign companies saw these challenges to Porfirio Díaz first as an opportunity to expand their economic turf. Now, it was argued, disgruntled and disunited Mexican elites might be willing to make new concessions to foreign economic interests and perhaps reduce the influence of rivals. For example, U.S. oil interests reinforced Madero's reservations about British oil. By coincidence, this sentiment translated into a rise in German financial influence within the strengthening Madero camp. Not surprisingly, British and French companies backed the status quo in Mexico City, hoping that the iron fists of Porfirian soldiers and rural militias would eventually overturn U.S. and German gains.

In contrast, the leaders of Mexico's regional revolutions were much more realistic about their links with foreign interests. For Pancho Villa, access to the U.S. hinterland guaranteed the flow of American weapons to his and other Chihuahuan rebels. For Francisco Madero, temporary exile in San Antonio, Texas, provided safety and the chance to reorient his previously reformist urban political challenge to Porfirio Díaz toward an alliance with the rebels in Chihuahua. The Zapatistas in Morelos distinguished themselves through their very lack of foreign support and therefore felt the full brunt of governmental repression in an emerging race war in Morelos. Ironically, in Yucatán the profitable links with markets in the United States and Europe cemented the social and political status quo, therefore avoiding the outbreak of sustainable revolutionary movements.

Mexican rebels appreciated how foreign money, weapons, or access to a logistical hinterland could be as important as ideology and social bonds if their rebellions were to last longer than a few days and stand a chance against the government in Mexico City. For the counterrevolutionaries in Mexico City, control over the ports in the Gulf of Mexico and continued tax income from the British petroleum industry provided sufficient money to initiate a hastened modernization and military deployment.

The political collapse of the Porfiriato in 1911 and the reluctance of Mexican revolutionaries in all regions to trade in their weapons or join the federal army of Madero's newly created government suggested to domestic and foreign observers that something radically different was emerging in Mexico. It was clear that these developments were more than an average rebellion or a fight between national rivals that could usefully be exploited by foreign business interests. Foreign interests and domestic elites alike agreed that the continuously expanding power of the lower classes and their increasingly unchanneled political activity needed to be stopped.

Suggestions for solutions to "the problem" differed sharply from camp to camp. European governments and company representatives favored straightforward violent repression and, unsurprisingly, backed the person they perceived to be the neo-Porfirian counterrevolutionary, Victoriano Huerta against the rebels of the north and in Morelos. In the middle stood U.S. ambassador Henry Lane Wilson, who mostly followed his own objectives and disregarded the directives of the newly elected Woodrow Wilson White House. Still, he played a critical part in enabling General Huerta to realize a coup against Madero, during which the Mexican president and his vice president were assassinated.

In Washington, D.C., President Wilson began to see Mexican developments as an exemplar for his idealistic, yet naive, efforts to turn Latin America into another part of the Americas governed by democracy. After several months of failed efforts to gain control over Huerta or at least to reach a modus vivendi with him, President Wilson turned into a determined opponent of Huerta's emerging military dictatorship. Left with few alternatives, Wilson moved his backing to the revolutionary coalition of the Constitutionalists in the north. Wilson's universalistic idealism had elevated the conflict into a regional Latin American issue.

In 1914, the outbreak of World War I in Europe and the accompanying establishment of the British economic blockade of the Atlantic Ocean again reframed the international context of the Mexican Revolution. For Europeans, Mexico's oil reserves and its proximity to the United States suggested a manipulation of the revolutionary factions as an indirect tool to deprive their enemies of valuable strategic resources and manpower for future battles. For example, German war planners theorized how a possible U.S.-Mexican war might tie up U.S. troops in Mexico and thus guarantee the continuation of U.S. neutrality in World War I. Also, sabotage in the Mexican oil fields could deprive the British navy of an important source of fuel for its defense against Germany. In turn, British war planners debated how they could protect British oil production in Mexico against German attacks without inviting rival U.S. companies to help. For the British navy a critical issue was how to maintain control over Atlantic shipping routes so that it would not be deprived of a critical fuel source.

There was also the issue of whether and how to drag the United States out of neutrality and into the war on the Allied side. Having the United States on the side of the Allies would certainly tip the strategic balance against Germany within months and keep the Germans from rising to the status of world power. U.S. planners watched with great concern the activities of German and other European agents in the various Mexican revolutionary camps. For different reasons the continuation of the Mexican Revolution was in the interest of all the major foreign powers. By then, the domestic Mexican conflict over national development had become a bilateral U.S.-Mexican issue, a Latin American concern, and an increasingly important sideshow for European and U.S. military strategists.

The Mexican rebels, too, recognized their growing importance and, in turn, tried to sell their involvement as expensively as possible. Short-term military gains began to replace national long-term political plans. For the Constitutionalists the internationalization of the Revolution offered critical foreign allies for their fight against the Huerta dictatorship in Mexico City. When President Wilson ordered a limited intervention by U.S. troops in 1914 and landed in Veracruz, President Victoriano Huerta suffered a decisive humiliation. Eventually, the combined pressure of domestic revolution and U.S. opposition forced him to accept a negotiated end to his attempt to turn back the political clock in Mexico. The internationally sensitive situation demanded that President Wilson engage in political negotiations with every major revolutionary faction to determine Huerta's successor. In the end, the expanding world war and the links of its European players with revolutionary factions made it impossible for U.S. planners to pick a Mexican president. Instead, Argentina, Brazil, and Chile acted as mediators in the ensuing competition over the presidency. The unexpected winner was the nationalist politico Venustiano Carranza, certainly not a comfortable candidate for Wilson. After Carranza's rise to the presidency the nature of the Revolution changed into a civil war between members of the previously united anti-Huerta revolutionary coalition. In addition, Mexican regions that had not participated in the Revolution were occupied by the Carrancistas and forced to bring their regional politics and economics in line with the changes in Mexico City.

The intensification of fighting in Mexico offered only more options for renewed behind-the-scenes European and U.S. manipulations. Pancho Villa felt so betrayed by President Wilson's reluctant but expanding support for the Pax Carranza in Mexico that the Chihuahuan decided to violate U.S. territorial sovereignty and attack the small U.S. border town of Columbus, New Mexico, on March 9, 1916. Villa hoped both to bring about a shift of popular nationalist support away from Carranza and to provoke the United States into invading Mexico. Immediately, a U.S.-Mexican war would demonstrate the limits of Carranza's power vis-à-vis the United States. Villa expected that Carranza's predicted helplessness could bring about a revival of Villa's rebellion in the north. Then Villa would fight simultaneously against Carranza and the United States, hoping to reenter the battle for the presidency. Within this provocative scheme rumors of secret German involvement abounded.

Villa's action failed to provoke a full-fledged U.S.-Mexican military confrontation. Yet, angry U.S. popular opinion demanded from President Wilson some public punitive action against Villa's violation of U.S. territory and the murder of U.S. citizens. Wilson chose to placate popular anti-Mexican sentiment by sending General John J. Pershing and 10,000 soldiers on a punitive expedition into Chihuahua with the task of capturing Pancho Villa. During the following months, Villa eluded U.S. pursuers in the impenetrable mountains of Chihuahua. More important, Carranza turned the crisis in his favor. An unexpectedly aggressive diplomacy and a confrontational press policy, as well as determined Mexican soldiers at the Carrizal garrison, brought about the withdrawal of U.S. forces. General Pershing's failure was somewhat hidden by a prolonged encampment on the Mexican side of the U.S. border, followed by an impressive but unjustified triumphal return to U.S. territory. The relationship between Carranza and Wilson had sustained lasting damage. Carranza recognized that in the years to come he could not expect any U.S. financial or political help for the reconstruction of his nation. Thus, ironically only Germany, if it had won the war, could have been a possible friend to Carranza's government.

The emergence in 1916 of unrestricted naval warfare between Germany, Britain, and the United States only confirmed the continuing international significance of the Mexican conflict for the European great powers. Germans pondered how to entangle U.S. resources in the Americas so that they could not be deployed on European battlefields. One option under consideration was the creation of a German-Mexican military alliance that would turn Mexico into enemy territory for the United States. Germany tried to entice Carranza into considering the offer seriously by suggesting the return of Mexican territory lost to the United States during the mid–19th–century U.S.-Mexican war after a victorious conclusion of World War I. When the discussion of the offer between German minister to Mexico Arthur Zimmerman and German foreign minister Heinrich von Eckardt was intercepted by British intelligence forces, luck provided the Allied powers with a propaganda weapon that would be remembered throughout the 20th century. The announcement of the so-called Zimmerman Telegram reinforced deep suspicions among Washington policy makers about Carranza's loyalties and the possible motives behind his nationalism. Not surprisingly, Carranza's insistence on Mexican neutrality during the war was interpreted in the U.S. Congress as nonbelligerency on behalf of Germany. More damaging for Mexico was the subsequent U.S. refusal to provide relief or help for Carranza's reconstruction of civil war-torn Mexico.

Carranza did not confuse German involvement with genuine interest in Mexico. He had no illusions that the Germans saw in Mexico anything more than the back door to the United States, a potential strategic hinterland and an ideal staging ground for secret attacks that exploited Mexico's neutrality during the war. Carranza, however, could not simply reject German approaches. Any openly negative attitude toward Germany might encourage German agents to abandon their careful consideration of Mexican sensitivities and initiate sabotage activities in the oil fields to damage Allied naval warfare capabilities. Most likely, sabotage in the petroleum fields would trigger a U.S. intervention that would reduce Mexico to a mere battlefield for Allied-German military campaigns. For the remainder of World War I, German-Mexican relations remained officially friendly and engaged. At the same time, in Washington, U.S. observers continued to characterize any German-Mexican interaction as a national security issue and considered the possibility of confronting German forces inside Mexico before their agents could reach U.S. soil. Only the German defeat in 1919 freed Mexico and Carranza from this very dangerous geostrategic dilemma.

In retrospect, Carranza deserves to be recognized as Mexico's greatest foreign policy maker of the 20th century. Under the most difficult revolutionary circumstances he succeeded in keeping his country and its citizens out of direct military involvement with both the German and the Allied sides during World War I. His skillful diplomacy prevented a devastating U.S.-Mexican war or a longer U.S. military presence on Mexican soil. Meanwhile, he succeeded in assuring Germans of enough Mexican interest in future cooperation to avoid sabotage against the British and U.S. petroleum industries in Mexico. He also isolated Pancho Villa in Chihuahua, as well as his German manipulators, in addition to confronting U.S. president Wilson vigorously through diplomacy, propaganda, and a very symbolic display of Mexican military courage. In the midst of this explosive context, he and representatives of other revolutionary factions passed the Constitution of 1917, which created the legal foundation for subsequent presidents to achieve true Mexican sovereignty over national territory and domestic natural resources.

Finally, Carranza developed a set of principles—later called the Carranza Doctrine—that guided Mexican foreign relations through several decades of the 20th century. Its most important points were the rejection of the Monroe Doctrine; a demand for foreign respect in regard to Mexico's economic and territorial sovereignty; an insistence that all foreign powers accept the concept of nonintervention in Latin America; and, finally, an emphasis on the importance of negotiating alliances with European and Latin American countries that could counterbalance Mexico's geographic fate of bordering on the United States. Under the most difficult domestic and international circumstances Carranza had broken with Porfirian laissez-faire and established a distinct nationalistic Mexican centrist postrevolutionary agenda that sought domestic solutions to the international challenges of expanding capitalism and century-old great-power rivalries in Europe.

Carranza's dogmatic insistence on Mexican self-definition turned out to be timely. Following World War I, the United States replaced Britain as the most important economic and political power in Latin America. And the newly founded League of Nations recognized the validity of the Monroe Doctrine in Latin America, refusing to aid Latin American countries against short-sighted and amateurish U.S. policies of big-stick and dollar diplomacy and big stick during the Republican presidencies of the 1920s.

By 1921, Pancho Villa's retirement from revolution, the assassinations of Zapata and Carranza, and Wilson's retirement from the White House provided a new opportunity for Mexican and U.S. representatives to forge a closer, more constructive relationship. And yet the next four years remained as difficult for the emerging Mexican postrevolutionary state as the previous years had been. A sharp break with Wilsonian universalism and moralistic determinism by newly elected Republican president Warren Harding brought relief from the naive perception that democracy could be decreed overnight in postrevolutionary Mexico. Other possible benefits from the United States' turn toward isolationism, however, did not materialize. U.S. racial discrimination against Mexicans continued and even intensified within the context of the xenophobic immigration debates of the 1920s. The Republican political and economic laissez-faire stance only made U.S.-Mexican bilateral relations more difficult. Now that the U.S. government was only one among many laissez-faire political interests in Washington, U.S. contacts with Mexico diversified to the point of destructive chaos. A cacophony of voices claiming to represent the one authentic U.S. position demanded from the new Alvaro Obregón administration satisfaction of their particular interest, whether they were the U.S. State Department; the chauvinistic and militantly anti-Mexican secretary of the interior, Senator Albert B. Fall; the U.S. Department of Commerce, the U.S. Army and Navy; the U.S. Treasury; the White House, U.S. Protestant groups; the U.S. Catholic church; nondenominational U.S. religious groups; U.S. multinational companies; U.S. private banks (in particular J. P. Morgan & Co.); the U.S. mining industry; U.S. state chambers of commerce; small and midsize U.S. businesses; U.S. newspaper organizations; or U.S. mayors from U.S.-Mexican border towns. How could the postrevolutionary Mexican state identify the seat of power in the United States and lobby for diplomatic recognition under these circumstances? The situation was made even more difficult because the power of the Sonoran dynasty in Mexico City was by no means secure, thus making it desirable to continue the World War I tactic of forming business alliances with potentially influential revolutionary groups in Mexico, again creating numerous opportunities for U.S. manipulators to challenge and undermine the Obregón presidency.

For several years, Senator Albert B. Fall managed to dominate official U.S. foreign policy emanating from the Department of Interior until he was disgraced by being convicted of bribery in the Teapot Dome oil scandal of 1923. Backed by U.S. and British oil companies, Fall tried to force Obregón to accept an intolerable diplomatic quid pro quo: U.S. diplomatic recognition of Mexico in exchange for the repeal of Article 27 of the Constitution of 1917, which gave ownership over subsoil rights to the state. U.S. and European banking circles also appreciated Mexico's difficult financial situation during this period and hoped that the ongoing refusal of diplomatic recognition would bring about a more favorable settlement of Mexico's foreign debt, which had been acquired during the Porfiriato and the Revolution. At the same time, Fall and the multinationals encountered vehement opposition from U.S. small and midsize companies, chambers of commerce, and mayors of the U.S.-border region. All of them favored a rapid recognition of Mexico to bring about a revival of the Mexican economy, which they hoped would increase wholesale and retail business with Mexico. The Department of Commerce under Herbert Hoover also argued for quick diplomatic recognition.

The Obregón administration reacted with a three-pronged foreign policy approach. Gaining U.S. diplomatic recognition and debt settlement was a priority, because that would be followed by European diplomatic recognition and therefore Mexico's official readmission to the bodies of international politics. This meant resisting diplomatic pressure tactics, accepting painful compromises on minor issues, and being open to de facto, temporary concessions while remaining determined to insist, in principle, on Mexico's national rights as spelled out in the Constitution of 1917. Within the Americas, Obregón tried to influence the development of the Pan American Union to avoid the creation of an exclusive institution through which the United States could pass down its preferred political stances toward Latin America. As long as the European-based League of Nations respected the Monroe Doctrine it made no sense to apply for membership in this global institution.

Finally, in the Central American region Mexico's tradition of dominance resurfaced. This time Mexico supported individuals and social movements that could bring about a second successful Latin American social revolution, thereby ending Mexico's political isolation among the conservative Latin American elite. In sum, long-term approaches, concentrating on creating international

Albert B. Fall, Secretary of the Interior under President Warren G. Harding, for years was the mouthpiece of United States business interests—especially oil interests—in Mexico. He was discredited for his role in the Teapot Dome scandal in the United States, which removed him as an obstacle to reasonable relations between the two nations.

legitimacy for the new postrevolutionary state were beginning to replace the short-term foreign relations typical of the revolutionary period and World War I. Nevertheless, the diplomats of the new Mexican revolutionary state accepted the century-old customs and rules of the Western diplomatic game, unlike their revolutionary cousins in the Soviet Union.

Between 1910 and 1917, the fluid nature of revolution had made it impossible to conduct one Mexican foreign policy out of one location. The pressures of civil war, with its shifting alliances and constantly changing linkages with foreign manipulators, had factionalized foreign relations. Links with other nations had had to run through the field headquarters of various rebel groups as well as a disoriented Foreign Ministry in Mexico City. Personal emissaries of Villa, Zapata, Huerta, Carranza, and Obregón had conducted separate private missions for the particular interests of their leaders. After 1920, Obregón faced a different context. The exile of Huerta, the assassinations of Zapata and Carranza, and Pancho Villa's withdrawal to Chihuahua to take up ranching allowed the reinstitutionalization of diplomacy in one central location. Obregón charged his close aide Eduardo Pani with the administrative rebuilding of the Foreign Ministry in Mexico City. Pani secured a permanent budget for the ministry and systematically recruited well-educated members of the small urban middle class with generous pensions. He standardized professional expectations, issued rules for civil service members, and spelled out the responsibilities of lower-ranking diplomatic personnel. This also included a reduction of favoritism on that level. Higher-level Mexican ambassadors continued to be mostly political appointees who served

Mexico abroad any way their personal style motivated them. Next, Pani purchased embassy buildings in Washington, Hamburg, Berlin, Geneva, London, and Paris to represent revolutionary Mexico in First World style.

Obregón's multilevel approach produced some early successes. Mexico's diplomats forged important linkages with U.S.-business groups and others along the U.S.-Mexican border. Also, U.S. intellectuals and artists supported Obregón, voicing alternatives to dollar diplomacy and big-stick approaches. In the meantime, Mexican minister of hacienda (treasury) Adolfo de la Huerta negotiated revolutionary debts in New York with international bankers under the leadership of the J. P. Morgan's chief negotiator, Thomas Lamont. Unfortunately, de la Huerta was a politician, not an international finance expert. Thus, European and U.S. bankers gained significant advantages. The lesson for Obregón from this experience was that revolutionary politicians do not necessarily make good international financial negotiators. Just as the Porfirian state had needed its professional scientific advisors, the revolutionary state needed professional experts to represent the interests of the new state in international diplomatic, economic, and financial circles. The Mexican institutionalization and professionalization of international economic and political negotiations had begun just in time to deal with the complex international economic environment of the late 1920s.

In negotiations about diplomatic recognition Obregón remained stubborn, refusing to give in to threats and harassment from the U.S. State Department, Senator Fall, or foreign oil companies. He could not give in to the violation of Mexican legal sovereignty and provoke the animosity of many relatively independent revolutionary warlords in Mexico's regions. Besides, the next presidential election was only a few years away. Popular Mexican hostility resulting from U.S. interventions continued, preventing Obregón from pursuing a less nationalistic, more pragmatic relationship with the United States for the sake of rebuilding the Mexican state. In the end, Obregón's gamble worked.

When Senator Fall became discredited in the Teapot Dome scandal and de la Huerta challenged Obregón with a dangerous nationwide military rebellion on the eve of the 1924 presidential elections, the U.S. State Department changed course and recognized the Obregón government. True, Obregón made significant de facto concessions, many of them controversial and offensive to popular Mexican sensibilities. At the same time, he saved the de jure sanctity of the Constitution of 1917 against considerable U.S. and European diplomatic and big-business pressure. Domestic opponents of Obregón and Plutarco Elías Calles, his designated successor, welcomed the endorsement of the United States as a critical resource. Regional warlords had to recognize that while the United States could not impose a president on Mexico, certainly no Mexican opposition leader could successfully challenge Calles without at least U.S. toleration of it. This time, the U.S. military and government had protected the Mexican status quo with critical military support and the unique legitimacy that came with diplomatic recognition. Obregón was able to hand his successor the Constitution of 1917 as an untouched and therefore powerful legal tool to further cement

Mexico's economic sovereignty. Now Mexico had been admitted to the international diplomatic and financial community and would henceforth suffer less from the ups and downs of confusing and conflicting ideas about Mexico within the United States. Despite the damage to domestic economic reconstruction and the deepening poverty of Mexico's population during these years, the revolutionary state had successfully maneuvered the antirevolutionary Western diplomatic establishment into a position where it had to grant recognition to a political regime in Latin America that had come to power neither through monarchic inheritance nor through the democratic ballot box. From then on, with Mexico as a recognized member of the Pan American Union, newly elected president Calles could carry Mexico's fight for legitimacy and revolutionary movements into the Latin American diplomatic setting.

Now that the United States had replaced Britain as the premier foreign power exerting influence in Latin America, the vaguely defined but effective tool of the Monroe Doctrine had to be challenged more than ever before. Mexican foreign minister Genaro Estrada carried the familiar theme of diplomatic recognition to a new level, demanding that in the future any new government should receive diplomatic recognition, regardless of how it had come to power. If this initiative were successful, Mexico could thus recognize any new revolutionary administration and end its ongoing political isolation in the Latin American setting. Thus, one central policy goal of the U.S. and conservative Latin American nations would be defeated. The emergence of a revolutionary alternative à la Mexico south of the Mexican-Guatemalan border would be impossible to stop by diplomacy and aboveboard political means. Estrada's effort was an understanding that the uncontrolled entry of popular forces, peasants, and working classes as independent political actors into 20th century Latin American politics had to be recognized.

President Calles went further within the Central American setting. Based on his personal initiative, an aggressive propaganda campaign was waged against U.S. gunboat diplomacy and the work of U.S. Marines in the Caribbean and Central America. Also, Mexico developed a special relationship with Cuba at a period when this Caribbean island was struggling to redefine its relationship with the United States. Moreover, Calles backed diplomacy and propaganda with action, as in providing support and later asylum to the Nicaraguan revolutionary Augusto César Sandino. Ironically, when it came to domestic Mexican affairs Calles went to great lengths—even terror and violence—to avoid the establishment of political alternatives at home.

When he was governor of Sonora under President Carranza, Calles had obsessively tried to eliminate the remaining influence of the Catholic Church there. His adoption of 19th–century Mexican anticlericalism coincided with a Vatican effort to revive the institution and the power of the Catholic Church on a global scale. In reaction to the ideological innovations of Marxism, social democracy, natural science, and, later, the Soviet Revolution, the pope had backed the development of a more radical Catholic labor policy, hoping to regain influence with workers and employees of the industrialized nations and urban centers in Latin

America. More frightening for the postrevolutionary regime was the fact that the Cristero movement gained a significant popular following in Mexico's heartland and in the West. The movement's mysticism made it an ultimately futile but psychologically rewarding approach to providing protection against the continuing upheavals after the 1920s, the commercialization of agriculture, the ups and downs of international economic cycles, and the artistic innovations that had emerged with the muralist revolutionary symbolism. The fusion of millennarianism, a sort of community spirituality, and the institutional Catholic revival promised powerful relief and thus a serious challenge to the bitter and continuously violent politics of 1920s state building.

Calles, using the legal provisions of the Constitution of 1917, forced the existing tensions to the point of direct confrontation with the Vatican. For example, the number of Catholic priests that could officiate was reduced, the Spanish-born church leadership was vilified as a foreign anti-Mexican force, and, most importantly, Calles revived efforts by 19th–century president Benito Juárez to found a national Mexican church, independent of Rome and in imitation of Henry VIII and his Anglican Church. The Vatican responded in kind and, together with the Spanish-born church leadership, suspended religious services. Many priests, fearing for their lives, abandoned their parishes to seek protection in the anonymity of large Mexican urban centers and across the U.S. border. Mexicans for whom Catholic ritual and practice remained the cornerstone of their belief system were caught between the two extremes represented by the Vatican and the National Palace. The absence of baptism, marriage, confession, and funeral services and the cancellation of village feast days and celebrations of local patron saints triggered a massive popular psychological emergency. Immediately, the confrontation mushroomed into the third most powerful civil war since the beginnings of Mexico's independence movement in 1810. At stake were traditional customs of Mexican regions and the modernizing pressures exercised by governments in Mexico City. The bloody Cristero rebellion that followed lasted three years and drained the reserves of the postrevolutionary state. Once again the push for national economic development slowed down.

U.S. Catholics, Protestants, and other religious people became the Cristeros' most important pressure group outside the country, aside from the Vatican, to confront the Calles administration. This movement represented a different type of U.S. intervention in Mexican affairs. From the Cristero rebellion on, U.S. ambassadors to Mexico had to represent popular U.S. concerns about the violation of religious freedoms in Mexico. U.S. citizens who had never heard of the complexities of the century-old struggle between church and state in the former Spanish colonies equated events in Mexico with Marxist anticlericalism as applied in the Soviet Union. Suddenly, U.S. Protestant and Catholic congregations found themselves in the company of aggressive, deeply conservative big-business groups who were only too happy to find Calles in yet another domestic crisis that could be used to weaken Mexican resolve to challenge Article 27 of the constitution. In the end Calles had to realize that he could not continue the state-building project while persecuting a significant part of Mexico's population. Gradually, the religious conflict deescalated over the next few years, and a modus vivendi emerged for both sides. Religious services resumed slowly, the presence of the Spanish leadership in the Mexican Catholic church was reduced, and the violent persecution of clergy was halted. It took until the 1940s, however, for a Mexican president to identify himself as a Catholic in public. The rupture of diplomatic relations between the Holy See and the postrevolutionary Mexican state lasted until 1992.

In comparison, Calles's engagement with Leninism, Stalinism, and the Soviet Union was much less contentious. The Soviet Union's ideological claim to having had the first and only genuine revolution of the 20th century presented an uncomfortable symbolic challenge to Mexico's postrevolutionary leadership and their state-building project. The Mexican revolutionary propaganda claimed that, because all popular grievances were being addressed by the postrevolutionary state, there was no need for a future Communist movement inside Mexico. Whatever minor potential threat might have come from the Comintern at that time, Calles answered this challenge with greater skill than he had the Catholic issue. First, he backed the organization of Mexico's still small, but growing, industrial workforce into the conservative Regional Confederation of Mexican Workers (CROM) union movement. Quickly, Calles's labor leader, Luis Napoleón Morones, built a powerful co-optive union structure that systematically confronted independent alternative unions and funneled a small amount of benefits to labor groups that aligned themselves with CROM.

In Mexico's rural areas, the Catholicism of agricultural workers made Soviet-style organization ineffectual. In the meantime, the Soviet Union challenged traditional gender roles in Mexico by sending the first female ambassador from any nation to travel to Mexico, who argued for greater female rights and emancipation. The as yet unsubstantiated claim was made that Soviet agents were interested in exploiting domestic Mexican tensions to destabilize the United States. Then Mexico used a minor occasion as a pretext to break off Mexican-Soviet diplomatic ties. This was no sacrifice for the Mexican administration and could only impress the groups inside the United States who were concerned about the influence of Communist activity.

The arrival of Dwight W. Morrow in 1927 as the new U.S. ambassador to Mexico brought a significant shift in U.S.-Mexican bilateral relations. Unlike Ambassador James Sheffield between 1924 and 1927, Morrow preferred quiet nonconfrontational diplomatic approaches that moved serious tensions between the two countries out of the eyes of the nationalistic public. During the last year of Calles's presidency, Morrow built a special relationship with the Mexican president that moved difficult discussions into the back room of the National Palace. Publicly, Morrow moved away from pointing out differences and emphasized commonalities between the two countries. This special ambassador-president relationship became a U.S.-Mexican diplomatic ritual that continued during the next three administrations. Morrow was helped by the presence of Genaro

Notwithstanding U.S. Ambassador Dwight Morrow's (right) years as a Wall Street banker with J. P. Morgan, President Plutarco Calles (center) considered him an amiable diplomat, eager to work toward removing the major obstacles in Mexican–United States relations. Morrow played a role in the negotiations that ended the Cristero Rebellion. He and Calles met regularly, even after Calles formally left the presidency.

Estrada, an accomplished diplomatic professional who rose to be head of the Secretaria de Relaciones Exteriores (Foreign Ministry) in 1930. Together, Calles, Morrow, and Estrada realized a second important change in Mexican foreign relations by the end of the 1920s: Mexican foreign relations moved onto the global stage. After focusing during most of the 1920s on U.S.-Mexican issues and the Pan American Union, Mexico prepared for its membership in the Europe-based League of Nations.

This development coincided with the U.S. stock market crash in October 1929 and the subsequent depression. From then on, U.S. political attention was refocused on domestic issues, and the pressure on the U.S.-Mexican relationship eased even further. Whereas earlier the League of Nations had respected the Monroe Doctrine and therefore U.S. dominance in Latin America, it now became active within the Western Hemisphere. Also, the depression forced Britain, France, and Germany to neglect great-power rivalries in Latin America and make domestic issues their own number one policy priority. Suddenly, new room for independent activity opened for Mexico. As the Pan American Union had before, the League of Nations now challenged the United States in the Western Hemisphere and strengthened Mexico's continuously precarious position as the only revolutionary country south of the Rio Grande.

Increasingly, Mexico's maxim of unconditional respect for national boundaries and self-determination echoed within a dramatically changing world. No longer were violations of national borders limited to U.S.-western European-Latin American relations. Fascist and militaristic movements in Asia and southeastern Europe soon became aggressive authoritarian empires. Consequently,

Mexican diplomats added attacks against Italian, German, and Japanese behavior to the protests against U.S. and British aspirations south of the equator. Mexican ambassadors to the League also offered themselves as intermediaries for intrastate conflicts within South America. These occasions were always a welcome opportunity to reinforce the idea of Mexico's political and social distinctness within Latin America. Thus Mexican diplomats became active in international labor questions, women's rights, white slavery, environmental issues, and the mediation committee of the 1932–35 Chaco War between Paraguay and Bolivia.

Mexican economic planners saw the depression as the most important capitalistic crisis of the century. To their dismay, they observed how all the traditional economic measures to revive national economies were failing. Increasingly it seemed possible that capitalism and free enterprise might be challenged successfully by Communist or fascist alternatives. Mexican diplomats in the League of Nations reacted to this crisis of the 20th–century liberal state by considering the lessons of other countries in a Mexican context. They studied Italian experiments with exchange rates; British experiments with the new, unproven tool of deficit spending; Soviet experiments with agricultural collectivization and state-directed industrialization; the devastating effects, of German hyperinflation; and finally the U.S. New Deal. It was obvious that the postrevolutionary state, too, would have to develop its own distinct developmental path to deal with the dramatic reduction of international agricultural trade and the continued absence of foreign investment for Mexican development.

Against this background, Abelardo L. Rodríguez assumed the Mexican presidency in 1932. When he arrived in Mexico City he could count on a national financial structure that had been created in 1927 and on the existence of various ministries that had tried to modernize Mexico's agriculture as a cooptive measure to strengthen the control of the state over regional peasant organizations. In 1933, Rodríguez charged Foreign Minister José Manuel Puig Casauranc with a second round of reorganization of the Foreign Ministry. Its goal was to turn Mexico's consuls and diplomats abroad into economic and developmental scouts. Whereas in the 1920s Foreign Minister Eduardo Pani's reorganization had forged the Foreign Ministry into a tool of the state to confront anti-Mexican policies in the Americas, Puig Casauranc shifted the focus toward an improved professional reporting service that confirmed the role of the state as the central national agent in development for years to come. The Foreign Ministry was becoming an information service to observe world developments systematically and to discuss their economic, political, and social implications for Mexico's development.

To achieve this goal, the ministry introduced professional standards and schedules for diplomatic reports from abroad. Sometimes the foreign minister himself edited and evaluated the diplomatic reports to upgrade the quality of the political and economic information coming from abroad. Often incoming reports contained suggestions about the strengths and weaknesses of foreign powers, allowing Mexicans to evaluate whether European gestures were idle threats or serious issues. Increasingly, foreign policy and trade decisions were influenced as much by professional information as by the political leanings of presidents and other Mexican political players. Outwardly, postrevolutionary rhetoric continued to dominate daily events; behind the scenes, however, professionals and technocrats had joined politicians in the conduct of national affairs.

By the early 1930s, privately based U.S.-Mexican interactions occurring through the avenues of tourism, culture, literature, music, and the other arts were augmenting Mexico's official world linkages in diplomacy, finance, the military, economics, and politics. A continuously flowering cultural dialogue between Mexico and the world had begun in the early 1920s, when the end of the violent phase of the revolution allowed a revival of travel to Mexico by U.S. intellectuals and writers such as Frank Tannenbaum and Carleton Beals. U.S. citizens sought refuge and alternatives in Mexico to the modernizing pressures of U.S. society. On the surface, Mexican postrevolutionary society seemed to offer alternative political directions as well as deeper, more meaningful emotional satisfaction than that provided by the U.S. consumer culture. By the end of the 1920s, U.S.-sponsored archaeologists and scientists were joining this group of early academic and journalistic cultural bridge builders. When Charles Lindbergh undertook to do an aerial survey of Mexico after his famous transatlantic flight, his airplane was popularized in the U.S. media as an innovative, useful vehicle to fuse scientific pursuit and travel. A popular exhibit at the Chicago Century of Progress brought Mexican gold and jewelry discoveries from Monte Albán's Tomb No. 7 to a wider U.S. public. Additional exhibit stops in Washington and New York spread firsthand experiences with Mexico. And Mexico's public postrevolutionary discussion about the role and contribution of Native American society to contemporary culture was followed by an interested U.S. public.

The relationship between Mexican artistic developments and the U.S. artistic community forms a special chapter of this expanding, multifaceted cultural interconnection (see Chapters 17 and 20). The Mexican muralist movement, in particular paintings by Diego Rivera and José Clemente Orozco, suggested to U.S. artists a viable alternative to European modernism, abstraction, and lack of political engagement. Mexican muralism excited with its use of color and a representational style that engaged the average viewer while also making a powerful sociopolitical statement. With the discovery of pre-Hispanic artifacts at archaeological excavations, U.S. artists saw Mexico as an inspiration for form and design. Just as African art had inspired European painters, Aztec, Maya, Olmec, Toltec, and Mixtec pottery and jewelry influenced U.S. popular viewers and artists alike.

Mexican painters in turn increasingly saw the U.S. artistic environment as a safe place to work, free of the volatile political setting of Calles's Mexico. When the postrevolutionary state tried to separate itself from the activism and utopianism of the muralists, the U.S. "cold" consumerist, capitalist environment suddenly appeared as a pleasing refuge. Now that the National Palace in Mexico City had begun to restrict opportunities for painters such as Orozco and Rivera, they continued their artistic rivalry in the United States, one mural at a time. Thus, most U.S. painters who had not traveled to Mexico could gain a chance to study Mexico's contributions to world art at galleries in New York and California.

But there the circle of the U.S.-Mexican cultural exchange closed. Personal impressions of Mexican culture gained at art exhibits, through newspaper articles, and via the mass medium of radio reinforced the insight that Paris, London, and Berlin were no longer the only places worthy of artistic attention. In Mexico the fusion of centuries-old Italian fresco techniques, artistic revolutionary nationalism, and pre-Hispanic designs was producing a new art form equal to if not better than the artistic innovations taking place in Europe during the 1920s.

A more troubling aspect of this widening popular artistic interaction was the lasting creation of stereotypical caricatures of Mexicans. During World War I, the absence of European films had reoriented the Mexican market toward showing films produced in the United States. In the 1920s, U.S. nativism and racism reinforced the characterization of Latin Americans as lazy peasants, emotionally unbalanced childlike characters, and sexually crazed people without cultural values. The influential stereotypes of the Mexican peasants on infinite siestas, romantic but violent bandit-revolutionaries, and Latin lovers joined Mexican archaeologists and painters in the pantheon of popular perceptions about Mexico. Representatives of the Foreign Ministry and the country's consuls fought U.S. nativism and racism through innovative propaganda departments and public statements along the U.S.-Mexican border that emphasized the complexity of Mexican society. From there it was only a small step to confronting U.S. officials on the state level who were only too eager to use nativist laws to deport Latin American-looking people into the Mexican desert, violating human decency and the U.S. Constitution at the same time. Popular fascination in the United States with the European discovery of Mexico undoubtedly had a troublesome, obsessive racist undercurrent. And the yearning of U.S. exoticism had its own dark cultural undercurrent.

At the same time, Mexicans and the Mexican government itself wrestled with their own racist and cultural xenophobia. During the 1920s and 1930s, U.S. popular music and dances, in particular jazz and the Charleston, were condemned as a decadent art form that threatened the Spanish social values of Mexico's establishment and small middle class. The open display of artistic exchange and pleasure across racial and social divides was too much of a challenge for most Mexicans who followed foreign music trends. European-based concepts of high versus popular art rejected U.S. multiracial, cross-class artistic popular expressions as being menacingly decadent and un-Mexican.

Individual, folk-based cultural exchanges along the U.S.-Mexican border simply disregarded these cultural battles. On the Mexican side, migrant workers returning from U.S. agricultural work and Midwest industries pursued their own cultural experiences and expressions without apology. On the U.S. side, people who wanted to escape the Protestant moral boundaries of small-town life crossed the Mexican border to seek escape, release, and pleasure in gambling, drugs,

During the Great Depression, United States policies at the national, state, and local levels attempted to block immigration from Mexico. This resulted in the deportation of thousands of Mexicans from the southwestern states to remove them from U.S. welfare support. Nevertheless, daily border crossings continued with great frequency.

prostitution, and alcohol. Sometimes such crossings also provided the only opportunity to practice homosexuality. The area along the U.S.-Mexican border remained a unique cultural zone shaped by distinct cross-cultural realities, technological advances, and the accelerating commercialization of agriculture as well as the politics of Prohibition.

In 1934, Abelardo Rodríguez handed over the Mexican presidency to Lázaro Cárdenas. By then Mexican relations with the world were significantly different from the days of the struggle for diplomatic recognition in the early 1920s. A multitude of revolutionary short-term concerns had been replaced by more centralized, long-term issues. The Mexican postrevolutionary state had asserted itself successfully against U.S. dollar diplomacy, Soviet manipulations, and religious reactionary forces in contact with the Vatican. Within Latin America, revolutionary Mexico had prevailed with a distinct political presence that differed sharply from the conservative policies of other nations. As a permanent member of the Pan American Union and the League of Nations, Mexico continued to project a politically innovative and socially progressive image without becoming restricted by a dogmatic ideological system. U.S.-Mexican relations had become more predictable, centralized, and respectful since the 1927 arrival of Ambassador Dwight Morrow and the faint beginnings of the Good Neighbor policy under President Hoover. No longer did Mexican diplomatic efforts focus exclusively on defending the national sovereignty. The pressing need for national economic development and for protection against alternative foreign ideologies, as well as the fight against human rights violations of Mexicans inside the United States, had become as important. Now the continuing crisis of the depression and the weakness of Mexico's private industrial sector confirmed the pivotal role of the state as the agent for national economic development in the years to come. Mexico's international relations encompassed traditional diplomacy, economic policy, financial relations, cultural policy, Mexican Americans in the United States, and popular culture in newspapers, art, film, and music.

Today the presidency of Lázaro Cárdenas is known for its progressive social and labor policies. These were part of a larger effort to industrialize Mexico and move its still predominantly agricultural society toward a consumer culture that could sustain an independent Mexican industry. Most Mexican private entrepreneurs and elites rejected state-driven development out of ideological principle. Not surprisingly, the technocratic elites of the administration thus had to act as nationalistic entrepreneurs.

Mexico's economic planners from the ministries of Hacienda, Foreign Affairs, Agriculture, Communication and Infrastructure, and National Economic Development and from the Bank of Mexico devised an experimental developmental policy that envisioned a time when Mexico could stop being a raw-material exporter and sustain a self-supportive circle of industrial growth. In particular, the minister of hacienda, Eduardo Suárez; the head of the Bank of Mexico, Eduardo Villaseñor; and Cárdenas's friend and minister of national development Francisco Múgica supported the idea in a very nonideological, pragmatic manner. In 1934 and 1935, a Mexican experimental developmentalism emerged that promised to use the global crisis of the depression to realize deep structural changes in Mexico's national economy. To the dismay of progressive Mexican government planners, the only foreign interests eager to offer developmental assistance were authoritarian and fascist countries. Through the use of exclusive cash-free barter arrangements, Italy, Germany, and to a limited degree Japan sought to reduce British and U.S. dominance over Latin American markets. In Mexico, Germany easily assumed during those years the role of Mexico's second most important trading partner.

U.S. president Franklin D. Roosevelt and Secretary of the Treasury Henry Morgenthau recognized that there was occurring a quiet financial reorganization of the flow of trade into Latin America according to fascist economic terms. However, antinationalist policies of multinational companies and their self-defeating sense of cultural superiority limited the power that official U.S. policy could exercise against this trend. Because the change in U.S. policy was mostly crisis driven, the Roosevelt administration had to wait for an emergency. At the same time, British economic policy toward Mexico was weakened due to Hitler's imminent threat and Britain's own continuing domestic economic crisis.

Nazi Germany used barter trade exchanges to gain a foothold in Mexico's emerging industrial sectors of electricity, pharmaceuticals production, fertilizers, small property mining, automobiles, and railroad construction. Mexicans tried to limit German involvement by approaching Italians to help with the silk industry, Soviets with agricultural machinery, the Japanese with airplane technology, and Spaniards with the creation of a national merchant marine. U.S. companies were asked to help with steel production, the creation of a national airline system, military hardware, and petrochemical know-how.

When Cárdenas began to commercialize Mexico's *ejido* program—communal ownership of land, borrowing from Aztec legal concepts—Germany's role in Mexican development became even more important. The success of the ejido commercialization effort depended, among other factors, on an ability to market the expected higher agricultural production on the continuously depressed international agricultural markets. Only Germany was seriously interested in importing Mexican agricultural products on a long-term basis, as part, of course, of its preparations for war. Once again, Mexican long-term developmental needs ran up against political and personal rejection in dealing with national socialist Germany.

Between 1934 and 1936, a bifurcated Mexican-German relationship emerged. It was a pragmatic economic cooperation combined with a determined, very personal political fight by Cárdenas himself against the global rise of fascism. As early as 1934, Cárdenas had eagerly supported Mexico's leftist unions under the rise to prominence of Vicente Lombardo Toledano and his public fight against Nazi persecution of German union members, Communists, socialists, and Jewish people. Mexico's Jewish organizations had been one of the first groups inside Mexico to use economic boycotts in their efforts to mobilize against German fascist representatives and interests inside Mexico. Cárdenas personally guided the antifascist political campaign by Mexican ambassador to the League of Nations Isidro Fabela. Mexico attacked in the League of Nations the fascist and authoritarian aggression in Ethiopia, the German Ruhrgebiet (industrial region), and the Japanese conquest of Nanking. Cárdenas also made a personal statement in 1937 when he provided asylum for Leon Trotsky in Mexico.

From 1936 on, Cárdenas recognized that Franco's increasingly successful revolt in Spain could lead to the formation of a Spanish brand of fascism and the creation of a dangerous bridgehead for future fascist expansion into Latin America. Therefore, Cárdenas helped embattled Republican Spain with military aid and provided exiled Spanish Republicans with asylum in Mexico. With them came much of the Republican Spanish gold that had been earmarked to create an economic base for a future Republican insurgence against Franco. Cárdenas's determined fight against any type of violation of national boundaries was also confirmed by the Mexican mediation in the Paraguayan-Bolivian Chaco War and his sharp condemnation of the Japanese looting of Nanking. Even before the oil expropriation, Cárdenas had sent pleas to President Roosevelt inviting him to launch a joint diplomatic initiative against the threat of global violence before another world war could break out. His statesmanship was disregarded.

Mexicans, especially in the capital, shared the tensions Europeans endured as Nazi Germany and Fascist Italy rose to power. While the Mexican government supported Republican Spain, the Nazis and Fascists supported the Spanish Falangists of General Franco. After tearing down the Nazi flag in Mexico City on October 8, 1935, these demonstrators proceeded to tear down the Fascist flag at the Italian embassy. Conservative Mexicans leaned toward the Fascist regimes, fearing the rise of communism in Mexico.

The other side of this policy was an intensification of economic interactions with Germany, Italy, Japan, and any other country willing to help Mexico with its national economic development. As long as democratic governments in Europe and capitalistic multinational companies remained unwilling to reward Mexico's determined public antifascist political stance economically, the Mexican developmental technocrats had no choice but to exploit the emerging tensions between the fascist and liberal political-economic orders for Mexico's national development. In the United States, a small group around President Roosevelt—Secretary of the Treasury Henry Morgenthau, Undersecretary of State Sumner Welles, and ambassador to Mexico Josephus Daniels—made an indirect but important contribution to Cardenismo. U.S. Treasury purchases of increasing amounts of Mexican silver at above public market prices indirectly fueled a boom in Mexico's mining industry. This in turn translated into a growing amount of tax income which, between 1934 and 1937, provided the Mexican state with pivotal income to function as an economic engine and public works project employer. This U.S.-Mexican silver purchase agreement created an unprecedented U.S.-Mexican interdependence in international financial relations. Another important link in this invisible connection was Mexican state-sponsored infrastructure programs that financed employment for tens of thousands of Mexicans whose government paychecks reinforced their psychological links with Cardenismo. All this together prevented Mexico from experiencing a deeper political crisis, which would have offered an opportunity for manipulation by extreme right-wing political organizations that were only too eager to seize upon any and all conspiracy openings that came with the turmoil south of the U.S. border.

From a 1930s macroeconomic perspective, Cárdenas's development policy showed encouraging results. Despite increased labor agitation, government support for unions, and more radical social policies, the economic barometer in Mexico remained optimistic. Although almost no foreign investment was flowing into Mexico to finance development projects, the economy was expanding, diversifying, and moving toward a more integrated national economic unit. Compared to the continuing serious economic troubles in the United States, Britain, and France, Mexico was weathering the time after 1935 with much greater optimism. Mexican developmentalists were using the global economic crisis to realize significant structural economic reforms.

In 1936, the available indicators suggested that it would be desirable to move ahead with the reorganization of some of Mexico's commercial sector based on communal concepts of property. The ejido program required even more government revenue to finance necessary tractors, seeds, and fertilizers. At the same time, Cárdenas's *sexenío* (six-year term) would end in four years, which gave barely enough time to make the ejido program a political, social, and commercial success. Thus, the minister of hacienda decided to force extra loans unsupported by collateral on the accounts of the Bank of Mexico. In theory, an expected good harvest would repay the loan before the end of the fiscal year, and the government's budget would close the year with an appropriate balance.

According to this ministerial developer's vision, the following year German-Mexican petroleum joint ventures and increased production and sales of petroleum from state-owned oil fields would generate more than enough new money to provide a more solid financial base for years to come. Then Mexico would collect direct income from raw-material exports, not just taxes on exports. It was reasonable to assume that this would provide enough money for continuous financing of highways, railroads, and the expansion of the ejido system. Of equal importance, Mexican developers could evade the pressure of unions to expropriate the foreign petroleum and mining companies, a step that would have assured the continued absence of private foreign investment from Mexico for years.

But suddenly, between May and December of 1937, these optimistic developmental plans and Mexico's foreign economic relations experienced a dramatic collapse. When the country recovered, in 1939, the domestic and international situations had changed so radically that this domestically based developmental strategy from the 1930s had to be abandoned.

President Lázaro Cárdenas nationalized the foreign oil companies on March 18, 1938. The oil companies' refusal to adhere to a Supreme Court ruling in favor of the workers provoked his action. Here the president meets with a group of oil workers during his inspection of the nationalized oil fields in Tamaulipas.

In retrospect, it is easy to identify the first snowball that, half a year later, would grow into the devastating avalanche that destroyed so much of what had been created in the previous years. As planned, in early 1937, Minister of Hacienda Eduardo Suárez forced new loans on the Bank of Mexico to finance the expanding ejido program. He suggested using the expected harvest at the end of the year as collateral. Its sale on European markets would, he argued, make enough money before the end of the fiscal year to balance the Bank of Mexico's books. A hypothetical bountiful harvest was now securing Mexico's state-sponsored program of agricultural commercialization. From the perspective of May 1937, Suárez's action was a reasonable calculated risk. By the end of the year it proved to traditional, anti-Cárdenas forces that state-sponsored agricultural commercialization with a communal base could work.

By coincidence, Mexico's oil workers began a highly symbolic emotional strike against the British- and Dutch-owned El Aguila petroleum company in May. Most Mexican union members did not take into consideration the forces of macroeconomics. Instead, they saw Cardenismo's support for labor unions as an opportunity to force the government to support their nationalistic, long-term traditional fight against the arrogant and imperialistic British-Dutch petroleum multinational. This strike was as much about wages as it was a demonstration of popular national economic self-determination and an assertion of the growing political role of the leftist political union, outside of the political control that President Calles had previously woven around Mexico's union movement. The symbolism of this strike was understood by all social groups within Mexico. In particular, private banks, midsize companies' owners, and small merchants interpreted it as a potential watershed for Mexico's economy. Several years of increasing labor agitation and a political atmosphere full of expropriation rumors, along with their cultural conservatism, led them to a paranoid interpretation that Communism was advancing inside Mexico. From that perspective, only a wait-and-see attitude was wise economic behavior. Overnight, psychological factors began to exert a strong influence on decision making in Mexico's private economic sector.

Next, the infusion of large amounts of ejido funds into the Mexican financial system triggered unprecedented inflationary surges that expressed themselves in rising prices of everyday food items and other basic consumer goods. This time, average Mexican consumers understood that something was changing in the economy. Now, their experiences, too, counseled caution in the near future. Consumption and therefore overall retail business began to slow. In the petroleum-producing regions the continuing oil strike led to a more immediate dramatic economic decline. First, fuel shortages suggested to regional manufacturers that the strike might affect their enterprises even more seriously. The basis for private industrial production might be endangered if the strike was not resolved in the immediate future. A destructive economic-psychological cycle was forming that steadily changed public and private perception of the economic viability of Cardenismo. This tension among domestic developmental policy, the perceptions of private business and consumers, and the reverberations of the petroleum strike were beginning to challenge the economic base of Cardenismo.

The crisis deepened when foreign-owned companies moved their international currency reserves out of Mexico to prevent their potential loss in case of a possible expropriation. Now Mexico's exchange rate came under pressure, thus changing the costs of production and sale prices in Mexico's private industry. Merchants, entrepreneurs, and bankers decided to play it safe and called in their outstanding loans. As a result, domestic private investment in Mexico's economy became a trickle. In the near future, this combination of lack of investment, fuel shortages, and inflation would make it impossible to have a growing, developing economy. Thus the necessary tax income to finance development would decrease, and the Cárdenas administration would have to cut its infrastructure programs. Everybody understood that Mexico's economic ship was in very troubled waters. All social groups were beginning to rethink their political and social relationships with the administration, further fueling the existing tensions between the postrevolutionary state and the extreme right- and left-wing alternatives.

Cárdenas's political opponents welcomed this crisis. A demand for immediate political and economic change was heard increasingly in popular discussions. Left-wing unions advocated class struggle, while right-wing private business owners pointed to Franco's civil war in Spain and debated the exclusion of peasants and workers from the political system. The conservatives' preferred model was to return to the hierarchical social and gender values of the early 19th century. Mexico's unresolved historical debate about the form and purpose of an independent nation was resuming. Unlike before, opposition forces now found willing listeners among European fascist and orthodox Catholic circles in Spain.

Cárdenas's economic planners tried to reverse this trend by hurrying Mexico's state-owned petroleum reserves into earlier production. This they hoped would again produce fuel for domestic industry, earn new foreign exchange to support the fledgling peso exchange rate, and produce new government income to jump-start the shrinking economy. Cárdenas even went so far as to offer extensive production increases to the British-Dutch oil company, which continued to humiliate Mexican workers.

But nothing helped. The German-Mexican petroleum joint venture negotiations had not yet progressed far enough. Mexican state petroleum reserves could not be rushed into production, because the government had run out of money. Minister of Hacienda Suárez refused to burden the Bank of Mexico with more bad debt. In London, private financiers refused to finance a joint venture that would have created a Mexican tanker fleet for the sale of Mexican petroleum independently of the multinational tanker fleets. And Japanese interest in Mexican oil proved to be only lukewarm, as long as cheaper U.S. oil could reach Japan without going through the costly Panama Canal route. Certainly, the multinational companies were committed to obstructing Mexico's economic nationalism every step of the way. Even though the spread of nationalism could not be prevented in Mexico, the Mexican case could serve as a warning to politicians in Latin America and the Near East.

Cárdenas's situation became desperate when nature conspired against his government and the projected ejido harvest fell far behind expectations. The forced loan of early 1937 could not be repaid. From the 1930s perspective of limited experience with deficit spending Mexico's domestically driven development was racing toward a public crash. By the end of 1938, the Mexican government had to admit that its financial reserves were not enough to continue the previous development course. For the first time government-sponsored infrastructure projects had to stop construction. Government accounts for contractors and the salaries of public workers went unpaid for the first time in a generation. Some ejido farmers recognized that there would be no credit in 1938 to plant the next harvest. Soldiers in the military learned that the lack of money endangered the promised social security system for the professionalizing army. The precarious political coalition of army, workers, and peasants that had supported Cárdenas politically from 1934 on began to unravel. The loss of its economic base was threatening Cardenismo's political collapse.

Minister of Hacienda Suárez tried to forestall the pending emergency with a plea for help to the pro-Mexico group in the U.S. Treasury. Indeed, Secretary Morgenthau and the White House helped Suárez and Cárdenas with special silver purchases and access to U.S.-dollar stabilization funds. In Mexico City, this unprecedented show of U.S. support for Mexico failed to impress. Private Mexican banks refused point blank to cooperate with Suárez. Urban and rural

Mexican extremists on the right and left organized during the 1930s. Here Mexican communists battle mounted Mexican fascists known as the "Gold Shirts." This confrontation in the Zócalo, November 22, 1938, resulted in two deaths and 47 injured persons.

Mexicans suffered from skyrocketing prices and food shortages. Workers' wages went unpaid; unemployment increased. Ejido peasants had no money to buy seed for the new planting season. In San Diego, California, conservative Mexican exile groups conspired with anti-Communist domestic Mexican entrepreneurs against Cárdenas. Warlord Saturnino Cedillo from San Luis Potosí courted foreign oil companies, foreign fascist groups, and Mexican small-property agricultural owners to support a coup against Cárdenas. In Mexico's western states orthodox Catholic communities, influenced by pro-fascist Catholic interests, marched against Cárdenas's agricultural government. A multitude of voices demanded that the Cardenistas publicly recognize the failure of their policies. The prospect of civil war in Mexico was within sight.

The nationalization of foreign oil property in March 1938 was Cárdenas's way out of this emergency. Overnight it ended the oil worker labor issue and strengthened this vital bond of the oil industry with the Mexican government, while assuring that the state would control the workers in the future. The resumption of oil production brought new fuel to an industry revitalizing its domestic production. Domestic entrepreneurs knew where they stood overnight and resumed economic activity. The revival of retail business was now in sight. Most important, the nationalization served as a smoke screen for the necessary peso devaluation that made Mexican goods cheaper and more attractive for future exports. Government control over the petroleum sector meant immediate guaranteed income for the administration without having to rely on taxes or foreign middlemen. The unprecedented amount of popular nationalism that resulted from the expropriation temporarily covered the serious divisions that had emerged between Cardenismo and all social sectors during the previous nine months. It bought enough time until macroeconomic changes could produce enough positive economic results for Cárdenas to finish his term in office. Most significant for the government's development planners, nationalization was the only way to resume a corrected development course.

Mexican diplomatic observers and the Mexican Foreign Ministry had told the government that nationalization would be a calculated risk. Reports from London predicted that the British government's representatives would care mostly about Hitler's military threat in Europe, not multinational petroleum reserves in Mexico. The British ambassador in Mexico City was disliked among the British citizens and companies in Mexico and lacked any real power. U.S. Ambassador Josephus Daniels was pro-Cárdenas and was willing, in principle, to defend the expropriation, with compensation for the oil multinationals. Enough independent oil merchants and shipping company owners existed in 1938 to make the reasonable assumption that Mexico would be able to market its oil after expropriation in spite of the multinational boycott efforts. Finally, there was the spread of war on all continents, promising foreign petroleum orders for the international war machine regardless of the economic principles of the multinational companies. The Mexican decision to expropriate the property of the industry thus marked a desperate rescue attempt but also provided proof that the emerging world war was once again changing the international context of Mexico's economic development. Only for foreigners was the oil nationalization an unimaginably daring step.

The integration of the nationalized petroleum sector into Mexico's economy between 1938 and 1940 proved this point to all those involved. Immediately following the expropriation, government officials and Cárdenas supporters from all political and social spheres offered petroleum reserves to foreign buyers. Hopes that Republican Spain would help were frustrated because of the Spanish Civil War. The French declined Mexican oil purchases because they feared that doing so might see them cut off from British oil supplies in a future German-French war. And initially Germany refused to buy Mexican oil because Shell and Standard Oil were promising to supply Germany in case of a future war. The first, and only, breakthrough for the Cardenista oil merchants came in the fall of 1938 when the German navy experienced inexplicable petroleum delivery problems during the German conquest of the Czech Sudety region. German navy circles recognized then that, in times of real crisis, the petroleum multinationals might side with the Allied powers.

From then on, German government bureaucrats no longer objected to an expanding importation of expropriated Mexican petroleum products through the independent U.S. oil man William Rhodes Davis. Subsequently, middleman

Davis and his independent oil company sold enough expropriated petroleum for Mexico to survive the economic boycott of the petroleum multinationals. Ironically, some of the Mexican oil was used in the Spanish Civil War on the side of Franco. Once Germany provoked war against Britain and France in 1939, Mexican oil flowed to Mussolini's navy. Suddenly the Japanese navy purchased increasing amounts of Mexican petroleum to strengthen its fuel situation. The growth of regional wars in Asia and Europe helped Cárdenas hold out against the oil multinationals.

Cárdenas exploited the relationship with Davis by ending Britain's diplomatic presence in Mexico. As a result little direct British pressure against the Mexican government could be applied from within Mexico. At the same time, he offered U.S. president Roosevelt Mexican oil and diplomatic cooperation against the Axis powers. It was becoming obvious that in the not too distant future U.S. companies would become the major foreign technological group to help Mexicans operate their nationalized industrial sector.

In early 1940, an agreement between the small U.S. oil company Sinclair and the Mexican government broke the united front of expropriated companies and proved that Mexico was willing and able to pay compensation. By then the regional conflicts in Europe had become one European war and multinational companies had to confront how their "profits above nationalism" strategy was only helping the rise of world fascism. In 1941, the other U.S. oil multinationals reached an agreement concerning compensation with the newly elected Manuel Avila Camacho administration.

Finally, Mexican oil was allowed to flow again into the United States and help the democratic defense against the Axis powers. Just as Cárdenas had promised for years, oil deliveries to Germany, Italy, and Japan stopped and Mexico's four-year-old economic offer to the cause of the democratic powers was now taken seriously. British oil interests continued to hold out against Mexico until after World War II. By then, U.S. oil companies had established themselves as Mexico's future partner in developing the nationalized properties.

The resumption of Mexican national economic development within a context of war in Europe and Asia proved more difficult. German companies had admitted in January 1940 that the increasing requirements of war production made it impossible to deliver Mexican prewar orders for infrastructure projects until after a final German victory. Although Mexico had paid for all orders up front with oil, Germany would deliver nothing in return for years to come. Next, the Italian entry into World War II in June 1940 eliminated the remainder of Mexico's previously critical European oil market. With it also disappeared the rest of Mexico's agricultural markets in Europe. The European war had closed one-third of Mexico's prewar markets. In the years to come European technology and know-how would not help Mexico's continuing quest for industrial development. Temporarily, Mexican planners sought an intensification of trade and technological exchange with Japan. However, a Mexican trade commission that traveled to Japan in the spring of 1940 returned with only contracts for oil exports. There could be no doubt that Japan, too, was interested in Mexico only as a raw-materials exporter, not as a country that was trying to make itself economically independent from the First World. No doubt as long as World War II lasted the only country left as a partner for Mexican development was the United States of America.

Before the Mexican technocrats and U.S. government groups could work together more closely on economic matters, presidential elections had to be won in both countries. Only after the election of the official Mexican presidential candidate, Manuel Avila Camacho, in Mexico City and of Franklin Delano Roosevelt in Washington, D.C., would a continuation of the Good Neighbor policy be guaranteed. However, a victory of opposition candidates Juan Andreu Almazán or Francisco Múgica in Mexico or a Republican U.S. president would once again worsen U.S.-Mexican relations. In the worst case, Mexico would break into quarreling political factions and offer its territory as a vehicle for foreign manipulations, just as in World War I.

To understand the situation better, one has to examine the activities of the Cardenista opposition groups in Mexico between 1937 and 1939. German national socialist representatives had made contact with every major Mexican opposition group by 1937. In addition, Japanese and German professional spies were using Mexico as a center for gathering information to be used against U.S. and British shipping in Mexico and Central America during the next war. Just as dangerous were Mexican right-wing Spanish circles, who established a new focus in a newly founded Mexican anti-Communist group and the ongoing rebellion by Franco in Spain. Franco's increasingly successful blend of authoritarianism and Catholicism offered pro-fascist Mexican groups for the first time a distinctly Spanish version of extreme right-wing social policies, something that Hitler's anti-Catholic national socialism and Mussolini's fascism had not been able to provide. Representatives of Mexico's main veterans organization were so enamored with Franco's rebellion that they asked the Cárdenas administration to establish a fascist state in Mexico. These groups were loosely connected with anti-Cárdenas exiles living in California.

Fortunately for Cárdenas, Franco's victory was not certain until 1939. By then the German government was willing to disregard subversive plans of local German Nazis and their Mexican right-wing supporters. The flow of Mexican oil to Europe was more important for the conquest of Europe than was a premature revolution in Mexico. Hitler himself urged members of the Nazi Party and the German secret services to suspend violent activity in the Americas until a German-dominated Europe was assured.

Against these developments the Mexican presidential campaign got off to an early start following the 1938 expropriation of the oil industry. Many Mexican entrepreneurs and owners of small businesses and midsize companies saw this election as the last opportunity to undo the changes in social, labor, and agricultural policy that had occurred during the first four years of Cardenismo. Inspired by Franco's victory in Spain, Mexico's conservative and Catholic opposition

The 1940 presidential race between the official candidate Manuel Ávila Camacho and the conservative choice, Juan A. Almazán, resulted in widespread violence and corruption. Almazán may have been the popular choice in Mexico City and may have won the most votes there, but when the results were announced, Ávila Camacho won the race. Here supporters march through Mexico City with banners proclaiming that "Almazán is already President."

forces gathered around the regional strongman General Juan Andreu Almazán. Almazán himself hoped for the election of a Republican president in the November 1940 U.S. elections.

Before the tensions between Mexico's extreme right and left could further polarize Mexico's electorate, the Cárdenas administration won a much-needed reprieve with the announcement of the Hitler-Stalin pact. The sudden cooperation of the historical archenemies Communism and fascism was ideologically incomprehensible for most politicized Mexicans. Overnight, the potentially explosive tensions between Mexico's left and right imploded and were replaced by deep personal ideological introspection. Hitler and Stalin's game with the ideological identities of their sympathizers caused rank-and-file sympathizers in Mexico to fall into a deep political paralysis. Average followers on both sides deserted their leadership. This flow translated into an automatic weakening of the anti-Cárdenas forces. Then Germany's attack on Poland and the Soviet Union's invasion of Finland further alienated Mexico's popular leftist and rightist groups. These events were too reminiscent of great-power behavior against smaller countries in the 1920s and 1930s. Cárdenas declared Mexico's official neutrality in the European conflict, suggesting a distinct Mexican political stance that would avoid close cooperation with Britain, France, and Nazi Germany alike. Once again the political momentum had shifted in favor of Cárdenas and the official presidential candidate, Ávila Camacho. The benefactor of this development was the existing status quo in Mexico, whose distinctive Mexicanness suddenly made extreme leftist and rightist political and social alternatives less attractive.

Only the leadership of the most rabid Mexican anti-Communist conspirators and exiles in California proceeded with their subversive work against Mexico during this time. In late 1939, Mexican conspirators made their first indirect contact with Franco's new state in Spain. On the Spanish side, Minister of the Interior Ramón Serrano Suñer and his supporters in Spanish secret security forces identified the upcoming Mexican presidential election as a unique chance to create a first pro-Franco bridgehead within Latin America. Suñer and his followers fantasized that a pro-fascist Mexico after 1940 would deliver to them the large number of Republican exiles in Mexico and take away those exiles' remaining financial resources. In addition, a pro-Spanish Mexico could be offered as an operational base for German, Italian, and Japanese forces against the capitalist, Protestant United States. It might even be the first falling domino in the establishment of a new Spanish colonial empire in Latin America. Drunk with dreams of victory for the global fascist movements following dramatic German war victories in the first half of 1940, Suñer and Franco already fantasized themselves as future lords of a reassembled Spanish colonial system reaching from Madrid through Acapulco all the way to Manila in the Philippines.

On the Mexican side, right-wing conspirators saw this opportunity as a cultural war that would reverse the social and political gains of the Revolution and move Mexico closer to colonial times. After their victory, a traditional Spanish social hierarchy would put the mestizos and Indians back into a social space of limited importance in all spheres of life. Once again, Spanish seigniorial culture would put the importance of high-class social representation above the "shallow glow" coming from capitalistic, nouveau riche social groups and revolutionaries whose social status was based exclusively on force and money. The reestablishment of a conservative, orthodox Catholic hierarchy in Mexico would reinforce an idealized colonial moral code and gender roles. In this dreamy scheme the very modern, capitalistic, industrial Texas Oil Company would play a critical role as operator of the expropriated petroleum reserves of the U.S. Standard Oil and British Shell Oil companies.

An important part of this historical *imaginarium* was the separation of the United States from Latin America. In the eyes of the conspirators, the United States would become a singular democratic state north of the Rio Grande that slowly would be forced into subservience to world fascism. Eventually, this remnant of the liberal political and economic order would be eliminated and the world would return to the times before the Spanish independence movement, free of capitalism, modernity, democracy, and the secular form of statehood.

Opposition candidate General Juan Andreu Almazán lost the presidential election in July 1940. However, the inauguration of president-elect Avila Camacho would not take place until December 1940. This hiatus offered the right-wing opposition forces almost five months to change the course of Mexican history. As expected in 1939, Almazán did not accept defeat in the presidential election without a serious challenge. Almazán left Mexico for the Caribbean, whereupon his supporters organized a publicity campaign in the United States and Central America, challenging the outcome of the election. Inside Mexico, a small number of Almazán followers who had lost races for local and regional offices staged limited uprisings. Another group, in contact with former Mexican president-in-exile Calles, bought arms on the U.S. market to supply a larger military uprising. From Spain, Serrano Suñer announced the departure of Spanish Falange agents to promote subversive activities in Mexico. Germany was approached to contribute a small number of tanks, heavy weapons, and airplanes. Delivery to the Pacific Coast of Mexico was supposed to be made via Japan.

Fortunately, this effort failed, because of unprecedented cooperation between U.S. and Mexican security forces, the reelection of President Roosevelt, and the German refusal to act at that particular moment. President-elect Avila Camacho's supporters systematically enlisted the help of U.S. supporters, asking for early diplomatic recognition by that country and therefore giving international legitimacy to Avila Camacho as the official winner of the 1940 Mexican presidential election. Avila Camacho's campaign manager, Governor Miguel Alemán, succeeded in obtaining this recognition in the early fall of 1940. The White House and the State Department recognized Avila Camacho even before the U.S. presidential elections and the Mexican inauguration. After losing the political battle over recognition, the Almazanistas moved toward large-scale armed rebellion. However, with the help of the FBI, U.S. military intelligence, and Mexican agents supplied by the Ministry of Finance, the Ministry of the Interior, and the military, the Almazán conspirators in the United States, along the U.S.-Mexican border, and inside Mexico were systematically shadowed and their preparations disrupted. The Mexican military quashed local uprisings in the Mexican north and patrolled Mexican coasts to prevent the landing of revolutionary troops or weapons deliveries. When Almazán wanted to slip into the United States to spearhead the next phase of his rebellion, the U.S. Immigration and Naturalization Service gave him a public welcome. The White House and the State Department refused to meet with the Almazanistas, who wanted to make their case in favor of their candidate. The German Foreign Ministry decided against joining Spanish efforts opposing Mexico, because Avila Camacho seemed to be more pro-German than the outgoing Cárdenas. Hitler himself preferred a neutral Mexico over a revolutionary one at that time. Consequently, the Almazanistas in Mexico never received the heavy military hardware necessary to mount and sustain a serious military operation inside Mexico.

Finally, the reelection of Franklin Delano Roosevelt in November 1940 guaranteed a continuation of the pro-Mexico policy in the White House over the next four years. To make this point President Roosevelt appointed U.S. vice president-elect Henry Wallace to represent the United States at the Mexican presidential inauguration in December 1940. This was the first public demonstration of how close the Avila Camacho camp and the Roosevelt administration had become during the joint U.S.-Mexican battle against pro-fascist forces during the past five months. It also suggested a major break with the Cardenista foreign policy that had preferred Carranza's ideal of Mexican cooperation within a multilateral Latin American framework against the United States. In the end, defeated Mexican presidential candidate Almazán recognized reality, publicly admitted his defeat, and returned home to Mexico to join the economic elite of the postrevolutionary state. Mexico's private economic sector quickly saw an opportunity to profit from the expected U.S.-Mexican wartime economic cooperation. The last major Mexican regional revolutionary warlord turned entrepreneur. Postrevolutionary politics and development had finally completely replaced the era of violent revolution.

As early as 1936, Mexican domestic observers had suggested that during the next global war U.S. and European military powers would be more dependent on Latin American raw materials to sustain a long-term fight. Therefore, Mexico might find itself in the unique position of being able to sell its raw materials more expensively than in peacetime and generate new state income to finance domestic development. Petroleum sales after 1938 had confirmed the expected effect that international rearmament was having on the international oil trade. It took until the spring of 1939 for Mexico to return to more planned national industrial development. A few months later Europe and Asia were ablaze in war. Now the engine that would fuel the industrialization of Mexico would be the external stimulus of rearmament and wartime raw-materials needs. As soon as the Roosevelt and British administrations would accept Cárdenas's offer of supplying democratic countries with petroleum, Mexico's planners could use the money to acquire U.S. know-how and technology to expand Mexico's manufacturing base. If everything went according to plan, at the end of the war Mexican factories could satisfy the pent-up demand for consumer and durable goods, freeing foreign currency for other developmental needs.

However, the step from policy idea to economic reality was much more complex. Even before Avila Camacho's inauguration on December 5, 1940, U.S. undersecretary of state Sumner Welles and Mexican government representatives had agreed in principle to use the coming months to reach comprehensive settlements on the most critical unsolved bilateral issues. Indeed, from December 1940 on, an unprecedented degree of Mexican-U.S. diplomacy unfolded. Bilateral committees negotiated terms of cooperation in the areas of military, naval, and air defense. A planned exchange of Mexican raw materials for U.S. manufactured goods and industrial technology was organized according to Washington's bureaucratic war economy rules. One commission resolved the continuing oil expropriation conflict with U.S. oil multinationals. Additional groups discussed bilateral water rights, agrarian expropriation, agricultural labor, revolutionary claims, the joining of U.S. armed forces by Mexican citizens, and other wartime financial issues. By November 1940, most of the major U.S.-Mexican conflicts of the previous 20 years had been resolved. War in Asia and Europe had given the U.S. government unprecedented clout to pressure unpatriotic multinationals into

complying with national war needs. And exceptional diplomatic goodwill on both sides had cleared the road for even deeper bilateral cooperation in the years to come.

Mexican developers organized their concessions to the United States in such a way as to produce the greatest economic benefit for their developmental vision. For example, an April 1940 flight agreement opened access to U.S. Lend Lease funds as well as bringing military planes to modernize Mexico's air force. The seizure of German and Italian boats in Mexican harbors brought overnight previously unavailable, nationalized tanker space to export Mexican oil to the United States and earn foreign currency. The enactment of the Allied Blacklists in July 1940 provided a powerful legal smoke screen to move Germany's chemical and pharmaceuticals industrial facilities and patents into national guardianship and to prepare for the later final expropriation of the German monopoly after the war. On July 15, 1940, Avila Camacho's negotiators signed an all-encompassing U.S.-Mexican commercial treaty guaranteeing Mexicans a U.S. market at protected prices for the surplus production of 11 strategic materials. From the beginning of the depression, Mexico had not enjoyed a similar preferential situation. In addition, Mexico reached special silver purchase agreements and gained access to U.S. currency stabilization funds. The agreement over the nationalization of the oil industry in November 1940 made the Mexican action legally irrevocable. More important, it isolated the British oil claims in Mexico even more and confirmed Cárdenas's idea that the expropriation had been a sound risk. War had forced the multinationals to give in to Mexico's economic nationalism. Critical

U.S. petroleum technology and expertise were again allowed to enter Mexico, helping with the development of the nationalized property. The Roosevelt administration also provided Avila Camacho with a much-needed overhaul of Mexico's expropriated railway system as well as financing for the continuation of the Pan American Highway, Baja California road projects, and Mexican harbor modernization.

Most important from a long-term perspective, Mexico's national foreign debt was reduced by almost 90 percent. Mexican minister of finance Eduardo Suárez decided that Hitler's complete control over Europe warranted the cancellation of most of Mexico's European debt. As expected, the external stimulus of the war was providing financing for vital national infrastructure projects and the Mexican equivalent of Works Progress Administration job programs. If Mexico could escape the war without experiencing fighting on its own territory, it would emerge with a strong national infrastructure and an attractive financial position vis-à-vis international investors and banks. Brilliant negotiators were repositioning Mexico's international macroeconomic position to accelerate development with foreign loans after the end of the war.

The creation of advantageous macroeconomic features did not translate, into improvement for workers and peasants. To the contrary, in some agricultural sectors the United States requested crop changes that caused famine and regional economic dislocations lasting for years in previously functioning local markets. Only the determined personal intervention of U.S. Ambassador George Messersmith avoided a more serious hunger disaster and a public relations nightmare. A torrent of financial flight from the United States and Europe, as well as massive financial reimbursements for Mexican raw materials, created an expanding inflation that ate away at the already meager purchasing power of workers. Labor rights were even more restricted, and many of the political freedoms that union members had gained in the 1930s were repressed. In short, the war became a pretext to attack Mexico's political left. Also, U.S. government bureaucrats were far less demonstrative in their support of Mexico than were the White House and the U.S. ambassador to Mexico. The relocation or construction of manufacturing plants and sophisticated technology failed to materialize. U.S. economic war needs remained more important than Mexican development. Few U.S. planners acknowledged that Mexico's raw-materials deliveries fueled 40 percent of the U.S. war industry. It was the most significant Latin American contribution to the fight against the Axis powers. Finally, U.S. military support for financing projects in Mexico ended overnight when victory in the Battle of Midway made a landing of Japanese troops on Mexico's Pacific Coast unlikely.

By 1943, experienced Mexican economists realized that the enthusiastic U.S.-Mexican wartime economic cooperation of the last three years was becoming less and less justified. Minister of Hacienda Suárez reminded the cabinet that bilateral wartime cooperation had been a temporary exception, not the beginning of a long-term U.S.-Mexican relationship. To the political left, former Cardenistas and more radical politicians resumed their criticism that U.S.-Mexican wartime cooperation was little else than a simple pretext for U.S. imperialists to establish a lasting hegemony over Latin America. As early as the course of the war allowed, Minister Suárez and the head of the Bank of Mexico, Eduardo Villaseñor, resumed their prewar outreach toward their European, Asian, and Soviet economic partners, exploring alternatives to U.S.-Mexican economic exchanges. The traditional Mexican diplomatic stance between the United States and Europe was being reconstructed, only now within the context of the expected winners of World War II: Britain, the Soviet Union, the United States, and the soon-to-be-reconstituted countries of France, Poland, Czechoslovakia, the Netherlands, Belgium, and Scandinavia.

Reacting to the growing nationalist frustrations in Mexico, presidents Roosevelt and Avila Camacho made determined personal efforts to continue the early positive wartime cooperation into the postwar era. During a presidential exchange visit in 1943, a special bilateral study commission was created that sought solutions to the problems that came with uneven wartime development. The bilateral bureaucratic rules and inertia were more powerful. Still, Mexico was the only Latin American country that received such special attention and genuine U.S. goodwill from the White House.

With the majority of Mexicans continuing to be apprehensive about U.S.-Mexican wartime cooperation, President Avila Camacho and Foreign Minister Ezequiel Padilla could not push openly for a Mexican declaration of war against the Axis powers. In the fall of 1941, the German decision to close Latin American consulates in occupied Europe had given the National Palace the opportunity to close Axis consulates in Mexico. This step eliminated many clandestine bases for secret Axis subversive operations. Following the Japanese attack against Pearl Harbor in December 1941 and the German declaration of war against the United States later in the same month, the Avila Camacho administration broke diplomatic relations with Germany but did not declare war against it. And while smaller Latin American countries did declare war against all the Axis powers, it took repeated German submarine attacks against Mexican ships in the Gulf of Mexico after February 1942 to create a strong enough case for Padilla and Avila Camacho to overcome popular reservations and convince Congress to enter the war formally on the side of the Allied powers.

Avila Camacho strengthened this fragile domestic front by inviting former Mexican president Plutarco Elías Calles to return from exile in California, by naming the nationalist former president Lázaro Cárdenas as minister of war, and by entrusting the defense of the Gulf of Mexico to conservative former president Abelardo Rodríguez. The labor union caudillo Vicente Lombardo Toledano was further constrained through restrictive labor-government agreements that forced him to become active outside Mexico as a Latin American labor union leader, certainly a project doomed to fail in light of the continuing political conservatism of the rest of Latin America.

By then, popular cultural exchanges, nurtured by a relentless Allied propaganda in all the media—print, radio, movies, even postage stamps—had brought some sense of wartime emergency to the small but important Mexican urban middle class. U.S., British, and French propaganda machines took over the reporting of all foreign affairs. Those who could not read learned about the war in public spectacles, such as dramas performed in the Zócalo (central plaza) in Mexico City following the sinking of the Mexican tanker *Potrero de Llano* by a German submarine. Special propaganda aimed at priests enlisted the small number of pro-Allied priests to influence their local parishes. Almost surreal civil defense "emergencies" and real-life military war games engaged Mexicans against the Axis powers long after the Axis forces had the resources to launch a sustained attack against Latin America. Never before had the postrevolutionary elite and its foreign supporters enjoyed so much influence over the political opinions of its citizens. The threat of an Axis invasion gave the Avila Camacho administration the opportunity to promote a new conservative national consensus that tried to bridge serious divisions of geography, race, and class.

The Avila Camacho administration feared a possible German or Japanese landing on Mexican soil, a surprise act that would have been answered immediately with an invasion by Allied forces that would have turned the country into a battlefield. To ensure that the Axis powers would stay away from Mexico's shores, Avila Camacho allowed extensive operation by U.S. secret forces in Mexico. Under the leadership of FBI agent Gus Jones, U.S. advisors trained and cooperated with Mexico's counterintelligence forces. These advisors also helped in writing Mexico's first law against espionage, subversion, and sabotage. In addition, a stream of U.S. undercover agents from naval military intelligence and the Office of Strategic Services toured every bay along the Mexican Pacific and Atlantic coasts, investigating rumors of German and Japanese landing preparations. None of these searches found foreign troops on the beaches.

Nevertheless, U.S. secret forces and representatives of the Mexican ministries of government and Treasury, the military, and the presidential security service unmasked Germany's, Italy's, and Spain's most sophisticated network of agents and saboteurs north of the Panama Canal before Hitler could change his mind and order large-scale sabotage operations in the Americas in 1941 or cooperate in a Pearl Harbor-like attack on the Americas. Because Axis subversion systematically exploited ethnic groups to prepare for a full-scale military invasion, the Mexican government removed the Japanese, Germans, and Italians from Mexico's coastal zones. As long as Spain remained neutral, the presence of pro-Franco Spaniards along Mexico's coasts had to be tolerated. Following the arrest in 1942 of the Japanese naval attaché and German spies in Mexico, U.S. and Mexican investigators learned of contingency plans to attack and conquer the Mexican port of Acapulco, damage U.S. airplane production in San Diego, and attack the Panama Canal. Indeed, after the 1942 Mexican declaration of war, German foreign minister Joachim von Ribbentrop angrily suggested sabotaging Mexico's oil fields. After 1942, Mexican vigilance kept the remaining Axis amateurs from trying to inflict serious harm on the country. Just as Venustiano Carranza had protected Mexico from the dangerous consequences of German subversion and sabotage during World War I, Avila Camacho's cooperation with U.S. and British secret forces protected the Mexican state and everyday Mexicans from German designs for the second time in this century.

Mexico's declaration of war in June 1942, following the sinking of the *Potrero de Llano*, embarrassed U.S. military leaders in Washington into taking Mexico's military dedication more seriously and to admit at least a symbolic Mexican fighting force to a European or Asian war theater. The development of a modern Mexican air force emerged as a compromise that accommodated continued popular hesitation to fight abroad and promised respect and legitimacy to all of Mexico's professionalized armed forces. At a time when Brazilian forces were preparing for deployment in Italy and the Mexican military's official role in politics was being eliminated, World War II offered high Mexican officers much-needed glory. President Avila Camacho himself expressed a personal desire to fight abroad, saying that only the presidency was keeping him from action.

Mexican air force pilots received training in the United States during 1944 and fought valiantly in Philippine air battles in 1945. Mexican pilots that died in the campaign and Mexican air force squadrons came to personify Mexico's unwavering commitment to the cause of the Allies during World War II, and, as important, Mexico's rightful claim to sit at the side of the victors. In the United States the bad memories of Carranza's World War I policy were being replaced by a realization that without Mexican raw materials in U.S. factories, Foreign Minister Padilla's Latin American diplomacy, Mexican bracero workers in U.S. agriculture and industry, and Mexican soldiers, as well as Mexican-American volunteers in all branches of the U.S. armed forces, the war effort of the United States against the Axis would have been less strong and self-assured. Most likely, a politically weaker Mexico would have been tolerant of German anti-American activities carried out from Mexican territory. In Spanish-speaking Latin America, the Avila Camacho administration's relentless pro-democracy stance and action justified Foreign Minister Padilla's demand to act as mediator between the United States and Latin America but also came as a distinctly Latin American voice within the newly formed United Nations. Mexico's experiences and lessons from the Pan American Union of the 1920s and the League of Nations in the 1930s were now translated into the United Nations.

Then the sudden retirement of Undersecretary of State Sumner Welles and the death of President Roosevelt removed the staunchest pro-Mexico advocates from Washington. FBI head Herbert Hoover and other members of the U.S. State Department resumed the cold war against the Soviet Union within the Western Hemisphere as early as 1943. They revived unilateral pressure politics that failed to comprehend the particularities of Mexico's leftist political culture. Then the departure of U.S. ambassador to Mexico Messersmith removed the last remaining pillar of the special U.S.-Mexican wartime relationship. Ezequiel Padilla continued his tenure as Mexican foreign minister and represented Mexico with distinction during the creation of the United Nations at the conference at San Francisco in 1942. But his lone determination was not enough to avoid negative change.

Those in the United States who preferred to see the Western Hemisphere as one regional block, not as a set of discrete political entities with their own unique political agendas, were gaining ground in Washington. In the Western Hemisphere, World War II evolved into the cold war. Miguel Alemán defeated Padilla easily in the 1946 presidential election and established his own relationship with the Truman administration.

Fueling the popular Mexican love-hate relationship with its neighbor to the north, the war had given new proof of the financial possibilities of mass tourism. The closure of the Pacific and Atlantic, the overhauling of the Mexican railway system, and the opening of the Pan American Highway had brought an unprecedented number of U.S. tourists south of the border. The penetration of Mexican movie houses by Hollywood films also continued after 1945. There was no alternative. Britain was bankrupt. The economies of Germany, France, Italy, and Japan were destroyed, and the Soviet Union was not interested in industrializing Mexico. Raw materials from other Latin American countries continued to compete with those from Mexico. More so than after World War I and the Mexican Revolution, the United States was the focus of Mexican foreign relations. From then on, the new context of the cold war produced a new variation on an all-too-familiar theme.

Photo Essay:
Festivals of Mexico

Communities across Mexico celebrate civic occasions, church holidays (including saint's days), and local activities that promote pride among the residents. Here a young woman is dressed in traditional clothes for the Coffee Festival in the town of Puebla.

Towns, individuals, occupational groups, sports teams, and other social organizations have patron saints that they celebrate annually. Because of the role of the Franciscan order in the evangelization of Mexico during the colonial period, San Francisco has a widespread following on October 4. Here a participant prepares to parade in the San Francisco celebration in Puebla.

The celebration of the day of San Pedro, on June 29, a holiday usually shared with San Pablo, includes parades, masses, and vigils. This woman lights a votive candle before San Pedro's image in Durango.

Community dance groups make costumes using the colors of the patron saint and practice their dances all year to prepare for the holiday. Both of these girls are performing during the festival of San Miguel, celebrated September 29, in Tlacohahuaya, Oaxaca.

The Fiesta of Santa Cruz, the celebration of the Holy Cross on May 3, serves as the special devotion of carpenters and other construction workers. This celebration in Chatinos, Oaxaca, shows a special church service honoring the image of the cross.

San Isidro, the patron saint of farmers and irrigation, is honored on May 15, with a celebration and fair. Often communities have a parade with the saint's image that includes individuals dressed as devils who move through the crowd to maintain order and play jokes, giving a humorous character to the festival. This San Isidro devil comes from the state of Guerrero.

Mexico's most important civil celebration, Independence Day, begins on the evening of September 15 and continues through the next day. This photograph shows the riot of flags celebrating the day and reveals the transborder influence of television with the *Simpsons* T-shirt worn by a reveler.

Mexico's other popular civil celebration on May 5 (the Cinco de Mayo) commemorates the victory of Mexican troops over invading French soldiers at Puebla on May 5, 1862. The holiday, celebrated throughout Mexico and the southwestern United States, often includes a mock battle between French troops (shown here) and the Mexican victors.

Birthdays, such as the one this woman is celebrating, are often combined celebrations honoring the day's patron saint.

The passage from childhood to young womanhood comes on a girl's fifteenth birthday. The celebration of the Quincinera includes both a special church service (as shown here in the parish church in Morelos) and a family coming-out party.

Celebrations mark the passages of life in Mexico, many of which include the church. Here, a newly-married couple leaves a Mexico City church in a traditional carriage. The newlyweds must have a civil ceremony (signing the civil registry) to make the marriage legal.

Death demands somber celebration from both family and community members, as the village honors its members, both the living and the dead. Here villagers attend a funeral in Chiapas.

Mexican communities often offer special devotion to certain church holidays. The town of Tlacotlapan, Veracruz, has a national reputation for its celebration of Candelaria (Candlemas) each February 2. The activities include a procession of the image of the Virgin through town.

Carnival celebrations (often three days long) provide an opportunity for merriment and social reversals (here a young man has become a bull) before the forty days of Lent. This parade in Chiapas also includes raucous noise makers and a mock bull fight.

Holy Week celebrations range from the appropriately somber Mass on Good Friday, with the altar and images shrouded and the bells silent, to processions through the streets by church groups (called cofradías). The procession includes images that portray the passion of Christ. Here girls from a catechism class precede an image of Christ in San Luis Potosí.

During Holy Week, performances of passion plays tell the story of the life of Jesus Christ, and conclude with a re-enactment of the crucifixion by villagers dressed as Roman soldiers. This play occurred in Zacatecas.

Until the middle of the nineteenth century the holiday of Corpus Christi included displaying the Eucharist. National laws attempting to reduce the influence of the church halted this practice, resulting in parades of groups in indigenous costumes and conquistador clothing retelling the story of the bringing of Christianity to Mexico. This participant in the Corpus Christi parade comes from Veracruz.

The voladores, or flyers, from Papantla, Veracruz, form part of the traditional town celebration of Corpus Christi. The voladores practice a ritual that extends back to the pre-Columbian culture. The flyers astonished the Spaniards when they first arrived.

Day of the Dead festivals (marking the holidays of All Saints and All Souls) combine both pre-Columbian and Catholic rituals. The festivals include the construction of elaborate home altars, such as this one in Santa Fe de la Laguna, Michoacán, and the gathering of family members around graves in the cemetery.

During Day of the Dead festivities, family members clean grave sites, decorate them, often with the favorite foods of the deceased, and hold all-night vigils waiting for the return of departed souls. This grave-side gathering comes from San Miguel de Allende, Guanajuato.

Christmas season in Mexico includes the traditional celebration called Posadas in which neighbors go house to house, re-enacting Mary and Joseph's search for lodging, until the evening's host admits them for a fiesta that include breaking a piñata. The posadas take place during the two weeks before Christmas.

December 12 marks both a major religious and national holiday with the celebration of the Day of Virgin of Guadalupe. Many pilgrims make the journey to the Basilica of the Virgin, where dancers representing communities from across Mexico perform dances in the Virgin's honor. This dancer from Michoacán has worked the Vigin's image into his dance costume.

17

Mexican Culture, 1920–1945

HELEN DELPAR

In September 1921, Mexico City saw a month-long celebration of the centenary of the consummation of its independence from Spain. More than 100 events were scheduled, despite the somewhat equivocal nature of the anniversary, which commemorated the deeds of Agustín de Iturbide, who marched into Mexico City on September 27, 1821. But the motives underlying the centenary celebration were related only tangentially to the events of 1821. The observance was intended to be a proclamation of Mexico's resurgence from a decade of civil war as well as an affirmation of Mexican culture, designed to contrast with the lavish celebration mounted in 1910 by the regime of Porfirio Díaz to commemorate the start of the independence movement 100 years before. Alberto J. Pani, the secretary of foreign relations in 1921, later recalled, "In contrast to the Porfirian festivities eleven years before, which stood out for their aristocratic tone and indifference to our traditions, arts, and customs, those of 1921 were equally accessible to all social classes and exhibited a marked nationalist color."

The program for 1921 included exhibits of Mexican art, a procession of decorated canoes in honor of the Aztec goddess Xochiquetzal at Xochimilco, and an excursion for diplomats and foreign guests to the newly excavated ruins at Teotihuacán, ending with a luncheon at which barbecue, turkey with *mole* sauce, and beans were served, along with *pulque* and beer. The festivities culminated with a "Mexican night" in Chapultepec Park, supervised by the painter Adolfo Best Maugard. Featuring fireworks and regional dances and music, it was intended, according to the program, to have "an essentially Mexicanist character" composed "entirely of the different national arts."

Pani exaggerated the antinationalist aspects of the 1910 centenary celebration, which included inauguration of a museum at Teotihuacán and dedication of monuments to independence and to Benito Juárez, hero of the mid–19th–century

Robert Montenegro painted the mural entitled *Reconstruction* at the former Convent of San Pedro and San Pablo that had become Public School No. 6 in Mexico City. This detail from the mural presents *The Mexican Family*, the people for whom the revolution was fought.

reform movement. However, the 1921 festivities accurately reflected the cultural nationalism that was to characterize much of Mexico's artistic and literary production during the next two decades. They also foreshadowed an extraordinary flowering of art, music, and literature that would gain unprecedented international admiration, especially for the murals created by the three masters: Diego Rivera, José Clemente Orozco, and David Alfaro Siqueiros. To many contemporaries this cultural renewal was not only an expression of the forces and aspirations unleashed by the ongoing revolution but an integral, valuable part of the revolutionary process itself.

While nationalism can be seen as the primary theme of Mexico's cultural production after 1921, contemporary intellectuals, composers, and artists were by no means bound by ideology nor were they adherents of a single school or movement. José Vasconcelos, who as secretary of public education from 1921 to 1924 was the initial sponsor of the mural movement, was above all an admirer of Hispanic civilization. The muralists themselves, as well as other artists and writers, were steeped in European cultural styles past and present. All denounced the Díaz regime for its alleged disdain of native traditions, especially those originating in the indigenous population, which was seen as the intended beneficiary of agrarian reform and other policies of the revolutionary administrations. But even those who were most committed to improving the lot of the Indians, such as the anthropologist Manuel Gamio and the educator Moisés Sáenz, envisioned their assimilation into an integrated, Spanish-speaking nation. In reality, despite the affirmation of purely indigenous traditions, *mestizaje*—the blending of the Indian and the European—lay at the root of the cultural nationalism of the era.

A second prominent theme in the artistic discourse of the era was the obligation of painters and others to create work that would be accessible to all, not only in an aesthetic sense but also in a physical one. Out of this conviction grew the emphasis on the painting of murals in public places, where they could be seen by workers and peasants, who might thereby be instructed or moved by the nationalistic, sometimes revolutionary subjects of the murals. What, if anything, the murals signified to the working-class people who saw them cannot be determined, though Orozco doubted that art alone could spur the masses to rise up against their oppressors. Moreover, as the international fame of the Mexican muralists grew, it was the elites in Mexico and elsewhere that embraced them most fulsomely, and their easel paintings often ended in the collections of North American millionaires. Both Orozco and Siqueiros expressed concern that Rivera and other artists were overemphasizing the folkloric elements in their work—themes that Orozco and Siqueiros considered no longer relevant to Mexican realities but that appealed to foreign tourists and collectors.

A highlight of the 1921 centenary festivities was an exhibition of Mexican folk art organized by the painters Gerardo Murillo (better known as Dr. Atl, the Nahuatl word for water), Jorge Enciso, and Roberto Montenegro. President Alvaro Obregón himself attended the opening and was reported to have been "highly pleased" by the exhibit. After his departure, the remaining dignitaries moved to a nearby courtyard, where they sampled a collation of tamales and *atole*, a corn-based beverage. The exhibit grew out of a contemporary movement that championed folk art as the truest representation of the innate aesthetic sense of the Mexican people. An expression of this view can be found in the *Revista de Revistas* (*Review of Reviews*) in 1920: "Our manual and domestic industries . . . form a popular and handsome medium of expression that is truly indigenous, because behind the Spanish colonial and Oriental influences—Chinese, Korean, and Japanese—one perceives the spirit of [our] ancestors who produced objects in stone and clay more beautiful than those of any other people in the world except the Greeks." In connection with the exhibit Dr. Atl wrote *Las artes populares en México* (1922) in hopes of stimulating the study of what he called a quintessentially Mexican art. The exhibit traveled to Los Angeles, where it was seen by thousands. The U.S. writer Katherine Anne Porter, who had been living in Mexico, prepared an English-language guide to the exhibit, in which she noted that after independence, when it became fashionable to imitate

Europe, Mexico's folk art had "disappeared from popularity . . . and [was] used only by the Indio [Indian]."

Now, however, folk art experienced a resurgence in popularity with, as the historian Daniel Cosío Villegas recalled, every home acquiring a lacquered bowl from Olinalá in Guerrero or a pot from Oaxaca. Some Mexican artists, such as Rivera, Enciso, and Miguel Covarrubias, became serious collectors, as did two North American expatriates Frederick Davis and William Spratling. All five lent objects from their collections for the first important exhibit of Mexican art to be seen in the United States. Opening at New York's Metropolitan Museum of Art in October 1930, the show assigned a prominent place to folk art. According to the organizer of the exhibit, René d'Harnoncourt, Mexican folk art had reached "the highest plane of excellence" because of the "abundance of raw materials, a highly developed manual dexterity, the traditions of many centuries, and native taste. . . . These many articles of personal use remain the Mexican Indian's unique contribution to the civilization of his country."

Although artists and intellectuals treasured Mexico's folk art and lamented its likely demise as the country became industrialized, Orozco observed in his autobiography that it appealed mainly to the bourgeoisie. While they filled their dwellings with clay pots and tin candlesticks during the 1920s, workers were eager to buy mass-produced modern objects for their homes.

The 1921 folk art exhibition also led indirectly to the founding in 1925 of *Mexican Folkways,* a bilingual magazine that during the seven or so years of its existence carried articles, photographs, and artwork about many aspects of contemporary Mexican life, especially that of the Indian. Its editor was a U.S. citizen, Frances Toor, who had been so impressed by the exhibit that she decided to move permanently to Mexico: "I wanted to know more of the country in which humble people could make such beautiful things." Initially subsidized by the department of education, the magazine included leading Mexican and North American artists, writers, and scholars among its contributors.

Another important event during the 1921 centennial celebration was an exhibition of paintings produced by students at the Academy of Fine Arts under the inspiration of its director, Alfredo Ramos Martínez. When first elected to that influential post in 1913 during the regime of Victoriano Huerta, he outlined a program that was perceived as a radical departure for the academy. In a letter to the secretary of education, Ramos Martínez stated that he wished to take his students out of doors so that they could paint directly from nature. "The aim," he added, "is to awaken the enthusiasm of the students for the beauty of our own land, and to give birth to an art worthy of being truthfully called a national art." A house was rented in the village of Santa Anita, and students set up their easels in the patio to begin experiments in impressionism. Ramos Martínez lost his position after the fall of Huerta, but the teachers and students again elected him director in July 1920. He established another open-air school, this time in Coyoacán, where students resumed their observations of the Mexican landscape and its inhabitants. Dr. Atl, who had briefly succeeded Ramos Martínez as academy

director in 1914, spoke at the 1921 exhibit, which he called "a vigorous manifestation of art and will," adding that there was more of the latter in evidence than
the former. A critic for the newspaper *Excelsior* disagreed, praising signs of a new
orientation among the students that would help them break with traditional
teachings so that they could develop their own artistic personalities.

Although the artistic nationalism expressed by Ramos Martínez would be a
major theme of the 1920s, the emergence of a Mexican art can be traced to the
colonial period. From the earliest days of Spanish rule there is evidence for the
modification of European traditions by pre-Columbian techniques, especially in
the decorative arts. Moreover, by 1700, painters—many of them Mexican by
birth—were turning to local subjects. For example, Miguel Cabrera
(1695–1768), himself a mestizo, depicted the mixing of races, while Antonio
Pérez de Aguilar (flourished 1749–69) included in his *Painter's Cupboard* (1769)
the round wooden boxes in which the confection known as *cajeta* was sold.

This painting was presented to the gallery of the Academy of San Carlos soon
after its formal establishment in 1785. Although the academy staff was dominated by Spanish-born artists during its early years, a Mexican of indigenous
ancestry, Pedro Patiño Ixtolinque, became director of the academy in 1825.
Rivalry between Mexican artists and imported Spanish instructors was a constant
source of dissension throughout the 19th century. Regardless of their nationality,
most of those affiliated with the academy continued to produce paintings or
sculpture on historical and religious themes in accordance with prevailing trends
in Rome, the favored site for foreign study. An exception was the foremost
19th–century academic painter and teacher of Diego Rivera, José María Velasco
(1840–1912), whose landscapes of the Valley of Mexico demonstrate his mastery
of perspective and color. Meanwhile, outside the academy, provincial artists such
as Agustín Arrieta (1802–74) and Hermenogildo Bustos (1832–1907) painted
portraits and still lifes that captured an unmistakably Mexican reality.

Also unmistakably Mexican were the illustrated broadsides featuring *calaveras*
(animated skeletons) and printed on special occasions, such as the Day of the
Dead. These broadsides contained often biting text that commented on political
events or the inevitability of death but are remembered mainly for the illustrations attributed to the printmaker José Guadalupe Posada (1852–1913). Unno-
ticed in his lifetime, Posada was later hailed for his incisive portrayals of Porfirian
society and as an inspiration to the nationally oriented artists of the postrevolutionary era.

By 1910, an air of renewal pervaded the academy as younger artists forsook
Italy for France and Germany, where they absorbed modernist currents they then
disseminated at home. Yet artistic nationalism remained powerful. When the
Díaz administration sponsored a large exhibition of contemporary Spanish art as
part of the 1910 centenary celebrations, academy students led by Dr. Atl
protested. He asked the director of the academy, Antonio Rivas Mercado, for permission to use its walls to hang an exhibition of Mexican painting and sculpture.
Rivas Mercado, designer of the independence monument unveiled during the

Despite his later move to the political right, José Vasconcelos earned an honored place in Mexican history with his efforts as Minister of Education from 1921 to 1924.

centenary, readily agreed, and both he and the secretary of education, Justo Sierra, provided funds for the exhibit. It included paintings with consciously nationalist and indigenous themes such as José Enciso's *Anahuac*, which depicted an Indian silhouetted against a Mexican landscape. By 1910, Dr. Atl had also become an enthusiast of mural decoration, which he envisioned as a collective enterprise, and formed an artistic center to seek out walls on public buildings on which to paint murals.

Although the outbreak of the Revolution soon disrupted the work of Mexico's artists, the nationalist current that sought inspiration in indigenous themes and motifs remained strong as painters such as Montenegro, Best Maugard, and Saturnino Herrán portrayed scenes and personages derived from the pre-Columbian past or modern folklore. The Guatemalan-born Carlos Mérida, who settled in Mexico in 1919, went further, arguing that such paintings offered a purely literary or anecdotal form of nationalism. What was needed, he insisted, was an exploration of color and composition in a nationalist vein. This he did himself in his own decorative canvases. In short, the problems of developing a national art had long been debated in Mexico. As Orozco noted in his autobiography, "by 1922 the table had been set for mural painting."

The start of the mural movement is always associated with José Vasconcelos (1882–1959), who became secretary of public education when the department was reestablished in 1921. It was given jurisdiction over libraries and the fine arts as well as educational institutions at all levels, in which the federal government was to have an expanded role. Vasconcelos had no background as an educator but was one of Mexico's leading intellectuals, having been a founder in 1909 of the Ateneo de la Juventud, a forum for proponents of literary and philosophical renewal. He later claimed to have been guided as secretary by the example of the Soviet commissar of education, Anatoli Lunacharsky, though he did not share the latter's Marxist ideology. He championed rural schooling and indigenous education, even though his efforts to bring the classic works of Western civilization to the masses provoked derision from those who believed such a policy was absurd in a nation of illiterates. This effort reflected his belief in the superiority of Mexico's Hispanic and European heritage. He may have glorified the mestizo in his *Raza cósmica* (1922), but as art historian Leonard Folgarait has observed, "In this mixture . . . indigenous peoples were to be assimilated to the point of nonrecognition."

The first murals executed under the sponsorship of Vasconcelos were painted by Dr. Atl, Montenegro, Enciso, and others in the former Church of San Pedro and San Pablo in Mexico City, which had been acquired by the department of education. However, the beginning of the mural movement is usually dated from the decoration of the colonial building housing the Escuela Nacional Preparatoria (National Preparatory School), a secondary school preparing students for entrance to the National University. It was here that the three "great ones" of Mexico's artistic renaissance—Rivera, Orozco, and Siqueiros—were first employed in painting murals, along with several other artists. The murals at the Preparatoria would arouse both praise and outrage, a hallmark of the entire movement.

At the time Vasconcelos engaged Diego Rivera (1886–1957) to paint a mural in the auditorium of the preparatory school, he was probably the most accomplished and best-known painter in Mexico. After studying at the Academy of Fine Arts from 1898 to 1906, he traveled on a government fellowship to Europe, where he immersed himself in the new artistic styles of the day, especially Cubism. From 1913 to 1917, he painted approximately 200 Cubist canvases before shifting to a style strongly influenced by Cézanne. Before leaving Europe in 1921, he toured Italy and was dazzled by the art he saw there: frescoes, Byzantine mosaics, and Etruscan funeral vases and tomb paintings. Because of his long absence abroad, Rivera did not personally experience the turmoil of the Revolution, but he returned to Mexico with a desire to undertake large public projects accessible to the masses. This goal was strengthened during a trip to Yucatán as a member of Vasconcelos's entourage when he examined Maya monuments, including the frescoes of the Temple of the Tigers at Chichén Itzá.

Creation (1922–23), the mural Rivera painted on the arched wall of the Preparatoria's auditorium, differs from those he would paint later in that it was

Minister of Education José Vasconcelos was determined to educate the Mexican people about their history and culture. He launched a major school expansion program in the countryside and selected muralists to paint the nation's history on public buildings. In this mural at the Ministry of Public Education, *The Woman Rural School-teacher*, Diego Rivera portrays the revolution's educational campaign.

José Clemente Orozco, Diego Rivera, and David Alfaro Siqueiros were the three major muralists of the 1920s. This image is called the *The Banquet of the Rich,* a detail from Orozco's mural *While the Workers Quarrel,* at the National Preparatory School.

executed not in fresco but in gold leaf and encaustic, a method based on the application of pigment and melted wax to walls. Nor is it especially Mexican in theme. Instead, it is a complex allegory inspired by Vasconcelos and suggestive of the public art Rivera had seen in Italy, but with flattened figures reminiscent of his Cubist years. However, he gave mestizo features to female figures in the mural, and in a recessed area of the wall he painted a tropical scene of luxuriant vegetation and exotic fauna.

The early life of David Alfaro Siqueiros (1896–1974) foreshadowed the political activism that would characterize his adult years. As a 13-year-old student at the Academy of Fine Arts he took part in a 1911 rebellion against Rivas Mercado, the director. When Dr. Atl's tenure as director was cut short in 1914 by conflict among the revolutionary factions, Siqueiros and other students followed him to Orizaba in Veracruz, where an academy in exile was set up. Siqueiros later joined the staff of the Carrancista general Manuel M. Diéguez and thereby became familiar at firsthand with the casual cruelty and violence of the Revolution. From 1919 to 1922 Siqueiros was in Europe where he, like Rivera, had an opportunity to study the masterpieces of the past and become acquainted with the new aesthetic theories of the day. In Barcelona in 1921, he published a manifesto addressed to the painters and sculptors of America in which he extolled the dynamism of the machine age and expressed confidence in the art of the future, yet called on modern artists to seek inspiration in the works of their pre-Columbian predecessors.

Siqueiros, invited to participate in the Preparatoria project, began work in December 1922 on a mural in encaustic on the ceiling of a small stairway. Known as *The Elements*, it reflected his observation of Italian frescoes and was dominated by the figure of an angel. A second, unfinished mural in the Preparatoria, *Burial of the Sacrificed Workers*, marks this painter's shift to an openly political art, for it displays a hammer and sickle atop a coffin and is dedicated to Felipe Carrillo Puerto, the socialist governor of Yucatán who had been recently murdered.

José Clemente Orozco (1883–1949) was older than Rivera and Siqueiros. While attending the Preparatoria as a teenager, he had lost his left hand and damaged his eyesight and hearing in an accident. He had come late to art, having completed a course in agriculture before entering the Academy of Fine Arts in 1906. In 1914 he joined the exodus of Dr. Atl's students to Orizaba. Although Orozco painted a mural in Veracruz in 1915 that adumbrated his later work, he first distinguished himself for his acerbic political cartoons and his representations in various media of young girls and prostitutes. His first one-man show was not well received, whereupon he traveled to the United States, only to have some of his drawings destroyed by U.S. customs for their supposed immorality. Back in Mexico, he remained in relative obscurity until Vasconcelos invited him to join the other muralists at work in the Preparatoria in 1923. Orozco's intentions changed as he worked in the Preparatoria during 1923 and 1924, and he altered or destroyed several of his murals. The Botticelli-like *Maternity* evolved out of an elaborate plan for a series of allegorical paintings on the theme of the gifts of nature to man. Elsewhere the murals reveal the style and social commentary of Orozco's cartoons. *Revolutionary Trinity*, for example, depicts a central figure, carrying a rifle and blinded by a Jacobin cap, who is flanked by one figure praying for salvation and another whose hands have been severed.

Several other young artists were engaged to help decorate the walls of the Preparatoria, among them Fernando Leal (1896–1964) and Jean Charlot (1898–1979), a French-born painter of part-Mexican origin who would later become the historian of the early mural movement. A former student in Ramos Martínez's open-air studio, Leal painted in encaustic *Pilgrimage at Chalma*, in which he wished to show the persistence of indigenous beliefs within the Christian environment of modern Mexico. Charlot, preferring to work in fresco, chose as his theme an episode from the Conquest, the massacre of Indians at the templo mayor.

At the instigation of Rivera, in late 1922 the Preparatoria muralists formed the Syndicate of Technical Workers, Painters, and Sculptors. In keeping with the leftist ideology embraced by Rivera and Siqueiros, the organization, while not rejecting international models, was committed to the collective creation of art that would aid Mexico's masses in their struggle against oppression and would reflect the country's indigenous traditions. In 1924, the syndicate established a newspaper, *El Machete*, edited by Xavier Guerrero, who had assisted Rivera with his murals. According to the masthead, machetes served not only to cut cane but also "to humiliate the pride of the wicked rich." The newspaper contained articles championing the cause of workers and peasants but was notable mainly for its engravings and drawings by Guerrero, Siqueiros, and Orozco. The seventh issue contained an often quoted manifesto by the syndicate, which condemned easel painting and endorsed "monumental art in all its forms, because it is public property."

The syndicate would be most active in defending its members' murals when they were mutilated by Preparatoria students in 1924. Artistic conservatives had long expressed criticism of the murals, and on June 25 of that year students responded by throwing mud and stones at murals by Orozco and Siqueiros and scratching them. They also demanded that work on the murals be halted. Vasconcelos, who was himself unenthusiastic about the murals, quickly complied. The syndicate denounced the students' actions but also blamed many others: "reactionary teachers . . . the rich and their breed, who intrigue against all that comes from the people and is of use to the people . . . the reactionary press that shields them, the irresponsible revolutionaries who do not realize that their lack of affinity with revolutionary painting discloses within them a percentage of the bourgeois still rampant."

Replying to the syndicate, the Student Federation of Mexico asserted that the Preparatoria belonged to its students and that they had the right not only to criticize the murals but to demand that they be erased and replaced with paintings worthy of the school. A group of foreigners living in Mexico, among them the photographer Edward Weston and the journalist Carleton Beals, entered the fray by publicly condemning the mutilation of the murals. They believed that, even though they were foreigners, they had the right to speak out against the vandalism because the arts, "though deeply rooted in national culture . . . become the patrimony of the world at large. . . . Damaging the paintings of the Escuela Nacional Preparatoria injures our cultural assets as well as your own."

The suspension of the work at the Preparatoria ended the first phase of the mural movement. The artists dispersed and the syndicate soon disappeared. *El Machete* later became the organ of Mexico's Communist Party, of which Rivera, Siqueiros, and Guerrero were prominent members. José Vasconcelos also departed from the ministry of education at this time. Having alienated President Obregón because of his apparent opposition to the succession of Plutarco Elías Calles, Vasconcelos left his post soon after the mutilation of the murals to run unsuccessfully for the governorship of his native Oaxaca. Vasconcelos's successor and later foreign minister, José Manuel Puig Casauranc, introduced greater efficiency and a more bureaucratic orientation to the ministry, along with educational theories then popular in the United States. His second in command, Moisés Sáenz, had a master's degree from Columbia University, where he had been a student of John Dewey.

Rivera's work was little disrupted by the Preparatoria riot and the departure of Vasconcelos. Since 1923, he had been painting murals in the recently inaugurated ministry of education building and, despite the fact that they, too, had generated substantial criticism, Secretary Puig continued the project. Completed in

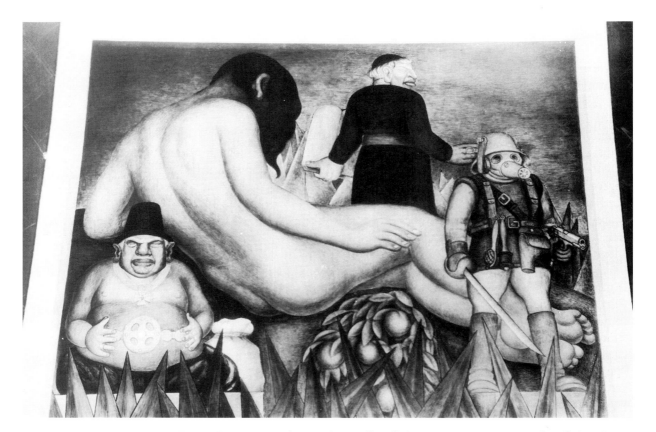

Among the lesser-known frescoes of the muralist school are the Rivera works at the National Agricultural School in Chapingo. This mural, *The Earth Surrounded by Enemies,* is in the school's chapel. The people's enemies are represented by the priest, the imperialist soldier, and the corrupt politician. The nude woman represents the earth.

1928, Rivera's 235 panels on the walls of the two open courtyards of the three-story building constitute his first great achievement in fresco, depicting both the popular culture of Mexico as well as the aspirations unleashed by the Revolution. The first courtyard is dominated by spare, somber scenes of Mexicans at work, while much of the second courtyard is devoted to more optimistic scenes of religious and political celebrations. On the third floor of the second courtyard Rivera painted panels illustrating verses from three *corridos*, or popular songs, of the revolutionary era. In the second courtyard the Mexican people fill every bit of space, as if Rivera were trying to create a panoramic image of the nation. Although all the murals are based on Mexican life and traditions, they are rich in allusions to European religious painting. Thus, the outstretched arms of the miner being searched in *Exit from the Mine* suggest the Crucifixion, while *The Burial of the Revolutionary* evokes El Greco's 1588 masterpiece *Burial of Count Ordaz.*

In 1924–26 Rivera painted murals on the walls of a new agricultural school at Chapingo near Mexico City (now the Autonomous University of Chapingo) that are considered among his finest works, especially those in the chapel. In a style similar to that which he used for the ministry of education, he painted on the west wall of the chapel a series of frescoes depicting the exploitation of the peasant and the struggle for agrarian revolution. Opposite these panels, on the east wall, Rivera used female nudes to represent the natural forces that govern the cycles of the earth, suggesting a parallel with the revolutionary forces shown on the west wall. On the altar wall of the chapel he painted his pregnant wife,

Guadalupe Marín, as "the liberated earth" attended by the forces of nature—fire, wind, and water—controlled by man.

Rivera's murals, like his political life, took a new direction as the 1920s ended. Continuing to enjoy official patronage even though revolutionary momentum had stalled by 1929 and the Mexican government had adopted an anti-Communist stance, he was commissioned to paint murals in the seat of government itself—the National Palace. There he filled three adjoining walls with his interpretation of Mexican history, depicting class conflict in the pre-Columbian past and tracing Mexico's trajectory through colonial oppression, imperialism, and revolution to a future inspired by Marx. The same year (1929) Dwight Morrow, the U.S. ambassador to Mexico, commissioned a series of murals for another important building, the palace of Hernán Cortés, in Cuernavaca, the capital of the state of Morelos. Here Rivera presented a regional history, again emphasizing Spanish brutality and exploitation and suggesting deliverance at the hands of Emiliano Zapata, a native of Morelos, and his peasant followers. Meanwhile, Rivera was expelled from the Communist Party in 1929, for reasons that remain unclear but are probably related to his Trotskyite leanings. Although he continued to consider himself a staunch Marxist-Leninist, in the early 1930s he was the target of attacks by Siqueiros and other Stalinists in Mexico and the United States who criticized him for accepting commissions from the seemingly reactionary Mexican government and from capitalists such as Morrow.

Both Orozco and Siqueiros painted murals after their dismissal from the Preparatoria, but relatively few opportunities came their way in Mexico. After completing murals entitled *Omniscience* and *Social Revolution* in Sanborn's Restaurant in Mexico City and the Industrial School of Orizaba, respectively, Orozco returned to the Preparatoria in 1926 at the invitation of Alfonso Pruneda, rector of the National University. Here he created powerful renderings of the revolutionary experience, as in *The Trench*, and ambivalent scenes of the Spanish Conquest, such as *The Franciscan and the Indian*, in which a robed friar appears to suffocate a naked Indian as he embraces him. In 1925, Siqueiros and Amado de la Cueva decorated the walls of the chapel of the University of Guadalajara. Otherwise, Siqueiros spent the years 1925–30 engaged mainly in trade union work on behalf of the Communist Party.

All three of these muralists traveled to the United States, where reports of Mexico's artistic renaissance had preceded them, and all three painted murals there, provoking criticism as well as admiration. Their very presence in the United States was sometimes denounced as an affront to native artists, who were being denied mural commissions at a time of economic hardship. Others condemned the political views of Rivera and Siqueiros and the incorporation of these views into their work. Orozco was the first to make the journey, traveling to New York in 1927 at a time when his prospects in Mexico looked bleak. He initially experienced hardship and neglect but eventually received mural commissions from three educational institutions: Pomona College in California (1930), the New School in New York City (1931), and Dartmouth College in

New Hampshire (1932–34). At Dartmouth, Orozco covered the walls of the Baker Library with his interpretation of the evolution of the New World. The civilizing Mesoamerican god Quetzalcóatl plays a central role in the mural, which offers a generally pessimistic view of both past and present.

Rivera arrived in San Francisco in 1930, where he painted murals in the stock exchange and the California School of Fine Arts. The following year he enjoyed a major triumph when the Museum of Modern Art in New York presented a one-man show of his work, including eight frescoes he painted on movable panels specially for this occasion. Attendance during the show's five-week run totaled more than 56,000, surpassing the number who had seen a recent Matisse exhibit at the museum.

In 1932, Rivera received a commission for a series of murals in the Detroit Institute of Arts. The resulting work, with its sinuous portrayals of science and technology, produced some controversy, but it was dwarfed by the celebrated Rockefeller Center episode. Having accepted an invitation to paint a mural in the RCA building on the theme of *Man at the Crossroads*, Rivera used his mural with this title to shore up his leftist credentials and placed Lenin in a central place in the mural. After he refused to excise Lenin's portrait, the nearly completed mural was destroyed in 1934.

Siqueiros went to Los Angeles in 1932 to give a course on muralism at the Chouinard School of Art. There he painted murals at the school, on an exterior wall of the Olvera Street Plaza Art Center, and in the home of film director Dudley Murphy. The Plaza Art Center mural, in the heart of the city's Mexican district, was the most ambitious of the three. This mural, titled *Tropical America*, proved controversial because of its symbolic portrayal of the oppression of the continent's indigenous peoples and was soon covered with several coats of whitewash.

In November 1932, Siqueiros left the United States after the authorities refused to renew his visa, and traveled to Argentina and Uruguay. In the country house of a Buenos Aires newspaper editor Siqueiros created a mural, *Plastic Exercise*, that was notable in several ways. Instead of conventional paint, he used nitrocellulose pigments normally employed for industrial purposes, which he applied with a spray gun and a drill. In addition, he attempted to create a "painted environment" in which the entire room would be an integral part of the mural.

Siqueiros returned to New York in 1936 as the official Mexican delegate to the American Artists Congress. He then organized a short-lived experimental workshop in which he and a group of like-minded artists attempted to create art for the people, achieved through posters and floats created for political events, and to develop modern art techniques and materials of the kind he had used in *Plastic Exercise*. What he sought was "a new plastic language, a new and infinitely more rich graphic vocabulary for the art of the epoch of the REVOLUTION."

Despite the controversy the Mexican muralists occasionally aroused in the United States, they had an immense impact on North American art at a time when it lacked strong direction or leadership. Their example helped inspire an upsurge of mural painting in the United States, especially under the aegis of the Federal Artists Project. They also influenced many individual artists, such as Ben Shahn, who assisted Rivera on the Rockefeller Center project, and Jackson Pollock, who was a member of Siqueiros's experimental workshop. Their reputations enhanced by their foreign successes, the Big Three resumed their work as muralists upon their return to Mexico.

In 1934, Rivera re-created in Mexico City's Palace of Fine Arts the destroyed Rockefeller Center mural. Replicating concepts he had incorporated into earlier murals, he portrayed both his admiration for advances in science and technology and his belief in the failings of capitalism. The figure of Lenin occupies a central place in this redone mural, joining the hands of a soldier and of black and white workers.

In 1938–39, Orozco painted what is considered to be his masterpiece, in the chapel of the Hospicio Cabañas (now the Cabañas Cultural Institute) in Guadalajara. Here, on the eve of World War II, Orozco created a somber but compelling portrait of humanity in both its benign and malevolent aspects. Several panels depict the violence of both the pre-Columbian world and the Spanish Conquest, while others take the dictators and the mechanized violence of the modern age as their theme. In the cupola a man on fire represents human creativity.

After spending a year fighting on behalf of the Republican forces in Spain, Siqueiros returned to Mexico to paint an innovative mural in the stairwell of the electricians' union in Mexico City in 1939–40. Creating a continuous pictorial surface in the cubed construction of the site, he and his assistants chose *Portrait of the Bourgeoisie* as the theme of the mural, which was painted in pyroxylin, another industrial pigment. While the electrical industry is portrayed on the ceiling, the main sections of the mural present capitalism as the source of fascism and war.

Despite the condemnation of easel painting by the painters' syndicate in the 1920s, Rivera, Siqueiros, and Orozco all painted in oil and other media during that decade and the next. Some of Rivera's best-known canvases of the era, such as *Woman Grinding Maize* (1924) and *Flower Day* (1925), depict scenes of indigenous life and recall panels in the ministry of education building. Siqueiros's *Woman with Stone Mortar* (1931), painted in oil and pyroxylin on burlap, emphasizes the sculptural qualities of its central figure. She is an Indian, but the viewer's attention is drawn to her apparent poverty rather than her ethnicity. Even less folkloric is *Ethnography* (1939), in which the face of a contemporary Indian is depicted as that of an Olmec deity. Siqueiros's *Echo of a Scream* (1937), painted in enamel on wood, was inspired by a photograph of the current conflict in China. It shows a wailing child atop a mound of modern detritus and is a chilling indictment of the violence that already gripped the world.

Like Rivera, Orozco painted many canvases reminiscent of his murals, such as *Barricade* (1931), which echoes *The Trench* in the Preparatoria. Then a series of paintings of New York, done in 1928–30, represented a thematic departure. Here Orozco delineated in somber hues the dehumanizing structures of the modern city, as in *The Third Avenue Elevated* (1928).

Many other artists, less celebrated internationally than the Big Three, produced distinguished work during the 1920s and 1930s. Francisco Goitia (1882–1960) is noted for his harrowing scenes of death based on his observations as a staff artist with Pancho Villa's forces during the Revolution, but his masterpiece is *Father Jesus* (1926–27). Its depiction of two indigenous women weeping over an unseen body can be seen as emblematic of the sufferings of the Mexican people. Antonio Ruiz (1897–1964) is best known for his small canvases, portraying in exquisite detail scenes from everyday life, as in *The Lottery Ticket* (1932) and *Schoolchildren on Parade* (1936). In a different, somewhat surrealistic manner, is Ruiz's enigmatic *The Dream of Malinche* (1932), which depicts the interpreter and mistress of Cortés, who lies asleep on her side. On the hill made by her hip a church overlooks a colonial village divided by a large chasm. Miguel Covarrubias (1904–57) painted a satiric yet affectionate portrait of a provincial schoolteacher, *The Bone* (1937), but was known in Mexico and the United States primarily as a caricaturist. In his later years he devoted himself to archaeology and anthropology, and amassed important collections of pre-Columbian and folk art.

These artists, as well as the Big Three and all the others mentioned here, were represented in a major exhibition, *Twenty Centuries of Mexican Art*, held at the Museum of Modern Art in 1940. The exhibition was cosponsored by the Mexican government, which viewed it as "an effective means of bringing about a better understanding of [Mexican] life, both past and present" in the United States. Describing Mexico's recent artistic output in the catalog, Covarrubias emphasized both its native roots and its relationship to the Revolution: "Thus the art of Mexico has reached a turbulent maturity, attained only after a dogged struggle against the bonds that held it fast to the decaying cultures of Europe. The artistic liberation of Mexican art runs closely parallel to the social and political liberation of the nation itself, and if the participation of the artists in this struggle had been less whole-hearted, perhaps modern Mexican art would never have shown its present freshness and vigor."

While Mexico's painters were interpreting their country's history and society, three outstanding photographers—Tina Modotti (1896–1942), Manuel Alvarez Bravo (1902–), and Lola Alvarez Bravo (1907–93)—were offering their own vision of Mexican realities. Their deceptively simple black-and-white prints captured many aspects of Mexican life, from its landscape to its anonymous workers. They also photographed the great murals of the 1920s and 1930s, helping to publicize them outside Mexico.

The life of Modotti has been veiled in a film of legend, due as much to her unconventional personal life and her political activism as to her achievements in photography. Although she was born in Italy and lived in the United States from 1913 to 1923, almost all of her photographs were produced while she lived in Mexico from 1923 to 1930. She moved to Mexico, recently widowed, as the companion of Edward Weston. Modotti and Weston had become acquainted with several Mexican expatriates while living in Los Angeles and had learned from them of the country's artistic renaissance. Weston, married and the father of four

Tina Modotti took this photograph entitled *Telegraph Wires* in 1925. It was printed in 1927 in a history of the *estridentista* movement and in Eugene Jolas's modernist journal, *Tradition,* in 1929.

Tina Modotti - 1925

sons, was also seeking to escape the confines of bourgeois life in California and was encouraged by the success of a 1922 exhibition of his photographs held in Mexico City.

In Mexico, Weston photographed the country's folk art, emphasizing its forms rather than its context, and made portraits, including one of Diego Rivera, which the painter then used as the basis for a self-portrait in the ministry of education building. Modotti, meanwhile, began to develop her own skills, her first dated photograph being a February 1924 portrait of Weston. Other early photographs, such as *Telegraph Wires* (1925), illustrated her links with Estridentismo (Stridentism) a short-lived avant-garde literary and artistic movement exalting the dynamism of modern industrial life as it was developing in Mexico.

Having shed her dependence on Weston, Modotti remained in Mexico when he returned to the United States in 1926. During this period she became deeply committed to the cause of proletarian revolution and joined Mexico's Communist Party in 1927. Her new romantic attachments were also with Communists, such as Xavier Guerrero and the young Cuban exile Julio A. Mella, who was murdered in 1929 while she was walking by his side. Many of her best-known photographs appeared in *New Masses*, a leftist magazine published in New York, among them a photomontage in the April 1928 issue of a worker below an advertisement of clothes for the elegant man. In the January 1930 issue her credo as a photographer is quoted: "I am anxious to make honest photographs without affectation and 'artistic effects' or in imitation of other mediums of graphic expression. The camera is a product of our mechanized civilization. I use it as a tool and a most satisfactory medium to portray the life we are living." Her career as a photographer, which had yielded some 250 images, would soon be coming to an end. In February 1930, she was deported by the Mexican government, then at odds with Communists, both foreign and domestic. For the next few years she devoted herself to political work, mainly in the Soviet Union and Spain, on behalf of the Republicans during the Spanish civil war. Their defeat brought her back to Mexico, where she lived quietly until her death in 1942.

In 1927, Modotti befriended Manuel Alvarez Bravo, who is considered Mexico's greatest photographer. Born in Mexico City, Alvarez Bravo was self-taught as a photographer and purchased his first camera in 1924. At Modotti's suggestion, he sent a portfolio of his work to Weston, who responded with enthusiasm. Some of Alvarez Bravo's early photographs, such as *Wooden Horse* (1925), suggest the influence of Weston, and others that of the French photographer Eugene Atget, who infused documentary photography with self-expression. Above all, however, the work of Alvarez Bravo was shaped by Mexican culture and by the artistic ferment of the 1920s and 1930s. While his photographs ostensibly present scenes and objects of ordinary Mexican life, they convey an ambiguity that renders them universal and timeless. In three photographs of the early 1930s—*Girl Watching Birds* (1931), *The Dancer's Daughter* (1933), and *The Crouched Ones* (1932–34)— the faces of the subjects are partially or completely hidden, creating an aura of mystery. In another celebrated image, *Striking Worker, Assassinated* (1934), the viewer sees only part of the dead subject's bloody face and torso, and the context is provided only by the title. Thus, though the work is not conventionally political, this worker can be seen as a symbol of the abused and martyred of his class everywhere. Lola Alvarez Bravo married Manuel in 1924 and separated from him in 1934. Like Tina Modotti, she was initiated into photography at the side of her male partner but soon developed her own artistic identity. Many of her photographs are documentary in nature, yet she endowed her scenes of urban and rural life with a poetic quality that transformed their mundane subjects. She also experimented with photomontage, as in *Dream of the Poor* (1935), which shows an obviously impoverished youth asleep below a fantastic machine that produces coins. Finally, she was a gifted portrait photographer, whose subjects included the painters Frida Kahlo and María Izquierdo, both of whom were close friends.

A regular participant in the 1921 centenary celebration was the Orquesta Típica del Centenario, conducted by Miguel Lerdo de Tejada (1869–1941), grand-nephew of the 19th–century statesman of the same name. As its name implies, this orchestra represented an extension of the cultural nationalism of the 1920s into the field of music. As in the case of art, Mexico's 20th–century musical nationalism had numerous antecedents dating back to the colonial period. The music composed in Mexico during the colonial period was primarily religious, closely following European models. However, hymns were written in Nahuatl, and the indigenous song and dance form called the *tocotín* was adapted for Christian purposes. The Spanish musical and poetic form known as the *villancico* acquired a local flavor in Mexico, where it enjoyed great popularity during the 17th and 18th centuries and became a joyous song to be performed on church feast days. The gifted poet Sor Juana Inés de la Cruz wrote the lyrics for many villancicos, some of which contained sections written in black dialect or Nahuatl. During the colonial era Mexico also produced a rich body of folk music and dance based on Spanish tradition.

European themes and forms remained dominant in the 19th century, but Melesio Morales (1838–1908) essayed a one-act opera, *Anita*, set in Mexico during the French intervention of the 1860s. Aniceto Ortega (1823–75) composed patriotic anthems and marches such as the "Marcha Zaragoza" (1867) in honor of the victory over the French on May 5, 1862, and the opera *Guatimotzin*. Relating the struggle between the Aztecs and the Spaniards for control of Mexico, this work was first performed in Mexico City in 1871 with Mexico's celebrated soprano Angela Peralta (1845–83) as an Aztec princess. It represented the first effort in Mexico to incorporate elements of pre-Columbian music into the prevailing Italian operatic styles.

Among the composers represented at the "Mexican night" in Chapultepec Park in 1921 was Manuel M. Ponce (1882–1948). Famous as the composer of the song "Estrellita" (1914), Ponce was a pioneer of musical nationalism who, like the Czech composer Antonin Dvořák, used Mexican folk music of Spanish origin as the basis for art music in a romantic vein. "I consider it the duty of every Mexican composer," he said in 1913, "to ennoble his country's music by giving it *artistic form*, attiring it in the garb of polyphony, and lovingly conserving the popular music that is the expression of the country's soul." The symphonic poem *Chapultepec*, written in the 1920s and later revised, is his best-known orchestral work in a nationalist idiom.

During the 1920s, Ponce's fame was eclipsed by that of Carlos Chávez (1899–1978), who became Mexico's leading exponent of musical nationalism by integrating popular and indigenous materials into a modernist style influenced by Stravinsky and other contemporary composers. Chávez, who studied piano and harmony with Ponce and other teachers in Mexico City, expressed his commitment to a nationalist orientation for Mexican music while still in his teens. His early work included arrangements of traditional and revolutionary songs, such as "Adelita" and "La Cucaracha" (1915). In 1921 Vasconcelos invited him to compose a ballet on an Aztec theme. The resulting work, *El fuego nuevo*, contains allusions to indigenous music he had heard in Tlaxcala as a child.

Travel to Europe and the United States in the 1920s exposed Chávez to modernist trends in music and acquainted him with other champions of musical nationalism such as Aaron Copland, who became a good friend. Chávez drew on his Mexican roots for many of the pieces he composed over the next two decades. For example, in the ballet symphony *H. P. (Caballos de vapor)*, which premiered in 1932, he used the music of Mexican folk dance to evoke the tropics, which he contrasted with the industrialized society of North America. The thematic structure of the one-movement *Sinfonía India* (1935–36), derived from Indian melodies from Sonora and Nayarit, is scored for indigenous drums, rasps, and rattles, as well as more conventional instruments. A short piece, *Xochipilli* (1940), also employs indigenous percussive instruments to create what Chávez called "an imagined Aztec music."

Chávez's influence on Mexican music during this period extended far beyond his own composition. In the mid–1920s, he organized a series of concerts that introduced Mexico City audiences to the work of Bartók, Stravinsky, and other modern composers. In 1928 he became director of the Symphony Orchestra of Mexico, creating an ensemble that won national and international plaudits for its quality and repertoire, which balanced new music with standard works. Determined to make fine music available to all classes, he initiated a series of free symphonic concerts for workers, first in a Mexico City park and later in the Palace of Fine Arts. He also revived and reorganized the National Conservatory of Music, which he headed from 1928 to 1934. Finally, he inspired and taught other Mexican composers who also embraced musical nationalism. The most distinguished of these was Silvestre Revueltas (1899–1940), assistant director of the Symphony Orchestra of Mexico from 1928 to 1935. During a decade of intensive productivity, Revueltas composed a series of nationally oriented pieces, such as the symphonic poem *Colorines* (1932), noted for their unique adaptations of the harmonic and melodic patterns of Mexican folk music. Revueltas also composed for several Mexican films, including *Redes* (1934) and *Vámonos con Pancho Villa* (1935).

Mexican literature experienced an era of rejuvenation after 1920 but was less dominated than the visual arts or music by a single school or movement and gained less international attention. The affirmation of nationalism was perhaps less pressing in literature, because 19th–century writers had produced a body of poetry and fiction that was uniquely Mexican in subject and theme if not in form, starting with the picaresque though moralistic tale *El periquillo sarniento* (1816) by José Fernández de Lizardi (1776–1827). Translated into English by Katherine Anne Porter as *The Itching Parrot* (1942), it is generally considered Mexico's first novel.

In 1871, Ignacio M. Altamirano (1834–93), a liberal activist and man of letters, called on his countrymen to declare their intellectual independence from Spain and create a national literature reflecting the language and environment of Mexico. He followed these prescriptions in his own work, notably the novels *La Navidad en las montañas* (1871), (*Christmas in the Mountains*, 1961) and *El Zarco: Episodio de la vida mexicana en 1861–63* (1901) (*El Zarco: The Bandit*, 1957). Other novelists followed suit, among them Federico Gamboa (1864–1939), author of *Santa* (1903), a naturalistic tale of a prostitute notable for its scenes of life in Mexico City. Shortly before his death, the poet Ramón López Velarde (1888–1921) wrote "Suave patria," which remained unpublished until 1932. López Velarde failed to mention the recent revolution in this lyrical paean to his native land but rather celebrated its natural setting and the traditions and folklore of its people.

After 1920, two new movements—Estridentismo and that associated with the review *Contemporáneos*—found inspiration at least in part in contemporary European and North American literary trends. However, the most significant development in literature during the 1920s was the emergence of the novel of the Mexican Revolution, which sought to document the violence and chaos of the previous decade.

Estridentismo was founded by Manuel Maples Arce (1900–81), a lawyer and poet who wished to renew Mexican poetry along lines suggested by the European avant-garde. In 1921, he published a manifesto, *Actual. Número Uno*, calling for a new literature to reflect the character of the modern machine age but be created out of native elements. He then became the nucleus of a small coterie of poets and artists who produced several short-lived magazines, of which the most important was probably *Horizontes* (1926–27). Published in Jalapa, Veracruz, it was distinguished by the graphic designs of Ramón Alva de la Canal and reproduced several photographs by Weston and Modotti. The best-known work by Maple Arce is *Urbe* (1924), a long poem exalting the dynamism of Mexico City and the struggles of its workers. It was translated into English in 1929 as *Metropolis* by the U.S. novelist John Dos Passos.

Of more lasting impact was the Contemporáneos group, which was associated with several literary reviews, notably *Ulises* (1927–28) and *Contemporáneos* (1928–31). The magazines carried writing by Mexican authors but devoted many of their pages to poetry and prose by foreigners, including North Americans.

The muralists dominated Mexican art into the 1930s, when some artists turned to new, nonrevolutionary themes. The publication *Contemporaneos* provided a medium of expression for modernist views in both writing and fine art.

Members of the group also attempted to reinvigorate Mexican theater, then dominated by Spanish impresarios and repertory, through staging plays by Eugene O'Neill, Jean Cocteau, and other modern dramatists. The group's cosmopolitanism and apolitical stance provoked criticism from nationalists and leftists, who denounced its efforts as reactionary and irrelevant to Mexican concerns. Aggravating this criticism was the fact that two of the most prominent members of the group—Xavier Villaurrutia (1903–50) and Salvador Novo (1904–70)—were known to be homosexual.

Villaurrutia wrote numerous works for the stage but is remembered mainly for his lyric poetry, especially the collection *Nostalgia de la muerte* (1938), translated as *Nostalgia for Death* (1993). With their melancholy and anguish over the nature of human existence, the poems confirm the U.S. critic Frank Dauster's assessment that Villaurrutia was "the first Mexican to give expression to man's radical solitude in our torn century." Novo wrote much poetry and nonfiction during his long career as a man of letters, but his greatest contributions were in the theater, as a producer and director and dramatist. His plays and novels include *Yocasta, o casi* (1961) and *La guerra de las gordas* (*The War of the Fatties*, 1963). The latter, a novel of the Mexican Revolution, is usually defined as a long prose narrative dealing with the revolutionary upheaval that started in 1910. Many such novels focus on the military aspects of the conflict during the succeeding decade, but others recount its effect on civilians or are set in the post–1920 period. These works are often described as episodic, and even cinematic, because of their short scenes and lack of psychological depth. They are frequently autobiographical;

indeed, some of the best-known works in the group are not novels in the conventional sense but are rather narratives of personal experience. Although all these works are nationalist in that their settings, themes, and characters are entirely Mexican, they by no means offer a positive view of the Revolution and its achievements. Their authors are likely to be critical or disillusioned or at best ambivalent regarding the people and events they describe.

Los de abajo (1915; translated in 1929 as *The Underdogs*), the first novel of the Revolution, is still considered the outstanding work in the genre. Its author, Mariano Azuela (1873–1952), was a medical doctor by profession who had published three novels by 1910 and served with the forces of Pancho Villa. *Los de abajo* was serialized in an El Paso Spanish-language newspaper in 1915 and published in book form in 1916, but it remained virtually unknown until it was rediscovered in the mid–1920s. Recounting the exploits of a band of peasant revolutionaries led by Demetrio Macías, the novel reveals Azuela's convictions about the futility of the conflict. In it Macías fights first against Huerta's *federales* and later against the Carrancistas without a clear motive. When his wife asks why he fights, he replies by throwing a pebble into a ravine and watching it roll down. Alberto Solís, a character often seen as Azuela's spokesman, answers the same question by comparing the Revolution to a hurricane: "The man who surrenders to it is no longer a man but a miserable dry leaf tossed about by the storm." Luis Cervantes, the only character who speaks of the Revolution as a struggle for freedom and justice, is an opportunist and turncoat who had opposed Madero and supported Huerta.

Azuela wrote several other novels that focused on middle-and upper-class civilians during the Revolution—among them *Los caciques* (1917; *The Bosses*, 1956), *Las moscas* (1918; *The Flies*, 1956), and *Las tribulaciones de una familia decente* (1919)—but he was as critical of the cynicism and venality of these groups as he was of the folly and brutality of the lower orders. He himself wrote of his attitude toward the Revolution that "my bitterness is directed against men, not against the idea—men who corrupt everything."

El águila y la serpiente (1928; *The Eagle and the Serpent*, 1930) was written by Martín Luis Guzmán (1887–1976) while he was living in Spain from 1925 to 1936. It is a novelized memoir of the author's experiences from 1913, when as a foe of Huerta he fled to the United States, to 1915, when he again left Mexico after the collapse of the government headed by Eulalio Gutiérrez. The book's dominant figure, however, is Pancho Villa, whom Guzmán regarded with a mixture of fear and awe. Later, in the semi-fictional *Memorias de Pancho Villa* (1951; *The Memoirs of Pancho Villa*, 1965), he would portray the northern revolutionary as a hero without flaws.

Guzmán's other major literary work, *La sombra del caudillo* (1929), was not published in Mexico until 1938. Unlike most other novels of the Revolution, this one deals with events after 1920, being a fictional account of a presidential contest in which the unnamed caudillo employs treachery and murder to install his chosen candidate as his successor. To Mexican readers the novel recalled actual events, particularly the unsuccessful revolt of generals Francisco Serrano and Arnulfo Gómez, who opposed the reelection of Alvaro Obregón in 1928. Guzmán decries dictatorship in the novel, but the flaws of his protagonist, General Ignacio Aguirre, and his supporters make clear his belief that the defects of Mexico's political system could not be blamed solely on the caudillo.

Often included in the canon of revolutionary novels is *Ulises criollo* (1935), the first volume of José Vasconcelos's five-volume autobiography, which traces his life until the death of Madero, of whom he had been a supporter. Vasconcelos chose the name Ulysses as his epithet because his career and that of contemporary Mexicans suggested an odyssey, while he added *criollo* (of European descent) in tribute to Mexico's Hispanic heritage. *Cartucho* (1931; translated 1988) by Nellie Campobello (1900–)—the only work in the group written by a woman—is also a personal narrative. It consists of 56 brief sketches purporting to be a child's account of the Revolution in her northern town. Campobello's simple, seemingly artless prose makes the stories of bloodshed and cruelty all the more compelling.

The accession to the presidency of Lázaro Cárdenas in 1934 and the emergence of a more pronounced *indigenismo* (Indian movement) coincided with the appearance of several novels in which the Indian assumed a central role. The most celebrated of these is *El indio* (1935, translated 1937) by Gregorio López y Fuentes (1897–1966), a journalist who had already published three revolutionary novels: *Campamento* (1931), *Tierra* (1932), and *Mi general* (1934). *El indio*, which won Mexico's first National Prize for Literature, combines ethnography and narrative to depict an anonymous indigenous community. Its members are secretive and distrustful of the whites and mestizos who invariably abuse or betray them. The Revolution brings them some land, but little change otherwise. *Resplandor* (1937; *Sunburst*, 1944), by Mauricio Magdaleno (1906–86) offers an even gloomier assessment of the Revolution's accomplishments to date. In it impoverished Indian villagers hope that the Revolution will enable them to acquire the underutilized lands of a neighboring hacienda, but they are deceived by a local leader who becomes governor of the state.

Disillusion with revolutionary promises of political reform is also evident in *El gesticulador*, a play by Mexico's leading dramatist, Rodolfo Usigli (1905–79). Written in 1938 but not performed until 1947, this play revolves around the metamorphosis of a failed university professor after he is mistaken for a legendary revolutionary general who had disappeared years before. The complex plot demonstrates the hypocrisy of contemporary politicians and the emptiness of their rhetoric.

During the 1930s and 1940s, some Mexican artists eschewed the didactic, overtly political themes characteristic of the muralists and produced paintings that, while identifiably Mexican, were informed mainly by personal or aesthetic concerns. This trend was furthered by the visit in 1938 of the French poet and essayist André Breton, spokesman for the Surrealist movement, which he introduced to Mexico. With the collaboration of the Russian Communist exile Leon Trotsky, who had found refuge in Mexico, Breton and Rivera drafted a manifesto

Following the muralists, Rufino Tamayo emerged as the first Mexican artist to capture world attention with his work. This is one of his masterpieces entitled *Portrait of a Woman*.

in which they condemned the restrictions imposed on artists in the Soviet Union and elsewhere. Arguing that the artistic imagination requires freedom from coercion, they maintained that artists had an "inalienable right" to choose their own subjects. Breton also helped organize Mexico's first International Exhibition of Surrealism, in 1940. Included in this show were works by Picasso, Hans Arp, and Giorgio de Chirico as well as by Rivera, Antonio Ruiz, and other Mexicans. Manuel Alvarez Bravo was also represented, and his photograph *About Winter* adorned the cover of the catalog. As a result of Breton's visit, Mexican art gained greater international exposure, and several European artists, such as Wolfgang Paalen, Remedos Vara, and Leonora Carrington, were encouraged to settle there during World War II. These developments heightened Mexicans' awareness of new approaches to art, though there is a debate over the extent to which they were influenced by Surrealism.

An early exemplar of the alternative trend was Rufino Tamayo (1899–1991), who studied sporadically at the Academy of Fine Arts from 1917 to 1921 and was later employed at the National Museum of Archaeology, where he had the opportunity to study folk art and pre-Columbian sculpture. In 1926, he went to New York with Carlos Chávez, with whom he shared a loft apartment. "Chávez composed jazz numbers," Tamayo later recalled, "and I once had to paint a restaurant kitchen for little more than my dinner. Those were hard times, and sometimes I lived for a whole week on seven apples." Tamayo returned to Mexico in 1928 but went back to New York in 1936, remaining for more than a decade and making periodic visits to Mexico. It was in New York that he was first exposed to recent trends in European art, and it was there that he first won recognition, during the 1930s.

Tamayo painted murals in both Mexico and the United States, but he is remembered above all for his easel paintings, which show the influence of Braque, Picasso, and other modern artists. Yet this artist's use of color, his modeling of the human figure, and his choice of motifs reveal his Mexican roots. A well-known early still life, *Mandolins and Pineapples* (1930), is an exercise in composition, though the musical instruments reflect his interest in music, and the pineapples and a lone banana recall his childhood days when he lived with an aunt who had a fruit business in Mexico City. By contrast, the Cubistic *Lion and Horse* (1942) has no apparent Mexican sources, the horse suggesting a similarly anguished beast in Picasso's *Guernica*. *Animals* (1941) may derive its inspiration in part from the work of Picasso, yet many have noted a kinship between Tamayo's creatures and carvings of pre-Columbian canines from western Mexico. Picasso's influence is also evident in *Woman Spinning Wool* (1943), but the subject and the coloring are Mexican in origin. Tamayo always acknowledged his Mexican roots, but he was critical of what he considered the narrow nationalism of the muralists. Toward the end of his life, he declared: "The painters before me, the muralists, tried to make the Mexican School of Art. For me that was phony. Art is universal, and any nationalistic kind of art means limitation. Apparently, the muralists did not care to be universal. This is pure chauvinism, and I was against it from the very beginning."

From 1929 to 1933, María Izquierdo (1902–55) was the companion of Tamayo, and the work she did at the time reveals thematic similarities with his. Avoiding political subjects, she infused her canvases with the shapes and colors of Mexican popular culture. She painted circus images, allegories, and portraits, mainly of women, such as *My Nieces* (1940), notable for its brilliant color and Rousseau-like background of foliage and flowers, but her most highly regarded works are probably her still lifes. Among them are brightly colored renderings of cupboards and household altars such as *Offering for Our Lady of Sorrows* (1943). She labeled some of her paintings *naturalezas vivas* ("living" still lifes) to suggest the sensuousness and fertility of the fruit, fish, and other organic objects she depicted, often against a background of desolation. In 1945, she was invited to execute a mural for the government of Mexico City. Two North American sisters, Grace and

Marion Greenwood, had painted murals in Mexico, but she was the first Mexican woman to receive such a commission. When the contract was canceled after the Big Three questioned her technical competence, she was indignant and publicly attacked the "monopoly of the triumvirate." Soon afterward she suffered a stroke that impeded her ability to paint.

The work of Frida Kahlo (1907–54) is also steeped in Mexicanness, though it is primarily a record of her difficult life, marked by pain, disappointment, and loneliness. The daughter of a successful photographer of German Jewish ancestry and his Mexican wife, she was one of the first women to attend the National Preparatory School. When her studies were cut short after a traffic accident in 1925 that fractured her pelvis, spine, and right leg and crushed her right foot, she took up painting during her convalescence and showed her work to Rivera, who encouraged her. In 1929 she wed Rivera, whose marriage to Guadalupe Marín had collapsed. Her parents are said to have described the union of Kahlo and Rivera, 21 years her senior, as a "marriage between an elephant and a dove." Their marriage was marred by his numerous infidelities, which caused her much distress despite her own extramarital affairs, and they were divorced in 1939, only to rewed in 1940. Her inability to bear children is also said to have been a source of anguish.

Kahlo's relationship with Rivera was a central theme in her painting. It can be seen in *Frida and Diego Rivera* (1931), painted in a naive 19th–century style. In it she depicts herself as much smaller in stature and is seen in native Mexican attire, which she began to wear after she met Rivera. Other portrayals of herself with Rivera are less cheerful. In *Self-Portrait As a Tehuana* (1943), she wears the headdress of the women of Tehuantepec, noted for their beauty and independence. On her forehead is a small portrait of an impassive, perhaps indifferent, Rivera. Another recurring theme was the physical pain she endured throughout her adult life as a result of the 1925 accident. *The Broken Column* (1944) is a self-portrait painted after one of her many operations, when she was confined in a steel corset to alleviate the pain in her spine. It eloquently conveys her pain, but without self-pity.

When André Breton saw Kahlo's work in 1938, he declared that it showed "pure Surreality," though she had not been previously acquainted with the movement. At all times, her Mexican identity is a crucial element in her painting. This is dramatically illustrated in *My Nurse and I* (1937), in which the artist—depicted as an infant with an adult's face—sucks at the breast of an Indian woman whose massive, expressionless form is reminiscent of pre-Columbian sculpture.

As the events of 1910–20 receded farther and farther into memory and severe economic and political problems persisted in Mexico, scholars and intellectuals came to question the entire revolutionary experience, often finding continuity rather than a sharp break with the Porfirian era. Even so, the Revolution remained a seemingly inexhaustible source of inspiration for writers and painters, though they often used new approaches or themes. *Al filo del agua* (1947; *The Edge of the*

Storm, 1963) by Agustín Yáñez (1904–80) was a stylistically innovative novel set in a Jalisco village in the months before the Revolution. By emphasizing the stultifying social milieu created by the village's puritanical priests and the tension produced by occasional intrusions from the larger society, the author minimizes economic and political oppression as a cause of the Revolution. Instead, it can be seen at least in part as a response to sexual repression.

Disillusionment with the outcome of the Revolution continued to be a frequent theme in literature. Mariano Azuela's last, posthumously published novel, *Esa sangre* (1956), revives the character Julián Andrade, a cowardly hacendado whom he had created in one of his first novels, *Mala yerba* (1909; *Marcela*, 1932), an indictment of the subjugation of the peasantry by powerful landowners. In the later novel conditions have changed, but the representatives of the post-revolutionary generation are morally little better than Julián. Perhaps the most celebrated indictment of the Revolution and the society it created was *La muerte de Artemio Cruz*, (1962; *The Death of Artemio Cruz*, 1991) by Carlos Fuentes (1928–). Combining interior monologue with third-person narrative, Fuentes depicts a revolutionary veteran on his deathbed as he recalls his rise to power and wealth through betrayal and opportunism.

The three great muralists remained active until their deaths, filling walls with their vision of Mexico and the Revolution in a generally affirmative vision lacking the bitterness expressed in contemporary writings. Returning to the National Palace in 1942, Diego Rivera began a series of fresco panels on the second level portraying in great detail scenes from an idealized pre-Columbian past. One of them, *The Great City of Tenochtitlán* (1945), can be contrasted with *The Disembarkation at Veracruz* (1951), which depicted Hernán Cortés as a deformed syphilitic. Also noteworthy among Rivera's late murals is a fresco painted in 1947–48 in the lobby of the Hotel del Prado, located near the park of the same name in Mexico City. Titled *A Dream of a Sunday Afternoon in Alameda Park*, this fresco depicts Rivera as a boy in Porfirian Mexico. He holds the hand of a calavera, which in turn holds the hand of José Guadalupe Posada, who is thus acknowledged as a mentor of the artist. Surrounding Rivera in the crowded scene are other figures from his personal life and Mexican history.

In 1947–48 in the open-air theater of the National Teachers' School in Mexico City, José Clemente Orozco painted his largest single mural, called *National Allegory*, which is 59 feet high and 72 feet wide. Using ethyl silicate paint to protect the mural from the weather, the artist created an abstract work that is brilliantly integrated into its architectural setting. More in keeping with his earlier works was the fresco *Juárez, the Church and the Imperialists* (1948), painted in the National Museum of History in Mexico City's Chapultepec Castle.

David Alfaro Siqueiros remained politically active in his later years, being jailed from 1960 to 1964 for his efforts on behalf of political prisoners and his criticism of the government. Two of his principal murals date from this period. In the National Museum of History he painted in acrylic the panoramic *From the Dictatorship of Porfirio Díaz* (1957–65). It contrasts the corrupt society of the

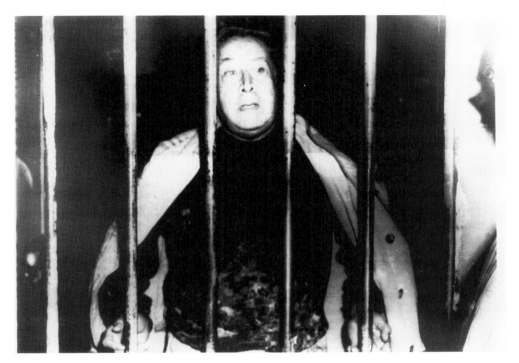

David Alfaro Siqueiros, the third of the muralist giants, took a leadership role in the Mexican communist party that ultimately led to his arrest. In August 1960, he was arrested after a two-hour running gun battle through Mexico City.

Porfiriato with the people in arms during the Revolution. A panel depicting the Cananea strike of 1906 in a border town near Nogales, showing a struggle for control of the Mexican flag, can be considered an allusion to Siqueiros's belief in the continuing reality of U.S. imperialism and thus a commentary on the unfinished work of the Revolution.

Leonard Folgarait has recounted in detail the controversy stirred by Siqueiros's last major murals, created for the Polyforum (1967–71) in Mexico City. Siqueiros and his associates decorated twelve massive exterior panels as well as the domed elliptical interior. The latter mural, called *The March of Humanity*, covers the entire surface of the interior except for the floor, so as to envelop the viewer. While some called this mural Siqueiros's greatest achievement, others found little of aesthetic or political significance in its swirl of abstract forms. Still others were critical of the fact that the Polyforum was constructed as part of a privately owned development project and that Siqueiros's interior mural would be seen mainly by paying tourists from abroad. The inauguration of the Polyforum on December 15, 1971, was attended by President Luis Echeverría and other dignitaries from Mexico's political, business, and cultural communities, who hailed Siqueiros's work as a fitting monument to 50 years of muralism in Mexico.

Despite the continuing popularity of muralism in Mexico after 1945, younger artists joined Tamayo in challenging the dominance of the nationalistic school of Mexican art represented by Rivera, Siqueiros, and their followers. In a 1956 essay, "The Cactus Curtain," José Luis Cuevas (1934–) charged that the continuing ascendancy of the Mexican school stifled creative freedom and kept the nation isolated from artistic developments in other countries. "What I want in my country's art are broad highways leading out to the rest of the world," he wrote, "rather than narrow trails connecting one adobe village with another." As the decades progressed, moreover, the rest of the world also reevaluated Mexican muralism, modifying the enthusiasm that had once surrounded the work of Rivera in particular. In 1974, Emily Gennauer, Tamayo's biographer, observed that his star had risen while the reputation of the muralists, except for Orozco, had fallen. "They are seen today as greatly gifted but bombastic, illustrative, rhetorical painters, more energetic than truly creative." Certainly in the era of abstract expressionism and cold war tensions the didactic, highly politicized murals of a Rivera or a Siqueiros were unlikely to win favor abroad. Frida Kahlo, meanwhile, had been transformed into an icon for feminists as well as art lovers everywhere, with her life story being told in a Mexican motion picture, *Frida, naturaleza viva*, in 1984.

Two years later, as part of the centennial of Rivera's birth, the Detroit Institute of Arts mounted a major retrospective of his work, which served as an occasion for a more favorable reassessment of his artistic significance. In 1990 workers in Los Angeles restored Siqueiros's badly damaged *Tropical America*, now recognized by many as an important work of art. Thus, as the 20th century came to an end and the centenary of the Mexican Revolution loomed, the work of Mexico's muralists as well as its writers and composers remained important not only as artistic achievements but also as an unforgettable record of the cultural nationalism that was one of the most enduring legacies of that upheaval.

Mexico in the Post-World War II Era

✦ ✦

The people and the needs of Mexico changed after World War II. The revolutionary reforms of the 1920s and 1930s could not provide for the vastly increased number of Mexicans, who had become greatly urbanized. The ruling regime renamed the official political organization the Party of the Institutionalized Revolution (referred to as the PRI) but resorted primarily to revolutionary rhetoric to explain its policies. In the aftermath of the 1968 student riots everyone could hear the hollow sound of these revolutionary phrases.

The postwar era saw the inauguration of civilian rule, new economic development, urban growth, and booming exports, especially of oil. However, the cost for these advances proved high. Civilian rule did not necessarily mean an end to bureaucratic corruption and the beginning of greater democracy. Urban and industrial growth provided some workers with good jobs and a sense of well-being but for many more brought only unemployment, underemployment, or survival through the underground (including the criminal) economy that operates outside government regulation and taxation. Industrial growth did occur, but the measure of its development after World War II became statistical indicators. Rather than examining real wages, real profits, or real benefits, the government looked to average increases in percentage terms. Anyone familiar with acronyms such as GDP (gross domestic product) knows the gap that exists between statistical and real measures.

Finally, Mexico's economic miracle was built on burgeoning exports, notably petroleum products. The miscalculation of the value of the 1970s oil strikes lured the Mexican regime into borrowing heavily on this promise alone. As a result, in the '70s Mexico had the largest foreign debt in the third world, which was overcome only with a savage austerity program.

Other changes in Mexico in the past half century resulted not from wishes but from hard work. The drive toward more representative, more responsive government progressed only in the tiniest increments with many setbacks, but by the end of the century more than half of all Mexicans were governed at the local level by politicians who were members of opposition parties. The national congress, until recently a presidential rubber stamp, has become since the mid–1990s an independent branch of government, even challenging on occasion the official party.

Paradoxically, Mexico today has a relationship with the United States in which the cultures are converging through mass media, tourism, and economics, yet it has become increasingly recognized throughout the world as a unique culture. Through it all, from the great encounter with Spanish culture to the present, the constant factor has been the resourcefulness and resolute character of the Mexican people. While Mexico has experienced a series of ups and downs as a political entity, its people have remained undaunted.

18

The Mexican "Miracle" and Its Collapse

JOHN W. SHERMAN

In 1947, Daniel Cosío Villegas, one of Mexico's most illustrious 20th–century intellectuals, published an article titled "Mexico's Crisis" in which he criticized the new presidential administration of Miguel Alemán. According to Cosío Villegas, after just one year under Alemán the so-called revolutionary government had ceased to be revolutionary. In a jarring about-face, it had abandoned the moderation of the Manuel Avila Camacho years (1940–46) and had begun to swallow up the advances made under the presidency of Lázaro Cárdenas (1934–40). In addition to these practical reversals, Cosío Villegas contended, the very heart of the revolutionary experience was about to be cut out of Mexican national life. Underlying commitments to ending foreign economic domination and addressing grossly inequitable wealth distribution were in danger of evaporating as Alemán and his cohorts redirected the country toward unbridled capitalist development. Though not without its flaws, "Mexico's Crisis" offered an astute evaluation of the regime and correctly prophesied many of its policies and their long-range consequences. In the late 1940s, a charismatic young president was setting Mexico on a new course. Gone were the days of revolutionary zeal that sought to modify the economic and political structures for the betterment of the "masses." Instead, a fresh approach envisioned such blazing success at wooing capital and fostering economic growth that wealth would trickle down and social harmony inevitably follow. In short, Mexico was looking for a miracle.

In December 1946, Miguel Alemán became Mexico's new head of state. At first notice some would have thought him an unlikely heir to the presidency. Only 46 years old at his inauguration, energetic, blessed with dashing good looks, he was something of a playboy who had frequented Hollywood social circles and nightclubs during the war years. His rise to power was unusual, given his family's political background: His father had fought with the winning Carrancista faction

Miguel Alemán, shown here voting in the presidential elections in 1946, won the presidency as a youthful civilian who personified the shift of national programs from the countryside to the city. He was later accused of great personal corruption.

during the Revolution, only to side with multiple losers in the 1920s and perish in Pablo Escobar's revolt of 1929. But Miguel Jr. capitalized on a friendship with a regional strongman, Cándido Aguilar, and obtained the governorship of his native state of Veracruz (1936–39) before serving as Avila Camacho's campaign manager in 1940 and minister of government during his term. Like so many of his successors, he found this post a natural conduit to the presidency.

Alemán is arguably the most important president in 20th–century Mexican history. He profoundly changed the nation's course by allying the state with mon-eyed interests, wooing foreign capital, accelerating industrialization, and undoing or mitigating many of the reforms promulgated by Cárdenas. He was corrupt, amassing a personal fortune even while overseeing unprecedented patronage to buy off and control rivals and manipulate vying political factions. Social scientists have given Lázaro Cárdenas disproportionate attention for crafting a political coalition under the auspices of his Party of the Mexican Revolution in 1938, but the real genius of modern Mexican political life was Alemán. While the Cárdenas coalition—rooted primarily in industrial labor and segments of the peasantry— faltered, Alemanismo rested on a new coalition of the formerly disassociated, including wealthy industrialists and the rising urban middle class. Alemán did far more than simply acknowledge a name change for the dominant Party of the Institutional Revolution (PRI), formerly the Party of the Mexican Revolution, in 1946, he turned Mexico's body politic on its head. And, unlike that of Cárdenas, his coalition endured, providing the nation with an era of relative consensus that lasted until near the end of the century. Although he left office in 1952, his successors held the alliance together easily until the late 1960s, when political and economic crises created tensions that forced some adjustment.

The most important component of the new coalition was the powerful industrialists located in Monterrey and Mexico City. The Monterrey group, tightly knit and extremely conservative, at first resisted the Alemán government's overtures, making peace with it only gradually. In contrast, Mexico City's wealthy private sector quickly settled into an alliance, taking a major step even before Alemán secured the presidency by signing an industrial-worker pact in 1945 with the Confederation of Mexican Workers (CTM). These ambitious capitalists, sometimes dubbed by Mexican scholars the forties faction, subsequently rose to prominence with Alemán, even joining him on campaign tours in 1945–46.

But Mexico City was about far more than the super-rich aiming to construct opulent homes in its Chapultepec Hills district. Much of the center of the city was occupied by an entrepreneurial middle class composed of small businessmen, shopkeepers, lawyers, bureaucrats, and professionals. Annoyed by labor unrest and inflation during the previous decade and scornful of Cardenismo, these city dwellers helped deliver the capital's electorate to Juan Andreu Almazán in the fraud-ridden 1940 presidential contest. Yet in a remarkable feat of political maneuvering, Alemán drew them into his new coalition by favoring conservative economic policies and addressing their political expectations.

The middle class, especially in the capital but also elsewhere, acquired political clout under the auspices of the National Confederation of Popular Organizations (CNOP)—the most important subsection of the newly reorganized official party. In Mexico City the PRI consolidated its allegiance largely through the governance of a conservative mayor for the Federal District, Ernesto Uruchurtu (1952–66), who was appointed by the president. Friends with Alemán since their days together at the Escuela Nacional Preparatoria, Uruchurtu appeased the middle class by subsidizing housing construction, initiating urban beautification projects, opposing disruptive downtown development projects, and combating— sometimes brutally—the myriad squatter settlements constantly popping up on the city's outskirts. His emphasis on law and order benefited from his close relationship with Carlos Serrano, head of the increasingly sophisticated, FBI-trained Federal Directorate of Security. Uruchurtu's policies were so fundamentally conservative that the right-wing National Action Party (PAN) attempted to recruit him as their presidential candidate in 1958.

Indeed, the hallmark of Alemanismo was a rightward shift that undermined the opposition and created a new national consensus. The former "enemies" of the Revolution (and under Cardenismo there had been many) were now its beneficiaries, and by the time Alemán left office the "institutionalized revolution" was one only in name. This was particularly frustrating for PAN, which had had to watch the PRI steal much of its natural political base. Women, for example, had rallied to the conservative opposition camp since the 1920s, largely in anger over the anticlericalism and "godlessness" of the revolutionary regime. At the outset of his term Alemán granted woman suffrage in municipal elections by amending the Constitution of 1917. But women still overwhelmingly voted for the opposition conservatives, nearly giving PAN an upset in 1948 in Monterrey by providing 70 percent of the vote for city council candidate José Guadalupe Martínez, a challenger openly backed by the local archbishop. By the time they participated in the first presidential election a decade later, women were no longer prone to support PAN or the right. Instead they were drawn into the PRI's consensus politics.

But the dominant party's tent was not big enough for everyone. The fabled Peace of the PRI probably involved a good deal more repression than scholars have thus far acknowledged. Organized labor in particular suffered profoundly under Alemán. The CTM, the umbrella organization of unions mobilized under Cárdenas, lost ground slowly during the Avila Camacho administration. In 1946, its leader, Vicente Lombardo Toledano, being miffed over a personal feud with presidential aspirant Ezequiel Padilla, threw the CTM's support behind Alemán and helped him secure the presidential nomination. Such a tactic proved to be an unmitigated blunder when Alemán returned the favor by effectively declaring war on organized labor. Even in his inauguration address he warned that the days of unauthorized strikes were over. When oil workers attempted a 24–hour work stoppage a few weeks later, the army rushed in and arrested the union's leaders, many of whom were jailed and beaten.

In Mexico City, the surviving Cardenista bureaucrats were coopted with new material incentives or quietly ushered into retirement. Those who balked or openly criticized the government, such as former socialist education secretary Narciso Bassols, faced ostracism and even surveillance by the security directorate. Many looked to Cárdenas himself for leadership, but the quiet-mannered former president refrained from political commentary. By 1952, it was widely believed that he tacitly supported the presidential candidacy of the reform-minded Miguel Henríquez Guzmán—an effort within the PRI that, given its dominance by Alemán loyalists, had no chance of winning the nomination.

The nature of repression in Mexico has always depended on one's money and status. Security forces monitored well-known critics, such as prominent Henriquistas (supporters of Henríquez Guzmán) in the capital, but did not risk the formidable ramifications of arresting them. A surprising number of well-placed opponents acquiesced to bribery and cooptation, including, apparently, Henríquez Guzmán himself. For those with slightly less political capital, such as students at the National University, repression took a more concrete form. When 4,000 youths staged an antigovernment protest in June 1951, Mayor Uruchurtu called out the riot police. Tear gas and billy clubs left 150 demonstrators injured, some of them hospitalized. For the working poor, the arm of the law exerted its muscle most overtly. Taxi drivers attempted a strike to protest their miserable working conditions in January 1950, only to see police raid their union headquarters and pummel their leaders in an orgy of violence that left two dead. When Henriquistas in the poor Indian state of Oaxaca orchestrated a successful general strike against the government in March 1952, the army moved in and crushed it, opening fire on a peaceful demonstration in Oaxaca City and killing an untold number of long-forgotten victims. Another small-scale massacre took place in Mexico City's historic Alameda Park. And when the Henriquista movement, known institutionally as the Federation of Parties of the Mexican People (FPPM), still refused to yield in docility to the dominance of the PRI, it was outlawed. Alemanismo was by no means placing Mexico on the road to democracy.

Still, despite the considerable repression, cooptation above all else marked political life in Mexico under Alemán and his successors. If the savageness of the Federal Directorate of Security or the military is at all shocking, so, too, is the quite amazing success of the PRI machine at compromising and manipulating its natural opponents. Take, for example, the case of self-professed Marxist and labor leader Vicente Lombardo Toledano. Even as the government persecuted oil workers, taxi drivers, and others into submission, he acquiesced to its dictates and chanted the official party line. When he finally broke with Alemán and created the "opposition" Popular Party (PP), something was still unnatural. The PP operated in fact as a dummy opponent, spouting blandly predictable discourse rhetoric about opposing "Yankee imperialism" even while it bent over backward to support the government on any substantive issues. (After it changed its name to the Popular Socialist Party in the 1960s, its rhetoric became, if possible, even more hollow.) In a similar fashion, the PRI coopted the right. The PAN played the role of a loyal opposition, fielding business candidates such as Luis Alvarez (1958) and José González Torres (1964) who railed as much against communism on the campaign trail as against their PRI opponents. Derisively labeled a banker's club, the party had little to oppose in terms of the direction the PRI was taking the country.

The PRI sanctioned and even encouraged the electoral straw-man competition of a whole host of minor parties, in large part because it provided a certain outward legitimacy to a political system that was in fact closed and rigid. Some groups, such as the Nationalist Party of Mexico (PNM), actually evolved with the establishment's blessing. Small and wholly fake opponents like the PNM and the misnamed Authentic Party of the Mexican Revolution (PARM) answered a long-standing need in the political culture for avoiding the appearance of a dictatorship akin to that of the vilified Porfirio Díaz. If the government happened to channel funds to these window-dressing opponents or grant them a few meaningless seats in the compliant national congress, as it usually did, all the better for the appearance of democracy. But the PRI itself headed in the opposite direction when, in 1950, it replaced the practice of selecting candidates through staged primary elections with the much more honest, though blatantly undemocratic, method of simply announcing them in public. The reality in postwar Mexico, and a defining feature of Alemanismo, was the truth of a maxim coined by an astute observer of Mexico two decades earlier: The party is the government, and the government is the party.

Following this simple equation was made easier by the centralization of political power in Mexico. The executive branch of government exercised enormous influence throughout the entire body politic. The strong presidency had predated Alemanismo, but the postwar years saw its enhancement. Legislative initiatives originating with the president received quick and often unanimous approval in Congress and faced no challenges from a compliant and feeble judiciary. In the rare instance that the Supreme Court did take issue with a measure, it invariably did so at the behest of the chief executive as a means of invalidating a measure proffered merely for appearance rather than implementation. The primary conduit of executive communication with the judiciary, Congress, various agencies, and the states was the Ministry of Government. Far and away the most important cabinet position, the ministry executed presidential orders, served as liaison to state and national officials, and even convened cabinet meetings (a rare phenomenon, as infrequent as three or four times a year). Not surprisingly, the post of minister of government became the stepping stone to the presidential palace. Ultimate authority rested there, as did leadership of the PRI. A confusing web of offices cloaked the party's hierarchy, but a seven-member executive committee closely tied to the president made all meaningful decisions. The PRI governed from the top down. Its control was so effective that from 1946 to 1973 it won 98 percent of all mayoral and congressional elections, with the controlled opposition winning the remainder. Potentially legitimate challengers from the left were persecuted into oblivion. Those on the right, namely PAN, were undercut by the conservative direction of the PRI.

The official party also won every gubernatorial race during the postwar era, there being only five truly competitive vote counts, making up less than 1 percent of the elections. As overwhelming as the state party's control was, on these rare occasions—usually in outlying regions—local political agitation sometimes nearly upset the status quo. The single remarkable instance of this phenomenon in the interior of the country was the case of Dr. Salvador Nava in the city of San Luis Potosí. An ophthalmalogist, Nava boldly ran for mayor of the state capital in 1958, generating widespread local support in a conservative region long resentful of the ruling party. When pro-Nava university students celebrated the Day of the Revolution by pelting the PRI governor with eggs, the army moved in and beat them. A general strike ensued, forcing Mexico City to acquiesce to Nava's election. In 1961, the doctor, having rebuffed offers to incorporate into the PRI, ran for governor under the banner of his Democratic Potosinan Party. The PRI lavishly outspent him but still had to rely on massive fraud to deny his election narrowly. Such a brazen challenge to the official party could not be tolerated, and after the PRI "won" the vote it was time to administer discipline. Hundreds of Nava supporters were jailed, and two years later security forces seized the once untouchable Nava himself, treating him to torture sessions until it was certain that he would completely withdraw from politics.

Genuine opponents faced the wrath of the stick, but most, whether in high or low places, accepted the incentive of the carrot. Nava and his followers stand out because of their steadfast refusal to cut deals with Mexico City. It has been argued, with some legitimacy, that the PRI gave postwar Mexico a benign, if corrupt, one-party political system. Rewards have awaited those willing to work from within the power structure. The ambitious young organizer who mobilized a community of poor, for example, could expect a small government position if he swung his followers in line with the PRI. Soon, some of the demands of the community would be answered, because the process of cooptation involved negotiation from both above and below. The government did indeed give, but it did so because it could also then take. This process is not to be confused with the grassroots empowerment of a democratic society. The powers that be invariably gave presumably less than would be due in a truly open society, and the heavy hand of terror was never far behind for those who persisted in dissent.

Not surprisingly, while the system offered incentives to those who bartered from the lower rungs of the ladder, it provided the greatest benefits to the few at the top. Another prominent characteristic of Mexico's postwar governance (and even its society) has been its landmark legendary levels of corruption. The *mordida* (bribe), which has long been practiced, is visible in a historical legacy stretching back to the Spanish Crown's sale of political offices during the colonial era. But with the presidency of Miguel Alemán the phenomenon of public enrichment reached stunning new proportions.

Ironically, Alemán began his term by announcing an anticorruption campaign—a political stunt that quickly evolved into a presidential tradition. Such rhetoric in fact reveals something of the man's cynicism. Although he managed much of his illicit wealth under a *prestanombre* (the "borrowed name" of the Spanish industrialist Manuel Suárez), even while he was in office his financial exploits were widely known. He amassed an astounding personal fortune, perhaps surpassed in real terms only by that of his distant successor Carlos Salinas de Gortari (1988–94).

Alemán had a particular penchant for real estate, gobbling up huge tracts of rich agricultural land in the newly irrigated northern state of Baja California and acquiring coastal acreage in his native Veracruz. And Alemán's inner circle of friends duplicated his ambition. Former president Abelardo Rodríguez, for example, who had lost his sizable holdings in gambling operations in the northwest under Cárdenas, recouped his wealth while serving in the cabinet and by managing the national telephone monopoly, Teléfonos de México. But whether powerful and vested or lowly and ambitious, corruption and cooptation were possible because from 1946 into the late 1960s the economic pie was, in fact, rapidly expanding. Thus, those in power had the resources with which to accumulate grand wealth for themselves even while buying off most of their potential rivals and enemies.

While in political matters the presidency of Miguel Alemán broke with the patterns of Cardenismo, in economics it continued the program, begun in the late 1930s, of state-guided industrialization. However, Alemán greatly accelerated and significantly modified the process. Both his and successive administrations aggressively wooed foreign capital in their zeal to industrialize, but they also suppressed organized labor and spent lavishly on mostly infrastructure-oriented public works. On paper, at least, their accomplishments looked noteworthy. A postwar "miracle" had indeed occurred, in which Mexico averaged nearly 6 percent annual gross domestic product (GDP) growth into the 1960s, one of the highest sustained rates recorded in the world. But statistical growth unfortunately does not always translate into on-the-ground well-being and stability. It is certain that the Mexican economic pie grew in size, but the poor received increasingly less of it. The bottom quintile—or lowest fifth of the population—which received 5 percent of the nation's income in the mid–1950s, garnered less than 3 percent two decades later. Much of rural Mexico in particular lagged badly behind urban pockets of development as agriculture, responsible for 10 percent of GDP in 1940, fell to 5 percent by 1973. The burgeoning population also mitigated the positive consequences of the highly vaunted economic gains.

Under Alemán, Mexico pinned its economic hopes on a process of rapid industrialization. Largely financed through U.S. capital, this strategy made close ties to American business interests essential. Those ties, which had been disrupted earlier in the century by the Revolution and the later, by the radicalism of Cardenismo, were rejuvenated during World War II and flourished anew in the postwar years. Although the United States prudently refrained from engaging in high-profile political and diplomatic interactions, in their economic dealings rich Americans and Mexicans united to a degree not unlike that seen during the Porfiriato. By the 1970s, as the Mexican political scientist Lorenzo Meyer has pointed out, U.S. economic control reached proportions similar to, if not greater than, that under Díaz. There were, however, significant differences. Joint cross-border ownership and the prominent role of the state made for the rise of a much more powerful domestic business class than had ever existed before.

During Alemán's term in office U.S. and Mexican elites joined hands in close partnerships. In 1944, a new law stipulated that 51 percent of an enterprise had to be owned by Mexicans. Several loopholes facilitated evasion of this requirement, including the option of creating subsidiary corporations with titular Mexican ownership. As U.S. business interests utilized these loopholes, the Mexican government looked the other way. A primary reason for both the law and its neglect was the emerging business alliance. The ownership requirement served as a way for wealthy Mexicans to draw their U.S. counterparts into a lucrative partnership, while the lack of enforcement tightened the bond. President Alemán himself was at the center of this entire process. Fluent in English and widely traveled in America the United States prior to his term, he enjoyed close relations with some of the country's most influential businessmen. Shortly after taking office he enhanced these links by a highly publicized, multistop U.S. visit that found him warmly received.

Historian Stephen Niblo has demonstrated that a relatively small number of men orchestrated the new alliance and carried out its major economic and investment decisions. Wealthy American U.S. and Mexican bankers negotiated enormous loans through myriad nascent international agencies, including the

World Bank, the International Monetary Fund, and the Export-Import Bank. U.S.-backed loans for industry-related public works projects such as hydroelectric dams received approval through the U.S. embassy where, after 1947, former ambassador to Mexico George Messersmith (president of the Mexican Power and Light Company) could exercise his influence in the process.

Meanwhile, the administration of President Harry S. Truman routed critical technical assistance through its Point Four program. Alemán mobilized domestic finances through the centralized Bank of Mexico and other agencies, providing for a mixed economy where a large segment of the requisite capital for industrialization—probably about one-third—came from within. The line between the private and public sectors was further blurred by the composition of corporate and government boards. Powerful Mexican politicians such as Alemán and Abelardo Rodríguez helped manage corporations, while President Alemán wooed formerly aloof Monterrey industrialists into positions of power connected to his government.

But before the hyperconservative Monterrey group—or, for that matter, many U.S. businessmen—could be drawn into backing the industrialization project, the Mexican government had to demonstrate its position on labor relations. The rise of powerful unions under Lombardo Toledano's CTM workers' umbrella group during the Cárdenas administration had deeply irritated management and had threatened to generate capital flight. In order to appease management, Alemán needed to recast completely the state-labor alliance from one designed to improve workers' lives to one that guaranteed their pacification. This he did with zeal. His crushing of a work stoppage by oil laborers in December 1947 signaled the end of labor's long decade in the sun. During the following year, Alemán skillfully played off factions within organized labor against each other in a strategy of divide and conquer that was facilitated by the limited political acumen of Lombardo Toledano. Eventually the renowned labor leader and other progressives were driven from the CTM, which fell to the leadership of the conservative and obedient "Don Fidel" Velázquez, who reigned as Mexico's official labor guru until his death in 1997.

Alemán and Velázquez divided labor by imposing on its unions compliant new leaders in a process that became known as *charrismo* (drawn from the word *charro*, or cowboy, the term evolved from the cowboylike, cavalier attitude of these new chieftains toward their rank and file). As industrial wages reached new lows in 1948, the workers found themselves left on their own. The government altered the 1931 labor law, sharply increasing its penalties for unauthorized strikes. The Supreme Court even ruled briefly that all strikes were illegal when contracts remained in effect, a dictum that could have kept labor perpetually on its knees, though even Alemán had to back away from this 1948 decision—one that, in all probability, he had sanctioned. Government arbitration, too, suddenly shifted in 1948 from a relatively neutral stance to a pattern of uniformly pro-business decisions. When one Monterrey firm summarily slashed wages by 50 percent, Alemán's labor ministry backed their decision. And when the Ford

Motor Company fired 400 workers without cause in 1949, again the government raised no objections. Millions of petition signatures poured into the presidential office from desperate workers, only to be ignored by Alemán. On the rare occasions when independent labor factions could still threaten an industry, the newly installed charro leadership invariably "won" modest wage increases for "their" workers. But once the threat of genuine labor agitation diminished, so too did the newfound benefits and concessions.

The workers, of course, resisted charrismo and fought to retain control of their unions. But many of their leaders simply could not refuse the bribes and rewards offered to turncoats. And, as awful as it was being part of a government-controlled union, the fate of the independents was far more grim. During Alemán's term in office free labor associations faced relentless and often brutal persecution, which the government justified in the name of fighting cold-war Communism. Even the famous and once influential Lombardo Toledano bore scorn and suffered threats of deportation when Velázquez betrayed his friendship and slandered him as a Soviet agent. It takes little imagination to envision what happened to the powerless and the poor who dared to strike but then fell into the hands of the army or the security directorate. Yet for Alemán the combination of charrismo and repression accomplished its task. As late as 1960 the real wages for industrial workers remained lower than in 1940 even as worker productivity nearly doubled. In terms of labor costs, postwar Mexico offered investors a favorable business climate.

Also essential to wooing both foreign and domestic private capital was a plethora of government incentives. The Mexican state was deeply involved in creating, promoting, and even capitalizing industry. First, it made sure that the tax structure favored business. High tariffs and protectionist policies incubated upstart start-up industries by guaranteeing them the domestic market, even while revenues from many export duties slowly declined. Archaic stamp taxes, literally paid in government-issued stamps, which were imposed on items ranging from legal documents to licenses, were phased out in the late 1940s. Then in the 1950s the tax burden shifted away from business with the steady increase of a personal income tax. And, in coordination with the Bank of Mexico, a credit institution called the Nacional Financiera (National Financier) aided investment by floating bonds and managing both public and private funds, including many of the major loans granted for public works.

Massive public works projects in fact offered a major incentive for industrialization. Mexico's government launched multiple initiatives to provide the infrastructure necessary for a manufacturing-based society. This challenge, as Alemán took office, was considerable. The railroads developed during the Porfirian era certainly had linked the major cities together and created swaths of development. But despite the slow advances made since the Revolution, Mexico was still largely a nation of isolated agricultural regions. Its new factories needed electricity, its new products needed a highway system with routes stretching from the interior to the United States.

The Pacific coast resort of Acapulco came of age with Alemán's support in the late 1950s and continued to expand with the steady rise in air travel over the next two decades. Although the presence of the rich and famous has defined much of its aura, the majority of Acapulco's clientele has always been Americans of the middle and upper middle classes who were drawn to its beaches, sparkling waters, and picturesque cliffsides. By the early 1970s, nearly the entire crescent-shaped lagoon was lined with highrise hotels such as the Hilton.

Accordingly, inspired by the success of the Tennessee Valley Authority, the Alemán government launched a similar program, albeit for different motives. Floodwaters were not much of a problem in mostly arid Mexico, but the need for irrigation and the benefits of hydroelectric power were visible to all. In the southeast, enormous dams rose on the Grijalva and Papaloapan rivers (creating enormous lakes named after Nezahualcóyotl, the ancient native poet-king, and Miguel Alemán). In the northwest, dams harnessed several of the rivers of Sinaloa, Sonora, and the Baja states, helping transform those areas into agricultural oases.

Bonds issued by the Nacional Financiera funded new roads, including the Christopher Columbus Pan-American Highway stretching from Ciudad Juárez across from El Paso to the Guatemalan border. Opened in 1950 and inaugurated by a 2,200–mile automobile race, it was followed four years later by the completion of a route from Nogales, on the Arizona border, to Mexico's second-largest metropolis, Guadalajara. Other superhighways linked Mexico City to Puebla, Cuernavaca, and a host of lesser cities in the Bajío (west-central plateau). By 1957, Mexico had 15,000 miles of paved roads, a testimony to both the government's commitment to road building and the technology of new paving equipment imported from the United States. Buses and trucks soon crisscrossed the country, with trucks soon challenging the railroads in some areas of freight hauling.

New highways not only facilitated the shipping of raw materials and manufactured goods but greatly aided a young industry destined to become one of the nation's top three moneymakers by the end of the century: tourism. Alemán saw to the construction of a four-lane road south from Mexico City to an idyllic enclave of beaches on the Pacific near the small fishing town of Acapulco. Investing himself heavily in beachfront property, he promoted the resort after his term in office by serving as his successor's minister of tourism. Though a few smaller hotels had already been established in the village that had catered to a rich clientele, which often arrived by yacht, the new highway and the aggressive promotion by Alemán converted Acapulco into a world-class resort by 1960. Plush highrises clustered along the seashore, hosting many of the world's rich and famous, including Hollywood personalities such as Rita Hayworth, Errol Flynn, Cary Grant, and John Wayne, some of whom had known the young Alemán when he had romped around the film capital as a young man.

Acapulco's growth also owed a debt to another booming transportation industry: aviation. In 1940, only 90,000 passengers went airborne in Mexico, but by 1952 the annual passenger count had reached 1 million. The three dozen airports in existence at the outset of the 1950s had been largely financed by private capital, many by the airlines themselves. Government funds came to the aid of the industry during the decade. A new airport opened to the southeast of Acapulco, while two 7,000–foot runways enhanced Guadalajara's airfield and a $5 million terminal improved service at Mexico City's Benito Juárez airport in 1953. Also in that year Mexico held its first National Tourism Congress, where businessmen and advertisers gathered to coordinate efforts to make the nation a major destination for American U.S. vacationers.

As impressive as infrastructure improvements such as airports, highways, and dam construction were, they ultimately served the process of industrialization— the heart of the Mexican economic "miracle." After Alemán tamed labor, sidestepped ownership laws, and courted American U.S. capital to enter into an investment alliance, new factories sprouted up, especially in the industrial parks on the north side of Mexico City. Annual industrial output rose an average of 7.3 percent during the 1950s, fueling a sharp but stable rise in gross domestic product. This growth led to tens of thousands of rural Mexicans flocking to the capital in search of jobs. These new factories, along with the public works designed to support them, gave Mexico in the 1950s an image of a rapidly modernizing nation. Yet as visible as many of the changes were, the development taking place ws exceedingly uneven. Only a small minority of Mexicans found work in the industrial sector, and the modernization was not eradicating poverty.

The coastal boulevard that arcs through Acapulco bears the name of Miguel Alemán, but the secondary streets honor his two successors, Adolfo Ruiz Cortines (1952–58) and Adolfo López Mateos (1958–64). It was Alemán who redirected the political and economic course of postwar Mexico, whereas the subsequent two presidents both held his coalition together and followed the major contours of his policies. It fell to Ruiz Cortines and López Mateos to complete much of what Alemán had begun. While major highways linked Mexico to the United States by the mid–1950s, for example, during the next decade the paving of countless rural

The Institutionalized
Revolutionary Party (el
Partido Revolucionario
Institucional, or PRI) has
dominated Mexican
politics and the federal
government since its
creation from earlier
official parties in 1946.
The PRI has demon-
strated great ability to
mobilize Mexicans to
affirm their support for
the party.

routes continued. Small roads cut through the jungles of Yucatán, finally tying
that remote peninsula to the populated heartland. Although it was Alemán who
moved the National University to a sprawling new campus on the outskirts of
Mexico City, it was left to his successors to build the myriad apartments and dor-
mitories around it. But although the two Adolfos were political heirs of Alemán,
they practiced his policies with less zeal and somewhat more moderation than
their flamboyant mentor. They also toned down the excesses of Alemanismo, created some (albeit limited) space for dissent, and exercised slightly more restraint
than had Alemán in the use of repressive force.

The hallmark Alemán policies of favoring capital, fostering industrialization,
and dividing labor continued, however. Ruiz Cortines, Alemán's friend and fellow
veracruzano who had served as his minister of government, inherited a restless
industrial working class when he became president in 1952. It did not take long
for workers in the early 1950s to recognize that charro leadership rarely acted on
their behalf. Accordingly, in part due to the new president's leniency in terms of
repression, independent unions grew. Although precise calculations are impossible, by the end of the decade approximately one-third of the organized workers
belonged to what can be termed independents. Facing potential worker agitation,
the Ruiz Cortines administration followed Alemán's example and attempted to
play different factions off against one another. The obedient umbrella group
CTM, under Velázquez, rivaled the more belligerent but still coopted Revolutionary Confederation of Workers and Peasants (CROC), while genuinely non-
governmental unions tended to coalesce under the auspices of the General Union

of Workers and Peasants of Mexico (UGOCM). This strategy of division kept the peace with relative success until the close of Ruiz Cortines's term when, ironically, his youthful secretary of labor succeeded him as president.

López Mateos, elected by the customary PRI landslide in July 1958, faced labor unrest in the form of gradually accelerated work stoppages by railroad workers. Long on the front lines of the labor struggle, the railroad union had in August elected the outspoken Demetrio Vallejo as its head, who in turn pleaded the workers' cause for wage increases after years of steady real-wage declines. The showdown with the government drew to a climax in March 1959 when the union staged a major strike on the eve of Holy Week, a time when hundreds of thousands of Mexicans relied on trains for affordable travel. A vengeful Mexican government responded. Raiding the strike headquarters under the pretext that Vallejo and his cohorts had ties to the Soviet Union and world Communism, security forces arrested labor leaders while the army seized the major rail lines. Declaring the strike illegal, the administration filed conspiracy charges against the workers and shipped many of them, including Vallejo, off to serve long-term prison sentences.

Despite the ugly repression of this railroad strike, historians have generally viewed Adolfo López Mateos as a well-intentioned reformer. To the surprise of many, after this inauspicious start to his term, he seemed to shift ideologically leftward. His administration oversaw the acquisition of a controlling government interest in electrical works, the initiation of a modest profit-sharing plan for corporate workers, and the nationalization of the failing motion picture industry. His term happened to coincide with the dramatic unfolding of the Cuban Revolution, at which point he opted to strain diplomatic relations with Washington by refusing to break off relations with Fidel Castro. He and his cabinet ministers frequently traveled abroad, often advocating nonalignment among nations caught in the middle of superpower rivalries. With the United States itself he negotiated the transfer of a long-disputed tract of land in El Paso, Texas. Chamizal, as it was known, had passed from Mexican hands after the Rio Grande River had changed its course. The 1963 treaty arranging for its return served the rekindled nationalist rhetoric of the Mexican government well.

The tone of the López Mateos administration compares favorably to that of Ruiz Cortines. There is little doubt that López Mateos was far more adept at employing populist rhetoric than his refrained more restrained predecessor, but when all is carefully analyzed, it may well prove true that the first Adolfo was every bit as moderate as his more famous successor. Indeed, many of López Mateos's most significant programs actually began under Ruiz Cortines. It was the latter who began to accelerate funding to the Ministry of Education after a sharp lapse under Alemán. By 1963, education had become the largest single item in the national budget as the government aggressively promoted rural school construction and distributed free textbooks—which, not surprisingly, tended to praise the current government. Ruiz Cortines launched the construction of rural health clinics, hospitals, and initiated social security system—programs expanded under López Mateos. Even the López Mateos's independent foreign policy owes a debt to the prior administration, which voted to defend the reform regime of Jacobo Arbenz in Guatemala in the face of U.S. aggression, then gave him sanctuary when he was forced to flee Guatemala. Yet all the moderation of the two Adolfos aside, the broad patterns of development begun under Alemán surged ahead unabated. The "miracle" continued, but even with reform and increased social spending it was leaving a large number of Mexicans by the wayside.

Both Ruiz Cortines and López Mateos faced the most acute challenge of poverty in the countryside. Despite the national emphasis placed on industrialization, factories still employed only a small fraction of Mexico's burgeoning workforce. Even by the early 1960s Mexico was predominantly rural. Yet under the postwar development model isolated villages lagged badly behind the modernity gripping the cities. Although paved roads and even electricity arrived in most outlying regions, these were proved no substitute for good jobs and adequate incomes. Aggravating the problems of the countryside was an accelerating birth rate and a declining death rate as immunizations now protected Mexican children from many once devastating diseases. In fact, postwar Mexico had one of the highest growth rates in the world, averaging approximately 3.5 percent, which caused its population to double between 1940 and 1964, to about 40 million.

Ruiz Cortines recognized the problems besetting rural Mexicans and, though he would not swerve from Alemán's industrialization model, resolved to at least address them. Simply distributing land, though politically attractive given the legacy of the Revolution, did not completely answer the needs of the poor. Increasingly, in the money-driven economy of the late 20th century, access to plots of land could not ensure physical material well-being. Instead, Ruiz Cortines identified the necessity of cheap basic food. He greatly expanded the role of the Mexican Exporting and Importing Company (CEIMSA, established in 1949 with quite different objectives), using it to control prices on essential foodstuffs by dealing in commodity trades on such items as milk, cornmeal, eggs, and grains. As a result, food prices dropped in Mexico during the 1950s, if over the objections of the multinational agribusinesses.

Capitalizing on Ruiz Cortines's initiative, López Mateos replaced CEIMSA with the National Company of Popular Subsistence Foods (CONASUPO) in 1961. CEIMSA had begun an innovative program of delivering basic foodstuffs to remote, impoverished villages by mobile vans. CONASUPO aggressively expanded this popular program, reaching millions of Mexico's most needy villagers through a network of mobile units and stores in a system that was further improved by bureaucratic decentralization in the mid–1960s. Subsidized corn, beans, rice, wheat, and other essentials ensured that the vast majority of Mexicans, even the poorest of the poor, could eat regularly. Both CEIMSA and its

The national program to provide basic foodstuffs at reasonable cost to the nation's peoples (called CONASUPO) relied on mobile supermarkets such as the one in the photograph. The trucks carried packages of rice, beans, bread, sugar, flour, soap, coffee, and dried fish. CONASUPO also sold milk in disposable cartons. Costs averaged about half the cost of these items in markets.

offshoot CONASUPO garnered tremendous gratitude for the government and the PRI from rural Mexicans.

Some small farmers also enjoyed the benefits of government intervention, because CONASUPO purchased their goods. But although its sources of produce and its program variations were myriad, CONASUPO tended to manipulate the market at the point of consumption rather than of production. Even in the late 1950s its predecessor, CEIMSA, began the practice of importing cheap grains from overseas. Thus, unlike the price supports buttressing production in western Europe and the United States, Mexican grain prices steadily declined into the mid–1960s, driving tens of thousands of peasant farmers out of business or into other crops. Corn, the most important foodstuff and the centerpiece of the peasant diet, made up two-thirds of the cultivated land in 1940, but only about half of it some 20 years later.

The primary reason grain prices fell was a dramatic increase in productivity attributable to the so-called green revolution. The effect of this revolution was that, even though less acreage was now given to corn, that which remained produced far larger harvests. Initiated in Mexico through the generous funding of the Rockefeller Foundation and other U.S. philanthropies, the green revolution involved the use of fertilizers, insecticides, and hybrid seeding to enhance production, augmenting these resources with new technologies and a wide range of educational programs designed to instruct peasants in the new methods of planting, sowing, and reaping. There is no doubt that through the green revolution food production rose sharply in Mexico: Corn alone surged upward by 250 percent. Between 1950 and 1970, Mexico's wheat crop rose from 300,000 to 2.6 million tons, while beans increased from 530,000 to 925,000 tons. These impressive gains came from increased yields per acre because the amount of land used in wheat and bean production, like that of corn, actually declined.

In technological and statistical terms, then, the green revolution was an astounding success. But scholars over a range of disciplines have been divided as to its net benefits. The most succinctly argued downside of the dramatic increase in agricultural productivity is that it ultimately put millions of rural Mexicans out of work. Aided by science and technology, one farmer (or, more properly, one worker on a large commercial farm) could replace a half dozen or more other farmers. As prices on a whole range of basic foodstuffs dropped, so, too, did the number of producers. Despite its surging population growth, Mexico had fewer farmers in 1970 than it had had two decades earlier. And as the pool of unemployed rural labor increased, daily wages also moved downward. Mexico now had more food, but less work. The ever growing ranks of the displaced in the countryside sought relief by migrating to the cities or to the United States, or by filtering into what economists dub the "informal economy"—selling crafts and consumer goods to passersby on the streets. Hundreds of thousands of teenage women turned to domestic servitude or prostitution or, in some cases, something akin to a combination of both.

The promises of the green revolution could not save Mexico from other damaging long-term trends. Eventually, with fewer farmers, ever more people, and government intervention at the buying end of the market, grain prices reversed direction and went up. After 1965, Mexico, finding itself increasingly troubled by foodstuff inflation, again turned to grain imports. The caloric intake of the average citizen declined by 10 percent between 1967 and 1976 as the heyday of low-cost food passed. Ironically, the simultaneous trend toward export agriculture continued. Huge commercial enterprises cultivated a host of specialty crops for grocery stores catering to the middle class or to North Americans: strawberries from Guanajuato, plums from Chihuahua, pineapples from Veracruz. Many products were marketed by huge, vertically integrated, U.S.-owned firms such as Continental Grain, Cook Industries, and Ralston-Purina. As in manufacturing and tourism, U.S. capital joined its Mexican counterparts in managing the nation's agricultural resources.

When shoppers purchased groceries, only a fraction of their payment returned to the farmer who had produced them. And by the 1970s the "farmer" was usually not the simple campesino or *ejidatario* (collective farmer) living on a government-managed collective farm. At the center of food production were large commercial estates capable of producing bumper crops cheaply by enjoying access to capital with which to finance the needed technology. In contrast, the government *ejidos* (collective farms) lagged behind badly in both productivity and profits. Strapped by their lack of capital, bureaucratic corruption, and managerial inefficiency, many of the grand estates established under Cardenismo slid into bankruptcy and disrepair during the postwar era. Although the Constitution of

1917 forbade their alienation as repayment for incurred debt, many ejidos were in fact rented out. Their discouraged inhabitants often departed voluntarily for wage labor elsewhere in Mexico or in the United States. Similarly, small peasant farmers could not compete with the enormous profitable agribusinesses that were producing over half of Mexico's marketed crops by 1970.

Agricultural prosperity became restricted to a few well-capitalized regions. The data reveal that in 1970 a mere three states—Sonora, Sinaloa, and Veracruz—held nearly 40 percent of the nation's tractors and yielded one-third of the value of its agricultural production. In these areas large commercial operations specialized in export agriculture, because that was where the most money could be made. Truckloads of tomatoes, grapes, winter vegetables, and citrus fruit rolled north into the United States, passing hungry Mexicans on the way. In a marketplace determined by money rather than by need, it was inevitable that the vested agribusinesses would follow the culinary tastes of their wealthier consumers at the expense of others.

Consequently, Mexico underwent a "second" green revolution in the 1960s, experiencing a sharp rise in cattle, hog, and poultry production as its producers catered to the dietary tastes of the booming middle class. The demand for meat in turn inspired the conversion of croplands from wheat and corn into animal fodder. Sorghum production, for example, rose from almost nothing to 2.7 million tons by the end of the decade.

Fodder production for calorie-consuming animals meant that staple production slowed. But the poor could not afford a meat-based diet. By the early 1970s, then, Mexico was experiencing a strange phenomenon—exporting increasing amounts of beef even while basic grains had to be imported. By 1974, according to data from the National Institute of Nutrition, 18.4 million Mexicans were severely malnourished and 90 percent of the rural population was experiencing serious dietary deficiencies. In the early 1970s, more than 350,000 children died annually due to malnutrition. Poverty persisted in a host of interior states, with despair gripping Tlaxcala and much of the Bajío region east to Puebla. Chronic unemployment ravaged the Indian-dominated south. Except for its tourist resorts on the Pacific and, later, the development of oil fields in Tabasco, southern Mexico languished. Interior villages in Guerrero, Oaxaca, and Chiapas sagged stagnated during the decades of the economic "miracle."

Such neglect fueled despair and, occasionally, revolutionary anger. A pattern of low-level repression in the Indian south emerged as the PRI coerced those who would not cooperate with it and eliminated those who could not be coerced. The most famous case of agrarian unrest was that of Rubén Jaramillo and his followers in Morelos. Waging intermittent guerrilla warfare since 1943 and unappeased by government rhetoric, these neo-Zapatistas served as an embarrassing reminder of the many unkept promises of the Revolution. After Jaramillo laid down his arms under an amnesty proffered by the administration of López Mateos, security forces apparently seized the day: His body, and those of his family, turned up dead shortly thereafter. López Mateos, with much flourish, promised to reinvigorate

After World War II, the movement of Mexicans from the countryside to cities, especially Mexico City, accelerated. Because cities could not keep pace with the burgeoning population, newcomers often eked out life in the expanding slums.

land reform during his term, though he ultimately distributed only 8 million acres of the more than 28 million acres he had vowed to deliver. Few poor Mexicans attempted to change their situation by taking up arms; many simply opted to evade their poverty by leaving. One avenue of exodus was to the United States, which continued to allow migrant workers into its own agricultural fields under the auspices of the bracero program until 1964. Initiated during World War II, when the United States was experiencing an acute shortage of manpower, the bracero agreement granted worker permits under a system of contract labor. During its 22–year history, 4.6 million Mexicans participated, mostly laboring during the harvest season in Texas and in California's Imperial Valley under subpar working and living conditions that Americans would not accept. Still, organized labor in the United States steadfastly opposed the program on the basis of Mexicans' supposedly taking American jobs, finally winning the battle for its termination during the administration of Texas Democrat Lyndon B. Johnson. Few Mexicans were disappointed, however. The contract labor program had always been marred by endemic corruption and mindless red tape. For every one legal migrant worker a half dozen or so had simply opted to enter the United States illegally. In the late 1960s, after the bracero agreement ended and as the Mexican economy slowed, the numbers of illegal immigrants soared. Though the nature of the migration makes statistical precision impossible, the U.S. Immigration and Naturalization Service's apprehensions of aliens classified by them as illegal along the Mexican border reflect the dramatic influx: 55,000 undocumented

Mexicans were returned in 1965, some 277,000 in 1970, and an astounding 680,000 in 1975.

While the United States was an attractive option to some, far more Mexicans yielded to the lure of the big city, with 3 million migrating into urban areas during the 1960s alone. Secondary cities such as Guadalajara and Monterrey, as well as numerable numerous state capitals, experienced sharp growth, but the mecca that welcomed the largest number most of the newcomers was Mexico City itself. By 1990, one-fourth of the nation's population would call the capital home. The draw, of course, was the hope of finding good work. Most migrants undertook this dramatic move by following immediate or extended family members into the city, for few would risk uprooting themselves without some communal support.

For millions, though, the experience was initially disillusioning. The noise, lights, commotion, and crowds of the city were overwhelming, and decent-paying steady work was, even in the best years of the "miracle," hard to find. Soon both the capital and other urban centers were encircled by infamous "misery belts." The newcomers, unable to find affordable accommodations in the city itself, resorted to squatting on the urban outskirts—usually on hillsides, in ravines, or on undesirable land such as the lava flows south of Mexico City known as the Pedregal. Attracted by the expectation of rent-free living, squatters invaded land that was often privately owned, sometimes en masse but at other times gradually.

The authorities inevitably called upon riot police, bulldozers, and even arsonists to combat squatter settlements, but persistence usually paid off. Once they became reasonably secure, these haphazard communities of the damned took shape, with shanties of cardboard and plywood being slowly upgraded into huts of cinder block and concrete, roofs of wooden sticks converted to sheets of tin, and paths of dirt eventually smoothed out and paved. Squatters illegally tapped into nearby electric lines, creating a *telaraña* (cobweb) of wires above them. But even long-established settlements frequently lacked running water and sewers, and disease and premature death often followed for some inhabitants.

For most of the newcomers urban life was a difficult struggle just to survive. The bustle of a great metropolis such as Mexico City constituted a strange world to those who had known only the relative tranquillity of the countryside. Encounters with authorities frequently fueled anxiety and frustration. And yet there were diversions. One of the most popular came by way of Salvador Lutteroth, a colonel in the Revolution who had spent time in the United States, where he discovered the unique phenomenon of professional wrestling. Lutteroth determined to import these colorful theatrics to his native land. At first, in the mid–1930s, his matches featured second-caliber U.S. athletes who drew mixed reviews from often bewildered audiences. But it was the colonel's good fortune that one of the early spectators was a young man by the name of Rodolfo Guzmán Huerta, himself a rural migrant newly arrived in the capital.

Guzmán Huerta took to professional wrestling with boyish enthusiasm and was instrumental in converting it into a major national pastime (by the 1980s,

The Pasquel brothers challenged major baseball in the United States by creating a new professional league. Jorge (left), president of the Mexican Baseball League, and his brother Bernardo (right) aggressively recruited professional ball players from both the Major Leagues and the Negro Leagues to play in Mexico. Eventually, the United States baseball owners halted the flow of players to Mexico and dismantled the upstart league.

second in attendance and viewership only to soccer). He first climbed into the squared circle during the war years, donning a silver-teared mask and christening himself El Santo (The Saint). His adoption of a mask was nothing new: Several American performers had worn masks over the previous decade, the first uncreatively calling himself El Enmascarado (The Masked One). But Guzmán Huerta was different. He was Mexican, understood the hard lives of the immigrant poor, and participated in the formation development of several innovations that made *lucha libre* (professional wrestling) not only widely popular but also distinctly Mexican.

El Santo never removed his mask, generating an element of mystery that helped elevate him into a legendary figure in the popular culture. He became not only the most famous wrestler of all time but also something akin to a Mexican Superman, with admiring fans throughout much of Latin America. Whether in the ring or in the dozen movies about him, El Santo was a tragic but noble figure: the honest, hardworking "little guy" who battled the injustices of the corrupt powers seeking to destroy him. In the ring such evildoers took the form of *los rudos*—a team of arrogant bullies willing to betray and cheat in order to reign supreme. Invariably, during the "brawl" of high-flying acrobatics, events initially went badly for El Santo and his allies. But by courage and determination, good turned the corner on evil. The lesson was not lost on the crowds, who by the 1950s flocked to Mexico City's austere concrete arenas in warm appreciation of the spectacle. They jeered the ugly, brutish rudos, who sometimes donned animal costumes or even police uniforms, and wildly applauded their modest, child-loving heroes, foremost among them El Santo.

Lucha libre was not the only urban pastime imported from the United States. Baseball, brought into Mexico during the Porfiriato by American U.S. workers and visitors, reached a new plateau in the postwar era. The Mexican League, composed of eight teams by 1946, briefly flourished under the tutelage of Jorge Pasquel, who aggressively promoted it. A businessman and close friend of Miguel Alemán who built a staggering personal fortune by cornering the fuel distribution market and, according to the U.S. embassy, by dealing in illegal narcotics, Pasquel owned the most successful franchise of the league, the Veracruz Azules (Blues). His club faced particularly talented opponents in Puebla, which fielded a team owned by General Motors investor Castor Montoto, and Mexico City. Many of the teams, including the capital's Diablos Rojos (Red Devils), enhanced their play in the late 1940s by recruiting off-season U.S. players from both the majors and the Negro League. Catcher Mickey Owen of the Brooklyn Dodgers moved south, as did Sal Maglie of the Giants and Max Lanier of the Cardinals. These infamous "Mexican jumping beans" were joined by Negro League stars such as shortstop Ray Dandridge and pitcher Leon Day. Twenty-six black Americans circled Mexico's baseball diamonds during the 1947 season alone.

In the postwar years, Mexico City residents could enjoy pastimes such as baseball, but they could also admire a host of new civic landmarks. The 1940s and 1950s saw the revitalization of the Paseo de la Reforma, the capital's spacious main boulevard, with the construction of massive banks and hotels along its curbsides and new monuments gracing its traffic *glorietas* (circles). For example, near the entrance to Chapultepec Park, the monument to Los Petroleros honored Lázaro Cárdenas and his nationalization of foreign oil properties. In the park itself, both residents and tourists flocked to the stunning National Museum of Anthropology, home to priceless pre-Columbian treasures in a modernistic structure designed by the noted architect Pedro Ramírez Vázquez that had been dedicated in 1964. Nearer the old center of the city, the sparkling Latin American Tower rose above all else when it opened in 1956, a triumph of engineering—given the problems of construction on moist, sandy subsoil. Its 46 stories swayed without incurring damage the following year during a moderate-sized earthquake. In what many considered a bad omen, however, these tremors toppled the capital's most endearing symbol, The Angel, atop the column honoring the nation's independence heroes.

Perhaps Mexico City's most noteworthy improvement came a decade later, when the city fathers opened the gates on the first line of an innovative subway system. The high-rise businesses taking over the center of the city were not only driving middle-class residents into the suburbs but were creating a logistical and transportation nightmare. Traffic jams ensnared commuting workers, frustrated visitors, and played havoc with plans to develop the old city's tourism potential. The idea of a subway had been kicked around since the days of Alemán, but the unstable lakebed subsoil with its high water content dissuaded all but the most visionary advocates. Mayor Ernesto Uruchurtu, loyal to a middle class that generally resented the growth of their city and the loss of its colonial charm, stubbornly opposed the idea. Into the center of the debate, however, came the powerful engineering and construction firm Ingenieros Civiles Asociados (Associated Civil Engineers, or ICA). A huge conglomerate, vertically integrated and heavily vested in Mexico City real estate, the ICA recognized the windfall profits it could reap through the project. And it had friends in high places. Carlos Abedro Dávila, president of the chamber of commerce, was a member of its board, and Angel and Gilberto Borja de Navarette were among its founders. A Borja de Navarette daughter was married to Gustavo Díaz Ordaz, Mexico's president since 1964.

Not surprisingly, Díaz Ordaz became one of the most outspoken supporters of the Metro, as the subway was called. He apparently helped orchestrate a prolonged bus strike in 1965–66 that greatly aggravated tensions in the capital and dismissed longtime subway opponent Uruchurtu in its wake. To no one's real surprise, the ICA won the contract for the undertaking after its final approval. Cost overruns and the need to import expensive foreign technology complicated the Metro's construction, but the physical accomplishment cannot be denied. By 1968, Mexico City had a state-of-the-art subway, with its sleek trains speeding visitors in and out of downtown during that summer's Olympic Games.

Quality hotels, such as the stylish Camino Real that opened the same year, pampered guests as the capital itself joined Acapulco as a tourist mecca. Car-owning locals, however, still tended to prefer the increasingly tedious drive to work. Middle-class commuters from the south and west sides traversed from suburban dreamlands such as Ciudad Satélite (Satellite City), a bedroom community also constructed by the ICA. Unfortunately, working-class poor from eastside barrios such as Ciudad Nezahualcóyotl did not completely benefit from the subway. Although the subsidized fares were low, the lack of a direct line to the northern industrial parks complicated the commute to those areas. In short, born of elite political power and financial opportunism, a product of foreign technology and a boon for tourism, the Metro was an imperfect blessing to the mass of urban dwellers. Its clean stations and French-built cars communicated the promising ideas of development, but within months of its opening the Metro was overburdened by crowds pushing the system to the breaking point.

The advent of the subway and other changes in Mexico City complicated the lives of those most visibly benefiting from the Mexican economic "miracle"—the middle class. As the 1960s drew to a close, political discontent among these rising urbanites festered. For, while modernization had introduced the families of small businessmen, bureaucrats, and educated professionals to the comforts of consumerism, it had led to no concomitant increase in political power. Despite serving as an integral faction of the Alemán coalition that had dismantled Cardenismo, the middle class had still failed, by the mid–1960s, to move beyond rudimentary participation in a political structure ultimately beholden to the nation's vested elites. As the political scientist Lorenzo Meyer has argued, even though Mexico's bureaucrats have risen from within the political system, the president has ultimately had to forge a relationship with the nation's elites in order to govern successfully (and to enjoy fully the fruits of office upon the expiration of his term). Not surprisingly, in the first major challenge to the Peace of the PRI, the politically frustrated middle sectors began to splinter away from the ruling party as the era of sustained economic growth slowed.

The fissures in the Alemán coalition opened only gradually as the middle class gained confidence in its place in society and as hopes for reform passed it by. In the early 1960s it appeared briefly that the powers that be would understand the need for political modernization. The appointment of the young, reform-minded Carlos Madrazo to the presidency of the PRI in 1964 especially held promise. Madrazo proposed the democratization of the candidate selection process through establishing open primaries. Two years later powerful figures in the party and government saw to his removal; in 1969, he was dead in a plane crash that many Mexicans viewed with suspicion. In the same year Madrazo lost his post, 1966, the PRI ousted the conservative mayor of Mexico City, Ernesto Uruchurtu, in a power struggle with the president, which was yet another blow to the two-decade-long alliance with the middle class. By 1967, especially in the northern states, the discontented began to swing out of the party and into the ranks of the opposition. At the same time, the small and heretofore largely compliant National Action Party (PAN) began to come to life. Winning a mayoral race in Hermosillo and scoring upsets elsewhere—especially in the state of Baja California—it forced the PRI to annul election returns and orchestrate blatant fraud in order to retain its monopoly on power.

It was in Mexico City where by far the largest concentration of middle-class Mexicans resided, that confrontation with the authoritarian government ultimately matured into serious violence. The avenue to the showdown lay in the lives of middle-class youth. Ironically, the sons and daughters of the middle class were among the most favored beneficiaries of development, for in the postwar years they—and especially the sons—attended university in large numbers. In the capital most enrolled in the National Autonomous University, popularly known by its acronym UNAM, located just beyond the comfortable southern suburbs on rocky, volcanic terrain. UNAM's sprawling modern campus, begun under Alemán, blossomed in the 1950s and 1960s as its student body soared from 23,000 in 1949 to nearly 80,000 by 1968. Statistics show that in the mid–1960s roughly 60 percent of these students not only lived in the Federal District but had been born there. Nearly 80 percent of them commuted to classes from home, mostly by bus. Second to UNAM, and also a product of liberal government funding, was the National Polytechnic Institute (IPN), with a 1968 enrollment of 55,000. Neither campus had proven particularly political, and on the few occasions in the postwar era in which major protests had ensued, the causes had almost always been localized issues such as bus fares or the quality of campus facilities. But in 1968, the nature of events would be different.

Opposite the student protagonists of change stood Gustavo Díaz Ordaz. Born of a wealthy family with a long history of service in government (his grandfather had been governor of Oaxaca), Díaz Ordaz obtained the presidency in 1964 after tenure as minister of government under his friend and mentor Adolfo López Mateos. Contrary to the conventional wisdom in the wake of events, he did not enter the highest office with unusual conservative credentials that were out of step with those of his peers. On the campaign trail he made agrarian reform and the alleviation of rural poverty his themes, and the press willingly portrayed him as a centralist (Díaz Ordaz was fond of comparing himself to the sonar device on a submarine, able to know by the voices of critics on the right and the left that his course was correct). In his 1963 nomination speech he vowed to protect civil liberties. Once in office, he largely continued the policies of his predecessor. Four López Mateos cabinet officers served under him, while the novelist Agustín Yáñez oversaw a Ministry of Education that still received a disproportionate share of the federal budget. It is true that Díaz Ordaz curtailed agrarian reform, but this appears to have been more the result of a shortage of distributable land than an ideological objective. As he insinuated he would in his inauguration speech, he preserved formal relations with Fidel Castro's Cuba, to the chagrin of the United States, and his Ministry of Foreign Affairs spearheaded a drive to make Latin America a nuclear-free zone.

Díaz Ordaz, then, was not an unusual president out of step with Mexico's political establishment. Yet his term in office, marred by a series of events destined to vilify him, was atypical. The paranoia of the powerful elites he represented collided with the aspirations of idealistic middle-class teenagers.

The origins of the crisis were amazingly simple. In July 1968, after months of mindless juvenile petty crime driven by gang allegiances and interschool rivalries, Mexico City's crack riot police badly overreacted to a street melee between competing students from two downtown preparatory schools. The Granaderos, as these troops were called, had had a long history of abusive treatment of civilians since their founding under Alemán in 1949. After roughing up multiple teens and bystanders, the Granaderos themselves became a cause of protest, upon which, perhaps to the surprise of everyone, tens of thousands of angry citizens took to the streets. On July 26, 1968, three days after the altercation, the anti-Granadero march meshed together with a smaller, simultaneous demonstration celebrating the Cuban Revolution. A strong police presence helped fuel tensions. Soon the very center of the capital erupted in chaos as tear gas canisters and attempts to disperse both crowds spawned barricades and full-scale riots.

At this juncture the situation was still largely controllable, but again government decisions fell prey to the impulses of panic. Díaz Ordaz and his cohorts were well aware that soon the eyes of the world would rest on Mexico, for the opening of the summer Olympics in the city was merely two months away. Deploying army troops, the regime forcibly seized four preparatory schools occupied by recalcitrant students, arresting and hauling them off to prison. These strong-arm tactics backfired, however. The popular anger filtered into the college ranks and the student bodies of both the IPN and UNAM—usually fierce rivals— united in indignation. Different coordinating committees issued demands to the

Soldiers rounded up protesters in the Zócalo the night after the massacre of students at Tlatelolco. This event totally discredited the national government and official party. The army's massacre of protesters stunned the Mexican people, and the event remains the great tragedy of Mexico's post–World War II history.

government, the most common being to release those arrested and to abolish the Granaderos. Both the students and their many sympathizers soon returned to the streets in massive demonstrations. On August 1 some 100,000 marched into the downtown area. The numbers rose throughout the month, quadrupling by August 27, when the organizers announced that they would post several thousand vigilantes in an around-the-clock occupation of the Zócalo, the spacious plaza in front of the National Palace.

The occupation did not last long. At midnight on the same day the lights went off in the center of the city and the police and army attacked, beating demonstrators and rounding them up by the hundreds. A few days later, Díaz Ordaz took to the airwaves in an address to Congress, stating categorically that Mexico had no political prisoners and that persistent unrest would not be tolerated. The compliant media pressed ahead with government assertions that "Communists" and "foreign infiltrators" stood behind the recent events, a propaganda technique probably designed, at least in part, to prevent the spread of antigovernment unrest to the conservative countryside. To buttress their case, the authorities used the tumultuous season as an opportunity to again persecute the minuscule Mexican Communist Party, raiding its headquarters and demolishing the offices of its press organ. For many of the demonstrators, the government warnings and knowledge of the nighttime roundup at the Zócalo sufficed to temper their passions. Although 250,000 participated in a silent march in early September, the numbers of the protestors began to dwindle.

Luis Echeverría and Chairman Mao. During the last year of his administration in 1976, President Echeverría traveled widely in an effort to enhance his reputation as a leader of the third world. He met with dozens of world leaders as part of an indirect, and ultimately unsuccessful, campaign for election as secretary general of the United Nations.

In this context, Mexico's political elites saw an opportunity to punish those whom they viewed as the prime instigators of the turmoil and provide a lasting message to those who might dare to push the system too far. Accordingly, on October 2, when only a few thousand of the most diehard advocates of change were gathered in protest at historic Tlatelolco Plaza, the authorities quickly surrounded them with security forces and the army. Given the signal by flares from a military helicopter circling overhead, the troops advanced and opened fire. Machine guns rattled and soldiers cut down civilians at their knees. Others pounced on the crowd with small arms and rifle fire as foreign press correspondents recorded the massacre until harassment forced them to retire. For those in the crowd there was little chance of escape. Security personnel trapped, hunted, and arrested thousands. Many of the several hundred bodies of those murdered were trucked off to Camp One, a military installation near Chapultepec Park, where funeral pyres lit up the night sky.

Thirty years after the massacre, in 1998, scholars finally obtained sensitive U.S. government documents under the auspices of the Freedom of Information Act. Authorities in Washington were kept well informed of events in Mexico City during 1968, largely through a network of FBI agents operating out of the U.S. embassy. Intelligence analysts advised their superiors that Mexico's unrest was homegrown—that, despite official pronouncements about "Communist subversion," no genuine leftist threat existed. They reported on the sophisticated countermeasures of the Mexican government, including its creation of the well-funded

Committee of the Authentic Student Body that worked to divide the opposition and undermine the protest movement. Officials high in the U.S. government were told in late summer that a crackdown was imminent, and the still-partial paper trail suggest that they at least tacitly acquiesced.

Beatings and torture at countless police stations and army posts continued for weeks. Some of the most significant student organizers abducted at this, the Tiananmen Square of Mexico, never again resurfaced. Dazed victims of the Tlatelolco slaughter later recalled wandering the rest of the great city in amazement that life continued as though absolutely nothing had happened. Indeed, television and radio broadcasts continued uninterrupted, and the next day the docile print media reported that "exchanged shots" and "foreign agitators" had caused some "disturbances" that, according to the widely read *Excélsior*, had left 20 persons dead. Within a few days a calm Díaz Ordaz opened the summer Olympics as Mexico hosted the world. But the image of the country had been badly stained by the blood that was quietly washed away with fire hoses in of Tlatelolco Plaza.

The closing months of Díaz Ordaz's term in office were overshadowed by the collective national shock over the events at Tlatelolco that were gradually revealed. Though the antigovernment demonstrations had ended, the tensions in the political climate seemed to be palpable. Simultaneous with this pressure came added economic uncertainty as the remarkable postwar era of sustained GDP growth wound down. Inflation had crept into the Mexican economic machine during the mid–1960s and had eroded the strength of the peso. An overvalued peso (set at a ratio of 12.5 to the U.S. dollar since 1954) made exports too expensive, fueling a negative trade balance, which in turn contributed to Mexico's growing but still relatively modest public and private debt. The dual storms of political despair and economic pressure required that the ship of state sail under a steady hand. Unfortunately for Mexicans, Díaz Ordaz chose a man to succeed himself who was inferior to the task.

Luis Echeverría Alvarez ascended to the presidency in 1970 with a background typical of the nation's ruling political elites. A lawyer, college professor, and PRI administrator, he climbed his way to the top, serving in the Ministry of Government under López Mateos and obtaining the ministership itself under Díaz Ordaz. In the public mind, because his office's portfolio included internal security matters, he was associated with the massacre and repression. At a youthful age of 48, Echeverría took to the campaign trail like no other presidential nominee had since Lázaro Cárdenas, perhaps hoping to redefine his image. His inevitable victory came, however, with a sharply lower voter turnout, as 58 percent of eligible voters, recognizing the futility of democratic practices in Mexico, stayed home.

If many Mexicans did not necessarily believe in Luis Echeverría, it can at least be said with a fair degree of certainty that the man believed in himself. Once in office, he exhibited great energy and confidence, and soon became one of the most activist-oriented chief magistrates in the nation's history. He attempted to restore the public's lost faith in the political system and vigorously labored to revive the ailing economy. Politically he was shrewd. He launched a significant political tradition: that of breaking with his predecessor and blaming the nation's woes on him, a tactic destined to be refined, to Echeverría's chagrin, by some of his own successors. Even during the campaign he infuriated Díaz Ordaz by pausing for a moment of reflective silence in honor of the victims at Tlatelolco. He was clearly intent on taking his own course.

In seeking to renew the nation's political integrity, the young president followed up his dramatic campaign stunt with concrete overtures to the ranks of the disillusioned. In particular, he wooed the nation's intelligentsia back into the system's fold. It seemed that academics were particularly ready to be bought. In exchange for new funding and opportunities to advise Echeverría (with suggestions that were, in turn, almost uniformly ignored), they heaped praise on his "enlightened" leadership and joined him on the presidential jet during his many worldwide outings. Novelist Carlos Fuentes, who had been so perturbed by the repression under Díaz Ordaz, became the ambassador to France. David Alfaro Siqueiros, a Communist mural artist jailed during the 1960s for his political beliefs, received the new administration's nationalistic praise. Yet the same patriotic rhetoric that suddenly honored compliant former dissidents was also utilized to silence new critics. When, for example, the U.S. scholar Kenneth Johnson began interviewing survivors of the 1968 repression for an edition of his book *Mexican Democracy*, the government arrested his family and promptly deported him.

Despite the high-profile co-optation of some intellectuals, Echeverría's ploys to restore the stability of the Alemán-era coalition largely failed. The broader middle class, whose political frustration had helped fuel the unrest in Mexico City, was not appeased. On the contrary, it continued to wander out of the arms of the PRI and, into the 1980s and beyond, into the hands of the surging resurgent PAN. Some segments of industrial labor also remained largely estranged from the political establishment. Nor could Echeverría win over the government's student critics. Shortly after taking office he sided with student strikers at the state university in Nuevo León, effectively forcing the PRI governor there to resign.

But this gesture was quickly undone with new developments in Mexico City. Students and sympathizers, determined to test the nature of the new apparent political opening, staged a march on June 10, 1971. Even before the crowd had fully assembled, right-wing thugs appeared, courtesy of free transportation on city buses. Police stood by and watched as these gangsters savaged the unarmed protestors with knives and light weapons, killing two or three dozen. There was little doubt that the massacre had been carried out with orders from the top. Hence, though the university campuses remained mostly quiet during his term, Echeverría had few student admirers on them. When he finally made an appearance at UNAM, hooded students tossed bottles at him until one hit its mark.

A very small minority of disillusioned students and their cohorts turned to guerrilla activity in the early 1970s, hoping to spark an armed uprising against the government. In Mexico City an urban cell known as the Movement of Revolutionary Action arose, while spin-off factions staged some noteworthy kidnappings in other cities, such as the abduction of U.S. consul general Terrance Leonhardy in Guadalajara. In the countryside, a disjointed guerrilla movement formed in the impoverished state of Guerrero, where dense undergrowth and mountainous terrain seemed to offer the prospect of a sustainable struggle. These incipient guerrilla bands proved no match for state-coordinated repression, however. Labeling them Communists and expelling some low-level Soviet diplomats for good measure, the regime went after these homegrown revolutionaries with a vengeance.

With 15 percent of the army effectively sealing off parts of Guerrero in 1971, authorities used torture and extrajudicial killings to snuff out the insurgents there. For an ally in its fight against subversion, the government turned to the extreme right. The most important counterterror organization was Los Tecos, a secretive society of neofascists organized in a layer of cells at the Autonomous University of Guadalajara (UAG). The UAG had remained an obscure and minor institution of higher learning until the early 1960s, when an infusion of funds from U.S. philanthropies, including the Ford and Rockefeller foundations, as well as U.S. Aid for International Development, converted it into a haven for devout middle-class Catholics. Fiercely anti-Semitic, Los Tecos distributed tracts that blamed Jews for world liberalism and set up innumerable fronts, including the Mexican Anti-Communist Federation, which conveniently came to the defense of the status quo. Most ominously, beginning in the early 1970s the federation emerged as a terror group, spawning death squads that helped purge the nation of "dangerous" leftist elements.

Yet even while Echeverría's administration was sanctioning the elimination of the regime's most committed opponents, the president himself was increasingly embracing a "radical" foreign policy. Even more than López Mateos, Echeverría longed to dance on the international stage. He frequently traveled the world, by the end of his term clearly trying to capture headlines as well as the general secretariat of the United Nations. In 1972 he ventured to Chile, where he consulted with socialist president Salvador Allende. The following year he headed to Asia for state visits in China and the Soviet Union. He also frequented nonaligned countries during his term, providing the press with countless photo opportunities as he hobnobbed with the likes of Indira Gandhi and Pierre Trudeau. He publicly articulated a policy of nonalignment and often criticized the United States. While some of his many travels involved the promotion of new trading partnerships, as much as anything Echeverría seemed intent on promoting himself.

But to Mexicans at home, what their president did or said abroad mattered very little. The overwhelming concern of both rich and poor was the state of the economy, which after 1971 was showing signs of strain. The inflationary trends evident since the mid–1960s began to spiral upward, which, in conjunction with the lopsided ratio of 12.5 weak pesos to the U.S. dollar, was fueling incipient capital flight. A carefully crafted financial package of new investment incentives and cautious adjustments to spending and the money supply might have smoothed out the bumpy economic ride, but Echeverría was not a cautious or particularly careful man. He tackled economic issues with the same relentless energy that he displayed in political and foreign policy matters, though again largely without an ideological focus or positive results.

Instead of allowing the peso to float against the dollar and thereby find its real value, Echeverría stubbornly refused to devalue the currency and instead allowed exports to plummet. Then, unwilling to stand by and watch as Mexicans lost their jobs, he had the government invariably step in and nationalize whole industries and myriad failing businesses. In 1971, nationalization "saved" the copper industry; then in 1972 it rescued tobacco, the national telephone monopoly Teléfonos de México, and much of the banking sector. As these trends continued, the public debt soared. Unwilling to raise revenue by significantly taxing powerful private interests, the administration opted for price hikes in gas and utilities, which in turn spawned inflation. By trying to counter inflation, the government set price controls on many basic commodities. When an exasperated finance minister, Hugo Margáin, advised Echeverría in the spring of 1973 about the impracticality of continuing his unorthodox economic course, he was promptly fired and replaced by a compliant José López Portillo, who continued the damaging practice of covering deficit spending by printing money and taking out more foreign bank loans.

Echeverría himself became focused on the plight of those in the countryside. Frustrated by the decline in basic grain production and at the prospect of continued massive imports, he authorized dramatic increases in spending on agriculture. Few easy solutions presented themselves. The administration recognized many of the shortfalls of the Alemán-era model of agricultural development, with its emphasis on modernization and commercial farming that had bypassed the small farmer and the landless peasant. The disparity between different regions of the country was also obvious; the languishing central and southern states needed help. But by the 1970s, the most convenient solution—continued land reform—was no longer viable. Very little even quasi-arable land was left to give out. Many of the heavily populated rural regions of Mexico had crossed the line to a predominance of *minifundias* (small plots of land unable to sustain their holders), and what little land Echeverría's government did find to distribute was generally of such low quality that it could barely serve as pasture. Hence, the administration turned to an ambitious program of farm credits, price supports, market management, and technical assistance. An enormous infusion of funds turned CONASUPO into one of the nation's largest bureaucracies, while a new web of lesser agencies also set out to revitalize the peasant agrarian sector.

Unfortunately, adding bureaucrats and money provided no lasting solutions. Initiatives, many of them hastily conceived, were often hampered by mismanagement. Petty local and interagency rivalries frequently disrupted their implementation. And the expense involved in raising this expanded bureaucracy deepened the national fiscal crisis that hurt everyone as inflation accelerated in 1973 and the federal deficit soared. The infusion of funds into new and preexisting agencies alike provided new opportunities for graft. Under Echeverría corruption reached a scale not seen in Mexico since the days of Alemán as archaic accounting methods failed to monitor cash flows adequately. The president himself left office a very wealthy man (some allege that his net worth equaled $1 billion), and his penchant for personal enrichment seemed to inspire many around him.

Endlessly searching for new economic panaceas, the Echeverría government supported rapid border development. The northern borderlands had begun to undergo transformation in the mid–1960s with the launching of the Border Industrialization Program under Díaz Ordaz. The centerpiece of this initiative was the maquiladora industry named for plants that assembled goods along the border. Raw materials emerged from U.S. factories, were assembled by low-wage workers on the Mexican side, then returned duty-free to the United States as finished products. Building on this promising start, Echeverría's administration aggressively pushed it forward, cutting bureaucratic red tape and much of the legal paperwork that had slowed the establishment of new plants. By 1974, more than 70,000 Mexicans, mostly young women, labored in 450 maquiladoras. Conditions in the plants were primitive, with dismal safety and environmental standards and abusive male supervisors availing themselves of opportunities for sexual exploitation. Wages were so low that the maquiladoras did little to elevate alleviate poverty. When Echeverría attempted to rectify this problem by doubling the minimum wage, this had the unintended effect of cooling the industry's growth until a peso devaluation in turn reversed the slowdown in 1976.

An unforeseen consequence of the renewed emphasis on maquiladoras and the borderlands was a new migration northward in the early 1970s. The growth of the border cities was astounding. Ciudad Juárez, opposite El Paso, watched its population surge to 700,000 by 1975. Most of the newcomers were poor. Occupying acres of dusty barrios surrounding the city on hillsides to the south and west, they hoped for jobs in the assembly plants, sought green cards for work in the United States, or, more often, contemplated illegal border crossings—U.S. Immigration and Naturalization Service apprehensions rose from 277,000 in 1970 to 680,000 in 1975.

While new initiatives transformed the face of the northern borderlands, Echeverría's administration managed a new megaproject at Mexico's southeastern extremity. In 1967, a group of investors and developers had circled above the primitive jungles along the Yucatán's coastline in search of an idyllic setting for a beach resort. It was in not until the early 1970s, however, that the tourist mecca of Cancún began to take shape. The crystal-white sands and deep blue waters of an L-shaped peninsula formed a perfect setting for what would become Mexico's largest tourist draw by the 1990s. In the early 1970s, job-seeking Mayas poured into the area, and by 1974, the first hotels opened their doors to the mostly North American tourists who arrived via an airport eight miles south. In spite of building codes and beaches that remained in the public domain, Cancún was soon on its way to becoming a pocket of that singularly un-Mexican tourist culture that features gift shops full of sombreros and other "native" crafts that are just as frequently assembled in China.

Despite tourism in the Yucatán and assembly plants in the border cities, Echeverría's myriad attempts to restore the Mexican "miracle" all failed. The possibilities of state-driven capitalism had been pressed to their full advantage by the time he entered office, and as early as 1973 his presidency was largely in tatters. The glitter and gloss of the previous three decades of economic growth were gone. The political stability spawned by Alemán's masterful use of co-optation and repression had also vanished, having eluded Echeverría's grasping hands. The economic and political accomplishments of postwar Mexico had always rested on a bed of contradictions—capital-intensive industrialization in a nation of unemployed masses, the green revolution and commercial farming in a land of peasants, political rigidity in the face of a rising middle class—and by the early 1970s these contradictions could no longer be contained. Recognizing the futility of attempting to find answers in the past, Mexicans looked warily to the future. Perhaps new economic panaceas and fresh political promises could resolve the contradictions shadowing the nation's quest for modernity.

19

The Time of the Technocrats and Deconstruction of the Revolution

RODERIC AI CAMP

Most observers of Mexican political history since World War II have noted the expansion of the state, both in broad political terms and in the degree to which expansion influenced economic growth. During the heyday of Mexican state, the 1950s and 1960s, Mexico's political stability and continuity were complemented by a so-called economic miracle based on the macroeconomic philosophy of import substitution industries, during which time growth reached rates of 6 percent annually. To the degree that Mexicans attributed this growth to a strong state, its legitimacy benefited substantially.

The post–World War II expansion of the Mexican state was not a purely economic phenomenon, nor can it be attributed primarily to Mexico's industrialization in that era. An explanation of the state's role in regard to expansion encompasses many variables that are historical, cultural, psychological, and political. From a historical perspective it is essential to recall the influential heritage of the indigenous cultures as well as that of the Spanish colonialists. Their institutions, political and religious, were authoritarian in construction and application, concentrating decision-making powers in the hands of few individuals. Thus the practice of allocating power to a central state authority has a long tradition in Mexico in its pre-Columbian, colonial, and independent periods. Concentrating the state's power in its executive authority limited the degree to which political decisions were shared, thus developing a foundation for a strong executive branch and an even stronger presidency and weak competing institutions.

Mexico also offers a long tradition in which important sectors of the population were allies or partners of the state. The symbiotic relationship between church and state in the colonial period, and the weak development then and later of a strong private sector, established conditions favoring cultural dependency on the state. Therefore, as in other Latin American and emerging nations,

The American Smelting and Refining Factory, Monterrey, in 1958. The growth of industry and tourism in Mexico after World War II resulted in a wave of economic expansion known as the Mexican miracle. Outside of the national capital, northern entrepreneurs made Monterrey a major beneficiary of the boom, and they emerged as a powerful economic and political bloc known as the Monterrey Group.

most cultural leaders found employment in state agencies or state-supported institutions. This does not mean that intellectuals never criticized the state, but it tempered the criticisms of some groups and altered the content and application of their political criticisms.

Ironically, the symbolic decline of the Mexican state occurred long before its economic influence waned. The state began its political decline in 1968, whereas it continued to increase its control over the economy, indirect and direct, through 1982, when President José López Portillo (1976–82) nationalized all the domestic banks, expanding indirect state control over the economy to a figure estimated at nearly 80 percent, a level never achieved before or since.

The events of October 2, 1968, when the Mexican army violently suppressed student demonstrators protesting government intervention in student affairs in Tlatelolco Plaza in Mexico City, marks a psychological departure in which Mexicans—particularly urban, well-educated citizens, intellectuals, and even government officials themselves—began to question the efficacy and morality of an authoritarian state that required violence against middle-class students to maintain its position of authority and legitimacy to govern. This departure produced a political crisis of major magnitude. Although the government appeared to survive it intact, cracks in civil society and levels of dissent emerged in renewed, vociferous forms. The president, Gustavo Díaz Ordaz (1964–70), represented the last of his generation to govern and proved to be the last of a certain breed of politician, a man having roots in the provinces, with strong ties to the governing party and experience outside the state bureaucracy.

When Díaz Ordaz designated Luis Echeverría Alvarez to be his successor as the Party of the Institutional Revolution (PRI) candidate for president in 1969, he believed Echeverría, a product of years in the government secretariat (the state's primary intelligence and political agency), to be a clone of his own approach and philosophy. Instead, as Judith Hellman suggests in her interpretation of his administration, Echeverría, who was sensitive to the underlying currents set in motion by the events of 1968, responded differently from his predecessors.

Echeverría believed that a culturally and economically expanded state could solve some of Mexico's most significant social inequalities. He accordingly made overtures to intellectuals and members of the generation of students affected by government actions in 1968, attempting to coopt potential critics by giving them positions of influence in his administration. He cultivated the friendship of Bishop Sergio Méndez Arceo of Cuernavaca, Mexico's foremost representative of Catholicism's "church of the poor," and established closer, if informal, ties to the Vatican. On the economic front, he encouraged his secretary of government properties, Horacio Flores de la Peña, former dean of the economics school at the National University, to expand state ownership of private enterprises and businesses.

Politically, Echeverría pursued a mixture of contradictory policies that somewhat enhanced the give-and-take in Mexican politics. On the one hand, he reallocated political influence among groups associated with the regime such as organized labor, favoring the interests of one union over another. On the other, he ordered the army to pursue Lucio Cabañas, the commander of rural guerrillas who had kidnapped the Guerrero state governor, and successfully eliminated his movement in 1974. It was under Echeverría that Mexico witnessed for the first time the growth of urban terrorists, as well as the rise of the organized political left.

Echeverría's attempts to cope with the influential actors on the national stage, including business, labor, and intellectuals, failed to alter significantly the balance of power among them or between them and the state. The president left his administration in disarray when he decided at the last minute to nationalize agricultural property in northwestern Mexico, leaving him the last president to do so in Mexican history. Naturally, by doing so he alienated many businessmen and their supporting organizations and left his successor with the difficult task of wooing support for the state from the business community.

That successor, José López Portillo, a boyhood friend of President Echeverría's who grew up with him in a suburb of Mexico City, can almost be described as an

José López Portillo, president from 1976 to 1982, told the nation that his government would use recently discovered oil fields to fund a campaign of industrial expansion, social welfare, and high-yield agriculture. In an effort to fulfill these goals, his administration borrowed huge sums at high interest, only to learn the oil was generally of low grade. The program left Mexico with the world's largest foreign debt.

intellectual-cum-politician, a Johnny-come-lately to public life. Initially, the president saw himself as someone who could achieve some degree of compromise between the conflicting interests in Mexican society. Although he faced a difficult political situation, with state and private sector interests in disarray, López Portillo entered office in an era in which crude oil prices reached their apex. He and his closest advisors viewed this state-controlled resource as a means by which Mexico could develop its economy and solve many of its social problems.

President López Portillo's administration can be characterized as the golden age of state expansionism. Using the sales of its proven oil reserves as financial collateral, the Mexican government began to borrow from foreign banks, particularly U.S. and European institutions, at the frightfully high interest rates typical of that period. As money poured into the economy in infrastructure expenditures and other government-financed projects, Mexico's annual economic growth rate averaged 6.5 percent.

López Portillo temporarily reversed the declining image of the presidency during the years 1977–79 and, in tandem, that of the state. But when oil prices dropped, toward the end of his administration, Mexico found itself with an overvalued peso, an extraordinarily high level of debt, soaring interest rates, and a declining economy. The president, seeing most of his positive achievements and his prestige crumbling, responded by nationalizing the private domestic banking sector, thus alienating in far stronger terms the private sector, and sowing distrust between businessmen and the government.

López Portillo's actions produced a stronger state in an economic sense, because its control over the nation's financial institutions and their loan portfolios meant control over most of the economy. But the prestige of the state lost out in many other respects. The Mexican people responded by heaping blame on the state, believing it to be responsible, directly and indirectly, for their declining economic fortunes.

When López Portillo designated Miguel de la Madrid, his former university student and programing and budgeting secretary as the presidential candidate of the Party of the Institutional Revolution (PRI) in 1981, he significantly altered Mexico's political leadership and its government's macroeconomic policies. As a presidential candidate and then as president, de la Madrid inherited a political situation that had deteriorated substantially beyond the successions of 1970 and 1976. López Portillo had become the most reviled president in recent memory. He was accused of huge amounts of fraud and was the butt of many vicious jokes. De la Madrid therefore decided to pursue a strategy of setting Mexican expectations rather low so that any disparity in their actual fulfillment would not generate even more frustration.

De la Madrid, the first Mexican president with a graduate degree and the first to have studied in the United States (at Harvard), did not believe that a state-led economic strategy would solve Mexico's problems. He represented a younger generation from that of Echeverría and López Portillo, both of whom had witnessed President Lázaro Cárdenas's nationalization of the petroleum industry, the symbolic high point of state power and sovereignty, in 1938 as young students. De la Madrid, however, who was born in 1934, grew up in an era when Mexico stepped more vigorously into an international arena marked by world war and followed by the intensity of the cold war during the 1950s.

In 1982, president de la Madrid entered office facing a minus 0.6 growth rate, which increased dramatically during his first year in office to minus 4.2 percent. Mexico was facing its worst recession since the Great Depression of the 1930s. The presidency, however, continued to retain most of its influence, and de la Madrid successfully achieved a social pact to control prices and begin the long, difficult path of reducing inflation and attracting domestic and foreign capital. Politically, de la Madrid initially opened up the system to strong competition from the opposition parties. His early promise of fair elections soon led to opposition party successes in local elections. As Wayne Cornelius and his colleagues have argued, the government, afraid of those electoral victories, retreated to the familiarity of its more traditional political strategies.

De la Madrid was successful in mending relations with the private sector and made it clear that it would only be a matter of time before the banks would be privatized. On the other hand, he pursued an active strategy of selling back to the private sector many of the enterprises that had become state owned under his two predecessors. Despite his efforts to remove some of the obstacles to an improved private sector-state relationship, groups within the private sector increased their public criticism of the government and of de la Madrid's administration. Furthermore, elements in the private sector decided to pursue a strategy of political partisanship, supporting opposition parties and candidates financially in hopes of achieving their policy preferences.

As the administration struggled to cope with the political fallout from its economic austerity strategy, Mexico City experienced a natural disaster that would itself produce consequences of considerable political magnitude when a major earthquake struck on September 19, 1985. From the public's point of view the earthquake revealed the president as distant and overly cautious. Instead of allowing the army to follow the agreed-upon national emergency plan, the president and his head of the Federal District relied on civilian relief workers, who proved insufficient to the task. In an extraordinary display of community self-help and collaboration, the residents themselves led the efforts to rescue victims, and the Catholic Church was instrumental in organizing relief aid.

The displaced residents, along with those who lost their employment, finding themselves unsatisfied with the government's efforts to cope with their problems, formed grassroots organizations, leading to a flowering of civic action and other types of interest groups. Popular figures such as the masked Super Barrio, a neighborhood hero dressed as a wrestler, a representative of good to the poor, took on huge symbolic importance in the effort to end government corruption and inefficiency. These groups anticipated those that would later become part of a larger grassroots movement of human rights and civic action groups in the late 1980s and 1990s.

In effect, Miguel de la Madrid became a transitional president in the same way that Manuel Avila Camacho (1940–46) provided a bridge between the populist Lázaro Cárdenas (1934–40) and the pro-business Miguel Alemán (1946–52). De la Madrid lacked the resources to engineer major economic changes. The end of his administration witnessed an intense struggle for power among those harboring presidential ambitions. Much of their struggle can be attributed to pure personal ambition, but the ideological agenda became equally important, as was the case in the 1940 succession.

From a policy perspective, two issues were at stake in the 1987–88 presidential succession: a choice between the more traditional state-led deficit spending strategy, or economic liberalism, and all that it entails, and political liberalism, which in Mexico referred to an increased democratization in the electoral process as well as within the governing PRI; or a continuation of the political status quo. Although he was never a leading contender for the nomination, given the fact that Mexico's incumbent president had until then chosen his successor from his own cabinet, Cuauhtémoc Cárdenas, son of the former president, and Porfirio Muñoz Ledo, a former party president and cabinet member, led a reformist movement within Mexico's leadership known as the Corriente Democrático (the Democratic Current). As Peter Smith has illustrated in his work, they attempted to reform the party and influence government policies as insiders but were ultimately forced to leave the party.

In the same way that 1968 can be considered a benchmark year in the evolution of Mexico's political system, 1988 can be seen as a newer point of demarcation in what has happened since. In the latter year de la Madrid selected as his candidate his secretary of programing and budgeting, Carlos Salinas de Gortari, replicating his own bureaucratic origins as a presidential candidate. The selection of Salinas, who in this cabinet-level post was most identified with the government's unpopular (in average citizens' eyes) economic strategy, and who had little support among party politicians, led to a further division within the party. Cárdenas decided to oppose his former party and colleagues as an independent presidential candidate. Initially, he ran on the ticket of one small opposition party, the Authentic Party of the Mexican Revolution (PARM), but before election day three additional parties—the Cardenista Front for National Reconstruction Party (PFCRN), the Popular Socialist Party (PPS), and the Mexican Socialist Party (PMS)—chose him as their candidate.

Cuauhtémoc Cárdenas surprised most observers with an extraordinary vote-getting performance, winning 38 percent to Salinas's 50 percent. And legislative candidates sympathetic to the Cárdenas ticket won numerous legislative seats, especially in urban centers, but also in states that had been recognized for their opposition to the government since the 1940s. Some observers believe that only widespread fraud prevented Cárdenas from achieving victory in the election.

It would be fair to say that the election of Carlos Salinas to the Mexican presidency in 1988 marked the low point of that office as well as of the declining legitimacy of the state. It is remarkable, therefore, that in only five years Salinas was able to reverse this pattern, achieving a level of popularity for himself and the presidency unmatched by recent administrations while strengthening the state's power. He accomplished this initially through some dramatic political decisions, cementing his initial popularity in a National Solidarity Program (Pronasol), a government-funded grassroots development agency. As numerous studies have concluded, this agency did help to alleviate the level of poverty in certain situations, but it also proved an effective tool in obtaining electoral and popular support. In a number of bold moves, the president privatized a range of companies owned and operated by the state, including the banks nationalized by his predecessor José López Portillo, significantly altered the constitutional relationship between church and state in 1992, and effectively ended the government land distribution program and the structure of *ejido* (village-owned land) agriculture.

On the surface, the changes under President Salinas, which in part undermined the long-standing corporatist framework on which the Mexican political model had been constructed since the 1930s, appeared to have reduced state influence. While it is true that direct state control over the economy declined, its influence—as a more streamlined political vehicle—remained, and indeed can be said to have been strengthened. The Salinas administration conceded some important electoral reforms, strengthening opposition parties and increasing

President Carlos Salinas de Gortarí delivers his fifth review of the nation in 1993. Salinas introduced innovative grassroots reform programs through his "Solidarity" campaign, but his reputation suffered because of rampant governmental and family corruption and extortion. Today he lives in self-imposed exile from Mexico.

their ability to defeat the PRI at the polls, but Salinas simultaneously concentrated more power in the hands of the presidency, using it to solve political disputes, including those between his own and opposition parties.

The revival of the state and the strengthening of the presidency continued on a steady path under Salinas until January 1, 1994, when a movement of indigenous guerrillas calling themselves the Zapatista Army for National Liberation (EZLN) made their dramatic appearance in and around San Cristóbal de la Casas, in the southern state of Chiapas. Initially, the president responded with military repression, but the domestic and international media, which immediately began reporting human rights abuses and excessive use of violence, turned national and international public opinion against the government, forcing a reversal in government policy and cabinet resignations among the responsible agencies.

In the midst of the 1994 presidential campaign the PRI candidate, Luis Donaldo Colosio, was assassinated on May 23, forcing the president to choose a replacement in a transparent display of presidential intervention. The party, already divided over other issues, further splintered when Salinas's choice became public: Colosio's campaign manager and former cabinet secretary Ernesto Zedillo Ponce de León.

Ironically, Zedillo was perceived in the same light as Salinas when he became the candidate in 1988: weak, lackluster, and a technocrat. Unfazed by these perceptions, Zedillo began to solidify a number of themes during his campaign that served as a foundation to his presidency. One of them was the decentralization of the presidency and, in conjunction, a declining role for the state. Politically, Zedillo's most important contribution to reducing the state's role was to separate the government from the party, specifically to decrease presidential influence over the party. The president sought to accomplish this difficult separation by increasing the party's autonomy in the candidate selection process. More important, and in a move producing longer-term structural consequences, in 1995, Zedillo instituted reforms strengthening the judicial and legislative branches.

Zedillo's first reform gave the culture of law, a favorite presidential theme, a more influential role and potentially favors individual versus state power. His second reform strengthened the only national institution in which the opposition parties had achieved considerable success, the Chamber of Deputies. Zedillo's purposeful strategy of weakening the presidency also contributed to the perception of a declining state, however, given the association between the presidency and the state in the eyes of the average Mexican citizen.

Few political themes in Mexico since the early 1970s have attracted more attention and provoked more discussion than the increasing role of technocrats and their influence on government policy and leadership trends. The rise of the technocratic politician is not, however—media interpretations to the contrary—a recent phenomenon. Its antecedents can be found as far back as the 1940s, when some of the same characteristics of the present-day technocrats began to appear among politicians. The quality that most easily distinguishes the rise of a technocratic leadership is the increased importance it attaches to higher education. Mexican politicians as early as the administration of Miguel Alemán (1946–52) stressed college education, especially in the field of law. Alemán also marked the shift from military-dominated to civilian-dominated leadership in Mexico.

Alemán's colleagues were significant to the technocratic trend because they provided an influential generation of politician-teachers who sought out disciples to replace them in their classes at the National Autonomous University (UNAM), the locus of the vast majority of successful Mexican politicians since the 1960s. This generation was important for three reasons. First, they valued higher education and teaching, qualities they passed on to succeeding generations. Second, none of them were formally trained in the field of economics, but they perceived its importance, and contributed to the development of an economics school located initially within the law program and subsequently as an independent school at UNAM. And third, although most of them were educated in Mexico, several key individuals shared experiences studying abroad, particularly in economics, experimenting with the economic philosophies of Europe and the United States. Notable among them was Ramón Beteta, a University of Texas-educated "whiz kid" and Alemán's secretary of the treasury, who produced a generation of influential disciples, including his own nephew, an early mentor of President Miguel de la Madrid, and Hugo B. Margaín, another treasury secretary.

The early Mexican technocrats can be found primarily in economic-oriented agencies, particularly those for industry and commerce, where Carlos Salinas's own father, Raúl Salinas Lozano, himself a disciple of Beteta with a Harvard M.A.

in economics, introduced numerous disciples in the 1960s. Among the key agencies in this regard were the treasury secretariat, where Hugo Margaín recruited his colleagues in the 1970s, and the Bank of Mexico, the core agency in pushing economists to the forefront of Mexican politics.

Luis Echeverría represented the last of the pre-technocratic presidents, yet he himself displayed two characteristics that quickly became mainstream qualities of the younger generations that arose to replace him. Echeverría became the first Mexican president in recent times to have been born and raised in the Federal District. He also was the first to become president without previously having held elective office. In the Mexican context, a technocratic leadership is symbolic of the decline of regionalism and the dominance of the capital city, as well as the decline of electoral experiences (such as holding elective posts) and the rise of bureaucratic careers. On the other hand, Echeverría fell back on his long experience inside the government party, having held numerous administrative positions and worked on many political campaigns.

José López Portillo, Echeverría's designated successor and boyhood friend, provided a bridge to the new technocratic leadership characterizing his successor's administration. López Portillo became the first president to have a postgraduate degree (Doctor of Jurisprudence), the first chief executive to have earned a college degree abroad (a law degree in Chile), and, most important, the first president in postrevolutionary times to come from the treasury secretariat. The source of the country's presidential leadership, given the one-party control of the Mexican political model, has been an essential variable in the structure of the nation's political recruitment patterns.

López Portillo's presidency marks a shift in importance away from the political agencies, notably government (the source of presidents Gustavo Díaz Ordaz and Echeverría), to economic agencies. When Miguel de la Madrid became the next candidate, he cemented the importance of these agencies, because his entire political career was in financially oriented positions in the Bank of Mexico, Petróleos Mexicanos (Pemex), the treasury, and programing and budgeting. Equally important, he became the first president with a foreign graduate degree, an M.A. in public administration from Harvard.

The technocratic leaders that emerged under Miguel de la Madrid, who were born in the late 1940s and early 1950s, were characterized by their big-city origins (typically Mexico City), their lack of electoral experience, their inexperience with the party, their education in nontraditional fields (notably economics), their graduation increasingly from private universities rather than the more traditional public institutions, their graduate-level educations, their study abroad (not in Europe or Latin America but in the United States, particularly in prominent institutions such as Harvard, Yale, MIT, and Stanford), and their professional careers within the national bureaucracy—but among a narrow range of agencies, typically treasury, the Bank of Mexico, and programming and budgeting. Carlos Salinas and Ernesto Zedillo personally represented these experiences, as did dozens of their important collaborators. Mexicans who have provided the leadership of the national government since 1982 from the departmental level on up also share many of these features, deemphasizing regionalism, traditional educational disciplines, and party and electoral experiences.

On a philosophical level, the technocratic political leadership in Mexico also represented significant influential policy trends. Most decidedly, this group, to a large degree based on their intellectual experiences abroad, became convinced that the import substitution strategy (subsidizing domestic industries to reduce imports of foreign manufactured products) was no longer viable for Mexico. They also felt that a neoliberal approach stressing greater foreign capital investment, declining tariffs, increased trade, competitive industries, and economic blocs would be the long-term solution to Mexico's persistent economic problems. They further believed that a smaller role for the state, conceptualized as an owner-operator of businesses, was essential. This did not mean, however, that they advocated in theory or practice a less influential state, but rather one whose economic control differed from that of its predecessors.

Politically, the technocratic politicians were also divided, even among the leaders who governed Mexico. Although the popular perception is that the true technocrat favors political liberalization, including electoral reform and a competitive party system, many technocrats associated with Salinas followed the president's posture of preferring a decisive economic strategy over a realistic political opening. These differences in approach, which are more fully developed in the discussion that follows, produced a schism within the leadership.

The most dramatic example reflecting the differences between the technocratic political generation and its nontechnocratic peers emerged during internal debates at the PRI assembly in the fall of 1996. There delegates attending the party convention imposed a recommendation on the party's leadership setting forth provisions that only an individual who had previously held elective office could become the party's presidential candidate and that the party's presidential candidate would be required to have been an active party member and to have served in a party office post prior to his designation. These requirements were a slap in the face to the current trend in technocratic leadership and the qualities these leaders represented under Salinas and Zedillo. This dramatic change is reinforced by the fact that as of mid–1999, no technocratic candidates were competing for the PRI presidential nomination, and the leading candidate, favored by Zedillo himself, was his secretary of government, marking a return to the importance of politically oriented cabinet governments.

At the end of the century, the PRI is playing an increasingly significant role in the competitive political environment that has been generated by electoral reforms since the 1970s. For many decades the party, while successfully engineering its candidates' election, including to the office of the presidency, performed an insignificant role as a source of government leadership. The recommendations just described altered the balance of power between the government bureaucracy and the party, enhancing the influence of the party and guaranteeing that it would expand its role in the recruitment process and thus in policy making. The requirement to hold elective office not only increased the party's importance, which was necessary for successful competitive campaigning, but more importantly redirected attention back to the legislative branch of government. The rise of the bureaucracy as a source of Mexican political leadership corresponds with the increasing importance of the state and the growth of the presidency as the source of policy and personnel decision making since the 1940s.

The origins of political liberalism extend back to the late 19th century, to the disciples of the orthodox liberals and Benito Juárez, who objected to Porfirio Díaz's authoritarianism and centralization of power, and to its postrevolutionary revival. Formally, the political model that evolved in the 1930s, when the government party dominated the electoral scene despite the founding of the National Action Party (PAN) in 1939, did not change significantly until the 1960s. At that time the government altered the legislative elections to create minority party seats, allocated proportionally on the basis of the votes these parties earned in national races. Nevertheless, the opposition parties never occupied more than 20 percent of these seats from 1964, when the law first went into effect, until 1977.

In 1977, under President López Portillo, his then secretary of government, Jesús Reyes Heroles, who has been recognized for his intellectual contributions to 20th–century liberalism, introduced a major electoral reform known as the Federal Law of Political Organizations and Electoral Processes (LOPPE), the first of many subsequent reforms fostered through the Zedillo administration. Under the new law, in addition to the 300 seats in the lower chamber elected on the basis of single-district competition, an additional 100 seats were guaranteed to the opposition, to be divided up on the basis of the national vote totals. Thus, in effect the law guaranteed opposition parties a minimum of 25 percent of all seats, in addition to any remaining seats they could win in district-by-district competition. This so-called plurinominal deputy system (providing seats based on national rather than district vote totals) provided the opposition with a core group of seats, not only giving it a voice in the lower chamber but providing an incentive for politically active Mexicans to run as candidates on opposition party tickets. Nevertheless, given the overwhelming weight of history favoring the PRI, including its consistently favorable media coverage and overwhelming financial resources, the opposition parties achieved little growth after the 1977 law's implementation.

In 1982, when Miguel de la Madrid became president, he appeared to indicate a changing attitude toward political liberalization, specifically electoral competition. Initially, state and local elections held during the first two years of his administration were largely free of fraud. Unfortunately, however, once the opposition demonstrated that they could defeat the PRI under such conditions, many of the traditional practices perpetrated by the government party returned.

Seen from a brief historical perspective, the most important contribution the de la Madrid administration made to political liberalization, though unintentionally so, was to reactivate the politically dormant Catholic Church. The highpoint of electoral fraud committed during his administration occurred in the northern state of Chihuahua in 1986. The level and nature of the fraud were so blatant on this occasion that the state's bishops felt it necessary to make a public appeal, which they did in a full-page ad in the leading Mexico City newspaper, *Excélsior*, to the government to reject the election's outcome and hold a new one. When this appeal did not produce a response from the government, the bishops took the extraordinary step of threatening to shut down all masses in Chihuahua. Their threat, had it been undertaken, would have forced the church and state into a confrontation, if on a smaller scale, similar to that which provoked the Cristero rebellion, the result of severe application of constitutional restrictions on the church, in 1926. In the end, the Vatican delegate intervened, persuading the bishops to withdraw their threats.

Although the northern bishops failed to force the government to overturn the Chihuahuan election results, 1986 marks a significant point at which bishops throughout Mexico then, and in succeeding years, repeatedly advocated the importance of civic responsibility and fair elections in pastoral letters circulated among the faithful in their dioceses. Adolfo Suárez Rivera of Monterrey, who became the leader of the Mexican episcopate, authored one of the most influential of these letters, "Pastoral Instruction on the Political Dimensions of Faith." Interviews with the Mexican episcopate demonstrated that, regardless of their theological position on the church's socially responsible position, they took an unequivocally strong collective position on representing the laity in their complaints directed toward electoral fraud, as well as fraud-related human rights abuses. Consequently, the church became a significant ally of Mexican citizens and politicians pushing vigorously for a rapid electoral opening.

Although President de la Madrid did not fulfill his pledge to clean up elections, he did, as had his predecessor, further advance the electoral process, through overseeing passage of the 1986 electoral code. This code expanded the plurinominal basis for legislative elections by increasing the total number of congressional seats from 400 to 500, for a total of 200 plurinominal seats to be allocated by a complex mathematical formula. Anticipating a decline in support for the PRI, the law allowed the majority party—in this case the PRI—to also win for the first time some of the plurinominal seats.

Specifically, the law was designed to guarantee that the party winning the largest number of single-member district seats (out of a possible 300) would receive a sufficient number of plurinominal seats to give them at least a simple majority in the chamber. While it was true that the law reduced the importance of the single-member district seats (which the PRI typically won) and increased the percentage of total seats controlled by the opposition, to 30 percent or more, as electoral expert Silvia Gómez Tagle has argued, the government essentially allocated the opposition a greater, but limited, role rather than altering the conditions that would have allowed the minority parties a chance to compete fairly against the PRI.

The 1988 presidential election, the first held under the auspices of the new electoral code, unexpectedly provided the most important impetus toward future electoral reforms. In that election Cuauhtémoc Cárdenas not only succeeded in reducing the PRI's presidential margin to its smallest-ever vote—51 percent—but, more important, the PRI captured only 50.4 percent of the congressional vote. This translated into 233 majority and 27 plurinominal seats. For the first time, the PRI had to rely on plurinominal seats to achieve a majority in the Chamber of Deputies: 260 out of 500 seats.

The success of the opposition parties in 1988 appeared to foreshadow an end to the PRI's dominance and the continuation of the one-party system. It also suggested, for the first time, that the legislative branch might become a more influential voice in the decision-making process. Unfortunately, the opposition parties were not able to capitalize on their initial victories. The PRI successfully reincorporated many voters who had left their fold to vote for the opposition in 1988, winning 61.4 percent of the vote in 1991, thus once again achieving its majority party status. PAN retained its strength from 1988, making the Democratic Revolutionary Party (PRD), an amalgam of parties that had originally supported Cárdenas in 1988, the primary loser. Its support declined from nearly a third of the electorate in 1988 to only 8 percent in 1991.

Once he had achieved a substantial level of popularity in the first year of his administration, President Salinas decided to pursue the same cautious strategy of slow political reform that had characterized his predecessors. When questioned about his commitment to political reform, Salinas made it clear that his ideological commitment and preferences favored economic liberalization. As a witness to what had occurred in the Soviet Union and Eastern Europe, Salinas viewed rapid political change as a path to political instability and an obstacle to achieving permanent economic reforms. Consequently, he considered political reforms secondary to his macroeconomic policy strategy.

The slow pace of political reforms characterizing the Salinas administration has been blamed on political forces within the party that were resistant to change. It is crucial to understand that two political forces existed within the government and party leadership on the issue of political liberalization. As noted above, however, it is too simplistic to suggest that a group of nontechnocratic, traditional politicians, popularly considered dinosaurs by the Mexican press, were the sole source of resistance to such political changes and that a younger group of government technocrats, surrounding the president, were the enthusiastic advocates of democratization, especially in terms of electoral reforms.

Salinas personally was not committed to encouraging reform. An assessment of his political decisions reveals a strongly authoritarian presidency, rather than actions designed to generate a firm basis for political reform. Mexico's government leadership, technocratic and nontechnocratic alike, was similarly divided in its support of political reforms. Reformists could be found equally among both groups, in the federal bureaucracy as well as the party.

The 1988 election, and the opposition parties' initial success in it, expanded the number of Mexican political actors. The most important of these new figures was the PRD, which provided an organizational catalyst for formerly uninfluential leftist parties, as well as for dissident populists no longer comfortable with the PRI. Given its diverse ideological origins, this party was not inclined to compromise with the PRI on policy matters or even on electoral reforms, since it considered the PRI's pace to be painfully slow. In numerous elections at the state and local levels from 1989 to 1993, the PRD offered contentious competition that led, in some cases, to violent confrontations with PRI partisans, as in Michoacán and Guerrero. The degree to which the PRD was threatening the PRI's interests can be measured by the number of party activists who were victims of physical abuse and violence at the hands of government officials and police.

The PAN, which had long functioned as the only serious alternative to the PRI but which had never been able to attract large numbers of voters to its ideological banner—having been perceived as a pro-business, pro-Catholic, pro-middle-class party—was reinvigorated as a consequence of the increasingly competitive electoral environment. Having had considerable strength in the north, the west, and the Bajío region of west-central Mexico, it capitalized effectively on the changing electoral environment. In 1989, for the first time since the PRI came to control Mexico's electoral fortunes, the government recognized an electoral defeat at the regional level, the gubernatorial race in the important border state of Baja California. PAN was able to duplicate its success elsewhere, winning the state of Chihuahua in 1992 and having one of its members appointed governor of Guanajuato in 1991 after the national government nullified a disputed PRI victory. But despite these significant victories on the local and state levels, by 1993, the PRI seemed well on its way to continuing its control over most national offices and state races.

Major political events conspired to alter the balance of power in 1994, significantly reconfiguring the political landscape and bringing an end to the immense popularity enjoyed personally by President Salinas. On January 1, 1994, the Zapatista Army for National Liberation attacked army posts and seized several communities in Chiapas. In its own published statements in the December 1993 issue of *El despertador mexicano* it described its movement as indigenous in origin and interested in righting wrongs committed by local officials and property owners against Indian peasants. Among its many goals it sought autonomy from state and national governments, social spending for education and health programs, and redistribution of agricultural lands. The date of their attack, the same as that on which the North American Free Trade Agreement (NAFTA) went into effect, was, as Tom Barry suggested in *Zapata's Revenge*, a symbolic but also real protest against the potential effects of this agreement on the fortunes of small farmers in Mexico.

The guerrilla movement's appearance in southern Mexico drew attention away from the ongoing presidential campaign, although the confrontation between the guerrillas and the army quickly shifted from one of violence to a Catholic Church-mediated negotiation between government and guerrilla leaders.

As negotiations continued between the two antagonists, an equally dramatic turn of events drew public attention back to the presidential campaign. Luis

Donaldo Colosio, the PRI's candidate, was assassinated in Tijuana, Baja California, on March 23, 1994, in the midst of campaigning. The death of a presidential candidate, unheard of in Mexican politics for more than half a century, produced serious political repercussions. Other than the immediate problem of replacing the party's candidate, Colosio's death, combined with the Zapatista uprising and the earlier May 1993 assassination of Cardinal Juan Jesús Posadas Ocampo in Guadalajara, suggested to many Mexicans and the outside world that Mexico was facing a period of genuine political instability. Public opinion polls in early 1994 confirmed this assessment, revealing that 69 percent of the urban residents interviewed believed Mexico's political situation to be grave or very grave.

The selection of Ernesto Zedillo to replace Colosio boosted the opposition's fortunes. Zedillo's selection deeply exacerbated the differences among the factions within the PRI in a way that was reminiscent of the insider battles in the 1928 and 1988 successions. Among these groups was a strong party faction identified with Fernando Ortiz Arana, the party's president, and with Manuel Camacho, the former head of the Federal District Department and a failed presidential contender who bridged the divide between the political technocrats and the traditional party types. Furthermore, politicians, the media, and the public viewed Zedillo as a stiff, relatively unknown, politically unskilled campaigner.

The PRD had redesignated its cofounder and original standard-bearer, Cuauhtémoc Cárdenas, to be its candidate. PAN chose a charismatic speaker and legislator named Diego Fernández de Cevallos. In the initial months of the campaign the PRI candidate continued to maintain a lead, followed by Cárdenas and

Fernández de Cevallos. But the fortunes of each party changed dramatically after May 12, 1994, when Mexico held its first-ever presidential debate. Capitalizing on his engaging personality and an aggressive, critical strategy, Fernández de Cevallos overwhelmed Zedillo's more statesmanlike posture and completely surprised Cárdenas by attacking his record as a former governor of his home state. Watched by an estimated 30 million Mexicans, Fernández de Cevallos suddenly captured the imaginations of the voters and swept into first place in the polls, slightly ahead of Zedillo. Cárdenas suffered a precipitous fall to third place, from which he never fully recovered.

In the final analysis, the instability provoked by the assassinations and the guerrillas contributed to the victory of the PRI and Ernesto Zedillo at the polls. Fernández de Cevallos never capitalized on his popularity, inexplicably tempering the intensity of his campaign in the remaining weeks. In the final months before the elections, the electoral code was altered still another time. Among the most important electoral changes in 1994 eliminated the winning party's right to a guaranteed simple majority in the chamber of deputies, limited any party from winning more than 315 of 500 seats, and established the Federal Electoral Institute (IFE) to supervise the election itself, giving the balance of power among its 11 members to 6 independent citizens.

Zedillo was able to capture the same percentage of votes on August 21, 1994, as had his predecessor: approximately 50 percent. The most significant change between 1988 and 1994 was that PAN replaced the PRD as Mexico's second-most-influential party, winning 26 percent of the vote. The PRD came in in third place, obtaining only 17 percent of the vote, a huge decline from its second-place finish in 1988. The 1994 elections also were among the fairest, attracting the largest turnout ever among registered voters, 78 percent.

Electoral reforms, and the performance of the two opposition parties from 1989 to 1994, contributed positively to increased political liberalization. The advance of these two parties, and the structural alterations in electoral practices, were achieved largely as a result of adverse political events and opposition demands, not because President Salinas willingly initiated these changes. In 1994, Mexican voters basically decided in favor of gradual change, and of having those changes occur in the hands of their traditional leadership, the PRI. Contrary to some predictions, the huge ranks of new voters who came to the polls voted largely for the government party, not the opposition.

Political liberalism received a significant boost following the presidential elections in 1994. This boost came from two sources. First, unlike Salinas, president-elect Zedillo offered a differing philosophy of governance and political development. While he believed in pursuing the broad outlines of a macroeconomic strategy similar to Salinas's, albeit with a much stronger intended emphasis on equitable distribution of income, politically Zedillo proposed willingly to implement changes that no predecessor thus far had ever publicly promised. He offered, surprisingly, to reduce presidential authority and specifically (in terms of political liberalization) to separate the state from the party or, more precisely, the

National Action Party (PAN) members, supporters, and sympathizers, numbering in the thousands, demonstrated in 1986 in front of Chihuahua's capital to protest state elections in which the official Party of the Institutionalized Revolution (PRI) claimed victory. Church leaders threatened to suspend Masses in support of the protesters. This action helped bring about the first small steps toward reform of the political system, especially at the local and state levels of government.

presidency from the party, authorizing the party to develop its own candidate-selection process at all levels.

Confronted within days of taking office by a financial crisis of greater proportions than those faced by de la Madrid or Salinas, Zedillo nevertheless stuck doggedly to decentralizing presidential power. Widely denigrated by the media and public as a weak president, he is in fact partly responsible himself for this perception, having divested himself of powers traditionally ascribed to or expected of a Mexican president.

After many months of negotiations among the three leading parties, they finally agreed in 1996 upon a new electoral package designed to further level the political playing field and encourage greater pluralization. Among the actual reforms having important consequences for political liberalization is the changed electoral status of the Federal District, which for the first time, in 1997, would elect its own governor instead of having a cabinet member appointed to this post. A second significant reform consisted of all members of the IFE becoming independent of any political party and separating themselves from the secretariat of government.

This Federal District election became particularly significant to the fortunes of the various opposition parties and to the process of increasing pluralization because PAN has had grassroots strength in the Federal District for decades, the PRD's elections have been cleaner and better supervised in the capital than almost anywhere else in Mexico, and, most important, nearly a fifth of Mexico's population resides in the Federal District.

President Ernesto Zedillo, First Lady Nilda Patricia Velasco de Zedillo, and Secretary of Defense Enrique Cervantes review military troops on parade in Mexico City during the Independence Day celebration on September 16, 1999.

The president approved these and other reforms and sent them to the legislative branch in the fall of 1996. Instead of accepting the presidentially approved package, the lower chamber, controlled by a PRI majority, offered them in a watered-down version. Instead of vetoing the revised version, Zedillo approved it. He has since been the object of severe criticism in the press for not insisting on stronger reforms, but the longer-term implications of his allowing the legislative branch to alter significant legislation, essentially unheard of in Mexico, has major structural consequences for executive-legislative decision making and pluralization. Because the opposition parties' greatest chance for success nationally in electoral politics has been in the legislative branch, strengthening this branch's decision-making influence, even under PRI control, is supportive of longer-term political liberalization.

It is equally important to remember that an increase in competitive elections, which did occur under Salinas and Zedillo, is not in and of itself sufficient for democratization, as Jonathan Fox and others argue, and that little is known about the linkages between electoral competition and other features of pluralism.

After the presidential election, history tended to repeat itself, in the sense that political events rather than legislation served as the catalyst for the changing electoral landscape. The political scene continued to be precarious in the remainder of 1994. José Francisco Ruiz Massieu, the PRI secretary-general (in effect the party's vice president) and former brother-in-law of President Salinas, was assassinated in September 1994, shortly before Salinas left office. Subsequently, the president's own brother, Raúl Salinas, was arrested on suspicion of involvement in the slaying, as well as for allegedly laundering millions in drug money, and was eventually convicted on the first charge. And even worse for the incoming president, just days after his taking office on December 1, 1994, Zedillo's administration faced a serious run on the peso that led to an extraordinary level of capital flight, both domestic and foreign, and thus to a tremendous financial crisis, requiring the joint intervention of the United States and the World Bank to stabilize the Mexican currency.

The PRI, poised to continue its strong showing in the presidential elections by beating back a PAN victory in the state of Jalisco and retaking ground in Chihuahua in 1995, instead found itself facing major defeats in gubernatorial races in Guanajuato, Jalisco, and, for an unprecedented second time, in Baja California. By mid–1995 the two major opposition parties governed nearly a third of Mexico's population on the state and local levels. As the government continued its harsh economic austerity program and unemployment and inflation took their toll, both PAN and the PRD continued their electoral victories in 1996, especially in the influential state of Mexico.

The electoral pattern begun in 1995 continued through 1997, when for the first time in Mexico's political history, the opposition parties won control of the Chamber of Deputies (with 60 percent of the votes) in the midyear elections. Moreover, Cuauhtémoc Cárdenas, the PRD's two-time presidential candidate, swept to an overwhelming victory as the elected head of the Federal District, the seat of Mexico's capital city. By 1999, the opposition controlled 10 governorships (including the Federal District), and on the state and local level controlled elective offices representing more than 60 percent of the population.

As Mexicans prepared for the 2000 presidential race, the influences of pluralization continued. The PRI announced a national primary process to select its presidential contender, open to registered voters from any party, and PAN, which until 1999 had used a democratic nomination process among party delegates, opened up their voting to all party members.

The United States has been viewed as a significant actor in the political path Mexico has taken. It has seemed ironic to many observers that a country bordering the United States should still be in the process of democratization while other nations in the region can boast more rapid liberalization and electoral reform. Three U.S. actors have involved themselves significantly, directly or indirectly, in Mexico's political evolution: the Congress, the media, and the financial community.

The significance of these three actors was most evident after 1988. When President Salinas and the United States and Canada began negotiating in earnest toward a free trade agreement, certain Republican members of Congress, led by Senator Jesse Helms, began to raise serious questions about forming a partnership with a government they perceived as authoritarian, compromised, and corrupt. Recognizing the obstacles that these congressmen's supporters could place in the path of approving NAFTA, especially once it became a U.S. presidential campaign issue in 1992, Salinas attempted to respond to their criticisms of electoral fraud and human rights abuses.

The U.S. media exerted an even more profound influence. For example, the army's violent repression of the Zapatista rebels, resulting in numerous human rights abuses, produced an immediate response in the media and on the Internet, documented by Denise Dresser, a professor at ITAM (Instituto Tecnológico Autónomo de Mexico), contributing significantly to the Salinas administration's policy reversal. Finally, the decision to rely heavily on foreign—particularly U.S.—investors for capital made both the Salinas and Zedillo administrations susceptible to the whims of this community. Zedillo's firing of his first treasury secretary, Jaime Serra Puche, on December 29, just days after the crisis began and after less than a month in office, has been attributed to Wall Street's loss of confidence in Serra Puche.

When President Echeverría took office on December 1, 1970, Mexico's economy was dominated by the agricultural sector, which then accounted for 39 percent of the economically active population and was more than twice the size of the next-largest sector, manufacturing. By 1996, midway through the Zedillo administration, the economically active part of the population had nearly tripled since 1970. But more strikingly, agricultural employment increased only 64 percent over those two and a half decades, whereas manufacturing grew 263 percent, services 473 percent, and transportation 355 percent. Agriculture's proportion of the economically active population working in it declined nearly by half, to only 23 percent, exceeded in size by services and closely followed by the commerce sector.

Not only did Mexico's economy change dramatically from the 1970s through the 1990s, but the influence of foreign investment, accompanying a growing economy and the Mexican leadership's evolving philosophy toward international economic linkages, also increased, in equally dramatic increments. Under President Echeverría, the most nationalistic and state oriented of presidents since 1970, foreign investment totaled only $1.6 billion. Under his successor, López Portillo, foreign investment more than doubled, to $5.5 billion. But if we examine the years of de la Madrid, Salinas, and Zedillo combined, during which time Mexican economic neoliberalism flowered under their macroeconomic strategies, foreign investment totaled an estimated $91 billion by 1997, for a sixteenfold increase in less than 15 years.

It was Miguel de la Madrid who introduced the most important characteristics of the neoliberal economic strategy: international economic cooperation (illustrated by Mexico's decision to join the General Agreement on Trade and Tariffs in 1986); heavy reliance on foreign investment; acceptance of International Monetary Fund guidelines for inflation, prices, debt repayment, and growth; and privatization, or the resale of businesses owned and operated by the state, many of which were acquired under his two immediate predecessors. By the end of 1988, when de la Madrid left office, he had divested the government of 706 companies,

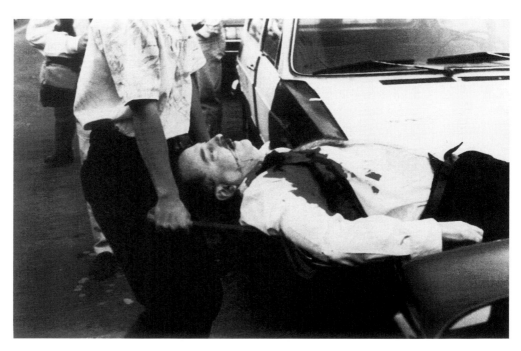

which accounted for 25 percent of the value of nonpetroleum manufacturing and 30 percent of the nation's total employment.

By selecting Salinas as his successor, de la Madrid ensured a continuation of economic neoliberalism because it was Salinas, with his programming and his budgeting secretary, who had been the most outspoken advocate of this policy strategy in the economic cabinet. Salinas had thus positioned himself as an increasingly influential figure after the resignation of de la Madrid's initial, popular treasury secretary, Jesús Silva Herzog, in July 1986.

As president, Salinas committed Mexico even more fully to the tenets of economic neoliberalism. He highlighted de la Madrid's privatization program by selling back the banks that López Portillo had nationalized in 1982. Furthermore, he began selling some of the major companies that had been symbolic of government monopolies for decades, including Teléfonos de México, Mexico's sole telephone company.

Salinas further cemented Mexico's neoliberal strategy by cultivating President George Bush's personal friendship and seeking a long-term economic relationship with the United States in the form of the North American Free Trade Agreement, designed to create an economic bloc among Canada, the United States, and Mexico. This agreement, concretely and symbolically, stood as the centerpiece of Salinas's macroeconomic strategy, a philosophy he successfully sold to the Mexican public despite vociferous opposition from the media and the academic community, as well as from the leadership of the DRP.

During his administration Salinas could point to economic statistics as evidence of the successful implementation of his neoliberal strategy. He claimed a decline in public-sector expenditures of 25 percent in 6 years, a gross domestic product growth rate of 2.9 percent, and a 67 percent decrease in state-owned companies. But Salinas's policies did not benefit the Mexican people equally. If the distribution of family income is examined from 1984 to 1992, from the administrations of de la Madrid through Salinas, the data reveal a persistent decline of the percentage of the national GDP among lower-income families.

In fact, if the population of the period were to be divided into ten equal income groups from lowest to highest, nine out of ten groups would show declining real incomes during those eight years of neoliberal economic policies. The worst declines occurred among the middle- and lower-middle-income groups. The only group that benefited from economic liberalism was Mexico's wealthiest families, whose income as a group increased 16 percent. These data tend to support the charges by critics that many individual capitalists were the direct beneficiaries of the reprivatization program and that government policies beneficial to private-sector interests mostly favored the rich.

If the quality of life is measured in much broader terms, using a "well-being index" constructed by the National Bank of Mexico of 19 variables ranging from health to food consumption to income, the track record of neoliberalism from 1980 to 1995 averages less than 1 percent improvement, compared to a 2 to 3 percent rate of yearly improvement in the 1960s and early 1970s.

According to plans he outlined shortly before taking office, President Zedillo intended to improve both economic growth and distribution. But the economic policies pursued by Salinas and his advisors in the final months of his administration, allowing the peso to become highly overvalued, led to a financial crisis of epic proportions that generated a run on the peso in mid-December 1994, forcing the Zedillo administration to devalue the peso against the dollar. President Bill Clinton, using his executive powers, created an emergency rescue package of up to $50 billion to stabilize Mexico's currency. Investors on Wall Street and elsewhere, as well as Mexican capitalists, withdrew billions of dollars, sending Mexico's economy into a tailspin.

By the end of 1995, after less than a year in office, Ernesto Zedillo and his economic advisors were faced with negative economic growth, a rise in inflation to 50 percent yearly (levels that had not occurred since the de la Madrid era), a loss of hundreds of thousands of jobs, a huge increase in interest rates on bank loans, a weakened banking system with a dangerously high level of bad loans, and numerous bankruptcies. As de la Madrid had done during the years of severe recession in the 1980s, Zedillo pursued a tough, IMF-supported austerity strategy. By the end of 1998, Zedillo had successfully reduced inflation, restored stability to the peso, strengthened the banks, and—after two years of negative economic growth—by mid–1996 even achieved forecasted growth rates of 3 to 4 percent.

Moreover, Zedillo continued other hallmarks of the neoliberal economic strategy. Emulating several South American countries, the government established a private pension system designed to strengthen the retirement program and

Children march in an Immunization Day Parade in Mexico City. Improved public health can be claimed as one of the major achievements of the government the Mexican Revolution created. Improved drinking water, better general health care, and widespread immunization against common diseases have resulted in reduced childhood mortality, improved life expectancy, and enhanced quality of life for Mexicans. The use of the Salk vaccine against polio nearly eliminated that disease in Mexico.

increase domestic savings. The administration also opened the natural gas sector to private investment. More important, Zedillo pushed for reclassification of the petrochemical sector to take it out of the traditional state-operated, sacrosanct petroleum industry. Although the petrochemical industry was to be privatized, the PRI party leadership rejected the proposed change. In the fall of 1996, Jesús Reyes Heroles Jr., the energy secretary, in fact backed off from full privatization.

At this writing President Zedillo appears to have turned the economy around from its deepest recession since the 1930s. But he accomplished this task at an enormous political price, both in terms of his own popular image—initially the lowest of any president since public opinion polls were instituted—and serious divisions within his own party (especially between the party leadership and the political-technocratic leadership in charge of economic policy). The opposition parties' success at the polls has been due in large part to the effects of the economic crisis and the government austerity program on employment, income, and future opportunities.

Furthermore, the rise of subsequent guerrilla groups since the Chiapan rebels, most importantly the Popular Revolutionary Army (ERP), which made itself known in the summer of 1996, suggests the degree to which frustration is widespread and the legitimacy of traditional political channels is inadequate. It is unclear whether Zedillo has sufficient political space and the necessary skills to achieve sustained economic growth through the remainder of his administration, to implement government policies aimed at enhancing a more equitable distribution of income, and to alter citizens' outlooks sufficiently to translate them into political votes for the 2000 presidential race.

As Mexico begins the 21st century, it is faced with a difficult legacy. Mexicans are confronted with a changing political and economic landscape. In numerous public opinion polls, Mexicans have suggested throughout the 1990s that they wanted to achieve two major goals: economic growth and higher incomes, as well as increased political democratization. Do Mexicans want democracy more than they want economic stability and an improvement in their standard of living? The answer is no. When given a choice, they resoundingly are concerned with typical bread-and-butter issues such as employment, household income, inflation, credit, interest rates, and growth. In 1995–96, more than four-fifths of all Mexicans considered economic issues to be the major problem facing the country. Fewer than one in ten mentioned any form of political concerns.

The linkages between economic and political liberalism have been a major intellectual issue of this era, but it is not clear that the average Mexican views these as connected in any way. The reason is that, given the history of the PRI's political monopoly and the abuses of power within successive governments, Mexicans attach little credibility to government generally, to the PRI specifically, and for that matter to political parties of all stripes. While Mexicans in increasing numbers have turned to PAN and the PRD as alternatives, they do not necessarily believe in their integrity or capacity to govern well.

In the 1990s, many Mexicans questioned Zedillo's credibility and ability to govern. They further viewed his government as contaminated by higher levels of influence among drug traffickers than were its predecessors. They were extremely pessimistic about their economic situation throughout his term and were not optimistic about their personal security, which they associated directly with the dramatic increases in urban crime. Indeed, many Mexicans consider corruption and crime to be serious obstacles to achieving a democracy (36 percent) in 1999.

Mexicans in general believe that their government has failed them miserably on two fronts. Economically, half of all Mexicans rate the government's performance as terrible. Politically, they are much less critical of weak or watered-down electoral reforms or the day-to-day management of government affairs but highly critical of the government's attempts to fight drug corruption. This view is highlighted by the number of unresolved political assassinations, some of which are allegedly connected to drug money, and the high-profile case of Raúl Salinas, the president's brother, who had unexplained assets totalling more than $100 million. The U.S. government estimated that 30 percent of the cocaine entering the United States in 1989 passed through Mexico. Just six years later, in 1995, Mexico accounted for 80 percent of those drugs and had become the major transit country for South American shipments.

The way in which Mexicans hope to solve their economic and political problems is unclear. It appears that their strategies are changing as the legitimacy of the political and economic model itself is in flux. On the economic side, most

Mexicans view the influence of the United States as excessive. Although they attribute the lion's share of blame for their economic crisis since 1995 to what they see as President Salinas's inaction, they also place some blame on U.S. investors. The party's rejection of reclassifying the petrochemical industry as acceptable for privatization suggests a stronger resistance toward Mexico's international economic linkages, especially on symbolic issues affecting their sense of nationalism.

Mexicans also reject, in large part, the inequitable distribution of income that the government's neoliberal economic policies up to 1996 reinforced rather than reduced. When Mexicans were questioned in the Latin Barometer poll in May 1995, 78 percent considered the distribution of wealth unjust. This largely explains why most Mexicans express considerable sympathy for the stated goals and programs of the Zapatistas, if not for their means.

What is most striking about Mexicans' perceptions—and disturbing, given their desire for increased pluralization—is their view of preferable political models. In a 1999 poll, only 50 percent of Mexicans believed democracy to be the preferable form of government. Ironically, the Mexicans with the lowest incomes, who are theoretically those with the most to gain from an altered political model, provided the least support for this alternative. Although, not surprisingly, Mexicans supportive of PAN gave stronger support to the democratic model than those favoring the PRI, by 62 to 57 percent respectively, those favoring the PRD responded with less enthusiasm than citizens supporting the PRI.

A deeper exploration of Mexican attitudes toward democracy suggests that the vast majority are very dissatisfied with the system's performance. Remarkably, in 1999 only 41 percent of Mexicans claimed any satisfaction with it. Why is this the case? Other questions in the 1995 poll reveal that the respondents did not believe democracy had been effective in solving Mexico's problems. Despite having participated in what has been described as Mexico's cleanest election, in 1994, for which they turned out in unprecedented numbers, an overwhelming 78 percent of Mexicans believed elections generally to be fraudulent. In 1999, in spite of dramatic opposition victories, 61 percent still consider elections to be fraudulent. Moreover, they have deep-seated doubts about the efficacy of the voting process: Only half of all citizens believe that their vote affects future policy.

These responses raise two serious questions about Mexico's future. First, what process do Mexicans actually favor? Their attitudes are in flux in part because of the perceived illegitimacy of the present model and because their experience with a more democratic version of that model is not necessarily an experience with a real political democracy. Thus, Mexicans have become more open to other means of change, the most significant and unpredictable of which is violence. Although most Mexicans remain opposed to political violence, its increasing use by various guerrilla groups contributes to some degree to its legitimacy, given the citizenry's sympathies for these groups' demands. For the first time in recent decades, approximately a third of Mexicans now admit that they support the use of violence to achieve political and economic goals under certain circumstances.

Elderly beggars in Mexico City's Zócalo. The U.S. government agreed to bail out the Mexican economy but insisted on rigorous austerity measures, including high interest rates and prices, to help the peso recover. The program increased the already high rates of poverty and incited a crime wave across the city that has only slowly abated.

The second issue these responses raise is, what institutions would Mexicans rely on to achieve their demands? When Mexicans are asked to rank their country's institutions according to the level of respect and trust they would assign them, the Catholic Church overwhelmingly scores above all others, while large companies, the armed forces, entrepreneurial organizations, the press, and television are lumped together midway up the ladder. The strictly political institutions themselves, including political parties and Congress, that were formed expressly to carry out these tasks are ranked at the bottom of the list. However, most Mexicans now believe that the executive branch should share power with Congress, probably the result of opposition party control of the legislative branch since 1997.

Today Mexicans face a difficult dilemma. They are not at all clear about a democratic path as their choice of a political solution. Indeed, surprisingly, only

31 percent expressed satisfaction with democracy, suggesting the tenuousness of the democratic model among citizens. The majority of Mexicans expect equality and economic progress from democracy, not liberty or fair elections. It is likely that more Mexicans will not learn to associate democracy with economic well-being in the new millennium unless the administration that follows Zedillo is able to demonstrate a connection between government policy, government performance, and increased income. If that occurs, and at the same time the legislative branch increases its ability to initiate legislation and the opposition parties also increase their representation—possibly even to the extent of winning the executive branch—then a stonger possibility exists for a redefinition of democracy's ills and strengths in the Mexican mind.

20

Mass Media and Popular Culture in the Postrevolutionary Era

ANNE RUBENSTEIN

By 1940, Mexico's postrevolutionary government had settled into the form it was to retain for the next 55 years. Yet Mexico's biggest transformation was just beginning. Most Mexicans in 1940 lived in the countryside or in small towns, could not read, and thought of themselves less as citizens of the nation than members of their small communities. Fifty years later, the majority of Mexicans were city dwellers, literate, more prosperous than their parents, and well aware of a national identity. Industrialization, urbanization, migration, the self-conscious creation of a single nation from many disparate regions, and the growth of consumer culture: These processes were as revolutionary as the Revolution itself.

Daily life for most Mexicans changed radically in the decades after World War II. Mass media and popular culture portrayed this sometimes painful, sometimes exhilarating transition. More important, they helped to create it. The media, together with older forms of expression and ritual, provided a means for people to understand their new circumstances. Sometimes ordinary people could use mass media and popular culture to build alliances (both within the various sectors of Mexican society and between Mexico and the world) and to legitimize its rule. And at times, mass media seemed to act almost autonomously, pulling Mexicans willy-nilly into an international culture with new technologies, new styles, and new ways to behave. Culture became the most important arena for political struggle in the postrevolutionary era.

Novelist Carlos Fuentes described the transformation of postrevolutionary politics and everyday experience in his 1962 novel *La muerte de Artemio Cruz* (The Death of Artemio Cruz). The story's anti-hero, Artemio Cruz, is a revolutionary soldier who becomes a corrupt, wealthy businessman and politician. In the middle of the 1950s, as he lies on his deathbed, Cruz muses on the daily life of less ambitious men: "Waiting forever on every corner in town for a bus . . . working in some shop, in an office, typing . . . saving up to buy a car on the installment plan, lighting candles to the Virgin . . . sighing for a refrigerator . . . sitting at a neighborhood movie on Saturdays, eating peanuts . . . having to shout there's no country like Mexico to feel yourselves alive; having to feel proud of serapes and Cantiflas and mariachi music and *mole poblano* just to feel alive.*

This is Mexico in the midst of its modernization: A new national identity was forged from new consumer goods (or the advertisements for them), recent history (or the official version of it), Catholicism, commodified folklore, and folkloric mass media. Fuentes makes Artemio Cruz speak contemptuously of those who partook of such new forms of pleasure and enjoyed such modest economic security. The novel protests the betrayal of the Revolution for the sake of peace, material well-being, and the hope of economic development.

The North American ethnographer Oscar Lewis described the material culture and leisure activities of poor urban Mexicans in his extraordinarily influential study, *The Children of Sánchez*, and his conclusions were similar to Fuentes's. Examining the least fortunate of Mexico's denizens at the same moment when Futentes dissected the elite and middle classes, Lewis found poor people sneaking into movie theaters and onto buses, dancing to music from the single radio that many families had to share, passing used comic books from hand to hand. The famous anthropologist expressed disgust with the materialistic, apolitical life of the urban working class; he felt that Mexican modernity had created a "culture of poverty" that was shortsighted, hedonistic, and ultimately self-destructive.

Most of the indigenous population outside the booming cities of this time remained far outside of this postrevolutionary prosperity. Yet economic and political change also transformed indigenous cultures. As anthropologists Guillermo Bonfil Batalla and Nestor García Canclini pointed out, the Mexican government and the international tourism industry made entrepreneurial enterprises out of traditional crafts and rituals. Long-standing localized methods of expression shaped themselves to the idiosyncratic demands of a global market for quaint or campy souveniers, and for objects that somehow represented "Mexicanness" or "nativeness." At the same time, mass media—especially radio, television, and comic books—spread into the most remote corners of the nation, while many indigenous people migrated to urban areas in Mexico or the United States. These movements broadened the range of goods, ideas, and images available to indigenous people. Cultural borrowing, appropriation, and misreading characterized ethnic relations in this era. Anthropologists and tourists alike indignantly reported such confusing phenomena as Mayan women offering bottles of Coke to the Virgin and weaving images of helicopters into their textiles, while mestizos in Mexico City boasted of the "authenticity" of the dances they had invented for their "native" performance troupes. A perceived lack of tradition or authenticity, then, has been another long-standing critique of Mexican mass culture in the postrevolutionary era.

---

* (Fuentes, *The Death of Artemio Cruz*, trans. Alfred McAdam, New York, 1991 [1962] pp. 79–80).

Examining movies, popular music, tabloid papers, religious movements, novels, poetry, comic books, fashions in food and clothing, radio and television, burlesque theater, folklore, sports, fine arts, dances, artisan goods, and other forms of media and culture from this era, we can see the strains that modernization placed on Mexican society and the demands that it made on individuals. Mexicans used all these cultural forms (as well as arguments about culture) to fight for power or just for survival, to define themselves and others, to resist categorization. And yet something else is also visible in all these cultural forms: They remind us by their very profusion that the postrevolutionary era has—on the whole—been a time of national confidence, of growing prosperity and broader opportunities for many. That era ended with the collapse of the Mexican Miracle. But the closing of this period only makes the optimistic, self-confident, and joyful tone of its cultural productions more apparent.

Much of the material and legal infrastructure necessary for the cultural transformation of Mexican culture was in place by World War II. The family enterprises that would grow into Mexico's enormous media empires already existed. A set of basic genre conventions, metaphors, organizing themes, and stories had developed that would set patterns for a great deal of mass media narrative and spectacle over the next five decades. Some entirely new forms of mass culture appeared after 1940—above all, television. But the cultural transformation of Mexico after that date was, for the most part, the culmination of long-term developments.

Of all mass media, print has the deepest roots in Mexico's past. Mechanical reproduction of imagery came early to Mexico: Daguerreotypes were first exhibited there in 1840, only a few years after they had debuted in France and Germany. Lithography began enlivening newspaper and magazine pages shortly thereafter. By the 1890s, although literacy rates were very low, an illustrated press had found a market for itself. The Revolution was predicted, interpreted, and to a certain extent created by a multitude of daily and weekly papers of all political persuasions, mostly aimed at the upper and middle classes. A few papers were written for urban workers, too, including a few dozen cheap weekly magazines of political satire. Many of these staunchly opposed the Porfirian regime, such as the famous *El Hijo de Ahuizote*, but they generally did not argue for the violent overthrow of the government; their preferred weapons were parody, caricature, and bad puns. This "penny press" spread the use of skull and skeleton imagery—*calaveras*—to mock the living, as in the famous woodcuts of José Guadalupe Posada.

The combination of words and pictures to tell stories did not always have a political purpose. Compulsory public education and adult literacy campaigns had, after 1930, produced a significant number of Mexicans who could read at least a little. Unreliable census figures indicated that in 1930, about 33 percent of the population over the age of six was at least minimally literate; by 1950, that statistic had reached 56 percent. Economic expansion meant that many more Mexicans could afford to buy papers and magazines. Using new, cheap printing and distribution technologies, publishers competed to sell all sorts of periodicals to this new audience. By 1940, every good-sized town in Mexico had its newsstand, while Mexican cities could boast of a newsstand on practically every corner. Women's magazines, true-crime tabloids, illustrated collections of song lyrics, movie magazines, sports papers and—above all—comic books all shared space with the daily papers.

The first effect of this boom in potential readership was the growth of daily papers. Between 1920 and 1940, newspapers grew enormously in size and many new ones appeared. Although not all were entirely aligned with the government, none offered full, accurate, or critical reporting on politics. In 1940, the government invented a subtle but powerful tool to ensure that the print media's political quiescence would continue. A new state-owned business, Productora e Importadora de Papel, S.A. (PIPSA, or Paper Producer and Importer, Inc.), supplied publishers with newsprint paper at cut-rate prices. This mattered enormously because paper was the single biggest expense in manufacturing a periodical. Mexico produced little paper and relied on imports from Canada, the United States, and (to a lesser extent) the Scandinavian countries; like many international basic commodities, paper's cost fluctuated in response to the strength of the peso and the vagaries of transport. World War II made paper especially scarce and expensive. The government, by providing a steady supply at a steady (and low) price, made continued operation possible for otherwise marginal periodicals. But the government could always threaten to withdraw the right to buy paper from PIPSA; almost always, such a threat convinced a paper to rein in its reporters. Between 1940 and 1976, the newspapers that were independent of PIPSA never lasted more than a year.

As an unintended consequence of improved printing technology and government support for the newspaper business, Mexico developed an advertising industry. The years after 1930 saw a rapid expansion of the amount of commercial graphics, an expanding number of goods being advertised, and a shift in the rhetoric advertisers used. Advertising before 1930 had been relatively dry and informative. The chants of vendors, some dating back to colonial times, remained an important means of selling goods. The department stores and cigarette manufacturers of the late Porfirian era, appealing to a relatively elite audience through their displays of goods and their packaging, sold fewer goods to fewer people but did create a reservoir of marketing techniques and images. All that changed with the advent of easy, cheap mechanical reproduction of imagery, and the arrival of mass-produced consumer goods. Advertising now underlined the general benefits of goods—appliances, automobiles, new forms of entertainment—rather than touting the specific virtues of a particular product. Very few Mexicans could afford to buy these goods at the moment when advertising for them first appeared. Advertisers intended to appeal to that small number of people, but in doing so they also created a consumer culture, persuading a far larger group that they wanted such things as refrigerators but could settle for buying chilled bottled sodas. And by the 1940s, the rhetorical and graphic techniques that had been invented to sell large appliances were being applied to the increasingly competitive marketplace for small-scale industrial products such as cigarettes, processed foods, and clothing.

Advertising in postrevolutionary Mexico fell into three broad and overlapping categories, all responding in some way to the intellectual currents that flowed out of the Revolution. First, some ads associated products with revolutionary nationalism. For example, in the 1930s, a newspaper ad for electric lamps told parents they had to provide good lighting so that their children could do the homework required by the new public schools, thereby enabling the family to participate in Mexico's revolutionary transformation. A second category of advertising referred to modernity without the patriotic overlay, deploying images and metaphors connected to technological progress, such as airplanes and the Eiffel Tower. Advertisers frequently used this style of persuasion in selling products that seemed connected to the new roles that urban modernity had opened to women—lipstick, high-heeled shoes, Parisian-style dresses—but it also appeared in advertisements for imported household appliances and automobiles. Finally, a third category of advertising associated products with racial and regional pride, especially the idea of "Indianness," *indigenismo*. Beginning in the 1920s and continuing through the 1960s, "Indian" and folkloric imagery decorated advertisements for such incongruous objects as automobile tires and mineral water. Eventually this type of imagery and rhetoric came to dominate the advertising presented by the Mexican tourist industry both inside the nation and in Europe and the United States, but until about 1960, Mexico preferred to present itself (at least to foreigners) as a series of up-to-date urban destinations.

By the mid–1930s, print advertising—signs, billboards, and ads in periodicals—covered the urban landscape and left a substantial mark on the countryside; these were the most ubiquitous forms of pictures in the nation. But other kinds of print were at least as influential upon and equally representative of Mexican modernity. Most of all, comic books shaped the expectations and imaginations of their readers, and by 1940, half the population seemed to be reading them. Comic books evolved from newspapers. Since they would not or could not vie with one another on the basis of which had the best investigative reporting or political commentary, newspapers competed by carrying new and entertaining features:sports sections, Sunday supplements, gossip columns, ever bigger and more lurid headlines, and plenty of eye-catching advertising. The Sunday supplements (known as *dominicales*) of any newspaper that could afford them always presented translated versions of comic strips from the United States; "Tarzan," for example, ruled the front page of *El Universal*'s weekly color comics section for almost 40 years, during which period the paper was the best-selling newspaper in Mexico City. Some papers retaliated by hiring Mexican cartoonists and then boasting of their patriotism in doing so. But cartoonists found that their best opportunity lay in quitting the dominicales altogether; funded by the newspaper publishers, they moved into the comic-book business.

In 1934, *Chamaco*, the first successful Mexican comic book, appeared. It was soon joined by two others, *Pepín* and *Paquín*. By 1940, the popularity of these three periodicals (together with three or four others of much lower circulation) made them the most important form of media in the country, rivaled only by radio. They were so popular that they soon started appearing daily, and after 1940, *Pepín* published eight issues a week, with a second Sunday edition. Such was their influence that they gave their names to the form of graphic narrative in general: Although these first comic books stopped publishing in the mid–1950s, even today Mexicans sometimes refer to comic books as *pepines* or *paquines*.

Mexican comic books did not resemble the comics that were becoming commonplace in the United States at the same time. Another Spanish name for the medium—*historietas*, literally "little stories"—suggests something of their form: These comic books were more like extended versions of the Sunday comic supplements than anything else. Every issue contained installments of 8 to 12 different continuing serials. These serials were sometimes comedic, in which case they could extend indefinitely (this was the origin of *La Familia Burrón*, which began as a regular feature of *Chamaco* almost 50 years ago and was published as a stand-alone comic book through 1997. More often, *Pepín*, and the rest offered melodramatic tales that concluded after 6 to 18 months of daily episodes. The abundance of stories—along with contests, advertising, and sometimes chapters of novels without pictures—meant that every issue could promise something that would entertain any reader. Unlike their English-language cousins, Mexican comic books did not assume that their audience would be young and male. Publishers designed them to appeal to anybody who could read even a little Spanish.

Furthermore, almost anybody could afford to buy them, at least once in a while. Despite their typical length of 64 pages, the *pepines* were small and lightweight, made with the cheapest available paper. Despite their lurid color covers, they were printed as cheaply as possible, always in monochrome and often with sepia ink. So the pepines were very inexpensive, usually costing less than half the price of a movie ticket. Yet they were made durably enough to be passed from hand to hand. Families shared them; men expected to find them in barbershops, schoolchildren traded them, and marketplaces throughout the country usually included at least one used-comic-book stall.

Sometimes their melodramatic stories based themselves in revolutionary or 19th–century ballads (such as "Adelita" or "Chucho el Roto") or in history (Maximilian and Carlota's story offered fodder for costume drama). But even when the names and the settings belonged to an earlier time, the plotlines followed contemporary models rather than relying either on historical fact or the stories told by the *corridos*. The basic plot of these melodramas, no matter what their settings, nearly always involved the destiny of a family. This family may be threatened or challenged by economic adversity, the greed or selfishness of some of its members, or sexual predations by powerful outsiders. Often, the plot is set in motion when one or more family members move away. If there is a romantic couple, much of

Comic books remain the most popular form of reading material in Mexico. Although Yolanda Vargas Dulché no longer writes scripts for the extremely popular comic book *Lágrimas, risas y amor (Tears, Laughter and Love)*, she and her husband still own the publishing house, and one of her sons manages it.

the time the plot begins with them already married, and in the course of events their union will either dissolve or be strengthened. In the end, the family is restored even when some of its members die. This happy ending often requires the intervention of a powerful or wealthy figure: the good boss, the good mayor, the priest, the Virgin. But sometimes the crucial intervention comes from a returning family member who has grown rich through talent, hard work, virtue, or dumb luck.

Some comic books and photo-novels underlined the realism of their stories by insisting that they were only lightly fictionalized versions of "true-life" tales that readers had contributed. The aura of reality was even stronger in a slightly less popular genre, the cheap true-crime tabloid. First appearing in the mid–1940s, sensationalistic dailies such as *¡Alarma!* borrowed photographs (and sometimes facts) from ordinary newspapers and constructed lurid tales around them. Murder—especially crimes of passion—was the most common theme of these tabloids. But they also printed heart-wrenching stories of innocent young women forced into prostitution, families separated by migration, comfortable households destroyed by drugs, alcohol, or simple economic misfortune. The tabloids told stories that were no different than comic-book melodramas, except that they rarely had happy endings.

Stories like these appealed strongly to Mexican audiences because they resonated with the difficulties, dangers, and pleasures of postrevolutionary life. Migration (either to Mexico's booming cities or to the United States) offered opportunity for exciting new experiences but also threatened family solidarity. The continuation of revolutionary ideology, consumer culture, and an increasingly vocal Catholic Church, created a far wider range of acceptable gender roles for men and women, which could be liberating—or confusing. The pace and structure of most people's working day changed dramatically as the plurality of jobs shifted from the agricultural to the industrial sector. And the "economic miracle" that brought a degree of prosperity to many Mexicans could also be disorienting, even frightening. Small wonder, then, that by 1940 a seemingly insatiable demand had developed for mass-media melodramas, whether in periodicals, on the radio, or in the movies.

The stories told by comic books and tabloid newspapers closely matched the narratives of *radionovelas*, radio soap operas. Often the same writers worked in both media. For example, Yolanda Vargas Dulché earned her fortune and fame as the prolific author of the comic books *Memín Pinguín* and *Lágrimas, risas y amor* (tears, laughter, and love), both still in publication in 1995, after lasting decades and peaking with sales of more than a million a week apiece in the 1970s. But she began her career as a short-story writer for newspapers, briefly sang in Cuban nightclubs, and wrote many radio soap operas and screenplays even as her comic-book stories were beginning to find their audience. Moreover, many of the melodramas she constructed for *Chamaco* or her own periodicals eventually found their way to radio, film, and television. This was not unusual: Useful plots or characters often passed back and forth among historietas, radio dramas, movies, and eventually televised soap operas, too. The Cuban radionovela *El derecho de nacer* (The Right to Be Born) did so well when first broadcast in Mexico in 1951 that it was remade with Mexican actors, then turned into a comic-book serial, then redone as a film with different Mexican actors—all within ten years of its first Mexican broadcast. Since then it has been recast into comic-book form again, been the basis for a televised soap opera and another film, and appeared as a photo-novel.

Radio soap operas did not catch on quite as quickly as magazine melodramas because it took some time for broadcasts to reach as far as print could. In 1935, when the comic books first became popular, Mexico's population was over 10 million, but there were only 600,000 radios in the whole nation—and barely 80 radio stations. The basic legal, economic, and material structures that would become the national radio system had been in place since the 1920s, however, and public interest in the new medium was already running high.

The mechanical reproduction of sound entered Mexican life with the first sale of a gramophone, in 1893. The first experimental radio programming was transmitted in 1923, and it featured speeches by President Obregón and president-to-be Calles. Thus broadcast media—in Mexico as in the rest of the world—was politicized from the moment of its inception. In 1923, the brothers Luis and Raúl Azcárraga persuaded the Mexico City newspaper *El Universal* to put up the money

This advertisement for "Radio" cigarettes produced by the Buen Tono company in the late 1920s makes reference to air travel, polar exploration, and radio communication to suggest a connection between the product and modernity.

for a commercial station, beginning a multimedia business empire that evolved into the present-day giant Televisa. This station had as one of its major sponsors the department store Sanborns, which capitalized on the association by inventing a new brand of soda called Radio. Not to be outdone, the cigarette manufacturer El Buen Tono invested in a radio station of its own and started selling El Radio cigarettes. By 1926, Mexico could boast of 13 stations. But the biggest moment in radio history came in 1930, with the inauguration of the 200–kilowatt station XEW. This station, owned by Emilio Azcárraga Vidaurreta, was the most powerful in the Western Hemisphere; listeners could tune it in from as far away as Havana. Though XEW was affiliated with the RCA network from the United States, it carried relatively little foreign programming because the technology was not yet available for simultaneous transmission. It concentrated, instead, on Spanish-language songs, and by doing so it became the most popular station in Mexico. Building on this success, Emilio Azcárraga launched a radio network that included 15 stations by 1938.

The political importance of radio became obvious in 1928, when news of Obregón's assassination spread via the airwaves long before newspapers could report it. Canny politicians used the new medium to their own advantage. Like Franklin Roosevelt in the United States, Lázaro Cárdenas was especially gifted at reaching the public through radio. His popularity owed much to the broadcast of his campaign speeches and rallies, and he used radio to announce the nationalization of oil, helping to create Mexicans' strong support for the move.

The connection between the government and the new media barons grew even closer because they needed each other. (Their ideological differences counted

for nothing, though Emilio Azcárraga was so conservative that in 1941 the FBI investigated the possibility that he was a Nazi sympathizer, or so the rumor ran.) A series of new laws, promulgated in 1932 and 1936, traded 50–year concessions of the radio spectrum for a demand that at least a quarter of the music carried by the stations consist of "typically Mexican" songs, a ban on political advertising, and a requirement to air a certain amount of government-produced programming every day. After 1936, government-made programming came to a half hour a day, plus a ten-minute daily health bulletin; in 1938, the weekly *Hora nacional* (National Hour) program joined the list of programs that the law insisted every station carry. This show was intended as part of the government's cultural project to build national consciousness, but it also supported the burgeoning tourist industry as it introduced Mexicans to the folkloric traditions of various regions.

Radio's beginnings—especially the legal requirement for "typically Mexican" music—created a huge demand for new songs. Sometimes these new songs were recorded, but often they were simply sung as part of live radio broadcasting. Many singers and songwriters gained lasting fame, especially those such as Guty Cárdenas and Lucha Reyes who died early and violently. But the undisputed king of the new songwriters was Agustín Lara (1897–1970). Lara wrote beautiful songs, and he wrote a lot of them: Between 1926 and 1968, he published roughly 200. His waltzes, tangos, *pasodobles*, and *danzones* often declared his love for the city of Veracruz or for one or another of his four wives and additional muses, most notably the lovely 1947 ballad "María bonita" celebrating his marriage to movie star María Félix.

But Lara also invented a whole new genre of song, the sad Mexican *bolero*, which was closely related to the kinds of melodramatic story that other forms of mass media were popularizing at the time. Lara's version of the bolero first appeared in his 1928 hit "Imposible." This new type of song was rooted in a Cuban song style of the same name but used a small ensemble of musicians instead of a solo guitar, and—unlike its Cuban ancestor—placed the singer's voice and the song's painful lyrics in the foreground. Lara's sad boleros, critics said, gave listeners the choice of dancing or weeping. These songs, set in the underworld of brothels and dance halls where Lara first performed, tell the sort of tales in which a young man hopelessly loves a prostitute, or a prostitute yearns for redemption. They often seemed to be musical expressions of the most tragic episodes from radionovelas, but without the uplifting conclusions. The story-telling component of Lara's songs helped him fit naturally on the airwaves next to all the radio soap operas, and in September 1929, XEW gave him his own weekly show, *La hora íntima* (The Intimate Hour).

The melodrama of his music also made Lara a natural for film work, and he began contributing songs to movie sound tracks beginning with the 1931 film *Santa*. He soon began appearing in movies, too, eventually participating in more than 30 productions, including a 1959 biographical film, *La vida de Agustín Lara*. His movies belonged to the popular genre known as *cabareteras* (cabaret stories) in which innocent young women come to the big city only to be forced into work-ing as dancers (*cabareteras*) or, more bluntly, as prostitutes. Lara nearly always played a semi-autobiographical role as a musician in this urban underworld. His voice on the sound track or his on-screen character warned the young migrant what to expect, explained to the audience that she was lovable despite her sins, and mourned her fate. Lara became a prototype for Mexican celebrity, famous all at once as a songwriter, musician, and movie star.

The Mexican movie industry, at the moment when it recruited Agustín Lara, was entering its golden age. In 1931, Lara's first film project, *Santa*, was also Mexico's first musical and one of its earliest talkies. Its production marked the beginning of an era in which Mexican filmmakers could invest a reasonable sum in their work—enough to deploy recent technological innovations such as sound and (after 1942) color—confident that they had a good chance of finding an audience. Film production seemed like a risky gamble in the early 1930s, how-ever, because the conditions for Mexican cinema had been so dismal. The movie audience developed very slowly; in 1938, there were still fewer than 500 movie houses in the entire country. And the film industry grew even more slowly than its audience.

In the waning years of the Porfiriato, Mexico's first cameramen and movie producers were engineers, full of ideological sympathy for the positivist philoso-phy of the day, and the Mexican film industry (like the radio industry decades later) was closely connected to the Mexican state from the moment of its birth.

One of the first Mexican movies—so primitive that it mixed still photography with short black-and-white, silent sequences—documented a journey Porfirio Díaz made to Yucatán in 1906. Another recorded Díaz's meeting with President Taft of the United States. But the chaos of the Revolution meant that film production did not move far beyond this newsreel style. Many people believed that cinema would eventually be an important, and profitable, medium. One hopeful soul even opened Mexico's first film school in 1916. The Madero regime had set up a system of movie theater inspection and was discussing the question of film censorship when it fell in 1913. As late as 1930, however, only two full-length movies per year were made in Mexico. This was due, in part, to a lack of state support, exemplified by a comment José Vasconcelos made in 1927, while he was minister of education: Cinema, he said, was "typically North American." Therefore, the revolutionary state would offer its citizens alternative art forms, such as murals, that were less subject to cultural contamination. The revolutionary state would not help a local film industry compete with foreign cinema.

The indigenous film industry's growth was most challenged by the unfortunate proximity of Hollywood. From the earliest days of silent film, Hollywood producers favored "picturesque" and cheap northern Mexican locations. Some of the earliest successful full-length English-language documentaries covered Pancho Villa's campaigns, and Villa was not above restaging battles fought on cloudy days for filmmakers whose cameras required better lighting. As Hollywood moviemakers came to understand the export potential of film, Mexico evolved into a major secondary market for them. Hollywood lured Mexican actors such as Lupe Vélez and Delores del Río, hoping that their presence (even in supporting roles, and often racist ones that conformed to the Latin spitfire stereotype) would bring their Hollywood films bigger audiences throughout the Spanish-speaking world. Between 1927 and 1932, Hollywood studios even made a few movies every year in Spanish, intended directly for the Latin American market. The first fan magazine sold in Mexico, *Cine Mundial*, was imported from New York City. Strategies like these, combined with the high production values and cultural prestige of Hollywood, worked well. Between 1930 and 1939, even as the local film industry was reviving, 76% of all films premiered in Mexico City had been made in the United States. (And another 17% were made in other foreign countries.) Most Mexicans, over the course of a lifetime, would see far more Hollywood films than any other kind—and this continues to be true today.

The audience not only had to arrive in the movie theaters, it had to decide on movie-viewing etiquette. Mexico had a long tradition of urban vaudeville theater called *carpa*, which transgressed sexual and social norms, mocking all forms of polite behavior and all the clichés of political rhetoric. (The great cinematic comedians Tin-Tan and Cantinflas began their careers in these theatrical revues.) Such theaters were well known as places where otherwise illicit acts could be performed in public places a respectable woman might hesitate to enter. In the early days of film exhibition in Mexico, these theaters were sometimes converted to cinemas, carrying their aura of masculine adventure and rule-breaking with them. To add to movie exhibitors' problems, one of the earliest available genres of film was pornography; in Mexico as in the rest of the world, pornographers were among the first to profit from new communications technology. In 1940, a highly publicized crackdown in which most of Mexico City's illicit movie houses were shut down helped the reputation of other cinemas and their patrons, as did the promulgation of film censorship in 1941. But on the whole, the potential uses of moviegoing and the acceptable forms of behavior for moviegoers was not a question for the state; it had to be worked out by the exhibitors and their patrons.

Ordinary movie theaters tried many strategies to differentiate themselves from burlesque houses and from the movie theaters that showed pornography. In the 1930s, a few cinemas offered special screenings just for women. Most had ushers who were supposed to enforce good manners. And all of them—following the logic of bullfights and wrestling arenas—carefully segregated their audience by class by varying the ticket prices for different sections of the movie house. The fancy names and elegant decor of first-run movie houses, too, suggested that moviegoers should behave well. Some of the houses had layers of thick red velvet curtains, elaborately carved balconies, and names such as The Palace, hinting that their audience was made up of aristocrats; others had streamlined architecture, chrome fittings, and names such as The Modern, to imply that their audience should be as disciplined as factory workers. But the audience rebelled. By the mid–1930s, it was clear that cinemas, like vaudeville theaters before them, would remain sites for all kinds of transgressive behavior. In the increasingly crowded cities, they were among the few places where courting couples could find privacy. Sneaking past the ticket takers became an accepted part of life for impoverished urban youth, and sometimes gangs of teenage boys staked out balconies of particular theaters as their havens. Eventually, too, movie theaters became a useful platform for other kinds of marginality, such as the teenage rock-and-roll fans whose rioting during a 1959 showing of an Elvis Presley movie shocked the nation.

Mexicans found many uses for movie theaters, and because of this (or in spite of it) the Mexican movie business grew significantly between 1930 and 1950. It made many more pictures—from 5 in 1930 to 125 in 1950—in response to a mushrooming audience. (By comparison, Argentina, whose film industry had been the most active in Latin America before 1940, made fewer than 30 feature films in 1950.) In 1950, there were 1,070 movie theaters in the country; that meant that every good-sized town had at least one cinema. Most of these screens were showing Hollywood films most of the time, but Mexican movies did travel the country and occasionally made a big splash.

The 1936 movie *Allá en Rancho Grande* (Over on Big Ranch) was the first real hit movie made in Mexico, a *comedia ranchera* (ranch comedy) that set a pattern for the genre. Its descendants included one of Mexico's first color films, *Así se quiere en Jalisco* (That's How They Love in Jalisco, 1942), another major hit. *Allá en Rancho Grande* involved romantic complications among a benevolent ranch owner newly returned to the small town, his loyal but proud young lieutenant, and a beautiful and innocent maiden, all caused by her meddling godmother; there were fistfights, misunderstandings, a great swooning scene, plenty of song and dance, and, of course, a happy ending. In a way, *Allá en Rancho Grande* was the obverse of the cabaretera films: It involved the preservation of female purity and the return of urban migrants to rural life, and nobody died.

Other hit comedies of this era could be seen as determined rejections of the melodrama that prevailed in popular song, radio soap opera, and comic-book serials. *En tiempos de don Porfirio* (In the Days of Porfirio Díaz, 1939) and *¡Ay, qué tiempos señor don Simón!* (Such Times, Mr. Simon, Sir!, 1941) both offered audiences a benevolent vision of the years before the Revolution, allowing them to imagine themselves as belonging to the nation's miniscule elite. On the other hand, *Ahí está el detalle* (This Is the Point, 1940) was the last in a series of films in which the comedian Cantinflas played a peladito, a harmless urban bum. It ridiculed the hypocrisies of the nation's new urban middle class through a complicated plot involving the hero's love for a servant girl. Cantinflas, unjustly accused of murder, triumphs through his use of rapid-fire wordplay. All these hit films provided audiences with a temporary escape from their social or economic troubles.

A few films of the 1940s—beginning with *Ahí está el detalle*—achieved a reasonable degree of popular success while also joining the canon of classic Mexican cinema. For the most part these were melodramas, compressed versions of the stories from radionovelas and comic books. They starred the giants of Mexican cinema: María Félix, Delores del Río, Pedro Armendáriz, Pedro Infante, Jorge Negrete. In 1943—an astonishingly productive year for film in Mexico—four dramas appeared that set the aesthetic and narrative boundaries of the art form. *María Candelaria*, set in prerevolutionary Xochimilco, starred Delores del Río; she played an Indian girl unjustly accused of big-city corruption. This movie ended tragically, but the other great movies of 1943 had more ambiguous conclusions. In *Doña Bárbara*, a historical drama set in Venezuela, María Félix played an "unnatural" woman rancher who will not submit to male authority; she finally decides to disappear into the plains so that her daughter can find happiness by marrying a neighborhood rancher. *Flor silvestre* (Wildflower) was a tale of the Revolution, in which the hero (Pedro Armendáriz) dies but his egalitarian ideals survive, as do his wife (Delores del Río again) and his child. Finally, *Distinto amanecer*—like Cantinflas's films—criticized postrevolutionary materialism but ended on a hopeful note: It shows Pedro Armendáriz losing his best friend, an assassinated labor leader, but eventually exposing the corrupt politician responsible for the crime.

The year 1943 produced an unusually large number of brilliant movies, but the '40s as a whole mark the maximum achievement of Mexican cinema. The flowering of film was no accident; it responded to changes in the financial, technological, and legal framework that supported the industry. Besides the advent of sound and color cinema, and the booming numbers of movie houses, the most important material change was the construction of enormous new studios in Mexico City. Emilio Azcárraga played a major role in this cultural industry, as he did in radio, publishing, and recorded music. He was forced to sell his movie-theater chain in 1944 by another powerful media mogul, the Puebla-based Manuel Espinosa Iglesias, who convinced Hollywood distributors not to send their movies to Azcárraga's cinemas (though the two men, along with Espinosa's silent partner William O. Jenkins, later developed a television network together). But Azcárraga remained active in film production: In 1944, he used financing from the Hollywood film company RKO to build the Churubusco studio, the most modern facility then available in Mexico, and six years later he merged Churubusco with the equally up-to-date Azteca studio, establishing the physical site for most Mexican film and television production.

New organizations, too, made film production, distribution, and exhibition much easier and much less risky. After 1936, a syndicate organized filmmakers and distributors. A small group of actors and directors (including Jorge Negrete and Cantinflas) split with this group in 1945, complaining that it had failed to understand their artistic needs. After grueling labor conflict that brought all production to a halt for months, the government brokered a resolution: A second syndicate, the Union of Cinema Production Workers, would take over responsibility for feature film production while the older Union of Cinema Industry Workers remained in charge of newsreel production, as well as distribution and exhibition of all Mexican film. As an aid to movie production, the new Mexican Academy of Cinematographic Arts and Sciences inaugurated the annual Ariel awards—a local version of Hollywood's Oscars—in 1946. All these groups enabled filmmakers to compete more effectively with Hollywood.

In any case, World War II temporarily made Hollywood a less dangerous competitor. With most of the European market closed to it, Hollywood needed the Latin American market more than ever. But United States policy makers worried that Latin Americans would ally themselves with Germany and Japan in the war, and their efforts to build and maintain alliances against that possibility included a cultural dimension. They were especially concerned that the Spanish-speaking world would be watching movies made in fascist Spain or neutral Argentina. Hiring Mexican advisors, U.S. cultural diplomats set Disney studios to making Spanish-language cartoons that would be tools for literacy campaigns. More important, they provided economic and technological assistance to Mexican filmmakers, they aided in opening Hollywood-dominated distribution networks in Latin America to Mexican films, and they encouraged Hollywood companies to work in partnership with Mexican producers. The Mexican film industry thrived due to this unusual political opening.

A series of Mexican government actions supported the rapid expansion of the Mexican film industry in the '40s. After 1934, the state experimented with different forms of aid for the film industry. Lázaro Cárdenas recognized that movies, like radio, had their political uses. In his first year in office he used government money to rescue the brand-new studio Cinematográfica Latinoamericana from bankruptcy (it was then the largest and best-equipped studio in the nation). This studio then went on to make the state-funded epic *¡Vámonos con Pancho Villa!*

(Let's Go with Pancho Villa!). Its million-peso budget ($200,000 U.S.) made it by far the most expensive Mexican movie of its time. Cárdenas himself was said to have edited—or censored—the final scene, complaining that it was too bloody. The movie was a catastrophic failure at the box office, although recently it has received much critical acclaim. After this economic fiasco, the Cárdenas administration limited itself to encouraging cooperative production ventures and funding newsreel and documentary films. The administration of Avila Camacho was less interested in making movies to express its ideological stances and more determined to control film content and support local industry. Thus it passed laws authorizing censorship of film scripts, but it also sponsored the Banco Cinematográfico. Beginning in 1942, this key institution provided low-cost loans to filmmakers, solving the single biggest problem the industry had ever faced—access to capital. Moreover, Avila Camacho made another protectionist gesture in favor of the local film industry by exempting it from income taxes after 1945.

The film industry came to depend on the state, in ways both obvious and subtle. Besides the crucial financial support it offered, government regulated every aspect of the industry, from the content of the scripts to the cleanliness of the movie houses. Such regulation in itself supported the industry by making both the movies themselves and the venues in which they played seem relatively wholesome, even patriotic, and thus more appealing to audiences. Moviemakers, usually without much conscious thought on the matter, found it natural to support the state that supported them; most of the classic films of the 1940s echoed the conservative nationalism that characterized the governments of Presidents Avila Camacho and Miguel Alemán. President Alemán himself delivered this message when he appeared (as himself) in the opening scenes of the 1947 movie *Río escondido* (Hidden River), lecturing rural schoolteachers on the dangers the nation faced from ignorance, disease, and poverty. The melodramatic and comic movies of this era—even the greatest of them—tended to sentimentalize rural oppression and urban poverty. They described, or invented, quaint regional traditions. And with few exceptions Mexican movies depicted the most powerful national institutions—local and national governments, the police, the church, the wealthy, the patriarchal family—as benign if not altogether above reproach.

Cultural innovations such as cheap periodicals, radio, and cinema received an enthusiastic welcome in postrevolutionary Mexico. But they had their critics, too. And the more that mass culture appeared to align itself with the political status quo, the louder the criticism grew. Protesting against media, like protesting against compulsory public education, was a relatively safe way for conservatives to express dissent. Furthermore, the narratives in these new media described (in idealized or melodramatic form, to be sure) how economic and political change, new technology, urbanization, and shifting gender roles affected Mexican lives; thus, to protest against new media was to demonstrate dissatisfaction with modernity itself.

Ironically, the most persistent and vocal protesters against mass media and consumer culture belonged to the new urban middle class, which was also the biggest beneficiary of modernization. The loudest complaints came from Mexico's biggest cities: Monterrey, Guadalajara, Puebla, and Mexico City. And among the most visible protesters were high school and university students. Sometimes the people who engaged in this form of protest were led by politicians, especially the fascist opposition of the mid–1930s through the mid–'40s and, more recently, by the National Action Party. More often they followed church leaders. But these protesters were not simply following anyone's party line. For the most part protesters expressed concerns that were widely held among otherwise apolitical Mexicans.

The question of gender was especially urgent, and the conservatives who complained about the mass media often did so in the name of female purity. Depictions of fallen women, they felt, could lead other women to fall. The prostitutes and dance-hall girls who peopled cabaretera films and Agustín Lara's boleros were exceptionally offensive. In 1936, the secretary of public education in the Cárdenas administration made a conciliatory gesture to the right by banning Lara's songs from being performed in the public schools. This move created little controversy within the ruling party, as conservative concern over sexual morality was not altogether different from the reformist zeal of the previous administration, which had been reflected in its attempts to control gambling, prostitution, and public spectacles. And the Department of Public Education under Cárdenas was, at this point, slightly more willing to compromise with its opponents; it had already backed off from an extraordinarily controversial attempt in 1933–34 to institute sex education in the public schools and suffered through a brief spate of violent resistance to its 1936 attempt to enforce the "socialist education" clause of Article 3 of the constitution.

Sexuality was not the only gender issue to trouble conservative protesters against mass media. The mere depiction of women at work rather than in their roles as wives and mothers also angered some members of the audience for radionovelas, historietas, and film. These melodramas frequently portrayed the workplace as fraught with sexual danger for vulnerable working women; they certainly did not serve as cheerleaders for women's entry into the paid workforce. But some protesters explained that the idea of women working was in itself a threat to family stability and national morality, and therefore it should not appear in the media even to be criticized.

The question arose, too, of who the ideal Mexican woman was; new media and the cultural ferment of the 1920s and '30s offered women a much broader range of models to chose among. The new tabloid press made the lives of powerful or talented people accessible, or seemingly accessible, to ordinary people. So María Félix might play a chaste and heroic schoolteacher, for example, but her audience would know something of her scandalous love life and multiple divorces. The lives of such unconventional figures as artists Frida Kahlo and Tina Modotti were also fodder for gossip columns, even if few ever saw Kahlo's paintings or Modotti's photographs. Fictional characters, too, helped to suggest that there was more than one way to be a good Mexican woman. Between 1935 and 1950, comic books and radio serials often toyed with the image of the *chica moderna*, the "modern girl," who stubbornly insisted on marrying for love rather than for family duty, who wanted to earn her own living before marriage, who wore sexy and fashionable clothing, and who unabashedly expressed her own opinions. She was a comic stereotype at times, but an affectionate one. Her most durable incarnation was in an extremely popular historieta *Adelita and the Guerrillas*, which featured two girl detectives. The resonant title made reference to the popular ballad "Adelita," a song describing a revolutionary's love for the prototypical woman soldier, suggesting that the cartoon character was also a figure of national pride.

Conservatives especially resented attempts to valorize the image of the *soldadera*, protesting even the singing of this corrido as well as the concept of a holiday in her honor. But they did more than protest; they tried to reinvent Mexican womanhood on their own "traditional" terms. They proposed that Mexico should borrow the celebration of Mother's Day from the United States (which it did, informally, from about 1920 onward). The Catholic Church used the pope's declaration of the Virgin of Guadalupe as Queen of the Americas in 1945 to reassert her importance to the Mexican imagination through massive celebrations. A decade later, the church enlisted the singer and actor Pedro Infante—an idol of the Mexican public—to raise funds for the restoration of the Virgin's basilica through Mexico's first telethon. And through new publications and organizations especially for women, the church concentrated on maintaining their allegiance and shaping their ideals.

Conservatives subjected all kinds of media and popular culture to close scrutiny and to protest. Comic books and film, especially, seemed to offend people. But urban space itself was also contested in a number of ways. Mexicans argued over what types of imagery posters and billboards could display in public, as in a 1996 uproar over a lingerie ad that showed a woman in her bra. (The caption read, "How do you like me?" and when the offending billboards were replaced by an almost identical picture of the model in a blouse, the new caption asked, "Now how do you like me?") Questions of public behavior—what kinds of dancing were or were not moral, whether or not men could be expected to restrain themselves in close proximity to strange women on buses, trains, and sidewalks—often spilled into demands for government regulation. Thus theaters and dance halls came under increasing scrutiny after 1940; and the Mexico City metro (which began construction in 1967) offered separate cars for women during rush hour.

Arguments over urban space were often veiled fights over the legitimacy of the Mexican state. When Catholics demonstrated in protest of blasphemous images in Diego Rivera's murals, and when *sinarquistas* beheaded a statue of Benito Juárez in the Alameda of Mexico City during 1948 riot, they expressed political dissent against the government that manipulated the pantheon of heros that these public artworks portrayed. Dissent was not always dramatic or obvious. Some people made a point of refusing to use the new names that revolutionary governments had given to existing streets and plazas, so that in 1945, the Avila

Camacho administration was only bowing to reality when it restored to the Mexico neighborhood around the basilica sacred to the Virgin of Guadalupe its old title of Villa de la Virgin.

Methods of protest against mass media and consumer culture depended on the target of the protest. Objections to media did not always lead to public demonstrations or even to boycotts. The Catholic Church recognized that parishoners were unlikely to give up moviegoing. Instead it tried to guide them to the least harmful films by handing out a weekly leaflet at Sunday mass (beginning in 1934 and continuing to 1950) that contained ratings of every movie showing in the diocese, sorted by the type and degree of sin visible in each picture. Additionally, some parishes organized boycotts of movie theaters that persistently offered "immoral" films. And at least one suburb of the capital—Coyoacán, in the 1940s—set up an alternative neighborhood cinema to show "clean" pictures. Similarly, many people tried to start up alternative children's magazines to compete with *Pepín* and other popular comic books. The first of these efforts had the backing of Lázaro Cárdenas himself but failed quickly all the same. Others lasted longer because they had financial support from the church. One children's magazine of the 1950s, *Tesoros* (Treasures), was so slickly produced that the only visible difference between it and commercial comic books was that *Tesoros* sometimes inserted photographs of its editors shaking hands with politicians and bishops. In 1980, the government sponsored another attempt at an alternative comic: *Episodios mexicanos*, a series of stories from Mexican history researched and (to some extent) written by historians but drawn and produced by professional cartoonists. Newsstand operators outside of Mexico City could not be induced to carry it, so the government resorted to transporting and selling the comic through the distribution network of Pan Bimbo, the extremely popular processed white bread manufacturer. (This relatively successful project ended in 1982 with the close of the López Portillo administration.)

The growth of demand for "moral" entertainment looked like an opportunity for profit in some culture industries. In 1934, a radio manufacturer's newspaper ad suggested to parents that they should buy a radio for the sake of their families, since children who ran home after school to listen to music or radionovelas would not linger in the streets, where they might be corrupted by "bad companions." Radio station XEX was struggling to define itself in a market dominated by the Azcárraga network until 1947, when its managers hit on the notion of advertising the station as the clean alternative to racy popular music. The station distributed a list of songs, soon reprinted throughout the country, which it called "obscene" and vowed never to broadcast. Prominent among the blacklisted tunes were Agustín Lara compositions such as "Mujer," some of the most popular records in Mexico. Nonetheless, this effort at niche marketing worked well. Similarly, comic-book publishers—especially those selling translated versions of comic books for children from the United States, like Disney cartoons—often sold their wares by advertising them as "clean," "wholesome," "healthy," or "educational."

Protestant missionaries attempted to convert Mexicans whom the revolutionary government had attempted to separate from the Roman Catholic Church. Despite the efforts of missionaries such as this Seventh Day Adventist, Mexican culture remains essentially Catholic.

Commercial efforts such as these ensured that conservatives did not unilaterally oppose all mass media or consumer culture. Sometimes church publications endorsed movies, particularly Disney cartoons. The modernization of consumer goods appeared harmless to the church hierarchy, or even beneficial, so that in 1949 the archbishop of Mexico City opened the first Sears store in Mexico with a special blessing. A preference for imported goods and imported culture, in itself, could mark an implicit resistance to the Mexican government and its efforts to invent a national mythos and a national culture.

By the 1960s, the Catholic Church in Mexico faced greater challenges than the temptations of mass media. Although Protestants remained a small minority in Mexico, their numbers increased as Mormons, Jehovah's Witnesses, Seventh-Day Adventists, and other groups sent increasing numbers of missionaries to Mexico after World War II. Many households posted signs on their doors announcing that "This is a Catholic home" to discourage proselytizing, a ubiquitous sight all over the country by the 1980s. In the south after about 1970—especially in Chiapas—conversion led to violent conflict within and between villages whose religious calendars, family groups, and economic cycles had been tightly intertwined through a system of rotating responsibility for expensive annual fiestas.

The Catholic Church in Mexico had internal as well as external problems. Many more Mexicans retained their allegiance to Catholicism than officially converted to Protestant denominations; as of 1900, more than 80% of the population called itself Catholic. But just as some indigenous groups did in colonial times, the new urban working class added other spiritual practices to their lives that the church, though not the practitioners, officially regarded as superstitious if not blasphemous: seances to consult with the spirit of Pancho Villa, the informal addition of U.S. president John Kennedy to the pantheon of saints, and (more recently) similar veneration in the north of Tejana singer Selena, and the use of healing techniques and divination methods attributed to pre-Hispanic cultures or a vaguely defined Asian wisdom. Meanwhile, the church throughout Latin America nearly split after Vatican II and the Cuban Revolution of 1959 as the new doctrine of liberation theology—the ideal of a socially engaged church that preached that God "had a preferential option for the poor"—took hold. In Mexico this division eventually separated the church in poor regions, especially Morelos and Chiapas, from the more traditionalist hierarchy in Mexico City and the north. In Cuernavaca in 1968, the new experimental spirit led the head of a monastery to send all the monks to a Freudian psychoanalyst and announce that fact to the press (in the ensuing uproar, he was defrocked). More serious expressions of liberation theology in Latin America included strong support for social movements, including armed ones; for example, the diocese of San Cristóbal in Chiapas provided crucial political support for the Zapatistas beginning in 1994, with the local bishop acting as a mediator between the guerrillas and the government.

Under these circumstances, it seems surprising that protests against media continued sporadically into the present day, but they did. In part this can be explained by the fact that the Mexican state began to encourage them by appearing to agree with conservatives on cultural matters. For instance, in 1944, President Avila Camacho reacted to a particularly strong wave of indignation against comic books by creating the Comisión Calificadora de Publicaciones Ilustradas (Classifying Commission for Illustrated Publications, later renamed the Classifying Commission for Publications and Illustrated Magazines), which was supposed to levy fines against publishers whose periodicals encouraged superstition, criminality, disrespect for established Mexican institutions, disdain for the Mexican people, sexual promiscuity, or the use of slang. This new bureacracy had few powers of enforcement; it never made much of an impact on the contents of comic books, photo-novels, or other Mexican periodicals. (The government could and did practice censorship of periodicals it felt presented a political—rather than moral—threat, but it used extra-legal mechanisms for that purpose.) Every few years after the promulgation of this law, new conservative protests arose against the increasingly daring magazine industry. But the existence of the law—like the similar regulations governing cinema and broadcasting—told protesters that the government was on their side. Beginning with the Avila Camacho administration, the government embarked on a project to co-opt conservative protest and convince citizens that it had nothing to do with the less acceptable forms of modernity in Mexico while still deserving all the credit for those changes in material existence that everyone enjoyed. And on the whole this project succeeded.

After 1940, the government of Mexico, while continuing to call itself revolutionary, demonstrated an increasingly single-minded focus on self-preservation and capitalist economic development. With the departure of Lázaro Cárdenas, it ceased to be a simple matter to locate a single official culture. Strands of earlier ideologies, continuities from the liberal, Porfirian, or revolutionary movements of the past: All these influenced government policies toward education, the arts, city planning, rural development, transportation, and media. Moreover, as the reach and power of mass media grew, consumer culture competed with official ideology in shaping the experiences and imaginations of Mexican citizens.

President Avila Camacho deliberately and publicly abandoned the cultural politics of his predecessors. Except for his sponsorship of a literacy campaign, he left the creation of national mythologies to the burgeoning culture industries and the church. He preferred to control the industries' output (or at least, as in the case of comic books, to have the appearance of control) rather than to involve the state directly in producing culture.

The accession of Manuel Avila Camacho marked a watershed in Mexican culture as well as politics—some historians regard it as the end of the Revolution—but the new president also learned from previous ones. He manipulated his public image through a use of media that was at least as adroit as that of Cárdenas had been, as in his post-election renunciation of revolutionary anti-clericalism: The president-elect got his point across simply by telling an interviewer that he was "a believer." The new president and his family enacted the gender stereotypes that the mass media (and media's conservative critics) were popularizing at the time. His wife Soledad, presumably with the president's approval, played the role of the prudish housewife to perfection: In well-publicized incidents, she first insisted that a nude statue of Diana the Huntress be removed from a central avenue of Mexico City and then rejected a painting by María Izquierdo because it, too, contained an image of a nude woman. Meanwhile the president's brother Maximino acted the part of the violent, powerful, and manly rancher as well as Jorge Negrete ever could. Maximino's affairs with such exotic conquests as a Spanish flamenco dancer and a woman bullfighter entered public consciousness through rumor, rather than the scandal sheets. But his 11 children (not all from his two marriages) were a matter of public record, and so were his takeover of the Ministry of Communications at gunpoint, and his jeweled pistols, and his temper. The public image of the president himself—the Catholic patriarch, firm, calm, and prudent—could have been the stereotype of the good father from any of a thousand radionovelas and comic-book melodramas. After 1940, politics became yet another entertaining melodrama, played out through the medium of jokes, rumors, gossip columns, interviews, and public pronouncements.

Successive administrations often tried to define themselves and leave their mark on the nation's culture through the construction of some monumental work, almost always a variation on the theme of Mexican modernity. The presidency of Miguel Alemán was exceptionally active in building highways, railroads, bridges, and airports. Members of the Alemán administration, alongside members of the Alemán family, took active roles in the lucrative development of

Acapulco as an international tourist resort. But President Alemán's administration reserved its maximum effort for a huge new school project, expressing an association of the state with education, and education with progress, that had by then become a reflex. So, in 1951, President Alemán opened the new campus of the National Autonomous University of Mexico.

Ciudad Universitaria, as it was named, joined in the expansion of Mexico City toward the south, moving students up and out from the center of the capital into their own sprawling suburb of undergraduate and graduate schools, libraries, galleries, and an enormous stadium. The architecture of the new campus rejected the relatively compact, highly decorative colonial splendor of the old. It favored stripped-down, functional, modernist buildings decorated with enormous paintings and mosaics—some of Mexico's last major murals in public spaces—as a visible sign of the university's commitment to progress. The design of the campus also demonstrated national pride through landscaping (supposed to look as "natural" as possible) and the use of the local black volcanic rock in many of the buildings. A large statue of President Alemán in academic garb stood at the center of the entire complex; nobody needed to ask the symbolic meaning of that architectural detail.

The National Museum of Anthropology, which opened in 1954, memorialized the presidency of Adolfo Ruiz Cortines. Its fabulous collection of pre-Hispanic objects was juxtaposed with examples of contemporary indigenous crafts and clothing, suggesting an unbroken connection between past and present reminiscent of 1920s indigenismo. The design of the building, with its two stories opening onto an enormous courtyard, referred back to the glories of colonial architecture. But the museum became an important participant in one of Mexico's most important industries: tourism. Guidebooks extolled the wonders on display in the new museum, and a long visit seemed obligatory to every foreign visitor. In keeping with this very 20th–century function, the museum's design used the visual and symbolic vocabulary of modernism: streamlined, minimalist, with relatively low ceilings for its sprawling exhibition halls, and plenty of plate glass and poured concrete.

Tourism, like other cultural industries, had a close and complex relationship to the state. The source of immense riches, it tempted politicians; presidents made a practice of placing close friends or family members in charge of the government office that supervised the industry. The tourist industry required government support, in the forms of a transportation infrastructure and advertising abroad. Spectacles such as the major exhibits of Mexican art that traveled the world in 1940 and 1990, the World Cup soccer tournaments (held in Mexico in 1970 and 1986), and the Mexico City Olympics of 1968, should be understood as—among other things—massive ad campaigns to sell Mexico to the world. The bloody repression of the student movement just prior to the 1968 Olympics occurred in part because public protests, in the eyes of high government officials, would ruin the event's potential as a promotional tool.

The extremely popular sport of *lucha libre* (professional wrestling) made celebrities of such wrestlers as Blue Demon and Black Shadow. The only wrestler to earn greater public acclaim was El Santo.

Spectator sports were a way for Mexico to present itself to the world, and they were also the source of immense national pride. In 1946, the nation watched with amusement as baseball impresario Jorge Pasquel filled his team with players poached from the major leagues of the United States, signing up players as they returned from World War II by offering better deals than their former teams were willing to make. In the relatively quiescent 1950s, student demonstrations were limited to support for their university teams; the design of Ciudad Universitaria, with its grand outdoor arena, recognized that fact. (U.S.-style football was especially popular in this venue, though nowhere else in the nation.) Soccer was the most beloved of all team sports. The whole nation seemed to come to halt every four years for the World Cup, in which Mexico was a perennial contender, though never a serious challenger, for the title.

Soccer and baseball are still enjoyed all over Mexico. But they require open space, so participants and spectators tend to live outside the largest cities. Another important sport, rodeo, has a regional base in the north. It owed much of

its popularity to the *ranchera* movies of the 1930s and '40s, and like them it involved highly stylized competitive displays of masculine prowess. (Women began competing in 1989, but their events were carefully distinguished from the men's, emphasizing grace, charm, and appearance above all else. Mexican rodeo continued to reinforce the gender ideology that had shaped it.) The gorgeously arrayed male athletes, or *charros*, demonstrated their abilities at training horses, handling long ropes, and subduing animals without hurting them. In contrast to U.S. rodeo, Mexican *charreada* competitions required far more skill and attention to appearance than strength or brutality. And like other forms of individual athletic competition that mattered in postrevolutionary Mexican culture—especially boxing and wrestling—the publicity that attended the sport and the form of the sport itself connected the spectacle to the familiar melodramatic stories that audiences knew from print and broadcast media.

Urbanization helped popularize other kinds of spectator sports suitable to crowded cities. Beginning in the 1920s, jai alai players from Spain (including women) played in frontons in most major Mexican cities, cheered on—for the most part—by the local elites who also watched horse racing. Boxing captured the working public's imagination in the '40s when Mexican bantam weights and welter weights began winning championship bouts in the United States. Innumerable radio and comic-book melodramas used the figure of the struggling young boxer as their hero, a kind of super-migrant who must seek his fortune across the border. Boxing mattered so much to some spectators that, when El Ratón Macías lost the world bantamweight title in 1957, they rioted. The combination of intense nationalism with the desire to succeed in the (presumably English-speaking) international arena can be glimpsed in the very name of an especially famous and successful boxer: El Kid Azteca.

Even more than boxing, professional wrestling—*lucha libre*—was a product of urban modernity. Its rules were first formalized in 1933; within a few years, a circuit of wrestling arenas offered bouts all around the nation. Lucha libre competed with the movies for an audience, and like the movies it was a cheap form of entertainment that offered satisfying melodramatic narratives far more complex than the simple question of victory or defeat. Every wrestler belongs to one of two categories: the rudos and the técnicos. Técnicos are the good guys; they do not cheat, they treat their opponents fairly, and they frequently lose. Rudos, on the other hand, make a show of rule bending and rule breaking. They suborn referees, use illegal holds, and gang up on opponents. Often, técnicos can win only by imitating rudo tactics. Audiences cheer when a starring técnico, at the end of an evening's competition, makes a theatrical display of losing his self-control and finally defeats his opponent (and sometimes the referee as well) with the rudo's own tricks. Both rudos and técnicos wear costumes that are as elaborate as any charro's, and the ultimate defeat—though this happens rarely—is to be unmasked.

Lucha libre closely resembles the popular understanding of Mexico's political system. Wrestlers who oppose each other in the arena can be seen to be complicit

outside it. The outcome is always fixed, though some viewers and most participants insist that this is not the case. The rules are clear but unevenly enforced,
and the representatives of authority—the referees—can be bribed. Many fans feel
powerful loyalty to favorite rudos, who represent the ability to bend an unjust
system to one's will. Both sexes participate, though not on equal terms (women
could not wrestle in Mexico City arenas from about 1950 to about 1980). The
law-abiding individual loses unless she or he gets help from friends or ceases to
obey the laws. And sometimes, bouts get out of hand: When the system breaks
down, participants can be badly injured, even killed.

The most important of all the parallels between radio and television was the
Television and lucha libre could have been made for each other. Lucha offered
broadcasters its long-running rivalries to provide dramatic interest, its eye-catching outfits, its bounded locations, its huge fan base, and its short spurts of violent
action. Television offered lucha libre the chance to reach an even wider audience,
and gave wrestlers the chance at celebrity that went far beyond the confines of the
arena. (El Santo, the most popular of all wrestlers, starred in more than 50 movies
as well as a best-selling photo-novel that appeared weekly—sometimes daily—
over a period of 30 years.) So wrestling was among the first sports to be broadcast
on Mexican television. Even though it was not broadcast between 1956 and 1990,
televised lucha libre succeeded so well when it returned that it threatened the
health of the sport; by 1995, audience preference for watching the sport from
their living rooms was so strong that wrestling arenas all over the country were
threatened with bankruptcy.

Television's development in Mexico followed a pattern set by the introduction
of radio. As with radio, its first broadcasts were either musical or political; the
first commercial programming began in 1950 with a speech by President
Alemán. As with radio, television soon fell into the hands of the family enterprises (most of all the empires of the O'Farrills and the Azcárragas) that already
dominated other media industries. And as with radio, television broadcasting was
well developed in Mexico City before it became available anywhere else. Television developed more quickly than radio had, however, thanks to the booming
economy of the 1950s and '60s that made investment capital easy to acquire and
created a large pool of potential consumers. The first Mexico City station
appeared in 1950; by 1954, stations had opened in Puebla and Nogales; by 1959,
20 states had at least one TV channel; by 1963, more than a million Mexicans
owned TV sets; by 1966, color broadcasting had begun.

The most important of all the parallels between radio and television was the
prominence of soap operas. Mexican television began experimenting with serial
drama in 1952, including somewhat abridged live performances of Shakespeare
and Beckett produced and directed by playwright, gossip columnist, poet, and
empresario Salvador Novo; in its early years, television was a site where high and
low culture could intermingle. In 1957, the first true daily *telenovela* was broadcast. Radionovelas and telenovelas shared the same basic structure: They were
family-based melodramas that, unlike soap operas from the United States, always

came to a predetermined conclusion after a period of months or years. Telenovela characters, in general, were at least a little richer than those in other mass-media narratives, since (at least in the first few years of TV production) the TV audience was also somewhat wealthier than average. More recently the range of characters has gotten wider, and audiences have devoted themselves to the stories of servant girls as well as heiresses. Mexican audiences have enjoyed locally made products, but imported telenovelas, often somewhat racier, from Venezuela and Brazil have been popular in Mexico too.

Around 1960, the history of television in Mexico began to diverge from radio and all other media industries. Rather than having to fight for its position against competition from abroad, Mexican television not only came to dominate its own market but also spread rapidly around the rest of the world. In 1961, the Azcárraga family purchased a TV station in San Antonio, Texas, the beginnings of what became their Spanish-language U.S. network Univisión. For legal and administrative purposes Univisión and Televisa did very well in Spanish-speaking markets, and the Mexican networks had global hits, too. Televisa exported the soap opera *Los ricos también lloran* (The Rich Cry, Too), which had been popular in the late 1970s, to Europe and Latin American in 1986. By 1990, it was the most popular program, a national obsession in Russia, and the following year Vietnam, too, succumbed to its charms. Nobody could explain quite why this particular soap opera meant so much to these audiences, but its popularity made it difficult for its star, Veronica Castro (who had subsequently become a broadcast journalist in the intervening years) to work in either country, because of the adoring crowds that followed her everywhere.

Such was the power of soap operas that the government attempted to use them to address social problems. Televisa cooperated, since it was heavily dependent on the lack of state intervention to maintain its near monopoly on comercial broadcasting (a monopoly that it lost when some educational stations were privatized in 1993, creating a second private network called TV Azteca). In 1970, for example, writer Daniel Cosío Villegas proposed a sweeping revision of the Constitution of 1917; the state responded by adding the constitution itself to the national pantheon of revolutionary heroes, and as part of this effort encouraged an especially lavish production of a soap opera, starring the much loved María Félix, called *La constitución*. The Department of Public Education supervised a 1975 telenovela called *Ven conmigo* (Come with Me) that was supposed to encourage students to stay in school, and a 1977 soap opera *Acompáñame* (Accompany Me) promoted family planning.

The rise of the telenovela contributed to the decline of Mexican cinema. By 1950, the glory days of the local film industry had passed, in part due to a shift of resources toward television. In some cases this movement had aesthetic purposes. Gifted director Julio Bracho, for example, first directed a soap opera in 1962 because it seemed that he would never be able to express himself on film; his 1960 film *La sombra del caudillo* (The Shadow of the Boss), a lightly fictionalized

Octavio Paz, Mexico's foremost literary figure, earned his reputation with his book-length meditation on the national character entitled *The Labyrinth of Solitude*. Throughout his career, he served as the literary conscience of the nation. He received international recognition when he was awarded the Nobel prize for literature. Here the Nobel laureate autographs copies of his last book, *Bislumbres en la India* (*Glimpses of India*) in 1995.

account of an ugly struggle among ex-revolutionaries for political power, was immediately censored and remained unseen for 30 years. More often, though, film industry resources were moved into television because TV was not in direct competition with Hollywood and thus its profit margins were considerably higher, as in 1968 when San Angel Inn studios—one of the nation's best filmmaking facilities—switched to video. Another of the historic production facilities in Mexico City, Churubusco, survived through the 1980s by renting itself out to Hollywood moviemakers: David Lynch made *Dune* there, for example.

Movies continued to be made in Mexico after 1950. In fact, production peaked in 1958, when 138 movies were produced. Even at its least active moments in the early 1970s and mid–1990s, the Mexican film industry still produced more movies than any other Latin American nation's. The problem was that the quality of Mexican cinema declined precipitously as movie producers tried to maximize profits under increasingly competitive circumstances. Oligopolistic chains of movie houses strongly preferred to show Hollywood movies, so Mexican films had trouble finding audiences unless they were significantly cheaper. Even then, owners of theater chains demanded that the movies all aim themselves toward the broadest possible audiences. The state was increasingly enmeshed in the industry through the Banco Cinematográfico and other agencies, but its efforts were directed at the protection of the wealthy few who had already grown rich in the movie business (including the theater owners) rather than at improving the quality of Mexican film. Between 1960 and the present, a few directors—notably Jaime Humberto Hermosillo, Alfonso Arua, and María Novaro—have managed to make serious films and have earned international reputations in doing so. But they are exceptional and for the most part their work is rarely seen in most of Mexico.

Viewers began to refer to many movies made in Mexico as *churros* as early as 1950, comparing them to the machine-made crullers for sale on many city street corners: Like churros, Mexican movies were enjoyable but not nourishing, rapidly made, soon forgotten, identical to one another, and cheap. (Churros' vaguely fecal shape may also have contributed to the comparison inherent in this bit of slang.) Churros helped sell other kinds of mass culture. As the Azcárraga family's power in media grew, more and more movies starred soap-opera actors or pop-music singers associated with their other businesses. In 1954 alone, for example, more than 30 movies were based on the new dance, the *cha-cha-chá*. Churros were generic, and the genres included not only the familiar Hollywood categories of horror or science fiction but also truck driver and lucha libre films. The exploits of a lady truck driver, Lola la trailera, formed the basis for an especially popular series of the 1960s and '70s; another, more recent series of comedies records the mishaps of a rural woman, la India María, a wise innocent who gives city slickers their comeuppance; but the most successful of all probably was the series of movies starring the wrestler El Santo. Sometimes churros could be quite pleasurable, but even participants recognized their low quality: El Santo, for one, claimed to believe that his fans attended his movies out of pity.

Mexicans purchased more and more material comforts after 1940, as the amount of domestically made media available to them grew exponentially. Radio, television, film, and print all told audiences what they already seemed to believe: Though Mexico still had its problems, its past was glorious and its future was bright. But in the middle of the 1950s, dissenting voices made themselves heard, first in the realm of the fine arts and then in mass culture, too. This dissent took the form of a multifaceted critique of official nationalism and an attempt to adopt contemporary European and American philosophies and culture. Some such movements inevitably achieved respectability and became part of Mexico's official culture themselves. More recently both low and high culture have involved themselves with reformulating the now outmoded icons of national identity, recycling them as a way of remaking Mexico's social and political reality.

One shocking moment of dissent from the official culture of the Revolution came from a group of young painters in 1954, when it published a manifesto denouncing the muralist movement as compromised, sentimental, and lacking in aesthetic standards. One of these painters, José Luis Cuevas, restated this critique in a 1957 essay wittily titled *La cortina de nopal* (The Cactus Curtain). Diego

Rivera had painted his last murals in 1953; an era had ended. With these texts the new generation of artists had announced itself as committed to abstraction and self-expression, just like the leading artists of Paris and New York.

Even more important was the 1950 publication of a brilliant essay by the young poet and diplomat Octavio Paz, *El laberinto de la soledad* (The Labyrinth of Solitude). The French existentialists, especially Sartre and Camus, strongly influenced Paz; his essay adapted their ideas to the course of Mexican history. Paz posed the question of the origin of Mexican national character, which he called violent, solitary, and misogynist. This problematic character resulted from the formative influence of male shame, Paz decreed, at the origin of Mexico in the treachery of Malinche, the indigenous woman without whom Cortés could never have conquered Mexico. According to Paz, all (male) Mexicans felt themselves to be "hijos de la chingada," sons of the raped woman, and the Revolution was best understood as an outburst of this isolated masculine shame transformed into a moment of communal violence. Thus Mexican history in general and the the Revolution in particular were both masculinized and depoliticized in Paz's influential essay. And although Paz spent much of his career in the diplomatic corps and did engage with the oppositional politics of 1968 (he resigned his ambassadorship to India in protest of the Tlatelolco massacre), he generally stood outside government, neither to the left nor the right but—like the antimuralist painters—arguing that real art could not be politicized at all.

Existentialism spread more broadly through Mexican intellectual society through translation projects undertaken in the magazine *El Corno Emplumado* after 1959, the same year in which the first Parisian-style "existentialist cafés" opened in Mexico City. Meanwhile, other philosophical currents from abroad also influenced Mexican intellectuals, especially the ferment of decolonization in Africa and the Cuban Revolution. The existentialist cafés soon had competition from folk music cafés, which drew inspiration equally from North American beatniks and from the "new song" movement that accompanied the Latin American revolutionary movements of the era. More seriously, the revolutionary movements of the era led novelist Carlos Fuentes (also a member of the diplomatic service) to reevaluate the Mexican Revolution and its aftermath in a series of novels that described the gradual betrayal of a grand social movement. Fuentes stayed well to the left of Octavio Paz, supporting the Cuban and Nicaraguan revolutions abroad and the Democratic Revolutionary Party at home; eventually their rivalry evolved to include their separate groups of supporters and disciples (referred to as "mafias") and two separate literary magazines. The rivalry ended with Paz's death in 1998, but the magazines remain as a memorial to it.

The United States also exerted its influence on intellectuals of the time. In 1964, positivist social science made an impact when the government-sponsored publishing house Fondo de Cultura Económica translated Oscar Lewis's ethnography of a Mexico City family, *The Children of Sánchez*. The book's notoriety grew when the government withdrew it from circulation as an insult to the nation and the much respected head of the publishing house, Arnaldo Orfila Reynal, lost his job. Orfila Reynal went on to found the publisher Siglo XXI with financial support from prominent Mexican authors, and a 1966 Supreme Court decision allowed another publisher, Editorial Joaquín Mortiz, to reprint Lewis's book. The hullabaloo helped make the reprinted version the best-selling book the publisher ever had. Meanwhile, writer Elena Poniatowska adapted Lewis's style of ethnography, which used his (generally poor and often illiterate) subject's own tape-recorded words to tell their stories. Lewis used his method to reinforce the appearance of scientific objectivity, but Poniatowska transformed it into a vehicle for social and political outrage on behalf of the powerless. Her novels mixed interview material with her own imagination to describe the lives of soldaderas (in *Hasta no verte Jesús mío*) and artists (in *Tinísima*); her book-length journalistic essays (*La noche de Tlatelolco* on the 1968 massacre, and *Nada, nadie* on the 1985 Mexico City earthquake) mingled many people's words—including ironic quotations from government officials as well as the survivors' voices—to provide moving accounts of these events.

The strongest influence of the United States, however, came through the power of mass media. The teen-rebel movies of the 1950s and '60s (such as *Rebel without a Cause* and *Jailhouse Rock*) fascinated young audiences precisely because their narratives of generational tension were so different from the family melodramas of Mexican film, radio, television, and print. Rock music, on the other hand, initially entered Mexico because it fit the familiar category of the dance craze; it seemed no different than the mambo, rumba, and cha-cha-chá, all of which had been imported from abroad and adapted to local tastes in the 1940s and '50s. Thus the first Mexican rock records (from 1959) were called *refritos*, as in "refried beans," because bands like Los Teen Tops and Los Rebeldes de Roc carefully reproduced hits from the United States with Spanish-language lyrics. Mexican television quickly picked up on this new trend precisely because it seemed no different from any other fashion in music and dance. Shows such as *Orfeón* a go go presented even those bands that rejected the refritos model and sang their own songs (sometimes in English for the sake of authenticity), such as Los Dug Dugs and Three Souls in My Mind, as if they were oddly dressed versions of the Caribbean groups popular in the 1950s.

All this changed with the advent of *la onda* (the wave), a cultural movement that began around 1965, loosely analogous to the French New Wave or the counterculture of the United States. *La onda* novelists such as José Agustín ignored local dance music but wove the rebellious lyrics of The Beatles and the Rolling Stones into their prose. *La onda* director Alejandro Jodorowsky made dreamy, mystical films and theater pieces that seemed more than a little influenced by drugs. Writers such as Carlos Monsiváis and José Joaquín Blanco invented *la onda* journalism, full of references to imported rock music and rigorously irreverent toward anything that smacked of official culture. *La onda* fashion required long hair on boys and longer hair on girls—which, satisfyingly, shocked the respectable opinion that had been quite willing to absorb rock music. There were even *la onda* comic books, as Rius (Eduardo del Río) produced first Los supermachos and then, after that was censored, Los agachados, both witty, didactic, and up-to-date versions of comedia ranchera, but from a strongly left-wing perspective.

La onda participants flocked to see whatever versions of the U.S. counterculture arrived in Mexico. Often these were events that the government shut down before many people could attend them, such as a series of concerts by the Doors in Mexico City in 1969. Also in 1969, the musical *Hair* was closed in Acapulco after the actors added references to Tlatelolco to the script. Local events, too, faced censorship; the Echeverría administration stopped a 1971 rock festival called Avándaro, a self-conscious attempt at creating a Mexican Woodstock, before it could get fully under way. In any case the attraction of rock music from England and the United States for the angry youth of the late 1960s and '70s was that it was *not* Mexican. Participants in la onda reacted angrily to the bankruptcy of government rhetoric and expressed disgust with the sentimentality of Mexican commercial culture: They turned to artistic movements from abroad as the absolute opposite of these unacceptable discourses. Mexican imitations of U.S. music and fashion would not do. (Ironically, at the same moment a folkloric, "authentic" image of Mexico had become quite fashionable among participants in the counterculture of the United States.)

La onda had vanished from public view by the mid–1970s. Student protests had, for the most part, been smashed. The artists and writers associated with the movement had either transcended it (as with Monsiváis), left the country (like Jodorowsky), or stopped working. The Zona Rosa of Mexico City, the geographic center of the movement, evolved into an expensive tourist trap. Rius abandoned the comic-book business and began producing unique *info-libros* for a much smaller audience (one of the first is available in English as *Marx for Beginners*). The best band of the era, Three Souls in My Mind, survived into the '90s; in fact, its popularity grew from year to year, but it achieved this feat by renaming itself (in Spanish) El TRI. But the movement had a lasting impact on Mexican cultural life. The advent of neoliberalism in Mexican political discourse, in a sense, could be described as the ultimate triumph of this sensibility. President Salinas belonged to the same generation as the rebels of la onda, and though nobody would suggest he shared their tastes in any other respect, he, too, was willing to break with decades of rhetorical *mexicanidad* and legitimize his ideas by emphasizing that they came from abroad.

Whatever its origin, the wave of privatization and deregulation of the Salinas years had enormous impact on Mexican mass media and popular culture. Decreasing support for the film industry threw it into a crisis that could well mark its death throes. Privatization did not threaten the dominance of the media conglomerates (and, reciprocally, in 1991 they were discovered to be among the multimillion-dollar supporters of the PRI). But by ending most public broadcasting and opening up the cable business, the government made far more imported television from the United States available and allowed the arrival of the slightly more critical TV Azteca, a second private network. U.S. series such as *Beavis and*

Butthead and *The Simpsons* soon found an audience, although they may have been understood differently in Mexico than they were in the United States. The bootleg Bart Simpson souvenirs sold throughout urban Mexico in 1992 did not have the kinds of sarcastic slogans attached that English-language Bart spouted; instead, they showed Bart pronouncing such sappy proverbs as "You only have one mother."

The Salinas administration substantially loosened controls on print journalism, primarily by doing away with the government paper wholesaler PIPSA. This may have resulted from a cynical calculation, on the part of the government, as to the relative unimportance of the written word compared to broadcast media. And a shift toward independent investigative journalism had already begun with the founding, in 1976, of the weekly *Proceso*. Journalism remained a dangerous career in Mexico—human rights organizations regularly complained that reporters are threatened, beaten, kidnapped, tortured, and murdered—and bribery was even more common, a more or less accepted way to supplement extremely low salaries in print media. The Mexico City daily *La Jornada*, for example, has sometimes printed government press releases almost verbatim, but it used an italic typeface on the headlines of those pieces so that the readers can be on their guars. However, in the capital and a few other cities, reliable daily papers finally appeared in the 1990s.

Finally, the 1990s saw Mexican culture—high and low—turning away from the melodramatic formulas of earlier years as the audience for both telenovelas and comic books shrank drastically. But artists, writers, musicians, painters, and actors also refused direct adaptations of models from abroad. Instead, they mined the language, mythologies, and iconography of the past to comment (frequently with some irony) on the present. Upscale restaurants stopped serving French cuisine and instead began inventing highly refined versions of local dishes. Carlos Monsiváis began writing a hilarious newspaper column that was a pitch-perfect parody of the voice of officialdom. Avant-garde rock band Cafe Tacuba (named after a historic hangout turned tourist destination) played tunes dedicated to comic-book villainess Raratonga, and reconfigured versions of mariachi standards; the more popular band Maldita Vecindad borrowed its look from the British punks but melded Mexican instrumentation with electric guitar and bass. Starlet Gloria Trevi reveled in scandal (producing a series of nudie calendars, for instance) but also announced with apparent seriousness that she intended to be president someday, playing cleverly with the normal expectations for Televisa-supported pop stars. A film called *Adiós, adiós, ídolo mío* (Farewell, My Idol) affectionately imagined the wrestler El Santo, star of innumerable churros, as a fat old man who could not accept retirement; meanwhile, a community organizer who called himself Superbarrio and always appeared in full lucha libre costume, mask and all, became an important figure on the Mexican left in the aftermath of the 1985 earthquake, bringing the political subtext of wrestling into the open.

The ultimate in this turn toward the postmodern in Mexican culture was the appearance of the Zapatista guerrillas in Chiapas on New Year's Day, 1994.

Rather than directly proclaiming their grievances against the Mexican state and transnational enterprise, the Zapatistas spoke in a playful, metaphorical style through the charming written pronouncements of their leader, Subcomandante Marcos. Though their name—and even the fact of their armed rebellion—was in itself profoundly nostalgic, they quickly asserted their attachment to modernity through their practice of communicating via the Internet. (Whether or not Marcos really used a solar-powered laptop with a satellite uplink did not matter as much as the idea that this might be plausible.) The masks they always wore, like Superbarrio's outfit, referred to the beloved sport of lucha libre but also made an implicit promise that they would not allow themselves to be co-opted or used by the state. A much photographed 1999 game of soccer, played by the rebels (in their trademark ski masks) against a group of professionals, underlined the playfulness and mexicanidad of the movement.

With Superbarrio and the Zapatistas, as with the less overtly political forms of Mexican postmodernity, popular culture had made a crucial leap. Performers and audiences had—at least temporarily—used such devices as parody, pastiche, and quotation to regain control of the collective memory from the state and the media. Whether or not they can continue to set the terms in which the past and future can be discussed remains an open question.

Glossary

✦ ✦

alcabala Sales tax imposed every time an item was sold or resold.

alcalde Local official charged with a wide variety of executive, legislative and judicial functions.

Ateneo de la Juventud Forum of intellectuals and artists calling for cultural renewal in the early twentieth century.

audiencia Colonial agency with multiple functions including serving as the highest court of appeals in the viceroyalty.

autos de fé Public punishments of different severity meted out by the Holy Office of the Inquisition for transgressions of orthodoxy.

ayuntamiento Municipal town council, also known as a cabildo.

Bajío Geographic region comprising the high plains of central Mexico, most notably the state of Guanajuato.

balche Intoxicating beverage which the Maya made from honey and flavored with a special bark.

Bases Orgánicas Constitution adopted in 1843.

beatas Women of piety, but not nuns, who were placed in charge of educating Indian girls during the colonial period.

Black Legend Particularly negative view of the Spanish endeavor in the New World espoused by England and other European rivals.

Bourbon Reforms Series of administrative readjustments and economic changes instituted for New Spain in the eighteenth century as the Bourbons replaced the Habsburgs on the Spanish throne.

bracero Literally, "those with arms." The term refers to Mexican farm laborers who worked in the United States during and immediately after World War II.

brigantine Small sailing ship, generally with two masts, used by Cortés during the conquest of Mexico.

cabecera Major town in an administrative district.

cacique Originally referred to local Indian chief but later applied to any political leader. The feminine variation is cacica.

calaveras Animated skeletons brought out for special fiestas such as the Day of the Dead.

camarilla Political interest group often pledging allegiance to a single individual.

camino real Royal road linking Mexico City and Santa Fe, New Mexico.

campesino Rural farm worker or peasant.

Capitulations of Santa Fe Written agreements concluded in April of 1492 between Queen Isabel and Columbus spelling out the rights he would enjoy by virtue of future discovery.

Cardenista Follower of Lázaro Cárdenas in the 1930s and of Cuauhtémoc Cárdenas in the 1990s.

Carrancista Follower of Venustiano Carranza.

casta Generic term referring to classifications of persons of mixed race.

caudillo Local, state, or national political leader who generally relies on force to remain in power.

causeway A raised roadway across a body of water such as the one Cortés marched across to reach Tenochtitlan.

CCM Mexican Peasant Confederation active in the 1930s.

Chaac Maya God of Rain.

charros Athletic rodeo performers dressed in highly stylized cowboy costumes.

Chichimeca Generic name for a variety of nomadic tribes some of whom migrated from the far north into Central Mexico.

chinampa Floating garden or raised agricultural field used by the Aztecs on the lakes of central Mexico.

científicos Positivist advisors to Porfirio Díaz.

Cinco de Mayo The Fifth of May national holiday commemorating the Mexican victory over the French in 1862.

Ciudad Universitaria Sprawling site of the National Autonomous University of Mexico.

CNOP National Confederation of Popular Organizations.

cochineal A brilliant red dye produced from the scale of an insect which thrives on the nopal cactus and is found primarily in Oaxaca.

comal Flat earthenware pan for preparing tortillas.

comercio libre Free trade within the eighteenth century Spanish American empire.

commadre, compadre Godmother or godfather.

criollo Person of Spanish parentage but born in Mexico.

Cristero rebellion Pro-Catholic and anti-revolutionary revolt in Mexico, 1926–1929.

CROM Regional Confederation of Mexican Labor, a national labor union established by Luis Morones.

cruzada Tax imposed by the Roman Catholic Church for the sale of an indulgence.

CTM Confederation of Mexican Workers, a union founded by labor leader Vicente Lombaro Toledano.

decena trágica Ten tragic days (February 9 to February 18, 1913) during which Mexico City became a revolutionary battlefield.

ejidatario Person who resides on and works on a communal farm.

ejido Communal farm which is worked in common and on which profits are shared.

El Aguila British owned petroleum company in Mexico until expropriated in 1938.

El Buen Tono Manufacturer of cigarettes and cigars.

El Hijo de Ahuizote Satirical newspaper highly critical of the Díaz regime.

encomendero Individual in the colonial period to whom an encomienda is awarded.

encomienda Grant of Indians for the purpose of collecting tribute and labor.

escoceses Scottish rite masons who supported conservative goals in the early nineteenth century.

federales Members of an armed military unit controlled by the national government.

First Chief Title awarded to Venustiano Carranza during the Constitutionalist Revolution.

fueros Special privileges granted to army officers and clergymen during the nineteenth century exempting them from the jurisdiction of civil courts.

gachupín Slightly derisive term referring to a peninsular or Spaniard residing in Mexico.

Grito de Dolores Call to arms made by Father Miguel Hidalgo de Costilla on September 16, 1910, initiating the struggle for Mexican independence.

hacienda Large landed estate devoted to agricultural production or cattle ranching.

hacendado Owner of an hacienda.

harquebus Heavy matchlock gun invented in Spain in the fifteenth century and used by the Spaniards during the conquest of Mexico.

hechicería Witchcraft often associated with an Indian medicine man or shaman.

henequen Tropical plant used for the production of coarse fiber and grown on large haciendas in southern Mexico.

hidalgo Member of the colonial aristocracy, sometimes holding titles of nobility.

hijo natural Child born out of wedlock.

Hill of the Bells Site of Maximilian's execution on the outskirts of Querétaro.

historietas Comic books, often containing serialized stories.

Holy Office of the Inquisition Ecclesiastical court of the Roman Catholic Church charged with enforcing Catholic orthodoxy.

Hora Nacional Weekly patriotic programming which all radio stations were required to broadcast under penalty of law.

Huertista Follower of Victoriano Huerta.

Huitzilopochtli Major Aztec deity. God of War and God of the Sun.

IFE Federal Election Commission.

indigenismo Indianist movement seeking to advance Indian cultural values.

intendancy Political subdivision instituted in the eighteenth century as part of the Bourbon Reforms.

jefe máximo Absolute leader and the popular term referring to the rule of Plutarco Elías Calles.

jefes políticos Political bosses or nineteenth-century provincial officials with duties similar to that of a governor.

jornalero Day laborer in both Spain and Mexico, primarily one who works in the fields.

latifundio Concentration of land into large holdings.

leva System of forced conscription employed to fill federal ranks during the Díaz regime and the Mexican Revolution.

limpieza de sangre Literally purity of blood, this concept was used in Spain and Mexico to justify the tracing of lineage to determine social status and class.

lucha libre Professional wrestling, Mexican style, playing an important role in popular culture and depicting the eternal clash between good (the técnicos) and evil (the rudos).

maguey Century plant of the genus agave.

Manga de Clavo Santa Anna's hacienda in the state of Veracruz.

manta Woven cloth, most commonly used as a blanket, shawl, or tapestry.

maquiladoras Twin plants straddling the United States–Mexican border where goods are assembled on the Mexican side for distribution on the United States side.

maximato Six year period (1928–1934) following the Calles presidency during which the former president ruled Mexico from behind the scenes.

Mesoamerica Embracing southeastern Mexico and western Central America, this region housed scores of vibrant pre-Hispanic cultures.

mestizaje Miscegenation or racial mixture.

mestizo Person of mixed white and Indian ancestry.

Metro Vast subway network of Mexico City.

milpa A small plot of farm land generally devoted to the cultivation of corn.

Mixton War Serious Indian uprising which occurred from 1540 to 1542 primarily in the modern state of Jalisco.

Monte Albán Zapotec capital in Oaxaca.

mordida A bribe offered to or demanded by a government official.

mulato Person of mixed white and black ancestry.

NAFTA North American Free Trade Agreement.

Nahuatl Uto-Aztecan language of the Aztecs and many other tribes of central Mexico.

New Christians Spanish Jews who converted to Christianity. Many migrated to Mexico in the sixteenth century.

Olmec Tribe considered the mother culture of Mexico and located primarily in the modern state of Veracruz.

obraje Colonial workshop or factory usually producing textiles and invariably with few, if any, protections for the workers.

Opata Indian tribe located primarily in the modern state of Sonora.

Order and Progress Positivist slogan utilized during the Díaz regime.

Otomí Indian tribe found today in much of central Mexico.

PAN National Action Party which in the 1990s gained strength and became the major conservative opposition to the PRI.

PARM Authentic Party of the Mexican Revolution.

patria Fatherland, a term Mexicans often use to designate their country or their place of local origin.

patria potestas Legal right of a father to control the life and property of his unmarried children.

peninsulares Persons born in Spain or the Iberian Peninsula.

Pimería Alta Territory occupied by the Pima Indians in northern Sonora and southern Arizona.

PIPSA State-owned company exerting tremendous influence over the press by virtue of its monopoly on newsprint until its dissolution in the 1990s.

Plan de Ayala Zapata's Plan calling for major agrarian reform.

Plan de San Luis Potosí Madero's plan calling for the overthrow of Porfirio Díaz.

PNR National Revolutionary Party which dominated Mexican political life in the 1920s and 1930s.

porfiriato Period of Mexican history encompassing the regime of Porfirio Díaz during the years 1876 to 1911.

pragmática Royal ordinance or decree.

PRD Revolutionary Democratic Party, an influential left-of-center opposition party.

PRI Revolutionary Institutional Party, the dominant political party of the second half of the twentieth century.

principales In Native American communities members of the nobility or other persons of high distinction.

PRM Party of the Mexican Revolution and successor to the PNR.

pronunciamiento Rebellion or military uprising.

Proceso Weekly news magazine to which leading intellectuals contribute regularly.

pulque Fermented juice made from the maguey and a source of intoxication among the poor.

pulquería Drinking establishment serving pulque.

Quetzalcóatl Feathered serpent and the benevolent Aztec God of Knowledge.

Radionovelas Radio soap operas.

ranchero Small independent farmer or rancher.

Regeneración The Flores Magón newspaper, important in the pre-history of the Mexican Revolution of 1910.

regidores Local officials sitting on the ayuntamiento, or town council.

repartimiento A division of goods or services. Also designated a system of forced labor for wages during the colonial period.

requerimiento A summons to the Indians informing them to accept Christianity and vow loyalty to the Spanish Crown. Failure to obey entitled the Spaniards to embark upon a "just war."

residencia Judicial inquiry conducted at the end of an official's term of office during the colonial period.

rurales Rural constabulary utilized to eliminate banditry and enforce law and order during the late nineteenth and early twentieth century.

Santanista Follower of Antonio López de Santa Anna.

SEP Secretariat of Public Education.

sexenio A six-year presidential term without possibility of re-election.

slash and burn An agricultural system in which the ground cover is cut back, placed in piles, and burned, leaving fields available for planting.

shaman Native American religious leader.

Siete Leyes Constitution of 1836.

Siete Partidas A thirteenth-century Spanish law code which considerable applicability in the Viceroyalty of New Spain.

soldaderas Female soldiers, some reaching officer rank, who served during the Mexican Revolution.

stelae Sculptured stone facings used for decorative purposes on some Indian buildings and monuments.

Tarahumara Indian tribes located primarily in the modern state of Chihuahua.

Tarascan Indian tribe located primarily in the modern state of Michoacán.

Tlaloc Aztec God of Rain.

Tecos A secret neo-fascist and virulently anti-semitic organization for many years based at the Universidad Autónoma de Guadalajara.

Tenochtitlán Aztec capital and site of modern-day Mexico City.

tertulias Social gatherings during which invited guests discussed literature and the arts as well as vital topics of the day.

telenovela Television soap opera.

Tenth Muse Title commonly used to describe Sor Juana Inés de la Cruz.

Tepehuán Indian tribe residing primarily in the modern states of Chihuahua and Durango.

Tezcatlipoca Smoking Mirror and Aztec God of the Night.

tierra caliente The warmer regions of Mexico, generally associated with the two coasts.

tierra fria The cooler regions of Mexico, generally associated with the mountains.

Totonac Indian tribe located primarily in the modern state of Veracruz and who became allies of Cortés during the conquest.

Treaty of Guadalupe Hidalgo Treaty ending the war between Mexico and the United States in 1848 in which Mexico was forced to cede half of its national territory to the United States.

Trigarante Iturbide's independence movement consisting of three guarantees—religion, independence, and unity.

Viceroyalty of New Spain Subject to the jurisdiction of a viceroy sitting in Mexico City this major administrative unit included all of present day Mexico, Spain's Caribbean Islands, most of Central America and the southwest and west coast of the United States.

Villista Follower of Pancho Villa.

Virgin of Guadalupe Patroness of Mexico who first appeared to the Indian Juan Diego in the sixteenth century.

visitas Tours of inspection for the purpose of examining officials during the colonial period.

Xochimilco Lake in the Valley of Mexico and site of the chinampas or floating gardens.

Yaqui Indian tribe located primarily in the modern state of Sonora.

yorkinos York rite masons who supported liberal goals during the early nineteenth century.

Zapatista In the early twentieth century follower of Emiliano Zapata and in the late twentieth century member of an anti-government rebellion in Chiapas.

Zipe Toltec Our Flayed Lord and the God of springtime, planting and renewal.

Zimmerman Telegram German proposal for an alliance with Mexico in 1917.

zócalo Mexico City's main central plaza known more formally as the Plaza de la Constitución.

Bibliography

✦ ✦

Aiton, Arthur S. *Antonio de Mendoza: First Viceroy of New Spain.* Durham, NC: Duke University Press, 1927.

Altman, Ida. *Emigrants and Society: Extremadura and Spanish America in the Sixteenth Century.* Berkeley: University of California Press, 1989.

Anna, Timothy E. *Forging of Mexico, 1821–1835.* Lincoln: University of Nebraska Press, 1998.

———. *The Mexican Empire of Iturbide.* Lincoln: University of Nebraska Press, 1990.

Bailey, David C *¡Viva Cristo Rey! The Cristero Rebellion and the Church—State Conflict in Mexico.* Austin: University of Texas Press, 1974.

Baudot, Georges. *Utopia and History in Mexico: The First Chronicles of Mexican Civilization 1520–1569.* Niwot: University Press of Colorado, 1995.

Bedini, Silvio A. *The Christopher Columbus Encyclopedia.* New York: Simon & Schuster, 1992.

Beezley, William H. *Insurgent Governor: Abraham González and the Mexican Revolution in Chihuahua.* Lincoln: University of Nebraska Press, 1973.

Berdan, Frances F., et. al., eds. *Aztec Imperial Strategies.* Washington, D.C.: Dumbarton Oaks Research Library and Collection, 1993.

Booth, George C. *Mexico's School-Made Society.* Stanford: Stanford University Press, 1941.

Bosques, Gilberto. *The National Revolutionary Party of Mexico and the Six-Year Plan.* Mexico City: Bureau of Foreign Information of the National Revolutionary Party, 1937.

Boyer, Richard. *Lives of the Bigamists: Marriage, Family, and Community in Colonial Mexico.* Albuquerque: University of New Mexico Press, 1995.

Brading, David. *Miners and Merchants in Bourbon Mexico, 1763–1810.* Cambridge: Cambridge University Press, 1971.

Brenner, Anita. *The Wind that Swept Mexico.* New York: Harper & Brothers, 1943.

Bricker, Victoria Reifler. *The Indian Christ, the Indian King: The Historical Substrate of Maya Myth and Ritual.* Austin: University of Texas Press, 1981.

Burkhart, Louise M. *The Slippery Earth: Nahua-Christian Moral Dialogue in Sixteenth-Century Mexico.* Tucson: University of Arizona Press, 1989.

Campbell, Randolph B. *An Empire for Slavery: The Peculiar Institution in Texas.* Baton Rouge: Louisiana State University Press, 1989.

Camp, Roderick Ai. *Crossing Swords: Religion and Politics in Mexico.* New York: Oxford University Press, 1997.

————. *Politics in Mexico: Democratizing Authoritarianism.* Third edition. New York: Oxford University Press, 1999.

Carr, Barry. *Marxism and Communism in Twentieth-Century Mexico.* Lincoln: University of Nebraska Press, 1992.

Centeno, Miguel A. *Democracy Within Reason: Technocratic Revolution in Mexico.* Second edition. University Park: Pennsylvania State University Press, 1997.

Cervantes, Fernando. *The Devil in the New World: The Impact of Diabolism in New Spain.* New Haven, Conn.: Yale University Press, 1994.

Chamberlain, Robert S. *The Conquest and Colonization of Yucatan, 1517–1550.* Washington, D.C.: Carnegie Institute, 1948.

Charlot, Jean. *The Mexican Mural Renaissance, 1920–1925.* New Haven, Conn.: Yale University Press, 1963.

Christian, William A. Jr. *Local Religion in Sixteenth-Century Spain.* Princeton: Princeton University Press, 1981.

Clark, Marjorie Ruth. *Organized Labor in Mexico.* Chapel Hill: University of North Carolina Press, 1934.

Coe, Sophie D. *America's First Cuisines.* Austin: University of Texas Press, 1994

Columbus, Christopher. *The Book of Priveleges Issued to Christopher Columbus by King Fernando and Queen Isabel 1492–1502.* Edited and translated by Helen Nader. Los Angeles: University of California Press, 1996.

Cook, Maria Lorena, Kevin J. Middlebrook, and Juan Molinar Horcasitas, eds. *The Politics of Economic Restructuring: State-Society Relations and Regime Change in Mexico.* La Jolla: U.S.-Mexico Studies Center, 1994.

Cook, Sherburne F. *Soil Erosion and Population in Central Mexico.* Berkeley: University of California Press, 1949.

Cope, Douglas R. *The Limits of Racial Domination: Plebeian Society in Colonial Mexico City, 1660–1720.* Madison: University of Wisconsin Press, 1994.

Cornelius, Wayne. *Politics and the Migrant Poor in Mexico City.* Stanford: Stanford University Press, 1975.

Cornelius, Wayne, Judith Gentleman, and Peter H. Smith, eds. *Mexico's Alternative Political Futures.* La Jolla: U.S.-Mexico Studies Center, 1989.

Cortés, Hernando. *Letters from Mexico.* New Haven, Conn.: Yale University Press, 1986.

Costeloe, Michael P. *The Central Republic in Mexico, 1835–1846: Hombres de Bien in the Age of Santa Anna.* Cambridge: Cambridge University Press, 1993.

————. *Church and State in Independent Mexico: A Study of the Patronage Debate, 1821–1857.* London: Royal Historical Society, 1978.

Cronon, Edmund David. *Josephus Daniels in Mexico.* Madison: University of Wisconsin Press, 1960.

Crosby, Alfred. *Ecological Imperialism: The Biological Expansion of Europe, 900–1900.* New York: Cambridge University Press, 1985.

Dabbs, Jack Autrey. *The French Army in Mexico, 1861–1867.* The Hague: Mouton, 1963.

Dauster, Frank. *Xavier Villaurrutia.* New York: Twayne, 1971.

DePalo, William A. *The Mexican National Army, 1822–1852.* College Station: Texas A&M University Press, 1997.

Díaz del Castillo, Bernal. Genaro Garcia, ed. A.P. Maudslay, trans. *The Discovery and Conquest of Mexico, 1517–1521.* New York: Farrar, Straus & Giroux, 1970.

Drexler, Robert W. *Guilty of Making Peace: A Biography of Nicholas Trist.* Lanham, Md.: University Press of America, 1991.

Dulles, John W. F. *Yesterday in Mexico: A Chronicle of the Revolution, 1919–1936.* Austin: University of Texas Press, 1961.

Eisenhower, John S. D. *So Far from God: The United States War Mexico.* New York: Random House, 1989.

Erfani, Julie A. *The Paradox of the Mexican State: Rereading Sovereignty from Independence to NAFTA.* Boulder: Lynne Rienner, 1995.

Farriss, Nancy M. *Maya Society Under Colonial Rule: The Collective Enterprise of Survival.* Princeton: Princeton University Press, 1984.

Fernández-Armesto, Felipe. *Before Columbus: Exploration and Colonisation from the Mediterranean to the Atlantic.* Houndmills, Basingstoke, Hampshire, U.K.: Macmillan Education, 1987.

Folgarait, Leonard. *So Far From Heaven: David Alfaro Siqueiros's The March of Humanity and Mexican Revolutionary Politics.* Cambridge, U.K.: Cambridge University Press, 1987.

Forbes, Jack D. *Apache, Navajo, and Spaniard.* Norman: University of Oklahoma Press, 1960.

Fowler Salamini, Heather. *Agrarian Radicalism in Veracruz, 1920–1938.* Lincoln: University of Nebraska Press, 1977.

Friede, Juan and Benjamin Keen, eds. *Bartolomé de las Casas in History: Toward an Understanding of the Man and his Work.* DeKalb: Northern Illinois University Press, 1971.

Garcia, Canclini, Nestor. *Transforming Modernity: Popular Culture in Mexico.* Austin: University of Texas Press, 1992.

Genauer, Emily. *Rufino Tamayo.* New York: Harry N. Abrams, 1974.

Gerhard, Peter. *A Guide to the Historical Geography of New Spain.* Rev. ed. Norman: University of Oklahoma Press, 1993.

———. *The North Frontier of New Spain.* Rev. ed. Norman: University of Oklahoma Press, 1993.

———. *The Southeast Frontier of New Spain.* Rev. ed. Norman: University of Oklahoma Press, 1993.

Gibson, Charles. *The Aztecs Under Spanish Rule: A History of the Indians of the Valley of Mexico, 1519–1810.* Stanford: Stanford University Press, 1954.

Giles, Mary, ed. *Women in the Inquisition: Spain and the New World.* Baltimore: Johns Hopkins University Press, 1999.

Gosner, Kevin. *Soldiers of the Virgin: The Moral Economy of a Colonial Maya Rebellion.* Tucson: University of Arizona Press, 1992.

Green, Stanley C. *The Mexican Republic: The First Decade, 1823–1832.* Pittsburgh: University of Pittsburgh Press, 1987.

Greenleaf, Richard E. *The Mexican Inquisition of the Sixteenth Century.* Albuquerque: University of New Mexico Press, 1969.

Gruening, Ernest. *Mexico and Its Heritage.* New York: D. Appleton-Century, 1928.

Gruzinski, Serge. *The Conquest of Mexico: The Incorporation of Indian Societies into the Western, 16th-18th Centuries*. Cambridge, Mass.: Polity Press, 1993.

Guardino, Peter F. *Peasants, Politics, and the Formation of Mexico's National State: Guerrero, 1800–1857*. Stanford: Stanford University Press, 1996.

Hale, Charles. *Mexican Liberalism of the Age of Mora*. New Haven, Conn.: Yale University Press, 1967.

———. *The Transformation of Liberalism in Late Nineteenth-Century Mexico*. Princeton: Princeton University Press, 1989.

Hall, Linda. *Alvaro Obregón: Power and Revolution in Mexico, 1911–1920*. College Station, Texas: Texas A&M University Press, 1981.

———. *Oil, Banks and Politics: The United States and Postrevolutionary Mexico, 1917–1924*. Austin: University of Texas Press, 1995

Hamilton, Nora. *The Limits of State Autonomy: Post-Revolutionary Mexico*. Princeton: Princeton University Press, 1982.

Hamnett, Brian. *Juarez*. London: Longman, 1994.

Hansen, Roger D. *The Politics of Mexican Development*. Baltimore: Johns Hopkins University Press, 1971.

Hart, John Mason. *Revolutionary Mexico: The Coming and Process of the Mexican Revolution*. Berkeley: University of California Press, 1987.

———. *Anarchism and the Mexican Working Class, 1860–1931*. Austin: University of Texas Press, 1988.

Hellman, Judith Adler. *Mexico in Crisis*. Second edition. New York: Holmes and Meier, 1983.

Harvey, Neil. *The Chiapas Rebellion: The Struggle for Land and Democracy*. Durham, NC: Duke University Press, 1998.

Herman, Donald L. *The Comintern in Mexico*. Washington, D.C.: Public Affairs Press, 1974.

Herrera, Hayden. *Frida: A Biography of Frida Kahlo*. New York: Harper and Row, 1983.

Hewitt de Alcantara, Cynthia. *Modernizing Mexican Agriculture: Socioeconomic Implications of Technological Change, 1940–1970*. Geneva, Switzerland: United Nations Research Institute for Social Development, 1976.

Hinds Jr., Harold E. and Charles M. Tatum. *Not Just for Children: The Mexican Comic Book in the Late 1960s and 1970s*. Westport, Conn.: Greenwood Press, 1992.

Hofstadter, Dan, ed. *Mexico: 1946–1973*. New York: Facts on File, 1974.

Hooks, Margaret. *Tina Modotti: Photographer and Revolutionary*. San Francisco: Harper, 1993.

Hu-DeHart, Evelyn. *Missionaries, Miners, and Indians: Spanish Contact with the Yaqui Nation of Northwestern New Spain, 1533–1820*. Tucson: University of Arizona Press, 1981.

Huppert, George. *After the Black Death: A Social History of Early Modern Europe*. Bloomington: Indiana University Press, 1998.

Hurlburt, Laurance P. *The Mexican Muralists in the United States*. Albuquerque: University of New Mexico Press, 1989.

Izquierdo, María. *The True Poetry: The Art of María Izquierdo*. New York: Americas Society Art Gallery, 1997.

Johnson, Lyman L. and Sonya Lipsett-Rivera, eds. *The Faces of Honor: Sex, Shame and Violence in Colonial Latin America*. Albuquerque: University of New Mexico Press, 1998.

Jones, Grant D. *The Conquest of the Last Maya Kingdom.* Stanford: Stanford University Press, 1998.

Jones, Oakah. *Nueva Vizcaya: Heartland of the Spanish Frontier.* Albuquerque: University of New Mexico Press, 1988.

Joseph, G. and D. Nugent, eds. *Everyday Forms of State Formation: Revolution and the Negotiation of Rule in Modern Mexico.* Durham, N.C.: Duke University Press, 1994.

Joseph, G. M. *Revolution from Without: Yucatán, Mexico and the United States, 1880–1924.* Cambridge: Cambridge University Press, 1982.

Josephus, Daniels. *Shirt Sleeve Diplomat.* Chapel Hill: University of North Carolina Press, 1947.

Katz, Friedrich. *The Secret War in Mexico: Europe, the United States and the Mexican Revolution.* Chicago: University of Chicago Press, 1981.

Kicza, John E., ed. *The Indian in Latin American History: Resistance, Resilience, and Acculturation.* Wilmington, Del.: Scholarly Resources, 1993.

Kirk, Betty. *Covering the Mexican Front: The Battle of Europe versus America.* Norman: University of Oklahoma Press, 1942.

Knaut, Andrew L. *The Pueblo Revolt of 1680: Conquest and Resistance in Seventeenth-Century New Mexico.* Norman: University of Oklahoma Press, 1995.

Knight, Alan. *The Mexican Revolution.* 2 vols. Cambridge: Cambridge University Press, 1986.

———. *U.S.-Mexican Relations 1910–1940: An Interpretation.* San Diego: Center for U.S.-Mexican Studies, 1987.

Krismaric, Susan. *Manuel Alvarez Bravo.* New York: Museum of Modern Art, 1997.

Lavrin, Asuncion, ed. *Latin American Women: Historical Perspectives.* Westport, Conn.: Greenwood Press, 1978.

Léon-Portilla, Miguel. *Aztec Thought and Culture.* Norman: University of Oklahoma Press, 1990.

Lewis, Oscar. *Five Families: Mexican Case Studies in the Culture of Poverty.* New York: Basic Books, 1959.

Levy, Daniel. *Mexico: Paradoxes of Stability and Change.* Second edition. Boulder: Westview, 1987.

Lipsett-Rivera, Sonya. *To Defend Our Water With the Blood of Our Veins: The Struggles for Resources in Colonial Puebla.* Albuquerque: University of New Mexico Press, 1999.

Lockhart, James. *The Nahuas After the Conquest: A Social and Cultural History of the Indians of Central Mexico, Sixteenth Through Eighteenth Centuries.* Stanford: Stanford University Press, 1992.

MacLachlan, Colin M. and Jaime E. Rodríguez O. *The Forging of the Cosmic Race: A Reinterpretation of Colonial Mexico.* Berkeley: University of California Press, 1980.

Mallon, Florencia E. *Peasant and Nation: The Making of Postcolonial Mexico and Peru.* Berkeley: University of California Press, 1995.

Mexico: Splendors of Thirty Centuries. New York: Metropolitan Museum of Art, 1990.

Meyer, Lorenzo. *Mexico and the United States in the Oil Controversy, 1917–1942.* Austin: University of Texas Press, 1977.

Meyer, Michael C. *Huerta: A Political Portrait.* Lincoln: University of Nebraska Press, 1972.

———. *Mexican Rebel: Pascual Orozco and the Mexican Revolution, 1910–1915.* Lincoln: University of Nebraska Press, 1967.

Meyer, Michael C., William I. Sherman, and Susan M. Deeds. *The Course of Mexican History.* 6th ed. New York : Oxford University Press, 1999.

Mora, Carl. *Mexican Cinema: Reflections of a Society 1896–1988,* 2nd.rev. ed., Berkeley: University of California Press, 1989.

Monsivais, Carlos. *Mexican Postcards.* New York: Verso, 1997.

Monter, William. *Frontiers of Heresy: the Spanish Inquisition from the Basque Lands to Sicily.* Cambridge: Cambridge University Press, 1990.

Morris, Stephen D. Political *Reformism in Mexico: An Overview of Contemporary Mexican Politics.* Boulder: Westview, 1995.

Nader, Helen. *Liberty in Absolutist Spain: The Habsburg Sale of Towns, 1516–1700.* Baltimore: Johns Hopkins University Press, 1990.

Nalle, Sara. *God in La Mancha.* Baltimore: Johns Hopkins University Press, 1992.

Newell, Roberto, and Luis Rubio. *Mexico's Dilemma: The Political Origins of Economic Crisis.* Boulder: Westview, 1984.

Niblo, Stephen R. *Mexico in the 1940s.* Wilmington, DE: SR Books, 1998.

———. *War, Diplomacy, and Development: The United States and Mexico, 1938–1954.* Wilmington, Del.: SR Books, 1995.

Nutini, Hugo G. *Todos Santos in Rural Tlaxcala: A Syncretic, Expressive and Symbolic Analysis of the Cult of the Dead.* Princeton: Princeton University Press, 1988.

Orozco, José Clemente. *An Autobiography.* Translated by Robert C. Stephenson. Austin: University of Texas Press, 1962.

Palmer, Colin A. *Slaves of the White God: Blacks in Mexico.* Cambridge: Cambridge University Press, 1976.

Paranagua, Paulo Antonio, ed. *Mexican Cinema.* London: British Film Institute, 1995.

Parker, Robert L. *Carlos Chávez: Mexico's Modern-Day Orpheus.* Boston: Twayne, 1983.

Patch, Robert W. *Maya and Spaniard in Yucatan, 1648–1812.* Stanford: Stanford University Press, 1993.

Paz Salinas, María Emilia. *Strategy, Security, and Spies: Mexico and the U.S. as Allies in World War II.* University Park, PA: Pennsylvania State University Press, 1997.

Perry, Mary Elizabeth and Anne J. Cruz, eds. *Cultural Encounters: The Impact of the Inquisition in Spain and the New World.* Berkeley: University of California Press, 1991.

Philip, George. *The Presidency in Mexican Politics.* New York: St. Martin's, 1992.

Phillips, William D., Jr. and Carla R. Phillips. *The Worlds of Christopher Columbus.* Cambridge: Cambridge University Press, 1992.

Pike, Frederic B. *Hispanismo.* South Bend, Ind.:University of Notre Dame Press, 1971.

Pike, Ruth. *Enterprise and Adventure: The Genoese in Seville and the Opening of the New World.* Ithaca: Cornell University Press, 1966.

Pletcher, David. *The Diplomacy of Annexation: Texas, Oregon, and the Mexican War.* New York: Columbia University Press, 1973.

Poole, Stafford. *Our Lady of Guadalupe: The Origins and Sources of a Mexican National Symbol 1531–1797.* Tucson: University of Arizona Press, 1995.

Poniatowska, Elena. *Massacre in Mexico.* New York: Viking Press, 1975.

Raat, W. Dirk. *Revoltosos: Mexico's Rebels in the United States, 1903–1923.* College Station: Texas A&M University Press, 1981.

Radding, Cynthia. *Wandering Peoples: Colonialism, Ethnic Spaces, and Ecological Frontiers in Northwest Mexico, 1700–1850.* Durham, NC: Duke University Press, 1997.

Restall, Matthew. *The Maya World: Yucatec Culture and Society, 1550–1850.* Stanford: Stanford University Press, 1997.

Ricard, Robert. *The Spiritual Conquest of Mexico: An Essay on the Evangelizing Methods of the Mendicant Orders, 1523–1572.* Berkeley: University of California Press, 1966.

Richmond, Douglas. *Venustiano Carranza's Nationalist Struggle, 1893–1920.* Lincoln: University of Nebraska Press, 1983.

Rippy, J. Fred. *The United States and Mexico.* New York: AMS Press, 1931.

Rivera, Diego. *Diego Rivera: A Retrospective.* New York: Founders Society, Detroit Institute of Arts, in Association with W.W. Norton, 1986.

Rochfort, Desmond. *Mexican Muralists: Orozco, Rivera, Siqueiros.* New York: Universe, 1993.

Rodriguez, Jaime O., ed. *Patterns of Contention in Mexican History.* Wilmington. Del.: SR Books, 1992.

Roeder, Ralph. *Juárez and His Mexico: A Biographical History.* New York: Viking Press, 1947.

Roett, Riordan, ed. *Political and Economic Liberalization in Mexico: At a Critical Juncture?* Boulder: Lynne Rienner, 1993.

Roth, Norman. *Jews, Visigoths, and Muslims in Medieval Spain: Cooperation and Conflict.* Leiden: E.J. Brill, 1994.

Rubenstein, Anne. *Bad Language, Naked Ladies, and Other Threats to the Nation: A Political History of Comic Books in Mexico.* Durham, NC: Duke University Press, 1998.

Ruiz, Ramón Eduardo. *The Great Rebellion, Mexico 1905–1924.* New York: Norton, 1980.

Russell, Jeffrey Burton. *Inventing the Flat Earth: Columbus and Modern Historians.* New York: Praeger, 1991.

Ryan, James W. *Camerone: The French Foreign Legion's Greatest Battle* Westport, Conn.: Praeger, 1996.

Sahagán, Bernardino De. *Florentine Codex: General History of the Things of New Spain.* 12 vols. Salt Lake City and Santa Fe: University of Utah Press and School for American Research, 1950–82.

Schele, Linda, and David Freidel. *A Forest of Kings: The Untold Story of the Ancient Maya.* New York: William Morrow, 1990.

Schele, Linda, and Mary Ellen Miller. *The Blood of Kings: Dynasty and Ritual in Maya Art.* New York and Fort Worth: George Braziller, Inc., and Kimbell Art Museum, 1986.

Schmidt. Samuel. *The Deterioration of the Mexican Presidency: The Years of Luis Echeverría.* Tucson: University of Arizona Press, 1991.

Schoonover, Thomas D. *The United States in Central America, 1860–1911.* Durham, NC: Duke University Press, 1991.

Schroeder, Susan, gen. ed. *Codex Chimalpahin.* 6 vols. Norman: University of Oklahoma Press, 1997–.

Schroeder, Susan, ed. *Native Resistance and the Pax Colonial in New Spain.* Lincoln: University of Nebraska Press, 1998.

Schroeder, Susan, Stephanie Wood, and Robert Haskett, eds. *Indian Women of Early Mexico.* Norman: University of Oklahoma Press, 1997.

Schuler, Friedrich E. *Mexico Between Hitler and Roosevelt: Mexican Foreign Relations during the Age of Lázaro Cárdenas, 1934–1940.* Albuquerque: University of New Mexico Press, 1998.

Seed, Patricia. *To Love, Honor and Obey in Colonial Mexico: Conflicts over Marriage Choice, 1574–1821.* Stanford: Stanford University Press, 1988.

Serrano, Mónica and Victor Bulmer-Thomas, eds. *Rebuilding the State: Mexico after Salinas.* London: Institute of Latin American Studies, 1996.

Sharer, Robert J. *The Ancient Maya.* 5th Edition. Stanford: Stanford University Press, 1994.

Simpson, Eyler N. *The Ejido: Mexico's Way Out.* Chapel Hill: University of North Carolina Press, 1937.

Singletary, Otis. *The Mexican War.* Chicago: University of Chicago Press, 1960.

Sinkin, Richard N. *The Mexican Reform, 1855–1876: A Study in Liberal Nation-Building.* Austin: Institute of Latin American Studies, 1979.

Smith, Lois Elwyn. *Mexico and the Spanish Republicans.* Berkeley: University of California Press, 1955.

Spicer, Edward H. *Cycles of Conquest: The Impact of Spain, Mexico, and the United States on the Indians of the Southwest, 1533–1960.* Tucson: University of Arizona Press, 1962.

Spores, Ronald. *The Mixtecs in Ancient and Modern Times.* Norman: University of Oklahoma Press, 1984.

Stein, Philip. *Siqueiros: His Life and Works.* New York: International Publishers, 1994.

Stern, Steve J. *The Secret History of Gender: Women, Men, and Power in Late Colonial Mexico.* Chapel Hill: The University of North Carolina Press, 1995.

Tannenbaum, Frank. *Peace by Revolution: An Interpretation of Mexico.* New York: Columbia University Press, 1933.

Taylor, William B. *Drinking, Homicide and Rebellion in Colonial Mexican Villages.* Stanford: Stanford University Press, 1979.

———. *Magistrates of the Sacred: Priests and Parishioners in Eighteenth-Century Mexico.* Stanford: Stanford University Press, 1996.

Taylor, William B and Franklin Pease, eds. *Violence, Resistance, and Survival in the Americas: Native Americans and the Legacy of Conquest.* Washington, D.C.: Smithsonian Institution Press, 1994.

Tedlock, Dennis. *Popul Vuh.* New York: Simon & Schuster, 1986.

Teichman, Judith A. *Policymaking in Mexico: From Boom to Crisis.* Boston: Allen and Unwin, 1988.

Tennenbaum, Barbara. *The Politics of Penury: Debts and Taxes in Mexico, 1821–1856.* Albuquerque: University of New Mexico Press, 1986.

Thomas, Hugh. *Conquest: Cortés, Montezuma, and the Fall of Old Mexico.* New York: Simon & Schuster, 1993.

Tutino, John. *From Insurrection to Revolution in Mexico: Social Bases of Agrarian Violence, 1750–1940.* Princeton: Princeton University Press, 1986.

Twinam, Ann. *Public Lives, Private Secrets: Gender, Honor, Sexuality and Illegitimacy in Colonial Spanish America.* Stanford: Stanford University Press, 1999.

Vanderwood, Paul J. *Disorder and Progress: Bandits, Police, and Mexican Development.* Wilmington, Del.: Scholarly Resources, 1992.

Vassberg, David E. *The Village and the Outside World in Golden Age Castile: Mobility and Migration in Everyday Rural Life.* Cambridge: Cambridge University Press, 1996.

Vaughan, Mary Kay. *Cultural Politics in Revolution: Teachers, Peasants, and Schools in Mexico, 1930–1940.* Tucson: University of Arizona Press, 1997.

———. *The State, Education and Social Class in Mexico, 1880–1928.* Dekalb: Northern Illinois University Press, 1982.

Vázquez, Josefina Z. and Lorenzo Meyer. *The United States and Mexico.* Chicago: University of Chicago Press, 1985.

Vigneras, Louis-André. *The Discovery of South America and the Andalusian Voyages.* Chicago: Published for the Newberry Library by the University of Chicago Press, 1976.

Walker, Geoffrey J. *Kinship, Business, and Politics: The Martínez del Rio Family in Mexico, 1824–1867.* Austin: University of Texas Press, 1986.

Weyl, Nathaniel and Sylvia. *The Reconquest of Mexico: The Years of Lázaro Cárdenas.* New York: Oxford University Press, 1939.

Winegardner, Mark. *Veracruz Blues.* New York: Viking, 1996.

Womack, John. *Zapata and the Mexican Revolution.* New York: Knopf, 1969.

Wright, Angus, *The Death of Ramon Gonzalez: The Modern Agricultural Dilemma.* Austin: University of Texas Press, 1990.

Zolov, Eric. *Refried Elvis.* Berkeley: University of California Press, 1999.

Contributors

✦ ✦

CHRISTON I. ARCHER, Professor of History, University of Calgary

THOMAS BENJAMIN, Professor of History, Central Michigan University

ROBERT M. BUFFINGTON, Professor of History, Bowling Green University

MARK A. BURKHOLDER, Professor of History, University of Missouri, St. Louis

RODERIC AI CAMP, Professor of History, Claremont College

LINDA A. CURIO-NAGY, Professor of History, University of Nevada

HELEN DELPAR, Professor of History, University of Alabama

WILLIAM E. FRENCH, University of British Columbia

VIRGINIA GUDEA, Professor of History, Centro de Estudios Históricos,
     Universidad nacional, Professor of History Autónoma de México

JOHN MASON HART, Professor of History, University of Houston

ROSS HASSIG, Professor of History, University of Oklahoma

ASUNCIÓN LAVRIN, Professor of History, Arizona State University

ELINOR G. K. MELVILLE, Professor of History, York University (Toronto)

HELEN NADER, Professor of History, University of Arizona

ROBERT W. PATCH, Professor of History, University of California, Riverside

ANNE RUBENSTEIN, Professor of History, Allegheny College

SUSAN SCHROEDER, Professor of History, Tulane University

JOHN W. SHERMAN, Professor of History, Wright State University

FRIEDRICH E. SHULER, Professor of History, Portland State University

PAUL VANDERWOOD, Professor of History, Emeritus, San Diego State University

JOSEFINA ZORAIDA VAZQUEZ, Professor of History, El Colegio de Mexico

Photo Credits

✦ ✦

and Photographs Division, LC–USZ62–61327: 323 (top); Library of Congress, Prints and Photographs Division, LC–USZ62–66216: 196; Library of Congress, Prints and Photographs Division, LC–USZ62–725: 353; Library of Congress, Prints and Photographs Division, LC–USZ62–75001: 473; Library of Congress, Prints and Photographs Division, LC–USZ62–75002: 516; Library of Congress, Prints and Photographs Division, LC–USZ62–79781: 272; Library of Congress, Prints and Photographs Division, LC–USZ62–80581: 439; Library of Congress, Prints and Photographs Division, LC–USZ9–162: 124; Library of Congress, Prints and Photographs Division, LC–USZ9–344–1: 190; From America by Theodor de Bry, Frankfurt 1595, courtesy Library of Congress, Rare Book and Special Collections Division: 186; From Atlas Pintoresco é Histórico de los Estados Unidos Mexicanos by Antonio García Cubas, Mexico City 1885, courtesy Library of Congress, Geography and Map Division: 283; From Civitates Orbis Terrarum by Georg Braun, Basel 1965, courtesy Library of Congress, Rare Book and Special Collections Division: 24; From Das Trachtenbuch by Christoph Weiditz, Berlin 1927, courtesy Library of Congress, Rare Book and Special Collections Division: 78; From Disertaciones sobre la Historia de la Republica Mejicana by Lucas Alaman, Mexico City 1849, courtesy Library of Congress: 279; From El Libro de Mis Recuerdos by Antonio Garcia Cubas, Mexico City 1905, courtesy Library of Congress: 335; From Escudo de Armas de Mexico by Cayetano de Cabrera, Mexico City 1746, courtesy Library of Congress, Rare Book and Special Collections Division: 167; From Frank Leslie's Illustrated Newspaper, January 10, 1862, Library of Congress, Prints and Photographs Division: 380; From Historia de las Cosas de Nueva España by Bernardino Sahagun, Madrid 1905–7, courtesy Library of Congress: 82, 108, 224, 234; From Homenaje á Cristóbal Colón, Mexico City 1892, courtesy Library of Congress: 89, 93, 96, 100, 126; From La Arquitectura Naval Española by Gervasio de Artiñano, Barcelona 1920, courtesy Library of Congress : 148; From Life in Mexico by Fanny Calderón de la Barca, Garden City 1966, courtesy Library of Congress: 331; From L'Illustration, courtesy Library of Congress: 384; From Los Conventos Suprimidos en Mexico by Manuel Ramirez, 1862, courtesy Library of Congress: 171; From Los Hombres Prominentes de Mexico by Ireneo Paz, Mexico City 1888, courtesy Library of Congress: 404, 408 (top); From Mexican Illustrations by Mark Beaufoy, London 1828, courtesy Library of Congress: 197; From México a Través de los Siglos by Vicente Riva Palacio, Mexico City 1887, courtesy Library of Congress: 297 (bottom), 291, 307, 312, 315, 331, 373, 408 (bottom); From Mexico Illustrated by John Phillips, London 1848, courtesy Library of Congress: 358; From Mexico Ilustrado by J.R. Southworth, Liverpool 1903: 417; From Mexico: Its Peasants and Its Priests by Robert Wilson, New York 1856, courtesy Library of Congress: 181, 320; From Oeuvres de Champlain by Samuel de Champlain, Quebec 1870, courtesy Library of Congress: 185, 229; From Praeclara Ferdinandi Cortesii de Nova Maris Hyspania Narratio, Nuremberg 1524, courtesy Library of Congress, Rare Book and Special Collections Division: 217; From Protest of Some Free Men, States and Presses against the Texas Rebellion, Albany 1844, courtesy Library of Congress: 344; From Recopilacion de Leyes de los Reynos de las Indias, Madrid 1681, courtesy Library of Congress, Law Library: 116; From The Adventures of Marco Polo by Marco Polo, New York 1902, courtesy Library of Congress: 13; From The Herball by John Gerarde, London 1597, courtesy Library of Congress, Rare Book and Special Collections Division: 137; From The Tlaxcalan Actas, edited by James Lockhart et al., Salt Lake City 1986, courtesy Library of Congress: 43; From Travels over the Table Lands and Cordilleras of Mexico by Albert Gilliam, Philadelphia 1846, courtesy Library of Congress: 357; Map by René Millon: 62; Museo de America: 246; Museo Franz Mayer: 249; Collection, The Museum of Modern Art, New York, Given Anonymously: 441; Courtesy Helen Nader: 41; National Archives, 306–NT–1174–9: 576; National Archives, 306–NT–1174A–11: 490; National Archives, 306–NT–1175–2: 523; National Archives, 306–NT–1175–MM–4: 520; National Archives, 306–NT–1175–Q–1: 484; National Archives, 306–NT–1175–S–1: 646; National Archives, 306–PS–D–58–8752: 610; National Archives, 306–PS–D–70–911: 585; New York Public Library: 645, 660; Courtesy Anne Rubenstein, 643; Watercolor copy by Antonio Tejeda, courtesy Peabody Museum, Harvard University: 54; UNICEF/Liba Taylor: 632; Robert Vose, courtesy Library of Congress, Prints and Photographs Division, LC–L9–58–7791–FF, #22: 656; Jeffrey A. Wolin, courtesy Helen Nader: 20.

Photo Essay: Latin Focus/ Lorenzo A.: 3, 4, 5, 9, (bottom), 11, 12, 13 (bottom), 14, 16; Latin Focus/ Mariana Dellacamp: 1; Latin Focus/ Jimmy Dorantes: 2, 8 (top), 15; Latin Focus/ Oscar Necoechea: 6, 7, 8 (bottom), 9 (top), 10 (top), 13 (top).

Index

✦ ✦

Page numbers in italic type indicate illustrations.